BIRTHDAY SECRETS

WHAT THE HEAVENS REVEAL
ABOUT YOU AND YOUR BIRTHDAY

Jill M. Phillips

Foreword by Kris Brandt Riske, M.A.
Professional Member of the American Federation of Astrologers

Publications International, Ltd.

Jill M. Phillips is the author of over two hundred published articles on astrology and related subjects, as well as over two dozen books, including *The Rain Maiden* and *The Fate Weaver*. She regularly writes forecast columns for *Horoscope Guide* and contributes to Globe's mini-magazine astrology series. Ms. Phillips works with clients through Moon Dancer AstroGraphics, her astrological counseling service.

Kris Brandt Riske, M.A., is an astrologer, writer, and editor who specializes in relationships, forecasting, and astrometeorology. Her articles have appeared in various astrological publications, including *Today's Astrologer* and Dell *Horoscope*. She is also the author of *Astrometeorology: Planetary Power in Weather Forecasting* and is a professional member of the American Federation of Astrologers.

Louis Weber, C.E.O.
Publications International, Ltd.
7373 North Cicero Avenue
Lincolnwood, Illinois 60646

Manufactured in U.S.A.

8 7 6 5 4 3 2 1

ISBN: 0-7853-3203-0

CONTENTS

FOREWORD
Astrology and You

Birthday Secrets is all about you, the inner core of your spirit, the guiding force of your personality—the real you.

Ever wonder why you love to cook, but your neighbor would rather weed the garden? Why you feel close to one sibling, but not another? Why some people are world adventurers and others like to stay home with a good book? Why no two people are exactly alike? Birthday Secrets reveals answers to those questions and more.

As you read, you'll learn about yourself, what motivates you, what challenges you, the talents and gifts that are yours alone because of the day of your birth. That, of course, is the fundamental tenet of astrology: opening the door to self-understanding and, through your planetary potential, fulfilling the promise of your birth. Astrology can show you how to make the most of you, how you can become the best you can be in every facet of your life.

More than 2,500 years ago, people first recognized a correlation between the placement of the planets in the heavens and which individuals became kings, warriors, merchants, lovers, physicians, and more. But only those in the highest echelon of society had access to astrologers and their marvelous insights into human nature.

Today, astrology is for everyone and is relevant in every life. Tens of millions of people read astrology columns in daily, weekly, and monthly publications, and others meet with professional astrologers for personal consultations. Why? It works! With uncanny accuracy, astrology can describe your personality as nothing else can.

More than that, it's fun and useful in your everyday life. Looking for insight into your boss, your coworkers, your mate, or your family? Birthday Secrets will open your eyes to what makes these people tick, their "hot buttons," and how to approach each one. Through that knowledge, you'll gain a greater understanding and appreciation of other people and your relationships with them. This is knowledge you can use to your advantage throughout your lifetime. After all, life is about people, and people are the core of astrology.

Birthday Secrets will pique your interest in astrology and in learning more about yourself. A professional astrologer can assist you in realizing your goals, in knowing when to act or maintain the status quo, and and deciding when to launch new endeavors. Of course, the word "professional" is the key, just as it is in other disciplines. To that end, astrological associations require their members to uphold certain ethics, and they certify only those members who successfully complete rigorous examinations after years of study. The American Federation of Astrologers, founded in 1938, was established with professionalism as one of its chief aims.

It is amazing, sometimes even to astrologers, that planets billions of miles away can affect our everyday lives, what we hope to become, and the goals we strive to achieve. Yet that is the truth of it and the wonder of it.

Welcome to the wonderful world of astrology!

—Kris Brandt Riske, M.A.,
Professional Member,
American Federation of
Astrologers (PMAFA)

INTRODUCTION

The Allure of the Heavens

We can safely say that astrology was born the first time people looked up at the stars and realized that those shimmering, distant orbs formed pictures in the heavens. It is a certainty that long before recorded history, when life was a succession of labor and tedium interrupted by the occasional terror of simple survival, the night sky was a source of profound interest to our ancestors.

AGES PAST The study of astrology—the prediction of personality traits and the divination of future events based on the relationship between the Sun, Moon, and planets—dates back thousands of years, to the ancient Egyptians, who were the first to make a science of it. The Babylonians, Greeks, and Romans also held it in high esteem.

Many people believe that the biblical Magi—the kings who brought gifts to the Christ child—were actually astrologers whose study of their art told them where to find the baby.

Although it is generally accepted that the Venerable Bede—that great English historian of the Dark Ages—studied astrology as a mystical discipline, it was not a popular art/science in Europe at that time. Later, during the great Crusades of the Middle Ages, the returning knights brought back many Eastern influences, including the study of astrology.

ASTROLOGY AND THE RENAISSANCE It wasn't until the European Renaissance of the fourteenth to the seventeenth centuries, when high learning and occult sciences were at their zeniths, that astrology came into its own in the West. Although it didn't coexist well with Catholicism, it was well received in Protestant countries. During this period in history, however, astrology was still the province of the rich and powerful. Kings, queens, and others of political and social significance were thought to be the only ones worthy to practice this mystical art.

In England astrology reached its high point during the reign (1558–1603) of Queen Elizabeth I. But with the discoveries and theories of astronomers Copernicus and Galileo in the sixteenth and seventeenth centuries, respectively, astrology and astronomy diverged, destined never to be reunited under the same scientific banner. Astrology eventually lost its strong association with mysticism and came to be regarded as a pseudo-science.

THE MODERN AGE The early twentieth century brought an astrology revival, particularly in the United States. Astrology's practical value as a predictor of stock-market gains and losses in the 1920s, for example, has been well documented.

Today, astrology is more popular than ever. This is largely due to two historical events, very different from each other, which overlapped one another. The first was the period of the late 1960s, characterized as the "Age of Aquarius," named for a song from a popular Broadway musical, *Hair*. That era of generational rebellion and social change downplayed materialism and urged people to embrace the mystical side of life. Astrology became a touchstone for this movement, as well as a forum for discussion of every aspect of human behavior, especially sexuality.

MEANING FOR THE MODERN AGE The second historical event, and greatest single force in the popularization of modern astrology, has been the development of the personal computer. Astrologers who once spent weeks casting and interpreting charts with accuracy that could not be assured can now compute and print out a chart in a matter of minutes, with no doubt as to its accuracy. Not only has this added to the number of people who can have their natal or transit chart analyzed quickly and for a moderate price, but it has also popularized astrology as a profession.

Astrology now has a much different use than it did in the ancient world. The rich and powerful still consult astrologers for clues to their future; the difference is that nowadays they are not alone, because everyone can do the same. But astrology is no longer about just love and money. Astrology answers many other questions. As in the past, there are astrologers who give stock market tips; and despite its ancient beginnings, astrology is now part of the New Age movement. Traditional predictive, transit astrology may still rule, but now there are just as many astrologers whose work involves past-life readings, next-life readings, marriage and family counseling, and questions of nutrition and health. There are now more working astrologers than at any other time in history.

And consider this: Two-thirds of people in the United States are said to have either had their charts read by an astrologer, or believe that astrology is a viable method of predicting and managing the future.

SUN SIGN ASTROLOGY
Sun sign astrology is the study of the twelve signs of the zodiac. Each of us fits into one of these twelve categories. (See the sample star chart on page 8.) You don't need to have your chart analyzed to discover a great deal about your natal (at-birth) characteristics, or to get a general idea of major influences at work in your life.

In this age of sophisticated computer software and complex relationship theories, Sun sign astrology has its detractors. Yet there is a great truth at its core. Sun sign astrology speaks to our understanding of and reliance upon ancient and modern archetypes, the basic character types we encounter over and over again. Although this sort of astrology deals

with only twelve basic character types, it offers the best overview of astrological characteristics, the most definitive measure of the self.

The ascendant table you'll find on page 9 of *Birthday Secrets* provides you with even more precise, individuated information. As with the star chart, the ascendant table does not provide a complete picture of your personality and destiny. For that, an in-depth analysis done one-on-one with a professional astrologer is best.

Regardless, the ascendant table will give you a reasonably precise idea of your Ascendant—that is, the sign of the zodiac other than your own that "colors" your personal nature and influences your future.

Each of us is much "more" than our sign suggests, and the ascendant table will help reveal it.

ELEMENTS AND NATURE
The twelve types are further divided into elements: Fire, Earth, Air, Water. Within each of these categories can be found three of the twelve signs. The elements help to describe the basic nature of a sign. For example, Fire signs (Aries, Leo, Sagittarius) have "firelike" characteristics: a hot temper, passion, creativity, and boldness. Earth signs (Taurus, Virgo, Capricorn) are stable, frugal, and sensual. People born under Air signs (Gemini, Libra, Aquarius) are intellectually inclined, changeable, and high-strung. Water-sign people (Cancer, Scorpio, Pisces) are intuitive, spiritual, and secretive.

THE LORE OF DAYS
Shakespeare asked "What's in a name?" Let us paraphrase that and inquire, "What's in a day?"

Each of us likes to believe we are unique, special in our own way. By studying the dates of our birth we can become aware of one aspect of that resolute uniqueness that separates us from people born on any of the other 365 days of the year.

THE ALLURE OF BIRTHDAYS
Why birthdays? Because they define us. They are

what we grow up with, grow old with—the common denominator of our hopes, dreams, and experiences. Birthdays have personalities, just like people. Events, both great and small, impress their own meaning upon each date, giving them renewed significance. Filled with promise, filled with potential, each date is a mixture of the mundane and the magical.

When millions of people from all cultures and walks of life share a birthday, can there be a common thread? Without a doubt. A look at a list of people born on a specific day gives us a clue to the amazing potentialities that exist for that particular date. In ancient times people looked to the gods and goddesses for answers. Today, our modern messengers are television and the tabloid press. Indeed, we are enmeshed in a cult of celebrity unlike anything ever witnessed in history. It is only natural that famous men and women should pique our interest. They invoke our envy, love, or pity. Many of us can quote the names of our celebrity astro-twins. But this is a phenomenon that speaks to us on a deeper, even more significant level.

THE POWER OF POTENTIAL
Celebrities are our living archetypes, the embodiments of our own dreams and desires, our fantasies and failures. In many ways they are us and we are them. This is not to say that celebrities are more important or even more successful than the rest of us. But famous people are famous for a reason. They may know what many of us do not—that we all have astonishing potential, but unless we believe in ourselves all of our best traits may go unrealized. For us to achieve our full potential and self-realization, we must summon a great sense of purpose, determination, and, most of all, belief. And while we can't all be famous, we can take the example of those who are. To believe in our abilities and our potential to succeed is the very best gift we can give ourselves.

USING THIS BOOK
Birthday Secrets is a carefully researched guide intended for use by the general public. Whether your interest in astrology is new or of long-standing, you'll find this book useful, fascinating, and fun.

Astrology is a complicated subject. Eventually you may wish to have your chart analyzed by a professional astrologer. But until that time you can learn a lot about your basic personality type—and the personalities of your family and friends—by reading and thinking about what you'll discover in *Birthday Secrets*. Sure, you may be a Gemini, but what special advice is appropriate for a *June 16* Gemini? And how does the day of a February 23 Pisces differ that of other Pisces people?

HOW WE DID IT
The exclusive insights you'll find in *Birthday Secrets* are based upon a variety of methods designed to analyze days within each Sun sign. First, careful examination was made of the traits and personality characteristics of the Sun sign itself, as well as the myriad associations related to its planetary ruler. Further division and definition of each sign was provided by the use of dwads (2.5-degree markers) and decanates (10-degree markers), which establish an even more specific profile within the Sun sign.

Finally, numerology (the study of numbers according to their divine and magical significance) and the Sabian symbols (a set of 360-degree symbols and meanings that describe arcane and modern symbology) have been used to attain even greater definition and accuracy.

YOUR SPECIAL DAY
Your birth date is something special because it is yours. Its number and characteristics should be talismans for you, symbols of what you are and what you can be. We are always in the process of *realizing*, but never fully attaining, our potential. But the adventure is in the search, and the meaning is in the doing.

Have fun with this book—and ponder what it says. Share the information with others and discuss what you've read. Use the *Birthday Secrets* as one step on your path to understanding all that you are, and everything you have to offer to yourself and others.

SUN SIGN BIRTH CHART

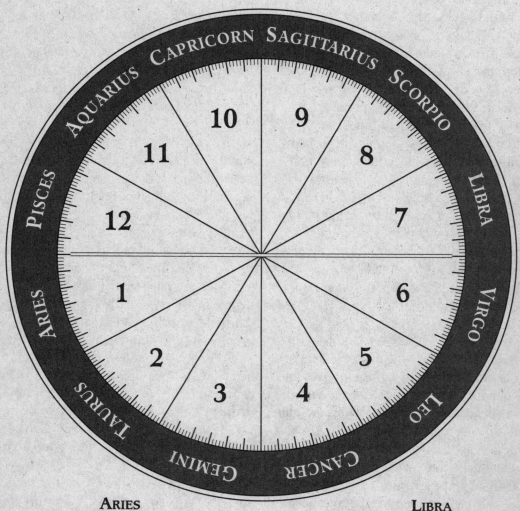

ARIES
March 21–April 20

TAURUS
April 21–May 20

GEMINI
May 21–June 20

CANCER
June 21–July 22

LEO
July 23–August 22

VIRGO
August 23–September 22

LIBRA
September 23–October 22

SCORPIO
October 23–November 21

SAGITTARIUS
November 22–December 21

CAPRICORN
December 22–January 19

AQUARIUS
January 20–February 18

PISCES
February 19–March 20

ASCENDANT TABLE

YOUR TIME OF BIRTH

YOUR SUN SIGN	6-8 A.M.	8-10 A.M.	10 A.M.-NOON	NOON-2 P.M.	2-4 P.M.	4-6 P.M.
ARIES	Taurus	Gemini	Cancer	Leo	Virgo	Libra
TAURUS	Gemini	Cancer	Leo	Virgo	Libra	Scorpio
GEMINI	Cancer	Leo	Virgo	Libra	Scorpio	Sagittarius
CANCER	Leo	Virgo	Libra	Scorpio	Sagittarius	Capricorn
LEO	Virgo	Libra	Scorpio	Sagittarius	Capricorn	Aquarius
VIRGO	Libra	Scorpio	Sagittarius	Capricorn	Aquarius	Pisces
LIBRA	Scorpio	Sagittarius	Capricorn	Aquarius	Pisces	Aries
SCORPIO	Sagittarius	Capricorn	Aquarius	Pisces	Aries	Taurus
SAGITTARIUS	Capricorn	Aquarius	Pisces	Aries	Taurus	Gemini
CAPRICORN	Aquarius	Pisces	Aries	Taurus	Gemini	Cancer
AQUARIUS	Pisces	Aries	Taurus	Gemini	Cancer	Leo
PISCES	Aries	Taurus	Gemini	Cancer	Leo	Virgo

YOUR TIME OF BIRTH

YOUR SUN SIGN	6-8 P.M.	8-10 P.M.	10 P.M.-MIDNIGHT	NOON-2 P.M.	2-4 A.M.	4-6 A.M.
ARIES	Scorpio	Sagittarius	Capricorn	Aquarius	Pisces	Aries
TAURUS	Sagittarius	Capricorn	Aquarius	Pisces	Aries	Taurus
GEMINI	Capricorn	Aquarius	Pisces	Aries	Taurus	Gemini
CANCER	Aquarius	Pisces	Aries	Taurus	Gemini	Cancer
LEO	Pisces	Aries	Taurus	Gemini	Cancer	Leo
VIRGO	Aries	Taurus	Gemini	Cancer	Leo	Virgo
LIBRA	Taurus	Gemini	Cancer	Leo	Virgo	Libra
SCORPIO	Gemini	Cancer	Leo	Virgo	Libra	Scorpio
SAGITTARIUS	Cancer	Leo	Virgo	Libra	Scorpio	Sagittarius
CAPRICORN	Leo	Virgo	Libra	Scorpio	Sagittarius	Capricorn
AQUARIUS	Virgo	Libra	Scorpio	Sagittarius	Capricorn	Aquarius
PISCES	Librd	Scorpio	Sagittarius	Capricorn	Aquarius	Pisces

How to use this table: 1. Locate your Sun sign in the far left column.
2. Look for your approximate time of birth time in a vertical column.
3. The intersection of your sign and your time of birth reveals your Ascendant.

It's impossible to determine your exact Ascendant without a complete natal chart. But this table will give you a useful approximation of your Ascendant. If you feel that the sign listed as your Ascendant is incorrect, try the one either before or after the listed sign.

ARIES
March 21 - April 20

Aries is the first sign of the astrological year and is known by its astrological symbol, the Ram. Aries individuals are willful, positive, and independent. With Mars as the ruling planet, people born under this sign are thought to be warlike and aggressive. They have amazing stamina and a potent drive to succeed.

THE ARIES MAN This man has a regal bearing. Even if he isn't handsome—though he usually is—he's the one noticed by everybody when he walks into a room. Although he may seem cool he actually has a very quick temper and can seem pushy, even rude at times.

Aries men are dedicated to their career aspirations and getting ahead. Their personal lives may be put on hold when they concentrate on their climb to the top. For this reason they are sometimes considered to be incompatible with family life, though this is an unfair assumption.

The ideal Aries man combines rugged masculinity with urbane charm. He may possess some old-fashioned views about his role as head of the household, but at heart he's a charmer.

THE ARIES WOMAN This lady knows what she wants out of life and isn't the least bit shy about going after it. She is independent and prefers supporting herself, no matter what her marital status. Aries women are often perceived as being "one of the boys" because they don't use their femininity in conventional ways. When they decide to turn on the charm it can be quite a revelation.

Like their male counterparts, Aries women have quick tempers and may often give the impression of bossiness, because they refuse to back down to anyone. These women have a bold sense of style that adds a fascinating new level to their natural beauty. They prefer to be noticed for their intellect and capabilities rather than for their good looks.

THE ARIES CHILD Anyone who has ever raised an Aries child knows that these determined little overachievers need a firm hand to keep them from getting out of line. Aries children often begin showing signs of leadership potential at a very early age. They tend to be the organizing force behind the play activity, often assuming an adultlike posture.

Aries youngsters are extremely self-possessed and prone to demanding their own way. Their temper tantrums are notorious, yet they can also be the picture of good behavior when they want to be. They may be especially troublesome during their teen years, but seldom take on the mantle of the "rebel without a cause." When Aries young people rebel, they generally have a very good idea of what they're rebelling against.

THE ARIES LOVER Aries natives have a powerful love nature and a strong sexual drive. These people inevitably take the initiative where love matters are concerned. Once they set their sights on a romantic interest, they go after that individual with all of the enthusiasm and purpose typical of this sign.

Some people may be surprised to learn that Aries men and women are not just sexual, but also highly romantic. These individuals have an extremely idealistic, even chivalric idea of what love should be, and they won't settle for anything less. But unfortunately, although Aries natives can be extremely single-minded during the dating stage, they often revert to type after they marry, devoting the greatest amount of their energy to career goals.

THE ARIES BOSS People who think they can stretch their 15-minute break into a half hour and get away with it have never worked for an Aries boss! These men and women are real sticklers when it comes to the rules and aren't likely to ignore them to benefit anyone. Although this sounds severe, these folks have their good points, too. They're interested in helping their workers attain their professional goals and will often act in the capacity of a mentor.

It is important that employees treat their Aries boss with utmost respect, if they expect to develop and maintain a good relationship. An Aries employer will always stand on ceremony and expects his or her workers to defer to knowledge and experience.

ELEMENT: Fire
QUALITY: Cardinal
PLANETARY RULER: Mars
BIRTHSTONE: Diamond
FLOWER: Hawthorn
COLOR: Scarlet

KEY CHARACTERISTIC:
Leadership

STRENGTHS: Intelligent,
Assertive, Adventurous

CHALLENGES: Trouble with
sharing, Too much ego, Vindictive

THE ARIES FRIEND With their powerful leadership potential, Aries natives make inspirational friends. They often act in a counseling capacity and will do what they can to help their pals achieve their dreams. These people are big on goals and want to promote this characteristic in their friends. The typical Aries friend will try to help his/her buddies become more successful and professionally centered. It's difficult for these driven individuals to understand anything but absolute dedication to career goals.

Aries people are interesting and enjoyable social companions. They make friends easily and show remarkable loyalty. Getting together with a bunch of pals to play competitive sports on the weekend is an Aries' idea of heaven.

11

MARCH 21

People born on this date have a proud and adventuresome nature, though this may not be displayed in conventional ways. March 21 individuals, though they are sure of themselves and their convictions, fear being ridiculed for their great dreams. For this reason they are likely to adopt a "who cares" attitude, when in truth they care very much.

March 21 natives have incredible emotional resilience and can bounce back from disappointment more readily than nearly any other individual.

FRIENDS AND LOVERS
March 21 people have a quiet intensity that is riveting. Although they do not make a great display of themselves, they draw others to them easily. Friends react positively to their bemused shyness.

March 21 individuals feel most secure about themselves when they are in love with a permanent partner. They require a great deal of affection and tenderness from a mate, since they may have been denied these comforts in earlier relationships. Because they are highly moralistic creatures, March 21 people often idealize their key relationship.

CHILDREN AND FAMILY
A childlike naivete about March 21 people allows them to understand the mysteries of childhood, whatever their age. Their own upbringing tends to be one of extremes—either emotional neglect or too much pampering. As a result, these individuals often enter adulthood with a great many unresolved feelings about the importance of being nurtured and understood.

With their own children, March 21 men and women seek to compensate for what they lacked during their own growing-up years. This generally has a healing effect.

HEALTH
People born on this date have to endorse a regular exercise regimen if they are to present a slim, fit appearance. They put on weight easily, especially around the hips and thighs, so cross-training and sculpting exercises may be beneficial in helping them to firm up problem areas. Weight gain is particularly likely late in life, so March 21 folks need to gravitate to a scaled-down diet at that time.

March 21 individuals are usually robust and possess a high energy level. It is rare for them to be sick, and they have the ability to work for long stretches without rest or sleep.

CAREER AND FINANCES
Positions of power come easily to March 21 individuals, who often flourish in business and management. These people have a natural ability to act as a mentor or guide to younger associates, and for this reason they also make excellent teachers.

March 21 natives have good financial instincts when handling their own money or that of a client. Money isn't really important to these people, though they do respond to the aura of power it provides.

DREAMS AND GOALS
Those born on this date can best facilitate their goals by learning to climb the proverbial ladder of success one rung at a time. March 21 individuals revel in their accomplishments but need to be reminded that, on occasion, a setback can be an even greater teacher than triumph.

MARCH 22

Instinct takes precedence over intellect in the lives of people born on March 22. They are impulsive, fun-loving individuals who see it as their mission in life to test boundaries and break the rules.

March 22 individuals are vibrant, exciting types who can draw people to them on the strength of their personality alone. They are natural leaders, yet not in the conventional sense. Their love of daring and risk-taking is the envy of others.

FRIENDS AND LOVERS
Relationships of all kinds play a turbulent role in the lives of March 22 people. They tend to fall in and out with friends on a regular basis, often under controversial circumstances.

The love life of March 22 natives is full of change and emotion. They are attracted to people who are their mirror opposite, which can create severe relationship problems.

Because it isn't easy for these people to keep ego issues out of their relationship with a mate, more than one marriage for them is not uncommon. They are passionate, entertaining, and never lack for warm attention from the opposite sex.

CHILDREN AND FAMILY
People born on this date enjoy the security of a large family and have a way of bringing distant relatives and even friends into their familial circle. They are bossy, loving, and always manage to keep track of what is going on in the lives of family members.

March 22 individuals make eccentric yet caring parents. They take such an active role in guiding their children that they may sometimes seem overbearing. If March 22 people have no children of their own, they have a way of inspiring a whole series of surrogates from their professional or personal circles.

HEALTH
High-strung and intense, March 22 individuals are workaholics who need to keep a handle on stress if they are to remain healthy and in good shape. Their kinetic lifestyle keeps them in a constant state of activity, which helps to ease work-related tension.

These people are careless where diet is concerned and do not always recognize the links between good health and good habits.

CAREER AND FINANCES
These people are the ultimate risk-takers, who put all of their energy and ability into getting what they want out of life. They are talented, sometimes brilliant individuals who have the potential to distinguish themselves in career matters. Good fortune, even fame, is well within their reach.

DREAMS AND GOALS
The sky's the limit for people born on March 22. They have the highest expectations for their own success and are unable to recognize the pitfalls that are possible when striving hard to reach a goal.

Even though they make a concerted effort to implement their dreams by accomplishing goals one step at a time, those born on March 22 can also depend on good luck to play its part. A strong belief in themselves is a key factor in their overall success.

EMBRACE
Quiet reflection
Doing good deeds
Accentuating the positive

AVOID
Personal obsessions
Needless worry
Bad habits

ALSO BORN TODAY
Singer/guitarist Jeremy Clyde; Senator Orin Hatch; mime Marcel Marceau; actor Matthew Modine; actress Lena Olin; evangelist Pat Robertson; composer/lyricist Stephen Sondheim; composer/producer Andrew Lloyd Webber.

MARCH 23

March 23 natives are self-deprecating, good-natured folks who can differentiate between taking their work and taking themselves too seriously. They approach life with gusto and are never at a loss to find new and interesting subjects to engage their intellect.

Talkative and outgoing, March 23 individuals give the appearance of being highly organized, though they actually prefer to take life as it comes. They have quick minds and are able to store facts on many subjects for use at later times.

FRIENDS AND LOVERS Friendship is an important factor in the lives of people born on this date, and they confide their deepest inner feelings only to those with whom they share a close relationship.

Because of their genial good humor they make friends easily, yet no one knows exactly how they stand in the affections of these complex people.

Their love nature is very similar. Although they may play the field for many years before settling down, once March 23 people commit to a relationship they are determined to make it work. Because their romantic nature makes them feel vulnerable, they guard that side of their personality.

CHILDREN AND FAMILY People born on this date have natural leadership abilities that affect their position within the family. Even if they have older siblings, they are likely to hold a place of honor and respect among the others.

March 23 individuals enjoy being parents, though they have a somewhat casual attitude toward this calling. They prefer setting an example for their youngsters in a quiet and unassuming way.

HEALTH March 23 individuals have a somewhat unorthodox attitude toward health matters. They enjoy gathering research material pertaining to unusual treatments and health practices. They take a holistic approach to keeping healthy and believe wholeheartedly in the adage "you are what you eat."

Since they have a great deal of nervous energy, people born on this day benefit from vigorous aerobic workouts as well as specific exercises to build physical endurance.

CAREER AND FINANCES People born on March 23 are drawn to careers that involve communication skills. They enjoy working with large groups of people, and they shine as part of a team. They make very fine teachers, lecturers, and news-gatherers. Writing and public speaking are good showcases for their intelligence.

They have the ability to make money quickly and are drawn to speculative opportunities. Unfortunately, their spendthrift habits often come back to haunt them.

DREAMS AND GOALS People born on March 23 have a tendency to take life as it comes, preferring spontaneity over any carefully orchestrated plan to succeed. They have high expectations but leave it up to Providence to make their dreams come true.

EMBRACE
Emotional depth
Spiritual goals
Destiny

AVOID
Excessive temperament
Ignoring details
Intolerance

ALSO BORN TODAY
Actress Joan Crawford; Princess Eugenie of England; figure skating champion Julie Lynn Holmes; figure skating champion Hayes Jenkins; film director Akira Kurosawa; singer Marti Pellow; actress Amanda Plummer; astrologer Dane Rudhyar.

MARCH 24

March 24 people are creative, sympathetic types who see their lives as an expression of their deep inner creativity. Their good nature extends to associations with everyone around them, and they are unlikely to have enemies.

Those born on this date possess a delightful naivete that in no way implies a lack of intelligence or sophistication. They manage to combine these qualities with a credible simplicity that attracts enthusiastic admirers.

FRIENDS AND LOVERS

The gentle nature of March 24 people encourages relationships with individuals who are emotionally stronger. They are often drawn into friendships with people several years older who may serve the role of mentor or advisor.

Love relationships may be equally complicated because March 24 individuals have a need to learn from each romantic encounter. Because of this, there is a tendency for them to lose interest in a partner once the "lesson" has been learned.

CHILDREN AND FAMILY

Because of their generally kind and docile personality, those born on March 24 often hold a special place within their family circle. They're likely to be the one to whom other siblings come when it's time to share a confidence.

March 24 individuals are tender, indulgent parents, and because they have difficulty enforcing rules and discipline, they may not be particularly successful in this role. What they do best is set an exemplary pattern of behavior for their youngsters, which can serve as a remarkable channel of unspoken understanding between the generations.

HEALTH

People born on this day have a natural enthusiasm about life that keeps them feeling emotionally energized no matter what stresses or tensions come their way. They are not especially active individuals and prefer to get their exercise from normal daily activity rather than an organized workout regimen.

People born on this date should drink plenty of water and stay away from heavily caffeinated beverages like coffee and soft drinks. Use of alcohol is not recommended.

CAREER AND FINANCES

Although March 24 individuals may achieve great success in their chosen field it is often due more to good luck than any clever planning on their part. These people prefer to follow a circuitous route to their accomplishments.

Any creative outlet makes a worthwhile career for those born on this date. They have a natural flair for color and make excellent decorators, designers, or artists. Handling money is not their forte, however, and they can benefit from professional attention to their expenses and investment opportunities.

DREAMS AND GOALS

For most March 24 natives, the concept of personal and professional goals may be an abstraction. They have a general idea of what they want to happen in their lives, but it is likely to be tempered by their wonder and enjoyment at watching events unfold in their own time.

EMBRACE
Hard choices
Spiritual harmony
Patience

AVOID
Losing momentum
Codependency
Negative thoughts

ALSO BORN TODAY
Bank robber Clyde Barrow; actress Lara Flynn Boyle; actor Robert Carradine; fashion designer Bob Mackie; actor Steve McQueen; artisan William Morris; author Malcolm Muggeridge; actress Donna Pescow.

15

MARCH 25

The inner nature of people born on March 25 is very different from their outer personality. They have strong social skills and may be considered by others to be the life of the party. But in reality these individuals draw strength from a rich and creative inner life.

March 25 natives are naturally shy, preferring their own company to crowds, even though they possess the ability to shine at any gathering.

FRIENDS AND LOVERS Given their emotional depth, it isn't unusual that people born on this date express much of their life-force energy through relationships with others. They may have a great many social friends, but very few close ones.

Romance is the focal point of life for March 25 individuals. Although their love life is often turbulent, sometimes even tragic, it is always their primary form of experience. They have the ability to bring out the very best qualities in a loved one. When a marriage or relationship breaks up, March 25 individuals are likely to remain friends with their ex-partners.

CHILDREN AND FAMILY Family life is not especially important to March 25 individuals, since they usually develop a social life outside of the family circle at a very young age. They do respect the traditions of family life and enjoy performing holiday rituals.

March 25 natives do not expect their children to follow in their footsteps. They much prefer championing independent-minded youngsters who have the determination to go their own way. They often develop a closer relationship with their grown children than they enjoy with little ones.

HEALTH People born on March 25 have little fondness for routine of any kind. They like to feel as if they are totally in charge of their destiny and for that reason may flout conventional wisdom about health and fitness.

March 25 individuals pride themselves on being able to get by with very little sleep, yet a lack of REM sleep can cause problems if it persists. Those born on this day lead a very active dream life and need to funnel their problems and stresses through dreaming.

CAREER AND FINANCES People born on this day have a great need to be famous. Of course, since it is not possible that everyone with this particular birthdate can have that wish, many of these individuals must be satisfied with being widely known within a small circle of professional associates. But one way or another, March 25 natives will make their mark.

DREAMS AND GOALS There are very few goals in life that March 25 people cannot achieve once they put their mind to it. Goals take on the weight of a quest, and dreams become vivid and dramatic. These are people who definitely believe in their ability to get what they want out of life.

Those who are born on this day have the ability to inspire others by the grandeur of their hopes and dreams. As far as they're concerned, anything is possible.

EMBRACE
Positive outflow
Emotional resonance
Being young at heart

AVOID
Pessimism
Looking back instead of forward
Being sullen

ALSO BORN TODAY
Singer Aretha Franklin; singer/songwriter Elton John; film director David Lean; actress Sarah Jessica Parker; actress Simone Signoret; feminist author Gloria Steinem; figure skating champion Debi Thomas; symphony conductor Arturo Toscanini.

MARCH 26

People born on this day are bright, cometlike individuals. On the surface they appear to be capable, even unflappable, yet there is a deep insecurity at their core that can create emotional distress.

March 26 people are unlikely to show their vulnerabilities to the world. They prefer to handle their own challenges, solve their own problems.

FRIENDS AND LOVERS Despite a well-earned reputation as leaders, March 26 individuals have a strong dependence upon the people they love and care about. True friendships, especially those lasting over a period of many years, have a valuable effect upon the lives of these people.

The love life of March 26 natives has an enduring quality. When these people fall in love it is likely to be a lifetime attraction. Because they have an uncanny knack for selecting just the right partner, their marital relationships are typically warm, long-lived, and fulfilling, both physically and spiritually.

CHILDREN AND FAMILY People born on this date have a unique link to family that they may perceive as karmic. No matter how often these people are separated from their family, or by whatever distance, they will always experience a tug of destiny that brings them all together again.

March 26 individuals may not feel a strong motivation to become parents, but if they do they will give the job their full attention.

HEALTH March 26 natives have a stern regard for matters of health and fitness. Although they may be blessed with only average good health, they are capable of developing a great deal of life-enhancing energy.

Although they can appreciate the occasional rare steak and good bottle of wine, March 26 individuals are extremely disciplined in their habits. They keep to a strict exercise plan and find considerable benefits from cross-training, since they appreciate variety in all things.

CAREER AND FINANCES Careers in productive, useful fields work best for people born on this day. They take great pride in managing the details of their profession and can always be counted upon to fulfill their work-related obligations.

March 26 people are experts at handling money. They have a strictly no-nonsense approach to managing their finances. When they set a limit for the family budget, everyone had better be in compliance.

DREAMS AND GOALS The personality of March 26 individuals is so completely integrated with what they want out of life that they find themselves living their goals nearly every day.

These people believe in their own ability to make things happen, yet they have a very strict set of standards and will never deviate from them in order to make their dreams come true. If something cannot be accomplished according to their own concepts of honesty and integrity, March 26 people would just as soon not see their goals come to fruition.

EMBRACE
Displaying sensitivity
A sense of beauty
Being happy

AVOID
Being secretive
Ignoring the needs of others
Sarcasm

ALSO BORN TODAY
Actor James Caan; poet Robert Frost; TV personality Leeza Gibbons; poet A. E. Housman; actress Vicki Lawrence; Supreme Court Justice Sandra Day O'Connor; singer Diana Ross; playwright Tennesse Williams.

17

MARCH 27

Strength, tenacity, and the ability to draw upon these abilities when needed characterize March 27 natives. They generally go their own way and make their decisions according to their impulsive nature. At times this impulsiveness can be a drawback in their relationships with others, since it has a tendency to make them seem bossy, even arrogant. In reality, nothing could be further from the truth.

FRIENDS AND LOVERS Despite their deeply romantic nature, March 27 individuals have a basically no-nonsense attitude toward all relationships. Though they value the opinions of others, they have a way of getting friends to appreciate their point of view with little effort.

March 27 people have a deeply sexual love nature that demands fulfillment. Although they appreciate the superficial and romantic aspects of togetherness, they need to feel as though the powerful physical attraction they feel for a partner is returned. People born on this day are intensely loyal and take marriage vows seriously.

CHILDREN AND FAMILY March 27 individuals often experience a tumultuous family life because they have a way of becoming involved in all aspects of their relatives' lives. They have amazing energy, which puts them at the center of things.

With their own children, March 27 natives create a bond of loving understanding, but there is never any doubt who is in charge. They encourage their children to take bold steps on the route to adulthood but are always ready to sympathize when there are disappointments along the way. This give-and-take relationship between March 27 individuals and their children continues throughout life.

HEALTH People born on this date have an amazing store of energy and vitality. They work and play with equal vigor and always have the endurance for both.

March 27 individuals are big eaters. They are often expert cooks as well, who enjoy whipping up tasty meals for themselves, friends, and relatives. Since it is the social aspect of eating that appeals most to them, they seldom have a weight problem.

CAREER AND FINANCES From the time they first decide upon a career path, people born on March 27 are primed for success. They often gravitate toward high-powered careers but can be happy in any area where they are able to pursue excellence and accomplishment.

March 27 individuals can be aggressive in their pursuit of financial success, but not for materialistic reasons alone. To them, professional acclaim and financial success go hand in hand.

DREAMS AND GOALS March 27 natives dream big dreams and expect them to come true. They work amazingly hard to achieve these ends, never expecting good fortune to come easily.

Because they understand the unpredictability of life, March 27 individuals know that all dreams don't come true. This knowledge gives them the flexibility to adjust their goals to the prevailing reality.

EMBRACE
Teamwork
True love
Lost causes

AVOID
Insincerity
Being disillusioned
Trying too hard

ALSO BORN TODAY
Musician Tony Banks; singer Mariah Carey; actress Judy Carne; actress Maria Schneider; actress Gloria Swanson; film writer/director Quentin Tarantino; singer Sarah Vaughn; actor Michael York.

18

MARCH 28

The personality of March 28 individuals is bubbly, excitable, and somewhat unpredictable. They can be argumentative, but never to the point where it diminishes their great personal charm. At their core these people are thoughtful, meditative, and spiritual. They spend a great deal of time and effort balancing these conflicting qualities.

FRIENDS AND LOVERS There is often a note of obsession in the lives of March 28 individuals, which shows itself in their relationships. Friendships can be as fervent as love affairs to these people, yet can often be troubled and complicated by frequent misunderstandings.

People born on this date find their true, core selves in love. They often love idealistically, only to be disappointed when they discover that the object of their romantic obsession is less than perfect.

CHILDREN AND FAMILY March 28 individuals are the keepers of family secrets. They have a sixth sense about such matters and possess the ability to anticipate the concerns and needs of those close to them.

People born on this date share an almost spooky closeness with their children, who see them from a somewhat exaggerated perspective. March 28 people may appear to be dominant in their maternal or paternal roles, but the purity of their motives can never be questioned.

HEALTH Any health problems experienced by people born on this date are likely to be the result of personal and work-related stress. If these individuals don't maintain a regular exercise regimen they could be troubled with insomnia or bad dreams.

March 28 individuals have extremely sensitive skin and can be troubled with rashes brought on by allergies. Women born on this date may have bad reactions to perfume or cosmetics. Drinking at least eight glasses of water each day helps to flush out toxins.

CAREER AND FINANCES Individuals born on this date have a reputation for changing jobs and even careers with great frequency. This is because they have an emotional stake in their profession, and if it ceases to resonate with the meaningfulness they need to feel good about themselves, it is time to move on to something else.

March 28 people have only the sketchiest idea of what constitutes good financial acumen, but they seem to have good luck with money despite this fact. This includes moderately profitable stabs at games of chance. An inheritance often plays a financial role in their later years.

DREAMS AND GOALS Many of the goals important to March 28 people are spiritual goals which, because of their deeply personal significance, may be kept secret from friends, family, and associates.

Though they may not have a specific goal in mind, March 28 people are on a constant pilgrimage to improve their lives in every way. They invariably draw others into this personal commitment to excellence, inspiring them in ways no one else could.

EMBRACE
Opportunity
Making good choices
Honest emotion

AVOID
Putting yourself first
Demanding perfection
Being petty

ALSO BORN TODAY
Novelist Russell Banks; actor Dirk Bogarde; actor Ken Howard; singer Reba McEntire; Renaissance artist Raphael (Raffaello Santi); actress Flora Robson; pianist Rudolf Serkin; actress Dianne Wiest.

MARCH 29

P There is a poetic quality to the people born on this day, a sense of combining the insubstantial with the corporeal. They have the ability to transcend the ordinary aspects of their personality by drawing upon a penetrating intelligence and extraordinary gifts of intuition.

March 29 individuals do not always realize they are making a determination by instinct rather than intelligence. Because they are so sensitive to the thoughts and projections of others, they operate on a level comparable to ESP.

EMBRACE
Treating others fairly
Being generous
Giving compliments

AVOID
Envy
Wishing ill to others
Wasting time

ALSO BORN TODAY
Composer Richard Rodney Bennett; tennis star Jennifer Capriati; actor Bud Cort; comedian Eric Idle; actor Christopher Lambert; pianist Rosina Lhevinne; baseball star Denny McLain; composer William Walton.

FRIENDS AND LOVERS Those born on March 29 are incredibly connected to the people in their lives. Friendship has a special meaning for them, and they wisely choose their friends from people who are as different from themselves as possible.

They are similarly attracted to romantic partners who have different life experiences and different values than their own. March 29 individuals see love as an opportunity to grow emotionally and spiritually, to learn lessons they may be unable to learn on their own.

CHILDREN AND FAMILY Individuals born on this date experience a close personal tie to their mother or a mother figure encountered later in life. The men are especially sensitive to feminine issues and are regarded by female relatives as something of a protector.

March 29 individuals take their responsibilities as parents very seriously. They are more than caregivers or authority figures to their children, preferring to be close on many levels.

HEALTH People born on this day have a tendency to suffer from nervous complaints like headaches, sleep disorders, and general malaise. Because they are not likely to be physically robust, they need to find ways to boost their endurance. Yoga offers just the right balance of physical and spiritual involvement to provide a harmonious blending of the two disciplines.

It is important for March 29 people to add fresh fruit and vegetable juices to their diet each day to ensure an abundance of vitamins and minerals.

CAREER AND FINANCES Individuals born on this day gravitate toward professions that allow them to utilize their powerful mental gifts and astounding nonverbal communication skills. Since they seem to almost read people's minds, they do well in professions that probe the human psyche: psychology, psychiatry, or marriage and family counseling. Their ability to divine the motives of others makes them especially good at management or supervisory positions.

March 29 individuals are not particularly adept at managing money, though their intuitive skills can pay off on occasion. However, gambling should be avoided.

DREAMS AND GOALS People born on this date want to understand life's mysteries. In order to make this dream come true, they spend a great deal of time reading and meditating. If religion is important in the lives of these individuals, they may seek to explore their life path through this means.

MARCH 30

People born on March 30 are renowned for their sense of humor. These are bold, generous people who live life to the fullest and who are never afraid to take chances on their self-appointed path to wisdom and enlightenment.

March 30 natives are enthusiastic and dynamic individuals who have the ability to spur others to action. They make fine mentors and will go to any lengths to help friends and associates attain their goals.

FRIENDS AND LOVERS The jovial countenance of March 30 people wins them friends from all walks of life. They seem to "collect" pals without considering whether or not they complement their own personality or character.

March 30 individuals are often very lucky in love, but they are also practical people who do not need to connect to a "soul mate" in order to be happy. Because of their sparkling personality traits, they easily attract the attention of potential love interests.

CHILDREN AND FAMILY People born on March 30 often come from a large and loving family circle. They take great pride in their heritage and may identify strongly with one or more of their interesting forebears.

March 30 individuals continue this cycle of ancestor appreciation with their children. They love to tell interesting stories from their own childhood. Since people born on this date possess a charming naivete, they have no difficulty becoming part of a child's world. Imagination and a genuine curiosity about life unite March 30 people with children of all ages.

HEALTH Individuals born on this date often behave as if they think themselves invulnerable to illness. They do everything in a big way, and to excess. But their habits, though extreme, are generally wholesome.

March 30 people have a competitive spirit and make laudable weekend athletes. They have strong legs and make especially good tennis and squash players.

CAREER AND FINANCES Entrepreneurial and ambitious, March 30 individuals set a professional course for themselves very early in life. They have a thirst for knowledge and flourish in an academic setting. These people make excellent teachers and have the ability to inspire others with their enthusiasm. On occasions when a love of food translates to gourmet skills, they can make top-flight chefs.

March 30 natives make no secret of the fact that they want money, and lots of it. Because they seem to have a golden touch where money is concerned, they make great financial managers.

DREAMS AND GOALS From the time they are children, March 30 people know what they want out of life. Even though they may end up taking a rather circuitous route to get where they are going, they have judgment enough to understand that sometimes the journey is more enlightening than the final destination.

March 30 individuals are emotionally flexible enough to understand that the dreams and goals of youth are sometimes replaced by other, more reachable ones later in life.

EMBRACE
Poignant reminiscences
Cheerfulness
Your special talent

AVOID
Hurtful criticism
Superficial friendships
Personality conflicts

ALSO BORN TODAY
Actor John Astin; actor Warren Beatty; musician Eric Clapton; singer Frankie Laine; actor Peter Marshall; playwright Sean O'Casey; actor Paul Reiser; artist Vincent van Gogh.

MARCH 31

The uniqueness of March 31 individuals owes itself in part to their ability to recognize unusual opportunities. These people always seem to be in the path of miraculous good fortune, but it is to their credit that when such a rendezvous takes place, they know how to benefit from it.

People born on March 31 have a great deal of charisma and can make things happen by the strength and force of their personality alone.

FRIENDS AND LOVERS People born on this date seem to draw controversy into their private lives without fail. They are natural rebels who attract eccentric, unusual types.

In romantic matters, March 31 people prefer the company of high-powered individuals who share their love of danger and the unexpected. At one time or another in life they are sure to make a totally unrealistic choice in a love match. When happily mated, they have the ability to keep even a long-running relationship fresh and exciting.

CHILDREN AND FAMILY March 31 individuals are basically unconventional in their approach to life, and this includes their dealings with family members. It is not unusual for them to be the standout in an otherwise mundane family group. They may even be characterized as the "black sheep" of the family.

Parenthood isn't compulsory for March 31 natives, but if they do choose to have children, they encourage them to be free-thinking and even a little rebellious. Although this sort of parent-child relationship may be contentious, it is never unrewarding.

HEALTH Given the unpredictability of their temperament, people born on this date have equally unconventional attitudes toward keeping fit. Their interest in maintaining healthy lifestyle choices seems to wax and wane repeatedly, often based upon their emotional state at the time.

March 31 people favor unusual diets and treatments to stay healthy. Vegetarianism, or at least a fondness for organically grown fruits and vegetables, appeals to their concept that "natural" is best.

CAREER AND FINANCES March 31 individuals do best in professions where their unique qualifications can be put to use. They work well on their own, or in situations where their talents can remain unsupervised.

People born on this date do equally well in artistic endeavors. They make fine actors, writers, craftspeople, and designers.

Money is rarely a consideration when these people choose a career. They prefer the freedom of setting their own standards, even if that means sacrificing potential financial gains.

DREAMS AND GOALS Although they may not always have specific goals in mind, March 31 individuals are ambitious about making their dreams become reality. They don't hold themselves to set standards, preferring to chart their own course.

Far from being concerned with their own success, March 31 individuals like to feel that their choices influence and even benefit mankind as a whole.

EMBRACE
Synergy
Faithfulness
Confidence

AVOID
Unpredictability for its own sake
Being late
Self-doubt

ALSO BORN TODAY
Musician Herb Alpert; actor Richard Chamberlain; designer Liz Claiborne; actor William Daniels; philosopher Rene Descartes; novelist John Fowles; actress Shirley Jones; athlete/actor Ed Marinaro.

APRIL 1

Despite their connection to this questionable "holiday," individuals born on this day are anything but fools. They are leaders, though not in the conventional sense of that word. Their quiet nature masks an ability to make the best of any situation, no matter how challenging or unpleasant it may be.

While April 1 people are frequently centered on their own concerns in the way most Aries natives are, they rarely ignore an opportunity to help or inspire others.

FRIENDS AND LOVERS

Those born on this day are sunny and enthusiastic about their relationships. They have a magnetic charisma; others feel good around them without even realizing why.

Romantic relationships are more complicated, but April 1 individuals never stop trying to make their love life work. They seem destined for disappointment on some level, since their idealism is rarely reflected in the actions of others. But despite such problems they continue to have an upbeat view of romance.

CHILDREN AND FAMILY

Individuals born on this day rely on the considerable love and support they receive from family members.

April 1 individuals make good parents. Even if they are not intimately involved in the day-to-day aspects of parenting, they never cease to act as emotional cheerleaders for their youngsters, though they are reticent about giving advice unless they are sought out to do so.

HEALTH

People born on this day don't know the meaning of the word relaxation. They are veritable human dynamos who were born with excess energy. Although they may not follow a prescribed health regimen, they are usually active, fit, and in excellent health well into old age.

The keynote to their physical well-being is their emotional health. If April 1 individuals lead unhappy or unfulfilled lives, their health is likely to suffer. Headaches, ulcers, and general malaise can result from emotional difficulties.

CAREER AND FINANCES

April 1 natives are natural go-getters who are adamant about making their mark. They generally have very definite career goals from an early age and will pursue these with amazing single-mindedness. Even if their path to success is rocky, they will keep on striving.

They have an ability for both making and losing a great deal of money. Their losses may come about because of their incredible generosity to friends and family members, and because they do not like to take advice.

DREAMS AND GOALS

"All the world's a stage" to April 1 individuals, who ultimately see themselves as players in a drama on a cosmic scale. They don't mind the ups and downs of life because they prefer to be caught up in extremes rather than dull routine.

April 1 natives have trouble admitting that certain goals have not materialized in their lives and may continue to expect success long after the cheering has died down and everyone else has gone home.

EMBRACE
Reality
Temperance
Generous impulses

AVOID
Being insincere
Hoping against hope
Valuing only what you can see

ALSO BORN TODAY
Guitarist Alan Blakley; comedian Sid Field; actress Ali MacGraw; actress Annette O'Toole; actress Jane Powell; composer Sergei Rachmaninov; actress Debbie Reynolds; mystery writer Edgar Wallace.

APRIL 2

Individuals born on this date walk a fine line between what they know of life and what they wish to be true. They possess uncanny powers of imagination and may spend a great deal of their life dreaming with eyes wide open.

April 2 people have a natural dignity that may cause them to seem standoffish to those who do not know them well. This reticence has a lordly resonance and creates an aura of specialness around them.

FRIENDS AND LOVERS

It is not easy for April 2 individuals to make friends. When they do, the relationship is often one-sided, with friends serving more in the role of loyal retainers instead of equals.

April 2 people are very discreet about their love life. They handle romantic disappointment well, looking at painful breakups as a way to learn more about themselves and their relationship to others.

CHILDREN AND FAMILY

People born on April 2 seem to sail through life without connecting deeply to others, particularly family members. Not given to emotional extremes, they are unlikely to cause either rancor or great love among siblings or other relatives.

These individuals have a casual, almost cold attitude toward their own children. Though they have great love for their offspring, they are more concerned with helping their youngsters to succeed on their own than in providing emotional support. While the children may appreciate this attitude once they're grown, they may feel emotionally neglected as little ones.

HEALTH

Those born on this date usually take a great interest in maintaining good health throughout their lives. They have the discipline that few others do, and will always find time to meet a workout commitment, no matter how many other things they have to accomplish.

They are not overly conscientious about diet, however, and may have an old-fashioned concept of what constitutes a proper eating plan. Too much red meat, alcohol, and rich desserts can be harmful to their skin and hair.

CAREER AND FINANCES

April 2 individuals are quite conservative in their approach to life. They don't like to take chances, and because of that their success is sometimes more limited than it should be. They are intelligent planners who don't mind taking the long route to their chosen profession. They believe that quality, not quantity, counts.

Because they can never quite believe in the constancy of their financial success, April 2 individuals are very careful about the way in which they handle money. They would rather save money than spend it.

DREAMS AND GOALS

As in other aspects of life, April 2 individuals keep a tight rein on their dreams and goals. They believe in their own ability to succeed and don't worry about how long it will take to achieve success.

They do not believe that anything happens by chance. A series of carefully planned moves and strategies helps them to achieve their life plans, and they will adhere stringently to those plans at any cost.

EMBRACE
Wholesome values
A spiritual path
Getting the most out of life

AVOID
Predictability
Jealous rages
Boredom

ALSO BORN TODAY
Writer Hans Christian Andersen; novelist Catherine Gaskin; Russian statesman Mikhail Gorbachev; actor Alec Guinness; actress Linda Hunt; actress Pamela Reed; musician Leon Russell; actor/director Jack Webb.

APRIL 3

People born on this date like to think of themselves as social rebels, but the truth is something quite different. These individuals always manage in some way to draw upon the resources of the status quo in order to fund or support their iconoclastic aims.

They have a broad view of life and see themselves as citizens of the world.

FRIENDS AND LOVERS April 3 people are never without friends. Their tolerant, positive attitude is an open invitation to everyone. Because of their great interest in helping the underdog, April 3 natives often surround themselves with people far less fortunate than themselves.

Individuals born on this day have considerable romantic appeal. They are great lovers who may have a difficult time settling on one special person as a companion. Though not naturally promiscuous, they do not like to limit themselves where love and sex are concerned.

CHILDREN AND FAMILY April 3 natives see themselves as part of one vast, collective, and extended family made up of relatives, friends, and even acquaintances. They do not normally distinguish between those individuals who are related to them by blood and others with whom they may merely share a special affinity.

Although they consider themselves excellent parents, April 3 people may fall short of their own expectations because they are far too idealistic. Since they are often very successful in business and social circles, these individuals can cast a long shadow. It may be hard for their children to escape it.

HEALTH Too much of a good thing is one way to characterize the health habits of April 3

people. They do everything in a big way, and that can include eating, drinking, and especially dieting. April 3 individuals seem to be on a perpetual diet. Because they love to eat, it is virtually impossible for them to adhere to a structured or limited eating plan.

People born on this day need to redefine their attitudes toward health and fitness, preferably by enrolling in a program that promotes moderation.

CAREER AND FINANCES Whether high rollers or two-dollar bettors, April 3 natives have a great love of gambling, and not just where money is concerned. They love taking chances in all avenues of life, and this includes the professional arena. High-stakes choices offer the thrills they seek and often dictate the type of career they will follow.

While April 3 individuals have the ability to make a great deal of money, they are just as likely to lose it.

DREAMS AND GOALS People born on April 3 find life's meaning through their cherished dreams. While others may find their life-goals far too ambitious, these individuals know better.

April 3 natives have a way of making the right choice at the right time. This often looks like good luck to others, but it is actually a sixth sense that is common to people born on this day.

EMBRACE
Empathy
Happy talk
Spiritual values

AVOID
An inability to love
Envy
Empty praise

ALSO BORN TODAY
Actor Alec Baldwin; actor Marlon Brando; singer/actress Doris Day; naturalist Jane Goodall; actress Marsha Mason; actor/comedian Eddie Murphy; singer Wayne Newton; musician Barry Pritchard.

25

APRIL 4

April 4 natives are marked from an early age by a quiet strength inherent in their personality. They possess the enviable talent of being able to be worldly and spiritual in equal measure. They inspire through example, yet never seek to force others into their way of thinking or behaving. A particular talent or ability is often the keystone of their nature, yet they prefer to see themselves as many-faceted rather than singularly directed.

FRIENDS AND LOVERS

April 4 individuals value their friends. They are far more likely to have a few close companions rather than large numbers of social acquaintances. Although they are kind and gentle, people born on this day do not share their feelings easily or comfortably with others.

Love is something of a mystery to these people. They don't like complicated relationships and often marry quite young. Their unflappable dispositions make them ideal companions, though they may be unable to detect boredom in their relationship after the flush of romance has worn off.

CHILDREN AND FAMILY

Those born on April 4 are often looked upon as "little mothers and fathers," even as children. They have a serious yet good-natured attitude that instantly commands respect. Their levelheaded way of dealing with problems belies their age.

Because of the heavy responsibilities placed on them in youth, many April 4 people do not seek parenthood, feeling that they have already experienced the event by proxy. Those who do have children of their own will usually be concerned with making their youngsters' lives less complicated and demanding than theirs were as children.

HEALTH

The health concerns of April 4 individuals can be traced to an inability to fully show or express their emotions. These individuals are generally so stalwart and uncomplaining that they rarely give their inner life the time and attention it requires.

Massage techniques, especially the treatment known as rolfing, can help April 4 individuals experience their true feelings and relieve their pain—and perhaps expel it forever.

CAREER AND FINANCES

Because April 4 individuals may not have a high opinion of their own abilities, they may settle for jobs that are far below their skill level. They are so accustomed to doing what is expected that they may not even realize that they are not living up to their full potential.

April 4 natives people can benefit from the attention of a mentor. They may also need financial advice, since they tend to have conservative views about money.

DREAMS AND GOALS

Those born on April 4 need to learn how to chase their dreams without feeling frivolous and self-centered. They are accustomed to doing what is right for everyone else; to deviate from this mindset can be a challenge. But once they untether their expectations, these individuals can soar.

April 4 natives respond well under pressure and can actually achieve more when the deck is stacked against them.

EMBRACE
Self-worth
Feeling good
The high road

AVOID
Trespassing on someone's feelings
Arbitration
Empty calories

ALSO BORN TODAY
Poet Maya Angelou; composer Elmer Bernstein; actor Robert Downey, Jr.; baseball star Gil Hodges; writer Kitty Kelley; actress Christine Lahti; actor Craig T. Nelson; actor/screenwriter Anthony Perkins.

APRIL 5

Those born on April 5 are the natural aristocrats among people. They have a high opinion of themselves and may even be self-centered to the point of egotism, although that attitude in no way influences their ability to interact with others or to be likeable.

April 5 individuals possess a sense of destiny regarding their actions and may often find themselves involved in unusual or extreme circumstances at some point in life. Their best trait is unabashed honesty.

FRIENDS AND LOVERS No matter how many friends April 5 individuals collect, they will always look to themselves for answers and inspiration. They value friends but are not likely to ask for or accept advice of any kind.

Temperamental by nature, April 5 natives make emotionally combative lovers. These people think nothing of fighting or reconciling with a lover in a public setting. They are honest about their feelings, and if they tire of a love relationship they will not hesitate to share that information with their lover.

CHILDREN AND FAMILY Individuals born on April 5 may have a contentious relationship with family members. This may be based upon an atmosphere of competition fostered during their growing-up years.

April 5 natives make loving but demanding parents. They have great plans for their offspring and may find it difficult to understand if a son or daughter harbors more modest aims. This could cause a period of estrangement between April 5 individuals and their adult children

HEALTH Those born on this day have a great abundance of energy, and illnesses are rare. They don't pamper themselves and enjoy flying in the face of controversy, often burning the candle at both ends.

Because of their mercurial disposition, overwork may bring migraine headaches or mental exhaustion.

April 5 individuals are moderate eaters, though they may overindulge in smoking or alcohol. To retain their natural good health they need to drink an abundance of water each day and refrain from taking in too much caffeine.

CAREER AND FINANCES Because of their ability to manage money, April 5 people often seek careers in accounting, bank management, or finance. They aren't as interested in accumulating money for themselves as they are in displaying their abilities in managing the financial affairs of others. Honesty and integrity underscore their professional efforts.

Money is an abstraction to these people and is rarely an enticement to follow a particular career path. They have a lively intelligence and curiosity, which makes them fine educators, particularly at the university level.

DREAMS AND GOALS April 5 individuals believe that there is nothing they cannot achieve if they work hard and plan well. They don't look for success and good fortune to fall from the sky; instead, they're willing to sacrifice to make their dreams come true.

EMBRACE
Vitality
Well-wishers
Your soul mate

AVOID
Self-pity
Capriciousness
Questioning existence

ALSO BORN TODAY
Writer Robert Bloch; film director/producer Roger Corman; actress Bette Davis; writer Mary Hemingway; actor Gregory Peck; U.S. Army General Colin Powell; poet Algernon Swinburne; symphony conductor Herbert von Karajan.

APRIL 6

Creativity and imagination of the highest level characterize those born on April 6. They are enormously talented and will use that talent as a means to express their life energy.

An element of illusion runs through their lives like a radiant thread. They have the ability to convince others of their opinions and aims, yet the manner in which they accomplish this is subtle, and generally is displayed rather than uttered. They have true "star quality."

FRIENDS AND LOVERS

Because of their pleasant nature, April 5 individuals have a genius for making friends. They are sociable people who enjoy, though do not require, the company of diverse companions.

April 6 individuals have an extremely powerful love nature; romance is often the central focus of their lives. They are romantics at heart who do not allow disappointments in love to amend their view that true love is not only possible, but necessary for their own emotional well-being. Even if they are not especially attractive they cast a spell over others and have the ability to draw the attention of many potential lovers.

CHILDREN AND FAMILY

Men and women born on this day have a deeply nurturing spirit. They revel in family life and often imbue it with their own deeply religious or spiritual qualities.

Even if April 6 individuals remain childless, they will in some way bring young people into their circle. This may be accomplished through adoption, foster-parent programs, or by shouldering the responsibilities of coaching a local sports team or dance program.

HEALTH

April 6 people have a delicate constitution, though they may appear vibrant. Often this natural glow is actually a reflection of a deep inner life. They crave harmony in all aspects of life and may become ill easily if they are placed in circumstances where their sensibilities are assaulted by anger, negativity, or emotional upset.

The skin is a good barometer for the health of April 6 people. If their diet is poor their skin will take on a dull or pallid appearance.

CAREER AND FINANCES

No matter what career April 6 individuals choose, there will always be some element of artistry involved, for they are naturally artistic and must find a way to express this attribute. Drawing, painting, dancing, acting, or design work of any kind suit their talents.

While they are not especially good handlers of money, they do have a sense of profound responsibility when it comes to managing finances.

DREAMS AND GOALS

April 6 individuals want to be happy. All other goals are secondary. They must feel as if they are contributing to the betterment of those around them, and that what they do touches others.

People born on this date are optimistic and see all goals as attainable. They have faith that the good they do will be returned to them, and for this reason they make it their business to promote a positive attitude in all areas of life.

EMBRACE
Good luck
Spiritual transcendence
Integrity

AVOID
Constant worry
Superficial relationships
Gossip

ALSO BORN TODAY
Comedian/magician Paul Daniels; actress Marilu Henner; illusionist Harry Houdini; actor Walter Huston; figure skating champion Janet Lynn; composer/conductor Andre Previn; musician John Stax; actor Billy Dee Williams.

APRIL 7

Individuals born on April 7 believe deeply in the ability of good to overcome evil. They are a fascinating combination of dreamer and doer, and will always put their talents to work in improving the conditions of those around them. They are incredibly involved with their inner life, yet may express themselves on a grand, even global scale. Because they are essentially without ego, they have the ability to understand the feelings of others.

FRIENDS AND LOVERS
Because they have the ability to become involved in the problems and concerns of others while withholding judgment, April 7 people often have a huge circle of friends. They inspire and in turn are inspired by the people in their lives.

April 7 natives may fall in love many times, yet each time it is a fresh experience. They will always place the feelings of a lover before their own concerns. When a romance ends they will grieve for it but will never hold a lover accountable.

CHILDREN AND FAMILY
Those born on this date have a way of rewriting the circumstances of their family life if the truth doesn't fit their mental image of how it should be. Because it is easy for these imaginative people to seek solace in fantasy, this method of dealing with the past can actually heal their emotional and spiritual wounds.

April 7 individuals like to feel as if they have the ability to inspire their children to live life on their own terms, and not those of the parents. Although this could mean their offspring follow a divergent path, they are accepting as long as it makes their children happy.

HEALTH
Though they are physically healthy, April 7 individuals can suffer moodiness and depression on occasions when their search for truth conflicts with reality.

These individuals benefit from vigorous exercise at least three or four times a week, in order to restore energy and lift boredom or gloom. Because they are extremely sensitive to the effects of pills and alcohol, they should stay away from both.

CAREER AND FINANCES
Great accomplishments and profound disappointments are often the experience of people born on this day. They seem unable to walk the middle road or take the path of least resistance.

April 7 individuals are climbers in the best sense of that word. They cannot be content simply having a job that provides the necessities of life. They need a career as a vehicle to project their will upon the world.

Politics is a good and satisfying arena for people born on this day.

DREAMS AND GOALS
April 7 individuals enjoy living large. Their dreams and goals, like every other facet of their lives, are played out on a huge scale and with drama to spare. Despite delays, they rarely lose sight of their ambitions.

Although practicality is not usually one of their virtues, April 7 people can put this skill to work if their desire to succeed is great enough. With a little patience and a lot of organization they can achieve their goals.

EMBRACE
A new you
Seeing the glass half full
Artistic integrity

AVOID
Empty promises
Selling yourself short
Fatalism

ALSO BORN TODAY
Film director Francis Ford Coppola; football star Tony Dorsett; TV host David Frost; singer Janis Ian; actress Elaine Miles; singer/guitarist John Oates; actor Andrew Sachs; poet William Wordsworth.

29

APRIL 8

Those born on April 8 are fighters. Despite a pleasing personality they have steel at their core, and they never miss a chance to learn from their mistakes or miscalculations. They may be regarded as potential movers and shakers, though their interests are often on a more limited scale. They don't see themselves as catalysts for change but will endeavor to right a wrong if an opportunity presents itself.

FRIENDS AND LOVERS Even though they make admirable friends and counselors, those born on April 8 never judge themselves by their ability to attract others. They may feel uncomfortable among those who regard them in a too-flattering or subservient manner.

April 8 individuals value love but will never place their complete faith in it. They are too self-sufficient to expect the love of another person to make them more fulfilled. Fidelity is an important factor in a relationship for April 8 individuals, and they will demand it from their mates. Once their trust has been breached, they will lose interest in the transgressor.

CHILDREN AND FAMILY Individuals born on this day see themselves as the ultimate authority figure. This may be a result of conditioning from childhood, when they were forced to grow up early and quicker than their years.

April 8 natives expect a great deal from their own children. They are strict disciplinarians who may occasionally seem cold and unforgiving of the mistakes of their offspring. Actually, this is only an affectation to help enforce the lessons they believe their children must learn to succeed and prosper in a difficult and challenging world.

HEALTH People born on April 8 are sticklers for good health and fitness practices. They possess a natural athletic ability as well as formidable mental and spiritual endurance. They can work for long stretches without taking a break and not feel the effects.

April 8 individuals require extra calcium to ward off brittle bones and arthritic conditions that may appear later in life. They benefit from a diet high in protein and B-complex vitamins.

CAREER AND FINANCES People born on this day are specialists. They may be good at many things, but they choose a career where they can achieve perfection, or something very close to it. Research, especially within the boundaries of science and medicine, appeals to their sense of order and balance.

Money is not a vital part of the equation for these people, but it does relate to their ambition to succeed. Practical in all aspects of life, they handle money well and with a certain flair, though they do not take risks with what they have worked so hard to earn.

DREAMS AND GOALS April 8 natives believe in their ability to accomplish whatever goals they value. Even though they face enormous challenges, they do not give up and they do not complain.

The moral and spiritual sturdiness of these individuals is a positive factor as they strive to achieve their life-dreams. They bow to Providence, but there is not one human being who can convince them that a goal is unreachable.

EMBRACE
Bonding with loved ones
Trust
Entertainment

AVOID
Promiscuity
Insensitivity
Burning your bridges

ALSO BORN TODAY
Actress Patricia Arquette; singer Roger Chapman; First Lady Betty Ford; basketball star John Havlicek; figure skating champion Sonia Henie; musician Steve Howe; singer/songwriter Julian Lennon; actor Edward Mulhare.

APRIL 9

Feisty and opinionated, people born on April 9 see life as a series of missions, some of which are successful, some of which fail. More pragmatic than idealistic, these people enjoy striving almost as much as the victories their efforts bring. When push comes to shove, April 9 individuals seem to be spoiling for a fight.

Their intrepid nature makes them virtual pioneers who are not afraid to challenge the status quo. April 9 people know what they want out of life and aren't afraid to go after it.

FRIENDS AND LOVERS

The gregarious nature of April 9 individuals goes a long way toward explaining why they are so often in demand, both socially and personally. These people are intensely loyal and will always stand by a friend, especially one who is in trouble.

The love nature of April 9 individuals is strong and uncomplicated. They exude a powerful sexual magnetism and have no trouble attracting lovers. Despite this, they are faithful mates who understand the consequences of dabbling in superficial sexual relationships.

CHILDREN AND FAMILY

People born on April 9 have a traditional, even old-fashioned view of family life. They enjoy being part of a domestic structure, and realize the importance of strong family ties.

April 9 individuals teach their own children the rules and values they were taught by their own parents. They like large families, feeling it is unfair for a child to grow up without siblings.

HEALTH

With energy to burn, April 9 individuals manage to enjoy exceptionally good health even though they seldom take care of themselves in any meaningful way. It is their positive attitude, rather than any systemized behavior pattern, which keeps them active and able when others their age have begun to slow down.

CAREER AND FINANCES

Individuals born on April 9 may not settle on a career until their middle or late twenties, after having tried a great many options. They like sampling jobs and careers, suspending judgment until they find something that suits their need for challenge and adventure.

Their ability to make money may also be latent during their youth. If they happen to inherit money or are the beneficiaries of family wealth, they are likely to use that money in ways other family members consider frivolous, even foolish. But these people know what they are doing and can eventually reap a fortune from a modest investment.

DREAMS AND GOALS

Despite their intellectual savvy, April 9 people have a naive and even childlike belief that dreams can come true. Because of their insistence on accentuating the positive, it often may not even occur to them that a much-prized goal may not materialize. When this does happen, as it must on occasion, April 9 natives are unruffled, considering this temporary setback as a mere inconvenience.

People born on this day have the instinct to challenge conventional wisdom.

EMBRACE
Going the distance
Peace and joy
Good taste

AVOID
Looking back
Saying, "I told you so"
Blaming others

ALSO BORN TODAY
Poet Charles Baudelaire; actor Jean-Paul Belmando; publisher Hugh Hefner; musician Mark Kelly; actress Michael Learned; singer/songwriter Carl Perkins; actor Dennis Quaid; actress Dorothy Tutin.

APRIL 10

April 10 people are fighters, though their sunny personalities may obscure this fact. These individuals have their own way of doing things and refuse to change their attitudes in order to accommodate others. Though they manage to accomplish their aims in the nicest possible way, there is never any doubt about how ambitious these people are.

Individuals born on this date have the capacity to see the world around them realistically, without letting that knowledge cause disillusionment.

FRIENDS AND LOVERS Joy is the keynote of the personal relationships of April 10 natives. They truly love people and consider their associations with friends, loved ones, and lovers to be among the peak experiences of their life.

Where romance is concerned, these people definitely have a penchant for experimentation. They aren't afraid to get involved with someone who is as different from themselves as day from night, and even when a romance fails they can see the value of lessons learned. People born on April 10 have no problem remaining friends with ex-lovers.

CHILDREN AND FAMILY April 10 people don't rely on family members to give them a sense of identity and value, yet they do experience a certain amount of growth through personal involvement with others. People born on this date make somewhat unconventional parents. They are loving and indulgent, perhaps to excess.

HEALTH A positive mental attitude is necessary for April 10 individuals if they are to create a healthy lifestyle for themselves. They are energetic, active people who generally look on the bright side.

Since April 10 people are somewhat excitable and high-strung, they should avoid talking about unpleasant subjects while eating, or shortly before bedtime. Because their dream life is an important factor in their physical and emotional well-being, people born on this date depend upon their nightly revels to keep their energies perfectly balanced.

CAREER AND FINANCES There is no doubt that April 10 individuals like to have attention paid to their efforts. They are not happy working alone or behind the scenes, since this offers virtually no chance for validation by colleagues or outsiders. As bosses, they are demanding, yet fair.

If April 10 people set out to make a large amount of money they are likely to succeed in doing it, yet if they are sufficiently fulfilled by the work they do, money may not be an issue.

DREAMS AND GOALS From the time they first decide upon a career, April 10 individuals have very specific goals and plans. This mindset may vary somewhat as time goes on, but it will never be abandoned.

April 10 individuals have more credulity than they will admit to, and they possess a considerable belief in the natural goodness of the universe to intervene on their behalf. When good things happen to them they feel obligated to bestow good fortune on someone else.

EMBRACE
Simplicity
Living in the now
Friendliness

AVOID
Manipulative people
Indiscretions
Giving in too easily

ALSO BORN TODAY
Ambassador/writer Clare Booth Luce; actor Peter MacNichol; coach/TV announcer John Madden; football star/TV announcer Don Meredith; actor Steven Seagal; musician Brian Setzer; actor Omar Sharif; singer Bobbie Smith.

APRIL 11

Good-hearted and daring, people born on this date have the potential to do a great deal of good in the world. Whether they seek the broad arena of political activism or confine their involvement to their proverbial "own backyard," April 11 natives display the care and compassion that is often missing from human endeavors.

FRIENDS AND LOVERS

Those born on April 11 have democratic attitudes regarding companions. They like to surround themselves with equals—partners who share their sense of commitment to their own goals and causes.

For these individuals there is a thin line between love and friendship. Friends may become lovers, and lovers may become friends.

When they do decide to marry, April 11 individuals make extraordinarily understanding and nurturing mates.

CHILDREN AND FAMILY

While they can't help trying to take the lead in all relationships, these individuals are also anxious to absorb the life philosophies of those who are closest to them.

As parents they prefer to let their children have an incredible amount of leeway. April 11 individuals believe in discipline, but not punishment. While others may question this method, it cannot be denied that people born on this date enjoy a close relationship with their children, even after the "little ones" have left the nest.

HEALTH

Few people can claim such vibrant good health as those born on April 11. They seem to radiate energy and high spirits from within, and rarely, if ever, seem to be their true age. In youth they appear wise and sophisticated beyond their years, but once middle age creeps up, they're active, wide-eyed teenagers again.

April 11 natives take particular care with their appearance and endorse a regular exercise regimen. Because of their highly excitable nature, they should refrain from drinking caffeinated beverages.

CAREER AND FINANCES

People born on this day treat their job as a crusade. Whether they are in a position to effect change on a minor level or a very large scale, they will do their best to make the world better through their actions.

April 11 individuals can become exceptional politicians, lawyers, social workers, and teachers. Generally, their career choice is determined by political or ethical considerations, but regardless of what position they hold, money is never a factor in determining their selection.

DREAMS AND GOALS

April 11 people believe in their own ability to change the world. When they are very young, they are overly idealistic, yet even as they mature and lose a few of their illusions these individuals retain a positive attitude.

Even if specific goals go unfulfilled, people born on this day know how to turn a negative experience into a lesson learned. April 11 individuals believe in themselves, but they are even more adamant about their belief in the basic goodness of those around them.

EMBRACE
The rights of others
The pleasure of giving
Enthusiasm

AVOID
Needing approval
Focusing on weakness
Controversy

ALSO BORN TODAY
Musician Stuart Adamson; designer Oleg Cassini; actor Joel Grey; actor Bill Irwin; Ethel Kennedy; actress Louise Lasser; actor Peter Riegert; singer/songwriter Lisa Stansfield.

APRIL 12

Armed with considerable intelligence, curiosity, and plenty of drive, people born on April 12 are in a class by themselves. They are philosophical types who prize learning, yet do not confuse it with wisdom. Students of the human condition, they are keen observers who can easily spot deception in a colleague or associate.

April 12 people have a genuine gift for enjoying life, and their ability to laugh at themselves is laudable and refreshing.

FRIENDS AND LOVERS

People born on this date make interesting choices in their relationships with others. They are often perceived as being the "senior partner" in a friendship or love relationship, generally because the avuncular or maternal role comes naturally to them. They thrive in relationships where mutual trust and emotional support are paramount factors.

These individuals are not the tragic-lover types. They seek joy and positivity in a romantic relationship and will leave any association that promotes dependency or misunderstanding. The typical April 12 native is likely to marry a much younger person.

CHILDREN AND FAMILY

Family life has a pleasant significance for April 12 individuals, who understand that their greatest life-lessons come through understanding and rediscovering their familial ties.

These people see parenthood as a sacred trust. No matter how much they love their youngsters, April 12 individuals understand that children are only lent, not given. When their children become old enough to register disagreement or even defiance, they accept it with grace.

HEALTH

Because they are such emotional creatures, April 12 natives draw energy from the influences that surround them. As long as they're happy and emotionally fulfilled, people born on this date need not worry about health problems, with the sole exception of possible effects from too much rich food and drink.

Moderate exercise is suggested to keep these individuals fit, since they may suffer from circulatory problems if they are sedentary.

CAREER AND FINANCES

April 12 individuals love the good life. They like nice things, comfortable surroundings, and all the benefits of traveling "first cabin." Because of this, they often pursue high-paying careers.

Money has great significance for these men and women, because they want to make a comfortable life for themselves and their family members. April 12 natives are extremely generous and aspire to give the people they love the best of everything. They tend to have a blind spot about investments and savings, and will benefit from advice from a professional.

DREAMS AND GOALS

People born on this day seek to coalesce their materialistic and spiritual aims, making them one. They do not see their life goals in terms of separate and distinctive endeavors, but as a broad system of experience.

When these folks decide upon a goal and make a commitment to it, they possess the will and ambition to make it a reality.

EMBRACE
The joy of giving
Graceful words
Daily affirmations

AVOID
Buying on credit
Placing blame
Seeing life from a single point of view

ALSO BORN TODAY
Playwright Alan Ayckbourn; personality Jeremy Beadle; actress Claire Danes; country singer Vince Gill; actress Shannen Doherty; dancer/actress Ann Miller; actor Andy Garcia; TV host David Letterman; dancer Ann Miller.

APRIL 13

There is definitely a spark of genius in those born on April 13. These are not showy individuals, but people who prefer existence in a humble, even obscure setting. Although they would never seek fame, it sometimes finds them, and when it does, it acts as a profound disruption in their lives.

There is nothing ordinary about these individuals, yet they have little ego about their talents. They consider themselves at the service of others.

FRIENDS AND LOVERS The analytic characteristics of April 13 individuals can make them seem rather cold in the way they interact with friends and romantic partners. Although this does not represent disinterest on their part, it is often perceived as such. Many April 13 people experience problems in a relationship because they're not as attentive as friends or lovers would like them to be.

Romance may not be the most important factor in the lives of April 13 people, but they do work very hard at it. They are happiest with a partner who understands their need to be free and autonomous.

CHILDREN AND FAMILY The iconoclastic, sometimes rebellious attitudes of April 13 people can be a bone of contention in family life. Because they are determined to walk their own path, they often find themselves in conflict with time-honored family traditions and values.

Although likely to be far more liberal in the way they bring up their own children, people born on this date may have a rude awakening when they discover that their kids are as anxious to do things their own way as they were!

HEALTH Nervous complaints, often stomach-related, are the typical health issues faced by April 13 people. Seminars in stress management can help these edgy people.

People born on this date have a tendency to eat on the run, which is very bad for digestive problems that may already exist. They do best on a bland and moderate diet.

CAREER AND FINANCES To people born on April 13, a career is more than a way to make a living or even express their own talents—it's a destination. Although not known for grandiose plans—indeed, there may be no plan at all—these folks have a burning sense that they must be allowed to learn, discover, and explore.

They may or may not be interested in making money through their efforts, but when they do, it often arrives as a result of a special gift they possess, which catapults them to success.

DREAMS AND GOALS Never passive, April 13 natives go after what they want. Success and achievement may be rather abstract and arbitrary terms to them, but they realize that life is a game with many rules.

Often these individuals pursue humanitarian goals that are unrelated to their own life or happiness. While it can be difficult for them to compromise their ideals, they will make small ideological concessions in the name of the greater good.

EMBRACE
An interest in others
Seeing life through rose-colored glasses
Long-range goals

AVOID
Family disputes
Being a people-pleaser
Arrogance

ALSO BORN TODAY
U.S. President Thomas Jefferson; playwright Samuel Beckett; actor Jack Cassidy; singer Al Green; singer/actor Howard Keel; British statesman Lord North; actress Jane Leeves; actor Paul Sorvino.

APRIL 14

The great desire of April 14 individuals is to forge a oneness between mind and spirit. They are highly evolved, emphatically intelligent people who are never afraid to question, to search, to dream.

They are capable of doing great things in life, yet they also have the ability to fail spectacularly, even foolishly. The importance to them isn't in the act, but in how they can translate the experience into an illuminating life lesson.

FRIENDS AND LOVERS
People born on this date seek out companions who can provide the experience they lack. For this reason they are likely to draw their friends from all walks of life.

In love matters they may be more conventional, choosing a partner who is sympathetic and tender. Men and women born on this date need to feel emotionally protected and nurtured by their mate, especially when a personal crisis threatens. They enjoy sharing an intellectual partnership with their lover.

CHILDREN AND FAMILY
This is an area of life that is exceptionally important to people born on this date. They draw a good deal of their strength from the family values they learned as children, and from the parents or parental figures who shaped their lives and choices.

April 14 natives are profoundly influenced by their own role as a parent and may consider it their most important and worthwhile undertaking. They expect a lot from their children but have the good sense not to be preachy.

HEALTH
They may bloom with vitality, yet there is a sense of fragility at the core of April 14 individuals that inspires friends and loved ones to care for them, even spoil them with acts of kindness.

Sleep disorders, particularly insomnia, can be a problem. To ease this condition, they should limit the amount of television they watch, especially in the evening hours. A half hour of meditation before bed is far more relaxing and beneficial.

CAREER AND FINANCES
The joy and turmoil of a professional career can be the spiritual undoings of April 14 people, and no matter how much they love their work it does have the potential to become a burden to them. Because of this, it's beneficial for these folks to change careers, perhaps more than once.

Money can be another complication, particularly if they have too much of it! April 14 individuals don't need a lot of material representations of success to make them feel good about themselves.

DREAMS AND GOALS
To be content, to be simply happy and at peace emotionally with oneself and the whole world, may seem a naive, even impossible set of expectations. Yet this is what April 14 natives crave above all else.

It isn't strange for these people to walk away from a successful career or relationship when they find it too stressful and complicated to maintain. It isn't about money or possessions or accomplishments; without the spiritual clarity April 14 natives require, they will never have what they truly want.

EMBRACE
A rage to live
Being yourself
Laughter

AVOID
Taking things too seriously
Antagonism
Brooding over disappointments

ALSO BORN TODAY
Haitian dictator "Papa Doc" Duvalier; actress Julie Christie; singer Loretta Lynn; actor Bradford Dillman; baseball star Pete Rose; actor John Gielgud; UFOlogist/writer Erich von Daniken; actor Rod Steiger.

APRIL 15

K eeping a balance between the need to be forceful and assertive, while making their world more beautiful and harmonious can be a tall order for those born on April 15. This trait draws these individuals into mild controversy their entire lives.

Gifted and intuitive, April 15 people gain inspiration from the natural world. Even though they have a tendency to accumulate material possessions, they are far more in tune with the meaningful aspects of life.

FRIENDS AND LOVERS
Those born on April 15 are inveterate people-pleasers who are sometimes willing to sacrifice honesty in a relationship in order to maintain the status quo.

April 15 individuals give their whole heart and soul to matters of the heart. They often marry young and experience a great deal of their personal growth and emotional maturation within the boundaries of a marital union. It is rare for these individuals to seek a divorce, even in extreme circumstances.

CHILDREN AND FAMILY
A childlike innocence in the character of April 15 people makes them the darlings of their family circle. Their sweetness, generosity, and kindness earn high points with loved ones.

As parents, people born on April 15 have extraordinary abilities, though they find it hard to enforce discipline and have a reputation for "sparing the rod." These individuals believe in total involvement with the social and educational portions of their children's lives.

Their only expectation is their children's happiness.

HEALTH
April 15 people have a propensity toward lethargy. Although naturally healthy and robust, they tend to favor a sedentary lifestyle. That's comfy in the short term, but can have negative long-term repercussions.

When attempting to lose weight, individuals born on this date should stay away from fad diets and other quick-fix solutions. A balanced diet high in protein and low in carbohydrates can be a successful alternative for them.

CAREER AND FINANCES
Even though April 15 individuals are not especially driven in career matters, they require a harmonious working environment with colleagues who are pleasant and helpful. Because of their creative streak and artistic aspirations, they do well in careers that allow them to exhibit these skills, such as advertising, architecture, and design.

April 15 individuals are fortunate where money matters are concerned. They have the ability to attract resources without working hard to obtain them, and they may benefit through a legacy or financial windfall at some point in their lives.

DREAMS AND GOALS
April 15 individuals aspire to be loved. These people rely upon the acceptance of those who are dear to them.

People born on this date become more ambitious as they grow older; in later years they're likely to involve themselves in a succession of goal-oriented activities that could include going back to school, a radical career change, or a profound spiritual transformation.

EMBRACE
Cheerfulness
Forgiveness
Your own limitations

AVOID
Bragging
Self-absorption
Indecision

ALSO BORN TODAY
Novelist Jeffrey Archer; actress Claudia Cardinale; singer Roy Clark; artist Leonardo da Vinci; snooker champion Joe Davis; novelist Henry James; actress Elizabeth Montgomery; actress/screenwriter Emma Thompson.

APRIL 16

Individuals born on this date have a great need to explore their world through a prism of altered reality. This has a wide variety of possibilities, including the use of stimulants to achieve a level of imagined perfection.

April 16 people are never content to keep their life-view to themselves but must share it through career achievements or personal relationships.

FRIENDS AND LOVERS

It is through their relationships with others that people born on April 16 come to understand their own inner drives. They choose companions who have qualities that they lack and seek to incorporate into their own lives.

Love is an extended learning experience for April 16 natives. They may subconsciously draw difficulties into their romantic relationships in order to extract the maximum amount of wisdom from the experience. Even when they settle into a committed relationship they find themselves testing its boundaries, as if to discover how lasting it truly is.

CHILDREN AND FAMILY

The highly imaginative powers of April 16 individuals make them children at heart no matter what their age. Even if they are not the "baby" of the family, their ingenuous personality has a way of endearing them to even the sternest relative.

The powerful psychic bond that exists between April 16 individuals and their children serves to resolve some of the difficult issues from their own growing-up years. There may be periods of estrangement between April 16 people and their adult children, but never for very long.

HEALTH

Because their systems are extremely sensitive to pills and alcohol, April 16 individuals should keep their diet as pure as possible. The integration of mental, physical, and emotional health works best for them; the absence of one may create a harmonic imbalance that can lead to fatigue or imagined illnesses.

A positive mental attitude is a must for April 16 natives.

CAREER AND FINANCES

There is often a sense of destiny in the career choices made by April 16 people, almost as if the profession chose them instead of the other way around. They need to feel as if their personal vision is reflected in the work they do, and that the world—or at least their own particular corner of it—is enriched as a result.

April 16 individuals are notoriously unconcerned with making money and may even unconsciously subvert their own efforts in that regard. People born on this date should stay away from gambling, since it can become an obsession.

DREAMS AND GOALS

April 16 individuals need to shine in the spotlight, even if only on a very small scale. Because they believe they have a lot to offer, these people often seek to fulfill their goals via a public forum.

They have an agenda and aren't afraid to advertise it. They want to reach the top and will work very hard to do so. This includes their spiritual journey as well as lesser, material goals.

EMBRACE
Fantasies
Musicality
Taking chances

AVOID
Needing to win
Delegating authority
Jumping to conclusions

ALSO BORN TODAY
Singer/actress Edie Adams; author Kingsley Amis; actress Ellen Barkin; filmmaker/comedian Charlie Chaplin; actor Lukas Haas; singer Dusty Springfield; actor Peter Ustinov; singer Bobby Vinton.

APRIL 17

April 17 people seem to have an innate understanding of the world around them and all of its intricacies, and they are always ready for an opportunity that comes their way. They are equally adept at recognizing opportunities for others and invariably use this skill at some point in life.

When April 17 individuals have an opinion, everyone in their circle is certain to grasp its wisdom.

FRIENDS AND LOVERS
The brusqueness of people born on this date can be somewhat intimidating to others, including the people they love. From an early age they display a marked ability for leadership and tend to select like-minded friends.

April 17 individuals do not fall in love heedlessly. They cannot love someone they do not respect, and so they inevitably choose a partner who embodies their particular concept of integrity and intelligence.

CHILDREN AND FAMILY
Those born on this date have a very clear image of their place in the family and usually retain very close, lifelong ties to siblings and other relatives.

They make excellent parents, although rather controlling ones. April 17 individuals proceed from a clearly conceived code of conduct and expect their children to observe and follow that code. Yet these individuals are unusually fair-minded and are always ready to listen to an explanation.

HEALTH
April 17 individuals can be accident-prone and therefore, although they possess a sound physical constitution, may experience more than their share of twisted ankles and stubbed toes. They can be vulnerable to arthritis in later life and should compensate by taking calcium supplements and practicing weight-bearing exercise.

People born on this date are finicky eaters. They often follow a strict diet because of an aversion to being overweight. Smoking is an especially irritating factor and should be avoided. Red wine, consumed in moderation, can have a positive effect on their health.

CAREER AND FINANCES
Before April 17 individuals choose a career, they consider their own limitations. These men and women will never aspire to something that is beyond their capabilities, but they are willing to sacrifice a great deal to get where they want to go. These people are especially well-suited for the business world but can also distinguish themselves in medicine, science, or police work.

If April 17 individuals set their sights on making a great deal of money, they are likely to succeed. Financial security is very important to them.

DREAMS AND GOALS
The goals and expectations of April 17 individuals are in line with their abilities. They are hard workers, dedicated to carrying out their responsibilities as best they can. They have a realistic approach to making their dreams come true and will not lose faith in themselves if they are temporarily derailed from this purpose. Failure and setbacks only make them more determined to succeed.

EMBRACE
Confidence
Happy thoughts
Emotional stability

AVOID
Guilt
Self-criticism
Danger

ALSO BORN TODAY
Film director Lindsay Anderson; writer Isak Dinesen; actor William Holden; actress Olivia Hussey; TV journalist Harry Reasoner; musician Pete Shelley; novelist Thornton Wilder; archaeologist Leonard Woolley.

APRIL 18

People born on this date are eminent doers and achievers. When they set themselves a task they will go to any lengths to accomplish it. Opinionated and aggressive, they often find themselves at the center of controversy.

These individuals favor involvement on all levels of existence and are not the type to sit idly by, as long as there are causes to espouse and victories to be won.

EMBRACE
Fun
Personal accountability
Positive ambiance

AVOID
Anger
Hiding from the truth
Impugning the motives of others

ALSO BORN TODAY
Attorney Clarence Darrow; actress Hayley Mills; TV host Conan O'Brien; actor Eric Roberts; composer Miklos Rozsa; symphony conductor Leopold Stokowski; artist Max Weber; actor James Woods.

FRIENDS AND LOVERS
People who inhabit the circle of people born on April 18 inevitably become part of their entourage. The enthusiasm and energy with which April 18 people conduct their lives are infectious and draw others to them as admirers and friends.

The romantic life of people born on this date is often operatic in its intensity and drama. April 18 folks are often good-looking, charming individuals who have no difficulty attracting lovers. When involved in a committed relationship, they make loyal, supportive partners.

CHILDREN AND FAMILY
April 18 people are able to inspire incredible respect and affection from family members. Despite their self-sufficiency, these individuals frequently defer to the attitudes and opinions of authority figures, such as parents or elder siblings.

People born on this date take an almost sacred view of the next generation and feel that it is their responsibility to help nurture and support it. Those April 18 men and women who become parents take their roles seriously and strive to provide good examples to their offspring.

HEALTH
With their high energy and eagerness to extract the maximum enjoyment from life, April 18 people are vital and vibrant. Those who follow in their energetic wake find it hard to match their level of endurance.

April 18 natives feel best when they eat a high-carbohydrate diet made up of several small meals taken throughout the day. Since their metabolism is naturally high, they require only a modest amount of exercise a few times a week. Highly competitive, people born on this date make exceptional weekend athletes.

CAREER AND FINANCES
April 18 natives are predisposed to success in whatever field they choose. Yet despite their ability to turn ordinary circumstances into opportunity, these people are most interested in concepts, not the bottom line. Because of their ability to inspire others, April 18 men and women make impressive politicians, teachers, and entrepreneurs.

In keeping with their impulsive nature, these people may make questionable financial choices and should seek professional advice.

DREAMS AND GOALS
The goal of April 18 individuals is to open the eyes of those around them and create change in their own time. Whether they agitate on behalf of the environment, political awareness, spiritual values, or the arts, people born on this date put all their efforts at the disposal of their ambition.

In the rare event of a setback, April 18 natives shrug off their disappointment and begin again. An unswerving belief in their ability keeps them on track.

APRIL 19

Possessed with a deep sense of their own spiritual significance, people born on April 19 have the ability to do great things. They have absolutely no interest in making a public show of their very personal aims, yet the zeal that characterizes their ambition often gains them notice.

April 19 individuals have marked psychic ability. Whether or not they choose to make use of this talent, it serves as a method for them to make a majority of their intellectual decisions.

FRIENDS AND LOVERS
Nothing that these people do—including their relationships with others—comes about accidentally. April 19 people have a way of channeling their experiences and relationships to grow spiritually and intellectually.

Love is a transcendent experience for April 19 people. Although they may appear to choose lovers or mates who are wrong for them, they are actually responding to a profound inner need to learn a spiritual truth from someone very different from themselves.

CHILDREN AND FAMILY
People born on April 19 are the custodians of truth within their family circle. They understand their brothers, sisters, even their parents in ways that would be impossible for anyone else to comprehend.

When it comes to raising their own children, April 19 people have a great tolerance and sensitivity. Even though they may expect their children to mirror their own opinions and values, they will never imperil their relationship when differences arise.

HEALTH
Because of their incredible sensitivity, those born on this date need to adopt a healthly and active lifestyle. The worst thing they can do is become moody and lethargic. Regular exercise is a good way for people born on this date to expel their nervous energy and relieve tension.

Many April 19 individuals suffer from indigestion, especially when they eat spicy food. They may also experience migraine headaches brought on by overwork and stress. They should avoid working in crowded interiors.

CAREER AND FINANCES
April 19 individuals often take a circuitous path toward their eventual career destination, with plenty of stops made along the way. Because they are very sensitive to the influences of their youth, these people often make a career choice based upon their respect for an inspirational teacher or mentor.

April 19 natives hold financial security dear where their families are concerned, since people born on this day are adamant in their dedication to make their child's life more secure than their own was.

DREAMS AND GOALS
April 19 individuals seek unification between the spiritual and secular elements of their nature. They are constantly reminded of the duality that inspires all their actions.

April 19 individuals are not great planners, but they do have a natural instinct about what choices to make and when to make them. The decisions they make may seem curious to others, but the people born on this day never question what their intuition tells them is best.

EMBRACE
Second choices
A love of literature
Gentleness

AVOID
Putting things off
Being disorganized
Alibiing failure

ALSO BORN TODAY
Actor Don Adams; Renaissance personality Lucrezia Borgia; actor Tim Curry; actress Jayne Mansfield; writer Gladys Mitchell; actor Dudley Moore; designer Paloma Picasso; singer/songwriter Mark Volman.

APRIL 20

People born on this date are guided by their emotions. Even when they appear to make decisions based on logic and intellect, they are actually tapping into the rich pipeline of their subconscious mind.

Because of their rich inner life, people born on this date sometimes appear to live in a dream world. Although naturally contemplative, they can summon the social elan needed to shine when the occasion arises.

FRIENDS AND LOVERS
April 20 individuals project their own needs and perceptions onto the personalities of the people they love. Very often their closest friendships begin in youth and last a lifetime.

Romantic relationships offer a fair share of disappointments for April 20 individuals, who expect love to have a fairy-tale aspect. These folks put a great deal of effort into making a relationship work and can be devastated when it doesn't. Once April 20 natives come to understand that no romance or marriage can be as glowingly perfect as they imagine it, they can deal with whatever comes their way.

CHILDREN AND FAMILY
Family is a strong force in the lives of April 20 people, who may have a particularly close tie to Mom. There can be a great deal of pressure exerted on these individuals to conform to a set of rigid, preordained values that are restrictive or outdated.

If they do not resolve their family issues satisfactorily, these are likely to be factors in the relationships April 20 people have with their own children. Happily, though, when these individuals are able to sidestep those issues, the cycle is broken, to the benefit of all concerned.

HEALTH
As a result of their great sensitivity, April 20 individuals are prone to imaginary illnesses, usually brought on by an episode of depression or just the blues.

People born on this day are concerned with personal appearance and will go to considerable lengths, including surgical means, to retain a youthful, attractive appearance.

CAREER AND FINANCES
With his/her special gift for words and beautiful speaking voice, an April 20 individual can exercise his or her will over others. They make great orators, actors, public speakers, and members of the media.

The financial affairs of April 20 people are in a continuous state of flux. While they often experience good luck in money matters, they also find it easy to overextend themselves. Their generosity is well-known, though they are sometimes taken advantage of.

DREAMS AND GOALS
The goals of April 20 individuals are likely to undergo a series of changes reflective of the various cycles in their lives. At an early age their plans are generally outer-directed. Many April 20 individuals, in fact, have a desire to change society. Later in life these people amend their idealism to accommodate the disappointments they may have experienced.

Still, involvement in socially significant projects gives them a sense of helping to make the world a better place.

EMBRACE
Daydreams
Making intelligent mistakes
True love

AVOID
Being humorless
Distractions
Making enemies

ALSO BORN TODAY
Actress Nina Foch; dictator Adolf Hitler; actress Jessica Lange; actor Joey Lawrence; silent-film comedian Harold Lloyd; cellist Gregor Piatigorsky; actor Ryan O'Neal; singer Luther Vandross.

TAURUS
April 21 - May 20

Taurus is the second sign of the astrological year and is known by its symbol, the Bull. Taureans are loyal, thrifty, and kindhearted. With Venus as its ruling planet, people born under this sign typically possess great personal charm, good looks, and a lovely speaking voice. Luxury-loving and acquisitive, they also can be lazy.

THE TAURUS MAN He isn't talkative and he certainly isn't complicated, but he can be every girl's dream. This guy is definitely the strong silent type who lets his actions speak for him. Taurus men possess a great deal of what used to be called "animal magnetism." They are often dark and brooding in appearance, taciturn in speech. They become good husbands and fathers, cherish traditional values, and rarely lose their temper. But when they do—look out!

Most Taurus men are more concerned with achieving success in their personal life than their professional life. They support traditional family values and are not particularly amenable where change is concerned. These gents usually have a great deal of creative talent, though they may require some coaxing in order to display it.

THE TAURUS WOMAN She is stylish, well-groomed, and socially involved. Whether she turns her energies to domestic or professional aims, she is certain to give it all that she has. With Venus as their ruling planet, these women manage to hold their own against any man, professionally speaking, without ever losing their trademark femininity. Taurean woman possess spectacular color and fashion sense, and look stunning even on a shoestring budget.

Taurus women are stubborn, practical, and budget-minded. They have the ability to balance family and career life without losing their emotional equilibrium. These ladies have their feet planted firmly on the ground, proving that incredible charm and common sense can coexist in the same individual.

THE TAURUS CHILD These little ones can be sugar and spice one moment, then walking thunderclouds the next. Don't be surprised if they do things a little behind schedule; Taurean children often take their time learning to walk, talk, and integrate within a play group. Taurean youngsters are generally obedient, but they may become belligerent in adolescence if the rules made by their parents are too restrictive.

Many Taurean children show a marked artistic talent at a very early age, especially in music and singing. They have great color sense and are drawn to beautiful things, especially toys. These youngsters are very practical about money and often start saving their allowance while still in grade school.

THE TAURUS LOVER The men and women of this Venus-ruled sign know everything there is about love and romance. They are passionate individuals who prefer marriage or long-term relationships to the dating scene. The Taurean lover is persistent, consistent, and always eager to please his or her partner. The one drawback to their approach is inflexibility. An adventuresome person who enjoys a lot of experimentation and diversity may grow weary of their Taurean lover's practical approach. But for the full spectrum of wooing and winning a love interest, Taureans score full marks.

ELEMENT: Earth
QUALITY: Fixed
PLANETARY RULER: Venus
BIRTHSTONE: Emerald
FLOWER: Red rose
COLOR: Shocking pink

KEY CHARACTERISTIC:
Determination

STRENGTHS: Hard-working,
Honest, Brave

CHALLENGES: Intractable, Short-
sighted, Bullying

Like other earth signs, Taureans are detail-oriented. They never forget a birthday, anniversary, or other romantic occasion. They also understand the importance of the proper atmosphere. Fine dining and fine wine, followed by incense and silk sheets, is a Taurean ritual.

THE TAURUS BOSS Those who have worked for a Taurean boss will gladly attest to the fairness and loyalty of this individual. The typical Taurean boss is friendly, accessible, and almost always pleasant. Despite all these good points, the Taurus boss may also be excessively serious and stubborn. Things that another boss may overlook or ignore will rub this individual the wrong way. Like most earth-sign people, Taureans have a long memory. If they are displeased by the behavior of a subordinate, they will not easily trust that individual again.

The Taurean boss is a very good judge of character and is often instrumental in drawing out the hidden talents of an employee.

THE TAURUS FRIEND No one can ask for a better friend than a Taurus friend, for these men and women are exceptionally steadfast and loyal. They treat their friends with the kind of respect and affection that most people reserve for family members or lovers.

Taureans get along best with people who have the same interests as their own, but their sympathetic nature often helps to draw people from various walks of life into their circle. Because of their busy social schedule, Taureans are often placed in situations that test their loyalty to existing pals—but it takes more than charm and good conversation to sway the allegiances of a Taurus. These men and women often serve their friends in an advisory role; their advice is treasured.

APRIL 21

The dynamism and sociability of April 21 people make them special. They have interesting, spirited personalities that attract admirers in both their personal and professional lives. People born on this day are extremely opinionated and at times have a problem accepting other points of view. Although their buoyant nature generally keeps them from seeming dogmatic or pushy, it is important that they cultivate tolerance on as broad a scale as they can muster. People born on this date are often physically attractive.

FRIENDS AND LOVERS
Outgoing, old-fashioned, and utterly charming, the men and women born on this date have the ability to inspire great love and affection among others—and in selected cases, jealousy. April 21 people are likely to have a large circle of pals from a wide social group, though they may lack intimate friends.

April 21 individuals are incredibly sentimental and romantic and believe that love was meant to last a lifetime.

CHILDREN AND FAMILY
People born on this day have a hierarchal concept of family and feel enormous pressure and responsibility to fulfill their familial obligations. In some cases these pressures may be severe, even punishing, but whatever the circumstances, April 21 individuals take them seriously.

When it comes to raising their own children, April 21 natives have their hands full. For fear of being perceived as authoritarian, they have a tendency to be liberal, even indulgent parents.

HEALTH
Due to the fact that they are the embodiment of vitality, April 21 individuals have a habit of taking their good health for granted. They enjoy doing things to excess, which can include overeating, drinking too much, and generally burning the candle at both ends.

It isn't easy for these people to cut back on their favorite foods, but they should substitute low-fat and sugar-free desserts for richer fare.

CAREER AND FINANCES
With their cosmopolitan viewpoint and love of the finer things in life, April 21 folks are excellent exponents of capitalism. Although not entrepreneurs in the literal definition of the word, these people make capable company or departmental heads. They also have great success as bankers, brokers, investment counselors, and financial planners.

Interestingly, April 21 people do far better handling other people's money than they do looking after their own.

DREAMS AND GOALS
April 21 individuals are painstaking in their methods of building dreams and bringing goals to fruition. These people believe in careful planning and never let an opportunity go unfulfilled.

Although they have a gift for organization, April 21 people have also mastered the art of flexibility. When things don't go according to their carefully laid plans, they always have a contingency to put into action.

EMBRACE
The best of everything
Growing old gracefully
Letting go

AVOID
Fear of change
Ignoring lessons
Going for broke

ALSO BORN TODAY
Novelist Charlotte Bronte; Russian empress Catherine the Great; England's Queen Elizabeth II; actor Charles Grodin; singer/actress Patti LuPone; actress Andie MacDowell; director/actress/comedienne Elaine May; photographer Norman Parkinson.

APRIL 22

There is a certain level of instability inherent in the character and personality of April 22 individuals, which makes them oddly appealing and attractive. They possess a bright, brittle charm that works its magic in all aspects of life.

Unusual circumstances and coincidences are the spice of life for these people, who may unconsciously draw excitement and danger into their lives.

FRIENDS AND LOVERS
People born on April 22 are the ones everyone loves and wants to emulate. They are stars within their own circle, and sometimes even on a larger scale. They have scores of friends, yet always manage to hold something of themselves in reserve—something that they share only with a special, intimate pal.

As lovers, April 22 natives are in great demand. They are not primarily marriage-minded and have a tendency to play the field for many years before finally settling down.

CHILDREN AND FAMILY
The instability and occasional ripples of chaos that characterize the experience of April 22 individuals often has its beginnings in family life. If the upbringing is conventional, it is likely that these people will rebel against it.

April 21 individuals make good, if permissive parents. From an early age they encourage their youngsters to "do their own thing." People born on this date are typically much more liberal than their offspring, which can set the stage for some misunderstandings and a few periods of estrangement.

HEALTH
April 22 individuals rarely concern themselves with the state of their health until something is wrong, and then they turn to holistic medicine to effect a cure. These people are born naturalists whose radical religious and political views are likely to influence their fitness and nutrition habits.

Although these people are fond of New Age treatments that invoke mind/body harmony, they may indulge in an unhealthy habit, such as smoking.

CAREER AND FINANCES
Life is one long adventure to April 22 people, and that includes their search for a satisfying career. They are extremely talented individuals who can rise very high in the world. Yet, being unconventional, they may choose to ignore obvious opportunities in favor of something unusual and "fun."

April 22 natives are big spenders. Although they have considerable talent for handling money, they have very little respect for material things. People born on this date have phenomenal luck in money matters. Legacies, as well as lotteries and other games of chance, can yield major financial windfalls.

DREAMS AND GOALS
Quirky and unconventional, April 22 people take life as it comes. The idea of plotting a course for success seems alien, even foolish, to them. These people trust in their own ability to make random choices that will bring them the satisfaction and fulfillment they want, as well as providing the excitement they need.

EMBRACE
Starting over
A good attitude
Attention to detail

AVOID
Being afraid
Interrupting
Careless mistakes

ALSO BORN TODAY
Actor Joseph Bottoms; singer/composer Glen Campbell; opera singer Kathleen Ferrier; musician Peter Frampton; philosopher Immanuel Kant; actor Jack Nicholson; TV producer Aaron Spelling; film director John Waters.

APRIL 23

People born on this date have brilliant and original minds. Their opinions generally run counter to conventional wisdom and they don't care who disagrees with them. These are joyous, irrepressible individuals who have the gift of making other people happy.

April 23 people have so many interests that they give the impression of scattering their energies rather than channeling them. While this can be true on occasion, it suits their purpose, since variety, not constancy, is what makes their lives worth living.

FRIENDS AND LOVERS
Because they have distinct and singular likes and dislikes, people born on April 23 are particular about their relationships. Even though they have a wide variety of friends, there are very few people who truly know them.

People born on April 23 don't take love too seriously. They like having a good time and may feel stifled by marriage vows. When they do choose a life partner, they'll gravitate to someone who shares their love of fun and spontaneity. When it comes to fidelity, April 23 individuals favor a somewhat liberal interpretation of the concept.

CHILDREN AND FAMILY
The men and women born on this date have a considerable interest in their family history. Meticulous record-keepers, they enjoy collecting all the stories that were told to them as children.

When they become parents, April 23 people encourage their own children to learn as much as possible about their lineage. Family honor is very important to these people, and they will raise their youngsters to be aware of the profound variety in their past and its potential to influence their future.

HEALTH
April 23 individuals may suffer from repeated bouts of mental exhaustion brought on by a lifetime of overwork. This can be countered by exercise and meditation.

People born on this date have unique eating habits. They enjoy fasting for health purposes and yet have a great love for exotic and unusual foods. When they are preoccupied with work or personal concerns, they may lose their appetite altogether.

CAREER AND FINANCES
April 23 individuals make talented writers, journalists, and teachers. They are communication-oriented, and the performance of their work may be influenced by or dependent upon electronic gadgets.

April 23 individuals are extremely savvy about making money. They take their financial future seriously, and in order to master it they will seek out information from classes, seminars, and books.

DREAMS AND GOALS
April 23 individuals are ambitious about making a place in the world. They desire fame, and if they cannot have it they may feel as if they have not been given their due in life.

People born on this date take an active interest in helping people close to them realize their own dreams and goals. These extraordinarily generous individuals are always willing to assist and encourage friends and family.

EMBRACE
Industry
Willingness to work
Contentment

AVOID
Dishonest reasoning
Irreverence
Selfishness

ALSO BORN TODAY
Actress Valerie Bertinelli; actor David Birney; actress Sandra Dee; basketball star Gail Goodrich; actor Lee Majors; novelist Vladimir Nabokov; singer Roy Orbison; artist J.M.W. Turner.

APRIL 24

People born on April 24 have a flair for the good life and a love of glamour. These sleek, sophisticated men and women radiate a special glow, which makes them as attractive physically as they are by way of personality.

April 24 natives are practical people who play by the rules. They are also talented, with a good sense of humor and the ability to laugh at themselves.

FRIENDS AND LOVERS April 24 people have a great deal of personal charm, ensuring themselves a large social circle and plenty of admiring friends. These are people who enjoy taking care of their pals in a warm, almost maternal way.

The men and women born on this date are warm, affectionate, and loving partners. They can build extremely happy marriages, yet it is not difficult for them to be alone, for they are very self-sufficient in emotional matters.

CHILDREN AND FAMILY The conventional side of April 24 individuals likes being part of a family unit and revels in the traditions associated with it. But there is another aspect to the people born on this day: Mischievous, stubborn, and a little rebellious, they like to break old patterns and establish new ones.

April 24 natives make extremely protective parents who may have trouble allowing their children to make their own mistakes. This can become a point of debate between these individuals and their growing children—especially teenagers.

HEALTH It is very fortunate for April 24 individuals that they are attractive, since vanity can be a great motivator—and motivation is just what these people need. Like many of their fellow Taureans, people born on April 24 have an enormous love of good food. Yet, because they value their looks, these people are likely to adopt a regular workout regimen.

In rare cases where mobility is a problem in old age, they can be troubled by gout.

CAREER AND FINANCES These folks have keen instincts and usually manage to find a way to make their most cherished financial expectations pay off. It is almost as if these people are money magnets. They know what sells and what doesn't.

Because they have a great deal of creative talent, they often find themselves in great demand as artists, designers, decorators, architects, and instructors in multimedia arts. They can also make a good living as models or musicians. Good investment decisions are a snap for these savvy individuals.

DREAMS AND GOALS These energetic, irrepressible people have big dreams and the determination to mold those dreams into reality. They tend to formulate definite career plans at an early age. At the same time, they're practical and patient and don't mind making the sacrifices that come with high aspirations.

Money is very important to April 24 people because it allows them to indulge in the opulent lifestyle that is so important to them. Fortuitously, April 24 men and women are expert at managing their financial future without help from professionals.

EMBRACE
Holistic healing
Stylish apparel
Competition

AVOID
Getting even
Feeling unappreciated
Making excuses

ALSO BORN TODAY
Musician Doug Clifford; musician Glenn Cornick; gourmand Clement Freud; musician Billy Gould; actress Jill Ireland; novelist Anthony Trollope; actress Shirley MacLaine; actress/singer Barbra Streisand.

APRIL 25

People born on this date are the seekers of life's deepest mysteries, and this gives them a tolerance that few other individuals possess. At the center of their being is a great spirituality, which gives them amazing strength of character.

April 25 natives take life as it comes and do not consciously attempt to impose their will upon events. When disappointments come their way, these people don't lose their natural composure but see the challenges as a valuable learning experience.

FRIENDS AND LOVERS

April 25 individuals are introspective loners who don't need to find themselves through relationships. No matter how much these people love a mate, they hold something of their personality in reserve.

Because of their deeply spiritual nature, April 25 individuals may remain celibate for long periods of time when there is no one special in their lives.

CHILDREN AND FAMILY

A great many unresolved and painful issues from childhood are likely to influence the adult lives of April 25 people. These may involve an early breakup of the family or a complicated relationship with a parent.

Many April 25 adults seek to heal their emotional wounds by raising a family of their own. They may marry and have children when still teenagers. This can prove helpful therapy for them, as long as they understand that forgiveness for the past must precede healing in the future.

HEALTH

April 25 people do not have the robust health generally associated with Taureans, and they have a tendency to catch cold easily.

People born on this date can benefit from a simple diet that restricts sweets. Coffee and sugary, caffeinated soft drinks put a strain on their system. Mineral water and herbal tea will help flush toxins from the system.

CAREER AND FINANCES

Music plays an important role in the lives of April 25 people. Even if it does not become a career choice, people born on this date respond to music's natural resonance, which gives them physical grace and a natural sense of rhythm. When they do choose to launch a career from these abilities, April 25 individuals can become talented dancers, choreographers, figure skaters, musicians, and singers.

Although they are very intelligent, these people are not advised to handle a significant amount of money without some professional advice, since they have a tendency toward financial recklessness.

DREAMS AND GOALS

The chief aim of April 25 individuals is to understand themselves, even if to do so means learning some unpleasant things about their nature.

Success to these individuals has very little to do with accumulating worldly possessions or praise. It is the intangibles of life that concern April 25 people, since they have no need of external validation. In their quiet way these people can make extraordinary spiritual guides and mentors.

EMBRACE
Concentration
Pondering an answer
Playing for keeps

AVOID
Tension
Telling a hurtful truth
Worrying about death

ALSO BORN TODAY
Poet Walter de la Mare; English king Edward II; singer Ella Fitzgerald; basketball star Meadowlark Lemon; film director Paul Mazursky; journalist Edward R. Murrow; actor Al Pacino; actress Talia Shire.

APRIL 26

There is a serious side to April 26 individuals that isn't always noticeable beneath their amiable exteriors. They have fine judgment and seem to possess an instinct for making just the right decision at the opportune time.

There is likely to be some secret embarrassment or humiliation lurking in the past of April 26 people. They may have experienced considerable economic hardship while growing up, or suffered from a parent or other family member who brought hurtful scandal into their life.

FRIENDS AND LOVERS April 26 individuals take their relationships very seriously and continue to learn from them throughout life. Their ability to inspire sincere affection even from casual acquaintances helps to explain why their true friends are so devoted to them.

Partnership is a must for April 26 individuals, who never take a romantic relationship lightly. Even though their feelings run very deep, these men and women are practical and levelheaded, unlikely to become involved in a relationship that is emotionally stressful or too demanding.

CHILDREN AND FAMILY April 26 people often find themselves in a position of familial authority or responsibility at a very young age. This is not something that they resent, and in later years they are sure to look back at this

experience as having been a positive, formative factor in who they are.

Men and women born on this date are likely to impose their view of responsibility on their own children; conflict between the generations is inevitable.

HEALTH People born on April 26 are likely to have nervous complaints brought on by tension, overwork, and an inability to relax. If they have a particularly demanding schedule, their attention to nutrition is likely to suffer.

It's important that these individuals eat a high-protein diet. Vitamin supplements, with extra iron and calcium, will help to increase their endurance.

CAREER AND FINANCES April 26 people know from an early age how they want to spend their lives, and even as children they may show a true interest in a particular career path.

Because their early years are often burdened by financial difficulties, money is important to these people. It serves as both a reward for their many sacrifices and a validation of what they have accomplished through dogged determination. If they do not appear overly generous it is because they can never completely separate their present-day success from the struggles of the past.

DREAMS AND GOALS People born on April 26 believe in old-fashioned values. To them, success is always the result of hard work. They have a healthy respect for talent and ability, but do not think that anything meaningful can be accomplished without sacrifice.

April 26 natives have incredible imaginations and often use creative visualization techniques as a means of programming their goals for success. They believe very strongly in the ability of the mind to effect tangible results.

EMBRACE
Leisure
Giving yourself the benefit of the doubt
Spiritual thinking

AVOID
Self-interest
Emotional detachment
Snobbishness

ALSO BORN TODAY
Actress/comic Carol Burnett; artist Eugene Delacroix; swimmer Donna de Varona; musician Duane Eddy; writer Anita Loos; singer Bobby Rydell; writer Jess Stern; philosopher Ludwig Wittgenstein.

APRIL 27

People born on this date are a study in extremes. Their emotions run hot and cold, and they have a reputation for being temperamental when crossed. Though they are intelligent, these people are primarily doers, not thinkers. Instinct plays a big part in guiding their decision-making, and they are famous for saying what they think.

April 27 men and women are people-oriented and never seem to run out of enthusiasm. They are natural cheerleaders for worthy causes.

FRIENDS AND LOVERS April 27 people never fail to make a vivid impression on those who know them. Their personality is forceful, sometimes domineering, yet their heart is always in the right place.

Both the men and women are highly sexual, but they prefer a stable union to a series of superficial encounters. They take their marriage vows seriously and will work hard to keep the relationship fresh and interesting.

CHILDREN AND FAMILY April 27 natives are not likely to be the children that their parents expect, or the parents that their children expect. Tradition means little to these free-thinking individuals. Even though they are not rebellious for the sake of rebellion, they do prefer to map their own course in life.

As parents they have a tendency to be more demanding than their past history should allow, but they never expect blind obedience from their children.

HEALTH Due to their energetic nature, April 27 natives have a habit of displaying their emotions—joy, anger, sadness, and a range of other feelings. This behavior can actually have a positive impact on their health.

April 27 individuals have a few bad habits, which may include a fondness for red meat. Alcohol, except for wine, is not a good choice for these people, and smoking should be avoided completely. Competitive sports such as tennis or racquetball make ideal weekend recreation for April 27 men and women.

CAREER AND FINANCES Because April 27 people are so dynamic, they are on everybody's list of "the one most likely to. . . ." These individuals have a real desire to succeed and will work very hard to get to the top of their profession. They do best in work that allows them to make use of their incredible energy and organizational skills.

April 27 natives have some bad habits when it comes to handling money. They are spenders, not savers, and can benefit from professional advice.

DREAMS AND GOALS April 27 individuals believe fervently in their dreams and the ability to realize them. The only problem is a lack of consistency: They often run out of steam before their goals can be actualized.

Emotion plays a big part in the ability of April 27 men and women to stay focused on the day-to-day implementation of choices and decisions that may turn dreams into reality. If their enthusiasm wanes, April 27 people are liable to lose faith in their own abilities.

EMBRACE
High energy
Faithfulness
Charity work

AVOID
Boastfulness
Being argumentative
Making enemies

ALSO BORN TODAY
Actress Anouk Aimee; actress Sandy Dennis; singer Sheena Easton; U.S. President Ulysses S. Grant; civil rights activist Coretta Scott King; actor Jack Klugman; poet Cecil Day Lewis; writer Mary Wollstonecraft (Shelley).

APRIL 28

April 28 people bring joy to their world. They have an amazing capacity for living life to the fullest and never failing to recognize an opportunity that comes their way.

People born on this day are exponents of the "glass is half full" philosophy. They have absolutely no cynicism in their nature and can find logic and reason in even the most difficult and trying circumstances.

FRIENDS AND LOVERS People born on this date have no problem making friends. They love people and derive a great deal of happiness from experiencing, secondhand, their friends' joys and successes.

In love matters April 28 people like to think of themselves as more than just romantic figures. They view marriage as a true partnership—a meeting of minds, hearts, and souls. They expect a mate to share their own high standards.

CHILDREN AND FAMILY April 28 people have something of a Norman Rockwell view of family life. They want the reality to measure up to that image and when it doesn't they can be severely disappointed. If they experience a particularly difficult upbringing, April 28 individuals may "rewrite" the scenario to provide them with a more pleasant view of the past.

With their own children, April 28 men and women show themselves to be exceptionally understanding and indulgent. They may, in fact, be overly involved in the life of their children, unwilling to let them fail.

HEALTH A good mental attitude has a lot to do with the vitality of April 28 individuals. These people are models of positive thinking and good health habits. If they possess any bad habits they can easily be persuaded to break them, and they understand the importance of keeping active, involved, and motivated.

When they may find themselves gaining weight, it's necessary for them to cut back on rich foods, including dairy products and starches.

CAREER AND FINANCES April 28 people identify very strongly with their career identity. If there are other areas of their lives that are not yielding all the promise they expected, these individuals can still be secure in the knowledge that they have stability in their professional lives. Because they enjoy sharing their philosophical views with others, April 28 natives excel in teaching, counseling, and the ministry.

Although they may get off to a rocky start with their handling of financial responsibilities, April 28 people eventually become capable of parlaying a small amount of money into a healthy nest egg.

DREAMS AND GOALS April 28 people can be reticent about believing in their dreams. This attitude could be the result of their upbringing; perhaps they were taught that having grandiose plans for the future could lead to disillusionment.

The major goals of April 28 men and women are likely to be career-oriented, although they may harbor a secret ambition to transcend the restraints of a difficult personal relationship.

EMBRACE
Taking care of yourself
A good attitude
Time

AVOID
Self-pity
Laziness
Disenchantment

ALSO BORN TODAY
Actress/singer/dancer Ann-Margret; actor Lionel Barrymore; TV journalist Rowland Evans, Jr.; actor Bruno Kirby; novelist Harper Lee; TV host Jay Leno; U.S. President James Monroe; actress Marcia Strassman.

APRIL 29

People born on this date are concerned with how they are perceived by others. This isn't a result of an unhealthy ego; rather, April 29 individuals simply have a high level of sensitivity, and literally "feel" the approval or disapproval of those around them.

Part of the problem is the inability of these men and women to appreciate their own best character traits.

FRIENDS AND LOVERS

The emotional life of April 29 individuals is volatile and likely to affect their relationships with great intensity. These people don't believe in superficial attachments. They are very loyal to their friends and are willing to go to extremes to offer help and support.

Unfortunately, they are no wiser in love relationships. April 29 women, in particular, have a reputation for choosing partners who are unlikely to give them the emotional support they require. The people born on this date often have a sincere yet unrealistic idea of romantic love, which can lead to one or more unsuccessful pairings.

CHILDREN AND FAMILY

In the lives of these very impressionable individuals there is often an event that, at a very early age, affects their life for many years to come. In extreme cases this can be a death in the family.

There may be a few unstable elements at work in the relationship that April 29 people share with their own children, even though there is certain to be a great deal of love on both sides. People born on this date have a special relationship with their daughters.

HEALTH

Even if they are healthy, April 29 individuals constantly require treatment for any number of minor illnesses or injuries. Headaches and insomnia are frequent complaints, especially if regular exercise is not part of their lives.

The best thing April 29 people can do for their health is to relax. Meditation, especially while listening to soothing music, can help to calm these edgy individuals. They should never eat before going to bed, since this inevitably causes sleeplessness or nightmares.

CAREER AND FINANCES

April 29 individuals are happiest in careers that allow them to express their deeply spiritual nature. They do well in the medical profession, especially as nurses, therapists, or counselors.

People born on this date have a strong material streak, and may use shopping to assuage whatever isn't going right in other areas of their lives.

DREAMS AND GOALS

Though personal issues are likely to be at the head of their wishlist, April 29 individuals are far more ambitious than they feel comfortable acknowledging. These dreamy and sensitive souls may have been conditioned to believe they are destined to play a passive role in life.

April 29 individuals may initiate a career change in middle age, which will necessitate a whole new set of commitments. Learning to believe wholeheartedly in their own talents can be a tall order for these people.

EMBRACE
Liberality
Ethics
Being spontaneous

AVOID
Irrationality
Loose talk
Childish behavior

ALSO BORN TODAY
Tennis champion Andre Agassi; football coach George Allen; actress Celeste Holm; actor Daniel Day Lewis; singer/songwriter/poet Rod McKuen; symphony conductor Zubin Mehta; actress Michelle Pfieffer; comedian Jerry Seinfeld.

APRIL 30

People born on this day are often forced into leading life on different terms than may be their choice. Whether it is a question of family responsibilities or just an unusual set of circumstances, these individuals seem destined to have their life-path influenced from an early age by outside forces.

Men and women born on April 30 enjoy playing for very high stakes in all aspects of life. This natural tendency toward gambling is something that, despite its potential consequences, never leaves them.

FRIENDS AND LOVERS

April 30 men and women simply cannot have too many friends. These folks look to their close associates to help them through the emotional highs and lows of life.

People born on this day typically select a romantic partner who is already a pal. Romance is important to these people, but it must be supported by respect and the fact that they have plenty in common with their mate.

CHILDREN AND FAMILY

People born on April 30 have a generally favorable relationship with family members. There is often a strong tie between April 30 individuals and one elderly relative.

April 30 men and women are often surprised to find themselves well-suited to parenthood. They have a natural understanding of a child's world and may seem to be more of a pal than an authority figure. They aren't comfortable punishing their youngsters, but do provide a disciplined environment that teaches values and responsibility.

HEALTH

April 30 people are naturally sturdy and do not need to do much to enhance their good health. Like most Taureans they enjoy good food, with an eye toward gourmet fare.

Even though these individuals have a big appetite they can usually keep slim through exercise. April 30 people have an active lifestyle that often includes walking, hiking, biking, and competitive sports. Many have the potential to pursue an athletic career.

CAREER AND FINANCES

Career choices that result in financial security and the chance to travel grab the attention of April 30 people. If something they love to do is not financially rewarding they are likely to look elsewhere, and subjugate their original choice to hobby status.

It is not uncommon for the people born on this date to become fabulously rich. They have incredible instincts for making their money grow, and even though they have a reputation for spending money lavishly, they never fail to give equal attention to savings. Travel is one of their greatest interests and is often behind the biggest outflow of cash.

DREAMS AND GOALS

April 30 individuals enjoy living life on a big, even massive scale with hopes and dreams to match. They are ambitious and are continually working to make a success of their lives—both in the personal and professional sense.

Unlike many others, April 30 men and women aren't fond of making heavy sacrifices in order to make their dreams come true. They believe they can have it all and generally end up having exactly that!

EMBRACE
Exploration
Family values
Living in the present

AVOID
Wasting resources
Losing interest
Self-indulgence

ALSO BORN TODAY
Actress Eve Arden; actress Jill Clayburgh; Queen Juliana of the Netherlands; composer Franz Lehar; actor Gary Collins; singer Willie Nelson; basketball star Isiah Thomas; singer Bobby Vee.

MAY 1

People born on this date have an indomitable will and endless ambition. Their ambition has little ego attached to it however, and is primarily a vehicle for the expression of personality. The energy of these individuals inspires everyone around them. Because of this they make natural leaders.

May 1 people don't require a huge stage on which to play out their real-life drama—though they can command it if they choose.

FRIENDS AND LOVERS
For May 1 individuals, there are many flowers in the garden of friendship. These individuals bring out the very best in their compatriots and are often responsible for helping their friends to make important, even vital decisions.

Romance is a positive, energizing emotion in the lives of May 1 people. They don't just fall in love, they live through the experience with a vigor that has a transcendental effect upon themselves and their partner.

CHILDREN AND FAMILY
The ability of people born on this date to draw the very best from their familial experience has much to do with their generally happy and successful lives.

People born on May 1 take an energetic role in raising their own children but are unlikely to sculpt out any pathway for the kids to follow, hoping that the youngsters will be as fair-minded in assessing their performance as they have been with their own parents.

HEALTH
May 1 people know how to take care of their health. If everyone was as conscientious about eating well and exercising regularly as these individuals are, there would be a lot less sickness in the world.

People born on this day take good health habits as a matter of course, integrating them into their everyday lives. Instead of joining a gym or purchasing expensive in-home equipment, these men and women prefer to do their own housework, yardwork, and home repairs. It's all part of their desire to keep their lives as uncomplicated and "real" as possible.

CAREER AND FINANCES
With so many talents at their disposal, it's amazing that all May 1 individuals aren't stupendous success stories. These people don't just have a lot of ability going for them, they also possess a great deal of personal charm to sweeten the whole package. But despite all this, May 1 individuals don't generally like being the center of attention. They're much more at home delegating authority than taking it for themselves.

The same attitude applies to finances. Money is important to May 1 people only in the way that it can bring them security and provide for family and friends.

DREAMS AND GOALS
May 1 individuals embody their goals and strive to meet them every day of their lives. These are highly focused people who have always known what they want out of life and are determined to get it. Yet as serious as they appear to be, people born on this date have little if any interest in achieving success for themselves. They want to live up to their potential and see if others do the same.

EMBRACE
Prayer
Discipline
Belief in others

AVOID
Lack of communication
Competition
Loneliness

ALSO BORN TODAY
Writer Joseph Addison; actor John Beradino; singer/songwriter Judy Collins; novelist Joseph Heller; actress Joanna Lumley; TV personality Jack Paar; singer Kate Smith; fashion designer Valentina.

MAY 2

People born on May 2 are infinitely aware of their unique gifts and want to share them with the world. Creativity—both artistic and intellectual—is their personal hallmark, and the aspect of themselves with which they most closely identify.

Although they may seem cautious, even reticent, May 2 people are adventurous souls. They are brave about the choices they make in life. Although they seek acceptance from others, May 2 individuals understand that they must first learn to accept themselves.

FRIENDS AND LOVERS
May 2 individuals need the emotional support of a great many friends.

Love can be a complicated enterprise for May 2 folks. They have a habit of falling in love with people who do not share their deep sense of personal commitment. Although their highly idealistic view of love is often challenged, they never lose faith in it. Even May 2 people who experience several marriages are unlikely to become cynical about this institution.

CHILDREN AND FAMILY
Because May 2 men and women make such empathetic listeners, siblings and other relatives often seek out May 2 people to discuss problems and look for solutions.

This need to soften the problems of others is a recurring theme in the relationships of May 2 people, and continues in their parental role. Keeping the channels of communication open between themselves and their children—particularly adolescents— is a good way for May 2 parents to show their sensitivity and transcend basic generational differences.

HEALTH
May 2 individuals often suffer from sleep disorders brought on by a lack of attention to good nutritional habits.

Often it takes an illness to make May 2 individuals understand that they must be responsible for their physical well-being. Once they start taking vitamin supplements on a regular basis and eliminating all fast food from their diet, May 2 people can enjoy sound sleep and good health.

CAREER AND FINANCES
Communication and emotion are the keynotes to the talents and abilities of May 2 natives. It's impossible for these people to ignore their need to let others in on their deepest, most personal feelings. For this reason they make extraordinarily good writers, novelists, and artists in various media. They have a deep understanding of dream states and draw much of their creativity from this aspect of their unconscious mind.

Money can be an unstable factor in the lives of May 2 people since they often favor professions where income is constantly in flux. But that hardly matters, because when they're doing something they love, these men and women have little interest in what it pays.

DREAMS AND GOALS
Helping the intangible to become tangible is the major goal of May 2 people. These individuals exist on the strength of their inner vision, but it doesn't end there. In order to believe totally in that vision, May 2 people must see it manifested through an act of belief, a commitment to creativity.

EMBRACE
Partnership
Appreciation of beauty
Farewells

AVOID
Being docile
Deception
Incompatibility

ALSO BORN TODAY
Singer Jon Bon Jovi; singer Bing Crosby; singer Lesley Gore; columnist Hedda Hopper; socialite/activist Bianca Jagger; satirist Jerome K. Jerome; composer Alessandro Scarlatti; columnist Sidney Skolsky.

MAY 3

Power, and the means by which it is used and exchanged, are central factors in defining the lives of people born on this date. Throughout their lives they continually find themselves drawn to the very seat of power, though they may not desire to occupy it themselves.

May 3 people want very much to help others through their own life-experience, but first they must come to grips with some of the truths in their lives.

FRIENDS AND LOVERS Friendship isn't easy for May 3 people because they have a tendency to try to "run" the relationship. People born on this date generally take the initiative, and may be seen as demanding by someone who doesn't understand their true character.

May 3 individuals are happiest in a permanent relationship wherein the balance of power is continually in flux. They seek power over others, even people they love, yet they despise weakness. With a partner who feels as they do there is always a great deal of emotional push-pull.

CHILDREN AND FAMILY Family life is fraught with complications for May 3 people, who may unconsciously find themselves drawn into a self-sacrificing pattern of behavior. These men and women give considerable weight to their upbringing and may be unable to make a distinction between what they have been taught by their parents and what they have concluded on their own.

If they don't make these distinctions early in life, May 3 people may put the same pressure to follow convention on their own children that was put on them by their parents.

HEALTH Because they generally exhibit robust good health, May 3 people can become careless about their personal health habits. They are not the sort to seek medical help except in the most extreme circumstances. This illusion of good health needs to be buttressed by daily workouts, especially long walks and stretching exercises.

People born on this date have a fondness for gourmet food and are likely to be expert at food preparation. As long as they don't overindulge in their own goodies, they should be able to keep the weight off, but must guard against eating for emotional reasons.

CAREER AND FINANCES Not infrequently, May 3 people find themselves inadvertently drawn into a family-based career or business venture simply because their sense of responsibility is so great. When they pursue their own instincts, however, they're likely to cast an eye toward politics, the law, or police work.

While money may not be a factor in choosing a career, May 3 individuals have an instinctive ability for managing high financial stakes.

DREAMS AND GOALS The men and women born on this date want to improve the lives of those around them.

For themselves, May 3 people are determined to make good use of all the opportunities that come their way. Not particularly intuitive, they depend upon logic to point the way.

EMBRACE
Delight
A sense of community
Bliss

AVOID
Material gratification
Emotional isolation
Chaos

ALSO BORN TODAY
Singer James Brown; novelist Henry Fielding; magician Doug Henning; singer Christopher Cross; boxer Sugar Ray Robinson; singer/songwriter Pete Seeger; playwright William Inge.

MAY 4

May 4 individuals seek to distill from life its purest essence. Where most people have a tendency to complicate events, these men and women want to enjoy life in a simple and unadorned fashion. Although it may take many years for these individuals to throw off the burdens that keep them from exploring life on their own terms, they will eventually come to this point of view. Spiritually, these individuals set high standards for themselves.

FRIENDS AND LOVERS People born on May 4 have a charismatic personality that sets them apart. Because of this it is sometimes hard for May 4 people to know why people are drawn to them as friends.

Romance brings with it a similar dilemma. Because May 4 people are so attractive they naturally draw potential partners to their side. And since they are easily swayed by flattery, May 4 men and women need to use a great deal of discretion when choosing a life-mate; if they fail to do this, they eventually will have to face the consequences of bad choices.

EMBRACE
Interesting projects
Joy
Changes of venue

AVOID
Anxiety
Insecurity
Drawing conclusions

ALSO BORN TODAY
Actor Howard de Silva; actress Audrey Hepburn; artist Thomas Lawrence; singer Randy Travis; novelist Lucy Walker; singer/actress Pia Zadora.

CHILDREN AND FAMILY The deep spiritual values possessed by May 4 people are generally the result of some profound experience during their childhood years. Their upbringing is likely to be unusual or offbeat, though they may be unaware at the time that their life differs in the main from that of others.

May 4 people love children, and whether or not they have any of their own, they'll continually concern themselves with children's issues.

HEALTH People born on this day take an active interest in keeping themselves healthy. They eat well, exercise regularly, and rarely if ever have to worry about putting on excess weight.

May 4 people need to be aware of possible family-related health concerns that could put them in a high-risk category. Frequent checkups and the use of alternate remedies in addition to conventional ones can go a long way to ensuring the good health of May 4 people.

CAREER AND FINANCES With their dynamic personality and devotion to social causes, May 4 individuals prefer careers where they can make a difference in the world. They often have political aspirations, or favor the law.

Other likely careers for May 4 men and women include social work, family counseling, and religious work. People born on this day often put their money to work for others. If they have considerable financial power they may use it to garner support for worthy causes. These people have simple tastes and seldom make a show of what they possess.

DREAMS AND GOALS Those born on May 4 are philosophical types who ask "why not?" when contemplating a life change. Most May 4 people have a wildly optimistic view of life, believing that they can make the world a better place through their own efforts. No matter what kind of career they decide upon, these individuals are sure to favor humanitarian concerns.

May 4 people will always work harder in aid of others than for themselves. Just as they don't flaunt their possessions, neither do they make a great display of their charitable works. For them, it's best to do good work in silence.

MAY 5

People born on May 5 have a definite agenda in mind. These individuals are verbal, imaginative, and not at all shy about expressing their opinions. The men and women born on this date identify more with their intellect than with any other aspect of their nature.

May 5 individuals are extremely talkative, and an animated manner is their personal trademark. They are also good listeners, and despite their "chatty" reputation, can keep a secret better than most people.

FRIENDS AND LOVERS
May 5 individuals need a lot of people in their life—the more there are the better they like it. They are friendly and sociable, making their friends feel as if they serve a vital role in their lives.

People born on May 5 can be fickle in romantic relationships. They tend to fall in and out of love quickly, often basing their feelings on intellectual kinship more than on romantic compatibility. They can make a successful marriage with a partner who is very different from them, temperamentally, as long as there is sufficient intellectual chemistry.

CHILDREN AND FAMILY
Family life and background rarely play a major role in the lives of May 5 individuals. Because these people are so free-thinking and anxious to go their own way, they often break from the teachings of their youth. This is rarely done in a rebellious fashion, but merely to establish their own social and intellectual identity.

Parenthood is not high on the list of priorities for May 5 individuals. They often marry and have children after their primary career ambitions have been satisfied.

HEALTH
May 5 people have a difficult time slowing down. They do everything in a hurry, even when they don't need to rush. Because of this, the people born on this date experience more than their share of needless accidents.

It is important that May 5 people refrain from taking unnecessary medication since it has a negative effect on their system. Alcohol consumption should also be kept to a minimum.

CAREER AND FINANCES
Outspoken and opinionated, May 5 individuals see their career ambitions as something of a mission. These bright, curious, and eager people start making career plans very early in life. Because of their exceptional communication skills, they make fine professors, lawyers, writers, and journalists.

People born on this date are very clever with money. They have uncanny judgment and can turn a small inheritance into a healthy bankroll with a few smart investments.

DREAMS AND GOALS
People born on May 5 are intrepid students. They never stop learning, never want to close the book on achieving the very best they can. They are adventurous, often leaving the comfort and security of a job in mid-life to train for a new career.

Worldly success and money mean very little to the people born on this date. They are looking to establish a "personal best" that accords with their own standards—not those of anyone else.

EMBRACE
Self-motivation
Gladness
Justice

AVOID
Living in a dream world
Glib remarks
Apathy

ALSO BORN TODAY
French Empress Eugenie; actor Lance Henriksen; political philosopher Karl Marx; actress Cathy Moriarty; actor Michael Murphy; TV personality Michael Palin; actor Tyrone Power; singer Tammy Wynette.

MAY 6

There is a dark side to the intense and glamorous figures born on this date, but it is rarely visible except to those who know them best. These people have real star quality and know how to use it to get what they want out of life.

Men and women born on this date are attractive and charming—and extremely popular with the opposite sex. The challenge for these gifted people is to transcend their physical appeal.

FRIENDS AND LOVERS May 6 men have the ability to conduct platonic relationships with close female friends and passionate affairs with female lovers without confusing the issues inherent in both situations.

There is often a fairy-tale element in the romantic lives of May 6 people. They fall in love madly, often badly, and yet never lose their ability to believe in love's wondrous magic. Love and sexuality signal an extremely important influence in the lives of these individuals.

CHILDREN AND FAMILY Women play a major role in the lives of May 6 individuals, regardless of gender. Whether expressed via relatives or friends, the female influence will be experienced in singularly positive ways. May 6 people are very close to a mother or other maternal figure. The early separation from such an individual could prove traumatic.

Men and women born on this date have an almost hypnotic influence over their own children. If the professional accomplishments of May 6 people are extraordinary it could prove distracting—even disillusioning—for youngsters who fear they can never compete with that level of success.

HEALTH People born on this date are susceptible to colds and sore throats, often brought on by poor nutritional habits. May 6 individuals have huge appetites, and need to cut back on starchy foods and high-calorie desserts if they want to keep their weight under control.

Because of their proclivity to go from one romance to the next, the men and women born on this date should never have unprotected sex.

CAREER AND FINANCES The creative talents of May 6 individuals are unique. These people have special ways of displaying their artistic vision. They don't follow a conventional career path and are more likely to be trailblazers than traditionalists.

May 6 individuals love beautiful things and don't care how much they must spend in order to get them. This isn't generally a problem, unless these people use credit cards instead of cash to pay for their purchases.

DREAMS AND GOALS The good looks and sex appeal of May 6 people often work against them, when what they really want most is to be taken seriously. Their serious goals may relate to their professional lives, or it may represent a goal within their relationship.

Where life goals are concerned, May 6 people are late starters. They may be able to coast through the first half of their life on charm, and often don't begin to show their grit until after they've weathered a few disappointments.

EMBRACE
Smiles
Surprises
Happily ever after

AVOID
Pretense
Unkept promises
Casual sex

ALSO BORN TODAY
Actor George Clooney; founder of psychoanalysis Sigmund Freud; actor Rudolph Valentino; baseball star Willie Mays; film director Max Ophuls; singer/songwriter Bob Seger; actor/director Orson Welles; actress Mare Winningham.

MAY 7

May 7 individuals know how to love, how to serve, and how to wait. These are quiet people, highly principled, whose concern for others nearly always outweighs concern for themselves.

The men and women born on this date are uncritical in the extreme. Yet despite their seeming mildness, there is nothing weak or unreliable about them. Their ability to put their own quiet strength behind the people they love is remarkable. There are no more loved and loving individuals in the world than these men and women.

FRIENDS AND LOVERS
People born on this day love selflessly, often sacrificially. They have no ego issues within the boundaries of a relationship, whether it is with a friend or a romantic partner.

No matter how many love affairs May 7 people have, there is always one great romance, one grand passion that surpasses all the rest. People born on this date cannot settle for an "ordinary" love—they need to find a soul mate.

CHILDREN AND FAMILY
The relationship between May 7 people and their family members is a complicated and sensitive matter. There often is some form of estrangement between the individual and a parent or authority figure, making it difficult to retain a close familial relationship in later years.

May 7 people have a natural affinity for parenthood. Because they have never lost touch with the memory of their own childhood innocence, these individuals can easily identify with their youngsters' world. They have the ability to inspire a child's creative instincts.

HEALTH
The sensitive nature of May 7 people can affect their health in a negative way if these individuals do not take a strong interest in remaining fit. Vigorous daily exercise is the best way to expel the stress so prevalent in the lives of people born on this date.

Pills, alcohol, and nicotine are poisonous to their system and should be shunned.

CAREER AND FINANCES
May 7 people often find themselves drawn to a career by abstract circumstances rather than by deliberate selection. The very nature of these individuals is out of sync with the demands and stresses of career concerns. The men and women born on this date need more than a career—they need a calling. No amount of money can substitute for the satisfaction these individuals require in their life's work.

When it comes to managing money, May 7 people have a surprising flair sparked by their other creative energies. Yet if an inheritance is involved, they should seek expert advice.

DREAMS AND GOALS
People born on this date tend to keep their hopes and dreams to themselves. Generally, they wish to make a success of their important relationships and maintain the clarity of their creative inspiration.

May 7 individuals judge the success or failure of a venture in a purely subjective way. If it reinforces their dreams, they are content. These individuals have little regard for the financial ramifications of their endeavors.

EMBRACE
Diversity
Entertainment
Transition periods

AVOID
Unprofitable conversation
Envying others
Ill-mannered behavior

ALSO BORN TODAY
Actress Anne Baxter; composer Johannes Brahms; actor Darren McGavin; poet Robert Browning; actor Gary Cooper; actor Michael Knight; composer Peter Ilyitch Tchaikovsky; football quarterback Johnny Unitas.

MAY 8

Men and women born on this day are practical and intelligent in a common-sense way. They are rarely glamorous, yet they have the opportunity to make a name for themselves by the very nature of their capableness.

They are well-known for their earthy sense of humor. These men and women can recognize the funny side of any situation, and have a reputation for saying what they think, whether it's critical or complimentary.

FRIENDS AND LOVERS The people born on this date may give the impression of being too self-sufficient to need the support of others. But these steady people need friends, too. Even though they aren't demonstrative about their feelings, they let their friends know just how important a role they play.

May 8 people are very romantic, with charming personalities that easily draw the interest of the opposite sex. They tend to marry in their later years, often to someone in the same profession. Although they can appreciate the thrill of romantic love, what they really want is a solid partnership.

CHILDREN AND FAMILY May 8 people are the "old souls" of their family. As children, the personality of these individuals may have resembled that of miniature adults. They are so remarkably "together" that they may not experience the typical teenage rebellion period.

It isn't odd for May 8 people to have children of their own later in life, when they have already derived a full measure of satisfaction from their career. These individuals are very concerned about teaching their youngsters to become self-sufficient and free-thinking.

HEALTH People born on this day are serious and responsible about health issues. They eat right, exercise regularly, and never take chances with their safety.

Although they are blessed with robust health, these people can sometimes work themselves into exhaustion. Dedication to their career is commendable, but can become dangerous when it deprives them of much-needed rest and relaxation.

CAREER AND FINANCES May 8 people have the talent and credentials to turn any career choice into a success. They often decide very early in life what they want to do, and work toward that aim with unstinting ambition.

Because of their intelligence and sensible nature, May 8 people do best in positions of high-level stress, like medicine, police work, and air-traffic control. They simply don't know what it means to lose their cool.

DREAMS AND GOALS Individuals born on this date don't believe in waiting for goals to come true—they go out and grab them. These are exceptionally organized people who are likely to plan their goals carefully, and never expect anything to be given to them without some intense effort and a few sacrifices on their part.

Although they have the capacity to indulge their fondest dreams, May 8 people are sensible enough to understand that without hard work, few dreams can come true.

EMBRACE
Soulfulness
Intelligence
Love of nature

AVOID
Pressure
Nervousness
Feeling lonely

ALSO BORN TODAY
Naturalist David Attenborough; novelist Peter Benchley; actress Candice Bergen; opera singer Heather Harper; actress Melissa Gilbert; actor/comedian Don Rickles; singer Toni Tennille; U.S. President Harry S Truman.

MAY 9

People born on this date are warriors in every sense of the word. They possess a bold spirit that propels them forward toward challenges that other, more timid individuals would never face.

Despite the forcefulness of their personality, these engaging individuals are by no means pushy or even aggressive. Their enthusiasm level is extremely high and they have the ability to laugh at themselves. There is no hidden agenda with these individuals—what you see is what you get.

FRIENDS AND LOVERS Individuals born on May 9 have a genius for friendship. They don't seek out people like themselves only, but prefer a diverse group of pals. Because of their strengths, May 9 people tend to be the leader of their group, though they invariably invite the opinions of others.

In romantic matters May 9 people discover that opposites attract. Although they sometimes become embroiled in tempestuous relationships, May 9 men and women generally prefer a stable union that allows them to be happy at home while concentrating the greater part of their energy on career objectives.

CHILDREN AND FAMILY It's not unusual for people born on this day to have demanding, goal-oriented parents who expect exemplary behavior from their children. Though May 9 people usually rise to the occasion, parent-child relations can be stressful.

May 9 individuals are superb examples to their own children. They don't instruct their offspring but simply set a good example.

HEALTH The men and women born on this date live full and active lives on all levels. Since they are always occupied with projects—many

of them physical—May 9 people rarely need to make any adjustments to their health and fitness habits.

Though not particularly heavy eaters, these men and women prefer a diet rich in protein, especially red meat. Alcohol should be taken in moderation and smoking avoided entirely. Since their temperament is excitable, these individuals can receive considerable benefits from daily meditation sessions.

CAREER AND FINANCES May 9 individuals have a talent for leadership and always seek out careers that provide the opportunity to exhibit that ability.

Those who are born on this date have great entrepreneurial skills and may seek to start a business of their own. Besides a wealth of ideas, May 9 people also possess an amazing potential for raising needed capital.

DREAMS AND GOALS The ability of May 9 people to achieve their goals is almost legendary. In addition to their organizational gifts, these people have a wonderful talent for visualizing their future plans.

May 9 men and women leave nothing to chance. They know that if they are to be successful in bringing their dreams to fruition, the dreams must be manifested through the practical methods they understand best.

EMBRACE
Gentility
A sense of humor
Color

AVOID
Thoughts of death
Boredom
Pretentiousness

ALSO BORN TODAY
Playwright James Barrie; film director James L. Brooks; actor Albert Finney; actress/member of Parliament Glenda Jackson; singer Billy Joel; faith healer Kathryn Kuhlman; TV journalist Mike Wallace; dog trainer Barbara Woodhouse.

MAY 10

People born on this date have a special view of the world. They are cautious optimists who believe that if they try hard enough they can make a positive impact upon their world.

May 10 men and women travel a somewhat solitary road. Though they aren't naturally solitary people, they do require more than their share of privacy. They depend on their subconscious to give them the guidance they need.

FRIENDS AND LOVERS These discreet yet charming individuals have the reputation for being loners, and yet because of their genuine concern for others they cannot be classified as standoffish. Early in life, romance can offer disappointment to May 10 individuals, who are more likely to find their permanent partner during middle age or later. If romance or marriage goes badly, these philosophical people have the ability to bounce back and make a new life.

CHILDREN AND FAMILY The character and integrity of May 10 people is an inspiration to family members. The quiet purposefulness of these men and women sets a good example. Although they aren't necessarily close to family members, May 10 individuals feel a great sense of responsibility to them.

The men and women born on this date make excellent parents. They are affectionate but not indulgent; discipline-conscious but not strict. Unlike many parents, they do not expect their youngsters to be a carbon copy of themselves.

HEALTH Despite a somewhat deceptive civility, people born on this date have a tendency to go to extremes. This is often reflected in a devotion to a particular health regimen. May 10 folks don't handle change very well, and if it becomes necessary to readjust their habits in favor of new ones they could lose interest altogether.

May 10 individuals sometimes suffer from food allergies, and should make a point to wholeheartedly embrace a holistic health routine.

CAREER AND FINANCES When it comes to setting a career path for themselves, May 10 individuals often look for professions that allow them to work alone or behind the scenes. They don't really enjoy taking instruction from others and prefer to set their own pace and schedule.

People born on this date have a real talent with money. Their financial instincts are good, if a bit conservative, and they have the ability to handle their own financial affairs in business or personal life.

DREAMS AND GOALS May 10 people live out their dreams and goals on an everyday basis. It is their habit to see life as a continuum, without qualifying their experience by degrees.

The men and women born on this date want very much to make a success of their lives, though not necessarily according to worldly terms. They have very high expectations about their ability to turn failure into success, and may sometimes unconsciously subvert their own efforts in order to test their ability to "come back."

MAY 11

Few people have the overwhelming creative potential that is the gift of May 11 individuals. Whether or not these men and women turn their talents toward artistic expression, they will be known for their ability to turn the ordinary into the special.

Individuals born on May 11 are brilliant, talented—and somewhat unstable. Despite a reputation for being short-tempered, even critical, May 11 people command the loyalty and devotion of everyone who knows them.

FRIENDS AND LOVERS
People born on this date have an eccentric band of friends and followers. They like to be surrounded by interesting, clever people. They don't like the restriction or responsibility of close friendship and prefer more superficial ties with people who share their rarefied tastes.

There are a lot of emotional ups and downs in the love life of May 11 people. These folks may not always love permanently, but they love deeply and without regard to whether or not they may be hurt. Often there is an almost operatic glamour to their romantic escapades.

CHILDREN AND FAMILY
The familial connections of May 11 people are usually as dramatic as the rest of their relationships. The men and women often have very close relationships with one of their parents, or with a nonconformist-type relative.

May 11 individuals provide their kids with a fascinating and challenging life-view. These individuals want their offspring to be exposed to as many learning experiences as possible. They don't believe in enforcing parental discipline just because they are expected to do so.

HEALTH
People born on May 11 have some very unusual ideas about keeping fit. They tend to go to extremes in whatever they do, including health and fitness habits. Because fasting combines spiritual and physical benefits, it's a favorite health practice of May 11 people. Men and women born on this date also enjoy keeping their diet as natural as possible, with an emphasis on organically grown fruits and vegetables.

CAREER AND FINANCES
A great many people born on this date turn their considerable creative talents toward the arts. They make excellent writers, sculptors, musicians, and dancers. Even if their career paths take them in another direction, these men and women will find a way to exhibit their creative skills through a hobby or a vocation.

Where money is concerned, May 11 people have a little more difficult time shining. They have the ability to make a great deal of money, but handling it is something else. They are attracted to risky enterprises and may fall into gambling as a favored pastime.

DREAMS AND GOALS
There is no limit to how big May 11 people can dream. They believe in their talent, and although sometimes assailed by doubts of how strictly they can adhere to the practical demands involved in bringing goals into being, they have far more grit than is generally supposed.

EMBRACE
Permanence
Hidden talents
Graciousness

AVOID
Negative influences
Grudges
Favoritism

ALSO BORN TODAY
Songwriter Irving Berlin; actress Margaret Rutherford; musician Les Chadwick; artist Salvador Dali; dancer/choreographer Martha Graham; trend analyst Faith Popcorn; actress Natasha Richardson; satirist Mort Sahl.

65

MAY 12

People born on May 12 are not so much leaders as they are guides, eager to show others the world through their eyes. These jolly individuals appreciate the serious aspects of life, even though they seem to be caught up in the pure pleasure of living it.

May 12 men and women have boundless energy and give equal amounts to both work and play. Their enjoyment and enthusiasm shows in everything they do.

FRIENDS AND LOVERS Individuals born on this date revel in a closely knit circle of friends and admirers. Although they don't need to be the center of attention they generally are, and many of their associates try to emulate their charm and good-natured appeal.

As lovers, May 12 individuals are not as bold as they would like to be, and often find the love of their life among a group of friends. It is important to these people that a permanent relationship be based on more than simple attraction. They are happiest when it provides stimulus for their physical and mental appetites.

CHILDREN AND FAMILY The men and women born on this date draw considerable strength and inspiration from their family backgrounds. Because they place so much credence in family tradition, these individuals may accept responsibility for a business or concern that could take them away from their chosen field of endeavor.

With their own children, people born on May 12 are far more liberal. They expect their offspring to carry on tradition, but in their own unique ways.

HEALTH It is rare when anything more than a seasonal cold or the flu sidelines someone born on this date. Their happy attitude combined with a naturally robust constitution keeps May 12 people going strong; they remain active well into old age.

Though it may seem as if only their good attitude can be credited for their condition, May 12 people actually contribute to their own good health by subconsciously doing everything right. They eat well, and sparingly. They exercise, but don't recklessly push their bodies. Best of all, they keep a sound mental attitude and remain engaged in worthwhile activities.

CAREER AND FINANCES True to their native Taurean personality, individuals born on this date are quick to act but slow to decide. It may take them several jobs or career starts before they can put down roots in what will be their life's work.

Business management and the decorative arts are two distinct yet very plausible career possibilities for May 12 individuals. They have a good head for business, yet their artistic talents need to be satisfied, as well.

DREAMS AND GOALS May 12 individuals believe in setting reachable goals. That doesn't mean that they don't dream big— they do. But they don't like to be disappointed and would rather set their sights a bit lower than have to contend with failure.

People born on this date depend a great deal on the love and emotional support of others to give them the impetus to keep going..

EMBRACE
Clean living
Memory
Your own style

AVOID
Repetition
Sarcasm
Becoming notorious

ALSO BORN TODAY
Composer Burt Bacharach; actor Stephen Baldwin; poet Edward Lear; actor/director Emilio Estevez; actress Susan Hampshire; actress Katharine Hepburn; TV personality Tom Snyder; singer/songwriter Steve Winwood.

MAY 13

People born on May 13 are rare individuals who possess unique and special talents. There is a dark side to these people, yet they are rarely moved to show this aspect of themselves to anyone.

May 13 natives have great imaginative potential, which they may need to shape through learning and experience. While it is not necessarily true that these people will be unsuccessful without a specific direction in mind, they will certainly be better able to accomplish their aims with one.

FRIENDS AND LOVERS
May 13 individuals are well-suited for friendship. They have a naturally giving nature and the ability to put their trust in someone close to them. They are quick to reveal their thoughts and feelings, and enjoy talking about shared goals.

Love brings great joy and great disappointment to these folks in equal measure to these individuals. Because they judge with their heart and not their head, they often choose a mate who is totally unsuited to their temperament. Once they realize a relationship is not working, they'll end the union abruptly, since nothing displeases them more than wallowing in failure.

CHILDREN AND FAMILY
People born on May 13 generally experience a somewhat distant relationship with family members. Even as children they were probably the ones who never seemed to "belong." These people are not group-oriented, and their opinions are often at odds with those of the family unit.

May 13 people are not particularly attentive parents, though they have a great capacity for love and tenderness. They want to give their children a great deal of leeway and rarely institute strong discipline.

HEALTH
It is not easy for May 13 individuals to be sensible about health habits. They eat whatever they please, whether or not it is good for them, and are especially partial to convenience and fast food.

Although they enjoy exercise, May 13 folks rarely have the discipline to stick with a workout schedule. They would much rather play a rousing game of tennis or racquetball, and then remain sedentary until the next game.

CAREER AND FINANCES
May 13 individuals are very talented and can make a success of just about any career. Though they may be expert at a particular subject, they will most likely follow their heart and do what they love best. Many May 13 people change careers as middle age approaches, switching from a "safe" job to something they find more emotionally satisfying.

Money has little meaning for these people. They want to express themselves, and if that means giving up a potentially large income, they are unlikely to care.

DREAMS AND GOALS
People born on this date want to be happy. They don't like restrictions of any kind, and will always take the path that they believe will take them closest to living life as they wish to live it.

May 13 men and women don't compare their success with that of other people. If they compete, it is against themselves, not their contemporaries.

EMBRACE
Reliability
Pride
Kindness to animals

AVOID
Arguments you can't win
Lack of respect for money
Tension

ALSO BORN TODAY
Actress Beatrice Arthur; novelist Daphne Du Maurier; actor Harvey Keitel; boxer Joe Louis; singer Lorraine McIntosh; composer Sir Arthur Sullivan; singer/songwriter Ritchie Valens; musician Stevie Wonder.

MAY 14

hose born on this day are torn between the intellectual life they are drawn to and the active life they want to pursue. This dichotomy of choice and personality is the defining factor in the lives of these complicated people.

May 14 people have extraordinary artistic vision and can do great things if left to their own devices. These men and women don't know the meaning of the word "compromise."

FRIENDS AND LOVERS
May 14 individuals seek out friends who provide emotional and intellectual support. They love to bounce their ideas off others, enjoying the give and take of differing opinions.

People born on May 14 have something of a "love 'em and leave 'em" reputation. This isn't because they're fickle but because they have a restless nature that requires constant stimulation.

CHILDREN AND FAMILY
Due to their highly competitive nature, May 14 individuals owe a great deal of their success in life to their family background. They may have parents who fostered a sense of competition between siblings, a fact that can spur May 14 people throughout their entire life.

In their own role as parents, May 14 individuals have a tendency to adopt the "friend" approach. They dislike being an authority figure since it puts pressure on them to adopt a more serious persona than they like. These individuals usually have better relationships with their children when the youngsters grow up, as opposed to when the kids are small.

HEALTH
Happily, these busy, active people don't have to worry about keeping off the pounds, which is just as well since they are often devotees of fast food.

It is important that May 14 people get plenty of sleep. Insomnia and other sleep disorders should be treated with meditation and relaxation techniques instead of pills. Tapes of music played over ocean sounds create a peaceful atmosphere for sleep.

CAREER AND FINANCES
People born on this date have many talents and can pick from several basic interests including communications, media, and the arts. These men and women are likely to switch careers at least once.

The financial ups and downs of May 14 men and women can have a negative effect on their ability to achieve the level of career success they want. Usually these difficulties with money are caused because May 14 individuals delegate these matters to people who are either less knowledgeable than they should be, or less scrupulous.

DREAMS AND GOALS
Individuals born on this day have a very specific idea of what constitutes success. On the one hand they value their own assessment of personal achievement, yet they also value the approval of others, particularly respected colleagues.

May 14 individuals are self-critical and may not be able to appreciate their own achievements. Until they learn that external validation is not the true measure of their success, May 14 people may feel unsatisfied by their own efforts.

EMBRACE
The ability to apologize
Happy thoughts
Starting over

AVOID
Rage
Confusion
Lack of imagination

ALSO BORN TODAY
Figure skating champion Kurt Browning; singer Bobby Darin; actress Meg Foster; painter Thomas Gainsborough; film director George Lucas; comedian Eric Morecombe; singer Danny Wood; film director Robert Zemeckis.

MAY 15

The men and women born on this day draw inspiration from their physical and emotional surroundings. These people have a great need to distill their experience and share it with others through art or some other personal expression.

Individuals born on this date have a real need to involve themselves in the lives of others: These people are natural do-gooders, who like to feel as if they are thoroughly connected to the family of mankind.

FRIENDS AND LOVERS
May 15 people have an uncanny ability to draw into their lives the very types of individuals they need. Whether it is for spiritual or emotional purposes, May 15 people sense what lessons they need to know, and act upon that knowledge through their relationships.

Romantic partners often fill the same role in the lives of May 15 individuals. If it seems as if these people are constantly making curious choices in romance, it's because they are looking for someone who can teach them the life lessons they need to know.

CHILDREN AND FAMILY
There are likely to be complications in the family life of May 15 people, often stemming from the demands or misconceptions of a parent or guardian. Unfortunately, May 15 natives often find themselves in the middle of a difficult family situation, which can negatively influence their decision to have a family of their own.

If they do have children, May 15 men and women are adamant about not repeating the mistakes their own parents made. Although concerned with their youngsters' success in life, May 15 people want it to be on their kids' terms, not their own.

HEALTH
No matter how disciplined the eating habits of May 15 people, they may suffer from a weight problem because of an aversion to exercise. People born on this day often lack the discipline to maintain or even to begin a daily workout regimen. But unless they are motivated, these men and women easily fall back into poor health habits.

CAREER AND FINANCES
Many people born on this date have superior speaking and singing voices that prompt them to build a career around those talents. They also have a very good head for business and can make a successful career of managing a home-based business.

Though not money-oriented, people born on this date enjoy living a lavish lifestyle—and that requires money. Fortunately, these folks have good instincts for making investments; they're fearless and don't worry about risk.

DREAMS AND GOALS
Success has many faces and May 15 individuals are not always sure just which of these appeal to them. Those born on this date have many dreams, but it can be difficult for these men and women to focus on a definite plan to make their dreams reality.

Because of their laid-back attitude, it isn't easy for May 15 people to focus on goals to the exclusion of other concerns in life.

EMBRACE
Transcendental awareness
Mental energy
Ecstasy

AVOID
Bitterness
Emotional instability
Lies

ALSO BORN TODAY
Photographer Richard Avedon; baseball star George Brett; actor Joseph Cotten; film director David Cronenberg; actor James Mason; composer Mike Oldfield; author Katherine Anne Porter; playwright Peter Shaffer.

MAY 16

In matters of self-expression, May 16 individuals are among the most buoyant and fascinating personalities within the entire spectrum of astrology. They have their own view of life and their own style—both of which set them apart from people born on any other day.

May 16 men and women can seem argumentative because they enjoy exchanging opinions with others. They love the sport of debate and prefer a rousing argument to a quiet discussion.

FRIENDS AND LOVERS

There is a special aura about May 16 individuals, which makes them incredibly appealing. Friends are drawn to the eccentric persona and also to the grace and charm of these men and women.

They are romantics who don't always evidence the most intelligent choices when it comes to selecting a mate. For this reason multiple marriages are not uncommon for these people. Although they fall in love many times, May 16 natives bring the same joy and enthusiasm to each experience.

CHILDREN AND FAMILY

There is a great deal about their upbringing and family background that May 16 people do not wish to acknowledge. They seem to prefer to revise many of the flaws and faults inherent in their childhood scenario by forgetting the unhappy parts and concentrating on the pleasant ones.

As parents they may repeat some of the mistakes made by their parents, yet they are extremely loving and protective. If their upbringing was restrictive, May 16 men and women are likely to be extremely liberal with their own children.

HEALTH

Because they have a need of immediate gratification it is very difficult for May 16 people to be as vigilant as they should be about maintaining their weight. Alcohol is especially damaging to their sensitive systems and should be avoided.

Because they are not known for being the athletic type, May 16 people should be encouraged to take a brisk walk each day.

CAREER AND FINANCES

May 16 individuals bring a sense of imagination and daring to everything they attempt. They don't like to follow the conventional path and will inevitably put their own imprint on anything they do. They love being on public view and make exquisite performers of any art or craft.

Because of their great talent and ability to extract the maximum attention out of what they do, May 16 people have considerable earning potential. They can be extremely reckless with money and should consult a professional to manage their financial affairs.

DREAMS AND GOALS

People born on this date want to be noticed for their unique abilities. Intellectually, they present a somewhat odd perspective, and are happiest when others see things through their eyes.

May 16 men and women feel that they are successful if they can do what they love on their own terms. These people are innovators who value their freedom of choice above everything else. They see no point in maintaining tradition just for its own sake.

EMBRACE
A sense of history
Good sportsmanship
Belief

AVOID
Fights with friends
Attitude problems
Shallowness

ALSO BORN TODAY
Writer H. E. Bates; actor Pierce Brosnan; actor Henry Fonda; gymnast Olga Korbut; designer Christian Lacroix; pianist Liberace; tennis star Gabriela Sabatini; actress Debra Winger.

MAY 17

People born on this day enjoy the pursuit of excellence. They are self-starters who generally know very early in life what they want and how to get it. They are intelligent, though not showy about what they know, and for this reason may not be perceived as especially brilliant by others. And that's fine, since May 17 men and women are considerably less concerned with how their actions are perceived by others than with whether they themselves are content.

FRIENDS AND LOVERS Because they have considerable leadership potential, May 17 individuals are likely to surround themselves with more "followers" than equals. They are so strong-minded that to be with other people like themselves can create conflict. They make exceptional mentors and confidantes to their younger, less experienced friends.

People born on this date are very discerning partners. They know what they want in a mate and will not settle for anything less. Because they are so particular, May 17 men and women often marry later in life.

CHILDREN AND FAMILY May 17 men and women believe very strongly in family honor. They endorse the traditional values of family life and may act as a surrogate parent to younger brothers and sisters. During late adolescence there may be an element of conflict between May 17 people and one or both parents.

Individuals born on this date are strict parents. Even if they have a loving relationship with their children, May 17 people never fail to emphasize discipline.

HEALTH There may be a touch of hypochondria in the nature of May 17 people. They concern themselves with every aspect of being fit: exercise, diet, and relaxation techniques, including meditative states.

Although they keep themselves physically fit, May 17 men and women can develop problems with their joints in later years if they have not made weight-bearing exercises a part of their daily regimen. Calcium supplements taken every day can help.

CAREER AND FINANCES May 17 individuals are well-suited to careers in business and finance. Although they have a keen imagination, this talent is likely to be subjugated to their other abilities. These people like to be in positions of authority, yet they are not power seekers.

Few people possess such natural abilities with money as May 17 men and women. They have an amazing faculty for turning small sums into substantial earnings through wise investment decisions.

DREAMS AND GOALS May 17 individuals have very specific goals and will not allow themselves to be diverted from achieving them. Many of these people require a college education for the work they want to do.

People born on this date generally keep dreams of a more personal nature to themselves. These people are very concerned with self-improvement, and often count this among their most important achievements.

EMBRACE
Staying power
Morality
Daydreams

AVOID
Inconsistency
Guilt
Truculence

ALSO BORN TODAY
Drummer Bill Bruford; Watergate prosecutor Archibald Cox; actor Dennis Hopper; singer Pervis Jackson; boxer Sugar Ray Leonard; opera singer Birgit Nilsson; actor Bob Saget; composer Eric Satie.

MAY 18

A love of freedom and independence characterizes the people born on May 18. These individuals are temperamental, lovable, and exasperating; they make it impossible for others to be indifferent toward them.

May 18 men and woman possess extraordinary creative energy, and are never without an important cause to champion. These individuals enjoy taking risks, but only when they believe the risk "matters."

FRIENDS AND LOVERS The men and women born on this date favor a large circle of friends who share their love of sports and good conversation. They are likely to have only a few very close friends to whom they confide their deepest thoughts and most personal secrets.

May 18 people often have troubled love lives. Because they are extremely emotional, breakups are hard for them. Their strong sexual nature often leads them to make some poor choices in love matters, but these folks are usually wise enough to understand that heartache often brings a measure of wisdom.

CHILDREN AND FAMILY May 18 people often stand alone within the family. Either they distance themselves from the family at an early age or their chosen life-path creates a breach.

Parenting is not often at the top of the list of priorities for May 18 men and women. These dedicated, driven people often need to fulfill a personal or career ambition first. When they do choose to have children, individuals born on this date provide a stable influence.

HEALTH May 18 people have high energy and a strong constitution. They adapt well to a daily physical regimen of exercise and toning.

As is the case with many active people, May 18 individuals run the risk of being accident prone when their physical energy supersedes their better judgment. They should also be aware of the benefits of showing their emotions, especially anger. When May 18 people bottle up their rage they can experience headaches, indigestion, and other physical complaints.

CAREER AND FINANCES The men and women born on this date have a single-minded approach to career goals. As a rule, most decided very early in life what they wanted to do and are not likely to deviate from that path.

May 18 individuals firmly manage their career path. At times they will defer to the judgment of a mentor, yet ultimately the decisions must be their own. Their independent spirit makes them ideally suited to careers where they are their own boss, or are at least autonomous within a larger structure.

DREAMS AND GOALS People born on May 18 want to make it on their own. On principle, they will shun the help of family or friends. These individuals can never be accused of getting somewhere due to nepotism or favoritism.

No matter how successful these men and women become they never forget their roots, and may even draw upon them for inspiration. They are deceptively ambitious, a fact that may go unnoticed by everyone except those who know them best.

EMBRACE
Dreams
Good taste
Criticism

AVOID
Rationalization
Anxiety
Feeling guilty

ALSO BORN TODAY
Film director Richard Brooks; singer Perry Como; pianist Clifford Curzon; ballerina Margot Fonteyn; film director Frank Capra; baseball star Reggie Jackson; Pope John Paul II; singer Enzio Pinza.

MAY 19

The men and women born on May 19 come into this world wanting to change it. These people are extremely motivated, eager to put their personal stamp upon their environment. They have supreme confidence in their abilities and never shrink when it comes to doing what is expected of them.

May 19 individuals are loners, but not in the traditional sense. They enjoy being with people, yet they trust only their own counsel and rarely take advice. Resourceful? May 19 people are at the head of the line.

FRIENDS AND LOVERS May 19 natives make friends easily, and probably have more friends than they require. They generally prize a few close confidantes, people to whom they can disclose their hopes and fears, dreams and disillusionments. As friends themselves they are loyal, helpful, and willing to keep secrets.

When in love, May 19 men and women display the same stoicism they project in other areas of their lives. Though they can fall deeply in love, they find it difficult to trust their feelings.

CHILDREN AND FAMILY Men and women born on this date generally retain very close ties with family members. They enjoy being part of a large and fun-loving group of relatives. If they don't have this kind of family they will often search for a surrogate among friends.

May 19 people may not look forward to parenthood, but in the event that they do, they stress independence and integrity to their children.

HEALTH May 19 people need a few pointers about how to take care of their health. They have a habit of choosing convenience over nutrition, and opt for lunch at their favorite fast-food joint more often than they should. Although naturally robust, these folks tend to exercise on an irregular basis.

Because they are naturally competitive, May 19 men and women find satisfaction playing weekend sports. They can be accident prone, however, and should be certain to wear protective equipment and suitable shoes.

CAREER AND FINANCES People born on this date like to work with their hands. They crave active, physical work, and don't generally enjoy a job that keeps them behind a desk. Even if they have a supervisory type of position, they find ways to remain active.

May 19 people don't need money to validate themselves, but they like accumulating it for the sense of security it provides. They favor good, if not luxurious, surroundings. Giving those that they love all the material blessings of life is a predominant aim.

DREAMS AND GOALS That old adage "there are no small parts, only small actors" could have been written to describe May 19 individuals. For these people the prize is in the striving, not just what is ultimately achieved.

May 19 men and women are practical enough to understand that they may not achieve all their aims. They are good winners, yet philosophical about failure.

EMBRACE
Jokes
Simplicity
True love

AVOID
Bad dreams
Taking foolish chances
Losing faith

ALSO BORN TODAY
Member of Parliament Lady Nancy Astor; novelist Nora Ephron; actor James Fox; playwright Lorraine Hansberry; actor David Hartman; actress Nancy Kwan; musician Pete Townshend; comedienne Victoria Wood.

MAY 20

People born on this date have a streak of eccentricity in their otherwise conventional personality. Although they are very intelligent, May 20 men and women may suffer from a learning disability of some sort, which, though small, undermines their self-confidence, especially when they are young. Once their personality expands to encompass this they will display it as a badge of moral courage.

EMBRACE
Challenges
Good causes
Peace of mind

AVOID
Negative attitudes
Running away from problems
Questioning authority

ALSO BORN TODAY
Actress/singer Cher; singer/songwriter Joe Cocker; actor Tony Goldwyn; musician Hephzibah Menuhin; hockey star Stan Mikita; philosopher John Stuart Mill; baseball pitcher Hal Newhouser; actor Jimmy Stewart.

FRIENDS AND LOVERS It is almost impossible not to like the people born on this day. They seem to draw friends from all walks of life. May 20 people love to listen to anyone's story, and are famous for giving remarkably apt advice.

They are equally fetching as lovers. May 20 people have a great deal of charm, not to mention good looks. These individuals can easily rebound from a bad relationship and are rarely without a partner.

CHILDREN AND FAMILY May 20 individuals often come from a dysfunctional background. Remarkably, this does little to affect their love of family and the traditions associated with it. They have a surprising need to surround themselves with the conventional trappings of the nuclear family.

People born on this date are liberal, loving parents. They want to give their children every-

thing they didn't have, and yet want to teach them independence. There can be difficulties between the generations at times, yet eventually these are sure to be reconciled.

HEALTH May 20 folks have a real concern about their appearance and work very hard to maintain their special look into old age. This is even more important for them if their work or social standing is dependent upon how they look.

Many May 20 people are health food fanatics. They have no problem excising white flour and sugar from their diets, and often prefer organically grown fruits and vegetables. Where exercise is concerned they are especially dedicated to perfection and will drive themselves to keep fit.

CAREER AND FINANCES People born on this date have a need to display their talents on a very large scale. Yet this may be in conflict with their basic need for emotional privacy. If they work in a large office they may have many friends and take part in a great many office-related activities—yet very few people will know anything about their personal life.

May 20 people have a gift for making and handling money, even if they have virtually no background for doing so. They have their own ideas about how to make their money grow, and don't easily take advice from other people.

DREAMS AND GOALS Men and women born on this date may have an unrealistic attitude about what it takes to make their dreams come true. They are ambitious, yet may lack the emotional stamina needed to be successful in their chosen field.

They are often better at helping friends or colleagues attain their wishes, since May 20 people can look at others in an objective light.

GEMINI
May 21 - June 20

Gemini is the third sign of the astrological year and is known by its astrological symbol, the Twins. Gemini individuals are bright, changeable, and inquiring. With Mercury as the ruling planet, people born under this sign are considered to be quick-thinking and always in motion. They have many interests and great social adeptness.

THE GEMINI MAN Gemini men have a very special charm. These guys are the original Peter Pan, and it is this youthful, little-boy attitude that is part of their appeal. Like other air-sign men, the typical Gemini gentleman has strong intellectual inclinations but isn't the intimidating sort. He doesn't quote facts and figures or make a fuss about his knowledge.

These men are often dedicated to their career, seeing it almost as a calling rather than simply a way to make a living. Gemini men excel in advertising, media, politics, teaching, or any field where language and communication skills are useful. Gemini men are natural dilettantes who enjoy a variety of hobbies as well as competitive weekend sports like tennis, golf, and racquetball.

THE GEMINI WOMAN The typical Gemini woman is glib, self-assured, and sophisticated. Although she isn't a slave to fashion, she can carry off a way-out look with considerable panache. Gemini women have a real talent for conversation. Smart, sassy, and sarcastic, these ladies will always have the last word.

Even though they are often exceptionally good looking, Gemini women are more interested in showing off their brain power than their physical attributes. These women are often career-driven, and even when they marry and have children they are likely to seek a career outside their domestic circle. They make good mothers, always encouraging their children to get involved in a variety of interests and hobbies. Gemini women retain their youthful appearance and attitude well into middle age, and even beyond.

THE GEMINI CHILD Children born under this sign are usually very bright, and may show a talent for logic and language skills at an early age. There is a tendency for parents of these little ones to attempt to turn them into prodigies, but this is not wise, given the typical Gemini child's vulnerability to emotional and mental exhaustion when too many demands are made upon them. Allowing them to progress at their own speed, emphasizing the joy of learning for its own sake, is the best method to employ with these children.

Gemini youngsters require a great amount of social contact from the time they are toddlers. They mix well with other children and usually have a diverse and interesting group of friends by the time they reach their teens. Although they encounter the usual adolescent problems, Gemini teens are generally upbeat and positive.

THE GEMINI LOVER

Those who have never been romanced by a Gemini have missed a great deal. These versatile, witty, and fun-loving individuals possess so much charm they can be almost impossible to resist. Gemini natives are turned on by language and seldom get serious about anyone who doesn't feel the same way. To a Gemini, verbal communication is a big part of romancing a love interest. Whether a clever fax, a romantic letter, or just a few endearing words left on an answering machine, the Gemini lover understands the erotic power of language.

It takes a unique individual to get a member of this sign to settle down in wedded bliss. Even when a Gemini does tie the knot, he or she can lose interest quickly if the excitement wears off.

ELEMENT: Air
QUALITY: Mutable
PLANETARY RULER: Mercury
BIRTHSTONE: Agate
FLOWER: Lily of the Valley
COLOR: Yellow

KEY CHARACTERISTIC: Communication

STRENGTHS: Witty, Talkative, Versatile

CHALLENGES: Superficial, Fickle, Lack of commitment

THE GEMINI BOSS

It isn't always easy to read this employer. He or she is likely to display different personalities on different occasions. A pushover one day, overly critical the next, this boss can be something of a challenge. Fortunately, this individual is also a good communicator and encourages debate among employees. If someone has a comment it will be heard, and probably acted upon.

This is one boss who feels perfectly at ease in a social relationship with employees and understands that the more relaxed and happy his people are, the better their work habits will be.

THE GEMINI FRIEND

Gemini men and women make good friends. Their naturally sociable nature and love of conversation is a big plus in drawing people to them. They aren't snobbish about friends and don't attempt to choose their companions thoughtlessly, via the status quo.

Though these individuals have a love of gossip, they never indulge in it with malice. To the contrary, they're happiest when they can pass on good news about others. People who witness Geminis in action are attracted to them—which is why so many folks have at least one Gemini friend.

A sympathetic listener, the Gemini friend nevertheless likes to use humor to leaven the troubles of others. Geminis will not allow pals to wallow in self-pity.

MAY 21

Those born on this date have a great will to succeed, and bend all their efforts toward that aim. These men and women often develop a sense of mission when they are very young, feeling that they have a destiny to fulfill. They see things on a grand, even epic scale and live their lives in a similar fashion.

Because of their dedication and sense of purpose, May 21 people can be seen as ruthless, even dictatorial by others.

FRIENDS AND LOVERS
May 21 people don't make friends so much as they recruit them. These individuals want comrades more than they want buddies, but that doesn't keep them from being very good at practicing the art of friendship. They are extremely generous and always willing to help out in any time of crisis or need.

However, men and women born on this date are less successful at keeping romantic relationships healthy. Often they are too involved in humanitarian or social aims to make a firm commitment to a lover.

CHILDREN AND FAMILY
People born on May 21 consider themselves part of the family of Man. They have less confidence in the workings of a biological family, even though they may experience great closeness with one or more of their siblings.

They can be strict with their own children, though their sense of fun makes them good guardians of youngsters. They want to see their children succeed in the world and will coach and encourage them at every possible juncture.

HEALTH
Although they often appear robust and vital, May 21 men and women may have their share of health challenges, usually brought on through poor diet and an unwillingness to exercise on a regular basis. A great many of these individuals have food issues that complicate their ability to maintain a healthy lifestyle. Sensible eating, rather than dieting to reduce, is best.

The discipline that characterizes May 21 individuals does not seem to exist for them in this aspect of their lives. It takes a lot to change their attitudes, but with great motivation it can be done.

CAREER AND FINANCES
May 21 people are intelligent rather than bright, learned rather than educated. They prefer common-sense occupations and are often drawn to farming, mining, or high-ticket retail.

These people truly possess the golden touch. They may not go into a particular career to make money, but make money they will. May 21 individuals prefer saving money to spending it.

DREAMS AND GOALS
Although they may not be especially good at articulating their goals, May 21 men and women have a very clear idea of what they want out of life. Security is usually very high on the list, and these people will work hard to ensure the achievement of that goal.

They have creative abilities that they may not market through a career path, but that they enjoy displaying via hobbies or pastimes. May 21 women often pursue successful artistic careers when their children are grown.

EMBRACE
Sophistication
Physical exertion
Progressive thinking

AVOID
Back-tracking
Irascibility
Bombast

ALSO BORN TODAY
Actor Raymond Burr; singer Peggy Cass; singer Ronald Isley; football coach Ara Parseghian; Spanish King Philip II; actor Judge Reinhold; physicist Anton Sakharov; musician Fats Waller.

MAY 22

People born on this day are unique in the extreme. They have great charisma and the ability to draw attention to themselves. Also, these men and women possess something of a dual nature. They may be lofty and intellectual one day, earthy and intense on another.

These individuals have a deeply spiritual side that they seldom reveal to others. For this reason they usually keep their personal beliefs to themselves.

EMBRACE
A healing spirit
Perfection
Balance

AVOID
Being quarrelsome
Self-interest
Obsession

ALSO BORN TODAY
Actor Richard Benjamin; model Naomi Campbell; painter Mary Cassat; writer Arthur Conan Doyle; actor Sir Laurence Olivier; astrologer Lois Rodden; lyricist Bernie Taupin; composer Richard Wagner.

FRIENDS AND LOVERS May 22 individuals are generally seen as leaders by others, though they may not see themselves in this role. Even as children they seem older, more in charge than others, as if born to be authority figures. Members of their inner circle are very much in awe of them.

Love can be a complicated thing for May 22 men and women. They may be unwilling to see the problems and failings of a beloved individual.

CHILDREN AND FAMILY May 22 men and women believe in the traditional family values. This is especially true if they weren't involved in a close family unit as children. They may not always agree with the attitudes that were passed down to them, or even with the religious beliefs that were espoused, but they do understand that family members can disagree but still love one another.

People born on this date take a very active interest in the lives of their own children. They are strict disciplinarians, yet fair. They are likely to impress upon their youngsters the importance of honesty and integrity.

HEALTH The people born on this date are naturally healthy and work very hard to keep themselves in top physical condition.

May 22 men and women have hearty appetites. They like plain food, cooked simply. They require a lot of protein in their diet, especially the sort gleaned from red meat. Although alcohol is not troublesome to their system, they should make water their beverage of choice.

CAREER AND FINANCES The written and spoken word has great meaning for people born on this date. Even if they do not make their living in this way, language will continue to have power over them all through life.

May 22 people are intelligent in a very common-sense way. They don't flaunt their knowledge and could never be thought of as intellectual snobs, yet erudition is their trademark.

Money has an important place in the lives of May 22 natives. They generally have big plans in life and making a good living is part of it. May 22 people are generous to their friends and family members.

DREAMS AND GOALS People born on May 22 are proud to see their hard work rewarded. They don't believe in getting something for nothing and would not wish to have idle dreams come true. But when they work very hard toward a goal, especially if it requires the discipline of many years, they are ecstatic.

May 22 people do not look for or need the validation of outside opinion. If they feel they have done a good job, that is reward enough.

MAY 23

People born on May 23 are known for their sense of humor and sense of style. They are fun-loving, free-thinking people who enjoy life on their terms. Even more than most Gemini natives, the men and women born on this date embody a youthful attitude that corresponds to their youthful good looks.

FRIENDS AND LOVERS

The men and women born on this date love to surround themselves with good company. They enjoy being around people and usually have a very active social calendar. They often select friends from every strata of life.

They are equally ecumenical when it comes to selecting lovers. Although May 23 people have a reputation for being frivolous when it comes to romance, they actually take their vows of love very seriously. But when they see that a relationship is going nowhere, they have the good sense to get out before it's too late.

CHILDREN AND FAMILY

May 23 natives need the support of a loving family group. Although they may have grown up as part of an unconventional family, they tend to keep in close touch with their parents and grown siblings.

Despite their own need for freedom, men and women born on this date can be demanding, even critical with their children. They foster a sense of competition among children that can at times be detrimental, and they may struggle to relate to a child who is self-conscious and shy.

HEALTH

Like many Gemini natives, May 23 individuals have a high metabolism, which causes them to burn calories easily no matter what they eat. Because they usually lead busy, active lives there should be no problem about getting enough exercise.

What these folks really need is a way to relax. That can best be achieved through yoga and meditation.

CAREER AND FINANCES

People born on May 23 have many talents and because of that fact it may be difficult for them to settle on a career. They may change their plans many times before finally deciding how they want to spend their lives. Yet it is more than likely that sometime during middle age they will pull up the proverbial stakes again and start anew.

Money flows in and out of the lives of May 23 people with considerable ease. Whatever their talent for accumulating money, the men and women born on this day have very little talent for saving it. Professional advice regarding investments is vital.

DREAMS AND GOALS

Even though May 23 individuals have very high ideals, they rarely have a clear concept of just what they want to accomplish in life. These are highly idealistic people whose talent for daydreaming outstrips their gifts for concrete planning.

When a goal is very important to these men and women they will work very hard to make it come true. Despite a reputation for being a dilettante, the average May 23 person has a great deal of emotional staying power.

EMBRACE
The will to win
Life-lessons
Loss

AVOID
Flirting with danger
Bad memories
Artifice

ALSO BORN TODAY
Singer Rosemary Clooney; actress Joan Collins; pianist Alicia De Larrocha; silent film actor Douglas Fairbanks, Sr.; actress Betty Garrett; musician Bill Hunt; chess champion Anatoli Karpov; physician Franz Anton Mesmer.

MAY 24

Despite the pleasant face they turn to the world, May 24 natives have a strong intellect and rock-hard opinions. These men and women are ably suited to handle the stresses and strains of life, even though they may appear to be emotionally fragile.

May 24 individuals nearly always manage to get their way, yet they do it with subtlety and diplomacy. It's rare for someone born on this day to be demanding, loud, or argumentative.

FRIENDS AND LOVERS

May 24 natives get along well with others. They have great social elan and enjoy being surrounded by an admiring group of friends. With their good looks and nice manners they are usually the center of attention in their particular social group, and are the member everybody else wants to know well.

These individuals have no problem getting the opposite sex to notice them. Although they have the potential to draw many admirers to them, May 24 men and women are likely to have only one great love in a lifetime.

CHILDREN AND FAMILY

Although on the surface it may appear that May 24 people have a close relationship with their family, there could actually be some problems lurking beneath the surface.

There can be some powerful issues in the relationships May 24 men and women share with their own children.

Since these individuals usually give more of themselves to a spouse than a child, the offspring of May 24 people can often feel ignored.

HEALTH

Because they care about their appearance, May 24 individuals generally take very good care of themselves. They like to eat, yet this is tempered by good sense and plenty of exercise. In the rare case that a May 24 man or woman feels unloved or unattractive, food, alcohol, or pills could become dangerously indispensable to them.

It is very important that these people get plenty of sleep or they will look puffy and pale.

CAREER AND FINANCES

Men and women born on this date can never be happy unless they pursue the career of their choice. Just "any job" won't do for these people. They have a great deal of creative talent that will find an outlet in writing, advertising, and music. Because of their diplomatic talents they make fine politicians.

May 24 individuals aren't interested in money, yet they like the fancy lifestyle it can buy. They prefer spending other people's money and for this reason both the men and women often marry well.

DREAMS AND GOALS

May 24 people compete against themselves, not others. They don't seek great material gain, but may have great personal dreams of success in an artistic field.

The men and women born on this date are generally fatalistic, believing that if something is meant to be, it will happen. Because of this fact they usually think it useless to strive for worldly success. Their personal vision is more important to them, and they will strive to realize it at all costs.

EMBRACE
Plentitude
Joint ventures
Negotiation

AVOID
Emotional temptation
Ego trips
Writer's block

ALSO BORN TODAY
Singer Roseanne Cash; politician Coleman Young; singer/songwriter Bob Dylan; actress Priscilla Presley; guitarist Derek Quinn; musician Rich Robinson; film director Joan Micklin Silver; England's Queen Victoria.

MAY 25

People born on May 25 are energetic and focused individuals who enjoy being in life's fast lane. They have enormous ambition to succeed and often put career plans ahead of their personal relationships.

May 25 natives are creative in an offbeat way, preferring to put their own ironic spin on events rather than allow themselves to be ruled by any given situation. That can mean taking big risks, but these men and women can take just about anything in stride.

FRIENDS AND LOVERS Although they are not loners in the traditional sense, May 25 natives don't have a strong need for the company of others, and seek their own counsel most of the time.

The road to romance can be a difficult one for May 25 men and women because they refuse to give up their independence in order to form a relationship. Anyone who falls in love with a May 25 individual must be prepared to play second fiddle to career goals a great deal of the time.

CHILDREN AND FAMILY May 25 individuals often seek to break free from the restraints of family life at a very early age. These people are extremely self-sufficient and don't like to follow the crowd.

If they opt for parenthood, May 25 individuals tend to be distant. They can be affectionate, yet may be preoccupied with career considerations. Often there is a better relationship between May 25 people and their offspring once the children are grown.

HEALTH May 25 individuals like to keep themselves in good physical condition. Since they may not be especially athletic by nature, it is necessary for them to hone their skills by frequent workouts and great attention to diet.

Most Gemini natives have a lot of nervous energy; in the case of May 25 men and women this needs to be either expelled through exercise or channeled toward some other pastime. It is important that these individuals have an active and satisfying love life. When they don't, May 25 people often distract themselves with alcohol or too much food. They are happiest in a committed relationship.

CAREER AND FINANCES May 25 natives are very career-oriented. They feel the need to expend the greatest amount of their energy on getting to the very top of their profession. These people set very high standards for themselves and may not be able to accept anything but the pinnacle of success.

Money is secondary in importance to May 25 individuals, but they do see it as some measure of their achievement. For this reason they will work very hard to make a great deal of money.

DREAMS AND GOALS Though their primary goals tend to be professional ones, May 25 individuals have other, more fundamental goals in mind. Their fierce struggle for success often embodies an "I'll show them" attitude, but they may actually be trying to erase the memory of hard times when they were young.

EMBRACE
Symbolism
Appreciation of nature
Knowledge

AVOID
Carelessness with money
A messy house
Jealous tears

ALSO BORN TODAY
Composer/trumpet virtuoso Miles Davis; actor Justin Henry; novelist Robert Ludlum; actor Ian McKellan; film director Frank Oz; actress Connie Sellecca; opera singer Beverly Sills; singer Leslie Uggams.

MAY 26

The natural character of May 26 individuals is hard for others to divine. Outwardly they appear serious, even stoic. Yet underneath this facade the men and women born on this day are warm-hearted, kind, and even funny when the mood strikes them.

May 26 people are very aware of their own dignity. Even the way they carry themselves seems to proclaim a sense of decorum.

EMBRACE
Comfort
Conversations with yourself
Solitude

AVOID
Pragmatism
Estrangement from friends
Self-pity

ALSO BORN TODAY
Actor James Arness; singer Peggy Lee; actress Helena Bonham-Carter; singer Stevie Nicks; actor Peter Cushing; TV sportscaster Brent Musburger; actor Robert Morley; actor John Wayne.

FRIENDS AND LOVERS Friendship is one of the most important factors in the life of May 26 people. Men and women born on this date have the ability to make very close friendships, which often last a lifetime. They are extremely loyal people who would do anything for a friend.

There is a lot of stress in the love life of May 26 people. These otherwise intelligent folks have a bad habit of falling in love with people who are wrong for them. Often they will try to make a success of an impossible relationship, giving up only when they realize they've made a mistake.

CHILDREN AND FAMILY May 26 people often have extraordinary responsibilities placed on their shoulders from a very young age. They may help with younger children in the family, or even fulfill the role of surrogate authority figure.

May 26 men and women may be excessively strict with their own children. Although they prefer discipline to punishment, their

overriding goal is to teach their youngsters the ethical principles of life. They need to be more willing to show their affection.

HEALTH May 26 people are very concerned about their health and fitness. They have excellent dental hygiene and may even be a bit obsessive on the subject. Because they have great pride in keeping themselves slim and active, they are careful to exercise on a regular basis. Aerobics, weight-training, running, and body sculpting are all a part of their routine.

People born on this date eat to live, not live to eat. They are scrupulous about eating plenty of fresh greens and fruits and may become vegans in middle age.

CAREER AND FINANCES May 26 men and women prefer "serious" careers. These people have very good business sense and do extremely well in retail. It may take them some years to learn that they have what it takes to be an entrepreneur, but once they accept that fact that can be very successful in a home-based business.

Individuals born on this date have great respect for money and may even lean toward frugality. Their ability to predict trends in economic life makes them admirably suited to handle their own, and other people's money.

DREAMS AND GOALS Nothing is more important to May 26 individuals than that they be seen to do their best. Although they may seem to lack the imagination of grandiose dreams, they are simply practical enough to know that reaching too high can sometimes mean the dream's death.

Men and women born on this date understand that very few goals can be achieved overnight. They have the foresight and patience to achieve their dreams one step at a time.

MAY 27

Men and women born on May 27 are masters at reinventing themselves. Time after time, without a thought to their last incarnation, these people will strip away the old facade, only to replace it with a new one. This is their way of remaining interesting to themselves and others.

May 27 people never quite let anyone see their true self, not even those individuals who are closest to them. They revel in maintaining a sense of mystery and intrigue.

FRIENDS AND LOVERS
May 27 men and woman love the spotlight and enjoy an active social life. They especially enjoy situations where they can meet new and interesting people. They like eccentric people who share their love of good food, good wine, and smart conversation.

Romance is a favorite pastime for May 27 individuals. They are natural flirts and generally prefer "the chase" to any other aspect of love. They may marry often, or not at all, simply because they enjoy playing the field.

CHILDREN AND FAMILY
Like many Gemini natives, May 27 people never quite grow up. They remain in touch with that magical land of childhood and take spiritual refuge in it when the realities of life grow too hard to take.

May 27 people may not be excellent parents in the conventional sense, but they can bond with their kids in a way that many parents cannot. Men and women born on this date are pals more than parents.

HEALTH
May 27 individuals have a high-strung, nervous temperament. This can cause them to fall into bad health habits like smoking or alcohol as a means to quiet their nerves. In rare cases they may be affected with bulimia or other food-abuse illnesses.

Headaches and insomnia may be problems for May 27 people. They can remedy these by learning how to relax, which can be difficult for any Gemini native.

CAREER AND FINANCES
People born on this day love to exhibit themselves. They adore fashion and are often impeccably dressed, making them an asset in any profession. These individuals are naturally artistic yet they may prefer a career that exists on the fringes of creativity. They have a great talent for language and have the ability to become the sort of teachers every student remembers.

May 27 people are not particularly good with money. They spend it far too freely and sometimes foolishly. On rare occasions their spendthrift habits may bring them to the edge of bankruptcy. Yet for the most part they are simply generous in the extreme.

DREAMS AND GOALS
People born on this date want to be noticed. They have the feeling—generally correct—that they are not ordinary individuals but someone very special. It is that special self that they wish to share with the world.

Even if their stage is smaller than the entire globe, they still need to be at the center of things. May 27 men and women will usually find a way to shine, since anything else is unbearable for their ego.

EMBRACE
Emotional restoration
Quiet joys
Mystery

AVOID
Intimidation
Snobbishness
Misinformation

ALSO BORN TODAY
TV personality Cilla Black; dancer Isadora Duncan; actor Louis Gossett, Jr.; writer Dashiell Hammett; U.S. Vice President Hubert Humphrey; actor Christopher Lee; actor Vincent Price; novelist Herman Wouk.

MAY 28

May 28 men and women possess the pioneer spirit. They have absolutely no sense of danger, no fear of failing. These people don't wait for life to happen to them—they go out and wrestle with it.

Individuals born on this date have a bold personality yet there is nothing egotistical about them. They are adventurous types who never lose interest in life or confidence in their ability to conquer it.

FRIENDS AND LOVERS Enthusiastic and fun-loving, May 28 people make great friends. They love people and enjoy getting involved in the personal lives of their friends. May 28 men and women treat their friends like family and often have a houseful of visitors.

Romance is the single guiding factor in the lives of May 28 people. They are idealists, often unable to see the bad points of someone with whom they are romantically involved. This can lead to heartbreak on occasion, but more often than not May 28 natives are lucky in love.

CHILDREN AND FAMILY May 28 people place great importance upon their family background. Whether they came from a rich household or a poor one, these people relate strongly to their lineage. There is likely to be more than one scrapbook tucked away in their closet, packed with photos and clippings that tell the story of a family and growing up.

People born on May 28 make wonderful parents. They enjoy regaling their youngsters with tall tales of their own youth. Although they are essentially liberal in the use of discipline, May 28 men and women are sure to give their youngsters a good set of values.

HEALTH People born on this date are blessed with good health and the good sense to take care of it. Although they may possess a few bad habits, such as smoking or eating the wrong foods, for the most part they adhere to a healthy lifestyle.

May 28 individuals could use more exercise, since they tend to have sedentary jobs. Food preferences tend to be simple, though these people should stay away from fried foods and too much red meat.

CAREER AND FINANCES The career path of May 28 individuals is often circuitous but always interesting. The men and women born on this date may be unsure of what they want to do with their lives until well into adulthood. They believe that variety is the spice of life.

May 28 individuals care more about what job they're doing than how much money they can make doing it. They're often lucky in games of chance.

DREAMS AND GOALS People born on May 28 believe that their life is a success if they are happy. Material goals mean very little to them. They count their successes according to the number of lives they touch and people they inspire—and how much fun everybody has along the way.

May 28 men and women believe very strongly in performing selfless acts of charity that improve the lives of others. This, combined with unstinting good humor, is their trademark.

EMBRACE
Safe arrivals
A happy heart
A winning spirit

AVOID
Bad dreams
Revenge
Nervousness

ALSO BORN TODAY
Actress Carroll Baker; writer Ian Fleming; singer/songwriter John Fogarty; England's King George I; baseball star Kirk Gibson; politician Rudolph Giuliani; singer Gladys Knight; actress/director Sondra Locke.

MAY 29

There are few more dazzling characters than those born on May 29. These individuals possess a star quality that is virtually unrivaled by others. Their ability to sway the opinions of others is nothing short of miraculous.

May 29 men and women have charm, intelligence, and wit. If they lack for anything it is an introspective side. These highly social individuals prefer not to analyze their feelings except on rare occasions. They gravitate to risk and can even be foolhardy at times.

FRIENDS AND LOVERS May 29 individuals make a big hit with everyone and they are not ashamed to use their considerable charm to their own advantage. They are personable and have the ability to make an individual feel as if he or she is the most important person in the world.

Men and women born on this date often have a frivolous attitude toward love. They shy away from intense affairs or individuals who try to "own" them.

CHILDREN AND FAMILY May 29 individuals have a tendency to adopt the role of family "black sheep." This can be surprising, since the charm of these individuals cloaks a decidedly rebellious nature.

The men and women born on this date make tender, sympathetic parents. Like all Gemini natives, they have an instinct for childhood and can relate well to little ones. While they are careful to nurture a sense of family pride in their children, May 29 people will always strive to develop a child's sense of independence.

HEALTH Despite the lithe, youthful image they represent, May 29 men and women may actually do very little to support a healthful lifestyle. They are the sort who can eat all the wrong things, yet remain imperiously slim, mocking the efforts of others who will never look like them no matter how hard they try.

Since they tend to keep their emotions to themselves, these people can find outlets for their anxiety through meditation or periodic sensory deprivation exercises.

CAREER AND FINANCES People born on this date have a complicated nature and are drawn to many different subjects, but prefer to learn through books rather than firsthand experience. They are extremely analytical and have a habit of looking at things abstractly.

May 29 men and women are not known for their ability to handle money, though they may be able to make it easily enough. They make excellent teachers, realtors, and attorneys.

DREAMS AND GOALS Individuals born on this day are extremely goal-oriented. They will work very hard to make a goal become a reality, but if they get bored along the way—always a possibility with a Gemini individual—they will toss all their hard work to the wind without a second thought.

May 29 individuals have high ideals, yet enough wisdom to know that there are times when those ideals need to be temporarily sacrificed in the name of friendship, love, or simple common sense.

EMBRACE
High style
Wholeness
Humility

AVOID
Self-parody
Aloofness
Sins of omission

ALSO BORN TODAY
Actress Annette Bening; England's King Charles II; singer Melissa Etheridge; actor Anthony Geary; American patriot Patrick Henry; comedian Bob Hope; singer LaToya Jackson; U.S. President John F. Kennedy.

MAY 30

May 30 people are like artists who see the entire world as their canvas. Their paints are the experiences and emotions of everyday life. These individuals are virtuosos when it comes to putting their imprint on the world around them.

The men and women born on this date have considerable mettle and can overcome adversity with ease. Their will to succeed is strong, but never ruthless.

FRIENDS AND LOVERS May 30 individuals bring a great sense of joy to all of their relationships. They are curious about people and never allow their own egos to get in the way of a friendship. The ability of May 30 men and women to commiserate with a friend's problems is one of the reasons they are well-loved.

They are equally thoughtful in love relationships. May 30 lovers have a knack for keeping their marriages fresh and interesting, even after many years with a partner.

CHILDREN AND FAMILY Although May 30 individuals are generally easy to get along with they often find themselves locked into a serious disagreement with a family member. This may be related to a religious matter or a basic life-philosophy change that does not jibe with the way in which the May 30 person was brought up. Conflict may be inevitable.

Since education is highly prized by these people, they may have a problem with offspring who do not want to attend an institution of higher learning.

HEALTH Where exercise is concerned, May 30 people may be more talk than action. They know the value of regular exercise and may even go to great lengths to accommodate it—purchasing expensive home gym equipment or hiring a personal trainer. Yet they often fail to follow through on their professed good intentions.

May 30 individuals are intrigued by fad or specialty diets. Because of their expansive and generous natures, self-discipline is not one of their strong points.

CAREER AND FINANCES People born on this date are natural organizers who use this talent in every aspect of life. To organize the office softball team is as important to them as the career work they perform during the day.

May 30 men and women often gravitate to positions of power. They have exceptional ability with money and are scrupulously honest, whether a situation involves their own or someone else's funds.

DREAMS AND GOALS People born on this date have high expectations and often have secret dreams of becoming rich and famous. Even if this doesn't come true for them they will always seek to be a high-profile member of their own circle.

May 30 men and women live by very high standards of personal conduct, and may conform to a particular religious code. They are proud of their ethics and may feel a need to convince others to follow a similar path.

EMBRACE
Good grooming
Riches of the soul
Attention to detail

AVOID
Indifference
Sleeplessness
Poor choices

ALSO BORN TODAY
Actor Keir Dullea; clarinet virtuoso Benny Goodman; film director Howard Hawks; singer Wynonna Judd; cosmonaut Aleksei Leonov; Russian Tsar Peter the Great; football star Gale Sayers; actor Clint Walker.

MAY 31

People born on May 31 like to push the proverbial envelope, always looking for ways to get close to dangerous circumstances without actually getting hurt. They like to give others the impression that they have a "bad" streak, but generally they're not as unconventional as they may appear.

FRIENDS AND LOVERS
Men and women born on May 31 usually contrive to be the most popular person within their circle. Whether it is their charm, good looks, talent, or temperament, there is always something that distinguishes them from other people.

Because of their appeal and reputation—which is often self-generated—May 31 individuals are very popular with the opposite sex. In youth they may be attracted to a somewhat promiscuous lifestyle, either their own or someone else's. In later years they grow more conservative.

CHILDREN AND FAMILY
May 31 men and women are very much a product of their upbringing. If born to privilege, they have a great deal of trouble understanding what life is like for those in less fortunate circumstances. If they are born poor they cannot resist carrying a chip on their shoulder.

Individuals born on this date can truly "find" themselves in parental roles, especially if they have children later in life. They experience great joy through their children's accomplishments and show considerable restraint when it comes to discipline.

HEALTH
People born on this date may be casual, even careless where their health is concerned. Their sense of personal invincibility allows them to feel as if nothing bad can happen to them. Unfortunately, this attitude may result in frequent accidents or unusual ailments, which can be forestalled by more practical attention to safety and health.

May 31 men and women are not big eaters, yet their dietary habits may still be wanting, since their energy level is often in flux. Several small meals, rather than three moderate or large ones, will increase stamina.

CAREER AND FINANCES
Folks born on this date are naturally drawn to jobs or careers that offer an element of danger. Even if they do not need to put their career and financial safety at risk they will do so gladly, as if to prove their invulnerability.

A careless way with money combined with great generosity often lands May 31 people in financial distress.

DREAMS AND GOALS
People born on this date like to feel as if they are living in the "now." They have little care for the future and even less for the past. They dream of a lifestyle capable of sustaining this level of freedom and intensity.

May 31 natives are not deliberate planners. They like to take life as it comes and not worry about the consequences. Success is an abstract concept to them, defined more by attitude than capitulation to a set of prescribed rules.

EMBRACE
Putting first things first
Following your dream
Being at ease

AVOID
The need for validation
No-win situations
Giving up

ALSO BORN TODAY
Actor Tom Berenger; football star Joe Namath; actor/director Clint Eastwood; actor Denholm Elliott; actress Sharon Gless; Prince Rainier of Monaco; actress Brooke Shields; actress Lea Thompson.

JUNE 1

The men and women born on this day have a great need to bask in the sun of approval. They value their talents and abilities and yet may constantly look to their peers for validation and advice. Feeling that they have the power to please others is as seductive to them as their own success.

June 1 individuals wear the thin veneer of Gemini superficiality well, yet they are more complicated than they seem. These people can be their own best friend or worst enemy.

FRIENDS AND LOVERS Like many Gemini natives, June 1 men and women crave the constant attention of friends and associates, and yet no one may know them intimately. They demand considerable loyalty from their friends and will always respond in kind.

The romantic life of June 1 individuals is likely to have its peaks and valleys, but these people are never afraid to take a chance on a new relationship. Everything they have learned from a love affair or marriage is taken into the next one.

CHILDREN AND FAMILY Even as little ones, June 1 people are seekers of attention. If they are an only child they may be excessively demanding of the parents' time. If there are siblings they may connive to receive the lion's share of attention.

An understanding of their own childhood is important for June 1 people before they become parents. If they felt emotionally neglected they need to work through the anger and refocus it in a way that is helpful to their own children.

HEALTH June 1 natives have good health and a high level of vitality. The nervous energy that is so common to Gemini natives is better channeled in these individuals than many others of their sign, and often allows them to work for long periods without sleep.

Diet is rarely a problem for June 1 natives. They can eat anything, at any time of the day or night, and not be bothered with indigestion.

CAREER AND FINANCES June 1 individuals are first and foremost "communicators." Though that generally means via speech it also predisposes them to expression through other means. They are drawn toward any career that facilitates their need to communicate with others on either a personal or nonspecific level.

People born on this day make excellent writers, teachers, newscasters, and dramatic performers. Although they have a talent for research, they prefer to be in the foreground of their field. Endowed with the natural hand-eye coordination possessed by most Gemini natives, they also make excellent painters, decorators, and architects.

DREAMS AND GOALS Men and women born on this day crave achievement and attention. They are wedded to the idea that success equals happiness and are often unhappy with life if they feel it doesn't measure up to their youthful goals.

June 1 natives possess incredible optimism and are likely to hold out for their dream job rather than take something that is not to their liking. It is difficult for them to compromise, though on occasion this may be necessary.

EMBRACE
Lightening someone's burden
Higher education
Posterity

AVOID
Interdependence
Worthless promises
Scheming

ALSO BORN TODAY
Actor Rene Auberjonois; singer Pat Boone; actor Morgan Freeman; poet John Masefield; novelist Colleen McCullogh; screen legend Marilyn Monroe; musician Ron Wood; actor Edward Woodward.

JUNE 2

People born on this date live more through their emotions than their intellect. This may not be readily apparent, since they are bright achievers with a quiet personality that discourages them from "opening up"; they reserve their real selves for those closest to them.

June 2 people have a more serious disposition than many Geminis. They give the impression of being emotionally fragile but actually are very strong-willed and independent.

FRIENDS AND LOVERS June 2 people are not interested in superficial relationships of any sort. To the contrary, they seek out friends who can share their need for emotional intimacy. Men born on June 2 often count a woman as their closet confidante.

People born on this day have an extremely romantic nature and are often disappointed in love. They may be reticent about marriage since it conflicts with their notion of a grand passion.

CHILDREN AND FAMILY June 2 people find it hard to disassociate themselves from traumas experienced in their childhood. This is especially true if there was an early separation from a parent figure or a favorite sibling.

Because of their sensitivity, June 2 men and women often form extraordinarily close emotional ties with their own children. People born on this date are sometimes overprotective of their offspring.

HEALTH June 2 natives are basically strong but can often find their health adversely affected by emotional issues. This is especially true if they happen to go through an unhappy or unfulfilled period of life. During such a time they may be bothered with headaches, digestive problems, and sleepiness.

There is a tendency for June 2 men and women to find solace in "comfort foods" if things go wrong. Fortunately, this rarely leads to being overweight since, like most Geminis, they have an active metabolism.

CAREER AND FINANCES Because of their quiet, introspective natures, June 2 men and women are attracted to thoughtful occupations that give them an opportunity to use their intelligence and sensitivity. They have great empathy for people and do very well as therapists, nurses, and veterinarians. They also make fine teachers, particularly of the very young.

June 2 people are apprehensive about handling money. Their eccentricities may include a dislike of banks or an unwillingness to deal in anything but cash transactions.

DREAMS AND GOALS People born on June 2 rarely disclose their personal goals to others. Generally modest in their desire for obvious trappings of success, June 2 people have a desire to "fit in" because their sensitive nature often makes them feel like outsiders.

June 2 natives place considerable significance on their personal relationships; when these are successful, they enjoy a great sense of personal accomplishment. Other goals may include travel to exotic, faraway places.

EMBRACE
Acts of daring
Professional advice
Adaptability

AVOID
Doubts
Constant criticism of yourself and others
Gloating

ALSO BORN TODAY
Film historian Kevin Brownlow; composer Edward Elgar; singer William Guest; composer Marvin Hamlisch; novelist Thomas Hardy; actress Sally Kellerman; actor Jerry Mathers; musician Charlie Watts.

JUNE 3

People born on June 3 are extremely intelligent, though their brilliance is likely to be analytical rather than creative in nature. They are much more at home solving abstract problems than handling life's more commonplace problems.

June 3 men and women have considerable nervous energy, which can manifest itself as ill temper. Although they can be argumentative at times, these individuals are much more likely to keep their feelings to themselves.

FRIENDS AND LOVERS

June 3 individuals do not have the usual Gemini need for making friends, although others are easily attracted to them. There is an element of egotism in these folks, yet it does not detract from their likableness. June 3 people are held in great awe by friends who admire their intellect.

June 3 people can be demanding partners in romance because they need constant reassurance that their mates are devoted to them.

CHILDREN AND FAMILY

People born on this date tend to come from an extreme background—either very fortunate, or the opposite. In either case they have a difficult time reconciling their adult feelings with the emotions they experienced as children. Instead of trying to rechannel their experience as parents, people born on June 3 often back off from the challenge, fearing it will exert unhealthy pressure on the relationship. These individuals generally remain in close contact with their grown children.

HEALTH

Those born on this date have a strong constitution and amazing good health, especially in view of their tendency to overindulge. June 3 people have a great fondness for food and can eat virtually anything without ill effects, yet they should beware of eating for purely emotional reasons.

It is important that June 3 individuals balance their intake of sugar and starches with plenty of fresh vegetable juice and purified water. A diet too rich in carbohydrates can promote weight gain in later years.

CAREER AND FINANCES

June 3 individuals do best in careers requiring extreme mental discipline and study. They have tidy minds, and make excellent students. True to their Gemini versatility, these men and women may change careers more than once. These people are very sensitive to economic trends and have the ability to make excellent employment choices.

The financial fortunes of June 3 folks rest upon how motivated they are to achieve all that they can. They need to be very careful about investment opportunities that appear too good to be true.

DREAMS AND GOALS

June 3 individuals wish to achieve a level of independence in their economic and personal lives. Although they work intermittently and with some dedication to bring this about, they may lack the discipline to achieve their ultimate goals.

Also, people born on this date may have set unrealistic personal goals. They can ignore their loved ones, and realize the value of those people only when they are no longer part of their lives.

EMBRACE
Intellect
Making others happy
Egoless love

AVOID
Selfish concerns
Emotional power plays
Fear

ALSO BORN TODAY
Choreographer Martha Clarke; actor Tony Curtis; actress Colleen Dewhurst; artist Raul Duffy; actor Maurice Evans; English King George V; poet Allen Ginsberg; actress Paulette Goddard.

JUNE 4

People born on this date combine daring with practicality, discipline with artistry. These folks cleverly manage to reinvent themselves from time to time. It's all part of their incredible ability to see things from multiple perspectives.

June 4 people have a sparkling personality and are very much aware of the effect they have on others. They need to be honest with themselves in order to keep from using this talent to unfair advantage.

FRIENDS AND LOVERS June 4 men and women express a great deal of their life-energy though friendships. They are fascinated by people whose backgrounds are very different from their own, doubtless because this provides, albeit secondhand, an avenue of new experience for them.

June 4 men and women adore taking chances, especially romantic ones. They are quick to fall in love, and quick to fall out of it. Knowing their own nature, they may put off marriage as long as possible, fearing it will not live up to their expectations. Yet if they do choose marriage, they make excellent, if unconventional, mates.

CHILDREN AND FAMILY These people are often at odds with their upbringing: If it was repressive, they opt for eccentricity and rebellion; if it was liberal, they seek conventionality.

This opposition to the prevailing norm continues when June 4 people become parents. Attitudes and platitudes they have reviled in the past suddenly begin to make sense, and they find themselves rebelling against their own rebellion!

HEALTH People born on June 4 tend to be extreme in their attitudes about health and fitness. Whether fad diets, fasting, or foods

taken in combination, these folks always seem to be at least one step ahead of the current health trends. Health aside, they favor hot and spicy foods. Consumption of alcohol should be kept to a minimum.

June 4 men and women have a great love of sports and may pursue them on a professional or semiprofessional level.

CAREER AND FINANCES June 4 individuals have a hard-science bent, and may look for a career in which they can practice one of the scientific disciplines. Careers in defense work or communications are profitable choices for these individuals. Since June 4 men and women have a crusader's instinct for doing good works, they can also find great satisfaction in police, fire, or rescue work.

The financial fortunes of people born on this date tend to rise and fall depending upon their ability to manage things.

DREAMS AND GOALS People born on June 4 think of life as one big series of exciting surprises. They love spontaneity and would rather be caught off-guard by circumstances than plan for them. This can be a rather untenable situation if they need to achieve a series a standards in order to get what they want most out of life.

These individuals are great humanitarians who feel it is their duty to give of their resources and talents to help those who are less fortunate.

EMBRACE
Charity
Quietude
Turning the other cheek

AVOID
Disillusionment
Machinations
Co-dependency

ALSO BORN TODAY
Actor John Drew Barrymore; opera singer Cecilia Bartoli; film director Henning Carlsen; actor Bruce Dern; English King George III; opera singer Robert Merrill; actress Michelle Phillips; actor Parker Stevenson.

JUNE 5

Those born on this date believe in the natural goodness of the world around them. They are more than merely optimistic—they are altruists who draw their greatest inspiration from the everyday miracles that others may not perceive.

June 5 individuals often exhibit a take-charge attitude that may seem authoritarian. They have quick, mercurial movements and always seem to be in the midst of performing some physical task.

FRIENDS AND LOVERS June 5 natives have a great love for their fellow man. They like being surrounded by good companions, and rarely prefer their own company to that of friends.

These folks make affectionate romantic partners. They often marry at a very early age; for this reason they may spend a great deal of their life with a single partner. In the case of multiple marriages they generally remain on good terms with a former mate, and have nothing but nice things to say about that person.

CHILDREN AND FAMILY June 5 men and women are close to their family members, especially siblings. Even as adults they are likely to carry on warm relationships with sisters and brothers, regarding them more as friends than relatives.

Those born on this date make fantastic parents who, despite professional demands, involve themselves in every aspect of parenting. Like so many Gemini individuals they have the gift of entering into a child's mind, reliving the joy and innocence of that time of life.

HEALTH These active, mercurial people have a high level of energy and never seem to sit still. Although this is indicative of good health, it also displays a high-strung nature. June 5 natives often suffer from sleep disorders because they find it impossible to relax.

Diet can be a challenge to the men and women born on this date, because they seem to prefer "junk food" to balanced meals. They often require a high carbohydrate diet.

CAREER AND FINANCES Because of their great ability to get along with others, June 5 people excel in professions that showcase their engaging personality traits. Sales, public relations, and the media are good career choices for these individuals. Note that because they are emotionally fueled by their relationships with others, they do not work very happily or easily on their own.

Although money is not usually a big consideration in choosing a career, the men and women born on this date do enjoy a lavish lifestyle that requires a good salary. They do not have difficulty accepting that a spouse may make more money than they do.

DREAMS AND GOALS June 5 individuals are excited about life and want to experience everything it has to offer. Their goals are optimistic in nature, sometimes impossibly so. But this does not deter these energetic people.

Those born on this date have a remarkable ability to see only the positive side of life. If a cherished dream does not come true they simply turn their attention to yet another goal.

EMBRACE
Fantasy
Tears of joy
Patience

AVOID
Wasting time
Judging others
Feeling overburdened

ALSO BORN TODAY
Novelist Ivy Compton-Burnett; musician Kenny G; playwright David Hare; economist John Maynard Keynes; novelist Margaret Drabble; actor Robert Lansing; journalist Bill Moyers; film director Tony Richardson.

JUNE 6

People born on this date have a need to express themselves through artistry and words. They are remarkable individuals for whom the world is one gigantic wonder to be explored. These men and women have unbounded curiosity and never tire of learning new things.

FRIENDS AND LOVERS Individuals born on this date have a talent for drawing to them the individuals best equipped to teach them what they need to learn about life. It is almost as if they act as a psychological magnet. Yet on another level these people may feel quite alone, and may count their true friends sparingly.

Where love and marriage are concerned, the men and women born on this date have their share of misfortune. This is due to the fact that they tend to fall in love very deeply, and if they are severely disappointed it can take them a lifetime to get over it.

CHILDREN AND FAMILY Family life has a very powerful effect on these individuals, although they may not always be able to see all of the values it brings to their life. As children they were no doubt highly imaginative and may have been left to their own devices on far too many occasions. This tendency toward escapism is evident in their behavior even as adults.

With their own children they will behave in one of two ways. Either they will discourage too much play-acting, or they will recognize it for the emotionally enriching experience it is and encourage their children to participate.

HEALTH These people require a very powerful spiritual interest in life to maintain their emotional equilibrium. Meditation, prayer, and even fasting can help them to center themselves.

Light to moderate exercise plays a big role in keeping June 6 people in fit condition. Walking is best, since it allows them to commune with nature.

CAREER AND FINANCES With so many artistic talents at their disposal, these people can easily make a place for themselves in some creative field. Since the performing arts are extremely competitive, they may find more success behind the scenes. Those June 6 men and women who opt for a different type of career should still make some artistic hobby a priority in their lives.

True to their creative heritage, June 6 individuals are not particularly adept at handling the financial side of life. They are often willing to turn that duty over to a spouse or business partner.

DREAMS AND GOALS People born on June 6 are dreamers. They often set goals for themselves that seem to be impossible, and yet on some level they seem able to hit their mark. June 6 individuals understand what many people do not: that the journey is more important than the destination.

The men and women born on this date aspire toward a high level of spiritual perfection. The ways in which they seek this goal are sometimes as questionable as the goal itself is laudable.

EMBRACE
Contentment
Spiritual peace
Tradition

AVOID
Tension
Negativity
Hopelessness

ALSO BORN TODAY
Russian Empress Alexandra; comedienne Sandra Bernard; singer Gary Bonds; tennis star Bjorn Borg; actor Robert Englund; actor Harvey Fierstein; composer Adam Khatchaturian; actress Amanda Pays.

93

JUNE 7

People born on this day have the desire to make their presence felt in the world. They have considerable star quality and can get far in life just on their charm.

June 7 men and women are curious and vibrant, with an ability to keep their level of enthusiasm high no matter what goes wrong. They have a deservedly high opinion of themselves and will go to great lengths to make themselves seen and their views heard.

FRIENDS AND LOVERS

Because June 7 natives are constantly surrounded by people attracted to their winning personalities, they choose their close friends with great care. In a friend, June 7 people look for someone whose motives are honest.

The men and women born on this day can take their pick of romantic partners. They enjoy being in demand and may delay marriage because they don't want to be taken out of circulation.

CHILDREN AND FAMILY

People born on this date are accustomed to being the pampered ones in the family. Their charm and sweetness usually guarantees this favored status, although their family environment may have been more restrictive than they would have preferred.

June 7 men and women have a real talent for getting along with children—their own or those of other family members or friends. They stress to their own children the importance of learning to be independent.

HEALTH

Those born on June 7 have an undisciplined attitude about health and nutritional concerns. They tend toward extremes and excesses, and may sometimes overeat because of boredom or insecurity. When they diet, June 7 people often follow fad regimens or radical eating plans that can do them more harm than good.

Individuals born on this date can benefit from an exercise regimen that emphasizes weight-bearing exercise and aerobics.

CAREER AND FINANCES

June 7 men and women do best in careers that allow them to make use of their winning personality. For this reason they make excellent sales representatives, Realtors, and front-office personnel. Their creative abilities can be put to good use in careers in the arts or humanities.

Although not particularly good at money management, June 7 men and women have amazing luck with money. It's almost as if they have a sixth sense about investment opportunities, for though they often make the wrong choice, they never seem to suffer from it.

DREAMS AND GOALS

Most June 7 individuals would like to be rich and famous, but since that isn't something that all of them will achieve, they're content to be the star of their own circle.

Men and women born on this date need to express the deeply spiritual aspects of their personality, and may opt for periods of worldly abstinence. Although this may seem extreme to friends and family members, June 7 people understand the importance of occasionally setting their sights on nonmaterialistic goals.

EMBRACE
Affection
Spiritual escape
Wondrous memories

AVOID
Greed
Enviousness
Dishonor

ALSO BORN TODAY
Pianist Philippe Entremont; film director James Ivory; singer Al Jolson; actress Jessica Tandy; singer Tom Jones; actor Liam Neeson; singer Prince; symphony conductor George Szell.

JUNE 8

The men and women born on June 8 are survivors, with considerably more emotional stamina than the typical Gemini native. No matter how many times they suffer setbacks or disappointments, they come back and start again.

June 8 people are hard workers who put their whole heart and soul into everything they do. Their level of commitment is amazing.

FRIENDS AND LOVERS June 8 men and women do not strive for the huge circle of friends favored by many Gemini people. Instead, they prefer to cultivate a few very close friendships that last for many years. They generally pick friends who are as serious-minded as they are themselves.

June 8 people may experience more than their share of romantic disappointments, often because they misjudge the level of commitment possible by the other individual. When they do find someone who is caring and considerate, June 8 natives are likely to enjoy a most rewarding partnership.

CHILDREN AND FAMILY People born on June 8 may shoulder great responsibility in youth, or they might have found themselves forced to live up to the image of a dominating parent or other family authority figure. This can have a negative effect on the ability of these people to achieve their true destiny.

Because of the great pressures they may have experienced during their growing-up years, June 8 men and women are often very lenient toward their own children. Although they are certain to instill values in their youngsters, they're wise enough not to expect their kids to be carbon copies of themselves.

HEALTH Those born on June 8 have a generally strong constitution, although they may be somewhat lacking in stamina— the result of a sedentary lifestyle or a poor diet. June 8 people are often light eaters who are unduly committed to staying slim.

June 8 men and women can jack up their energy level by increasing the amount of protein in their diet. They should also take vitamin and iron supplements. Drinking a glass of fresh vegetable or fruit juice each day can help to combat a desire for sweets.

CAREER AND FINANCES People born on June 8 are immensely intelligent and have a great gift for managing other people. They are adept at bringing out the best traits in others because they constantly emphasize the positive rather than the negative aspects of any given situation.

Further, these folks are clever when it comes to making money. This is especially true if they have their own business, since they possess the ability to spot trends in the making.

DREAMS AND GOALS The way in which they appear to others, especially their superiors, is a key concern of June 8 natives. For this reason their goals may reflect a need to live up to the expectations of someone they admire.

When they do concern themselves with more personal goals, June 8 men and women often set themselves a humanitarian task. If they are well-off financially, this project will usually depend on their own money.

EMBRACE
Confidence
Wholesome enjoyment
Conversation

AVOID
Pretense
Subjugating your goals
Disappointments

ALSO BORN TODAY
Actress Kathy Baker; composer Robert Schumann; actress Melissa Gilbert; singer Millicent Martin; comedienne Joan Rivers; singer Nancy Sinatra; actor Jerry Stiller; director/actor Keenan Ivory Wayans.

JUNE 9

People born on this date are motivated to succeed in every aspect of life. They are excitable and imaginative, with a great sense of humor. Like most Gemini natives they are talkative and enjoy a rousing debate about a variety of subjects.

June 9 individuals are pleasant people. They can have a good time in just about any situation, and are often the proverbial life of the party. These individuals also have a serious side, but usually keep it hidden.

FRIENDS AND LOVERS Although they enjoy being surrounded by a large circle of friends, these folks are also anxious to claim their time in the spotlight. They have a highly developed ego and need to feel as if they are on the same level of achievement as their pals.

June 9 individuals are flirty, romantic souls who have no problem attracting the interest of the opposite sex. Because they enjoy the dating scene they may marry late in life or not at all.

EMBRACE
Innovations
Courage
Ethical behavior

AVOID
Self-pity
Bossiness
Manipulative people

ALSO BORN TODAY
Musician Trevor Bolder; actor Robert Cummings, comedian Jackie Mason; actor Johnny Depp; writer Nell Dunn; actor Michael J. Fox; musician Billy Hatton; songwriter Cole Porter.

CHILDREN AND FAMILY June 9 natives enjoy the close relationships that can result from large families. Whatever place they have within that group, these individuals are likely to be the family favorite. Their good nature and happy-go-lucky attitude enchants everyone.

Because they never really grow up themselves, June 9 men and women make sympathetic and fun-loving parents. The only challenge June 9 parents may face is an inability to be a strong disciplinarian.

HEALTH Like most other Gemini natives, June 9 people have a high-strung nature. They seem to be constantly in motion. They sometimes suffer from sleep disorders, usually brought on by an inability to relax.

Since they are likely to have an active metabolism, June 9 people rarely have a weight problem, even though they never seem to stop eating!

CAREER AND FINANCES People born on this date usually gravitate toward careers that allow them to showcase their bright and exuberant personalities. They do very well in communications, media, and sales. Telephone sales jobs or realty work can also be good choices.

Despite their seemingly carefree attitude toward life, these individuals have good money sense. They can operate very efficiently on a tight budget, but also have the talent and vision to handle complicated investment programs. Generosity with money is one of their more noticeable traits.

DREAMS AND GOALS June 9 people use bold intelligence to put their plans into action from a very early age. They are often "whiz kid" types who have the daring to undertake risks that would intimidate other people.

People born on this day are driven to succeed on both a personal and financial level. They aren't interested in making money in jobs they don't like, but are sensible enough to understand that sacrifices may be necessary from time to time.

JUNE 10

P eople born on this date have a highly emotional nature. They may seem to be on an endless roller coaster of highs and lows, which can amaze and alarm those who known them well.

June 10 men and women are acutely aware of the expectations of others and may often go to great lengths to live up to them. Being at ease with who they are is a trait that they need to cultivate.

FRIENDS AND LOVERS
Men and women born on this date have some challenges with their choice of friends. Because they are vulnerable and kind they often choose people who are having trouble in their life. June 10 individuals love to help people with their problems, even when it isn't a good idea.

June 10 people are somewhat more successful in their choice of romantic partners, though they are wildly romantic and even a bit idealistic where love is concerned. Sometimes they are unable to see the negative qualities of a love interest, and are surprised to discover these characteristics when they marry. Despite this, they make loyal and loving mates.

CHILDREN AND FAMILY
June 10 people love family life. Whether a big family, a small family, or something in between, these people love all the accompanying ritual and tradition. Once they begin their own families, June 10 men and women often borrow ideas of their parents to celebrate in much the same way as their folks did.

Men and women born on this day are involved, caring parents. They are very conscious of the psychological needs of their youngsters and will work very hard to meet those needs, creating an atmosphere of trust and friendship.

HEALTH
These people are amazingly vital and active. They have a high energy level and never seem to run down. But only a part of their energy is physical—the rest is emotional. June 10 people are permanently high on life and never seem to come down. They can eat almost anything and usually do, but their diet, fortunately, is varied enough to keep them healthy.

CAREER AND FINANCES
The men and women born on June 10 want to set the world on fire with their talent—which is considerable. They love to "perform" so they often gravitate to careers that put them in the spotlight. When this isn't possible they prefer jobs where their charm, good nature, and good looks are showcased.

People born on this date have good math skills and may become successful accountants, engineers—or astrologers! Yet they are not as good at managing their own finances and usually look to their mate to handle the family's money matters.

DREAMS AND GOALS
Although they seem very secure with their self-image, June 10 people actually need to have their ego carefully nurtured. They have a great many goals and plans, yet may not always feel as if they have what it takes to bring them about.

June 10 individuals cannot be truly happy unless they feel fulfilled on an emotional level as well as a spiritual one.

EMBRACE
Joy of living
Moderation
Quiet times

AVOID
Excesses
Unwise love affairs
Depression

ALSO BORN TODAY
Defense attorney F. Lee Bailey; supermodel Linda Evangelista; singer/actress Judy Garland; actor Lionel Jeffries; Olympic figure skating champion Tara Lipinski; fashion editor/publisher Grace Mirabella; England's Prince Philip; playwright Terence Rattigan.

JUNE 11

People born on this date have a strong personal vision about what they want their lives to be. These individuals have the ability to move beyond the commonplace. Even though they need a great deal of personal validation from others, they generally possess an ego strong enough to support their grandiose ambitions.

Many June 11 men and women have leadership qualities that are second to none. Properly focused, they have the potential to make a real difference in the world.

FRIENDS AND LOVERS June 11 people don't make friends easily. They are basically loners, sometimes even misfits, who prefer the company of a few close friends to a wide variety of pals.

These folks are extremely romantic and fall in love a great many times. Even though they generally seek a stable or committed relationship, they are not always lucky in this way. June 11 people want love to be more than it is, and frequently draw controversy into their love lives without even realizing what they are doing. Multiple marriages are not uncommon.

CHILDREN AND FAMILY People born on this date have a great belief in family values. This is especially true if they come from a very traditional family themselves. They tend to pursue a strong interest in family matters long after they have left home and begun their own domestic life. June 11 people often have a strong relationship with one of their parents, especially the mother.

As parents themselves, June 11 men and women are concerned about doing their best. Although they may be committed to career responsibilities, they try very hard to make time for family life.

HEALTH Because of their somewhat moody disposition, June 11 people may suffer from any number of real or imagined ailments brought on by their emotions. Headaches, mild depression, and skin rashes are often indications that all is not right in their world. These health problems usually abate when June 11 people are happy.

Some men and women born on this date deal with their emotions by eating or drinking too much. It is important for them to learn to protect their emotional well-being from these tendencies.

CAREER AND FINANCES June 11 individuals like to lose themselves in creative occupations that give them the opportunity to express their deepest inner dreams and fears. They will usually gravitate toward such a career choice very early in life, perhaps even in childhood. Because they are not ambitious in the traditional sense, these people can benefit from the help and advice of a mentor.

DREAMS AND GOALS People born on this date may not be particularly goal-oriented, but they do know what they want out of life. Since they are often daydreamers, they're more likely to "feel" rather than "know" how to go about making their dreams come true. June 11 men and women have a great deal of faith in their own abilities and will work very hard to make their dreams come alive.

EMBRACE
Calm
Happy memories
Yourself the way you are

AVOID
Going to extremes
Dogmatic behavior
Hypocrisy

ALSO BORN TODAY
Actress Adrienne Barbeau; photographer Julia Margaret Cameron; actor Chad Everett; football coach Vince Lombardi; composer Richard Strauss; novelist William Styron; football star Joe Montana; film director/actor Gene Wilder.

JUNE 12

These individuals don't do anything in a small way. They are big thinkers who possess the enthusiasm to go for all the marbles. June 12 people see the big picture and have a great love of life. These incredible optimists believe that everything that happens is for the best. When they must face a setback, they're never depressed. June 12 men and women are great self-starters who always seem to have a plan in mind.

FRIENDS AND LOVERS
The attitude of June 12 people is that no one can ever have too many friends. They have a genuine love of people, and value diversity in their circle of pals. They enjoy all aspects of friendship. People born on this day are romantic idealists who often marry early in life; their mate is likely to be a high school or college sweetheart. They are very serious about romantic commitments and seldom break them.

CHILDREN AND FAMILY
Family life is complicated for June 12 people. Though they try their best, they may not be able to meet the incredibly high standards set for them by a parent or parent figure. This difficulty can create lifelong estrangement between June 12 folks and family members.

These individuals are much more liberal with their own children. They like a large family and do their best to give an equal amount of love and attention to each child. If they cannot produce children of their own they are likely to seek alternatives, such as adoption.

HEALTH
These high-strung individuals enjoy generally good health, though they do have the propensity to worry more than necessary. They are always juggling a great variety of tasks, yet always seem able to perform well in all areas of life. Getting plenty of sleep and taking vitamins on a daily basis should be enough to give them the stamina and endurance they need.

Although they are usually very slim in youth, June 12 men and women have a tendency to put on weight in middle age.

CAREER AND FINANCES
June 12 people don't believe in setting limits. Whatever it is that they want in life, they have the vision and determination to go after it. They do exceptionally well in careers that allow them to act as leaders. Teaching, counseling, or the law are good avenues of endeavor for these people.

There are so many projects June 12 people wish to accomplish in life, and most of these ideas require considerable capital. Also, they are very concerned about maintaining an opulent lifestyle for their loved ones.

DREAMS AND GOALS
There are few individuals who have as many goals as June 12 people. They want the very best that life can offer. Sometimes though, details can derail their plans, since these folks tend to think in large, rather than small, terms. But once they grow to understand the importance of managing those small details, nothing can stop these individuals from making their dreams come true. June 12 people generally start working toward their goals at an early age and don't mind sacrificing their time and energy to facilitate their dreams.

EMBRACE
Advice
Work ethic
Sense of destiny

AVOID
Confrontation
Poor choices
Materialism

ALSO BORN TODAY
Film producer Irwin Allen; novelist Brigid Brophy; actor Timothy Busfield; U.S. President George Bush; singer Vic Damone; actor/author Peter Jones; singer/actor Jim Nabors.

JUNE 13

These people love adventure and prefer living life on the edge. They have no patience with people who make only "safe" choices. June 13 individuals will always set their sights on what they want and go after it, no matter what it takes.

The men and women born on this date have a kinetic kind of charm that easily draws others to them. They can even seem a little self-involved, but that is usually due to the fact that they are accustomed to causing a stir wherever they go.

FRIENDS AND LOVERS
June 13 individuals love making friends. They often enjoy success at bringing together people who might never have sought each another out otherwise. They prefer people who enjoy conversation as much as they do, and are seldom drawn to those who are quiet and introspective.

It is the same in love matters. June 13 men and women are attracted to people who are very much like themselves. They have a genius for making themselves appear attractive even if they are not, and can always gain the attention of potential dates and mates.

CHILDREN AND FAMILY
June 13 people sometimes have a dubious position of importance within their family. Either they are the proverbial "black sheep" or the one to whom all others come in times of trouble or worry.

The men and women born on this date are not particularly comfortable in the role of parent figure, since it conflicts with the rebel image they have of themselves. They are very good at fostering a child's independence.

HEALTH
Like many Gemini natives, people born on June 13 have an excitable, nervous nature. They may take their good health for granted, failing to eat correctly or get the rest and sleep they need. Most June 13 folks lead a very active life, but that doesn't mean they get all the exercise they need. A regular regimen, which includes weight-bearing exercise and stretching, is helpful in maintaining their strength and flexibility.

CAREER AND FINANCES
Because they are talented and intelligent, there are very few careers that are beyond the capabilities of June 13 men and women. If they have a creative temperament they can produce works that are quite extraordinary, even controversial.

June 13 individuals are not particularly effective at handling money, even though they are likely to make a great deal of it. Generally speaking, they have little interest in the practical aspects of life and may prefer to leave these details to a professional.

DREAMS AND GOALS
June 13 people do not usually follow their goals in a linear fashion. Instead, they seem content to zig-zag back and forth, enjoying the progress toward their goal as much as the eventual destination.

There are times when these complicated individuals seem to undermine their own success. This is not as strange as it seems, since they never do anything the easy way. June 13 people enjoy putting obstacles in their own path, since it makes their eventual success considerably more fulfilling.

EMBRACE
Self-expression
Sentimentality
Fame

AVOID
Doubts
Rage
Guilt feelings

ALSO BORN TODAY
Actor/comic Tim Allen; artist Caristo; actor Basil Rathbone; novelist Dorothy Sayers; actress Ally Sheedy; First Lady Martha Washington; actor Richard Thomas; poet William Butler Yeats.

JUNE 14

The men and women born on this day are in a class by themselves. They combine a winning personality with a penetrating intelligence that is truly disarming. These people are social gadflies who almost possess a great sense of their own importance.

June 14 men and women are "idea" people and enjoy communicating their concepts of life to others. They aren't shy about expressing their opinions, yet don't insist that people agree with them.

FRIENDS AND LOVERS June 14 individuals have great leadership potential, even in social situations. They always seem so "together," so well-informed, that people just naturally bow to their experience and knowledge. Partly because of this they are more likely to have admirers than friends.

The men and women born on this date can be fickle about love. They are incredibly attractive to the opposite sex, and it is difficult for these folks to limit themselves to a single love interest. For this reason they may marry rather late in life, or even several times.

CHILDREN AND FAMILY It's typical for June 14 individuals to disavow their own family background once they have achieved adulthood. They may feel as if their upbringing was too strict, or that their own parents did not appreciate their talents and abilities.

Because they are usually preoccupied with matters of business or lifestyle, June 14 individuals do not make exceptional parents in the usual sense. Yet when they choose to fully involve themselves in that role, they can be outstanding. They never seek to mold their children in their own image and are always ready to celebrate whatever successes their youngsters achieve.

HEALTH June 14 individuals are very healthy, though they may suffer bouts of mental exhaustion from time to time. These can easily be avoided by taking frequent work breaks and making sure that weekends are free from any professional responsibilities.

Those born on this date are sometimes bothered by tension headaches, which can be soothed by taking herbal teas on a regular basis.

CAREER AND FINANCES The men and women born on this date have many career choices. Their intelligence and curiosity often lead them to look for work in the scientific or medical community.

June 14 people have very creative ideas about making money. There is nothing traditional about the way they seek to invest their assets, since they seem to enjoy taking risks that would make other people shiver.

DREAMS AND GOALS Nothing is out of bounds for these ambitious individuals. June 14 people want it all, and they will bend all of their condsiderable efforts toward that end.

People born on this date dream big dreams. They have a great fear of failure, and yet they will put themselves "out there" in risky situations in order to capture the brass ring. These people are looking for validation, but only the sort that they can give themselves, not the sort that comes from others.

EMBRACE
Decisiveness
Organization
Spirit of leadership

AVOID
Egocentricity
Self-doubt
Being argumentative

ALSO BORN TODAY
Photographer Margaret Bourke-White; folk singer Julie Ann Felix; actress Marla Gibbs; tennis star Steffi Graf; guerilla fighter Che Guevara; actress Dorothy McGuire; singer Boy George; financial magnate Donald Trump.

JUNE 15

June 15 people know how to get their way with charm. Even though these individuals are tough, they are never rude or abrasive. They possess the proverbial iron fist in a velvet glove. Even when they choose to play hard ball with an opponent or rival, the individual in question may never realize that they've been in a fight.

The people born on this date are well-mannered, quiet, and seemingly shy, yet they usually manage to get their way without argument.

FRIENDS AND LOVERS
Everybody likes June 15 people because they are eminently lovable. For this reason they have scads of friends. Yet there is a private side to their nature that few people, even their closest friends, are able to see.

June 15 men and women are romantic types who are forever searching for their true love. While many Gemini natives are restless and have difficulties settling down, June 15 people are drawn to the idea of constancy in a relationship.

CHILDREN AND FAMILY
With their sentimental nature, June 15 men and women are likely to remain very close to their adult siblings, as well as cousins and other relatives. They draw strength and happiness from the continuity that these relationships bring into their lives.

June 15 individuals are soft-hearted, indulgent parents who may be a little too liberal in the way they rear their own children. These people cannot bear to see their little ones suffer in any way, and try as hard as they can to make things easy for them.

HEALTH
June 15 men and women often appear to have no bad health habits, but the fact is they may be closet overeaters.

The men and women born on this date need to formulate a serious exercise regimen that will improve their circulation and help them to feel good about themselves. Yoga provides a positive method of channeling their energy.

CAREER AND FINANCES
These pleasant, well-mannered people do very well in careers that require them to deal with the public. They make excellent salespeople, Realtors, counselors, and lawyers.

June 15 people are skilled at making money, although that's not always their principal aim in life. They are extraordinarily generous, eager to help friends and family members who may not be as well-off financially. Even though this cuts back on the amount of money they have available for savings, it fulfills the caring aspect of their personalities.

DREAMS AND GOALS
Those born on June 15 are free-thinking, positive people who have a strong can-do attitude. They will work very hard to bring a goal to fruition, but they may not be willing to sacrifice their private lives in order to achieve professional success.

June 15 folks understand that a happy personal life is more important than the achievement of career goals. For this reason they try very hard to maintain a balance in their lives that will accommodate all aspects of their existence.

EMBRACE
Variety
Focus
The joy of giving

AVOID
Playing favorites
Indecisiveness
Incompatibility

ALSO BORN TODAY
Astrologer John Addey; actor Jim Belushi; actress Courteney Cox; politician Mario Cuomo; composer Edvard Grieg; actress Julie Hagerty; actress Helen Hunt; singer Waylon Jennings.

JUNE 16

Enthusiasm and a genuine curiosity about life mark the personality of individuals born on June 16. These people are life's true adventurers. To them, every day is a potential voyage of discovery. They have strong opinions, yet are always open to new experiences.

Friendly and outgoing, June 16 natives have great "people" skills. They have the ability to rise to any social occasion are make exceptionally fine hosts and hostesses. They are perceptive, bright, and as interested in those around them as in their own concerns.

FRIENDS AND LOVERS
June 16 natives have no problem making friends—in fact they may actually find it difficult to handle the array of invitations they receive from existing friends and acquaintances. These people are usually the most popular individuals in their respective sets.

Love can be a rockier road for June 16 individuals, but when they meet that special someone they are quick to settle down. They make loving, loyal mates who know how to keep romance alive.

CHILDREN AND FAMILY
If June 16 folks experience any regret regarding their own upbringing and place in the family, it may be that they did not receive all of the nurturing and attention they needed. Anxious to maintain family ties, they are likely to act as people-pleasers long after that role is effective or necessary.

With their own children, they seek to heal their own emotional wounds from the past. They make strict but affectionate parents, eager to present the best possible example to their youngsters. These folks are well known for their ability to bridge the gap between the generations.

HEALTH
When very young, June 16 individuals see themselves as virtually invulnerable and therefore may not pay special attention to health matters. They possess considerable nervous energy and need to find a suitable means to channel it.

Since they tend to make food choices more from convenience than because of nutritional good sense, it's important that these people augment their diet with vitamins and other supplements. Sufficient amounts of calcium and iron are particularly important. Excitable by nature, June 16 people should stay away from caffeine.

CAREER AND FINANCES
Communication is the keynote to any career sought by June 16 people. Talkative and intelligent, they are happiest when pursuing careers related to the written or spoken word.

Because of a generous nature and seemingly cavalier attitude toward money, June 16 natives can give the impression of being spendthrift in their habits, though nothing could be further from the truth. They actually possess a keen money sense and a genius for spotting investment opportunities.

DREAMS AND GOALS
Those born on this date prefer spontaneity, and are often reluctant to plot a course of action. They believe very much in the benevolence of time and enjoy taking each day as it comes, knowing that it brings them one step closer to a cherished dream.

EMBRACE
The wisdom of time
Happy memories
Being yourself

AVOID
Manipulative people
Going to extremes
Bickering

ALSO BORN TODAY
Author Victor Canning; English King Edward I; newspaper publisher Katharine Graham; novelist Isabelle Holland; comedian Stan Laurel; actress Laurie Metcalf; writer Joyce Carol Oates.

JUNE 17

As Gemini natives go, these people born on this day are uncharacteristically serious. They are very concerned with making a success in life, yet a spirit of rebellion lurks behind their seemingly conservative and traditional facades.

June 17 people have a vision all their own, but aren't always sure just how to achieve it. They are concerned about stepping out of character and letting others see their vulnerabilities, yet this is exactly what they need to do in order to come to grips with their true nature.

FRIENDS AND LOVERS
June 17 people have difficulty confiding their feelings to others, even to close friends. These men and women are afraid that their friends will think less of them if they are honest about their emotional frailties. Love can be difficult for these folks. It's hard for June 17 people to trust, and love relationships are the ultimate test of that ability. For this reason they tend to be very cautious about choosing someone to whom they can give their heart.

CHILDREN AND FAMILY
June 17 people often have an unusual view of what family life should be, based on the way they were reared. It's likely that they had a great deal of responsibility placed on their shoulders when they were young, and this can affect their choices.

The men and women born on this date may shy away from having children if their own childhood was unhappy. Even if their childhoods were happy, they still may feel unequal to the task. When they do choose to become a parent, they need the full support and loving help of their mate in order to make them feel secure in handling the many responsibilities of parenthood.

HEALTH
June 17 people have a rather low level of resistance and may be likely to catch colds and flu easily. Although they have a healthy appetite, they may have trouble gaining weight. Dairy products and calcium supplements help to prevent bones from growing brittle.

CAREER AND FINANCES
June 17 people flourish in careers as physicians, surgeons, dentists, and nutritionists. These individuals also make good accountants, bankers, brokers, and lawyers.

The men and women born on this date may start saving money seriously at a very young age. Even as adults they would rather save money than spend it. Not particularly adventurous as investors, they prefer to take the safe route.

DREAMS AND GOALS
June 17 individuals are conservative about their life aspirations. They are ambitious, yet worry about overstepping their abilities and being disappointed. They need to learn that if they are ever going to get everything they desire out of life, they will have to take some risks.

People born on this date have a real need to help others. They are not particularly humanitarian in their aims, but have a natural understanding of the way in which each individual owes his or her good fortune to providence and mankind.

EMBRACE
Forgiveness
A joyous heart
Attention to detail

AVOID
Flights of fancy
Irresponsibility
Ingratitude

ALSO BORN TODAY
Russia's Grand Duchess Anastasia; artist M.C. Escher; actor Mark Linn-Baker; singer Barry Manilow; singer/actor Dean Martin; actor Jason Patric; actress Beryl Reid; composer Ivor Stravinsky.

JUNE 18

These people are practical, sensible individuals who have high ambitions and clear ideas about what they want to achieve. It is very important to June 18 people that they make a success of their lives on every level. Although they understand the need for strong family ties and the fulfillment of personal happiness, they will sacrifice that happiness in order to put their plans into action. June 18 men and women keep busy and never seem to have a moment of leisure at their disposal.

FRIENDS AND LOVERS June 18 individuals often flex their leadership muscles as children. These are the ones who organize the games, while other children willingly follow their lead. Although there is an element of ego involved in this, it is more the consequence of their incredible organizational abilities

These attractive, exciting people can be difficult to fall in love with because of the attributes noted above. They may not realize how bossy or demanding they seem to their mate. Fortunately, they are usually lovable enough to be forgiven.

CHILDREN AND FAMILY June 18 men and women often learn their leadership skills as children. Even if they are not the oldest, they may seem to fill that role. Models of good behavior and obedience, they make any parent proud.

People born on this date make strict but loving parents. They will not tolerate disobedience, yet they are understanding when accidents occur.

HEALTH June 18 individuals have impressive good health and have great powers of endurance. Because they have so much energy they can benefit from a regular program of exercise. They enjoy weekend sports, which showcase their competitive spirit.

Because of their active lifestyle, June 18 men and women have a tendency toward reckless injuries. They need to be especially careful when driving, and of course should never drink alcohol before getting into a car.

CAREER AND FINANCES People born on this date are rarely happy just sitting behind a desk. They prefer careers and jobs that give them a chance to be active and involved. Any profession that keeps them physically and intellectually challenged should be encouraged.

June 18 people are among those rare individuals who are acutely concerned about their own financial security and who are willing to take risks in order to improve upon it. They like to think of themselves as mavericks who aren't afraid to test their mettle in order to get what they want out of life.

EMBRACE
Sensitivity
Participation
Inner path

AVOID
Ruthlessness
Stubborn streak
Petulance

ALSO BORN TODAY
Actor Richard Boone; songwriter Sammy Cahn; film critic Roger Ebert; actor Louis Jordan; singer Janette MacDonald; actor E. G. Marshall; singer/songwriter Paul McCartney; actress Isabella Rossellini.

DREAMS AND GOALS June 18 individuals have far-reaching goals and endless ambition. Once they have achieved one goal they will go on to the next, always aiming higher than before, eager to climb to the very top.

People born on this date are gamblers about the future. They aren't afraid of failure. These individuals would rather lose out on an opportunity by failing, than simply because they did not try. These people have real grit and will struggle to succeed no matter what the odds.

JUNE 19

Those born on June 19 love being first in everything. They adore being in the spotlight and will fight to stay there. These men and women are goal-oriented rather than egotistical; they know their own worth and are eager to prove it.

June 19 natives are exuberant, creative people who seem to light up a room when they enter it. They have personality to spare and are not shy about displaying it.

FRIENDS AND LOVERS
Men and women born on June 19 possess a glamorous air that attracts friends and lovers. These people have a slightly idealized view of relationships of all types and may often be the one most in demand within their own circle.

June 19 individuals are the original party animals. They are social creatures who are usually linked romantically with like-minded individuals. It may take them a long time to find that special someone, but when they do they are happy to hang up their dancing shoes forever.

CHILDREN AND FAMILY
June 19 individuals have a habit of distancing themselves from their family upbringing, even if it was a pleasant experience. These people are famous for reinventing themselves on a regular basis.

People born on this date can be fine parents, though parenting is rarely a primary interest in their lives. In cases where they are in a position to act as a step-parent or guardian they are firm and loving without demanding the love that may be reserved for the child's true parent.

HEALTH
June 19 people have a golden glow of health. This is partly due to their natural good health, and also to their rigorous health and fitness regimen, which keeps them in fine condition.

The men and women born on this date are often excellent cooks and gourmands who are careful about what they eat. No fast food for these fussy people! They prefer lean meat, low-calorie salads, and vegetables, plus plenty of fresh fruit and honey.

CAREER AND FINANCES
June 19 individuals are natural actors and performers who cannot get enough public attention. They prefer careers that give them a chance to "show off" and are seldom happy in low-level positions. They have tremendous ambition and continually strive to improve themselves. Because of their taste for experimentation, it is not uncommon for June 19 people to change careers several times during their lifetimes.

Money matters are often delegated to their spouse, since June 19 folks are not particularly interested in handling their own finances.

DREAMS AND GOALS
Although they think big, June 19 people may not be very clear about what they wish to accomplish. They have the concept, but interpreting it may be a bit beyond them.

The high ideals and integrity of June 19 individuals keep them from going after goals just for the sake of achieving power. While they are very good at just about anything they try, they will never take advantage of a situation simply to make themselves look good.

EMBRACE
Moments of solitude
Autonomy
Kismet

AVOID
Sadness
Selfish motives
Being discouraged

ALSO BORN TODAY
Singer/dancer Paula Abdul; baseball star Lou Gehrig; bandleader Guy Lombardo; actor Malcolm McDowell; actress Phylicia Rashad; Duchess of York, Wallis Simpson; actress Gena Rowlands; actress Kathleen Turner.

JUNE 20

The men and women born on June 20 have a unique and interesting character. An attitude of emotional instability makes them very attractive to others who may feel a need to "take care" of them, although they are actually much more centered than they appear.

June 20 individuals are usually quite attractive and have a great deal of personal charm.

FRIENDS AND LOVERS

People born on June 20 possess a highly idealistic view of all relationships. They have no guile and will never choose their companions because of status or in order to enhance themselves in some way. June 20 individuals enjoy "hanging out" with their pals, usually in casual settings where good conversation dominates.

Men and women born on this date have a resoluteness about love that belies their casual nature. They seem to fall in and out of love with people who are not suited to them, yet they always manage to bounce back without allowing themselves to become disillusioned or bitter.

CHILDREN AND FAMILY

People born on this date have a great need to experience family life. This may reflect a happy childhood—or the total absence of one. One way or the other, these individuals seem destined to pursue family relationships that give them a sense of their personal worth.

June 20 individuals make excellent, willing parents. They may be too indulgent, yet they manage to instill strong values in the upbringing of their youngsters.

HEALTH

June 20 natives are not known for taking care of their health. Whether this lack of attention stems from laziness or a habit of self-indulgence where food and drink are concerned, they need to take a hard look at their habits and make some changes.

Therapy can be a wonderful tool in helping June 20 people learn to stop using external means in order to achieve the emotional and spiritual validation they may be missing.

CAREER AND FINANCES

June 20 individuals have a variety of talents, but handling money isn't at the top of the list. Even if they are lucky enough to earn a great deal of money in their career, June 20 men and women will almost certainly spend more than they can earn.

Because of their sensitive nature, it is important that these people pursue the type of career that makes them the happiest. If they allow themselves to accept anything less than their dream career, they will be unhappy and unfulfilled.

EMBRACE
Mysticism
Humor
Beautiful thoughts

AVOID
Temper tantrums
Bizarre behavior
Mood swings

ALSO BORN TODAY
Actress Olympia Dukakis; actor John Goodman; playwright Lillian Hellman; actor Martin Landau; singer/songwriter Cyndi Lauper; actor John Mahoney; composer Jacques Offenbach; singer Lionel Richie.

DREAMS AND GOALS

People born on this date need to feel emotionally comfortable and will put all other goals second to this one. They do not wish to pursue fame, fortune, or any of the material aspects of life. They want honest-to-goodness happiness and will unfailingly seek it out.

June 20 individuals have modest material needs, yet their spiritual and emotional needs are considerable. These can be met through marriage or friendship, but are most often achieved as the June 20 person moves along the path to self-discovery.

CANCER
June 21 - July 22

Cancer is the fourth sign of the astrological year and is known by its astrological symbol, the Crab. Cancer individuals are intelligent, organized, and generous. With the Moon as the ruling planet, people born under this sign are considered to be home-loving and tenacious. They are devoted to family members and provide enormous emotional support.

THE CANCER MAN The men born under this sign are something of an enigma. They can be loving and attentive one minute, remote and unreachable the next. They have the potential to be a bohemian or a devoted family man. Either way, even those who are closest to them can never really know them because, like all water-sign individuals, they keep their secrets well.

Cancerian men are very adaptable to family life, since family means a great deal to them. They cherish their children and often take a very active role in the children's upbringing. Even when wrapped up in career concerns, the Cancer father will drop everything to attend his child's ballet recital or baseball game.

THE CANCER WOMAN They are, arguably, the most womanly of all the signs. The Cancer woman has a strong maternal instinct and the desire to make her home a place of domestic bliss. Even an unmarried and childless Cancer woman is likely to be an incurable homebody.

Women born under this sign have a great loyalty to family members and close ties to their mothers. They also have a large circle of friends and associates. These ladies often feel a need to involve themselves in community projects, and spend a great deal of their free time organizing charity or social events. The typical Cancer woman always looks beyond her career or home-centered activities to find additional interests through which she can contribute to the benefit of others.

THE CANCER CHILD Little ones born under this sign are sensitive and shy. They are quiet, reflective children who prefer to be seen and not heard. It isn't odd for them to begin talking later than other children. They may have a difficult time being part of a group, allowing themselves to be dominated by more aggressive youngsters.

Parents of Cancerian children need to be especially helpful in their social development, teaching them to assert their individuality and independence. These children are rarely discipline problems, though they can become excessively moody and depressed during adolescence. During this period it is important that parents are especially under-standing, sensitive, and open to discussion about matters vital to teenagers, since these young people will never confide in parents who are judgmental or inflexible.

THE CANCER LOVER Cancerian individuals are extremely romantic and passionate people. Men and women born under this sign have an old-fashioned attitude toward love and romance. They enjoy all the traditional rituals of wooing and winning a sweetheart, and usually opt for marriage or a long-term relationship, not simply a short-term affair. They are serious by nature, and that attitude extends to romance.

People born under this sign make loyal mates. They will champion their spouse's career and expect the same in return.

These individuals are keenly attuned to the needs and wants of their partner; because of this they are exceptionally sensitive lovers. Once they feel that they can share their innermost feelings with a mate, the Cancerian man or woman becomes totally devoted and secure within the relationship.

ELEMENT: Water
QUALITY: Cardinal
PLANETARY RULER: Moon
BIRTHSTONE: Pearl
FLOWER: Larkspur
COLOR: Silver

KEY CHARACTERISTIC:
Emotion

STRENGTHS: Intuitive, Nurturing, Maternal
CHALLENGES: Controlling, Bossy, Manipulative

THE CANCER BOSS The typical Cancerian boss is gentle, but exacting. He or she demands perfection and loyalty from an employ-ee, as well as high ethical standards. If these attitudes are not adhered to, the Cancer boss loses respect for the worker.

In cases where a good relationship has already been established, the Cancer boss fosters an atmosphere of good feelings and positivity in the office or workplace. This is one employer who is very motivated toward helping workers move up in the world. Most Cancer individu-als have a mentor mentality, but when he or she is also in the position to inspire the people who work under them, they may become a pseudo-parent figure.

THE CANCER FRIEND Cancerians have a genius for friendship. With their gentle and caring spirit, they are the ones to whom others turn with problems, worries, and life-choice concerns. Cancer men and women often seem to possess an "old soul."

Despite their ability to support and nurture their pals, Cancerians do not make friends easily. This may be because they take friendship seriously, and don't bother to indulge superficial associations. They are often shy people who wait for friendships to develop instead of actively pursuing them. Because they believe so strongly in loyalty to the peo-ple they care about, Cancer men and women often maintain friendships with people they met in high school and college.

JUNE 21

People born on this day feel the need to do great good in the world. They are happy individuals with a genuine love for others. Fairness is a passion with them, and they have a personal need to live according to a set of ethical standards.

The men and women born on this date combine intelligence with a great sense of caring. They do not shrink from becoming involved in situations that put their reputations on the line.

FRIENDS AND LOVERS
June 21 natives need the closeness and emotional intimacy of their relationships. They usually have a wide and varied set of friends, who allow them to see life from ever-changing perspectives.

Where love and romance are concerned, June 21 men and women have quite a history. They are romantic souls who fall in love many times, always searching for perfection in their love relationships. Since they never reach the point where they believe this is impossible, June 21 people may marry several times.

CHILDREN AND FAMILY
If June 21 people lack the sort of family background they desire, they will sometimes concoct a new one. This is not done from a sense of embarrassment, or the need to make themselves seem more grand than they are. It is simply that they have a picture in their mind's eye of how things should be, and they will sometimes arrange the facts to fit that image.

These men and women adore children and make exceptional parents. They are loving, demonstrative, and quite liberal when it comes to discipline. June 21 men and women enjoy big families and often have a great many children.

HEALTH
People born on this date have naturally robust good health, although they may eat too many sweets and starches. Eating is often a passion with them, and in their middle years they can sometimes suffer the consequences of their indulgence.

Their upbeat, enthusiastic disposition goes a long way toward making these men and women healthy, and they believe very much in the adage that "a healthy mind makes a healthy body."

CAREER AND FINANCES
Although their personal lives are just as important to these people as their professional aspirations, June 21 natives are often very successful at making a living. They have a true entrepreneurial spirit and can be exceptionally creative in bringing their ideas before the public.

Money is a necessary fact of life to these people, yet they are not greedy or acquisitive by nature. They believe very much in bestowing their largess upon those less fortunate.

DREAMS AND GOALS
There is never a lack of dreams for these talented and far-thinking individuals. They live large and dream large, always believing in their ability to make their goals come true with the aid of providence and a little good luck.

June 21 men and women are happiest when putting together a plan for the future. To them, the journey is every bit as important as the eventual destination.

EMBRACE
Sensuality
Psychic awareness
A sense of history

AVOID
Pettiness
Revenge
Feelings of alienation

ALSO BORN TODAY
Actress Meredith Baxter; actor Michael Gross; novelist Mary McCarthy; actress Juliette Lewis; philosopher Jean-Paul Sartre; England's Prince William; actress Jane Russell; novelist Francoise Sagan

110

JUNE 22

People born on this date may be perceived as being sociable, but they are actually very shy and seek their own company as much as possible. They are extremely sensitive to the emotional climate around them and can be both positively and negatively affected by their environment.

These individuals have a secret side, which they show only to those closest to them. Not given to displays of ego, they prefer to remain in the background, where they perform their daily responsibilities expertly, and in their own quiet way.

FRIENDS AND LOVERS

Although they may seek out only a small circle of associates, June 22 natives value their friendship and derive a great deal of happiness from them. These people don't make friends easily, but when they do they are likely to keep them for life.

Love is also a very permanent and stable factor in the lives of June 22 individuals. They prize ethics and honesty far more than good looks or charm when looking for a partner. Once they find the person of their dreams, they're likely to be mated for life.

CHILDREN AND FAMILY

Maintaining strong family ties is important to June 22 individuals, who revel in all the trappings and traditions of family life. Because they fervently wish for things within the family structure to be perfect, they may dwell exclusively upon positive memories rather than allow their illusions to be banished by truth.

June 22 people are doting parents. Though they recognize the need for discipline, they prefer to set a quiet example, rather than aggressively manage their kids' upbringing.

HEALTH

Enjoying robust good health, June 22 folks do everything they can to maintain a wholesome lifestyle. They don't care how hard they must work in order to stay fit. Because of their disciplined attitude, they manage to keep up with an exercise regimen no matter what else is going on in their schedule.

There is sometimes a tendency for people born on this date to turn to food for comfort when things go wrong. But they can just as willingly bend to the discipline of a structured eating plan when necessary.

CAREER AND FINANCES

People born on this date are hard workers who don't mind sacrificing free time if it means moving up the ladder of career fulfillment. They do especially well in banking and retail sales.

Skillful handling of money is second nature to June 22 people. Although essentially conservative in their approach to investments, they have the good sense to take a financial risk once in a while.

EMBRACE
Truth
Understanding
Your own limitations

AVOID
Deception
Lecturing subordinates
Feeling superior

ALSO BORN TODAY
Designer Bill Blass; gangster John Dillinger; political figure Diane Feinstein; actor-singer Kris Kristofferson; writer Anne Morrow Lindbergh; singer Peter Pears; actress Meryl Streep; film director Billy Wilder.

DREAMS AND GOALS

One of the premier aims of June 22 natives is to do as much good for others as possible. They are happiest when they can use their personal or professional influence in positive ways.

No matter how much someone born on this day wants to succeed, they will never compromise their ethics in order to do so.

JUNE 23

The people born on this date know how to have a good time. They are likely to be less serious and sensitive than most men and women born under the sign of Cancer. They appreciate a funny story when they hear one and have the reputation for playing practical jokes on their closest friends and family members.

June 23 individuals are generous to others. They are intelligent, common-sense types with an unexpected streak of eccentricity.

FRIENDS AND LOVERS June 23 natives really know how to make friends. Not only are they good at the social aspects of friendship, but they have a heartfelt concern for those within their circle. They are loyal people who may keep the same set of friends over a period of many years.

These witty, socially adept folks can sometimes make foolish romantic choices. And yet, unlike some Cancer natives who allow a failed marriage or relationship to make them bitter, June 23 people keep coming back for more.

CHILDREN AND FAMILY Men and women born on June 23 may have a complex family background. One parent is likely to have a more profound influence over their lives than the other. If not emotionally satisfying, this relationship may still be one of the most important in the life of a person born on this date.

June 23 people make very good parents. They are strict, but never fail to impart real affection to their little ones. Since education is very important to these people, they will go to great lengths to make certain that their children go to the best schools and become involved in a number of worthwhile extracurricular activities.

HEALTH June 23 people are naturally healthy, and their positive mental attitude has a lot to do with it. They never believe in feeling sorry for themselves, and although they're physically active, they don't use this fact as an excuse for overindulging in rich or fatty foods.

Daily exercise helps them to maintain their emotional equilibrium. If sleep disorders occur, meditation before bed is helpful.

CAREER AND FINANCES June 23 people are success-oriented individuals who will work very hard to get to the top of their fields. They know how to put all of their energy to work for them. When young, they are excellent, motivated students.

Although money is seldom a symbol of status to these people, they do enjoy the security it brings. They are generous to others, yet do not indulge themselves except on rare occasions. They are fiscally clever and conservative, making good investment choices and then watching them keenly.

DREAMS AND GOALS June 23 people want all that life can give them, even if that comes at a price. Whether adolescents or senior citizens, they continue to be thrilled and challenged by their future.

The men and women born on this date have the patience to wait for their goals, understanding that much of what they desire must come over a period of time. They're never without a new dream.

EMBRACE
Punctuality
Logic
A sense of history

AVOID
Insensitivity
Lack of humility
Bossiness

ALSO BORN TODAY
Playwright Jean Anouilh; novelist Richard Bach; actor Bryan Brown; singer/songwriter Ray Davies; English King Edward VII; Empress Josephine; opera conductor James Levine; Supreme Court Justice Clarence Thomas.

JUNE 24

The men and women born on June 24 have a great need to break with tradition and the past. These creative, artistic souls have something to prove to themselves and others, and will not abandon that goal at any cost.

June 24 people have great personal charm, which may give others the impression that they are more mellow and less driven than they actually are. In fact, these folks are extremely career-oriented, and sometimes sacrifice personal happiness in order to achieve their aims.

FRIENDS AND LOVERS Relationships can be troubling for the men and women born on this day. They constantly feel the need to give of themselves in friendships and love relationships, but their feelings are often not reciprocated in the ways they hope.

June 24 people sometimes have problems succeeding at love, though they try very hard to do so. They are extremely emotional and can struggle to recover from a broken romance. When these men and women marry they want it to be forever. To this end, they do everything they can to keep the romance alive, no matter how long they and a spouse have been together.

CHILDREN AND FAMILY June 24 natives often have the good fortune to be the "fair-haired" child of the family. Their charm makes it easy for them to be loved by all, and when they are very young these people have a tendency to use this to their advantage.

Many men and women born on this date are not particularly interested in becoming parents, though they are exceptionally good at the job if and when the responsibility comes their way.

HEALTH Nervous complaints and stomach ailments can trouble men and women born on this date. Unless their lives are in harmonious balance, they may suffer these illnesses, which are exacerbated by a love of rich food and drink.

June 24 people are luxury-loving men and women who are likely to find it difficult to discipline themselves to exercise every day—yet their good looks and health depend on it.

CAREER AND FINANCES Despite their need for fulfilling and exciting careers, June 24 individuals do not always have the stamina or perseverance to follow through on their ambitions. They often feel driven to accomplish something in the artistic realm, as if they're on a mission.

These people spend money easily, even obsessively, then wonder why their finances are in a state of disarray. Professional help with these matters is advised.

DREAMS AND GOALS June 24 people often wish to succeed in a creative endeavor, even if their career ambitions lie elsewhere. They do not require a lot of attention for their efforts, only the knowledge that they have achieved a treasured goal.

People born on this date often take circuitous paths toward their goals, becoming involved in or distracted by other aims in the process. Yet once they see the possibility of a dream coming true, nothing can keep them from attaining it.

EMBRACE
Probity
A sense of decorum
Protective love

AVOID
Costly mistakes in love
Economic stress
Jealousy

ALSO BORN TODAY
Musician Jeff Beck; writer Ambrose Bierce; film director Claude Chabrol; boxer Jack Dempsey; singer Mick Fleetwood; actor Peter Weller; musician John Illsley; actress Michelle Lee.

JUNE 25

The men and women born on this date are unusually sensitive, and apt to find themselves at odds with their true nature and the bold persons they hope to be.

June 25 natives are dreamy and inexact, giving others the impression that they are not very focused in their life-paths. Actually, they are considerably more centered than they appear, although they can be easily distracted. They are charming people who are often physically attractive.

FRIENDS AND LOVERS

The personal lives of June 25 individuals hold the key to their abilities to express their talents. When they are happy and fulfilled in their personal relationships, June 25 men and women are able to transcend any other complications in their lives, which gives them the ability and strength to focus on developing and highlighting their natural talents.

The love lives of June 25 people can be challenging at times, especially if they are paired with someone who lacks the sensitivity to understand their true nature. Since they are not known for their communicative talents regarding matters of the heart, June 25 people often suffer their emotional pain in silence.

CHILDREN AND FAMILY

Because of their sensitive nature, June 25 people have a lifelong tendency to be drawn into quarrelsome family differences. These are people who never truly leave home, at least not in the emotional sense. When a family member is in trouble, they're quick to offer assistance, which does them credit.

June 25 individuals are intensely loving to their own children. They may suffer sympathetic "growing pains" as their kids try to make their places in the world.

HEALTH

Many June 25 natives suffer from uncertain health, although this most likely has to do with their attitude, since these people have a tendency to be fatalistic. If they can manage a more upbeat and optimistic state of mind, they are more likely to enjoy increased physical well-being.

June 25 individuals have a great sensitivity to alcohol and pills, both of which create problems for them and should be avoided.

CAREER AND FINANCES

June 25 people may try their hand at a great many jobs before they find the one that is right for them. These dreamy folks are sometimes passive when faced with important life-decisions. Eventually, they will find what they're looking for, but well-meaning friends and family members should not "push" them toward any goal.

People born on this date care very little for money. For that reason, they may have trouble managing it.

DREAMS AND GOALS

Although they experience great peaks of inspiration, June 25 individuals have ill-defined ideas of what they wish to accomplish in life. They are happiest when their love lives are full, successful, and satisfying.

June 25 people often aspire toward goals that showcase their creativity. They have considerable artistic talent and may wish to express some of their unfocused energy through these channels.

JUNE 26

People born on June 26 are blessed with brilliant and creative minds. These individuals have extraordinary potential. They enjoy conversation, yet feel frustrated with the limitations of verbal communication.

It is easy to mistake these loner types as being unhappy, since they are incredibly solemn in disposition. Yet under the calm and quiet surface is a wicked sense of humor that can cut their scholarly reputation—and the pretensions of others—to ribbons.

FRIENDS AND LOVERS The typical June 26 native has a powerful personality that attracts others. However, their complexity can be exhausting for all but those who love them best.

Love is an abstract concept to June 26 individuals. In some respects they are far too analytical to give themselves up to the uncertainties of romance; yet when they do fall in love it is an amazing revelation to them. Despite their bohemian nature, they thrive when part of a committed relationship or marriage.

CHILDREN AND FAMILY Unlike most Cancer natives, the men and women born on this date are not emotionally bound to their childhood experiences. They may even dismiss it as a somewhat irrelevant part of their lives, with a few meaningful exceptions.

Once they have their own children, June 26 individuals are quite different. They begin to put down emotional roots, and can actually find themselves through rearing their youngsters.

These formerly self-absorbed people become tender and vulnerable in their parental role.

HEALTH June 26 men and women can be quite fussy about their health, worrying that

their long hours at work will put an unavoidable strain on their physical constitution. For this reason they are careful to get plenty of physical exercise, as well as watch what they eat.

Because they indulge in a great deal of mental activity, there is a likelihood that sooner or later they will experience tension headaches or muscle spasms in the neck and back.

CAREER AND FINANCES June 26 individuals need to choose a profession that gives them the chance to make use of their powerful intellects. Verbal communication is their forte, and for this reason they make effective writers, public speakers, teachers, lecturers, and therapists.

Finances are another matter. Although these folks are intelligent enough to make good choices where money is concerned, they may have a chip on their shoulder that reflects their cynicism. No matter how much money they make, June 26 individuals are likely to feel as if they are not paid adequately.

DREAMS AND GOALS June 26 people wish to influence their world in a profound and meaningful way. They will actively pursue this goal throughout their lives, sometimes feeling cheated if they are not able to accomplish it. They have highly evolved souls, which can lead them to experience a transcendental reality.

EMBRACE
Forgiveness
Lasting love
Integrity

AVOID
Insincerity
Troubled heart
Wounded spirit

ALSO BORN TODAY
Symphony conductor Claudio Abado; poet Laurie Lee; symphony conductor Antonio Brico; singer Chris Isaak; musician Mick Jones; politician Stuart Symington; musician Larry Taylor; writer/philosopher Colin Wilson.

JUNE 27

Although they possess a great sense of their own importance, June 27 individuals are not naturally egotistical people. They have a strong, almost overbearing personality, yet they wear it with ease and grace.

June 27 people make a good impression upon all who meet them. They have a dynamic charm, which is unusual for Cancer natives, who are usually quiet and unassuming. The men and women born on this date have a lot to offer to others.

FRIENDS AND LOVERS June 27 natives are upbeat, friendly and devoted to creating meaningful friendships. They enjoy having a lot of people around them, yet it is more important for June 27 men and women to cement close personal relationships.

Because these men and women have a strong sexual nature, their love life is often fraught with considerable temptation. Yet, if they find their soul mate they are usually able to turn their backs on other potential romances, in order to nurture a meaningful love relationship.

CHILDREN AND FAMILY June 27 people may have a difficult time maintaining their ties to relatives who have hurt them in the past. Worse, negative childhood experiences may have left these people with misconceptions about the nature and value of family life. For these reasons, June 27 people may choose to remain childless. If they do have children they will encourage their youngsters to have plenty of outside-the-family associations, keeping them from suffering the same kind of familial disillusionment they themselves had to suffer.

HEALTH The people born on this date are often blessed with vibrant good health. They lead an active lifestyle that keeps them trim and toned, even though they have a great love of good food and frequently overindulge in such pleasures.

Many June 27 men and women have the natural ability to be professional athletes, yet if their tastes do not run in this direction they will certainly keep themselves fit by playing weekend sports. They need sports or exercise as emotional and physical outlets.

CAREER AND FINANCES Those born on this date have common-sense attitudes toward making a living. They tend to favor a job that provides the sort of financial security they have come to depend on, yet find it impossible to do work that does not satisfy their emotional needs.

The men and women born on June 27 are naturals at handling income and investments. They are practical, yet possess enough vision to be able to recognize a good thing when they see it.

DREAMS AND GOALS June 27 people are more ambitious than they may seem. Because they take a slow and measured approach to reaching their goals, more overtly driven types are apt to underestimate the drive of the June 27 person. But in truth, June 27 people have big dreams and are serious about making them come true. They are especially concerned with making a good and secure life for loved ones.

EMBRACE
Solace
Religiosity
Carefree spirit

AVOID
Envy
Lack of respect
Self-pity

ALSO BORN TODAY
Actress Isabelle Adjani; French King Charles IX; actress Julia Duffy; artist Philip Guston; writer Helen Keller; French King Louis XII; singer Lorrie Morgan; presidential candidate Ross Perot.

JUNE 28

June 28 people have a marvelous sense of fun. This isn't just a sense of humor, but a way in which they choose to live life. If they can't have fun with a situation, they don't want to be involved in it.

Although their attitude may shock others, these individuals are determined to wring every bit of humor out of even the most unlikely events; nothing is off limits. But they are democratic in their attitude and can laugh at themselves when they are the subject of somebody else's jokes.

FRIENDS AND LOVERS

It may be surprising to find that these jokesters are loners who do not easily make friends. They prefer to have a very few close confidantes, yet they seldom open themselves up emotionally, even to those closest to them. June 28 people are the perfect manifestation of the adage "comedy is serious business." These men and women may be witty and hilarious, but they are far from lighthearted at their core.

People born on this date may suffer many disappointments before they find their true love. Unfortunately, some June 28 natives don't recognize that marvelous opportunity when it comes because they are so accustomed to erecting emotional barriers. Although they seem practical, their hearts will always win over their heads.

CHILDREN AND FAMILY

If it is true that comedy equals tragedy plus time, then the family backgrounds of many June 28 people were comic in the extreme. These people have a lot of sensitive and difficult memories that they have not been able to shake easily.

When June 28 men and women have children of their own they seem to revert to childhood themselves. They are active parents who understand that sometimes a dash of silliness is needed in order to cope with all the trials that come with the job description.

HEALTH

June 28 people often suffer from minor stomach cramping or nausea, especially when overworked or excited. Unfortunately their "cure" for this is often to overeat. An occasional fast, supplemented by the juices of fresh fruit or vegetables, can put these people back on the road to recovery.

Nicotine, alcohol, and caffeine are extreme irritants to the sensitive constitutions of these people, and should be avoided at all costs.

CAREER AND FINANCES

June 28 individuals are extremely savvy about how to get to the top of their professions. Behind all the smart sarcasm and pretense at indifference, these people are determined to make their mark on the world.

The men and women born on this date have a good sense of how to manage money, and may continue to employ money-saving techniques long after they no longer need them.

DREAMS AND GOALS

June 28 individuals keep their goals to themselves. Although well aware of the steps that must be taken along the way, they treat the matter in a cavalier way—almost contemptuously. This is a mask worn against the possibility of failure, because failure is their deepest fear.

EMBRACE
Common sense
Good nature
Placidity

AVOID
Hasty actions
Hurting others
Mendacity

ALSO BORN TODAY
Actress Kathy Bates; comedian/film director Mel Brooks; actor John Cusack; football star John Elway; English King Henry VIII; actress Alice Krige; actress Mary Stuart Masterson; comedienne Gilda Radner.

JUNE 29

There is something almost preternaturally sensitive about the men and women born on this date. They are ruled more by emotion than reason, and refuse to give up their idealism even in the face of hard facts and realism. Yet they are far more determined than their nature would make them seem. June 29 people have a great reservoir of faith and strength, which allows them to move forward despite trouble.

FRIENDS AND LOVERS Where matters of friendship and love are concerned, June 29 people can sometimes be their own worst enemies. They have a tendency to surround themselves with false or fair-weather friends who do not deserve their patronage. Reason? Because June 29 people have a groundless fear of being lonely, and do not appreciate their own best traits.

It can be a similar story in love matters, though these folks seem to do better in this arena. They have a great capacity for love, but should be very careful to whom they give their heart.

CHILDREN AND FAMILY June 29 individuals are likely to have a powerful connection to their original family. They may be especially close to their mother, or a mother figure; this relationship has the potential to be one of the most powerful and inspiring of their lives.

In romantic matters, a June 29 man is apt to look for a wife who echoes the traits of his mother, while a woman born on this date may subconsciously seek to repeat her mother's actions.

HEALTH Weight gain can be a serious concern for June 29 individuals, since they have a tendency to eat heartily, especially "comfort food" that becomes appealing when they're feeling depressed. In order to cut back on unnecessary pounds, they need to ignore calorie-laden soft drinks or hot chocolate, and gravitate to fresh-squeezed juices and sparkling water.

Regular exercise is a must for these individuals. They may not enjoy doing anything too strenuous, but even a daily walk can help to keep them in good physical condition.

CAREER AND FINANCES June 29 people have a great many talents, yet are likely to remain undecided for years regarding a permanent career. Although they may wish to pursue a creative field, they may also be afraid that such an endeavor will not bring the sort of financial reward they require in order to feel secure. For this reason they may take many different "day jobs," while working at their true vocation off and on for years.

When they have saved enough money to invest in their creative future they are likely to strike out in new career directions.

DREAMS AND GOALS The most cherished goals of many June 29 individuals relate to their creative talents. Although they wish to perfect these talents, and believe in them, they often lack confidence in their ability to succeed.

June 29 people care about helping others. They are unselfish and always involved in some activity that brings hope or inspiration to others. If they become financially successful, they are quick to put some of their money at the disposal of those less fortunate.

EMBRACE
Time for yourself
Rules
Exhilaration

AVOID
Guilt
Self-doubt
Needy people

ALSO BORN TODAY
Actress Maria Conchita Alonso; composer Leroy Anderson; actor Gary Busey; singer Nelson Eddy; writer Oriana Fallaci; figure skater David Jenkins; singer Steadman Pearson; actress Ruth Warrick.

JUNE 30

June 30 individuals have an exceptionally well-balanced nature. They are materialistic, yet in a good sense because they wish to help others. At the same time, though, they'll never neglect the welfare of those closest to them.

Men and women born on this date are sensible, yet fun-loving. They strive for success, yet never lose sight of their personal commitments. They are strongly motivated to serve the greater good.

FRIENDS AND LOVERS
Although they love people and possess a genuine interest in those around them, June 30 natives understand that before they can establish worthwhile personal relationships, they first have to work on themselves.

June 30 folks are usually lucky in love. They often marry early, but even if more than one marriage is indicated they manage to stay friends with their ex without angering the new partner—a neat trick. They have a positive attitude about romance, and refuse to be drawn into the routine arguments and disagreements.

CHILDREN AND FAMILY
These people may be on the phone every other day to a sibling who lives half a world away, and they never forget to put that Mother's Day or Father's Day card in the mail.

When they have their own children, June 30 men and women are emotionally transported back to their own childhoods. These are "hands on" parents who leap and romp with their kids as if they were little ones themselves.

HEALTH
Like many other Cancerians, June 30 individuals need to watch what they eat. They have big appetites—and a bad habit of snacking on junk food. For their own health and the health of their families, these men and women need to organize and monitor their nutritional habits.

Playing sports on weekends can help to keep June 30 individuals reasonably svelte, but not necessarily healthy. They need to be aware of which illnesses are prevalent in their family history in order to make wise choices regarding health habits.

CAREER AND FINANCES
June 30 men and women make great entrepreneurs because they can see the big picture and the small details. They will never make a business decision based on a hope or a whim.

People born on this day need a lot of money because they are constantly spending it—on themselves or others. They'll work very hard to maintain the lifestyle they want, but they are not willing to cut into important family time in order to do it. This is one of the reasons they thrive when working for themselves.

DREAMS AND GOALS
June 30 natives believe they can achieve whatever they want in life. This positive attitude is a self-fulfilling prophecy, because the dreams of these folks often come true.

Whether working toward material or spiritual goals, June 30 individuals are more than equal to the task. In the rare instances when one of their dreams is not realized, June 30 men and women have the resilience to adopt a philosophical attitude.

EMBRACE
Peace
Ingenuity
Love of mankind

AVOID
Being judgmental
Greediness
Sense of superiority

ALSO BORN TODAY
Singer Florence Ballard; actress Nancy Dussault; actor David Alan Grier; actress Susan Hayward; singer Lena Horne; musician Hal Lindes; actor Tony Musante; singer Glenn Shorrock.

119

JULY 1

These are extraordinary people who spend their entire lives striving for perfection. Although they seem to court the status quo, they actually need to break free of all inhibiting restrictions. Men and women born on this day seem to have great emotional fragility, yet their spirit is actually very strong.

July 1 people have an unfortunate knack for being their own worst enemy. Even though they are good-hearted and generous, these people seem to draw complications and controversy into their midst.

FRIENDS AND LOVERS
July 1 individuals need a diverse group of friends who will understand their varied and sometimes dark moods, and sympathize with them. As with most Cancer natives, they are devoted to their friends and will go to any lengths to help them.

Because they have an idealistic view of what romance should be, they are sure to be disillusioned at some point in their lives.

CHILDREN AND FAMILY
These sensitive individuals are tied to childhood memories. It doesn't matter if the memories themselves are happy or unhappy—the July 1 person will hold on to them with determination and a measure of regret. If their upbringing was a positive one, they will relive it over and over again, savoring its sweetness. If the experience was negative, they will become obsessed with finding the flaws

and trying to reconcile them.

Despite this emotional baggage, July 1 men and women make excellent parents. They have a loving nature and a genuine sweetness in their character; this provides a happy haven for their own children.

HEALTH
Because July 1 people are concerned about their appearance, they are usually very serious about taking care of themselves. Regular exercise not only helps to keep these people in good physical condition, it also serves as a liberating factor in their lives. When they vent their emotionalism through a good workout, they feel healthy in body, mind, and spirit.

CAREER AND FINANCES
July 1 men and women often seek careers in the caring professions. They make excellent nurses, nutritionists, counselors, teachers, and members of the clergy. Because they are naturally shy, they often prefer to work behind the scenes, letting others take the bows they are too timid to take.

Finances are generally favorable for these individuals. They have a good head for business and can usually manage their own money without help from a spouse or accountant. They are especially clever with investments and may have very good instincts along this line.

DREAMS AND GOALS
The ambitions of July 1 individuals are usually quite modest and often revolve around personal rather than professional goals. They need to feel secure and happy in their domestic lives and will sacrifice a great deal to make this come true.

July 1 men and women are extremely humanitarian and often spend a good deal of their spare time helping friends or even strangers to better their lives. The gratification they receive by helping others is more valuable to them than any material consideration.

EMBRACE
Structure
Appearance
Appeasement

AVOID
Self-criticism
Self-consciousness
Destructive habits

ALSO BORN TODAY
Actress Karen Black; actress Genevieve Bujold; novelist Barbara Cartland; Princess Diana; film director Sidney Pollack; novelist George Sand; novelist Jean Stafford; film director William Wyler.

JULY 2

The people born on this date know how to use humor as both a tool and a weapon. Although their creative gifts may, out of necessity, be subjugated to the needs of their day-to-day existence, these people will always find a way to use their abilities to shine.

July 2 people often have marginal psychic ability, and are extremely adept at self-analysis. They want to know and understand their deepest and most profound inner drives, and will go to great lengths to dredge them up from their subconscious.

FRIENDS AND LOVERS
Those born on this date share a deep emotional bond with their friends. Although they are not likely to have a large circle of friends, those who are close to them are of paramount importance in their lives.

July 2 individuals require the undivided love, respect, and loyalty of their lover. These people are never happy being involved in superficial relationships. They must have assurance of a commitment or they can never give their whole heart.

CHILDREN AND FAMILY
These men and women have strong ties to their families and may even count family members among their closest friends. This is not to imply that their relationships with relatives are always pleasant or even positive. Because of the strong emotionalism involved, there are likely to be many incidents where July 2 people need to separate from their families for a while. But they will always return once the difficulties have been reconciled.

July 2 people make good, but anxious, parents. They are never quite confident of their own abilities as parents and may often err on the side of caution.

HEALTH
Because July 2 individuals tend to have a good sense of humor, they are unlikely to manifest the same problems with weight and diet that other Cancer natives may have.

If they have a sedentary job, these individuals may need to get involved in a serious exercise program. Walking outdoors or on a treadmill is just the sort of contemplative exercise July 2 people prefer.

CAREER AND FINANCES
July 2 individuals have good business skills and also excel in law, education, and any profession that makes use of their intellectual and analytical skills.

Money management is one of their strong points. These men and women are often self-made, and come from poor or otherwise disadvantaged circumstances, yet are able to do very well for themselves professionally and financially. Given this ability, they are unlikely to be frivolous about the family budget and may even be a bit parsimonious at times.

DREAMS AND GOALS
People born on this date are serious about making their dreams come true. They often set an educational or professional goal for themselves at a very early age.

There is little or no ego attached to the wishes and goals of July 2 people. They simply believe in themselves and try to do the very best they can to live up to their potential.

EMBRACE
Spirituality
Financial acumen
Integrity

AVOID
Stinginess
Lack of imagination
Stubbornness

ALSO BORN TODAY
Musician Johnny Colla; Archbishop of Canterbury Thomas Cranmer; model Jerry Hall; novelist Hermann Hesse; political wife Imelda Marcos; singer/actor Brock Peters; actor Ron Silver; musician/composer Paul Williams.

JULY 3

Though they may seem conventional on the surface, July 3 people have a deeply mystical nature. They live life according to their own personal vision. At once eccentric and blessed with exceptionally good taste, July 3 people enjoy living the good life, but never lose sight of their spiritual concerns. They always seem able to balance their material and more esoteric needs. This is good, because these people are forever seeking balance between the different aspects of their nature.

FRIENDS AND LOVERS
People born on this date may have a great many friends, yet few if any of those friends will truly know what a July 3 person is all about. These individuals guard their private life closely; even lovers may get the "mystery" treatment from these folks. One reason why is that July 3 people need their emotional space. Also, they have a desire to retain their sense of mystery. When July 3 men and women find themselves in a committed relationship, or when they marry, they still require a great deal of privacy and personal autonomy.

CHILDREN AND FAMILY
July 3 individuals may not have close relationships with family members, but this does not imply problems. As with all of their relationships, these people simply need to keep a little of themselves to themselves.

As parents, July 3 men and women are likely to be extremely indulgent and liberal; discipline is likely to be minimal. They may feel that they were not given enough freedom when they were young, and are determined to allow their little ones a greater margin for error.

HEALTH
Because they often have a disorganized lifestyle, July 3 people may not be careful about their health and nutritional habits. Like many Cancer individuals, they have a great fondness for good food and sometimes overindulge when they feel blue.

July 3 men and women are prone to yo-yo dieting. When they are young this isn't a serious problem, but as they approach middle age this bad habit can become dangerous, especially if they don't participate in a regular exercise program.

CAREER AND FINANCES
With their talent for introspection and self-study, July 3 individuals make fine counselors, therapists, and psychologists. They love to search out the truth and will go to great lengths to prove a point. Because of this turn of mind, academic research and law are worthwhile professions for them.

July 3 men and women may have bizarre attitudes about money. It is possible that they refuse to use anything but cash, for instance, or that they choose to keep their money at home rather than in the bank.

DREAMS AND GOALS
People born on this day change their priorities at regular intervals. A prized goal at one period of their life may give way to some other dream a few years later. Though they are not especially goal-oriented, July 3 people are idealistic and eager to bring more joy and good will into the world.

EMBRACE
Social responsibility
Tenacity
Precision

AVOID
Intolerance
Immaturity
Lack of focus

ALSO BORN TODAY
Singer/actress Betty Buckley; actor Tom Cruise; composer Leos Janacek; novelist Franz Kafka; French King Louis XI; film director Ken Russell; playwright Tom Stoppard; TV personality Montel Williams.

JULY 4

I t's not always easy to get along with people born on July 4. They are a strong-willed and determined bunch, dedicated to having their way. Yet they are also fair enough to admit when they are wrong, and even apologize once in a while.

July 4 men and women have a humanitarian streak and will do many good deeds in their life. Yet they prefer doing good works in secret.

FRIENDS AND LOVERS
People born on this date have a need to manage their relationships in a very specific way. They are generally regarded as leaders by the people in their circle of friends and associates, and may indeed seem somewhat distant because of this attitude of authority.

They are equally regimented in the way they handle their romantic affairs. These folks leave nothing to chance, and are forever trying to "manage" those they love. This can put a strain on their romantic relations, especially if they are not diplomatic in the way they behave toward a loved one.

CHILDREN AND FAMILY
July 4 people have a great deal of respect for their upbringing. Their ties to family members, particularly siblings, are likely to be strong—almost psychic—in nature.

As parents, July 4 people draw upon their background and pass on the values that were bequeathed to them. In most cases this is a good idea. Yet if there was a problem in a relationship they shared with a parent or sibling, they may be unable or unwilling to admit it existed, or exists.

HEALTH
These robust, vigorous individuals are often health fanatics. They consider exercise a necessity, not just a pastime. They are perennial dieters, yet usually settle upon a more realistic eating plan at some time in their experience, and then stick with it for life.

July 4 individuals are sometimes accident-prone. This is often because they have a tendency to hurry for no reason.

CAREER AND FINANCES
Men and women born on this day enjoy being in the public eye. They like to draw attention to themselves and will connive to do so whenever possible. Because they have a charismatic personality, they often gravitate to professions where they are "on display." The performing arts, modeling, public speaking, and media are all good avenues for them to follow.

There is no real financial stability in the lives of July 4 individuals. These people often make a great deal of money, yet are unable to hold onto it.

DREAMS AND GOALS
Living each day to the fullest is the goal of many July 4 men and women. They take pleasure from starting each new day and realizing its potential.

July 4 individuals need to find personal happiness in order to make their lives worthwhile. They have the good sense to be flexible in achieving their aims and know that they are just as likely to find the man or woman of their dreams through a trick of fate or good fortune as by searching for them.

EMBRACE
Discretion
Reasonableness
Emotional warmth

AVOID
Materialism
Ingratitude
Lack of character

ALSO BORN TODAY
President Calvin Coolidge; composer Stephen Foster; novelist Nathaniel Hawthorne; hotel figure Leona Helmsley; actress Gertrude Lawrence; talk show host Geraldo Rivera; playwright Neil Simon; New York Yankees owner George Steinbrenner.

JULY 5

People born on this date need a large stage on which to play their life-part. They have a profound need to live in the "now," and yet they desire to transcend time through their own actions and plans. Intelligent, shrewd, and canny, these men and women put their own stamp upon events.

July 5 natives have a great love for the art of conversation. They can talk themselves into almost any situation, and impress others with their insightful thinking.

FRIENDS AND LOVERS
July 5 people seem to have a nearly endless supply of friends. Despite a strong cynical streak in their nature, their innate openness to others makes it easy for others to like them.

Love is an exercise in mind games for these folks. Although they may seem to judge a love interest by physical appearance, they are actually indifferent to such things. But they are thoroughly turned on by wit and intelligence, and will usually select a partner who possesses these qualities.

CHILDREN AND FAMILY
Because they inevitably affect a disinterested, sophisticated manner, it's hard to know just how much of an influence family life has on July 5 natives. While they tell amusing stories relating to their childhood and growing up years, it's difficult to know if they're telling the truth or merely spinning one of their diverting yarns.

While they seem far too cosmopolitan to be the parental type, July 5 individuals are very good in that role. No matter how many protestations they may have made while single, once they are married with children of their own, their true Cancer nature kicks in and they find nurturing skills just beneath the veneer of their sophistication.

HEALTH
Many July 5 people can make the claim that they have never had a sick day in their life. With the exception of colds and flu, they are remarkably healthy, especially considering the fact that they are lackadaisical about maintaining it.

July 5 natives love collecting recipes of all types and sharing them with friends and family members. Compiling ever-growing personal cookbooks may be a favorite pastime.

CAREER AND FINANCES
July 5 individuals have a very social nature and need a career that allows them to indulge that characteristic. They have a real head for sales or any of the hospitality occupations, such as food service, catering, or hotel management.

Men and women born on this day like to live well, but they are more concerned with putting something away for a rainy day. They are talented money managers and have the ability to handle their own finances, no matter how complicated these matters may be.

DREAMS AND GOALS
July 5 natives are ambitious, but often do not possess the self-discipline to see goals through to fruition. Much of what comes to them may seem like good luck to others, since these individuals do not seem to work very hard at anything. But few people realize that it is clever behind-the-scenes operations by July 5 men and women that make their goals a reality.

EMBRACE
Gentle persuasion
Acts of kindness
Scruples

AVOID
Emotional encumbrances
Self-pity
Bluntness

ALSO BORN TODAY
Circus owner P. T. Barnum; poet/film director Jean Cocteau; actress Katherine Helmond; singer Huey Lewis; actress Shirley Knight; politician Henry Cabot Lodge; guitarist Michael Monarch; cellist Janos Starker.

JULY 6

July 6 men and women have a great love of comfort and beauty. They are extremely tactile and draw immense pleasure from a well-decorated and harmoniously maintained environment. While status often plays a big role in their need to be surrounded by luxury, these men and women are basically down-to-earth, and derive a great deal of pleasure from being able to help those with fewer resources.

FRIENDS AND LOVERS

People born on this date can be excessively demanding in their personal relationships. They don't like to share their friends with outsiders, and may seem bossy when it comes to giving advice or suggestions.

They can be manipulative in romantic matters and have a hard time regaining their confidence if a love match fails. Holding on to people they care about can become an obsessive habit that is difficult for them to break. Although they love deeply, they also require more love than many partners are willing to give.

CHILDREN AND FAMILY

A great deal of fantasy role-playing is involved in the way July 6 men and women see their family life. Because they want to believe that their familial relationships are good and satisfying, they will go to extremes to make themselves believe it. They may idealize their childhood, and especially their parents, into representations quite different from reality.

July 6 people have a tendency to use similar techniques as they raise their children. These individuals need to understand that their little ones are better off knowing a "bad" truth than a "good" lie.

HEALTH

Food issues often loom large with July 6 men and women, who may eat, drink, and party to escape their real feelings. It isn't so much their habits that are destructive but their attitude, since their insecurities may be the trigger for a great many of their food-related problems.

It's important that these people do some form of aerobic exercise several times a week in order to combat potential problems with their circulation.

CAREER AND FINANCES

July 6 individuals have a marked artistic ability and are often drawn to careers in the arts, though usually from a behind-the-scenes position since they are generally far too shy to be performers. They make talented designers, fashion consultants, carpenters, and decorators.

Although they are intelligent and able, these people are also generous to a fault. They're likely to spend money they can ill-afford on friends and loved ones. It may take a veritable "crisis" to alert them to their own bad financial habits.

DREAMS AND GOALS

July 6 individuals seek their happiness and accomplishment through relationships with the people they love. Even though they can be unintentionally deceitful in these matters, July 6 men and women are also intensely loyal. If they fail in a marriage or love relationship, they may feel their entire life has been a failure.

EMBRACE
Spiritual transcendence
Charity
Objectivity

AVOID
Pretense
Snobbishness
Needing to win

ALSO BORN TODAY
Pianist Vladimir Ashkenazy; actor Ned Beatty; TV personality Merv Griffin; actress Shelley Hack; rock and roll legend Bill Haley; actress Janet Leigh; first lady Nancy Reagan; actor Sylvester Stallone.

JULY 7

People born on July 7 understand that the greatest lessons in life take place on a subconscious level. These individuals are dedicated to self-improvement in all its forms, yet their most profound concern is to express themselves through group involvement.

These men and women have the potential for great spirituality but may spend a great deal of their lives confused as to what they actually believe. Since organized religion holds little allure for them, they are likely at some point to ally themselves with New Age studies.

FRIENDS AND LOVERS Friendship and love are the high points in the life of July 7 individuals, yet these things are just as likely to cause them pain as happiness. Friends may prove themselves false, which usually has a shattering impact upon these sensitive men and women.

When romance goes wrong, these people can grieve for months, believing that they will never again find someone who loves and understands them.

CHILDREN AND FAMILY Many July 7 individuals feel a need to "rewrite" their family history. This rarely has anything to do with a wish to impress others but is more of an attempt to bring the illusion into line with the reality. These people have a hard time dealing with truths that may be painful for them. Because of this, they are drawn to a more compassionate version of reality.

They make very fine parents but need to drawn the line where truth and illusion merge in the lives of their children. It is imperative that they teach their youngsters to value truth no matter how difficult it may be, or how painful.

HEALTH July 7 people often suffer from imaginary ailments. These may include headaches or feelings of malaise, usually brought on by boredom or a sense of helplessness. Unfortunately, these individuals sometimes turn to drugs and alcohol as a means to banish unhappiness or fear. These people should stay away from alcohol and certainly from drugs, even those which are legally prescribed or sold over the counter.

CAREER AND FINANCES July 7 men and women succeed in careers that carry with them an illusion of glamour. These people often feel ill at ease in the present day and prefer a simpler, more elegant time when craftsmanship and artistry were emblems of excellence.

Since they are often physically attractive, these people can make a great deal of money trading on their good looks. They are adept on both sides of a camera lens and may be as fine a photographer as a model. July 7 individuals who have the entrepreneurial spirit are likely to be involved with spiritual advice.

DREAMS AND GOALS July 7 men and women have the need to change the world they were born into. They are visionaries, illusionists, people with an artistic dream or a philosophical bent. Being able to share their special talents with others holds great excitement for them.

Even though they have a loner mentality, these men and women are not shy about letting others feel the influence of their own religious faith or spiritual conscience.

EMBRACE
Dedication to family
Glamour
Instinct

AVOID
Anger
Guile
Playing with people's feelings

ALSO BORN TODAY
Designer Pierre Cardin; painter Marc Chagall; film director Vittorio de Sica; actress Shelley Duvall; composer Gustav Mahler; composer Gian-Carlo Menotti; comedian Bill Oddie; musician Ringo Starr.

JULY 8

People born on July 8 are more serious-minded than they appear because their quirky personality gives them a carefree, eccentric aspect. But in truth, July 8 men and women have a powerful need to display their abilities. They believe in conquering the "impossible dream." Their idealistic streak is powerful, but they don't expect things to come to them easily. They want to earn everything they have—and they wouldn't have it any other way.

FRIENDS AND LOVERS
July 8 natives are very select in the way they choose their friends. These quiet, introspective people are often put off by people who chatter too much or are too curious. July 8 people feel completely at ease only with friends who are supportive yet know when to pull back.

Love is an extremely serious matter to these people. They aren't especially marriage-minded and may wait for years to wed. Even when they do find the right partner, July 8 men and women are likely to put career concerns and responsibilities first.

CHILDREN AND FAMILY
People born on this date have a strong connection to their family. They rely on relatives to be their support system in challenging times, and are likely to provide the same type of emotional closeness for family members. They are very involved in the lives of their siblings' children.

When July 8 people do become parents they are quite strict. They feel that to instill a sense of honor in their children is a duty.

HEALTH
Because of their disciplined nature, July 8 men and women are good about personal health and fitness. They're careful about their diet, with red meat their primary indulgence. Although they enjoy a social drink now and then, these people make water their number-one beverage.

July 8 natives are often fitness fanatics. They like the challenge of keeping their weight down and their energy level up. They find that meditation helps them manage daily stress.

CAREER AND FINANCES
Those born on this date have the talent and energy to make a success of their life, regardless of their career plans. They understand the need to pursue a strategy for accomplishment, yet also realize that often the best opportunities are the unexpected ones. To be able to take advantage of these lucky breaks can be worth more than all the planning in the world.

Smart investments are no problem for July 8 folks. They have good instincts and the discipline to put their money to work for them

DREAMS AND GOALS
These people understand that there must sometimes be a trade-off between what they want and what they can have. This is why the goals they set may be modest in contrast to their ambitions and abilities.

Although the men and women born on this date are often exceedingly career-oriented, they know the worth of personal goals. They understand that money and possessions mean very little unless loved ones are around to share these things.

EMBRACE
Moral character
Spiritual energy
Faith

AVOID
Prejudice
Patronizing remarks
Cheating

ALSO BORN TODAY
Actor Kevin Bacon; archaeologist Sir Arthur Evans; comedian Marty Feldman; actress Anjelica Huston; psychologist Elizabeth Kubler-Ross; guitarist Graham Jones; U.S. Vice President Nelson Rockefeller; actor Jeffrey Tambor.

JULY 9

Although the men and women born on this date are extremely ambitious, they're likely to experience a period in their lives when their greatest talents are subjugated to the daily needs of making a living. Because they have an exceptionally spiritual nature, they're usually able to grow as they meet this challenge.

July 9 people are great role models. They have the ability to be happy with very few material possessions, yet because they're willing to think more of others than themselves, they often receive blessings many times over.

FRIENDS AND LOVERS
The natural leadership and bold and kinetic energy of these people have a way of drawing friends easily. Their friends not only respect them, but often emulate them.

The men and women born on July 9 are passionate and exciting in love matters, yet because of their Cancerian nature they also cling to the object of their love. This can make a relationship unnecessarily complicated at times, especially if the other individual is unwilling to sacrifice his or her autonomy. If both parties have the ability to communicate well and often, there is less chance that the relationship will fall apart.

CHILDREN AND FAMILY
July 9 natives can be very secretive about their family backgrounds. This could be because there was serious upset in the family unit when they were a child—or perhaps they've simply managed to reinvent themselves in a way that's more pleasing to them.

HEALTH
July 9 people have a strong interest in taking care of their health. They eat well and love to exercise—the more the better. Because they're so active, July 9 individuals have a tendency to be accident-prone.

People born on this date need to supplement their diet with plenty of vitamins and herbal supplements. July 9 people are active and require at least eight hours of sleep each night.

CAREER AND FINANCES
July 9 natives are extremely career-dominated. They are concerned with making a success of their lives and are often determined to make a great deal of money. They have a good head for business, and climb the corporate ladder easily.

Since money is a great motivator for these men and women, they handle this resource carefully. Because many July 9 men and women come from poor circumstances, they know the value of a dollar; they're not likely to spend their hard-earned money frivolously. Happily, they have a reputation for being extremely generous to relatives and friends.

DREAMS AND GOALS
July 9 people are ambitious, positive, and eager to succeed. They will sacrifice a great deal of their time and effort in order to make their goals a reality. Because this sometimes results in time stolen from spouse and family members, people born on this day need to help their loved ones understand that these sacrifices are necessary for the time being, but will not be lifelong problems.

When July 9 folks reach their goals, especially financial ones, they are invariably generous to those they love.

EMBRACE
Fun
Good fortune
A sense of the ridiculous

AVOID
Negativity
Jealousy
Controversial issues

ALSO BORN TODAY
Actor Tom Hanks; artist David Hockney; actress Kelly McGillis; novelist Ann Radcliffe; composer Ottorino Respighi; actor Fred Savage; football star O. J. Simpson; actor Jimmy Smits.

JULY 10

People born on July 10 are far more conventional than they appear. Although willful, they also possess considerable self-discipline. A natural authoritarian streak is balanced by a need to have the good opinion of others in order to be happy.

They surround themselves with expensive possessions, yet it's not the things that dazzle them, but the realization that it's all been made possible by their hard work.

FRIENDS AND LOVERS
Friendships come easily to these folks. Although they may often find themselves involved with people who can "help" them professionally, they're just as eager to make friendships on the basis of personality.

July 10 people prefer stable romances. They dread having to deal with pangs of unhappiness or jealousy, and want to know from the start of the relationship just where it's going.

CHILDREN AND FAMILY
People born on this date often come from secure, stable families—but if they do not, they may "pretend" in later years that they did. This isn't because they're ashamed of their background in any way, but because these are the values they admire. Further, they like to present what is good in them as reflections of their parents.

July 10 people are active, loving mothers and fathers. Although they may be somewhat narrow-minded in their approach to parenting, their motives are always good. They're eager to give their kids a good start in life.

HEALTH
Good health comes naturally to people born today, though bad habits can put that health in jeopardy. Smoking is ruinous to their heart, and should be avoided at all costs. Rich, fatty foods, and simple overeating are equally harmful.

Rather than constantly put themselves at risk with one dubious diet after another, July 10 natives should select a sensible eating plan and stick with it for life. They should eat plenty of green, leafy vegetables and lean meat. Vitamin pills should be taken daily, along with the occasional iron supplement.

CAREER AND FINANCES
July 10 men and women often know from an early age which line of work they want to pursue, and begin to work toward it at that time. They're talented in many respects, and do especially well in work that makes use of their wonderful organizational ability, as well as their effective management of other people's resources and abilities.

People born today are equally skilled in making money. They aren't flashy about the way they handle it, and usually opt for a sensible approach.

EMBRACE
Dynamic change
Generosity
Positive energy

AVOID
Manipulation
Gossip
Bad manners

ALSO BORN TODAY
Newsman David Brinkley; politician David Dinkins; actor Ron Glass; folk singer Arlo Guthrie; guitarist Jerry Miller; novelist Marcel Proust; actor Max von Sydow; artist James Whistler.

DREAMS AND GOALS
July 10 men and women like to see solid proof of their efforts. While they can appreciate the value of "castles in the air," they prefer more tangible evidence. For this reason their goals are often material ones: a big house, a new car, good schools for their children.

When they do allow themselves to dream more aesthetically, July 10 people support goals relating to their own self-improvement. Good health and being a loving parent and faithful spouse are high on their list of aspirations.

JULY 11

The men and women born on this day utilize their extreme sensitivity to understand others; they are never victimized by their own finely tuned nature. These kind and generous people may not always appear to be on top of the world, because their happy nature is something they often keep within themselves.

July 11 natives have a great dichotomy in their nature: Although they love people, they have the temperament of a loner.

FRIENDS AND LOVERS Friends play a very important part in the lives of July 11 individuals. Self-sufficient, these people nevertheless need to reach out to others. The ability to get on well by themselves doesn't keep them from enjoying emotional intimacy.

Like many water-sign individuals, July 11 people look for more than a romantic partner—they want a soul mate, someone who can share their deepest feelings and fantasies. Yet despite their longing for someone special in their personal life, they're able to take what comes their way without feeling disappointed.

CHILDREN AND FAMILY Family life holds great importance for these people. Not only do they require the love and support of a strong family unit, but they're willing to give the same in return.

July 11 people make good parents, though they have a tendency to be staunch disciplinarians. They believe that children learn best when parents set a strong example and stick by it. They also feel that children need to follow the old-fashioned adage: "Seen and not heard."

HEALTH The health of July 11 men and women is tied to their emotional state. When they feel secure and at peace with themselves, they're ailment-free. But on those rare occasions when they feel unhappy or ill at ease, they're likely to experience headaches, a loss of appetite, and other symptoms of "the blues."

July 11 people have an emotion-based reaction to exercise and fitness. At times they're fanatics about getting fit, but they inevitably lose interest.

CAREER AND FINANCES People born on this date aren't always aware of the talents they possess. Often they have pronounced musical ability, though they may consider this to be little more than a hobby.

July 11 men and women need to feel emotionally involved in their work, and will never be happy with an unfulfilling job, even if it brings them a good living.

Money isn't a primary concern for most July 11 people, but they do like creature comforts. Sometimes they react to money in a very emotional way, using it as a way to fill an emptiness in their life.

DREAMS AND GOALS People born on this day are more concerned with how they feel about their lives than how successful they are, or how much money they accumulate. If they're content in their personal relationships and in the work they do each day, they feel as if their dreams have come true.

Like everyone else, July 11 individuals want their goals to become reality, yet they have the ability to be happy even if they do not.

EMBRACE
Realism
Encouragement
Great expectations

AVOID
Excessive solitude
Unhappy memories
Unprofitable associations

ALSO BORN TODAY
U.S. President John Quincy Adams; designer Giorgio Armani; actor Yul Brynner; boxing champion Leon Spinks; actor Tab Hunter; writer E. B. White; actress Sela Ward; figure-skating champion Kristi Yamaguchi.

JULY 12

July 12 natives are party-hearty folks who still manage to retain a wholesome set of values and a strong humanitarian streak. These men and women often have an inner emotional pain that encourages them to bring happiness to others. In this way, they're able to make themselves happy.

People born on this date have a great need to connect with others on a profoundly emotional level. Even though they have a love of material things, they understand the spiritual realm, as well.

FRIENDS AND LOVERS July 12 folks make friends wherever they go. They are energized by people and genuinely care for others. Much of their own life experience is transmuted through their dealings with their friends and associates.

People born on this date are romantic individuals who have an overly idealistic view of love. This mindset has the potential to create problems in their personal relationships, since these men and women look for a level of perfection in their union that is impossible to maintain, or even achieve in the first place.

CHILDREN AND FAMILY July 12 natives often experience extremes in their upbringing. They may have been emotionally neglected as children, or unwisely indulged. One way or another, they have a strong emotional tie to the past, which makes it difficult for them to break from their family.

Because they are deeply loving and giving, July 12 people make good parents, though they need to guard against using their insecurities to overindulge their children.

HEALTH People born on this date are often very heavy or very thin. This is because they give in to their love of food and drink—or are so afraid of their appetites that they remain on a perpetual diet.

July 12 people are sometimes troubled by allergies, especially skin rashes, which can be the result of their ambivalence toward their food habits. Once they come to grips with their true feelings, these physical symptoms are likely to vanish.

CAREER AND FINANCES Men and women born on July 12 have a deep and genuine love for others—a noble trait that's also beneficial professionally. Counseling, therapy, or the clergy are amenable career choices.

Because they enjoy living life on a grand scale, July 12 people need to make a good salary. However, they don't need money in order to be emotionally secure, and in fact can be quite content to live modestly.

EMBRACE
Your own limitations
Self-love
Direction

AVOID
Cynicism
Lack of focus
Fair-weather friends

ALSO BORN TODAY
Comedian Milton Berlé; film director Tod Browning; pianist Van Cliburn; actor/comedian Bill Cosby; lyricist Oscar Hammerstein II; actress Mel Harris; poet Pablo Neruda; diet guru Richard Simmons.

DREAMS AND GOALS July 12 men and women don't simply want to help others— they need to do so. These people often use their own pain to heal others.

These individuals are addicted to long-distance travel and often learn some of their greatest life-lessons in foreign cultures. Their tolerant viewpoint and appreciation and respect for the beliefs of others creates an environment in which many of their dreams can come true.

JULY 13

July 13 people are blessed with a charismatic personality that complements their gentle soul. Modest, they often receive far more attention than they are comfortable with. They have a fear of change, yet understand that it is only through change that they are able to discover their own true nature.

People born on this date realize that all experience is a rite of passage toward spiritual transcendence.

FRIENDS AND LOVERS

A rocky journey to satisfying relationships often awaits July 13 natives. Despite their intelligence, they often choose the wrong people to be their friends and lovers. On the face of it, that's not good, but on the other hand it's the sort of experience they need to learn lessons that can help them later in life.

Love affairs can be particularly difficult for these individuals, who are often disappointed. They love with a true heart, yet sometimes feel forced to compromise their life-view.

CHILDREN AND FAMILY

July 13 individuals may spend the major part of their lives trying to come to grips with their background. They may have a challenging relationship with parental figures, or it is possible that they did not have the kind of upbringing they needed.

With their own children, July 13 men and women may experience an early emotional separation. This is because they are likely to encourage youngsters to make their own choices and decisions from a very early age. July 13 people realize the benefits that flow from personal autonomy.

HEALTH

Good health undercut by poor health habits characterizes July 13 natives, who dislike monitoring their diet and tend to eat whatever foods they prefer. Although they usually have an active enough lifestyle to avoid putting on weight, they may be denying themselves some of the nutrients they need.

People born on this day enjoy playing sports in their spare time, though they may be prone to injury. It's much more beneficial for them to indulge in an exercise program on a daily basis.

CAREER AND FINANCES

July 13 folks do very well in professions where they must deal with people on a one-to-one basis. The charm and magnetism of their personality makes them both likable and believable. For this reason they do especially well in sales positions.

Money matters can be complicated for people born on this day. They either spend far beyond their means or have trouble maintaining a steady income. Fortunately, the acquisition of money isn't one of their primary aims, so this seldom makes a difference to them.

DREAMS AND GOALS

July 13 men and women have high ideals, and they're anxious to fulfill them. If they can influence others positively through their words or actions, they feel as if their fondest wish has come true.

When these people have a deeply personal goal, they're unlikely to share it with anyone else, even the individual it may concern. They want very much to have a strong and stable personal life.

EMBRACE
Truth
Mental toughness
Sophistication

AVOID
Vacillation
Foolish choices
Disapproval

ALSO BORN TODAY
Film critic Bosley Crowther; Renaissance astrologer John Dee; musician Lawrence Donegan; actor Robert Forster; comedian Cheech Marin; actor Harrison Ford; football star/politician Jack Kemp; actor Patrick Stewart.

JULY 14

People born on July 14 are quick-witted, highly verbal, and prone to react in a haughty manner when crossed. They may seem very social and fun-loving, yet are considerably more serious than their personality makes them appear.

July 14 individuals have a great understanding of the structure needed to maintain tradition.

FRIENDS AND LOVERS
July 14 people often make friends with professional associates who have profoundly and positively affected their lives on many levels. They're likely to feel especially close to someone who has acted as a mentor to them.

There may be a considerable fairy-tale aspect to the love life of interesting people born on this date. Either they met their partner through an unusual set of circumstances, or they persevered through difficult times in order to keep their marriage or relationship together. These people believe in the sanctity of marriage, and divorce only if their partner has ceased to care for them.

CHILDREN AND FAMILY
Whether they are aware of the fact, people born on July 14 have a desire to constantly reconnect with their upbringing. They have great respect for their parents. Even though they may have very different opinions and attitudes, July 14 folks respect the lessons that were taught to them.

As for their own abilities as a parent, July 14 natives are often far too permissive. They believe in allowing a child to have maximum freedom to develop to his or her own potential without interference from parents.

HEALTH
July 14 natives are very hard workers and may suffer the effects of stress as a result. They often complain of severe headaches—usually the result of too much work and too little recreation. During periods of calm, when the July 14 person takes time out for relaxation, the headaches generally disappear.

People born on this date may suffer from sleep disorders. These, too, are often the result of overwork. A regular bedtime and meditation before sleep can be a tremendous help.

CAREER AND FINANCES
With their gift of gab, July 14 individuals make very good lawyers, professors, and radio personalities. They may also distinguish themselves as journalists, especially when connected to periodicals covering politics and current events. Writers born on this date often occupy menial "day jobs" while practicing their art in their off hours.

Money does not come easily to these people—they may have to work very hard to achieve financial security. Yet once they do, their situation is likely to remain fixed, with very little variation in the future.

DREAMS AND GOALS
July 14 individuals are dedicated to public expression of their opinions. Whether or not others believe in what they have to say is not really of any great concern to them. As long as these people have a means to express themselves, they're content. If they do receive some measure of praise or acceptance for their beliefs, it's just frosting on the cake.

EMBRACE
Distinction
Dedication to duty
Acceptance

AVOID
Feelings of inferiority
Inertia
Doubts

ALSO BORN TODAY
Actress Polly Bergen; film director Ingmar Bergman; TV newsman John Chancellor; musician Chris Cross; U.S. President Gerald Ford; playwright Arthur Laurents; magazine editor Frances Lear; novelist Irving Stone.

JULY 15

July 15 men and women look to relationships to tell them who they are. These individuals understand better than most people just what the harmonics of day-to-day relationships signify in their lives.

These people are sensitive, yet strong. They have a powerful attraction to beauty in all its aspects and seek to replicate it in their own life. Despite their charming personality, these men and women are extremely sensitive and are easily hurt.

EMBRACE
Elegance
Fearlessness
Shared responsibilities

AVOID
Overwork
Destructive behavior
Crabbiness

ALSO BORN TODAY
Guitarist Julian Bream; architect Inigo Jones; football star/actor Alex Karras; novelist Iris Murdoch; actress Brigitte Nielsen; painter Rembrandt; singer Linda Ronstadt; actor Jan-Michael Vincent.

FRIENDS AND LOVERS
People born on this date have a genius for attracting individuals who can teach them the lessons they need to learn.

Romance has its snares for these sensitive folks. They continually find themselves involved with people who aren't right for them, yet once they settle down with that perfect someone, they may feel the first faint stirrings of boredom.

CHILDREN AND FAMILY
July 15 men and women harbor an exceptionally sentimental attachment for their growing-up years, and love to look back at the past. They have such an idealistic view of life that they can't often see that not everything in their childhood was as rosy as they would have liked.

Though they make very sensitive and caring parents, July 15 individuals need to be far more realistic in the way they present the world to their little ones.

HEALTH
The ailments usually experienced by July 15 people are often related to their overindulgences. These men and women have very little self-discipline where the good things in life are concerned, and that goes for their diet, too. July 15 natives love sweets, and all rich foods in general.

July 15 people are often reluctant to exercise. While they don't usually enjoy working out they can still reap the benefits of exercise while walking, either outdoors or on a treadmill.

CAREER AND FINANCES
Because these folks understand relationships, they are very adept at careers that require such skills. They make fine marriage and family counselors, members of the clergy, social workers, psychologists, and astrologers. No matter what their professions, July 15 men and women understand how to get along with their colleagues.

Since they enjoy living a sumptuous lifestyle, July 15 natives often choose lucrative careers. If they've inherited money or are in another situation that frees them from daily work, they'll often pursue a hobby instead of a full-time career.

DREAMS AND GOALS
To get along with others is the main goal of July 15 natives. Although this talent comes naturally to them, it doesn't always come easily, since there are always other people involved who may have few, if any, interpersonal skills.

July 15 men and women also set material goals for themselves. They are forever setting their sights on something new, something beautiful. This can be a real hurdle if money is a problem, since "saving up" for an item is difficult for these spendthrift people.

JULY 16

Those born on this day are very spiritual, with an innate sense of self. Although quiet, introspective, and seemingly shy, these men and women have a strong will. They use the power of their positive attitude to get them through tough times.

Happy, yet paradoxically fatalistic in their outlook, July 16 people have a common-sense approach to life: They hope for good things to happen, but are never surprised when the opposite occurs.

FRIENDS AND LOVERS July 16 natives

are not especially social, yet they seek out intimate friendships and love affairs with people whose lives they can affect positively.

Their love relationships are equally complicated. They are sometimes attracted to a lover for karmic reasons—perhaps to continue a spiritual tutelage from a past-life experience, or to give support and affection to an individual who did the same for them in an earlier incarnation.

CHILDREN AND FAMILY Reincarnation

is often the key element in the story of July 16 people and their families. Although this is a fairly common scenario played out between anyone and their relatives, only very sensitive people, such as July 16 natives, can learn from it. In cases where there has been unhappiness between parties in an earlier incarnation, the people involved in the current relationship will inevitably seek to work out their differences.

July 16 people often feel this powerful karmic tie for the first time when they become parents. The sense that they've known their children before can be very strong.

HEALTH Because of their extreme spiritual

sensitivity, July 16 men and women sometimes suffer from ailments that seem to have no cause, but that are actually created by past-life traumas. Of course, they should first look for answers on the current plane, but if these are not forthcoming, they need to consult a reputable past-life regression therapist who can bring the causes to their attention, and suggest a cure.

CAREER AND FINANCES July 16 people

have a great deal of artistic talent. They're often drawn to careers that allow them to express themselves creatively, although more commonly from behind the scenes rather than as a performer.

Money is relatively inconsequential to people born on this day. They are much more concerned with being able to express their sensitivity in a positive way than with the accumulation of money.

DREAMS AND GOALS July 16 natives

have the ability to reach the highest levels of spirituality. This is their quest, and if they are open to all the positive influences around them, they'll be able to leave this life even more enriched than when they came into it.

Material goals are rarely a strong focus in the lives of July 16 people, yet they do have a great need to connect with loved ones on an emotional level and make a difference in the lives of those who need their help.

EMBRACE
A joyful heart
Fortitude
Direction

AVOID
Isolation
A lack of commitment
Feeling blue

ALSO BORN TODAY
Actor Ruben Blades; painter Jorge Castillo; actress Phoebe Cates; artist Camille Corot; actor Corey Feldman; baseball star "Shoeless" Joe Jackson; actress Ginger Rogers; actor Mickey Rourke.

JULY 17

People born on July 17 are committed to excellence and achievement. They possess a high sense of honor and are sticklers for truth. Although they may have a decided weakness for flattery, they are not very self-assured, and often hide behind a facade of sophistication.

July 17 men and women have a wickedly entertaining sense of humor, and are often known for their seemingly uncharacteristic practical jokes.

FRIENDS AND LOVERS
July 17 natives are accustomed to being put in leadership roles from a very early age. Perhaps it's their serious nature and intelligence, or simply their respectability, which creates around them an aura of capableness. Whatever the reason, the friendships of July 17 individuals usually cast them in the additional roles of confidante and mentor.

Even in love relationships the typical July 17 man or woman will be admired for more than romantic eligibility. These highly competent people are sometimes drawn into relationships that challenge their philosophy and life-view.

CHILDREN AND FAMILY
July 17 people have a "firstborn" mentality. Even if they're not the oldest child in the family, they'll be looked upon by others as the most responsible, the most capable. This can create unfair pressures on them, which they may resent later in life.

Because of their upbringing, July 17 men and women are less likely to inflict similar pressures upon their own children. Indeed, they often overcompensate by giving their youngsters more freedom than they can handle.

HEALTH
People born on this date keep a close watch on their health; they're especially careful about what they eat, and cut caffeine, nicotine, and fat from their diet. They work out regularly and enjoy competitive sports.

The one thing often missing from the health regimen of July 17 people is a way to relax. These people are go-getters who are constantly striving for perfection, which can cause a lot of stress.

CAREER AND FINANCES
July 17 men and women are business-oriented, and keep an eye on the professional ladder. They have great emotional stamina and are very patient, understanding that they must wait their turn for success.

Few people are better able to manage their financial affairs than those born on July 17. They are scrupulously honest and want only what they've earned, yet are able to parlay this into a laudable income. July 17 natives are the sort who start to think about a retirement financial package when they're still in college!

DREAMS AND GOALS
July 17 folks want it all. Although they often grow weary of being told how capable and stable they are, these savvy types also realize they possess considerable brain power.

People born on this date plan their achievements in a very organized and efficient way. They realize that even though long-range goals are important, they can't ignore the day-to-day details.

EMBRACE
Individuality
Social skills
A happy disposition

AVOID
Procrastination
Judging others
Self-righteousness

ALSO BORN TODAY
Comedian Tim Brooke-Taylor; singer/actress Diahann Carroll; comedienne Phyllis Diller; writer Erle Stanley Gardner; U.S. naval hero John Paul Jones; TV personality Art Linkletter; singer Phoebe Snow; actor Donald Sutherland.

JULY 18

People born on July 18 are gifted and unusual. They are high-energy individuals with a psychic bent who understand the ways karmic forces can facilitate self-realization. Deeply in touch with their own subconscious drives, they're usually able to achieve their aims through focusing on the those inner desires.

FRIENDS AND LOVERS July 18 people
sometimes unintentionally intimidate those who would normally be their friends, simply because the force of their personality is so great. For this reason July 18 men and women often seek out other high-powered types who have nothing to fear from the "competition."

People born on this day are highly competitive, in love as well as other areas of life. They sometimes see a romantic conquest as a prize to be won, though this doesn't diminish their true feelings of affection.

CHILDREN AND FAMILY People born on
this date often come from a family where the parents encourage competition between siblings. Because they have a profound sense of fair play, these people can learn valuable lessons from this influence, but they must be careful not to become insensitive to others.

July 18 individuals make extraordinary parents. They love the rough and tumble aspects of playing with their children and are also eager to be involved in whatever activities their youngsters enjoy.

HEALTH July 18 natives usually enjoy robust
good health, though they're often guilty of overtaxing their physical resources. No matter what their age, July 18 men and women respond to the lure of competition. It releases their coiled energy and gives them a sense of purpose and resolve.

It's rare for July 18 people to have issues with food. They can eat anything and burn it off quickly. One thing they should be aware of is a propensity to scatter their energies. For example, a regimen of two or three kinds of aerobic exercise is likely to demonstrate the law of diminishing returns. It's best to concentrate on a more focused workout that incorporates aerobic, isometric, and breathing techniques.

CAREER AND FINANCES It doesn't usu-
ally matter to July 18 people if they have a high-powered job in the corporate world, or are involved in hands-on manual labor. They like to feel as if their efforts count.

July 18 men and women seem to have the golden touch when it comes to making money. They can start with very little money and turn it into a respectable sum—or better! They enjoy taking financial risks and don't flinch from losses. It's all part of the game to them.

DREAMS AND GOALS People born on
this date get as much fun from participation as they do from victory. Although they have a competitive streak, it's competition itself and not the results that turn them on.

The goals of these folks aren't written in stone. They change and intensify, ebb and resolve, just like the personality of the people involved. The number-one goal of July 18 people is simply to "go for it."

EMBRACE
Irony
Conviction
A dynamic spirit

AVOID
Fear of abandonment
Bewilderment
Self-blame

ALSO BORN TODAY
Figure skating champion Tenley Albright; actor James Brolin; figure skating champion Dick Button; astronaut/U.S. Senator John Glenn; actress Elizabeth McGovern; playwright Clifford Odets; novelist William Makepeace Thackeray; poet Yevgeny Yevtushenko.

JULY 19

Men and women born on this date are quiet and inscrutable, with a deeply sensitive nature. They possess a generally sweet temperament and a true love of people; they're easy to love. July 19 natives don't try to grab the spotlight, though they're often thrust unwillingly into it because of a colorful accomplishment or dramatic heroism.

FRIENDS AND LOVERS July 19 people are sentimental about their personal relationships, and constantly buy little tokens of affection for their friends. No birthday, anniversary, or other significant date goes unremembered. These people keep the same circle of friends for many years, sometimes even a lifetime.

Those born on this date often fall in love deeply and completely. They may marry young, perhaps to a high school sweetheart, and plan to stay with that individual forever. The only drawback to their attitude about love is an inability to leave the relationship if it turns sour.

CHILDREN AND FAMILY Family ties have deep significance for July 19 individuals, who have enormous respect for their parents. Often without realizing it, they style their own parenting habits accordingly. There can be some controversy regarding these people and their siblings, usually because the July 19 natives emerge as the parental "favorite." As a result, they may feel the sting of sibling envy.

July 19 natives make very good parents, though at times they may expect more of their little ones than the children are able to give.

HEALTH Health is generally good for those born on this date. These folks have a high energy level that's matched by their sense of emotional equilibrium. Further, they're often hip to the latest advances in nutrition and fitness, and put them to the test in their own lives.

July 19 men and women aren't fanatics about exercise. They like to keep fit by doing practical things that are a part of their daily schedule. They may park the car a few blocks away from a work destination, or take the stairs instead of the elevator.

CAREER AND FINANCES July 19 people have deceptively strong opinions that may not be noticeable under the veneer of their gentle personality. They have a great need to make their feelings known to others and may choose careers in communications, theater, or radio.

These men and women have a very sensible attitude about money. They know how to enjoy it, but they also realize the value of putting some aside for that proverbial rainy day. Because of their generous nature, July 19 people are also likely to give more than their share to charity.

DREAMS AND GOALS People born on this date want to feel good about themselves. They're usually able to achieve this by doing their best in everything they attempt and refusing to allow themselves to obsess over failure. These focused men and women realize that everyone has challenges in life, and that it is these difficult times that lead to important learning.

July 19 natives do have a fondness for travel, and may set some awesome goals for themselves related to trips in exotic locales.

JULY 20

People born on this date have an extremely strong sense of justice; integrity is everything to them. Although critical by nature, they never seem self-righteous. And although they love to get their own way, these people understand the power and importance of compromise.

July 20 men and women have a gentle yet determined nature. They also possess a loving heart, and because of this can see the positive side of any situation.

FRIENDS AND LOVERS Relationships are the life blood of July 20 men and women. These sensitive souls are the most intuitive of all those born under the sign of Cancer. For this reason they make excellent friends who have extraordinary concern and sympathy for the people they love.

Not surprisingly, July 20 natives are thoughtful lovers. Not simply highly romantic, they are utterly devoid of cynicism. They have an almost naive level of trust in their partner's goodness and fidelity, and have a great love of domestic life. With the right partner they can literally live happily ever after.

CHILDREN AND FAMILY People born on July 20 have a profoundly nurturing spirit. If they've been part of a loving family, they will continue to share close relationships with family members throughout their lifetime. In cases where their upbringing was difficult or unloving, July 20 people will seek to remake it through their relationship with their own children.

They are affectionate, perhaps overly cautious, parents who try too hard to shelter their youngsters from life's problems.

HEALTH Health problems of July 20 natives are often related to psychological or emotional trauma. When these people are unhappy or unfulfilled, they seem to lose interest in taking care of themselves.

While many July 20 men and women are unenthusiastic about exercise for its own sake, they do respond to more artistic endeavors, like dancing or skating. But their work may be undone by their fondness for "comfort food," which lifts their spirits when they feel blue.

CAREER AND FINANCES The men and women born on July 20 need to express their deepest inner drives through their work. They seldom take a job simply for financial considerations.

When these individuals are blessed with a good income, they exhibit incredible generosity. They also like to keep themselves in the lap of luxury. Working hard isn't really one of their passions, but July 20 people will do it if it can bring them what they want out of life.

EMBRACE
High ideals
Sensitivity
A broad viewpoint

AVOID
Periods of depression
Negative thoughts
Shyness

ALSO BORN TODAY
Silent film star Theda Bara; novelist Thomas Berger; mountaineer Sir Edmund Hillary; musician John Lodge; baseball star Tony Oliva; actress Diana Rigg; musician Carlos Santana; actress Natalie Wood.

DREAMS AND GOALS People born on this day have the desire to show their uniqueness to the world. They are extremely talented but are unlikely to realize their potential unless they have the approval and support of others.

July 20 natives are extremely dependent upon their emotional life to give them the satisfaction they need in order to make life worthwhile. The ability to sustain a happy personal life and successful professional life is one of their chief aims.

JULY 21

July 21 people experience a unique conflict between a need to be conventional and a desire to be original. Since their personality is usually larger than life, it can conceal their sense of insecurity with bravado. At the core of their being, July 21 people are extremely sensitive and may suffer much more than is apparent to others.

FRIENDS AND LOVERS Forging close relationships isn't an easy process for those born on July 21. Strongly competitive, they tend to choose friends who have a similar temperament. This makes it difficult for them to form a bond of trust, since both parties have a need to control the relationship.

July 21 natives may experience the same problem in their romantic involvements. The need to test the boundaries, to see just how secure the relationship may be, is the way in which July 21 people determine whether or not they can trust a love interest.

CHILDREN AND FAMILY Men and women born today usually bring a great deal of baggage from childhood into their adult lives. They may have experienced an unsatisfactory relationship with a parent who did not provide the validation required by the sensitive July 21 person.

If these people are able to reconcile their relationships with their parents, they have the chance to become happy in their own roles as parents. If not, they may elect to stay childless.

HEALTH People born on this date like to live and play hard. That can mean giving in to all forms of obsessive or addictive behavior, unless they can muster the self-discipline to say no to their cravings.

Smoking and drinking are two typical addictions that July 21 individuals must learn to give up. Alcohol is nearly as dangerous to their well-being. Learning to substitute fresh fruit juice—especially pineapple, which soothes the throat—and water for alcohol is a positive step forward.

CAREER AND FINANCES People born on this day are often exceedingly talented and capable of great things. But unless they match their abilities with discipline, they may never live up to their full potential. They are seldom without a book in hand, yet they understand the additional value of hands-on experience.

Money matters can be a source of considerable stress in the lives of these individuals. There is a tendency for July 21 natives to spend money heedlessly, even foolishly at times, with little thought to the future. Spending has a therapeutic effect upon them, yet for obvious reasons it can be potentially damaging.

DREAMS AND GOALS July 21 men and women may seem to believe in themselves and in their goals, yet a small core of doubt may reside deep in their hearts. These folks may know intellectually that they have what it takes to succeed, but emotionally they may be quite needy, requiring the validation of a friend or loved one.

People born on this date need to learn how to deal with minor failures without allowing these to discourage their pursuit of their goals.

EMBRACE
Acceptance
Flamboyance
Happy pastimes

AVOID
Destructive behavior
Bad moods
Fatalism

ALSO BORN TODAY
Actor Lance Guest; novelist Ernest Hemingway; actor Edward Herrmann; comedian John Lovitz; film director Karel Reisz; violinist Isaac Stern; singer/songwriter Cat Stevens; comedian Robin Williams.

JULY 22

The men and women born on July 22 are intellectually brilliant yet somewhat emotionally unstable. Their sharp wit and sharper tongue have a way of getting them into more than their share of verbal scrapes, especially with people they love.

They are bold, active individuals who go to great lengths to prove their abilities, both to themselves as well as to others. Their edgy charm makes them appealing, yet their personality is very much an acquired taste.

FRIENDS AND LOVERS
July 22 natives can impress others with very little effort. They have more followers than friends, yet when they put their mind to it they can command great affection, even love, from their colleagues and associates.

Romance is another matter. The eccentric, often caustic wit of July 22 men and women can work against them if a potential love interest grows weary of this constant verbal fencing. When July 22 people fall deeply in love they usually let go of their natural cynicism.

CHILDREN AND FAMILY
If July 22 people seem to have an "attitude problem," it's likely to have stemmed from their childhood upbringing. They may have been raised in an atmosphere of competition, where word battles were tolerated or even encouraged.

As parents themselves, July 22 men and women are determined to avoid the mistakes their own parents made. They want to foster an open dialogue so that their youngsters won't hesitate to come to them with problems.

HEALTH
Although July 22 natives have a very strong physical constitution, they're prone to a myriad of mystery ailments and injuries throughout life. These are often brought on by their indifference to common-sense habits, like wearing a jacket when it's cold.

They show restraint in habits like drinking, smoking, and over-the-counter medications. Their appetite is small, and they may favor a juice fast as a means to restore energy when they're feeling under the weather.

CAREER AND FINANCES
July 22 men and women have enormous ambition to succeed in their chosen careers. Because they have the ability to see small details as well as the bigger picture, they are very good at handling work-related tasks independently, with little or no supervision. These people like to feel that their efforts are appreciated and may change jobs or careers several times in their life in order to receive the sort of pay they believe they deserve.

DREAMS AND GOALS
The dreams of July 22 natives are limitless. When they see the vast potentials and opportunities open to them, they're challenged to go as far as their abilities will take them. Although honest by nature, people born on this date do have a habit of cutting corners if to do so will bring them a desired result.

July 22 people want success, but not in order to prove anything to themselves. They have old-fashioned values and believe that anything worth having is worth working hard to obtain.

EMBRACE
Career satisfaction
Candor
True self

AVOID
Bias
Gossip
Being too critical of others

ALSO BORN TODAY
Actor/director Albert Brooks; actor Willem Dafoe; fashion designer Oscar de la Renta; senator/presidential candidate Bob Dole; actress Louise Fletcher; film director Bryan Forbes; actor Terence Stamp; game show host Alex Trebek.

LEO
July 23 - August 22

Leo is the fifth sign of the astrological year and is known by its astrological symbol, the Lion. Leo individuals are dynamic, self-confident, and highly dramatic. With the Sun as the ruling planet, people born under this sign are considered to be good organizers, with an ability to lead and inspire others. They are talented people who find great happiness in self-expression.

THE LEO MAN Leo men are good-looking and personable, and they possess a certain swaggering grace that makes them attractive to women. These men are friendly and generally good-natured, although they have a tendency to sulk if they feel that loved ones aren't paying enough attention to them.

A great many Leo men have a macho persona, though they are usually quite gentle, even sentimental fellows. They have a very strong ego and can seem preoccupied with their own concerns at times. Image is important to these men, and they take great care in cultivating just the right one for themselves. They have a great love of athletics and probably played some competitive sport in high school or college. This athletic bearing is something that stays with them even into middle age.

THE LEO WOMAN The typical Leo woman is glamorous and regal, whether she is running a corporation or cleaning house. She isn't complicated—in fact she's more up-front and honest than just about any other sign. Leo women revel in the spotlight and often find themselves the center of attention at work, home, or within their social circle.

No matter how happy she is in her personal life, a Leo woman needs more. That usually means a career, or in some cases an involvement in social or community affairs that showcase her creative interests and organizational skills. Leo women have an innate talent for most philanthropic enterprises. It goes without saying that many women born under this sign have an amazing sense of style and can look as elegant in jeans and a sweater as other women look in an expensive designer dress.

THE LEO CHILD Leo children are so dramatic and outgoing that they can easily be classed as show-offs by parents who do not understand the necessity of their little one to "perform." It is a good idea to get these youngsters involved in some sort of creative enterprise even before they start school, since it offers them valuable training in focusing their talents in a positive way.

Since these children normally take on a leadership role from a very early age, parents need to prevent adversarial relationships between the Leo child and other siblings. These youngsters have a great need to win.

THE LEO LOVER From the amorous love letters of Napoleon Bonaparte to the liberated sexual antics of pop diva Madonna, Leos have always shown a driving need to express their true love nature. These men and women have a talent for blending the tenderest romantic sentiments with bold sexuality. They express their dramatic selves through every aspect of a relationship.

Leos are great devotees of the dating ritual. They love giving gifts and will go to almost any lengths to make their adored feel special. They retain their romantic persuasion even when they marry, and continue to "court" their spouse by showing just how thoughtful and generous they can be. Though they are perhaps too idealistic where love is concerned, Leos are definitely the lords and ladies of the art.

THE LEO BOSS Although his or her personal generosity is legendary, all an employee has to do is cross a Leo boss once to find out just how loud this lion can roar. Leo men and women put great emphasis on authority, and they do not like to be crossed, questioned, or disobeyed. The same employer who can seem so understanding and appreciative will not forgive a breach of work-related protocol.

In most scenarios the Leo boss is a creative, highly organized individual who has the ability to bring out the best in those who work for him. This individual has an eye for spotting untapped talent in employees and bringing it to the surface through encouragement and kinds words.

ELEMENT: Fire
QUALITY: Fixed
PLANETARY RULER: Sun
BIRTHSTONE: Ruby
FLOWER: Sunflower
COLOR: Gold

KEY CHARACTERISTIC:
Creativity

STRENGTHS: Courage, Integrity, Confidence
CHALLENGES: Egotism, Selfishness, Dominating to others

THE LEO FRIEND Despite their winning personality, it isn't always easy to be friends with Leo people, whose talent and self-confidence usually seem to place them at the center of things. That leaves a Leo's buddies always hanging out at the edge of the circle, waiting for someone to notice them. What makes it worse is the fact that Leo individuals thrive on all the attention paid to them, making them seem conceited and self-aggrandizing at times.

The Leo individual is best in a one-to-one friendship where his or her ego is less likely to intrude upon the relationship. Leo needs to be brought down to earth at times, and who better than a best friend to teach the Lion a few lessons in humility?

JULY 23

Like most Leo natives, July 23 people love being the center of attention. They have a pleasing personality and a good sense of humor. Even better, they love to tell jokes and use words in an unusual and memorable way.

It can always be said of July 23 natives that they do their homework. Whether a personal or a work-related project, these men and women are always prepared.

FRIENDS AND LOVERS July 23 individuals make friends effortlessly because they are such likable types. They're friendly and sociable, and have the heart to transform a frivolous relationship into a deep and satisfying friendship.

People born on this day are extremely romantic and cut a dashing figure. They do everything in a big way, and that means romancing a love interest with old-fashioned style. They're great believers in keeping the romance alive in a longtime relationship or marriage. These men and women feel that the romantic magic can—and should—continue over many years.

CHILDREN AND FAMILY July 23 people love their family, and remain in close contact with siblings, parents, and other relatives. Their spouse's relatives will become as dear to them as their own, and a close friend's parents or siblings are easily brought into the fold, as well. Because they can't wait to enlarge their clan, July 23 men and women often marry and start a family at a very early age. They make excellent parents because they combine lessons learned in childhood with their own instinct for doing a good job.

HEALTH There are few healthier specimens on the face of the earth than July 23 people. Their boundless energy and enthusiasm for life infuse their whole being with a sense of specialness and vibrancy.

These men and women love to eat, but they are also extremely health conscious and their meals are usually planned to encompass low-fat, high-protein specifications. On occasion they like to eat "junk food" but balance it with healthier choices. July 23 people love to look good—but health is even more important to them.

CAREER AND FINANCES People born on July 23 often experience their career success very early in life. This may seem like a blessing, but it's also a test. Retaining emotional and spiritual equilibrium as a "whiz kid" can be quite a chore.

Generally lucky where money is concerned, July 23 men and women have the potential to make—and lose—a great deal of money during their lifetimes. One of their few faults is a love of gambling.

DREAMS AND GOALS July 23 people never stop working toward their goals. Although they may change direction many times, they start out waiting for that brass ring to come around, and when it does they grab for it with enthusiasm.

Although career success and financial security come high on the list of goals for these folks, higher still is a desire to obtain the respect and love of those they care for.

EMBRACE
Constructive change
A happy heart
Methodology

AVOID
Being too analytical
Mental exhaustion
Looking back

ALSO BORN TODAY
Actress Coral Browne; writer Raymond Chandler; baseball star Don Drysdale; musician David Essex; TV personality Michael Wood; musician Martin Gore; actor Woody Harrelson; silent screen actor Emil Jannings.

JULY 24

Despite having many natural talents and abilities, people born on July 24 are not without life problems. It's possible that by succeeding in some way at a very early age they fail to see some of the pitfalls that await them. Optimism, erring and eternal, is the keynote to this personality from childhood to old age.

They're unwilling to acknowledge the possibility of failure, which is appropriate because they nearly always succeed.

FRIENDS AND LOVERS Those born on
July 24 have personality to spare and are often the center of attention among their friends. They like to surround themselves with plenty of happy people who know how to have a good time. Yet when they need to confide anything important and meaningful, they are likely to confide in just one or two individuals.

The love life of July 24 people is definitely adventurous. These folks will never be without a series of admirers and flatterers. Because they have charm in abundance, they are unusually appealing companions and lovers.

CHILDREN AND FAMILY July 24 natives
see themselves as central to their family's happiness. They have a rather old-fashioned view of family life and may continue to idealize their upbringing well into adulthood. As children they accepted responsibilities easily, and expect their own children to follow that example.

Because they have no difficulty relating to children on an emotional level, people born on July 24 make excellent parents. They may not fit the conventional image, preferring to be regarded more as a "buddy" than a disciplinarian.

HEALTH Not only do July 24 people enjoy
good health, they possess a remarkable athletic grace that is the envy of their friends. Unfortu-

nately, this gift is something they may take for granted. Excesses of all kinds are common to these people, due to a basically reckless nature.

Vigorous exercise is a favorite pastime of July 24 natives, yet it is hardly a constant factor in their lives. They will devote themselves to it at times, only to lose interest at some later date.

CAREER AND FINANCES Those born on
this date have a natural talent for making money so great that it could be considered a gift. They embrace the entrepreneurial spirit, and always look for an exciting new opportunity.

July 24 individuals are restless, impulsive people who may often change jobs and even careers, always searching for the perfect situation. Although nothing can live up to their expectations, they manage to extract amazing amounts of drama and intensity from their experiences.

DREAMS AND GOALS If July 24 natives
have one wish it is that they be able to shine via the force of their personality.

These folks live in a benign universe where all the pieces of the cosmic puzzle eventually fall into place. Because of this, they're unlikely to approach their goals in a linear, organized fashion. Although their successes may seem to be the result of careful planning, these are often nothing more than rewards of unshakable optimism.

EMBRACE
Sensitivity
New ideas
Commitment to excellence

AVOID
Instability
Breaking all the rules
Escapism

ALSO BORN TODAY
Feminist politician Bella Abzug; comedienne Ruth Buzzi; actress Lynda Carter; aviator Amelia Earhart; poet Robert Graves; actor Robert Hays; actor Michael Richards; pianist Peter Serkin.

JULY 25

July 25 natives are true trailblazers in the cosmic sense. These people are one of a kind, as their distinctive appearance often shows. They have a bold, even ruthless attitude toward life, and may seem overly ambitious to people who do not understand them.

But July 25 people are not simply adventurers. They have a fascinating brand of intelligence that is rooted in the subconscious and allows them to deal with people on many levels.

FRIENDS AND LOVERS

Individuals born on this date are leaders, and for this reason the friends they choose are often awestruck followers. Their closest friendships usually last a lifetime and may have roots in childhood.

July 25 men and women are not really the marrying type. Even when they find the man or woman of their dreams, they have a hard time making a commitment because they fear the loss of their independence. It takes a very special person to help them put their fears to rest. Once they do, July 25 people have a very good chance at marital happiness.

CHILDREN AND FAMILY

People born on July 25 have old-fashioned family values. They believe in maintaining a close relationship with family members throughout their lives. A father may have been an exceptionally strong influence.

July 25 men and women are good parents, though they may be overly strict. Learning that not all issues are black and white can help them to temper their attitude. Building trust in a parent/child relationship is key to their success as parents.

HEALTH

People born on this day usually possess superior good health, though they aren't especially careful about their diet. These people have gourmet tastes and may be talented cooks. "Fat-free" isn't in their vocabulary, so they must exercise in order to keep fit.

July 25 individuals need a varied and intricate exercise plan; without one, they'll grow bored. Since July 25 men and women often have extremely sensitive skin, they need to use a sunblock when out of doors.

CAREER AND FINANCES

July 25 natives often gravitate toward careers where they can be the proverbial power behind the throne. Unlike most Leo natives, they do not like to be the center of attention. But because these individuals have superior intelligence, they have a keen understanding of what people want. For this reason they do very well in market research, political campaign strategy, or entrepreneurial endeavors.

Moneymaking comes easily to July 25 men and women. They have a talent for managing finances—their own, as well as those of others.

DREAMS AND GOALS

Although July 25 people have the ability to reach the top with little effort, they can also be their own worst enemy, since an inability to follow through on their aims can spell failure. It's probably for the best that these folks are happy to see their ideas implemented by others.

With proper motivation, there's nothing that July 25 men and women cannot achieve.

JULY 26

The men and women born on July 26 have the genius to become archetypes in their fields. It's not only that they possess amazing star quality and an intriguing personality; these people also have the ability to draw attention to themselves without making an effort to do so.

July 26 natives often find themselves at the very center of controversy.

FRIENDS AND LOVERS July 26 natives
have a strong identification for the downtrodden, and may unconsciously choose their friends from an unglamorous strata of society. Whether or not they were born to privilege, they'll choose as a friend someone who does not possess their advantages.

People born on this date may be somewhat skeptical, even cynical, about love and marriage. When they do fall in love, they manage to keep their practical viewpoint.

CHILDREN AND FAMILY It's not uncommon for July 26 people to be the architects of their own backgrounds. If they're not in tune with the way they were brought up, they're likely to change its significance, even its substance, in their life.

Due to their conflicted feelings regarding authority figures, and their inclination to wait until later in life to begin their own family, July 26 individuals need to make some emotional and spiritual changes before they take on the role of parent.

HEALTH People born on this day have an eye on good health practices. Although they might indulge some bad habits in youth, they will most likely give these up well before middle age. Naturally dramatic and showy, these men and women like to project an image of carelessness, when in truth their energetic lifestyle is

carefully maintained by regular workouts and good nutritional sense.

July 26 natives understand the value of relaxation techniques.

CAREER AND FINANCES Despite an air of showmanship, July 26 men and women are far more practical than they may appear, and are likely to pursue a "serious" career in medicine or law. But whatever they choose to do for a living, these savvy people are unlikely to take advice from anyone. They seem to have an innate sense of what they must do in order to be a success on their own terms—and those are the only terms that matter to them.

July 26 people keep their eye on the bottom line. They're good money managers and never let a love of luxury interfere with their personal budget. They have the ability to earn a great deal of money and the good sense to hang on to it.

DREAMS AND GOALS People born on this date want very much to make a place for themselves in the world. They desire the material benefits that come with it, but more than that they want to enjoy the respect of their peers and colleagues.

July 26 people will work tirelessly in order to achieve their aims. Yet they will always strive for an unreachable goal in order to remain motivated and excited about what life has to offer.

JULY 27

Men and women born on July 27 embody a duality that's not strictly evident except to those who know them well. They appear to be entirely at peace with their emotional landscape, yet they possess a spiritual core of steel that allows them to "soldier on" no matter what is arrayed against them.

July 27 natives often hide an aspect of their personality from others, not because they are at odds with it, but in order to maintain a sense of control over their world.

FRIENDS AND LOVERS No matter how friendly and well-meaning July 27 individuals are, they always manage to hold something of themselves in reserve. They are personable people with very good social skills, yet at times they seem almost aloof, as if they're unwilling to undertake a friendship dialogue.

Even lovers and mates are kept at an emotional distance when July 27 people don't feel completely secure. They are determined to be loved for who they are and for no other reason. They have a great love of domestic life and settle into it with relative ease.

CHILDREN AND FAMILY The strong belief July 27 individuals have in themselves has its roots in their background. Their strength of purpose, and ability to meet the challenges of life head-on, can be traced to the values that were taught to them as children. July 27 people are traditional in their life-view, and are likely to replicate the views of their own parents when they have children.

People born on this date are sincere, committed moms and dads who instill integrity in their youngsters, along with a sense of wonder at the myriad opportunities that await them.

HEALTH Although they may not be fanatical about their health, July 27 folks come close to being so. They often develop a passion for exercise that, if they are very young, can become a lifetime obsession.

July 27 men and women actively maintain their physical well-being. They employ holistic as well as more conventional methods of staying healthy, and are very careful about what they eat.

CAREER AND FINANCES Whichever career they choose, July 27 people will throw themselves into it with vigor and enthusiasm. Since they're extremely organized, details related to their work will be handled skillfully and completely.

They're equally sensible in the way they handle money. Whether they have great resources or meager ones, July 27 men and women use what they have to maximize their hard work.

DREAMS AND GOALS People born on this date have a desire to be the best. This holds true no matter what their career aims may be. Whether they live out their life on the world stage or in one small neighborhood, July 27 individuals know their abilities and will put them to the test at every step.

Once they have achieved a goal, they move on to the next one. These people don't live in the past; rather, they seek to grow and mature in ways that make each challenge a little more special, a little more engaging than the last.

JULY 28

People born on July 28 understand the value of their own singularity. Haughty yet lovable, these men and women possess a personal code of ethics and a strong belief system. They have a great need to win, and often hide their emotional vulnerability behind this showy aspect of their personality.

July 28 people are likely to receive their greatest satisfaction in life when spiritual aims supersede materialistic ones, though they may have to experience a few lumps before they learn this lesson.

FRIENDS AND LOVERS
The people born on this date depend upon a support system of close friends and loved ones. They have a real talent for friendship, and although they get along with almost everyone, they put their trust in only a select few.

The love life of July 28 individuals can be uneven. Although possessed of a genuinely romantic nature, these folks often shy away from serious commitment because they fear losing their independence.

CHILDREN AND FAMILY
People born on July 28 believe in tradition, and are likely to have been strongly influenced by their parents. These men and women are very proud of their background and draw much of their strength from feeling a part of this heritage.

They take child-rearing very seriously, and fashion themselves into strict parents who demand good behavior and good manners. Even though they may seem to be overly concerned with discipline, they don't pursue it for their own gratification but for the well-being of their kids.

HEALTH
The considerable concern July 28 men and women have for their physical appearance acts as a great motivator for keeping themselves fit and in good health. They are careful about their diet, and exist mainly on lean meat, leafy green vegetables, and low-fat dairy products.

Regular, moderately paced exercise is one of the things that gives July 28 folks their characteristic glow. This, combined with an aversion to cigarettes and alcohol, helps these people to stay in shape well into middle age and beyond.

CAREER AND FINANCES
July 28 men and women have a fierce competitive spirit, which gives them an edge in almost everything they attempt. They are extremely intelligent and usually involve themselves in careers that push their abilities to the very limit.

People born on this date have a cautious attitude about money. Even though they have extravagant tastes, they make a point to keep a good amount of money in reserve.

DREAMS AND GOALS
July 28 men and women like to be noticed for their singularity of purpose. They are intensely goal-oriented.

Knowledge through education is one of the chief goals of July 28 people, who have a hunger to learn, and who will remain "students" throughout their lives. They are especially concerned with understanding history through the prism of experience, realizing that not all answers can be found in books.

EMBRACE
Wisdom
Fairness
Family life

AVOID
Self-centeredness
Greed
Ego issues

ALSO BORN TODAY
Actor Jim Davis; pianist Peter Duchin; poet Gerald Manley Hopkins; novelist Malcolm Lowry; symphony conductor Riccardo Muti; First Lady/book editor Jacqueline Kennedy Onassis; writer/artist Beatrix Potter; actress Sally Struthers.

JULY 29

People born on July 29 are intensely focused. They like to be involved on all levels of every endeavor, and are always willing to learn a little more about their world and the people in it. These individuals are quite set in their ways and aren't likely to be changed except by someone with exceptional skills of persuasion.

July 29 men and women understand the value of political activism. They very often becomes advocates for a particular cause that embodies their own adherence to a high standard of ethics.

FRIENDS AND LOVERS People born on this date are intensely personal and regard their relationships as opportunities to learn more about themselves and their motivations. July 29 natives don't make friends easily, but when they do it's usually with people who are as focused and committed as they are.

July 29 men and women hold their lovers to a high set of standards.

CHILDREN AND FAMILY People born on this date take great pride in their family tree. Whether they come from wealth, middle income, or poverty, these individuals understand just how valuable their heritage is. They draw many of their ideas from their upbringing and adapt them for use in their role as parents.

July 29 natives may have reservations about becoming parents, yet when they do

they're totally drawn into the experience. They may be indulgent of their children, yet have enough common sense to know when to draw the line.

HEALTH High energy and a strong constitution characterize most July 29 people. Although they may not enjoy physical exercise, they understand the need to follow a regular workout plan in order to remain healthy.

Diet can be a problem for those born on this date because they love food and often turn to it in times of frustration or unhappiness. They especially like the "comfort foods" they ate as a child: meat, potatoes, heavy gravy, and plenty of sweets.

CAREER AND FINANCES July 29 men and women like to be their own boss. For this reason they often start a home-based business or form a limited business partnership with a friend or colleague. It isn't money these individuals are looking for, but a chance to do what they wish, without the interference of outsiders.

Wealth isn't the real aim of July 29 people. They see money merely as a natural byproduct of their overall plan. These ambitious men and women care about putting their ideas to work for other people. If, in doing so, they have the good fortune to become wealthy, that's simply the icing on the cake.

DREAMS AND GOALS July 29 natives tend to take the circumstances they are given and remake them into a more personal reality.

They generally have a well-organized game plan for success, which includes working however many hours it takes to get the job done. Despite their attention to career goals, July 29 people recognize the importance of maintaining strong family ties.

EMBRACE
Assimilation
Strong opinions
Culture

AVOID
Intolerant people
Shyness
Inattentiveness

ALSO BORN TODAY
Actor Michael Biehn; singer Martina McBride; actress Clara Bow; filmmaker Ken Burns; U.S. senator Nancy Kassebaum; actress Thelma Todd; TV newsman Peter Jennings; actor David Warner.

JULY 30

People born on this date are creative in a spiritual as well as a tangible sense. Their almost otherworldly nature is fortified by a pleasant personality and a strong sense of self. Although they occasionally seem aloof and distant, they have a great love for humanity.

July 30 people have a genuine charisma that draws others to them. Whether or not they are physically attractive, they possess a singular charm that sets them apart from everyone else.

FRIENDS AND LOVERS Although loners by preference and temperament, July 30 men and women are intensely devoted to their friends. They may have a rather small circle of pals, but it is made up of people whom they love deeply.

With love and romance, July 30 individuals put themselves on the line. They often seem to fall in love with people who are very unlike them, and yet they manage to create a harmonious relationship.

CHILDREN AND FAMILY July 30 natives may harbor some serious doubts about their upbringing, and have a tendency to privately question the nature of their childhood. They usually feel as if their emotional needs were not met, and that their parents overlooked or did not properly validate their opinions.

As parents themselves, people born on this day seek to keep the lines of communication open at all times between themselves and their children. They don't want to be viewed by their little ones as unapproachable authority figures. July 30 people are good parents who try to make a harmonious environment.

HEALTH People born on this date have a love-hate relationship with exercise. They love the way it makes them look and feel, yet they can never quite muster any enjoyment from it. They may also find it difficult to make a place in their schedule for serious physical training, but when they do commit to a fitness regimen, they usually follow through.

July 30 men and women may have eating disorders that can lead to overweight, especially as middle age grows near.

CAREER AND FINANCES July 30 natives like to get to the bottom of things. They are expert researchers with a natural talent for turning up facts that other people may be unable to find. These people like to work behind the scenes, and for this reason they make exceptional writers, counselors, and scientists.

These people pay little attention to their financial status, and usually allow a spouse to handle the family money matters. Despite their seeming indifference, July 30 men and women actually have a very good instinct for making money.

DREAMS AND GOALS To learn as much as they can about the work they do is one of the major goals of July 30 individuals. These folks have a great need to work with creative, exciting concepts.

Getting to the top of the professional ladder isn't as important or meaningful to July 30 people as being able to have creative control over the projects they select.

EMBRACE
Mastering emotions
Desire
Self-esteem

AVOID
Fatalism
Manipulation of others
Intimidation

ALSO BORN TODAY
Singer/songwriter Paul Anka; film director Peter Bogdanovich; novelist Emily Brontë; actress Delta Burke; singer/composer Kate Bush; law professor Anita Hill; actor Ken Olin; actor Arnold Schwarzenegger.

JULY 31

People born on July 31 are natural trendsetters who have the ability to sway others to their way of thinking.

They are creative, friendly, and full of great ideas. These folks never play it safe, but put themselves out on a limb at every occasion in order to prove the worthiness of their positions. In more cases than not, their self-confidence and risk-taking are vindicated.

FRIENDS AND LOVERS July 31 men and women have an odd circle of friends. They seem to collect people, unaware of how different they may be from themselves. They like diversity because it gives them the chance to discover fresh points of view and life-choices.

People born on this date are extravagantly romantic and are likely to have a tumultuous love life. They often seek out partners who are eccentric or seemingly bizarre—another indication of their interest in novel points of view. Although they may appear to be fickle in their love relationships, July 31 natives are merely experimental.

CHILDREN AND FAMILY July 31 men and women are often the rebels of the family circle. They don't feel the need to conform to the traditions of their parents and siblings; because of this they may experience a temporary falling-out with other family members.

These people make liberal, but practical, parents. They're adamant about giving their children the freedom they feel they themselves missed, yet understand that children also need a firm and guiding hand if the little ones are to feel secure.

HEALTH July 31 natives have great spiritual and inner strength, which has an effect on how they take care of their physical self. They don't see mind-body-spirit as separate entities but as a synthesis that needs to be constantly maintained for maximum health and contentment.

Meditation and creative visualization are other effective methods for these folks to keep themselves thoroughly fit.

CAREER AND FINANCES Because people born on this date are highly creative, they need to express their inner vision through their work. These aren't people who can work all day at a job they hate or are bored with, then come home and labor over the artistic project that's their true passion. Instead, they need to do creative work every day, all day.

July 31 men and women have to put their dreams on the line, and if that means having a tenuous financial base for a while, it's a tradeoff they're willing to make. Money can be a good motivator for July 31 people, but it will never encourage them to compromise their values.

DREAMS AND GOALS July 31 natives are open to all forms of experimentation. They want to succeed, but not at the price of their deepest and most profoundly held beliefs. They don't like to make definite career plans because to do so can prevent them from taking advantage of the spontaneous choices that are bound to come along.

People born on this date never lose their enthusiasm for life. They're as excited about meeting personal goals in old age as they are when very young.

EMBRACE
Belief
Goals
The strength to dream

AVOID
Willfulness
Instability
Foolish choices

ALSO BORN TODAY
Guitarist Daniel Ash; actor Dean Cain; singer Norman Cook; actress Geraldine Chaplin; economist Milton Friedman; tennis star Evonne Goolagong; drummer Gary Lewis; actor Wesley Snipes.

AUGUST 1

People born on August 1 have heightened sensibilities, with a sense of style that reflects their inner and outer natures. Although they have a somewhat haughty personality, they are lovable people.

August 1 men and women need the validation of others, yet they are not likely to sacrifice their true self to that aim. These people set themselves a goal and go after it, with little thought of how much time or effort it will require.

FRIENDS AND LOVERS
Few other people can make and keep friends the way August 1 natives can. These people have a real genius for creating interesting and fulfilling relationships that have positive effects on their lives and the lives of the people closest to them.

The love life of August 1 people is varied and fascinating. These unique people have a difficult time finding partners who meet their needs, and may need years to come to grips with the idea of "settling down."

CHILDREN AND FAMILY
Because of their rebellious nature, August 1 individuals often separate early from their families. The reason could be a lack of love, or just an overwhelming sense of independence. They are not greatly interested in becoming parents, since they often have demanding careers that keep them well occupied. However, if they do make a commitment to parenthood, they tend to have a very liberal attitude.

HEALTH
Because they have such a busy life, August 1 people rarely have problems with weight, though they may have considerable difficulties with food. These men and women always seem to be on a diet, whether or not they need to reduce. If they wish to retain their good health, it's important that these folks grasp the dangers of diet pills and other weight-loss products.

August 1 people usually enjoy exercise, but may not have a regularly scheduled workout plan. A run on a treadmill for half an hour each day not only helps get rid of extra pounds, but reduces tension, too.

CAREER AND FINANCES
The people born on August 1 are highly competitive and go to great lengths to achieve their professional goals. They are determined to make it to the top of their field. They do very well in fast-lane professions, such as advertising, marketing, and high-level financial management.

Clearly, then, August 1 natives are dedicated to making a good living. They want the very best out of life, which includes being able to enjoy a great lifestyle and the security that comes with plenty of money in the bank.

DREAMS AND GOALS
August 1 men and women have great potential. Their well-developed ego tells them just how special they are; because of this they tend to set their sights very high. Professional goals are usually met with ease.

As for personal goals, however, the challenge is more severe. August 1 men and women are not at their best in the domestic arena, partly because they need time to figure out what they want.

EMBRACE
High energy
Pragmatism
Generosity

AVOID
Crass behavior
Intolerance
Poor personal choices

ALSO BORN TODAY
Actress Tempestt Bledsoe; comedian Dom DeLuise; singer/songwriter Jerry Garcia; novelist Robert James Waller; actor Arthur Hill; designer Yves Saint Laurent; novelist Herman Melville; cartoonist Tom Wilson.

AUGUST 2

The people born on this date have an edgy, unique personality that makes them interesting to others. They are often extremely good-looking individuals who have a desire to shock others with stories about their wild past. Even though these stories are often exaggerated, August 2 people see them as part of their "legend."

FRIENDS AND LOVERS Like many Leo natives, people born on August 2 believe that there is no such thing as having too many friends. Naturally, they enjoy being the center of attention, but because they dominate the spotlight in such a genteel and good-natured way, no one seems to mind.

August 2 individuals often lead an exciting yet troubled love life. They aren't really made for domestic bliss and seem to prefer playing the field for many years. They fall in love in a big way and often break up a relationship in a storm of recrimination or anger.

CHILDREN AND FAMILY Family is not usually a critical matter in the lives of August 2 individuals. They are fiercely independent types, though this is not to imply that they are in any way antagonistic toward family members. They may even have a close relationship with a sibling, which continues into adulthood.

As parents, August 2 men and women are in their element. They can indulge their own youthful nature by becoming part of a child's world, and reconcile unhappy memories from the past through the healing miracle of love. These individuals are very sensitive to the feelings of their little ones.

HEALTH August 2 people live life to the fullest. They are rarely careful about their diet, and seldom if ever get enough sleep. This can lead to periodic bouts of mild depression and crankiness.

People born on this date require plenty of vitamins and minerals in order to facilitate their good health. They should eat high-protein meals, and refrain from drinking beverages high in caffeine or sugar. They have a tendency to overindulge in alcohol, usually for social reasons.

CAREER AND FINANCES August 2 people like professions where they are on display. Because they are often extremely good-looking, these individuals have little trouble getting noticed for the job of their choice. They have an outgoing, joyous personality that lends itself to success as a performer, model, or attorney.

The typical August 2 native is very good at making money and even better at handling it. There is plenty of potential for becoming well-to-do, even extremely wealthy, as long as they have the discipline to follow through on their creative ideas and concepts.

DREAMS AND GOALS August 2 people see no barriers to making their goals come true. They want it all, and have the chance to achieve their dreams if they keep their enthusiasm at a high pitch.

Their one professional failing, lax work habits, must be corrected. Many of these folks talk a good game, but don't have the discipline to follow through on their plans.

EMBRACE
Acts of charity
A happy disposition
Imagination

AVOID
Antagonism
Bad money habits
Regrets

ALSO BORN TODAY
Novelist James Baldwin; actress Joanna Cassidy; film director Wes Craven; actress Myrna Loy; actor Gary Merrill; figure skating champion Linda Fratianne; actor Carroll O'Connor; actor Peter O'Toole.

AUGUST 3

People born on this date have star quality. Like most people who have an extroverted nature, these men and women are talkative and friendly. August 3 individuals are extremely ambitious. They work tirelessly toward their goals and do whatever they can to better themselves educationally and professionally. They possess great personal charm, and despite an appearance of self-absorption, they are deeply committed to causes that benefit others.

FRIENDS AND LOVERS

Even though they have an engaging personality, the men and women born on this date may have trouble making friends, usually because they have so many talents and so much appeal that it's easy for others to be jealous of them. August 3 natives may be blissfully unaware of this.

People born on this date often fall in love with love. They adore the courting ritual—wining and dining, buying gifts for their beloved. But when it comes to actually working at a relationship, they sometimes run into trouble. Personal commitment isn't their strong suit.

CHILDREN AND FAMILY

People born on August 3 have a tendency to idealize their family life. These people have enormous pride in their ancestors as well as the members of their immediate family unit. They identify very strongly with those who came before them.

August 3 men and women are usually very involved in the upbringing of their children. They especially enjoy setting a positive example for their youngsters.

HEALTH

Most August 3 people have robust good health. These men and women are good about sticking to an ambitious physical regimen. Although they may be less careful about their eating habits, people born on this date prefer a generally balanced diet.

August 3 natives sometimes suffer from chronic back trouble. If this is the case, they can find relief through yoga and meditation, in addition to conventional treatments.

CAREER AND FINANCES

The men and women born on August 3 have a great deal of creativity, and are likely to seek careers where they can indulge this ability. They are very good speakers and motivators, which makes them effective in any sales position. They also make exceptional actors, teachers, media personnel, and lawyers.

Although they enjoy living well, most August 3 natives are not especially concerned with making a lot of money. They love to dress well and drive an expensive car, and this is often where their money goes. But when it comes to making budgetary and savings commitments, they tend to be disinterested.

DREAMS AND GOALS

Career success is a must for the individuals born on this date, and it is to these ends that they are most likely to put their efforts. They may structure their potential goals from a very early age and attend to them with great care and self-discipline.

August 3 people often have the need to be a pillar of their community, and for this reason they are likely to become involved in local projects that give them the chance to shine even as they help others.

EMBRACE
Warmth
Good advice
Moderation

AVOID
Family discord
Jealous friends
Overindulgence

ALSO BORN TODAY
Football star Lance Alworth; singer Tony Bennett; poet Rupert Brooke; designer Anne Klein; film director John Landis; actor Martin Sheen; novelist Leon Uris.

AUGUST 4

People born on August 4 have considerable personal magnetism. Even if they are not particularly good-looking, they may seem to be highly attractive because their personality is so engaging.

These individuals are highly rebellious and may have a hard time fitting into a conventional mold. They prefer to do things their own way, even if this means hurting their chances for a promotion at work or receiving an accolade from friends.

FRIENDS AND LOVERS
When it comes to making friends, August 4 individuals are among the best. They have a genuine love of people and are virtually incapable of judgmental thinking.

Love is anything but conventional for these intriguing men and women. They are likely to have more than their share of heartaches, usually brought on by an overly idealistic view of romance and an inability to judge character accurately.

CHILDREN AND FAMILY
Because August 4 individuals are rebel types, family background actually means very little to them. They don't believe in having too much allegiance to family members. This doesn't mean they don't love their parents and siblings—only that they simply have little reason to emulate them.

August 4 men and women make somewhat distant parents to their own children. Because of their involvement in career and humanitarian concerns, these individuals may not be overly attentive to their own household.

HEALTH
Because they are almost always in a hurry, the people born on August 4 have a tendency to be somewhat accident-prone. They need to be especially vigilant while driving.

These people have plenty of nervous energy and are always looking for some way to expel it. They benefit from aerobic exercise at least four or five times a week. Stretching and deep breathing exercises can be helpful too, since August 4 men and women often suffer from stress and sleep disorders.

CAREER AND FINANCES
August 4 people have a love of science and other analytical studies. From childhood they enjoy working out formulas, adding figures, and stating hypotheses. They are highly intelligent men and women who make fine teachers, professors, chemists, health care professionals, and engineers.

Money is a fluid factor in the lives of these folks—it comes in and it goes out. Because August 4 people aren't particularly interested in holding on to their loot, they sometimes experience temporary financial shortfalls.

DREAMS AND GOALS
August 4 natives have an unconventional view of what constitutes success. They don't look to achievements to make them feel good about themselves, nor do they expect to find satisfaction through worldly things. Instead, they're more concerned with living up to a strongly prescribed code of personal conduct.

Because they have a great love of the unusual, August 4 natives delight in being able to contribute something unique to their world.

EMBRACE
Quiet times
Progress
Sensitivity

AVOID
Rash decisions
Idle promises
Egotism

ALSO BORN TODAY
Musician David Carr; baseball star Roger Clemens; England's Elizabeth, the Queen Mother; singer Frankie Ford; baseball manager Dallas Green; cartoonist Osbert Lancaster; hockey star Maurice Richard; poet Percy Bysshe Shelley.

AUGUST 5

August 5 individuals are intelligent and witty, with a flair for good conversation. They have a sublime sense of humor and are rarely without a clever quote or retort. On rare occasions they can be sarcastic, but they are generally good-natured and unwilling to use their wit to sting others.

However, people born on this date can be obsessively dogmatic about their ideas and will argue a point for hours in the hope of changing someone else's opinion to jibe with their own.

FRIENDS AND LOVERS August 5 men and women love to be surrounded by friends. They lack the temperament for solitude, and can usually be found in the company of others. Since conversation is their major form of entertainment, these people usually seek out friends who are smart and informed.

People born today have a reputation for being fickle in romantic matters. They fall in love easily, but find it difficult to commit to a long-term relationship. If they do marry, it's often to someone who started out as one of their buddies. They are definitely not the love-at-first-sight type.

CHILDREN AND FAMILY August 5 people often have a rather contentious relationship with family members, especially parents. While people born on this date are not typically rebellious, they do project a great deal of attitude, and this can be off-putting to relatives.

These men and women have a lot of fun teaching their youngsters to "be their own person." They have a loving yet casual attitude toward parenthood, believing that children are only lent, not given to them for keeps.

HEALTH August 5 people are often high-strung and obsessively active. They seem to get along on nervous energy a great deal of the time—which is quite likely, since their sense of proper nutrition is woefully inadequate. They often base their diet more on convenience than common sense.

Though always in motion, these folks don't necessarily get all the exercise they need. A walk once a day every day could be just what the doctor ordered.

CAREER AND FINANCES August 5 individuals live for communication, and they gravitate to jobs that let them indulge this passion. They enjoy any type of work that requires them to deal with people face to face. They're also adept at computer-related professions, especially software design or system analysis.

People born on this date have the ability to make money, though this is also tied to their ability to communicate.

DREAMS AND GOALS August 5 individuals have a great many goals, but may have trouble focusing their energy well enough or long enough to make them come true. They have incredibly high ideals, yet may not be sure just how to manifest them.

Given their pride in their intellect and their ideas, these people have a great need to inspire others. Whether or not this is something they can meld into a career option, they can be depended upon to state their opinions and follow their convictions.

EMBRACE
The entrepreneurial spirit
Praising others
Love

AVOID
Egotism
Forcing ideas on others
Misjudging people

ALSO BORN TODAY
Actress Loni Anderson; astronaut Neil Armstrong; archaeologist Jacquetta Hawkes; film director/screenwriter John Huston; writer Guy de Maupassant; astrologer Sidney Omarr; actor Jonathan Silverman; artist Louis Wain.

AUGUST 6

August 6 individuals are good-tempered and pleasant. From an early age they have a need to live up to their own potential. Although it may be hard for them to get their act together, once they set themselves a path they will follow it.

The people born on this date are exceptionally ambitious. They know the worth of self-actualization and are constantly looking for a way to train their talents and bend them toward something important and interesting.

FRIENDS AND LOVERS
People born on August 6 have a talent for making friends. They enjoy the social aspects of friendship, but they are more concerned with putting down emotional roots that will last a lifetime.

Love affairs are prevalent and usually happy for August 6 individuals. They enjoy playing the field, yet once they find themselves head over heels in love, nothing will keep them from walking down that aisle. If August 6 natives are disappointed in love it can take them a long while to learn to love again.

CHILDREN AND FAMILY
The men and women born on August 6 are affectionate by nature and are extremely devoted to their family. They are involved in the lives of brothers and sisters and have an especially good rapport with their parents.

August 6 people make very good parents, and if they have no children of their own they will often form close emotional bonds with nephews, nieces, or the children of good friends.

HEALTH
Even though they usually possess good health, people born today can easily undercut their energy with bad habits. They are extremely oral, with a powerful need to eat, drink, and smoke to excess. Yet despite these bad habits, August 6 natives want to look their best and will go to great lengths to achieve it.

Too much alcohol is especially dangerous to August 6 natives, who often suffer from poor circulation.

CAREER AND FINANCES
Because they are personally charming, August 6 people do very well in careers that put them in front of an audience. They usually have a pleasant, even exceptional appearance, and this, coupled with a friendly attitude, makes them very appealing.

The smart handling of money is not the strong suit of August 6 folks, who have a habit of spending the green stuff much faster than they earn it. They do possess a certain ability to attract material resources that can make up, in small ways, for their spendthrift habits.

DREAMS AND GOALS
Happiness and personal security are major goals of August 6 individuals. They want nice clothes, good furniture, and an expensive car, but they also prize whatever talents they may have. They are likely to be very artistic, and although they may not make a career of their abilities, they are always happy to show them off.

August 6 natives need the backing of loved ones and good friends to help them believe in their own abilities.

EMBRACE
Patience
Identity
Spiritual enlightenment

AVOID
Willfulness
Putting demands on others
Self-pity

ALSO BORN TODAY
Comedienne Lucille Ball; film director/writer Paul Bartel; actor Dorian Harewood; musician Pat McDonald; actress Catherine Hicks; artist/filmmaker Andy Warhol; actor Robert Mitchum; poet Alfred, Lord Tennyson.

AUGUST 7

August 7 men and women have a mysterious, somewhat enigmatic persona. They like to make great mysteries of even the smallest things and refuse to live their lives according to convention. These are attractive, magnetic people who have an unabashed need to play mind-games in order to seduce others, emotionally and spiritually.

FRIENDS AND LOVERS Friendships can be rewarding for people born on August 7, as long as they feel comfortable enough with their pals that they can express their deepest feelings. They have virtually no interest in casual relationships.

The mystery and intrigue of romantic and sexual relationships is the centerpiece of life for August 7 individuals. They have a tendency to enjoy clandestine love affairs, even when there's no reason for the affair to be secret!

CHILDREN AND FAMILY The family background of August 7 individuals is often a closely guarded secret. This may be for a very specific purpose, or there could be no logical purpose at all except for the need of August 7 people to maintain their image of mystery.

Men and women born on this date will always encourage their children to indulge their own uniqueness and special talents. There is often a very strong, even psychic, bond between these August 7 parents and their kids.

HEALTH August 7 natives should stay away from alcohol, drugs, and even the unnecessary use of prescription medicines. They have a very sensitive constitution and will invariably react negatively if they subject their bodies to great amounts of any of these.

These people may suffer from periodic sleep disorders, which can be doubly troublesome for them since they rely on a rich dream life to help them sort out emotional and spiritual concerns.

CAREER AND FINANCES People born on this date have a highly developed sense of creativity. They are drawn to drawing, painting, writing, photography, dancing, singing, modeling, or acting. If they do not pursue these avenues of creativity as a job option, they should at least have one or more of them as hobbies.

August 7 natives do not have a particularly good reputation for handling money, though they definitely have the talent to make a great deal of it. In such a case they should probably hire a reputable professional to handle their financial affairs.

DREAMS AND GOALS The dreams and goals of these mystical individuals can be as hard to define as the individuals themselves. They are not usually materialistic, and therefore are most interested in goals that are spiritually oriented.

Though not necessarily religious, August 7 men and women have a need to believe in something greater than themselves. Once they have established this connection they are more likely to see their goals become reality, since this gives them the strongly centered focus they need.

EMBRACE
Fairness
Reality checks
Authenticity

AVOID
Dark thoughts
Revenge
Selfish motives

ALSO BORN TODAY
Actor John Glover; spy Mata Hari; radio personality Garrison Keillor; baseball star Don Larsen; paleontologist Louis Leakey; astrologer Alan Leo; film director Nicholas Ray; singer B. J. Thomas.

AUGUST 8

People born on August 8 are often graduates from the proverbial school of hard knocks. They can seem unemotional or even distant, but are simply self-disciplined and in control of themselves.

Although August 8 individuals are often forced to climb the hard road to success, they actually wouldn't have it any other way. An eagerness to feel as if they have earned every opportunity they receive is very much in keeping with their character.

FRIENDS AND LOVERS

August 8 men and women are great role models for their friends. Because they represent the marriage of talent and discipline, these people are the envy of all who know them. Friendship is an important part of life for August 8 natives, but it doesn't keep them from speaking their minds about issues that could be a source of controversy between them and their pals.

People born on this date are strongly marriage-minded. Once they fall in love, they want to settle down and make a home for themselves and their beloved.

CHILDREN AND FAMILY

August 8 natives usually display their leadership ability while still children. Although their parents may discourage their intensity, these individuals are naturally serious. Because they may be very different from other children in the family, it's important that they be allowed to pursue their individuality.

Unfortunately, people born on this date may seek to impress their attitudes on their own children, who may be much more light-hearted.

HEALTH

August 8 people have a sensible approach to keeping fit, especially if they're at genetic risk for an illness or disease. Their eating habits are Spartan, and they are likely to shy away from alcohol and nicotine.

In order to guard against osteoporosis or other effects of bone-thinning during late-middle age, August 8 individuals need to make weight-bearing exercise, such as an aerobic workout, part of their daily routine.

CAREER AND FINANCES

People born on August 8 have a take-charge attitude and do well in careers where they are responsible for motivating others.

Most August 8 people are conservative about money matters. They don't believe in taking risks, even if the possible return is very high. For this reason they aren't likely to hit any financial jackpots. By the same token, they rarely make any serious mistakes concerning their financial position.

DREAMS AND GOALS

August 8 natives achieve success one step at a time. They don't look for shortcuts, believing that hard work and good planning are what make dreams come true.

The men and women born on this date have no illusions about life. They are uncharacteristically cynical for Leo natives and expect to succeed only to the extent that they seek to achieve. Because of this attitude, they're likely to achieve their dreams, though seldom go beyond them.

EMBRACE
Forgiveness
Sensitivity
Imagination

AVOID
Saying "I told you so"
A superior attitude
Bitterness

ALSO BORN TODAY
Actor Richard Anderson; England's Princess Beatrice; singer/actor Keith Carradine; film producer Dino De Laurentiis; actor Dustin Hoffman; singer/actress Connie Stevens; singer Mel Tillis; swimmer/actress Esther Williams.

AUGUST 9

The strong-minded people born on this day have the grit and ability to come back from difficult circumstances. They have a basic need to be challenged because it helps them to prove themselves on all levels of existence.

August 9 natives have great personal dignity, and carry themselves in a royal fashion. They are immaculate in their grooming habits and are always conscious of looking their best in any situation.

FRIENDS AND LOVERS
People born on August 9 have the unconscious desire to take the lead in all their associations. They are extremely proud individuals who can seem vain, though their friends understand it's just a pose.

August 9 men and women have high ideals in romantic matters. They can be badly hurt by lovers who do not have the same sense of honor that they possess. When they are happily mated, they're complete in mind, body, and spirit. They bring fidelity and honesty to their marriage, and demand the same from a partner.

CHILDREN AND FAMILY
People born on this date are model family members. They respect their parents and have deep affection for their siblings.

August 9 people aspire to parenthood with great enthusiasm and commitment. They adore children and are likely to indulge them, so it may be up to the spouse of the August 9 person to promote discipline and self-denial. These people have a genuinely close bond with their youngsters.

HEALTH
The typical August 9 person has a strong, compact physique that suggests athleticism. They have a high level of energy and are usually committed to some form of regular exercise. Since they enjoy pitting their athletic skills against those of other people, their regimen is likely to include competitive sports.

Individuals born on this date have a powerful appetite for good food, but are also careful about what they eat, and take particular care to stay away from fast food and packaged convenience snacks.

CAREER AND FINANCES
Men and women born on this day have boundless ambition and immeasurable integrity. Although those two qualities aren't often found in a single individual, August 9 people handle this dichotomy with amazing skill. They have exceptional management skills and the type of personality that easily motivates others.

August 9 natives work very hard to create a secure financial life for themselves and their families. They are not averse to working two jobs.

DREAMS AND GOALS
Getting to the top of their profession while still managing to retain their honesty and integrity is the dream of August 9 men and women. These people have a message to impart to others, and they'll work very hard to ensure their ability to do so.

They understand also how difficult it is to balance personal and professional responsibilities. They know that at times sacrifices must be made, but for the most part these folks manage to meet goals in both areas of their lives.

EMBRACE
Duty
Continuity
Spiritual transcendence

AVOID
Repetition
Health risks
Insecurity

ALSO BORN TODAY
Film director Robert Aldrich; basketball star Bob Cousey; poet John Dryden; actor Sam Elliott; actress Melanie Griffith; singer Whitney Houston; poet Philip Larkin; comedian David Steinberg.

AUGUST 10

August 10 natives are studies in contrasts. Although these people have talents or resources that mark them as different, even unique, their greatest wish is to be a part of the crowd. They have leadership skills, and yet they know they have the best chance to achieve personal goals through group activities.

FRIENDS AND LOVERS The positive mental attitude and intellectual resources of August 10 people make them a favorite rallying point for issues of all sorts. They don't so much have friends as followers.

People born on this date are usually lucky in love. They are romantic idealists who may endow their lover or partner with amazing characteristics that the other person may not possess. These individuals often experience a grand passion that stays with them for the rest of their lives.

CHILDREN AND FAMILY August 10 people often owe their great success in life to their fortunate beginnings. Even if they are born poor, there will always be resources at the ready to help these individuals to live out their dreams. They may also have the good fortune to find at an early age a mentor who is eager to guide them in their career or personal path. This mentor may be a parent or an elderly relative.

The people born on this date give the same sort of encouragement to their own children.

Although likely to be very busy, and at times even absent for protracted periods, these people do everything in their power to make a good life for their little ones.

HEALTH August 10 natives have remarkably good health, though they may not do much to maintain it. They seem able to eat and drink whatever they wish without experiencing any problems with weight gain or addiction—at least in their youth.

Things change somewhat as they approach middle age. At that time, August 10 men and women often pause to take stock of themselves and their habits. If they see that some of their health choices have not been good ones, they're sensible enough to realize that changes are in order.

CAREER AND FINANCES August 10 people seem to see themselves as first among equals. That's because, although they crave the spotlight, they also seek anonymity. This attitude often leads to a change in careers during their early to middle thirties. These folks know that they have talent, but they don't always know what to do with it.

People born on this date often make a great deal of money, but are just as likely to run through it. Foolish spending is, unfortunately, one of the traits of August 10 people, yet they do learn important lessons as a result.

DREAMS AND GOALS The goals of August 10 natives change so often that the people themselves may have difficulty remembering just what it was they originally wanted.

August 10 people gain their greatest satisfaction from their personal relationships, and have high hopes for the success and longevity of those unions.

EMBRACE
Productivity
Aesthetics
Idealism

AVOID
Underachievement
Laziness
Undue pride

ALSO BORN TODAY
Musician Ian Anderson; actress Rosanna Arquette; singer/actor Antonio Banderas; singer/sausage entrepreneur Jimmy Dean; U.S. President Herbert Hoover; singer Eddie Fisher; actress Rhonda Fleming; actress Norma Shearer.

AUGUST 11

People born on August 11 possess a great sense of curiosity about many aspects of life. These men and women have an analytical intelligence that prompts them to wonder how things work.

Often quiet and reserved personality types, August 11 people may seem distant and aloof in their personal and professional relationships, yet they are actually sensitive and caring. They have amazing patience and are rarely seen to lose either their temper or composure.

FRIENDS AND LOVERS
August 11 natives have a difficult time making close friends because it's hard for these people to show or share their deep emotions. They may want to confide their feelings, yet to do so makes them uneasy.

People born on this date have a similar problem with romance. They often look to a potential date or lover to make the first move. It is this very appearance of shyness that makes August 11 natives so appealing and attractive to the opposite sex.

These people are serious about relationships and unlikely to get involved in casual affairs. Love equals marriage as far as they are concerned.

CHILDREN AND FAMILY
People born on August 11 tend to have a lot of emotionally charged issues relating to their childhood and background. These may be tied to a rocky upbringing, or to a domineering parent. Once they reach adulthood, many August 11 people seek to put their past to rights by getting involved in therapy.

Happily, August 11 men and women make very good parents. They are able to put aside their own "invasion issues" and allow their own children to have a great deal of freedom.

HEALTH
If August 11 people have problems with their health, it is usually because of emotional reasons they are not ready to face. This can lead to stomach problems, headaches, sleep disorders—all very real, yet created out of depression or unhappiness.

While it is important that August 11 people pay regular visits to their doctor, they should also seek out a licensed holistic healer who may be able to link the root cause of their ailments to a workable cure.

CAREER AND FINANCES
People born on this date have a great capacity for kindness and care. They are often drawn to the caring professions such as nursing, therapy, social services, or the clergy.

August 11 men and women rarely go into a profession because of its monetary rewards. Although they enjoy nice surroundings and are not averse to the finer things of life—especially travel and luxurious clothes—these people are much more interested in helping others.

DREAMS AND GOALS
August 11 natives want to make a difference. They need to feel as if the service or friendship they provide to people is as invaluable as breathing. They don't expect their professional success to come overnight.

People born on this date do not possess some of the boastful characteristics of some other Leos. They meet their goals without personal fanfare.

EMBRACE
Intuition
Willingness to participate
Charm

AVOID
Emotional boundaries
Delays
Being too practical

ALSO BORN TODAY
Guitarist Erik Braunn; actress Arlene Dahl; TV personality Mike Douglas; TV evangelist Jerry Falwell; writer Alex Haley; playwright David Henry Hwang; ballerina Allegra Kent; writer Angus Wilson.

AUGUST 12

Men and women born on August 12 require a great deal of personal freedom. They generally know exactly what they want out of life and don't know the meaning of the word "quit." They go after their personal and professional aspirations with everything they've got.

Men and women born on this date have great artistic potential. They also know how to bring out the best in others, and act as an emotional bulwark to shy or insecure individuals.

FRIENDS AND LOVERS August 12 natives are keenly aware of their roles in personal relationships. They take friendship as seriously as they take romantic love, and seek to create true emotional empathy with the people they care about.

August 12 people believe in true love. When they meet someone who appeals to them physically and spiritually, they set out to create a magical emotional environment to protect their love and sense of togetherness. Of course, this sort of idyllic situation is unlikely to last for long, and when August 12 people suffer a broken heart they learn to chart a less-idealistic course in the future.

CHILDREN AND FAMILY If these folks enjoyed a particularly happy childhood, they will return to it in their mind during times of trouble.

August 12 natives have a real affinity for parenthood. They connect to their children on an amazingly deep level, almost with a psychic bond. Despite their tenderness, August 12 men and women are strict disciplinarians who want their children to learn useful life-lessons at an early age.

HEALTH People born on this date enjoy living well, and this includes sampling many of life's pleasures that aren't healthful. These people love rich food, especially sweets, and have a strong taste for sugary beverages.

While a regular exercise routine can help to offset some of their bad habits, August 12 people also need to make purified water their primary beverage.

CAREER AND FINANCES August 12 people have a great deal of artistic talent. They need to be proud of their craft and will hone it to perfection. Since they are decisive individuals, they often discover their true calling at a very early age. Once they've set upon a course, they're unlikely to change it for any reason.

Because of their determined approach, August 12 men and women usually find financial success, though it doesn't really matter to them. While their sumptuous tastes require a good financial base, they are more concerned with producing a worthwhile life than in capturing rewards, financial or otherwise.

DREAMS AND GOALS People born on this day have a very personal view of success, with goals directed more at process than product. These individuals see their work as a pathway to a spiritual destination that cannot be accomplished through compromise of any sort.

The personal goals of August 12 people have the same level of integrity. They want a shared closeness, but it must be real, not imagined.

EMBRACE
New horizons
Persistence
Details

AVOID
Stubbornness
Lack of humility
Being defensive

ALSO BORN TODAY
Film director Cecil B. DeMille; actor John Derek; English King George IV; writer William Goldman; writer Edith Hamilton; actor George Hamilton; poet Robert Southey; singer/songwriter Suzanne Vega.

AUGUST 13

August 13 natives have a deep need to connect with their own inner power. These eccentric and philosophical folks possess a kinetic energy that is the envy of all who know them.

These men and women are superbly talented individuals who have the ability to make a name for themselves in anything they attempt. Challenges seem to awaken their fighting spirit and give them the inspiration they need.

FRIENDS AND LOVERS

Despite their loner mentality, August 13 natives have a wide variety of friends. These men and women do not seek friendship as much for its emotional rewards as for the satisfaction it gives in allowing them to observe human nature.

Romantic involvements may encompass some of these identical needs, though in this area of relationships August 13 natives are more vulnerable. They have a very romantic spirit and may be much more sensitive and easily hurt than they appear to be. These men and women have a tendency to be drawn into unrequited love affairs at least once in a lifetime.

CHILDREN AND FAMILY

August 13 individuals often experience an unusual upbringing. The family may have relocated many times, forcing them to attend a variety of schools, each time making a new set of friends. Or a divorce or death could have robbed the August 13 native of a parent. These people learn their life-lessons at an early age, and it is from these challenging circumstances that they develop a great deal of their wisdom.

When August 13 men and women become parents they may adopt a somewhat distant attitude. Although they can be loving, they wish to teach their children hard lessons.

HEALTH

Nervousness and anxiety sometimes undermine the natural good health of August 13 individuals. These people worry about everything. Headaches and stomach trouble may be the result, as well as difficulty in learning how to relax.

August 13 men and women love to eat and may overindulge regularly, especially when they feel powerless in other areas of their lives. Since being overweight only adds to the problems, these people need to set aside some time each day for vigorous exercise.

CAREER AND FINANCES

People born on this date have a desire to transcend their own inner landscape. They are drawn to unusual, even dangerous occupations that give them the opportunity to experience a unique reality.

August 13 natives have a gift for making money, even when they don't set it as a priority.

DREAMS AND GOALS

August 13 men and women want to live life on their own terms. They gravitate toward the unique, the strange, the unusual because it allows them to play out their own inner conflicts.

An addiction to excitement also characterizes the personal lives of these lively people. They seek to push the level of their emotional involvement beyond mere commitment until it very nearly becomes an obsession.

EMBRACE
Adaptability
Graciousness
Mental quickness

AVOID
Holding grudges
A condescending attitude
Immaturity

ALSO BORN TODAY
Opera singer Kathleen Battle; actor/radio host Danny Bonaduce; Cuban dictator Fidel Castro; singer Dan Fogelberg; comic actor Pat Harrington; film director Alfred Hitchcock; singer Don Ho; golfer Ben Hogan.

AUGUST 14

Part mystery, part open book, August 14 individuals are perplexing, infuriating, and different. They usually manage to keep their true selves carefully hidden from even their closest friends. This is a subtle defense mechanism that allows them to retain their autonomy without sacrificing the illusions held by others. Their charm attracts people effortlessly. Everyone will feel as if they know the "real" person, yet almost no one will.

FRIENDS AND LOVERS Friendship provides a road of discovery for August 14 people by which they are able to find signposts to their own quixotic identity. Because of their deceptively strong personalities, the powerful impressions they make upon friends will be treasured for a lifetime.

August 14 individuals have a problem maintaining permanence in their love lives. Trust is a difficult issue for them, particularly if they've been negatively affected as children by poor parenting. Idealism can add a false note to a love match, but in the right hands it can lead to a rhapsodic relationship filled with passionate surprises.

CHILDREN AND FAMILY August 14 natives have a persistent need to remake the past, embellishing upon childhood memories until they barely resemble the original experience.

People born on this date are determined to give their own children a good start in life, often going to extremes in a sincere effort to see that their youngsters have everything. Tempered with a little discipline, this isn't a bad plan.

HEALTH Undisciplined and headstrong, people born on this date do not submit happily to any form of censure of the ways they eat, drink, and generally care for themselves. They are natural daredevils who enjoy beating the odds at any game, including their own well-being. Generally healthy, they are able to go for long periods without sleep; in fact, their powers of concentration may actually be greater at such times.

CAREER AND FINANCES People born on this date are late bloomers, and are often well into adulthood before they find their professional niche. It isn't a matter of indecision so much as an inability to focus their ambitions upon a singular pursuit.

Unfortunately, they have a cavalier attitude toward money. They spend generously on themselves and others, but are lax about putting money away for the future. They have good investment sense but need professional advice in order to keep from spending everything they earn.

DREAMS AND GOALS August 14 people do not rely on a succession of moves or a planned strategy in order to achieve their goals. They believe that fate, rather than effort, determines their future.

In the rare instances when they do address goals by plotting a careful course, they are able to draw upon amazing reserves of will power. In the professional arena they can be emotionally driven, but always measure success by their own standards, not those of others.

EMBRACE
The future
Faith
Nature's beauty

AVOID
Trying to rewrite the past
Doubting your ability
Revenge

ALSO BORN TODAY
Actress Halle Berry; singer Sarah Brightman; novelist John Galsworthy; basketball star Magic Johnson; cartoonist Gary Larson; comedian Steve Martin; actress Susan Saint James; novelist Danielle Steel.

AUGUST 15

August 15 men and women have enormous leadership potential. They may seem egotistical, but are simply very savvy about their own abilities, and can size up their accomplishments with great objectivity.

People born on this day feel they have many lessons to impart to others. They see the big picture better than almost anyone and yet can appreciate the value of details.

FRIENDS AND LOVERS August 15 individuals are devoted to their friends. They frequently pursue several distinct levels of friendship, some of which are primarily social, some of which are deep and personal. While it's not unusual for these men and women to project leadership qualities in their personal relationships, they do not try to "manage" their friendships.

People born on this date are extremely romantic and have a reputation for being great lovers. They often marry early, and often more than once. Scandal has a way of finding them, and their behavior may be called into question on many occasions.

CHILDREN AND FAMILY Family matters can be the thorn in the side of August 15 individuals. While they're likely to be intimately involved in family relationships throughout a lifetime, these individuals often find themselves drawn unwillingly into a center of controversy.

August 15 men and women are loving, involved parents who may not truly come into their own until they have children. They are unwilling to repeat the mistakes that may have been made by their own parents, and to this end are vigilant about their responsibilities.

HEALTH People born on this date have vigorous good health, which can be undermined only by their own bad habits. These individuals may be indolent and unwilling to get involved in a serious exercise program.

But if they wish to remain in good shape—and most August 15 natives do—they'll eventually find a workout regimen that's appropriate for them. This may include physical exertion that has a creative element, such as dancing or figure skating.

CAREER AND FINANCES August 15 people prefer careers that allow them to manage people as well as projects. These ambitious go-getters have a great desire to make it to the top of the professional ladder, but are equally concerned with the methods that may propel them there.

Big money is a definite goal for August 15 people. They like to live well, even sumptuously, and also enjoy the respect that comes from earning a good salary.

EMBRACE
Ceremony
Fastidiousness
Fair play

AVOID
A prickly personality
Rudeness
Dominating others

ALSO BORN TODAY
England's Princess Anne; French Emperor Napoleon Bonaparte; chef Julia Child; actor Mike Connors; journalist Linda Ellerbee; actress Tess Harper; film director Nicolas Roeg; novelist Sir Walter Scott.

DREAMS AND GOALS August 15 individuals never limit their goals. They have the ability to see beyond the infinite, and don't allow themselves to see any impediment to their success. Although their level of ambition may seem awesome to some, those who know and understand these amazing individuals expect nothing less.

These men and women are not afraid of failure. They know that everyone trips up at one time or another, but to them the stumbles are merely incentives to make them try harder.

AUGUST 16

August 16 people live their lives with the volume turned up. They're dedicated, disciplined individuals with a strong sense of personal destiny. While they absorb and listen to the criticism of others, it rarely causes them to change their game plan.

People born on this day are very concerned with their personal image. They often create a persona for themselves that is very much at odds with their true selves.

FRIENDS AND LOVERS

Relationships are a necessary lifeline for August 16 people, yet they can equal in importance the relationship these men and women have with themselves. This is not due to ego—it's simply because these people keep their own counsel and make their own decisions without advice from others. Socially, August 16 individuals are very much in demand, and many of their associations thrive in social settings.

August 16 people are extremely passionate. These men and women have great charm and considerable sex appeal, and when they fall in love it is a love that will last forever.

CHILDREN AND FAMILY

People born on this date often separate emotionally from their family at quite an early age. This may be brought about by their own uniqueness, which sets them apart from the family group.

August 16 men and women may be surprised by their genuine talent for parenthood. They have an ability to balance discipline with liberalness, letting their youngsters know how much they are loved.

HEALTH

Those born on this date are dedicated to keeping themselves fit and in good health. They love to exercise and are usually involved in some sort of cross-training program. August 16 people like their looks and want to retain them as long as possible.

Though they have the typical Leo appetite, people born on this day maintain a careful balance in their nutrition. Because their system may be sensitive, they need to balance the high fiber content in their diet with more than 100 ounces of water each day.

CAREER AND FINANCES

People born on August 16 have strong career ambitions and may begin putting together a professional game plan when they are very young. These people have solid leadership ability and do not thrive in positions of subservience.

Money plays a large part in the lives of August 16 men and women. They want to be more than just financially secure— they want enough money to exercise complete control over their personal and professional destinies.

DREAMS AND GOALS

It isn't characteristic for August 16 people to believe in luck— good, bad, or otherwise. They believe in making their own luck.

August 16 people manage their goals on two separate levels: "dreaming" and "doing." Both are needed to make their goals come true. These men and women have the rare ability to see details as well as the big picture—one of the keys to their success.

EMBRACE
Humility
Good manners
Stamina

AVOID
Prickly personality
Rudeness
Dominating others

ALSO BORN TODAY
Actress Angela Bassett; film director Bruce Beresford; ballerina Suzanne Farrell; sports commentator Frank Gifford; TV personality Kathie Lee Gifford; novelist Georgette Heyer; actor Timothy Hutton; singer/actress Madonna.

AUGUST 17

People born on August 17 possess enormous spiritual power. These are highly focused individuals who always follow their own paths. They are seldom influenced by trends, yet they may secretly ally themselves with the comfort of the status quo.

It is very hard to know these individuals. Although personable, they have an aloof quality. They appear steady and unflappable to others, but there are times when emotions get the better of them and their logic is useless.

FRIENDS AND LOVERS
August 17 individuals are extremely loyal to their friends. They are often in a working partnership with pals that spans many years and adds incredible richness to the relationships. They don't believe in superficial friendships.

Love and romance may elude these folks when they are very young, making them believe that they will never meet the person of their dreams. These people don't just want a love affair, they want to find a soul mate.

CHILDREN AND FAMILY
August 17 folks are often the black sheep of their family. They may rebel against the family's religious background or social status, creating a schism that can last for many years. Though there is often a reconciliation in later years, August 17 individuals may carry around a great deal of unnecessary guilt.

The men and women born on this date do not really have the proper temperament for parenthood. They can easily make some emotional adjustments if they have children, but are usually happiest when they remain childless.

HEALTH
People born on this date have a problem handling stress, which can affect their health. Because they always like to feel that they are in control, August 17 individuals may not be able to admit that they have this problem. Learning to relax can be a difficult proposition for these men and women, but once they own up to the situation they can begin to get help.

CAREER AND FINANCES
People born on this date have a loner mentality and enjoy working with as little supervision as possible. They make excellent researchers, especially in the realms of science or history. They also can be outstanding teachers.

August 17 men and women have some karmic lessons to learn regarding money. These may be manifested through periods when they have very little money, followed by financial success that tests their ability to remain spiritually unchanged.

DREAMS AND GOALS
People born on this day have a sincere commitment to making their dreams come true. They are extremely disciplined and can call upon great reserves of emotional and spiritual energy to sustain them during their climb to the top.

August 17 people have very little interest in fame and fortune, even as just an idle daydream. They want to do their very best at their job, in their relationships, and in their unending search for self-understanding. Whatever else they achieve is, to them, strictly superfluous.

EMBRACE
Originality
Technology
Free expression of emotions

AVOID
Brooding
Angry moods
Bad attitude

ALSO BORN TODAY
Figure skating champion Robin Cousins; actor Robert De Niro; musician Steve Gorman; poet Ted Hughes; actress Maureen O'Hara; actor Sean Penn; singer Kevin Rowland; actress Mae West.

AUGUST 18

People born on August 18 have great mental and physical endurance. They have a penchant for taking chances and get a thrill out of living dangerously.

These people have no hidden agendas. They know what they want and don't try to hide the fact. Their boldness is part of their attractiveness, which is heightened by their natural charm and good looks.

FRIENDS AND LOVERS August 18 people are extremely sincere in all their relationships. They don't have a great need for social acquaintances and prefer to keep their friendships on an intimate level. Because they have the ability to inspire others, August 18 individuals make fine mentors as well as friends.

The sincerity that marks the character of these people is also in evidence in their romantic relationships. They don't believe in playing a part and will always be honest in what they say to a date or mate. The term "sweet talk" was definitely not invented by these folks.

EMBRACE
Selectivity
Ebullience
Scruples

AVOID
Foolish risks
Confrontations
Irresponsibility

ALSO BORN TODAY
Actor Robert Redford; actor Patrick Swayze; First lady Rosalyn Carter; film director Roman Polanski; explorer Meriwether Lewis; actor Christian Slater; actress Shelley Winters.

CHILDREN AND FAMILY August 18 natives are likely to maintain close ties to their family, especially to a parent or other authority figure.

People born on this day take an active role in raising their children. Play time, discipline, learning experiences, and every other aspect of child-rearing is fascinating to these people.

Although they have an indulgent nature, August 18 men and women understand that it is better to err on the side of strictness.

HEALTH As with most Leos, August 18 natives have a genuine love for good food, which is surpassed only by their love of physical activity. These people like working with their hands and enjoy getting a workout by doing a lot of the household chores. They also have fun playing competitive sports with neighbors and friends.

August 18 men and women need to guard against muscle pulls and injuries caused during workouts, or from carelessness. Since some of these individuals attempt dangerous sports such as rock climbing, they need to be vigilant about their habits and their equipment.

CAREER AND FINANCES August 18 people shine in the spotlight. They enjoy any job or career that gives them chances to engage their leadership potential. These men and women are also extremely creative. If properly motivated they can excel in various artistic fields, including music, dance, or art.

People born on this day are not at their best when handling financial matters. They are often generous to a fault, and can make unwise decisions based more on optimism than good sense.

DREAMS AND GOALS August 18 men and women are eternally optimistic about their goals. They believe in themselves and know that they have the grit and determination to make their mark.

Even if a dream proves to be unrealistic or unreachable, the folks born on this date have too much innate stubbornness to quit. They will continue to work at their aims, doing everything they can to bring a dream to fruition.

AUGUST 19

People born on August 19 enjoy pushing themselves to the limit, both physically and mentally. They may have some awkward years before they decide how to focus their energies, but once they put it all together there is no stopping them.

Typically, August 19 men and women seek to focus their energy on great achievements, but egotism can get in the way of their common sense at times.

FRIENDS AND LOVERS
People tend to be drawn to the charismatic personality of August 19 individuals, wanting to bask in the sunniness of their nature. There is a tendency of people born on this day to take unfair advantage of this attitude, though they generally accept it as a show of friendship.

Although they are generally appealing, August 19 natives may have problems in love matters. They don't always meet their perfect mate until later in life and have often suffered more than their share of breakups by that time.

CHILDREN AND FAMILY
August 19 folks often have a great deal of responsibility thrust upon them at an early age. Although they are very adept at handling such pressure, it can cause them to miss out on some of the normal fun of growing up.

Because their own experience as children is often less than satisfying, August 19 people are very careful to give their own youngsters a considerable sense of security.

HEALTH
August 19 individuals have a big appetite for good food. Many of these folks are talented cooks, but more of them are inclined to have a less sophisticated palate. Unless they have an extremely active lifestyle, these men and women can expect to put on weight as middle age approaches—or even before. That's an unpleasant development.

People born on this date need to be motivated in order to commit to a regular exercise plan. Often this happens when they develop a minor health problem and are warned by their doctor to "exercise or else."

CAREER AND FINANCES
The greatest talent August 19 individuals possess is their ability to adapt. They are intelligent people with enough savvy to know how to make the very best of their abilities. Most people born on this date will have the canniness to understand that their personality can take them anywhere.

Money has the potential to be a problem in the lives of August 19 men and women. They need to learn the lessons of thrift and good financial stewardship, especially if they make a great deal of money. Credit spending could be a big problem if it isn't kept under control.

DREAMS AND GOALS
August 19 people have big dreams. They know that they are talented individuals, but parlaying that talent into success may not be easy because of circumstances arrayed against them. But these men and women are exceptionally tough and will work ceaselessly toward goals.

Once they achieve their dreams, August 19 people may be at a loss to find something to replace them.

EMBRACE
Restraint
Sincerity
Original vision

AVOID
Temper tantrums
Mood swings
Petulance

ALSO BORN TODAY
Musician Ginger Baker; U.S. President Bill Clinton; courtesan Madame DuBarry; actor Peter Gallagher; writer Ring Lardner, Jr.; actor Gerald McRaney; poet Ogden Nash; actress Jill St. John.

AUGUST 20

There is a dark side to the affable individuals born on this date. They like keeping secrets, even from those closest to them. Although this can be a reaction to their desire to maintain mystery, it generally responds to a deeper and more primal need. Simply put, these men and women are deeply self-protective.

People born on this day are extremely sensitive, and inevitably feel the disappointments and sadness of loved ones as keenly as they do their own.

EMBRACE
Education
Generosity
Optimism

AVOID
Alienation
Coldness
Inability to compromise

ALSO BORN TODAY
Actress Joan Allen; TV journalist Connie Chung; ballerina Carla Fracci; singer/composer/actor Isaac Hayes; poet Robert Herrick; writer H. P. Lovecraft; singer Jim Reeves; novelist Jacqueline Susann.

FRIENDS AND LOVERS

There is a genuine sweetness in the personality of August 20 individuals, which makes them easy to befriend. Even though they keep very much to themselves, these people have a real talent for making friends. They are especially good at helping shy people come out of their protective emotional shells.

Passion and obsession characterize the love lives of August 20 individuals. When these men and women fall in love they throw all caution to the wind.

CHILDREN AND FAMILY

August 20 individuals often conceal the true nature of their upbringing. Either they were part of a troubled family, or a relationship with one of their parents was intensely unsatisfying in a way that brought them great emotional pain.

Paradoxically, perhaps, it is their background that makes August 20 people such good parents. Although they seek to repair their relationships with their own parents through their own parenthood, they also bring their own special brand of love and caring to the job.

HEALTH

People born on this date may not possess the high energy level of other Leos. Bouts of mild depression and self-doubt can seriously harm their self-esteem. Even when they do feel good about themselves, August 20 men and women are somewhat indolent and may shy away from exercise.

In order to feel more energetic, these folks have to learn to get moving. They could also use a change in their diet, which could rely too much upon "fast" or convenience foods.

CAREER AND FINANCES

August 20 people need to be emotionally involved in their work in order to be happy. Just a job, even a well-paying one, doesn't cut it for these people. This is compounded by the fact that they may not find their true "calling" until adulthood.

Because of their unsettled circumstances it is possible that August 20 people may have to temporarily move back with their parents if finances become strained. This can really test the limits of the parent-child relationship, so it's important that during this period these people believe in themselves.

DREAMS AND GOALS

August 20 individuals are sometimes shy about letting others know about their deepest wishes, because they are afraid of the judgment that may come with it. This attitude could be a natural reaction to their upbringing, yet it is important that they learn to trust friends and partners.

The people born on this date have great determination and the will to succeed. As long as they retain these gifts they can look forward to the success they deserve.

AUGUST 21

Men and women born on August 21 have the need to live large. They are practitioners of conspicuous consumption and don't make any apologies about it. These people enjoy luxurious surroundings, and have a knack for accumulating material wealth and possessions.

August 21 natives are jovial and friendly, with a winning personality that endears them to others. A great love and respect for learning is a characteristic that may not be immediately apparent, but that is well-known to and applauded by people close to these folks.

FRIENDS AND LOVERS August 21 people
have a huge social circle that includes friends of all stripes. Although their personal beliefs and opinions are strong and unwavering, they have the ability to transcend their parochial views in order to accommodate others in personal relationships.

Love is almost always a positive experience for the men and women born on this date. They don't believe in being a victim and can bounce back from a breakup more readily than most people. It isn't uncommon for August 21 people to remain good friends with their exes.

CHILDREN AND FAMILY Family closeness is the cornerstone of life for August 21 natives. They get along well with their siblings and may count them among their best friends.

Being a parent is the emotional high of a lifetime for August 21 people. They understand how to enter a child's world, and how to bring a lifetime of experience to something as simple as a make-believe tea party. These people are more fun for kids than most adults, yet they are also firm disciplinarians.

HEALTH August 21 folks love good food and good wine, and sometimes have a hard time

knowing when to cut back. Although they are unlikely to have serious problems involving food, they may have unfortunate eating habits that will lead to overweight in later years.

People born on this date need to learn the importance of regular exercise. They like competitive sports of the weekend variety, but need to commit to daily aerobic-style workouts if they want to remain in good physical condition.

CAREER AND FINANCES August 21
natives like to be in the center of things. They prefer a demanding job that keeps them going at a hectic pace all day long. They don't enjoy working behind the scenes or in a small office. These people like the social give and take that comes with the activity in a large firm with plenty of colleagues.

The men and women born on this date have big plans that include making a lot of money. They have something of the entrepreneurial spirit about them, and may try starting their own business at some point.

DREAMS AND GOALS August 21
individuals have unflappable optimism. Their dreams and wishes are as concrete to them as any reality, and they don't allow themselves to be discouraged.

People born on this date have more than just a good attitude going for them. They are intelligent and capable, with just the right balance of naivete and common sense to get the job done.

EMBRACE
Scholarship
Rules
Psychic awareness

AVOID
Bragging
Selfishness
Questionable advice

ALSO BORN TODAY
Opera singer Dame Janet Baker; artist Aubrey Beardsley; actress Kim Cattrall; basketball star Wilt Chamberlain; England's Princess Margaret; football star Jim McMahon; singer Kenny Rogers; actor Clarence Williams III.

AUGUST 22

The men and women born on this date are thoroughbreds. They have good looks, personal charm, and plenty of class.

There is a certain instability in the personality of August 22 men and women that makes them intriguing. High-strung and somewhat nervous, they thrive on attention from others.

FRIENDS AND LOVERS Unlike most Leos, August 22 natives don't have a lot of "people" skills. They don't make friends easily, but are intensely loyal to the ones they have. It takes a great deal of trust in a relationship to allow August 22 men and women to confide their deepest fears and desires.

Love relationships can be immensely complicated for these individuals. They are critical by nature—a trait that can work against them at times. An inability to accept a lover or mate as those people are has the potential to break up romances. Once they learn to be more trusting and tolerant, their love life is sure to improve.

CHILDREN AND FAMILY There are strong ties between August 22 individuals and their parents, even if the relationship is overshadowed by conflict and controversy in later years. It is difficult for most people born on this date to separate emotionally from their parents.

Because of the dynamic characterizing the relationship with their own parents, August 22 men and women don't have a great deal of confidence in their parenting abilities. This changes when they have an opportunity to grow into the role.

HEALTH August 22 individuals may suffer from minor ailments like allergies or nervous stomach. Although these may merely be symptomatic of their generally high-strung nature, it's important that they take steps to improve their stamina and physical well-being.

Once they feel better able to cope with the tension in their lives, August 22 natives can focus all of their emotional, spiritual, and physical resources on getting what they want out of life.

CAREER AND FINANCES Those born on this date need to come to grips with their own talents and abilities. These are not always known to them because they are extremely modest people who may be unable to determine their own worth. For this reason they can benefit from the help and direction of a mentor who steers them during the early part of their career.

Money management is not the strong suit of the August 22 individual. These people have a hard time keeping track of their spending habits—particularly if they earn great amounts of money. Their difficulty stems from the fact that they don't really respect money.

DREAMS AND GOALS Before they can reach their goals, August 22 individuals need to learn to believe in themselves. This should not be a problem since they have so much going for them. Yet it often takes the personal validation of a close friend, family member, or colleague to make them see what is so obvious to everyone else—that they have talent. Once they have exorcised their doubts, August 22 men and women can climb as high as they wish to go.

EMBRACE
Good attitude
Belief in the future
Stamina

AVOID
Inner fears
Pettiness
Moodiness

ALSO BORN TODAY
Actress Honor Blackman; writer Ray Bradbury; composer Claude Debussy; actress Valerie Harper; singer John Lee Hooker; writer Dorothy Parker; actress Cindy Williams; baseball star Carl Yastrzemski.

VIRGO

August 23 - September 22

Virgo is the sixth sign of the astrological year and is known by its astrological symbol, the Virgin. Virgo individuals are intelligent, patient, and humble. With Mercury as the ruling planet, people born under this sign are considered to be quick-thinking, observant, and analytical. They possess an organized mind and have the logic to solve even the most difficult problems.

THE VIRGO MAN The typical Virgo man has a quiet dignity that sets him well apart from other men. He has discriminating tastes and an appetite for learning. Virgos make excellent students, a role that they seem to inhabit all of their lives. Virgo men are often extremely well-read and educated, but they may be averse to trumpeting these achievements.

Many Virgo men are stylish in an unassuming way. They are extremely concerned with their health and fitness and are very careful about their diets. Cooking for the Virgo man can be extremely trying, since he has a tendency to be quite fussy about what he eats and how it is prepared. But despite his eccentricities, the Virgo man is a gentle soul who actually possesses much more charm than men who have showier personalities.

THE VIRGO WOMAN The Virgo woman has discreet charm. She is intelligent, thoughtful, and very careful about her personal grooming. This lady is not the sort to neglect her personal appearance even when she has a day off. "Neat and tidy" describes her best.

Virgo women are efficient and hard-working. They are ethical and never put career achievements ahead of their own personal code of right and wrong. The want to feel as if they have earned what they get, and refuse to be manipulative or controlling. Because they are so well-organized, these women do a good job of balancing personal and professional responsibilities. Most Virgo women are especially adept at handling the family budget, because they have the patience to watch where every penny goes. Perfectionism comes at a price, however, and the Virgo woman needs to learn how to relax in order to ease the tension and stress that are brought on by adhering to her own high standards.

THE VIRGO CHILD These youngsters need a great deal of affection and emotional support, since they are likely to be extremely shy and may have difficulty developing friendships with other children. They are not naturally competitive, and because of this they may find it easier to give in to their more demanding playmates.

Virgo children are often studious boys and girls who have to endure the teasing of less talented schoolmates who resent their success. Parents should help their Virgo child develop an interest in at least one "cool" hobby or activity in order to help them fit in with the school crowd. Although they should be taught that being different is nothing to be ashamed of, it is also vital for these youngsters to develop a kinship with others.

THE VIRGO LOVER Virgo individuals may not be the most dashing romantic figures, but they offer their whole heart to a lover. There is no pretense involved in the way they act or what they say. When a Virgo is in love, he or she is completely devoted.

Because they are loyal in all human relationships, Virgos are big on fidelity. It takes a lot to make these people stray. They value more than the superficial aspects of a love relationship, and because of this fact they generally attract people who think and believe very much as they do. Marriage is a major commitment to these individuals, who value their union as both a love relationship and a working partnership.

ELEMENT: Earth
QUALITY: Mutable
PLANETARY RULER: Mercury
BIRTHSTONE: Peridot
FLOWER: Pansy
COLOR: Navy blue

KEY CHARACTERISTIC: Detail-oriented

STRENGTHS: Precise, Orderly, Efficient
CHALLENGES: Nervous, Sarcastic, Overcritical

THE VIRGO BOSS People who work for a Virgo boss soon discover that there are a million ways to do things wrong but only one way to do them right. Virgos are known for their perfectionist tendencies.

The Virgo boss is unlikely to establish anything more than a business relationship with employees. He or she isn't the sort to joke around or create an air of informality in the workplace. Yet despite these seemingly uptight attitudes, the typical Virgo boss is a fair and impartial individual who is never afraid to give an employee the credit and respect due to a good worker.

THE VIRGO FRIEND As a rule, shy, self-effacing Virgos have difficulty making friends, often because they lack the social skills involved in bringing people together. Virgo individuals may also lack the self-confidence required to meet new people. Yet when they do make the effort, these people are capable of achieving extraordinary things within the bounds of friendship.

Because they are incredibly loyal and caring, Virgos are likely to keep the same friends over a period of many years. They may not have a great many friends, but they cultivate the friendships that they do have, giving them a high priority in their lives. Often, Virgo individuals choose to befriend someone who has the showy personality they aspire to but feel uncomfortable assuming.

AUGUST 23

People born on this day have a mercurial, kinetic charm that brings them great affection from others. Their graceful bearing combines with a light touch of sophistication.

August 23 natives are guileless, genuinely nice individuals who are greatly concerned with other people's comfort. They have an almost preternatural ability as successful hosts or hostesses because they're constantly looking after the happiness and welfare of others.

FRIENDS AND LOVERS
Everyone wants to be friends with August 23 people. These friendly, energetic souls are so likable it's difficult to resist them. Thoughtful and kind, the people born on this date have a real hands-on approach to friendship. They unfailingly remember birthdays, and can be depended upon to send those touchy-feely cards to commemorate every conceivable anniversary.

Romance generally leads to marriage for August 23 men and women. They have a fairly conventional view of togetherness; once they fall in love, these people like to make it official.

CHILDREN AND FAMILY
Not every August 23 individual is the product of a *Leave It to Beaver* household, yet to hear them talk it may seem that way. These people are comfortable with their past and draw a great deal of wisdom from their own parents.

Parenthood is one of the great joys of August 23 people. They adore children and have a true affinity for them. If they're denied children of their own, these folks are likely to involve themselves with youngsters through humanitarian or charity organizations.

HEALTH
People born on this date have very definite ideas about health. Either they ascribe to a strictly holistic regimen or they conform to a more conventional outlook—but one way or the other they're sticklers for following a prescribed method. They're very big on exercise.

Because they often bring a philosophical approach to their physical habits, August 23 natives are likely to be casual vegetarians or even strict vegans.

CAREER AND FINANCES
People born on this date are team players. They rarely seek individual glory because they understand that they can make their greatest contributions as part of a group. Within this context they can accomplish amazing things, and usually do. If placed in a position of leadership, these clever people learn the ropes very quickly.

Financial success is not routinely part of the game plan of August 23 natives because they're good at getting along on a regular wage. But if they do happen onto a fortune, these people are sure to share it generously with family and friends.

DREAMS AND GOALS
August 23 men and women achieve their goals in an orderly, practical manner. These people learn from every experience, and use those lessons to their own best advantage in future situations.

Because of their enthusiastic nature, people born on this date never lose faith in their own ability to make things happen. If their goals are sidetracked, they look at it as a chance to regroup, rather than as a misfortune.

EMBRACE
Emotional depth
Self assurance
Nobleness

AVOID
Stubbornness
Stress
Burning the candle at both ends

ALSO BORN TODAY
Actress Barbara Eden; actor/dancer Gene Kelly; composer Constant Lambert; actress Shelley Long; French King Louis XVI; ballerina Patricia McBride; actress Vera Miles; politician Pete Wilson.

AUGUST 24

The greatest challenge for people born on this date is to be themselves. Because they may not have a lot of confidence in their abilities, they often look to colleagues or friends for validation. These men and women have discriminating taste and are best able to show their true character when they are loved.

The typical August 24 native is a real lady or gentleman. These people are known for their excellent manners, good disposition, and the generosity they display to those closest to them.

FRIENDS AND LOVERS

Friendships play an important part in the lives of August 24 people, inspiring them to aspire to and achieve goals they would not try to accomplish on their own. The basically shy nature of August 24 men and women makes them reticent to put themselves "out there," but with the encouragement of good friends, they're more likely to give it a try.

The love nature of August 24 natives is a complicated one. These people love deeply, yet they may not be able to achieve a close friendship with a lover or partner. If they wish to get beyond this emotional barrier, they'll need to break down a few walls.

CHILDREN AND FAMILY

August 24 men and women have a difficult time moving beyond the disappointments of childhood. They may have had an exceptionally strict upbringing that influences the way they regard their relationships as adults.

It certainly affects the relationship with their own children. August 24 individuals are not known for showing their emotions, and even though they love their children very much, it may be quite difficult for them to show it.

HEALTH

Because August 24 natives worry constantly about their health and fitness, it's not uncommon for August 24 individuals to be hypochondriacs. In truth, they're likely to be among the healthiest people on earth because they take very good care of themselves.

People on this day are particularly careful about the food they eat. They may give up meat quite early in life, and may also shy away from drinking and smoking. Vitamin and mineral supplements are a good idea, yet August 24 people often take them to excess.

CAREER AND FINANCES

Although certainly capable of handling whatever work is given to them, August 24 men and women prefer not to be in positions of great responsibility, at least not until they've been habituated to the task. These folks have a hard time believing in their own skills, and must feel that others have faith in them before they can have faith in themselves.

August 24 individuals are very cautious in the way they handle money. They may look to professionals for help if they feel insecure about making vital financial decisions.

DREAMS AND GOALS

August 24 natives have a great many personal goals, but in order to make them come true they must first come to grips with how they feel about themselves.

People born on this date are doers, and they will never stop trying to achieve their dreams. Once they learn to trust their own instincts they can go far.

EMBRACE
Inner drives
Communication
Sensuality

AVOID
Belligerence
Selfish motives
Pettiness

ALSO BORN TODAY
Musician Mark Bedford; singer Jeffrey Daniel; actor Steve Guttenberg; musician Ken Hensley; actress Marlee Matlin; French King Philippe II; baseball star Cal Ripken, Jr.; model Claudia Schiffer.

AUGUST 25

People born on August 25 have a complicated nature. On one hand they seem to derive a great deal of emotional sustenance from the approval of those close to them. Yet, they also qualify as true pioneers who are not afraid to accept the personal and professional challenges that come their way.

When August 25 folks find their niche in life they can be depended upon to make bold strides in whatever they attempt.

FRIENDS AND LOVERS
Friends are an important support system for people with an August 25 birthday. They are social creatures who prefer to conduct their friendships on deep, emotionally intimate levels. These individuals also enjoy being the recipient of a friend's knowledge and experience.

Love is always a serious matter to these folks, who make concerned, sympathetic, and loyal life partners. Relationship challenges never faze them. When problems arise within the marriage, August 25 people can be expected to deal with them in mature and selfless ways.

CHILDREN AND FAMILY
People born on August 25 feel incredibly connected to their childhood all their lives, and base many of their adult values on what they learned at their mother's knee.

They become involved, somewhat overly protective parents who are eager to give their youngsters all the material comforts they lacked as children. Yet they're careful to instill a sense of ethics as well. They believe that discipline, not punishment, is the key.

HEALTH
Individuals born on August 25 may find their health strongly influenced by emotional and psychological factors. A highly strung disposition could exacerbate nervous

conditions like skin rashes and even allergies. These people need to explore aerobic exercise, deep-breathing therapy, and other stress-busting activities. Frequent massage and meditation can also be of great value.

Because August 25 natives have a strong instinct to explore and learn about their inner drives, they often can benefit from various kinds of psychological therapy.

CAREER AND FINANCES
Because they are intelligent and very hard workers, people born on August 25 are likely to be successful in their career ambitions. Even if their goals tend to be modest, they have a good sense of their own abilities and always strive for improvement.

There is a tendency for August 25 individuals to be concerned about their financial security even if they are well-off—perhaps a reaction to an impoverished or otherwise disadvantaged childhood.

EMBRACE
A positive self-image
Happy memories
Learning

AVOID
Regretting the past
Finding fault
Worrying

ALSO BORN TODAY
Composer/conductor Leonard Bernstein; actor Sean Connery; singer/songwriter Elvis Costello; novelist Dorothy Dunnett; singer Billy Ray Cyrus; novelist Frederick Forsyth; TV personality Regis Philbin; former governor of Alabama George Wallace.

DREAMS AND GOALS
Although August 25 people may have worldly goals early in life, they will almost certainly turn their steps toward a spiritual path sooner or later. They are intrigued by life's mysteries, and want to know and understand their own motivations and those of people close to them.

Personal goals are usually met by August 25 individuals in a timely and consistent manner, based on stringent planning.

AUGUST 26

People born on August 26 possess a strong sense of purpose. They have a great devotion to fairness and a desire to apply their energies for the benefit of others.

These men and women are quiet and introspective. They don't make a show of themselves in any way, and prefer that others not attempt to put them in the spotlight.

FRIENDS AND LOVERS August 26 natives depend on their relationships to give them the emotional support that may be lacking in other aspects of life. In return, they give their friends unconditional love and support, as well as the occasional piece of good advice.

In romance, these folks are less sure of themselves. Although they make extremely loving helpmates and partners, they may be unsure of just how to meet all the emotional needs of the one they love. For this reason, they need to sharpen their communication skills and become better at perceiving what remains unspoken.

CHILDREN AND FAMILY August 26 people have a strong connection to their family, even though the relationship with their parents may have gone through some troubled times. These individuals want to maintain good relations with siblings, despite ill feelings that might be left over from adolescence, when competition was the rule.

Using what they have learned is their ticket to being a good parent. August 26 men and women are very sincere about what they bring to this job, and should learn to be more trusting of their instincts instead of expecting to make mistakes.

HEALTH Like many Virgo natives, these people are fanatics about their health habits. They usually strike a balance between conventional wisdom and the New Age approach, especially where nutrition is concerned.

Exercise is another key to the good health of these people. They understand the value of cross-training, and incorporate many different forms of exercise into their workouts. Stretching techniques keep the body supple and relieve stress.

CAREER AND FINANCES August 26 men and women have many talents, though they may need a great deal of encouragement in order to pursue them. They excel as teachers and professors, and in medical or scientific research, banking, or journalism.

Most Virgo natives are extremely conservative in the way they handle their finances, and August 26 people are no exception. They're not big spenders and are totally averse to credit buying. They prefer to save for a big purchase, rather than impulsively use plastic to buy it right away.

DREAMS AND GOALS August 26 men and women aren't as concerned with success as they are with getting things done the best way they can. They aren't competitive and prefer to take the middle road in their approach to most of life's challenges.

These individuals are careful planners, who take one step at a time toward making a dream come true.

EMBRACE
Solidarity
Passion
Impossible odds

AVOID
Transitory relationships
Worry
Prejudice

ALSO BORN TODAY
England's Prince Albert; musician Jet Black; newspaper editor Ben Bradlee; actor Macauley Culkin; singer Chris Curtis; Vice Presidential candidate Geraldine Ferraro; writer Christopher Isherwood; actor Michael Jeter.

AUGUST 27

People born on August 27 are practical and use their creative abilities to advertise a particular point of view. These men and women feel all of their responsibilities deeply. They have a social conscience and often involve themselves in useful projects that teach or otherwise help others.

Because August 27 people are bold and determined, they have a hard time taking orders from anyone. They steer their own course and take responsibility for their own mistakes.

FRIENDS AND LOVERS

At some point August 27 individuals usually find themselves at odds with close friends over a difference of opinion. These men and women wear their views like a badge of honor and refuse to defer, even to a close friend.

As with other relationships, romantic unions can be both satisfying and confusing for August 27 men and women. They want to put everything they have into a relationship, yet worry about being hurt. A part of these people fears falling in love because to do so forces them to give control of their life to someone else.

CHILDREN AND FAMILY

August 27 people have a great deal of respect for the traditions of family life. They are strongly influenced by their own upbringing, even if it wasn't altogether positive. They may be inhibited in their relationships with siblings, especially if they have unresolved issues from that period of their lives.

If they become parents, August 27 people will do their best to be conscientious and fair. However, they should strive to be more open and communicative with their kids. Once they manage an emotional breakthrough, they're apt to lose their inhibitions about parenting.

HEALTH

August 27 natives often suffer from sleep disorders brought on by stress and worry. These people take their responsibilities very seriously, which can translate to a high level of tension in their lives. For this reason they should be extra vigilant about their diet, ignoring caffeinated beverages like coffee and soft drinks, and spicy foods that affect digestion.

People born on this date can benefit from relaxation techniques.

CAREER AND FINANCES

August 27 people have a real way with words. These men and women make terrific writers, especially if they begin to practice their craft very early in life. Learning to have confidence in their abilities is the key to their success.

These people make good money managers. They have the ability to make sound and financially viable investments, and are willing to take risks.

DREAMS AND GOALS

The dream of August 27 men and women is to have as much control over their lives as possible. That can mean finances, career, or relationships. These bold individuals don't like to depend on others for help or reassurance, and are much happier when they make their own way.

Because they strive for self-sufficiency, August 27 people would rather have fewer material possessions and be their own boss than have a great deal and be in hock to others.

EMBRACE
Forgiveness
Sense of humor
Integrity

AVOID
Grudges
A wounded heart
Jealousy

ALSO BORN TODAY
Novelist Lloyd C. Douglas; U.S. President Lyndon Baines Johnson; novelist Theodore Dreiser; biographer Antonia Fraser; novelist C. S. Forester; actress Tuesday Weld; novelist Ira Levin.

181

AUGUST 28

The men and women born on August 28 have a strongly creative nature that needs to be addressed. They grasp the interdependence of nature and art—a sensitive side that's complemented by inner strength that lets them deal with life's demanding challenges.

Although August 28 natives have a good self-image, they can be deeply hurt by the bad opinion of others, especially those who are close to them.

FRIENDS AND LOVERS August 28 people have enough self-confidence to surround themselves with fantastically talented individuals. These creative men and women gravitate to people with similar tastes, and take a great deal of inspiration from these relationships.

Love affairs are a rich source of joy for August 28 people. They're sometimes reticent about settling down, and yet all that changes the moment they meet the person they know is their soul mate.

CHILDREN AND FAMILY August 28 men and women have a generally positive view of their childhood. They may have been the favorite child or perhaps the most talented and engaging member of the family, giving them a certain cachet that was resented by siblings. Nonetheless, these folks usually forge strong ties with relatives.

Although they make good parents themselves, August 28 people have a tendency to prematurely push their own children toward achievements and accomplishments. Once their children begin to rebel against their expectations, August 28 people will learn to make sensible adjustments.

HEALTH People born on this date are intriguing combinations of the careful and the carefree. They're watchful about what they eat, yet are unlikely to follow any strict, self-imposed diet guidelines.

They are definitely concerned about their appearance, which means a workout plan that keeps them feeling healthy and looking good. They aren't fond of anything too strenuous, preferring a moderately active aerobic workout a few times each week.

CAREER AND FINANCES August 28 men and women enjoy being in the professional spotlight. They have a real talent for managing people and bringing out the best in them, especially young people. For this reason, August 28 individuals make great mentors.

They have real ability to make money, and save and manage it wisely. They're often financially secure at an early age. This gives them the potential to take time off from their professional lives once in a while to indulge their love of an interesting avocation.

DREAMS AND GOALS The men and women born on this date have a lot of ambition, and work tirelessly toward a chosen goal. Their greatest talent in this area is their ability to know what they really want out of life. They understand the need to make sacrifices.

Where personal goals are concerned, August 28 people are never satisfied with just "getting by." They want to improve their mind, body, and soul in every aspect of life.

EMBRACE
A positive self-image
Lasting love
Decency

AVOID
Pretentiousness
Cynicism
Indifference

ALSO BORN TODAY
Poet John Betjeman; swimming champion Janet Evans; actor Ben Gazzara; actor David Soul; writer Johann Wolfgang von Goethe; figure skating champion Scott Hamilton; actor Jason Priestley; actress Emma Samms.

AUGUST 29

People born on this date have a strong life-force that's keenly expressed through their emotions. They have the potential to lead an extraordinarily spiritual life, though they must come to grips with all aspects of their personal relationships before this can be accomplished.

August 29 men and women need to follow their own paths, and will experience setbacks and disappointment if they allow themselves to be influenced against their better judgment.

FRIENDS AND LOVERS

Though they may have only a handful of friends, the ones that August 29 people do have are devoted to them. Since the people born on this day are not very adventurous, they are likely to befriend individuals who are very much like them.

August 29 people are often defined (or allow themselves to be defined) by their romantic associations. Because they are so emotional, these men and women experience profound joy and sadness in romance. Commitment can be difficult for them.

CHILDREN AND FAMILY

August 29 natives often have a troubled past that they would just as soon forget. Although this doesn't necessarily signify a bad or even disadvantaged childhood, there are certain to be some emotional scars that would have gone unnoticed by a less sensitive person.

In spite of their background, or perhaps because of it, August 29 men and women put all their energies toward being loving and sensitive parents. Yet they must learn to let their youngsters take a few emotional lumps now and then.

HEALTH

Individuals born on this date often favor a type of health and fitness program that seems extraordinary or strange to other people. They're sticklers for cleanliness, especially about food preparation.

August 29 people have an almost spiritual attachment to exercise. They do it for the sense of power and centeredness it gives them, not to look better in Spandex. Combinations of exercise and meditation give good results.

CAREER AND FINANCES

People born on this date are creatively intellectual. They seem to have the ability to extract the maximum amount of wisdom from every experience—whether it's reading a book or enjoying a conversation with a friend or loved one. They often pursue careers based in scholarship, or ones that require extensive academic training.

Money is just a means of exchange as far as August 29 people are concerned. They respond to more important things in life. If they have the opportunity to make big money, their intelligence and discipline will help them manage it well.

DREAMS AND GOALS

August 29 men and women try hard to come to terms with the difficult times in their past. This is their desire, even their mission in life, yet it's not an easy one. They need to become more secure in their ability to handle hurtful memories.

Personal relationships need special attention from these men and women, who can feel emotionally isolated at times.

EMBRACE
Clarity
Balance
Emotional transcendence

AVOID
Insecurity
Self-criticism
Compliance

ALSO BORN TODAY
Film director Richard Attenborough; actress Rebecca de Mornay; film director William Friedkin; actor Richard Gere; actor Elliot Gould; pop star Michael Jackson; TV personality Robin Leach; actress Isobel Sanford.

AUGUST 30

People born on this day have an overwhelming urge to express their individual identities. They have a great love of learning, travel, and the written word. These men and woman are known for their discriminating good taste and good looks, and always appear well dressed and attractive in public.

Although August 30 people seem calm on the surface, they're actually high-strung and excitable.

FRIENDS AND LOVERS People born on this date are sincere friends. They're extremely fun-loving and enjoy a vibrant social life. They like to spend time with good friends, and love to take trips, whether across the world or across town.

August 30 men and women are natural romantics who often fall in love with love. This can lead to disappointment in relationship matters, but it can also lead to great joy and happiness if they find the right person. The tumult that characterizes their relationships is usually of a positive nature.

CHILDREN AND FAMILY August 30 natives are often the beneficiaries of an extremely fortunate upbringing. They are dearly loved by family members, with whom they share a close and advantageous relationship.

As parents, August 30 men and women are very good at encouraging their little ones to express themselves as emotional and spiritual creatures who exist apart from their parents. This liberal approach brings children and parents together, rather than having the opposite effect.

HEALTH People born on August 30 are not overly concerned with the details of health and exercise. They have a great interest in food and make excellent cooks and nutritionists, but they are not averse to eating junk food at times, and may even have a powerful sweet tooth.

Though Virgo natives tend to be slim, August 30 people do have a tendency to put on weight if they don't participate in some sort of regular workout program. They may favor competitive sports, especially tennis and swimming.

CAREER AND FINANCES People born on this date have a broad view of their world. They like to express their expansive personality through their work, and often gravitate to professions that allow them to travel or study the culture of foreign nations.

Because they think big, August 30 individuals also have a tendency to spend big. They are incredibly generous people who can never resist buying gifts for friends and loved ones. Fortunately, these folks also have a talent for shrewd management of their finances.

DREAMS AND GOALS August 30 natives have such a positive attitude about life that even setbacks and delays don't worry them or deter them from going forward. These people have a high level of self-confidence and can envision their success even before it happens.

The men and women born on this date are ambitious on many different levels. They want to accomplish great things, but also want to live well and in a worldly manner.

EMBRACE
Self-esteem
Expectations
An open mind

AVOID
Ego issues
Self-criticism
Compliance

ALSO BORN TODAY
Writer John Gunther; actress Elizabeth Ashley; ski champion Jean-Claude Killy; actress Shirley Booth; baseball star Ted Williams; actor Timothy Bottoms; novelist Mary Shelley; actor Fred MacMurray.

AUGUST 31

People born on this date have a showy yet tasteful personality, and bask in the loving approval of others. Original and intelligent, they are often impractical. Their eclectic tastes display erudition and a great deal of originality.

August 31 people often find themselves in unusual circumstances. This suits their love of adventure quite well, and also gives them the opportunity to try out some of their latent talents.

FRIENDS AND LOVERS
As with every other aspect of life, August 31 natives show their unique nature through the friends they make. These broad-minded men and women don't have specific criteria for selecting companions. Instead, if they feel excitement in someone's company, or experience the miracle of instant communication with somebody, they've made a new friend.

Even in choosing lovers or a mate, August 31 people are likely to select someone who is unusual—even eccentric. The people born on this date are much more liberal than most Virgo natives and are romantically attracted to individuals who share this characteristic.

CHILDREN AND FAMILY
August 31 men and women have a mildly rebellious attitude toward the traditions of family life. Even though they generally end up very much like their own parents, they seem destined to go through a period when they are totally at odds with everything their background represents.

Fortunately for them, once they become parents they remember these attitudes, and are therefore prepared to accept the rebellious actions of their own children. August 31 people make very good parents because they combine the qualities of compassion and love with a good deal of common sense.

HEALTH
People born today revel in unusual health practices. They have a wide variety of special interests in these matters, which may include anything from chakra adjustments and aura cleansing to colonic washes and hands-on healing. It's rare for someone born on this day to take a conventional approach to anything, especially if it's health-related.

CAREER AND FINANCES
The individuals born on this day can make a mark in almost any career. These bright, iconoclastic people are exceedingly talented and make marvelous public speakers. They can also use their facility with words to become fine writers, journalists, teachers, lawyers, and members of the clergy.

Many August 31 people have a great desire to hit it rich and attempt to do so by way of risky planning. Sometimes this pays off— sometimes it fails spectacularly. Undeterred, the August 31 native tries again.

DREAMS AND GOALS
August 31 men and women may not think of themselves as being especially goal-oriented. They go after things in a big way, but often without making the necessary plans or considering details.

These individuals can make great personal and professional strides, due mainly to their ability to see things from a wide perspective, and to appreciate eccentricity and inventiveness.

EMBRACE
Organizational skills
Centeredness
High spirits

AVOID
Confusion
Domestic upheavals
Hasty actions

ALSO BORN TODAY
Actor Richard Basehart; hockey star Jean Beliveau; actor James Coburn; singer Debbie Gibson; actor Fredric March; singer/songwriter Van Morrison; violinist Itzhak Perlman; novelist William Saroyan.

SEPTEMBER 1

People born on September 1 have a practical approach to life that enables them to get things done. They take great pride in their ability to organize their activities, and although they keep up a steady pace with every project, they never hurry. Haste, to them, is definitely waste.

They have the same philosophical approach when it comes to life: "Do your best and leave the rest."

FRIENDS AND LOVERS

The attitude of people born on this date seems to be that no one can ever have too many friends. Despite having a large circle of acquaintances, September 1 individuals have the unique ability of being able to treat them all like family.

The men and women born on this date have an idealistic view of love, though this may not be apparent except to those who know them best. They will wait patiently for their turn at romance, unwilling to walk down the aisle unless they are 100 percent convinced it's true love. When they do meet that storybook lifemate, September 1 people plan to live happily ever after.

CHILDREN AND FAMILY

People born on this date see themselves as a continuation in a long line of tradition. Even if they have differences with their parents, they have an enormous amount of respect for them and for the value of their experience.

When they become parents, September 1 people put their whole heart into the job. They have a real affinity for youngsters, and although they have a reputation for being lenient, they're more likely to forgive a child's mistake than to scold the youngster for making it.

HEALTH

September 1 natives are cautious about their health. Even though they are generally robust, these people can never quite believe that everything is right with them. They are moderate in all things, and that includes their health practices.

Sleep is a critical factor for September 1 people, because of their essentially high-strung nature. They have a hard time learning to relax, which can lead to sleep disorders. Meditation before bedtime is the best cure.

CAREER AND FINANCES

September 1 men and women are witty, articulate people who can easily make their living with words. These individuals make exceptional writers, researchers, journalists, teachers, lawyers, and public speakers. They don't seek the spotlight, but they aren't averse to it, either.

Smart money management is second nature to September 1 people, who seem to have a sixth sense about such things. They have a real talent for taking a small amount of money and making it grow.

DREAMS AND GOALS

September 1 natives have fairly modest goals. They believe in making use of their best capabilities and will never sacrifice their own security or that of their loved ones to try something wild or unprovable.

The key to understanding September 1 people is to realize that they do the best they can, every day, on every project, without exception. To them, honest effort equals success.

EMBRACE
Freedom
Liberality
A sense of humor

AVOID
Overwork
Being too serious
Solitude

ALSO BORN TODAY
Novelist Edgar Rice Burroughs; actress Yvonne de Carlo; singer Gloria Estefan; symphony conductor Seiji Ozawa; singer Barry Gibb; composer Johann Pachelbel; comedienne Lily Tomlin; singer Dave White.

SEPTEMBER 2

People born on September 2 need to feel that they're in control in all aspects of life. These individuals are practical, serene, organized. They can always see the humor in things, though they don't often show that side of themselves to the world.

These men and women have exceptionally good leadership potential. They are devoted to their loved ones, although a quiet nature may give them the appearance of being somewhat unemotional.

FRIENDS AND LOVERS September 2
people are shy, and often find it hard to make friends. For this reason they tend to cherish the ones they have. Their friends often have qualities that they themselves do not possess.

Where romantic love is concerned, September 2 people are extremely vulnerable. They often experience a great disappointment in their early years, only to find the true love of their life years later.

CHILDREN AND FAMILY September 2
natives are extremely close to their family members. Indeed, they often have a difficult time separating from their family, even at the time of their marriage. This can cause problems with their spouses if they are not empathetic to the situation.

These individuals are good parents, though they may not be able to show their true feelings. Just being gentle with their children's feelings isn't enough. These men and women have to learn to communicate with their little ones in order to create a worthwhile relationship.

HEALTH People born on this date have a
sense of vulnerability about their health. It's possible that they were somewhat sickly as children; the attention they received as a result may have left conscious and subconscious marks.

Because they are not as disciplined as many Virgo natives, September 2 individuals need to be very careful about their dietary habits. When they cut back on calories and junk food, they'll find the energy they need. They can also benefit from a regular workout regimen, though they should be careful to keep their exercise in the light to moderate range.

CAREER AND FINANCES September 2
natives have a strong curiosity to discover how things work. For this reason they make good engineers, researchers, scientists, chemists, medical personnel, private investigators, law enforcement agents, and teachers. Whatever their occupation, these men and women put their talents to work with an admirable show of dedication.

Finances may be in flux for most September 2 people, because of their likelihood to spend money from a sense of emotionalism rather than with good sense.

DREAMS AND GOALS The people born on
this date tend to keep their goals to themselves. This doesn't indicate a lack of belief in themselves, but rather a fear of letting others down if they fail to achieve what they set out to do.

Yet quietly, without ceremony, most September 2 people do reach their ultimate objectives.

EMBRACE
Self-sufficiency
High spirits
Spontaneity

AVOID
Bad habits
Lack of focus
Mistakes in love

ALSO BORN TODAY
Football star Terry Bradshaw; tennis star Jimmy Connors; author Allen Drury; actor Derek Fowlds; singer Sam Gooden; actor Mark Harmon; musician Fritz McIntyre; actor Keanu Reeves.

SEPTEMBER 3

September 3 individuals are ambitious people who may be fortunate enough to achieve their ultimate goals early in life. If they do, they cannot be satisfied or happy until they also have a personal life that compares to the professional one.

These individuals have a great capacity for spirituality, yet this side of their nature may not come to the surface until later in life. They seem to be materialistic people, but that's only outward evidence of their natural practicality.

FRIENDS AND LOVERS People born on this date like having people around them, yet they have difficulty making close friends. This may be due to a strong level of competition that sometimes creates animosity. These people aren't always certain how to show their real feelings.

This competitive edge is even manifested in the love life of September 3 people. They have a great need to show that they can attract the most eligible partners, when what they really wish to do is find the man or woman of their dreams and settle down. Once they do, they have a capacity for true happiness and contentment.

CHILDREN AND FAMILY September 3 individuals have a somewhat grandiose view of what family life should be. This can be traced to their own growing-up years, which may have been less than idyllic. These people have a hard time coming to grips with the failure of their own parents to show genuine affection.

They feel similarly pressured when they become parents. It may be difficult for them to generate the level of commitment they believe is necessary to be a good parent, especially if it makes demands upon their professional life.

HEALTH September 3 people are devotees of good food and may have to adopt an exceptionally active lifestyle if they are going to stay slim. Good food makes them happy, and happiness is vital to their overall good health.

Because of their positive overall attitude, September 3 natives seldom experience nervous ailments. Although they may smoke or drink in moderation, they're wise enough to supplement their health with large supplies of green leafy vegetables and plenty of B-complex vitamins.

CAREER AND FINANCES People born on this date are sufficiently talented to find success in a great many fields of endeavor. They like to strike a balance between handling details and seeing the larger picture. They have a real capacity for learning and may often continue their studies well past college.

These people enjoy making money, and not just in order to buy themselves a good life. They're willing to gamble, but unfortunately they never become accustomed to losing.

DREAMS AND GOALS September 3 natives are incredibly goal-oriented. They don't believe in limitations and will pursue their dreams with every bit of energy and vitality they possess.

One goal common to many September 3 folks is to start their own business. These people have a strong entrepreneurial spirit and are always looking for ways to break out on their own.

EMBRACE
Family values
Good times
Domesticity

AVOID
Loneliness
Predictability
Boredom

ALSO BORN TODAY
Actress Eileen Brennan; singer Al Jardine; actor Alan Ladd; composer Pietro Locatelli; novelist Alison Lurie; actress Valerie Perrine; cartoonist Mort Walker; actor Charlie Sheen.

SEPTEMBER 4

September 4 people often display extraordinary bravery in the simple act of living their lives. They have the courage to scrutinize their own motives, and want to know the truth about themselves, whether positive or negative. Even though they have a great deal of common sense, they are also natural risk-takers.

Most September 4 men and women march to the beat of a different drummer. These unique, independent-thinking people possess a rare sort of charisma, which makes them appealing to everyone they meet.

FRIENDS AND LOVERS When it comes to making friends, nobody does it better than these people. They have a genius for companionship and live out many of their fantasies through associations with unusual and extraordinary individuals.

It's not unusual for the typical September 4 native to enjoy a colorful love life. They may be inclined to play the field for many years before settling down with a partner. These men and women have a problem giving up their autonomy, so any mate will have to give them a great deal of emotional space.

CHILDREN AND FAMILY People born on this date may have a difficult time getting along with family members who do not understand their need to break free of established patterns.

Because they dislike being molded into something they are not, September 4 men and women are especially liberal in the way they bring up their own children. These people understand the need of a child to disobey parental authority while attempting to become individuals and separate from the parents.

HEALTH September 4 people may not be as careful of their health as they should be. They always seem to be in a hurry, which makes them accident-prone. Since it's difficult for these kinetic types to slow down, they should at least be mindful of their safety, especially when in transit.

Because September 4 individuals have a tendency to go to extremes, they may dabble in unorthodox health regimens. This can include fasting, which should be discouraged since it can have an adverse effect on their health.

CAREER AND FINANCES September 4 individuals typically have difficulty being part of the nine-to-five set. They want something unusual and challenging, something that hints of danger or at least excitement. It's not uncommon for these men and women to change careers several times in the space of a lifetime, as they live out their fantasies more fearlessly than most people ever will.

People born on this date are apt to be unconcerned with how much money they earn; because of this indifference they're likely to do better financially than people who make money their chief goal.

DREAMS AND GOALS Every day seems to beckon September 4 people with new dreams, new goals. These amazingly driven people never stop being excited by life and all its myriad experiences. They have a strong curiosity about everything that surrounds them, and continue to look for answers as long as they live.

EMBRACE
Cooperation
Young ideas
Commitment

AVOID
Fixation
Obsessive love
Incompatibility

ALSO BORN TODAY
Guitarist Gary Duncan; drummer Greg Elmore; actress Mitzi Gaynor; astrologer Liz Greene; actress Judith Ivey; novelist Richard Wright; actress Jennifer Salt; actress Ione Skye.

189

SEPTEMBER 5

Because of their attitude and appearance, September 5 men and women stand out in a crowd. Intelligent and composed, they are usually in control of their emotions, no matter how severe their circumstances may be.

The aristocratic bearing of September 5 people is something to behold. They're not just physically attractive, but composed and dignified.

FRIENDS AND LOVERS

Relationships are the very essence of life for September 5 people, and they spend their entire life working to make them the very best they can be. Friends have a way of becoming family, while family members become true friends.

People born on this date have a real talent for making a marriage work. They are responsible and affectionate, and know how to keep the romance alive in well-established relationships. These people give their partners unconditional loyalty, and expect the same in return.

CHILDREN AND FAMILY

Family matters are generally favorable in the lives of September 5 men and women. They love to be a welcomed part of a group, and will stand by their relatives no matter what other differences may potentially divide them.

As parents, September 5 people are quite strict, though they also dispense a good deal of love and affection to their little ones. They are not indulgent parents, however, and make it clear to their spouse from the start that they will not tolerate any attempt to spoil the children.

HEALTH

September 5 men and women are generally healthy because they put so much time and effort into taking care of themselves. They maintain a low-fat, high-energy diet and usually practice a daily exercise program.

One of their secrets to good health is an ability to handle stress in a positive and life-affirming way. They don't believe in encouraging any sort of negativity. If they don't banish it with meditation, prayer, or exercise, they tackle it head-on through confrontational means.

CAREER AND FINANCES

People born on this date require a great deal of control over the work they do. If they don't feel passionately about their career goals, they'll look for something in another field that gives them the satisfaction they need. These people are often highly educated, yet many prefer to make their livings in nonacademic jobs.

September 5 men and women work very hard to achieve financial security. Their accounting and budgetary habits are extremely precise, and militate against a need for outside help with taxes, investments, or other financial concerns.

DREAMS AND GOALS

Although September 5 natives often satisfy themselves after attaining modest goals, it's not because they can't appreciate the big picture. Rather, it defines their notion that everything they put their hand to must be treated with equal conscientiousness and respect.

These men and women can balance professional goals with those in their personal lives without losing sight of either.

EMBRACE
Your muse
Special occasions
Individuality

AVOID
Dependence
Irrationality
Mood swings

ALSO BORN TODAY
Composer John Cage; actress Carol Lawrence; French King Louis XIV; composer Giacomo Meyerbeer; actor/comedian Bob Newhart; actress Raquel Welch; author Frank Yerby; guitarist Dweezil Zappa.

SEPTEMBER 6

People born on this date live life on the edge. They are not concerned for their physical safety and don't hesitate to take chances, including foolish ones.

September 6 men and women have a strong spirit and a gentle nature. They have a great love for beauty in all of its forms, and incorporate that characteristic into their lives, work, and relationships.

FRIENDS AND LOVERS People born on this date are highly social and usually prefer friends with a similar temperament. Although perfectly capable of establishing and maintaining close, intimate friendships, they prefer to confide their deepest feelings to a spouse.

Love can be complicated for these individuals, and yet September 6 natives never stop trying to make their love life work. They have a deeper nature than they generally show to others, and for this reason are often hurt more seriously by a breakup than they're willing to acknowledge.

CHILDREN AND FAMILY September 6 people love all of the traditions that surround family life, and usually have good memories of their own childhood. Even if they had conflicts with siblings, they're likely to forgive and forget.

As parents, September 6 people may seem more ceremonial than genuinely involved. They always indulge their children's goals—to the degree, in fact, that many women born on this day have the potential to become the proverbial "stage mother." Although they may sometimes implement the wrong methods, most of what they do seems to turn out right.

HEALTH September 6 individuals are very concerned with their appearance, a fact that affects their health habits. If they can eat a rich diet without putting on weight, they will not attempt to change their tastes to low-calorie food.

Women born on this date sometimes have serious food issues that can lead to bulimia or anorexia. They will benefit from advice offered by loved ones who are privy to their secret.

CAREER AND FINANCES Because of their tendency to be attractive and well-mannered, September 6 natives often make their living in a public way. They are exceptionally charming and do well in careers that require a pleasing personality. They are often drawn to fashion, retail, or the arts.

Many September 6 people are big spenders. They don't care about the status attached to making money, but they love the beautiful things it can buy. Since they may be fairly cavalier, or even foolish in their way with money, they should seek out a professional to help them make financial decisions.

DREAMS AND GOALS September 6 natives want to live the good life. From an early age they are fascinated by wealth and privilege. Style, art, and all things beautiful speak to them in a language few other people can understand.

Because they may lack self-discipline, some of their goals may remain little more than idle wishes unless they can learn to become more organized and aggressive.

EMBRACE
Respect
Inner voice
Career achievement

AVOID
Indecisiveness
Impatience
Emotional neediness

ALSO BORN TODAY
Musician Dave Bargeron; actress Jane Curtin; historian Page Smith; actress Swoozie Kurtz; American Revolutionary war figure Marquis de Lafayette; guitarist Claydes Smith; guitarist Paul Waaktaar; comedienne Jo Anne Worley.

SEPTEMBER 7

Although they may seem docile on the surface, September 7 men and women have a volatile inner energy that they use in their pursuit of achievement. These people are extremely ambitious, yet never ruthless. They believe in playing by the rules and will not change their attitude no matter how badly they want success.

September 7 people may seem to clamor for their place in the spotlight, yet are never so happy as when they're part of a loving family. They prefer security to unpredictable excitement.

FRIENDS AND LOVERS Because they are typically loners, September 7 natives don't make friends easily. Because they are shy, these men and women may appear snobbish or aloof, though they are actually in great need of finding people who understand them.

They may have an exceedingly romantic love life, but are very discreet about it. They are preoccupied with finding a soul mate, and will not be truly happy until they find someone who fills the bill.

CHILDREN AND FAMILY People born on this date have a great need to be part of an extended family. Relatives of all sorts, and even friends, become their familial support system. These folks seldom make a distinction between those related to them by blood, and others with whom they share a special, often privileged sense of kinship.

September 7 people may be unsure about their parental role and may look to a parent or sibling to give them guidance. The sense of being responsible for a life is overwhelming for them, yet because they are kind and caring they eventually succeed.

HEALTH People born on this date worry more about their health than is warranted. They often convince themselves that "something must be wrong," and perpetually search for miracle cure-alls. They waver between holistic and conventional methods, yet may be unsure and even untrusting of either.

These men and women need to learn how to manage stress and alleviate anxiety.

CAREER AND FINANCES For much of their lives, September 7 individuals may be undecided on which career they wish to pursue. This can lead them to experiment with many different jobs and professions.

Where finances are concerned, September 7 people can seem to be absolutely clueless. This has nothing to do with their intelligence, but because they have a hard time coming to grips with the finality of their decisions.

DREAMS AND GOALS September 7 men and women need to find the truth at the very core of themselves. If they can meet this goal fairly early in life, a great many of their later difficulties could be avoided.

People born on this date are extremely contradictory. What is an important goal to them one day can be overturned by the presence of a new religion, a new life partner, even a new hobby. Yet as long as they remain in touch with their inner-nature, they have accomplished their most important aim.

EMBRACE
Sensitivity
Good intentions
A crusading spirit

AVOID
Single-mindedness
Self-praise
Anger

ALSO BORN TODAY
Actor Corbin Bernsen; model/actress Susan Blakely; novelist Taylor Caldwell; England's Queen Elizabeth I; singer/songwriter Chrissie Hynde; actress Julie Kavner; French King Louis VIII; writer Edith Sitwell.

SEPTEMBER 8

People born on September 8 are inveterate searchers after truth. They may come to the deepest realization of self after suffering a great emotional pain or disappointment. September 8 men and women are determined to get to the heart of things. They have a practical view of life, which allows them to withstand difficulties without losing faith in themselves or their objectives. Knowing that they are better for having gone through their problems is a badge of honor to them.

FRIENDS AND LOVERS
Friendship means a great deal to the men and women born on this date. They feel a need to cultivate close relationships with people who share their values and beliefs, and may have a hard time connecting with those who see life differently than they do.

They have a similar feeling about romantic partners. People born on September 8 need the security of a lover or mate who will not challenge their life-view. Marriage is a logical step for them, since they appreciate the order it lends to their situation.

CHILDREN AND FAMILY
September 8 people are traditionalists in the way they look at life—this includes family relationships. They may have been given a great deal of responsibility as children and were doubtless molded by the experience.

When they become parents, September 8 natives tend to follow the ways of their own upbringing. If these tactics are questioned by their spouse, they may amend their behavior so that they're less strict and traditional.

HEALTH
People born on this date are constantly worrying about their health, even when there is very little, or even nothing, to worry about! This can lead to a fanatical approach to staying fit, which can actually be worse for them than doing nothing at all.

The biggest lesson that September 8 individuals can learn regarding health and fitness is that moderation is the key to their success. They can eat anything, as long as they don't eat everything. They don't have to burn every calorie they take in as long as they maintain a well-balanced workout program.

CAREER AND FINANCES
September 8 natives are often groomed to go into the family business, even if that isn't what they want out of life. For this reason they need to become more assertive and stand up to parents who may not understand where their true aspirations lie.

Thanks to sensible spending habits, these men and women have very few problems with money. Saving money is natural for them, and they are unlikely to take on debt through credit spending.

DREAMS AND GOALS
People born on this date want to know how they measure up to their ideal. They may have unwarranted doubts about themselves, but through a spiritual search they're often able to uncover the true essence of their being.

September 8 people are not motivated by worldly rewards, but by the realization that they have made a prized goal come true. Knowing that they possess this ability gives them the confidence they may lack.

EMBRACE
Identity
Loyalty
Inner path

AVOID
Feelings of betrayal
Destructive thoughts
Brooding

ALSO BORN TODAY
Comedian Sid Caesar; singer Brian Cole; composer Antonin Dvorak; novelist Grace Metalious; poet Siegfried Sassoon; actor Peter Sellers; musician David Steele; actor Henry Thomas.

SEPTEMBER 9

People born on September 9 are perfectionists—a fact that often makes their own life difficult while infuriating everyone around them. These people put incredible pressure on themselves, not so much to succeed as to be the best in their own eyes.

Expect amazing physical stamina from these folks, but beware of the perfectionism that can cause emotional turmoil in their lives. Because this is their nature, it's very hard to change them from this course.

FRIENDS AND LOVERS Relationships can be the defining matter in the lives of September 9 people. Only through their associations with others can these individuals learn how to be easier on themselves.

They also possess a strong love nature. They love deeply yet can often be fooled by someone with false motives. Their own great need for truthfulness in a relationship can cause them to be naive and overly trusting, though after one such disappointment they're likely to look at things in a new light.

CHILDREN AND FAMILY People born on this date often experience a falling-out with family members at quite an early age. This may be due to a lack of real love and affection shown to them by parents, or perhaps the family situation itself underwent radical, upsetting changes during their growing-up years.

September 9 men and woman often forge an extraordinary closeness with their own children. They make good parents, and are likely to learn more from their little ones than the children learn from them.

HEALTH These men and women usually lead an active lifestyle that makes it unnecessary for them to maintain a regular workout schedule. Yet true to their demands, they are likely to be involved in some sort of fitness program. September 9 people never believe that what they do is good enough.

September 9 individuals are often prone to sprains or muscle pulls suffered while working out. They may also experience tension headaches as a result of their hectic schedule.

CAREER AND FINANCES The men and women born on this date are doers, achievers. They don't wait for opportunity to knock on their proverbial door, but instead go out and seize it. This approach confirms their "type A" behavior. To them, there is no such thing as second place. There is only winning.

This all or nothing attitude has burnout written all over it. Although these people are capable of great achievement, they need to learn how to slow down. What good is their success if they are too engrossed in the competition of day-to-day life to enjoy it?

DREAMS AND GOALS September 9 people have definite ideas about what they want to achieve. Often their goals are not seen in detail but through the haze of their ambition. Once they begin to realize that they can still do all the things they want to do but without the perfectionist attitude, September 9 men and women will be on the road to happiness. These individuals need to learn that their goals should be spiritual as well as material.

EMBRACE
Virtue
Calm
A nurturing spirit

AVOID
Bickering
Scheming
Undue pride

ALSO BORN TODAY
Figure-skating champion John Curry; actor Michael Keaton; actress Sylvia Miles; musician Dave Stewart; actor Cliff Robertson; comedian Adam Sandler; novelist Leo Tolstoy; novelist Phyllis Whitney.

SEPTEMBER 10

The men and women born on September 10 have great personal flair and showy talent. They possess the ability to project their inner self through personality, giving them unique magnetism and charisma.

These individuals prize the intangible things in life, such as relationships, integrity, and learning. Although they may have difficulty reconciling the disparate sides of their nature, these men and women have a winning personality that makes them incredibly appealing to others.

FRIENDS AND LOVERS
Regardless of how many friends September 10 natives have, they inevitably look to themselves for answers. These people keep their own counsel and are likely to view friends from a social, rather than an intimate, perspective.

Because of their somewhat competitive nature, September 10 men and women are emotionally combative lovers. It may be a long time before they find the perfect mate, and in the interim they're likely to fall in love many times.

CHILDREN AND FAMILY
The people born on this date have a deeply nurturing spirit. They have a real belief in the traditions of family life and may even imbue it with a magic and specialness it does not possess.

As parents, they are forced to confront their unreality of their positive nature, which can be jarring. Yet, once they begin to feel more at home with a more pragmatic life-view, September 10 people can actually benefit from the experience.

HEALTH
These folks never do anything by half measures. If they are fitness-conscious, they're likely to go to extremes. If they're unconcerned about keeping fit, they may become actually indolent.

The one thing that can prompt these people to take care of themselves is a scary brush with mortality. Even a minor illness or ailment can cause them to reevaluate their attitudes.

CAREER AND FINANCES
For September 10 natives, the name of the game is style. Whatever they do, they have the ability to dazzle the eye and engage the senses. Sales, advertising, and retail management are good careers for these people.

Money management is quite another thing. Although intelligent, September 10 men and women are not particularly good at taking care of money. This is probably because it's impossible for them to separate their emotional reaction to it from the more common-sense concerns of budgets and investments.

DREAMS AND GOALS
People born on this day may not have clearly defined goals. The trip to their destination is likely to interest them more than the destination itself. Along the way, they become infatuated with many dreams, but often discard them just as quickly.

Once they find a goal that enthralls them, September 10 men and women give it their all. These people give new meaning to the word "enthusiasm."

EMBRACE
True motives
Authenticity
Psychic sensitivity

AVOID
Fear of change
Making demands
Irrational choices

ALSO BORN TODAY
Singer Jose Feliciano; actor Colin Firth; fashion designer Karl Lagerfeld; actress Amy Irving; journalist Charles Kuralt; baseball star Roger Maris; fashion designer Elsa Schiaparelli; actress Fay Wray.

SEPTEMBER 11

Folks born on this day need to believe in a cause or a mission in life. They may seem excessively emotional, yet they're actually very centered people who know exactly where they want to go in life and what they wish to accomplish.

Because their belief in themselves is generally strong and and unwavering, these men and women have the ability to withstand even the harshest forms of criticism.

FRIENDS AND LOVERS September 11 individuals will go to extremes in order to make their loved ones happy and secure. They possess an extraordinary sense of loyalty toward their friends, and consider them to be as close as family. Friends represent a strong support system for these people.

Love is a serious matter, as well. They are extremely concerned and sympathetic to the needs of their life mate, and for this reason make wonderful partners. These people are dedicated to the relationship and will go to great lengths to keep it healthy and meaningful.

CHILDREN AND FAMILY September 11 people enjoy the emotional comfort that comes from a large and happy family. These folks are traditionalists who are likely to want to re-create the style and tone of their own upbringing.

As parents, these men and women are extremely conscientious. They strike a good bal-ance between discipline and liberality; if they must punish a child, they are quick to show affection and respect afterward.

HEALTH September 11 individuals have amazing stamina and emotional endurance. Even when slight in build, these people are strong and youthful—even into old age.

Surprisingly, these folks do very little to maintain their good health, except the habit of moderation. They aren't big eaters and may often lose their appetite when under a great deal of stress. They generally prefer sports like swimming, tennis, or golf.

CAREER AND FINANCES People born on this date often enjoy working behind the scenes. They don't like to feel as if they are on display, and may have difficulty dealing directly with the public. Quiet, reserved, and typically well-educated, September 11 natives prefer the library or the laboratory to a crowded office. They work well with others, but feel most confident on their own.

Since they generally have rather modest needs and wants, they aren't concerned about maintaining a certain type of lifestyle. They make their lifestyle work whatever their economic situation.

DREAMS AND GOALS September 11 men and women want to be remembered. This may be through their relationships, or perhaps something more tangible like a poem, a book, or a painting.

Although not driven to succeed, September 11 men and women take each goal, one at a time, and quietly achieve it. They are sensible enough to realize that in order to make certain dreams come true, they must make sacrifices. Yet they never put their goals ahead of the people who are important to them.

EMBRACE
Artistic expression
A generous heart
Positive energy

AVOID
Temptations
Ambition
Dependence

ALSO BORN TODAY
Football coach Paul "Bear" Bryant; football coach Tom Landry; novelist D. H. Lawrence; actor Herbert Lom; singer Harry Connick, Jr.; actress Virginia Madsen; film director Brian De Palma; actress Kristy McNichol.

SEPTEMBER 12

People born on this date are much more jovial and relaxed than the typical Virgo individual. They are naturally happy, and habitually look on the bright side of things. Nothing gets these men and women down for very long. Whatever comes their way, they've got a smile and a parable to explain away the bad times.

September 12 natives seek to put their resources to work in helping others. Whether they possess a great deal of material wealth or only a nominal amount, they always find a way to give something to an individual who has less.

FRIENDS AND LOVERS

Friends are one of the most important factors in the lives of September 12 individuals. These people draw a great deal of inspiration from their pals, and may in turn serve as a counselor or confidante.

It is far more difficult for September 12 natives to trust a lover than a friend. These generally good-natured men and women have a hard time putting their happiness at risk, especially since they may have experienced more than their share of heartbreak in the past.

CHILDREN AND FAMILY

Even if they did not experience a particularly pleasant childhood, September 12 people have a fondness for remembering their youth. These optimistic individuals are likely to rewrite their upbringing in order to create a reality that reinforces their emotional needs.

They are more consistent in their own role as parents. These men and women often become parents quite late in life, and are able to draw upon a lifetime of experience in other relationships. They encourage the hopes and goals of their youngsters—so much so that they are often far too indulgent.

HEALTH

People born on this date need to watch out for health problems brought on by their love of indulgence. They enjoy all the good things that life has to offer, including excellent food and drink. They love the social atmosphere of fine restaurants, and may be especially partial to sweet desserts.

As long as they keep active, they'll have no trouble remaining healthy.

CAREER AND FINANCES

The men and women born on September 12 do not believe in setting limits on what they can accomplish. They are adamant about making their mark in life. Their career aspirations are often strengthened by the conviction that they have been "called" to follow a particular path.

Although money is not usually a deciding factor in choice of career, September 12 natives are eager to make a good life for themselves. They have a talent for working with money, and are exceptional accountants, bank employees, and investment counselors.

DREAMS AND GOALS

Getting to the top of the ladder is a common desire of people born on this date. But instead of being motivated strictly by self-interest, these men and women truly want to make a difference in the lives of others.

For this reason they often involve themselves in humanitarian issues.

EMBRACE
Originality
Imaginative people
Accountability

AVOID
Showing off
Need for constant approval
Personal fulfillment at the expense of
    others

ALSO BORN TODAY
Musician Barry Andrews; British politician Herbert Asquith; singer Tony Bellamy; actor Maurice Chevalier; singer/songwriter Barry White; actress Linda Gray; actor Peter Scolari.

SEPTEMBER 13

Men and women born on this date are style setters in their own way. They have a cool and collected attitude that marks them as winners. Their ability to make others feel comfortable and confident in any social situation is indicative of their natural talent as hosts or hostesses.

These folks do not typify the usual Virgo traits of caution and conservatism; they're more likely to walk on the wild side.

FRIENDS AND LOVERS
Loners by temperament, September 13 individuals have the need to surround themselves with quirky, interesting people. They don't generally encourage intimate friendships, but prefer just "hanging out" with a group of people whose company they enjoy.

They have similar taste in romantic partners, favoring people who have a sense of their own power and specialness. Yet they often find true happiness with someone who is quite different.

CHILDREN AND FAMILY
People born on this date are often diametrically opposed to the attitudes they grew up with. This life-view usually makes it hard for them to stay on good terms with family members.

September 13 men and women aren't drawn to parenthood. They feel uncomfortable giving instruction to anyone, and the idea of molding the character of a child from birth is hard for them to appreciate. Those September

13 people who do become parents are likely to depend on a spouse to maintain discipline.

HEALTH
People born on this date are high-strung and nervous. They may suffer from chronic tension headaches, and often wake up repeatedly throughout the night. Lack of sleep can have a cumulative bad effect upon their health.

In order to create a sense of calm that will allow them to fall asleep and stay asleep, September 13 natives need to restrict certain habits, such as playing video games or watching TV just before bedtime. The worst thing these people can do is have a television or computer in their bedroom!

CAREER AND FINANCES
People born on this date often choose unusual occupations or professions. They have absolutely no patience for status, and select their life's work with no thought of it. It's not uncommon for a college-educated September 13 person to spend years working at a job that requires only a fraction of their educational background or abilities, simply because they enjoy the work.

These men and women are uninterested in money, though they have a tendency to spend heavily at times. They may have a penchant for games of chance but should avoid this potentially destructive pastime.

DREAMS AND GOALS
The men and women born on this date change their goals almost as often as they change jobs. They have an overall sense of what they want to accomplish, yet their plans may be indefinite.

September 13 natives are happiest when left to pursue the lifestyle they feel is right for them. They prize independence, originality, and the ability to be themselves in any social or personal situation.

EMBRACE
Irony
High energy
Personal choice

AVOID
Conceit
Envy
Being overly sensitive

ALSO BORN TODAY
Actress Barbara Bain; author Roald Dahl; actress Jacqueline Bisset; B-movie actress Luma Driscoll; actress Nell Carter; author J. B. Priestley; singer Mel Torme; actress Claudette Colbert; pianist Clara Schumann.

SEPTEMBER 14

People born on September 14 embody the true spirit of Virgo perfectionism and criticism. They have extraordinarily high standards and refuse to settle for second-best. These complex and seemingly demanding men and women can be difficult to live with, but no one can doubt their sincerity.

September 14 individuals have a humanitarian streak and always like to feel as if they are making an important contribution to society through their work or life-efforts.

FRIENDS AND LOVERS
People born on this date don't ask a lot of their friends, but they do expect the same level of loyalty and concern they are willing to give. Friendship is not just a simple exercise in social involvement to these people. It is a real and serious commitment.

These men and women are equally steadfast in their romantic relationships. They are not interested in superficial charms or endearments. They want to hear the truth from their lover or mate. When these people decide to get married, they are completely secure about their decision.

CHILDREN AND FAMILY
Family life makes many demands upon September 14 people. Because they are concerned about doing the right thing, they often find themselves in a position where other family members are able to take advantage of them.

September 14 individuals are judicious parents. They are very concerned with teaching their children ethical behavior and a sense of obligation to others.

HEALTH
People born on this date are preoccupied with health and fitness matters. But while they are likely to epitomize good health,

they are constantly worried about it. Like many Virgo natives, they fear the unknown and may be emotionally torn between following a conventional or holistic regimen.

September 14 people believe in keeping fit. They usually favor a varied routine that includes aerobic and isometric exercise. They eat sparingly and are often vegetarians.

CAREER AND FINANCES
September 14 individuals have many talents. Because they are dedicated and professional, they do their jobs well and go to great lengths to be valuable to whichever company employs them. Once in a while these individuals wonder what it would be like to have their own business, though they may lack the confidence to strike out on their own.

These men and women may not have a very broad scope when it comes to money. If they invest, their instincts are likely to be good, if narrow.

DREAMS AND GOALS
September 14 individuals believe in doing a good job. They constantly aspire to perfection and feel insecure about their efforts if they fall short of that mark.

One of their goals is to harmonically balance the professional and personal sides of their lives. This is a difficult achievement, yet the people born on this date try hard to make it possible.

EMBRACE
Ambition
Crusading spirit
Vitality

AVOID
Stubbornness
Fear of commitment
Stress

ALSO BORN TODAY
Musician Peter Agnew; actress Faith Ford; feminist Kate Millet; singer/dancer/actress Joey Heatherton; actor/director Walter Koenig; actor Sam Neill; writer Larry Collins; actor Nicol Williamson.

199

SEPTEMBER 15

People born on this date have a natural talent for communicating with others. These affable individuals are scrupulously truthful, yet they need to find a personal dream world that allows them an escape from the harshness of reality.

Even though these men and women believe in putting their reputation on the line for a good cause, they are in no way controversial. They have a sensitive nature that may be obscured by a sparkling personality.

FRIENDS AND LOVERS
People born on this date enjoy meeting friends in social situations. They have a real love for people and can get along with almost anyone, as long as the relationship doesn't go too deep.

September 15 natives are romantic idealists who often choose their love interests superficially. They like to surround themselves with attractive, witty people who can make them laugh and feel good about themselves, yet when they meet their soul mate they are often surprised to find that this person in no way jibes with their "ideal."

CHILDREN AND FAMILY
Family life has a generally positive effect on the lives of September 15 men and women. These people are relationship-oriented and are likely to protect their family associations despite the personality differences they may have with particular members. September 15 people are likely to enjoy a close and rewarding relationship with siblings.

These men and women often "find" themselves spiritually when they have children. The ability to make their lives over again through raising a child has a wonderful effect on them.

HEALTH
People born on this date have a tendency to be ruled by their appetites. It's very hard for them to say "no" to their desires, and for this reason they may experience some self-created health problems. They enjoy good food, and have a tendency to put on weight once they reach middle age.

It takes a powerful motivation to get September 15 people to commit to something physical, since they are not exactly physical fireballs. However, once they experience the energizing effect of physical activity, they are sure to lock into better habits.

CAREER AND FINANCES
September 15 individuals are immensely talented, usually in an artistic way. Their ability to get along with people and to communicate on many different levels makes them good teachers, media consultants, therapists, and marriage counselors.

People born on this date have feelings of insecurity—generally unfounded—about their ability to handle money.

DREAMS AND GOALS
September 15 natives enjoy being in the spotlight and may chase that dream during adolescence and early adulthood. Once they begin to make a place for themselves in the world, however, their priorities and habits change. They begin to understand that the best goals are spiritual.

People born on this date want to understand their deepest motivations. In order to do so they must risk exploring their inner landscape.

EMBRACE
Vitality
Focus
Emotional security

AVOID
Inflexibility
Being judgmental
Pleasure-seeking

ALSO BORN TODAY
Novelist Agatha Christie; England's Prince Harry; actor Tommy Lee Jones; actress Margaret Lockwood; film director Oliver Stone; U.S. President William Howard Taft; film director Jean Renoir; symphony conductor Bruno Walter.

SEPTEMBER 16

September 16 individuals have a deeply spiritual nature that sustains them in times of trouble and confusion. Although these men and women tend to be very "together," they seem vulnerable, even fragile, to their acquaintances.

People born on this date are often deeply religious. This is not merely a hold-over from their childhood teachings, but a real and true belief that defines the way they look at the world around them, and life in general.

FRIENDS AND LOVERS To the men and women born on this date, relationships are an art. These people learn a great deal about themselves through their close associations with others, and usually grow spiritually as a result.

The love lives of September 16 people can be complicated. They look for perfection and commitment, and may have difficulty finding either, let alone both. When they do connect with a special someone, they usually find their lives transformed.

CHILDREN AND FAMILY The past may be a sensitive subject for these men and women. They may have experienced a great deal of indifference as children, or did not receive the guidance they needed in order to take them through the perilous route through childhood and adolescence.

September 16 individuals may overcompensate for what they did not receive as children, doting on their little ones to excess. Usually, though, the men and women born on this date see their mistake early and change their behavior accordingly.

HEALTH September 16 natives are generally unconcerned about their health. Like many people, they take it for granted until something goes wrong, and then they search for answers from a spiritual as well as physical perspective.

These men and woman can benefit from learning techniques of creative visualization, which allows them to bring positive energy into their lives.

CAREER AND FINANCES September 16 natives can never be happy in a profession that brings money and nothing else. They need to feel as if their work contributes something valuable to themselves and to others. For this reason, they often look to the caring professions: medicine, social work, therapy.

September 16 men and women don't expect to make a lot of money from their work. It's not uncommon for these folks to come from a somewhat privileged background, which they reject in order to live meaningfully.

DREAMS AND GOALS To September 16 people it's never about winning—it's about making a cherished dream come true. These people are not generally competitive, preferring to score a personal best rather than a victory over someone else.

They believe in the completeness of their acts. They want to savor the essence of their accomplishments, not simply applaud the end result. Once they have garnered the life experience required in order to understand their drives and needs, these people can count every positive move forward as a goal achieved.

EMBRACE
Intuition
Imagination
Determination to succeed

AVOID
Instability
Unrequited love
Solitude

ALSO BORN TODAY
Actress Lauren Bacall; magician David Copperfield; actor Peter Falk; actress Anne Francis; TV personality Allen Funt; baseball player Orel Hershiser; musician B. B. King; novelist John Knowles.

SEPTEMBER 17

September 17 natives are fighters and survivors who do not understand the concept of giving up. These men and women take life very seriously, approaching each obstacle in their path like a challenge.

It's sometimes said that these men and woman are old in youth and youthful in old age. They have real grit and remain true to their ideals no matter what.

FRIENDS AND LOVERS
People born on this date are loyal and steadfast, and expect their friends to be the same way. They enjoy, but do not overvalue, the social aspects of friendship; what really matters to them are the strong ties and intimacies friendship forges.

The men and women born on this date often find disappointment in their romantic choices, especially those made early in life. Once they begin to realize that everyone does not possess their high standards, they are more likely to find someone who fits into their romantic scheme of things. Because September 17 people support the status quo, marriage is very much a part of the picture for them.

CHILDREN AND FAMILY
One of the reasons September 17 men and women wear a serious face is because they were forced to shoulder immense responsibilities in their youth. For some, there may have been virtually no childhood at all. While this generally helps to mold their character in a positive way, it can also lead to an unrealistic sense of responsibility, as well as a lifelong feeling of being deprived.

September 17 parents are quite strict with their children, yet they know the value of showing affection. These people want their youngsters to experience childhood in a way they themselves never could.

HEALTH
September 17 men and women are usually quite healthy. They may require calcium supplements to guard against bone loss in middle age, but a program of weight-bearing exercise usually helps to keep them in good shape.

People born on this date are not big eaters; in fact, they may be constantly dieting to keep themselves slim.

CAREER AND FINANCES
September 17 natives like being in charge. This isn't a power trip, but merely an invocation of their very best qualities. They have a quiet, reassuring presence that's helpful in giving those under them a sense of confidence.

People born on this date are concerned about making a good living. They are very concentrated on security and have a real talent for making smart investment decisions. These people have a good chance of achieving financial success at an early age.

DREAMS AND GOALS
The men and women born on this date have an instinct for making the right move at the right time. They do not expect their success to come overnight.

September 17 individuals have the patience to wait for their moment in the sun. They have remarkable resilience in the face of disappointment.

EMBRACE
Good examples
Understanding
Spiritual riches

AVOID
Possessiveness
Superficial relationships
Fatalism

ALSO BORN TODAY
Actress Anne Bancroft; Supreme Court Justice Warren Burger; U.S. Senator Sam Ervin; actor Roddy McDowall; "Elvira" personality Cassandra Peterson; actor John Ritter; novelist Mary Stewart; country singer Hank Williams.

SEPTEMBER 18

People born on this date have great self-control, and an ability to use their energies for valuable achievement. They are dedicated to self-sufficiency, and don't like to rely on others.

September 18 people are serious and mysterious, and go about their lives with quiet precision. They have an inability to trust all but those closest to them, and may discreetly promote themselves as enigmatic, even eccentric.

FRIENDS AND LOVERS Although they sometimes seem emotionally cold, September 18 men and women are actually quite shy. They prefer to keep their own counsel, yet when they discover someone they can trust, they're immensely grateful to have a confidante.

In love relationships, September 18 people can appear illusive and glamorous to others. This "mask" is really nothing more than a way to hold something of themselves in reserve until they find the perfect person to whom they can reveal their true self.

CHILDREN AND FAMILY September 18 people often experience disappointment in youth, which springs from strained family relationships. Because they keep their feelings to themselves, it may not be evident to others just how deeply they have been hurt. Often it is not until later in life that September 18 people are able to confront family members with their feelings.

The men and women born on this date are sometimes tentative about becoming parents, fearful that they will repeat the mistakes that hurt them. If they do choose to have children, they try very hard to give their youngsters extra affection.

HEALTH September 18 natives are nearly fanatical about their health and fitness. They tend to follow a very strict routine that includes aerobic exercise and a sensible eating plan.

People born on this day have a great deal of nervous energy that needs to be channeled in a positive way. A hobby that is both enjoyable and relaxing can help them shift their focus from the stressful aspects of life to those with a calming effect.

CAREER AND FINANCES People born on this date are happiest when they can do their work in private, without the constant interference of a boss or supervisor. Because they have such a strong work ethic and good work habits, they do very well working as their own boss, or in a freelance capacity.

Although September 18 people may have problems with the big financial picture, they have very careful habits that can lead to financial security at a very early age.

DREAMS AND GOALS People born on this date usually have academic goals in youth that later blossom into career plans. These men and women know how to budget their time, and understand how to put all of their intellectual and spiritual resources into getting what they want out of life.

September 18 people sometimes struggle to make their personal life goals materialize until late in life, when they can finally turn their attention from career responsibilities.

EMBRACE
Emotional equilibrium
A love of nature
Laughter

AVOID
Passivity
Deception
Secrecy

ALSO BORN TODAY
Singer Frankie Avalon; actor Robert Blake; Renaissance personality Cesare Borgia; film actor Rossano Brazzi; film director Jack Cardiff; dancer Agnes de Mille; actress Greta Garbo; astrologer Walter Koch.

SEPTEMBER 19

ew people possess the charming personality and physical elegance of September 19 natives. They are elegant, classy individuals who always make a good appearance. Although they like being the center of attention, they can never be called egotists.

September 19 people are lifelong students who never lose interest in the mystery and beauty of life.

FRIENDS AND LOVERS September 19 people are generally loners, but they do rely on the judgment and advice of a few close friends. They have the ability to inspire considerable loyalty in their friends. These men and women have the potential to be good mentors to their young friends.

These folks exhibit great discretion when they select a lover or mate. Oddly, love may have very little to do with their choice, since they have very specific ideas of what they want in a partner.

CHILDREN AND FAMILY Family life is an important factor in the emotional life of September 19 people. They are extremely devoted to family members, and may count them among their closest friends. They may be especially close to a sibling or twin.

September 19 individuals make excellent parents because they have the ability to transcend the parental role and treat their children with the sensitivity of a close friend or peer. These men and women remember what it was like to be child, full of questions and worries about their place in the world.

HEALTH Good managers by nature, September 19 people are on top of health matters. They are extremely well disciplined and have no problem staying with a structured routine. These men and women benefit from moderate aerobic exercise.

People born on this date often maintain a restricted diet. They do not have large appetites so it's not difficult for them to banish things like sugar, white flour, or caffeine from their diets.

CAREER AND FINANCES September 19 men and women have a gift for organization. They are methodical, correct, and precise in whatever work they do, and are especially good at handling details. They're specialists who find meaning through their own areas of expertise. Because of their attention to grooming and natural good looks, September 19 people may choose a career in modeling or elsewhere in the public eye.

People born on this date are very careful with money but do not always trust their own judgment. For this reason they may look to a professional for advice on savings and investments.

DREAMS AND GOALS September 19 people are very concerned about appearances. They always take great care in how they present themselves, both physically and in the general tenor of their actions, so that what people see is a sleek and refined package.

If their vulnerabilities can be overcome through experience, these men and women can accomplish anything they wish. Their ability to believe in themselves is the key factor.

EMBRACE
Excellence
Innocence
A generous spirit

AVOID
Aloofness
Isolation
Excessive practicality

ALSO BORN TODAY
Singer Cass Elliot; novelist William Golding; actor Jeremy Irons; actor David McCallum; fashion designer Zandra Rhodes; model Twiggy; actor Adam West.

SEPTEMBER 20

People born on this date are the ultimate professionals in all they do. Practical and organized, they participate actively in life. These people are "doers," not "watchers."

September 20 natives are so frank and earnest about achieving their desires that they may appear to be opportunistic, but they're just being honest about their feelings. These men and women possess exquisite manners and impeccable good taste.

FRIENDS AND LOVERS September 20 individuals may have a large circle of friends but they are too canny and wise to trust anyone but those closest to them. Someone in their background may have breached their trust at one time, making them insecure about confiding their deepest feelings.

These people are highly sexual but they never allow that predilection to dominate their choice of a mate. Rather, they appreciate the partnership aspects of marriage that go beyond mere sexual attraction. Once in a committed relationship, they make every effort to keep it exciting.

CHILDREN AND FAMILY September 20 people are able to extract the very best of their background and use it to their advantage as adults. No matter what kind of upbringing they experienced as a child, they have the ability to transcend its limitations.

These men and women can be very exacting and demanding parents to their own children, but for good reason. They dislike spoiled kids and want their own little ones to develop good habits and proper behavior at an early age.

HEALTH September 20 men and women are the picture of health. They have a practical approach to fitness, which makes their habits a part of everyday life rather than a separate experience. Being careful about their diet is second nature to these disciplined individuals. They enjoy food—healthy food—and may be talented cooks.

These men and women understand the need to combine both the physical and spiritual aspects of good health. Meditation allows them to relax from the stress of daily life and also keeps them feeling and looking youthful.

CAREER AND FINANCES September 20 people are career-oriented, and may train for many years to perfect their professional skills. They have no problem adhering to the ritual of repetition and can seem to keep their interest in a project no matter how much of their time and effort it consumes.

People born on this date have remarkable money sense. Although they can operate on a very tight budget, these people want a lot more out of life than a regular salary can provide.

DREAMS AND GOALS People born on this date often put their plans into action early in life. They see achievement as a long process.

September 20 men and women show amazing single-mindedness about goals. They will gladly sacrifice their social lives, and even their personal lives, in order to make their dreams come true.

EMBRACE
Education
Recognition
Questioning authority

AVOID
Blunt speech
Emotional bullying
Disapproval

ALSO BORN TODAY
Basketball coach Red Auerbach; psychologist Dr. Joyce Brothers; fashion designer James Galanos; hockey star Guy Lafleur; actress Sophia Loren; composer John Dankworth; actress Anne Meara; actor Kenneth More.

SEPTEMBER 21

September 21 people are quiet and personable. They may be extraordinarily shy in youth, but sooner or later they learn to overcome this trait. Once they blossom, these men and women are really something special.

They have a tremendous fear of failure, and for this reason they may sometimes hold back their enthusiasm and sense of commitment. The ability to cross that divide is a real stretch for them, but when they make it they empower themselves as never before.

FRIENDS AND LOVERS Friendship is a vital component in the lives of September 21 natives. They need the external validation of people they trust, and yearn also for companionship that is uncritical and supportive.

In romantic relationships, these men and women also look for acceptance. They expect their own loyalty and thoughtfulness to be reciprocated, and feel left out of a relationship that fails to provide this kind of emotional support. These individuals value closeness on all levels. They do everything they can to keep the romance alive in their marriage or partnership.

CHILDREN AND FAMILY September 21 natives may have a great deal of emotional baggage left over from their childhood. These people do not readily show their feelings, and may have a hard time putting away painful memories from the past. To come to grips with the truth about relationships with family members can be difficult for them. September 21 men and women make loving parents who are not afraid to show their children just how much they are valued as individuals.

HEALTH Although possessed of a certain fastidiousness, September 21 people need to be reminded about taking care of their health on a daily basis. Dealing with stress can be a real struggle for them. Meditation and prayer can help, but these folks must also watch their diets. Spicy foods and caffeine bollix up their digestion and should be avoided whenever possible.

Moderate exercise practiced at least four times a week has the ability to quiet the anxieties of these individuals, and improve their sleep states.

CAREER AND FINANCES September 21 people value career choices that give them the chance to put their intelligence and creativity to work. These men and women are perfectionists who will labor over a project to make certain all the proverbial "tees" have been crossed.

People born on this date have a taste for the good life, but they rarely let it get in the way of making sound financial decisions.

DREAMS AND GOALS The most cherished goal of September 21 people is to give their family the emotional and financial security they need. If they can do this they feel free to concentrate on goals related to their professional status. These men and women are deceptively ambitious, and often begin to plot their career plans very early in life.

September 21 people may have a hard time finding their proper niche in life, but once they do they set themselves on a path that will take them anywhere they wish to go.

EMBRACE
Spiritual fulfillment
Ethics
Modesty

AVOID
Procrastination
Easy answers
Self-indulgence

ALSO BORN TODAY
Singer/songwriter Leonard Cohen; composer/astrologer Gustav Holst; novelist Stephen King; TV personality Ricki Lake; actor Rob Morrow; comedian Bill Murray; actress Catherine Oxenberg; novelist H. G. Wells.

SEPTEMBER 22

People born on September 22 have a powerful personality that exerts considerable influence over others. Although they may be drawn to scholarly pursuits, they almost always find themselves in demand to fulfill more worldly aims.

September 22 men and women are brainy individuals who have the potential to deflate the pomposity of others with their razor-sharp wit and critical opinions. They present a stylish, even elegant appearance.

FRIENDS AND LOVERS
Whoever becomes friends with September 22 people learns very early that these people expect complete and utter loyalty. Any breach of this can end the friendship. It is precisely because September 22 men and women are so demanding that they exert such a strong influence over others.

People born on this date have very little flexibility in personal relationships. They don't want any surprises in this aspect of life. The person they settle down with had better divulge any potentially damaging secrets early in the relationship, or it's unlikely to last.

CHILDREN AND FAMILY
September 22 people are loners who may not fit in comfortably with their birth family. For this reason, in adolescence they often seek out emotional surrogates to fulfill their need for family. Teachers, mentors, and friends may be taken into their confidence more regularly than parents or siblings.

Because of their own attitudes, September 22 men and women give their children great latitude. They understand the need of youngsters to find their own way of doing things, their own method of determining status. They seek to give their children many choices, not just the ones they favor—and are sufficiently broad-minded to live with the consequences.

HEALTH
People born on this date are a study in extremes. At times they are enthusiastic supporters of a healthful lifestyle, only to fall back on bad habits at other times. They favor New Age wisdom, yet they may not always practice what they preach.

One of the worse things these September 22 natives can do is pursue a "perfect" image of themselves. A simple exercise regimen and good eating habits will suffice to keep them healthy. Trying to make themselves into something they're not is foolish and doomed to failure.

CAREER AND FINANCES
September 22 people are often drawn to social or political activism as a means to display their humanitarian consciousness. They are unfailingly attracted to a crisis atmosphere and may seek out careers that put them in dangerous circumstances from time to time.

These men and women like to live on the edge, and their behavior with money expresses this attitude.

DREAMS AND GOALS
Those born on this date enjoy being singled out by fate. A situation may be good or bad, but they are more concerned with the potential magnitude of things than the ultimate consequences.

September 22 individuals like to be at the center of activity. At one time or another they will feel the need to explore the wide world.

EMBRACE
Graciousness
Setting an example
Knowledge

AVOID
Shiftlessness
Abandonment issues
A need for validation

ALSO BORN TODAY
Figure skating champion Tai Babilonia; actress Shari Belafonte; singer Joan Jett; baseball manager Tommy Lasorda; actor Paul LeMat; novelist Rosamunde Pilcher; film director Erich von Stroheim; novelist Fay Weldon.

LIBRA
September 23 - October 22

Libra is the seventh sign of the astrological year and is known by its astrological symbol, the Scales. Libra individuals are artistic, affectionate, and refined. With Venus as the ruling planet, people born under this sign are considered to be attractive and fashion-conscious. They seek peace and joy through personal and professional relationships.

THE LIBRA MAN When it comes to charm, there is no one more appealing than a Libra man. He is often the handsome tough-guy type, masculine but with a rare sensitivity that makes him utterly irresistible. The typical Libra man doesn't need to show off his manliness, because he is quite secure about who he is.

Men born under this sign are often drawn to artistic and creative careers. They usually marry, often at a very young age, because Libra is the sign of partnership and, indeed, these individuals seek permanency. Because they are generally good-natured and accommodating, Libra men are happy to do their share of household chores. They are enthusiastic about their spouse's career and willingly support her projects and interests with vigor and pride.

THE LIBRA WOMAN Because she is usually so attractive and charming, it is sometimes difficult for men to appreciate the talents and intellect of the typical Libra woman. In many ways she is the most feminine of all the zodiacal types. It has been said that although she thinks like a man, she reasons like a woman.

Women born under this sign have a natural ability to make relationships work. Even though they are extremely self-sufficient, they are not happy alone and usually have a permanent partner in their lives. The Libra woman is supportive of her spouse and is a great inspiration to him.

THE LIBRA CHILD Libra children are naturally sweet and obedient. In fact, these boys and girls may seem too good to be true. Even on rare occasions when their behavior is rebellious or aggressive, they are more well-mannered than other children. These sugar-and-spice little ones are often the "favorite" of family members, relatives, and teachers because they're too sweet to resist.

Adolescence brings big changes, and this is often the first time that the placid Libra child becomes difficult to handle. These youngsters usually manage to retain their lovableness, but their freedom-loving nature often draws them into the center of controversy.

THE LIBRA LOVER Libra men and women are the most romantic people among the zodiacal types. Venus-ruled, they have an idealistic view of love and togetherness. They are extremely relationship-oriented. Once these people fall in love, they start thinking in terms of marriage.

There is a strong sentimental coloring to the way Libra individuals look at romance. They have a storybook or Hollywood view, always with an eye to a happy ending. Libras don't enjoy romantic suffering. Whenever they are disappointed in a relationship, a Libra man or woman will spend a little time grieving, and then move on to another, hopefully more successful partnership.

THE LIBRA BOSS Fairness and impartiality are the hallmarks of the Libra boss. This individual never demands more than he or she is prepared to give, and is sensitive to the needs of employees. Although they want to be respected in their professional capacity, Libra bosses also have a need to be liked. This is something particular to Libras—they simply cannot bear to have people think ill of them.

The typical Libra boss can draw upon his or her impressive relationship skills in order to get along with employees; they're particularly adept at acting as a mediator between argumentative workers. The Libra boss's keen sense of justice informs the decisions he or she makes after determining who is a good worker and who's "faking it."

ELEMENT: Air
QUALITY: Cardinal
PLANETARY RULER: Venus
BIRTHSTONE: Opal
FLOWER: Pink rose
COLOR: Pale pink

KEY CHARACTERISTIC:
Harmony

STRENGTHS:
Diplomacy, Charm, Love of beauty
CHALLENGES:
Indecision, Narcissism, Superficiality

THE LIBRA FRIEND Because they are very social people, Libras make good friends on many levels. They are pleasant and fun to be with, but they also provide needed emotional support to friends who face problems or life-challenging decisions. Libras are great counselors because they have the ability to weigh the pros and cons of an idea fairly and without bias.

Libras enjoy being surrounded by a lot of people and make excellent hosts or hostesses. They love giving parties for friends and professional associates, and they have a great talent for making people feel at ease. These individuals make friends easily; their lively, outgoing personalities enthrall everyone. Although they may seem superficial at times, anyone who knows these charming men and women understands that they have an intriguingly profound side to their nature.

SEPTEMBER 23

Individuals born on this date are energetic fact-finders who seek answers to life's difficult questions. These highly verbal men and women combine a love of learning with excellent good taste—the hallmark of their sign.

September 23 people manage to project an image of seriousness while still maintaining their personal charm. Although they may seem indecisive, it is simply their nature to weigh all aspects of a question before making a decision.

FRIENDS AND LOVERS

People born on this date have a friendly, outgoing disposition that commands the love and respect of others. Not only do these individuals possess a wonderful sense of social decorum, they also cultivate deeply satisfying friendships.

September 23 folks show the same charm and discretion in love affairs that they exhibit in friendship. They generally look for and appeal to people who share their love of intelligent conversation and friendly banter.

CHILDREN AND FAMILY

September 23 natives retain a superficial attitude toward family life, choosing to remember the best of their upbringing while ignoring events that may not be as pleasant. These men and women have a hard time dealing with complicated familial relationships.

People born on this date need to feel as if they have a harmonious relationship with their own youngsters, and will work hard to accomplish this. This could lead to a lack of discipline on their part, which sends the wrong message to children.

HEALTH

September 23 individuals have an instinct for keeping their lives in perfect balance. They understand the need for moderation in all things and the necessity to combine mind-body-spirit harmony. For them a healthy regimen includes daily exercise, a balanced diet, and frequent periods of meditation or prayer.

These individuals are very concerned with their appearance, but will not sacrifice good health in order to look great.

CAREER AND FINANCES

September 23 men and women cannot work at a job they don't enjoy. These people find fulfillment working in the communications business or in positions that allow them to deal with the public on a daily basis. They require an atmosphere of harmony where the relationships between colleagues are pleasant.

These individuals have good financial habits. They prefer saving money to spending it, and are willing to save for a major purchase rather than using credit. September 23 people understand the value of being thrifty. They clip coupons, look for sales, and often do their holiday shopping year-round.

DREAMS AND GOALS

September 23 people need to speak their minds. They have an opinion about just about everything, although they are in no way controversial.

Because they have orderly minds and fastidious habits, these men and women have an easy time maintaining their focus on achievement. They can work slowly and patiently toward a goal without losing interest along the way. Their accomplishments are sweeter when savored with a partner.

EMBRACE
Permanence
Stability
Attention to detail

AVOID
Irresponsibility
Arguments
Mental exhaustion

ALSO BORN TODAY
Actor Jason Alexander; singer/composer Ray Charles; singer Ben E. King; actress Elizabeth Peña; actress Mary Kay Place; actress Romy Schneider; singer/songwriter Bruce Springsteen; artist/model Suzanne Valadon.

SEPTEMBER 24

People born on this day are dynamic, artistic, and luxury-loving. Possessed of a charming personality and a subtle intelligence, September 24 men and women are far more complicated than they seem to be.

Although their professional achievements provide a great deal of emotional transcendence, these people experience most of their satisfaction— and a great deal of their pain—as a result of personal relationships.

FRIENDS AND LOVERS Despite their charm, September 24 people are difficult to know. They seem to prefer keeping some part of their nature in reserve, fearful that no matter how they are to their friends, those friends may one day grow critical.

The love life of September 24 natives can be tumultuous. Even when they are truly infatuated, these men and women find that the course of true love never runs smoothly. Because of their need for a spiritual as well as romantic partnership, it's difficult for these folks to establish rules in a relationship.

CHILDREN AND FAMILY September 24 people believe in the traditions of family life. They may have grown up in a family situation that lacked total honesty, yet where a superficial spirit of calm prevailed. This is actually in their best interests because they prefer harmony— even the artificial variety—to confrontation of any kind.

People born on this date are loving parents, yet manage to keep a measure of emotional distance between themselves and their youngsters.

HEALTH These individuals have difficulty being moderate in anything, including their health regimen. While they can manage to put their eating habits into perspective—making a few beneficial changes here and there—it's next to impossible for these sedentary individuals to motivate themselves to exercise.

The strongest motivation for these people is their appearance. Because they want to look good, if they feel their slothful habits are interfering with that goal, they can rouse themselves to make important adjustments.

CAREER AND FINANCES September 24 men and women love beauty and harmony in all aspects of their lives and are often drawn to careers that allow them to express this facet of their nature. They have a great deal of creative talent that can be applied to various enterprises such as art, writing, dancing, photography, and fashion design.

Although September 24 people have the ability to make a lot of money, they are often less successful handling it. They are big spenders who often rely far too heavily on credit.

DREAMS AND GOALS In order to achieve the goals they set for themselves, the men and women born on this date must bring their common sense into line with their intelligence. Realizing that they cannot put off their responsibilities until another day forces them to draw upon vast inner resources they often ignore.

September 24 people want the world to value their talents, yet before this can happen they must become accountable to themselves.

EMBRACE
Family values
Personal excellence
Truth

AVOID
Restlessness
Appeasement
Dissatisfaction

ALSO BORN TODAY
Novelist F. Scott Fitzgerald; football star Joe Greene; actor Phil Hartman; puppeteer Jim Henson; singer Gerry Marsden; photographer Linda McCartney; TV sports announcer Jim McKay.

SEPTEMBER 25

September 25 people have a strong sense of personal honor and integrity. These sharply focused individuals expect a great deal of themselves. Opinionated and ethical, they also are highly motivated to achieve success on both a worldly and spiritual level.

And then there's a dark side that few people glimpse. These elegant, self-possessed men and women have a tendency to brood at times. Though lapses are rare, September 25 natives also have a reputation for carrying on clandestine love affairs.

FRIENDS AND LOVERS
September 25 individuals favor a small but select circle of friends. Although they aren't given to confiding in others, they're likely to display their inner feelings through a series of nonverbal clues or actions.

These men and women are often drawn to love affairs that are likely to end unhappily. They are highly romantic individuals who can be drawn into unwise relationships simply because the lure of excitement is too great to resist.

CHILDREN AND FAMILY
People born on this date have a need for emotional closure. For this reason they will seek as adults to mend familial relationships that were unsatisfactory years ago. This is not simply a forgive-and-forget proposition; these men and women genuinely need to understand what went wrong.

September 25 people never allow other areas of their lives to interfere with their parental responsibilities. They are completely dedicated to giving their children a more nurturing home environment than they experienced, and will do whatever it takes to ensure success.

HEALTH
People born on this date are in a constant state of trying to achieve balance in all areas of life, including health matters. They understand the value of exercise and may favor a cross-training approach. They also enjoy competitive sports on the weekends. Yet September 25 individuals understand that unless they also make time for meditation and relaxation they will not achieve the balance they're looking for.

CAREER AND FINANCES
Because September 25 people present a good appearance, they often seek careers that allow them to "show off" their looks. These men and women do very well in modeling, acting, or public relations.

People born on this date have a practical side that allows them to handle money matters well. They are generally more concerned with protecting what they have than attempting to make more, yet they have good instincts for investments.

DREAMS AND GOALS
September 25 individuals are interested in exploring the full spectrum of their own nature. This can be difficult for them because they are sometimes afraid of their own intensity.

These men and women may have to experience some life-milestones before they can truly understand what they are about. Marriage, children, and career changes all help these complicated individuals to define themselves.

EMBRACE
Satisfaction
Self-determination
Progress

AVOID
Limitations
Complicated relationships
Brooding

ALSO BORN TODAY
Symphony conductor Colin Davis; actor Michael Douglas; novelist William Faulkner; actress Heather Locklear; dancer/actress Juliet Prowse; composer Dmitri Shostakovich; actor Will Smith; TV journalist Barbara Walters.

SEPTEMBER 26

September 26 men and women are a study in contrasts and contradictions. They possess a sympathetic nature, yet have a strong will. Self-disciplined and practical, they are extremely romantic and given to periodic flights of fancy.

People born on this date appear reserved, yet they have a wonderful sense of humor that can diffuse any problem or touchy situation. They are self-starters who can set a task for themselves and rely on the results.

FRIENDS AND LOVERS Like most Libra

natives, September 26 individuals may have a large group of friends but only a few who are truly intimate pals. These men and women regard friendship as one of the most important relationship components in their lives.

Romance is serious, not superficial, to these folks. They value a strong partnership that has more going for it than mere physical attraction. September 26 natives look for a mate who is intelligent, funny, and focused. Once they are in a good relationship they will work very hard to maintain it.

CHILDREN AND FAMILY These people

have close relationships with their siblings, who are more like friends than family to them. Although there could be a period of estrangement with parents in early adulthood, September 26 natives always manage to reconcile any disagreements.

The men and women born on this date make excellent parents. They combine an ability to show affection with a genuine interest in being part of a child's world.

HEALTH While many Libra natives motivate

themselves to exercise and watch what they eat because of cosmetic reasons, September 26 men and women are genuinely concerned with health. These people are constantly looking for ways to add years to their life and life to their years.

September 26 people are very strict about their diet. They may have the same weakness for rich, sweet desserts as other Libras, but they have the willpower to resist them.

CAREER AND FINANCES The self-

discipline that so aptly characterizes September 26 people is a great asset to them in career matters. These dedicated men and women have what it takes to persevere in their education or training for a desired job.

Even though September 26 people have a love of luxurious surroundings, they are very careful with money and unwilling to take on more debt than they can realistically handle. Acknowledging the temptation of credit spending, these men and women are likely to limit themselves to cash-only purchases.

DREAMS AND
GOALS People born on

this date are goal-oriented, and work hard to make their dreams come true. Because they are not ambitious in the conventional sense, they are likely to be driven by a variety of motivations, not all of which are personal.

September 26 individuals take pride in a job well done. If they must sacrifice in order to reach a goal, they have the grit to do it, as well as the emotional and spiritual endurance to stay the course.

EMBRACE
Relaxation
Peaceful heart
Temperance

AVOID
Inhibitions
Restrictive measures
False hopes

ALSO BORN TODAY
Poet T. S. Eliot; composer George Gershwin; actress Linda Hamilton; philosopher Martin Heidegger; actress Mary Beth Hurt; singer/actress Julie London; singer Olivia Newton-John; actor George Raft.

SEPTEMBER 27

P eople born on this date see life as a battle to be won. They are determined, scrappy, and much more physically energetic than the average Libra individual.

These men and women live very much on the surface of things, never afraid to show their emotions. While they can seem a bit pugnacious at times, they never lose their sense of fairness. Personality is a big factor in the lives of September 27 people, gaining them recognition where other Libras may be content to fade into the background.

FRIENDS AND LOVERS September 27 natives are adventurous about all their relationships—both romantic and platonic. They pick their friends without trying to match them to their own personality traits and quirks.

In romantic matters September 27 men and women usually take the initiative. They enjoy the chase and aren't anxious to settle down. When they do, they want a mate who shares their enthusiasm and optimistic attitude, who is spontaneous and knows how to have a good time.

CHILDREN AND FAMILY For individuals born on this date, family matters are a complicated amalgam of love and guilt. Despite their independent nature, these people may have a difficult time breaking from the family, especially if there was a lot of turmoil during their growing-up years.

Because of unreconciled issues, September 27 people may opt not to have children of their own. If they do decide to opt for parenthood, they may first need to work out their problems with a therapist.

HEALTH September 27 men and women love good food, but rarely have to worry about it, since they lead an active lifestyle and are likely to burn off extra calories. What isn't as obvious is the fact that although they manage to retain a svelte appearance, these individuals may have negative food issues that date from childhood.

Learning to deal with the guilt and ecstasy that food can bring is a matter requiring professional help. There should be no shame connected with seeking help for this problem.

CAREER AND FINANCES Because of their feisty, outgoing nature, September 27 people often gravitate to careers that showcase their personality. They enjoy meeting the public, especially in jobs that require them to mingle on daily basis. Teaching, sports, and defense or military jobs are generally successful for these individuals.

September 27 people take an active interest in their financial future. These far-seeing men and women may begin saving for their retirement very early in their careers, and always have one eye on investment possibilities.

DREAMS AND GOALS People born on this date seem totally at ease with themselves, yet may have emotional demons that need to be tamed.

Coming to grips with the emotional baggage left over from childhood is part of asserting independence as an adult. September 27 people know this, and will always strive to move beyond any hurt they have suffered.

EMBRACE
Versatility
Fidelity
Imagination

AVOID
Penuriousness
Dogmatism
Mistrusting others

ALSO BORN TODAY
TV journalist Barbara Howar; chemist Adolph Kolbe; actress Jayne Meadows; film director Arthur Penn; violinist Jacques Thibaud; actress Sada Thompson; baseball star Mike Schmidt; dancer Heather Watts.

SEPTEMBER 28

People born on this date love being in the spotlight. They have an effusive, natural charm that they often use to achieve their aims in life. Artistic and sometimes eccentric, these men and women have the ability to communicate fluently via the nonverbal method known universally as "body language."

September 28 people are personality-heavy, and may be considered insincere or frivolous by others, who are jealous of their astonishing appeal.

FRIENDS AND LOVERS September 28 people have the ability to create a cult of admirers, no matter what their personal or professional situation may be. This is the girl who is a natural as homecoming queen; the woman who manages to retain her beauty and femininity while besting her male colleagues at work. The charm level is just as high with men born on this date.

Romantically, September 28 people can have their pick of admirers. This can have a negative or positive effect, depending on the personality of the individual, and his or her level of emotional security.

CHILDREN AND FAMILY September 28 people are generally beloved among family members, adored for their charm and happy disposition. Though there may be considerable sibling rivalry during adolescence, relationships between September 28 people and their brothers and sisters usually straighten out in later years.

People born on this date sometimes have a marginally adversarial relationship with their own children, though this too is likely to be just a transitory matter. Fortunately, these men and women understand that whatever conflict may exist can be smoothed over as long as the parties involved are talking to each other.

HEALTH Although dieting is a way of life for people born on this date, it isn't always done to facilitate good health. September 28 people are very proud of their appearance, and may find themselves drawn to fad diets that promise exciting results. These people are not big on patience, and will always go for the quick fix.

September 28 individuals can benefit from periods of enforced solitude, giving them the opportunity to reflect upon the nature of their lives.

CAREER AND FINANCES Despite the showy persona typical of people born on September 28, these people often look for professional challenges in fields that give them the opportunity to indulge their reflective side. This could mean taking a job behind the scenes, which allows these all-too-visible people to see things from a less lively perspective.

Learning to live within a budget can be a real challenge for these folks, but it's a lesson they need to master.

DREAMS AND GOALS These men and women need to learn persistence and the ability to withstand delays and disappointments. They have a great deal of enthusiasm, but many goals require more than that. When they maintain good work habits and refuse to obsess about how long it takes for a dream to come to fruition, they have already won half the battle.

EMBRACE
Talent
Self-respect
Devotion to duty

AVOID
Narcissism
A fickle heart
Superficial love affairs

ALSO BORN TODAY
Actress Brigitte Bardot; actor Peter Finch; actor Marcello Mastroianni; author/film director John Sayles; poet Stevie Smith; columnist/TV host Ed Sullivan; actor William Windom; singer Moon Unit Zappa.

SEPTEMBER 29

September 29 natives are deeply sensitive people who enjoy keeping secrets. They relate very well to others on a one-to-one basis, but have trouble getting along with them in a larger forum. These men and women have the typical Libra charm, yet may not possess the confidence to exhibit it.

People born on this date are extremely resourceful and have a talent for transcending the limits of circumstance. They value the experience of others and often owe their success to the help of a mentor.

FRIENDS AND LOVERS

These individuals depend upon their friends to help them through difficult times. While they can appreciate the social value of having good companions, they prefer to foster a more meaningful relationship with friends. September 29 people are loyal, and have long memories. Someone who was a close friend in youth is likely to continue to be one throughout their lives.

People born on this date are easily hurt in romantic matters. Their expectations are very high, and if not fulfilled may lead to a broken heart.

CHILDREN AND FAMILY

September 29 natives may find themselves in the position of reclaiming family life after years of emotional estrangement. This could be the result of divorce or some other unhappy circumstance from their childhood.

People born on this date are extremely protective of their own children, often as a result of their own childhood experiences. They may have a hard time allowing their youngsters to have the freedom they require in order to grow emotionally.

HEALTH

September 29 men and women are inconsistent in their health and fitness habits. Emotion is often a factor. They start a regimen with great promise and enthusiasm, only to let it slide when they lose interest.

Like all Librans, people born on this date are partner-oriented, and may do best on a fitness program if they have a buddy. Finding someone who can provide moral support is key. By sharing the experience, September 29 people can better handle the rigors of a diet plan or exercise regimen.

CAREER AND FINANCES

People born on this date have a great regard for knowledge. They are outstanding teachers who know how to draw others into their world of learning and wisdom.

Although they have very good financial and business skills, these individuals are not motivated by money. They are budget-minded, yet without being thrifty in the traditional sense.

DREAMS AND GOALS

September 29 individuals have a spirit of quiet determination that helps them to accomplish their aims with little fanfare. As adolescents, they may have trouble distinguishing goals from pipe dreams.

Where personal dreams are concerned, they need to learn to become more independent in their relationships. They want personal freedom, yet often struggle to separate emotionally from a mate, friend, or mentor. Once they feel their power, these men and women truly come into their own.

EMBRACE
Pioneer spirit
Communication
Illuminating truths

AVOID
Superstition
The dark night of the soul
Cynicism

ALSO BORN TODAY
Film director Robert Benton; actress Anita Ekberg; British Admiral Horatio Nelson; actress Greer Garson; TV journalist Bryant Gumbel; film director Stanley Kramer; singer/pianist Jerry Lee Lewis; actress Emily Lloyd.

SEPTEMBER 30

People born on this date appear to be emotionally detached and aloof, but their personality resembles a volcano under an iceberg. With all their good grooming and perfectionist tendencies, these men and women seem to have it all together, but they are actually much more explosive than they appear.

September 30 natives have the power to visualize their dreams. They are incredibly focused on achievement and are willing to put all else on hold while they are involved in a project that's important to them.

FRIENDS AND LOVERS
People born on this date are not as easy-going and accepting as most Libra natives—in fact, they can be headstrong and even a little unreasonable at times. They demand a great deal from their friends, including undying loyalty. In cases where a September 30 person divorces, they are likely to expect their friends to take *their* side, not that of the ex-spouse.

Romance comes with its own set of problems for these folks. They are romantic idealists who often fall for someone who is not right for them.

CHILDREN AND FAMILY
Whether or not they are the only child, September 30 people are often indulged, even spoiled as youngsters. They may enjoy a particularly close relationship with one of the parents, and discipline may be sorely lacking.

Once they become parents, people born on this date are forced to "grow up." This is their defining moment, and is often the critical point in their lives. Learning to be less self-centered, to care for the needs of someone else, is the very best lesson they can learn, and helps them to become nurturing and caring.

HEALTH
The health practices of September 30 people are generally motivated by their desire to remain as attractive as possible for as long as they can. Regular exercise and a diet rich in protein, calcium, and B-complex vitamins will bring the health and vitality they desire. Drinking an average of eight glasses of purified water each day is a good beauty secret.

CAREER AND FINANCES
People born on this date are effective bosses or supervisors because they can read a person's character, and they have the ability to motivate people and get the best out of them.

These men and women think big, and refuse to be limited by circumstance. For this reason they make great organizers who can head up a project and have fun while doing it.

September 30 people have the potential to make a great deal of money, but they frequently spend far more than they earn.

DREAMS AND GOALS
September 30 people are actually extremely focused, and know how to get things done. They refuse to see the negative aspects of any undertaking, which is one of the reasons why they seldom fail. Even if they do, they see it as a temporary setback, not a final condition.

September 30 men and women have an incredible appetite for life. They work hard, play hard, and never stop striving.

EMBRACE
Openness
A forgiving spirit
Erudition

AVOID
Being overly critical
Pretentiousness
Rivalries

ALSO BORN TODAY
Novelist Truman Capote; actress Angie Dickinson; TV personality Rula Lenska; actress Deborah Kerr; singer Johnny Mathis; singer Marilyn McCoo; actress Victoria Tennant; actor Jack Wild.

OCTOBER 1

People born on October 1 have a bold and uncompromising spirit, and an ability to come back from hard times and difficulties. They enjoy being in the spotlight, yet have far too much grace to appear egotistical or vain.

October 1 men and women understand the need to build their future on the successes of the past. Continuity is a big part of their life. They have an instinct for making the right decision in both personal and professional matters.

EMBRACE
Thoroughness
Acceptance
Happy memories

AVOID
A domineering temperament
Disapproval
Petty people

ALSO BORN TODAY
Singer/actress Julie Andrews; U.S. President Jimmy Carter; actor Stephen Collins; astrologer Marc Edmund Jones; actor Richard Harris; English King Henry III; fashion designer Mary McFadden; actress Stella Stevens.

FRIENDS AND LOVERS Friends play a pivotal role in the lives of October 1 men and women. These individuals have a wide variety of social contacts but they also have a small circle of very intimate friends with whom they share their innermost thoughts and feelings.

As with most Librans, October 1 individuals are extremely romantic. They fall in and out of love quickly. Once married, October 1 natives will always strive to keep the romance alive.

CHILDREN AND FAMILY Family life has a major impact upon the lives of October 1 individuals. They may have experienced an idyllic childhood that contrasts with the reality of their adult life, making them nostalgic for the past. People born on this date expect their spouses to be as indulgent as parents and other family members, and are often surprised if they are not.

October 1 people have the best intentions of fulfilling their parental roles yet may find themselves preoccupied with career responsibilities. Nevertheless, they manage to make an impact on their children, setting down rules of conduct that provide social and spiritual guidance.

HEALTH Because of their generally upbeat nature, October 1 men and women have little problem dealing with stress in their lives, which has a positive effect upon their health. Generally moderate in all things, these people usually manage to keep their weight down.

All Libra individuals are concerned about their good looks and October 1 people are no exception. Even though they hate to sweat, these men and women usually manage to keep up a regular workout program.

CAREER AND FINANCES October 1 individuals are often drawn to careers that give them a chance to show their commitment to the less fortunate. Politics, social work, and other humanitarian avenues are the perfect opportunities for them.

Despite being intelligent and clever, many Libra types feel insecure about their ability to handle money. Perhaps because they know only too well how much they enjoy spending hard-earned cash on beautiful things, they may not trust themselves.

DREAMS AND GOALS October 1 natives have the spirit to overcome adversity. Drawing upon this strength gives them great satisfaction because it allows them to demonstrate their true mettle to others.

These people seek harmony in all aspects of life. This can require some sacrifices in personal relationships, but October 1 folks are glad to make those sacrifices if it provides the peace of mind they require.

OCTOBER 2

People born on October 2 have personality plus. They are extremely charming and attractive to the opposite sex, and have a great capacity for learning. These men and women identify with the finer things in life. They take real pride in their appearance and have a strong sense of style.

October 2 natives are lovers of culture. They enjoy surrounding themselves with beautiful objects and may secretly yearn to be involved in an artistic enterprise.

FRIENDS AND LOVERS
Relationships are the most important factors in the lives of October 2 people. They understand themselves through their close associations with others, and continue to strive for even greater intimacy. Even though these people seem to be concerned with the more superficial aspects of life, they are actually devoted to friendship and other essentials.

Like all people born under the sign of Libra, October 2 men and women are romantics who wear their hearts on their sleeves. They may experience some major heartbreak in relationships but they never take themselves out of the running. Being in love is the greatest joy these people can experience.

CHILDREN AND FAMILY
People born on October 2 have generally favorable memories from childhood. They are likely to continue a close relationship with family members long after they have left the proverbial nest. These individuals may have a special closeness to their mothers.

As parents, October 2 men and women are concerned about meeting all of their child's needs. They are sticklers for discipline, yet manage to display a great deal of tenderness and affection in their relationship with youngsters.

HEALTH
Even though October 2 people have the best intentions on earth, they may fall far short of their aims in health matters. They mean to eat well, to exercise, and to take their vitamins, but unfortunately they have a hard time sticking with anything, even if it's good for them.

October 2 men and women know their limitations and for that reason don't attempt to put extra pressure on themselves by feeling guilty. They prefer to get their exercise by walking and feel absolutely saintly if they can manage to give up dessert a few times a week.

CAREER AND FINANCES
People born on this date are sensitive types who don't like to be in an environment that is noisy, ugly, or in any way unpleasant. Because they enjoy communing with people, it's difficult for them to work alone, or in a restrictive atmosphere.

October 2 people love to spend money on nice things, no matter how motivated they are to save.

DREAMS AND GOALS
The men and women born on this date have many artistic aspirations, though they may be shy about expressing them to any but their closest friends. These individuals often relegate their talent to hobbies, but with the good wishes and stout support of the people they love, these talents can blossom into something truly special.

EMBRACE
Transfiguration
Religiosity
Values

AVOID
Destructive impulses
Self-righteousness
Rages

ALSO BORN TODAY
Comedian/film star Bud Abbott; TV personality Anna Ford; novelist Graham Greene; fashion designer Donna Karan; celebrity photographer Annie Leibovitz; singer/songwriter Don McLean; film critic Rex Reed; singer Sting.

OCTOBER 3

People born on this date have great poise and composure. They are able to withstand difficult times without complaint and can learn major life-lessons without seeming to change in any noticeable way.

These people are often charming and extremely good looking. Although they have a very healthy ego, they're not vain. Although they may show a hint of the typical Libra frivolity, they possess great self-sufficiency and are incredibly logical.

FRIENDS AND LOVERS
October 3 men and women are first among equals. Although they try to integrate themselves into the mix, they usually end up having others look to them for answers. This could cut back on their friendship prospects but fortunately, they are exceedingly pleasant and good company.

In love matters, people born on this day have their emotional ups and downs. They are constantly looking for someone who shares their high level of commitment and high morals. Once they do manage to find such a person, they immediately begin thinking marriage. Like most Libra individuals, October 3 people experience life most fully through their personal relationships.

CHILDREN AND FAMILY
These positive people have only happy associations with childhood. They prize tradition and have probably inherited a great many of their parents' ideas and prejudices.

They have a real knack for being parents, though. These men and women are naturals at creating stable and loving relationships that offer their little ones plenty of spiritual and material comforts.

HEALTH
Few people have as positive an outlook on life as the men and women born on October 3. To these enthusiastic individuals, every cloud has a silver lining. They refuse to let setbacks or delays frustrate them, and for these reasons they are amazingly healthy.

October 3 people don't particularly enjoy exercise for its own sake, but they do have remarkably busy lifestyles, which keep them involved and active.

CAREER AND FINANCES
People born on this date are extremely intelligent and do well in careers that allow them to use their powers of analytical reasoning. Their persuasive attitude makes them adept at sales, real estate, the law, and marketing. They can also distinguish themselves as members of the clergy or other "caring" professions.

October 3 individuals are as skilled at handling money as they are at making it. They are extremely generous and therefore their resources always come back to them several times over.

DREAMS AND GOALS
October 3 natives want to live the good life. Though they may not be willing to bend all their efforts to this aim, they also understand the need to diversify their energies. These men and women want to succeed professionally, but also know that in order to be completely happy they must give at least equal time to their personal lives.

People born on this date understand that having money isn't the answer to everything.

EMBRACE
New ideas
Protocol
Taking risks

AVOID
Worry
Predictability
Empty praise

ALSO BORN TODAY
Singer Chubby Checker; stage actress Eleonora Duse; novelist Gore Vidal; actress Barbara Ferris; baseball star Dave Winfield; actor Michael Hordern; actor Jack Wagner; novelist Thomas Wolfe.

OCTOBER 4

Although Libra rebels are rare, October 4 individuals fall into this category. Of course, in the tradition of their sign they are well-bred and polite, yet they're rebels all the same. At times they can even get away with shocking behavior because they possess a likable personality and (when they feel like displaying them) exquisite manners.

October 4 people have respect for tradition, yet they enjoy deflating the pomposity of others. They make it a point to question social mores, especially outdated ones.

FRIENDS AND LOVERS
People born on this date draw a thin line between friends and lovers. Their friends often become lovers, and their lovers become friends.

October 4 people are among the most romantic on Earth. Even though they seem to be composed, they have a rapturous soul that sings a song of love. They will follow a lover halfway around the world if that is what it takes to maintain the relationship. Although they have a strong personality, they will defer to their mate or partner in order to strengthen their union.

CHILDREN AND FAMILY
People born on this date often show the same rebellious tendencies toward their family as they do the rest of the world. They may have experienced feelings of isolation in their youth, or they might have been the product of a broken home. One way or another, the experiences of youth stay with these individuals all their lives.

October 4 people are often, from necessity, absent parents, but that doesn't keep them from being good ones. These men and women are very sincere about making a positive impact upon the lives of their little ones, no matter how often they have to juggle their own schedules to do it.

HEALTH
People born on this date have a great deal of nervous energy. They understand that the only way to work this off is to be involved in a regular exercise program. They like to push their physical strength to the limit through aerobic routines, and also enjoy working out with weights. The ability to master their physical environment makes them feel spiritually and emotionally powerful.

October 4 people are often attracted to some radical diet. They may be vegetarians who also restrict sugar and white flour in their eating plan.

CAREER AND FINANCES
People born on this date have tremendous social awareness and may become engrossed in careers that bring them close to the underprivileged.

Money is important to these men and women only in the way it can sustain them in a reasonably comfortable lifestyle and give their family members a good life.

DREAMS AND GOALS
People born on this date are eager to make a difference in the world. When they see a job that needs to be done, they do it without question. Although their politics may seem extreme to others, these folks are sincere in all they do.

October 4 people believe that they can change the world. It is a sentiment they carry with them throughout life.

EMBRACE
Passion
Respectability
Good advice

AVOID
Trends
Scattering energy
Gossip

ALSO BORN TODAY
Actor Armand Assante; British designer Sir Thomas Conran; actor Charlton Heston; silent film actor Buster Keaton; U.S. President Rutherford B. Hayes; actor Chris Lowe; actress Susan Sarandon.

OCTOBER 5

October 5 individuals experience considerable conflict between their intellectual and spiritual goals. They value learning, yet understand that it is *experience* that brings true wisdom.

These personable men and women will not compromise their ideas, and pride themselves on their sense of social responsibility. They have the instincts of a reformer, yet never allow their political ideology or religious beliefs to get in the way of having a good time.

October 5 people seem to perceive their role as parents on two distinct levels—as authority figures and as friends. They have a real talent for parenthood and have the ability to positively affect the lives of their children.

HEALTH People born on this date are fairly unconcerned about health matters. They rarely subscribe to any particular regimen, preferring to live their lives in the way that makes them feel happy. Because they are naturally active, they are unlikely to have the problem with weight that dogs many Librans.

Being able to relax and beat stress can go a long way toward allowing these busy people to maintain their emotional and spiritual composure.

EMBRACE
Humor
A sense of the ridiculous
Simplicity

AVOID
Fear of change
An argumentative attitude
Disinterest

ALSO BORN TODAY
Actress Karen Allen; auto racer Mario Andretti; novelist Clive Barker; actress Glynis Johns; hockey star Mario Lemieux; singer Steve Miller; actor Donald Pleasance; football coach Barry Switzer.

FRIENDS AND LOVERS People born on this date have a high communication quotient. Although marvelous conversationalists, they're equally good listeners. They value friends who have the same interests as they have, yet they don't rule out getting close to people who function on different wavelengths.

Unlike most Libra natives, October 5 people aren't likely to make their love relationship the center of their existence. This isn't to say that they don't look for and find true love, but it's not their sole concern.

CHILDREN AND FAMILY Individuals born on this day have very clear memories of their pasts, which stretch back to infancy. Many of their beliefs and emotions are centered in the way they were raised; these beliefs are unlikely to be altered without great effort.

CAREER AND FINANCES People born on this date feel a great need to take control of their destiny through the work they do. This is often linked to a genuine need to make a difference in the world, so they may be drawn to careers where this can be achieved.

October 5 individuals handle their finances capably. They seem to have a knack for making good investment choices, and though they have the typical Libran love of beauty, they keep their spending to a minimum.

DREAMS AND GOALS The people born on this date are committed to making a difference. They have high ideals and realize that they have a very special talent for manifesting the essence of those ideals. These men and women don't require a lot of praise or encouragement for their efforts; they simply see what needs to be done and do it.

October 5 people aren't content to merely do the work they want to do. It is important to these folks that their message of reform is acknowledged and acted upon by others.

OCTOBER 6

The people born on this date are dreamers who have a great need to express their inner drives through imagination and creativity. They are less concerned with the reality of existence that with the essence of it.

October 6 people are lovers of fantasy and illusion. To their way of thinking, what appears to be true is much more interesting than what actually may be true. They are idealists who love beauty in all its forms.

FRIENDS AND LOVERS October 6 natives
make friends effortlessly. While they can be very helpful to the people they care about, they generally seek out people who can provide them with strength and emotional protection.

There are few people more romantic than October 6 people. These men and women perceive all their intimate relationships through the prism of their romantic idealism, and for that reason they are likely to suffer more than their share of heartbreak.

CHILDREN AND FAMILY October 6
people are so sensitive and vulnerable that they rarely look back at their childhood without some misgivings. It is possible that one parent was absent during most of their growing-up years, leaving the former child with a sense of loss.

Because of their background, it takes a firm commitment and a great deal of love for their spouse to prompt October 6 people— especially women born on this date—to seek out parenthood. Once they do commit to it, they are usually able to resolve their childhood issues through the love they feel for their own kids.

HEALTH October 6 individuals are basically
healthy but may suffer from a variety of ner-

vous disorders that keeps them from living life with vigor. While these symptoms are real enough, they are usually the result of feelings of unfulfillment.

Exercise is the best way these moody individuals can shake the blues. Working out on a regular basis helps them to shed unwanted pounds.

CAREER AND FINANCES Individu-
als born on this date usually gravitate to a career in the arts. Whether it is painting, writing, acting, dancing, design, or fashion, these incredibly talented men and women have an unfaltering concept of beauty and harmony, which finds its way into their work.

Money isn't usually an important factor in the lives of these folks, except as a means to provide them with the beautiful things and luxurious surroundings they desire.

DREAMS AND GOALS All October 6 indi-
viduals want to leave the world a more beautiful place than it was when they arrived. October 6 men and women attempt to bring positive energy to every aspect of their existence. Whatever their personal goals may be, these individuals will always make their choices according to the level of beauty and harmony they bring into their lives and the lives of others.

EMBRACE
Reality
Purposefulness
A plan of action

AVOID
Frittering away time
Escapism
Unwise love

ALSO BORN TODAY
English King Edward V; actress Britt Ekland; adventurer Thor Heyerdahl; actress Janet Gaynor; opera singer Maria Jeritza; actress Carole Lombard; French King Louis-Philippe; singer/ songwriter Matthew Sweet.

OCTOBER 7

The men and women born on this date need to come out of their emotionally protective shell in order to meet their real destiny. These individuals have a strong philosophical bent, which they often express through humanitarian activities.

There is a dark side to these people that may not be apparent to any but those closest to them. Because of their tendency to be extremely moody on occasion, people born on this date need to become involved in lighthearted, life-affirming activities.

FRIENDS AND LOVERS October 7 individuals rarely show all aspects of their nature to any one person. Instead, they compartmentalize their emotions and attitudes, sharing them with selected individuals only. This is not born of a desire to mislead their other friends, but merely because many October 7 men and women are extremely insecure about their feelings.

It may also be difficult for them to be completely honest with a lover or mate unless they feel an unparalleled closeness to that person. October 7 people look for a soul mate, not just a partner.

CHILDREN AND FAMILY October 7 natives draw great strength from their upbringing. Many of their humanitarian aims have a basis in the way they were raised. When these men and women become parents they are anxious to reveal the many aspects of life that might otherwise go unnoticed. Teaching their youngsters about compassion and caring from an early age will give them the same value system possessed by October 7 natives.

HEALTH Because of their deep concern for the environment, October 7 people often live a "green" lifestyle. This conservationist attitude also manifests itself in the way October 7 men and women look after their health. They may prefer to walk instead of drive, eat organically grown produce, or work out by doing chores. These men and women need to understand that their commitment to causes can lead to emotional exhaustion. Meditation helps to replenish their energies.

CAREER AND FINANCES October 7 men and women are committed to careers that allow them access to changing public opinion. For that reason they are often drawn to politics, the law, social services, and the media. They may also wish to use their artistic or creative vision as a means of changing people's attitudes. Filmmaking and writing are good career choices for these people.

October 7 natives have a very healthy attitude toward money. They aren't materialistic by nature, yet they have the ability to appreciate what money can do, especially for those less fortunate than themselves.

DREAMS AND GOALS It is the desire of October 7 men and women to use whatever influence they possess in order to help others. Although their opinions are often extreme, these people have the dedication and commitment necessary to make a difference.

Personal goals are also vitally important to these people. They know how difficult it is to balance personal and professional responsibilities, and try to strike a happy medium.

EMBRACE
Patronage
Relaxation
Holistic healing

AVOID
External pressures
Nervous tension
Sexual excesses

ALSO BORN TODAY
Actress June Allyson; singer Toni Braxton; cellist Yo Yo Ma; novelist Helen MacInness; singer Al Martino; singer John Mellencamp; political commentator Oliver North.

OCTOBER 8

People born on October 8 are level-headed types who cannot be swayed by personal flattery. They possess the usual Libra charm, and the power of their personality is felt by all who know them. Still, they don't trade on this talent.

October 8 men and women believe in paying attention to detail. They are personally ambitious, yet care more for relationships than any professional enterprise. An ability to balance both is one of their trademarks.

FRIENDS AND LOVERS

These people have a natural talent for making friends, especially through professional channels. They have a real interest in people and enjoy bringing new acquaintances into their circle.

They have a very serious approach to romance and often marry their first love. If they divorce, they may have trouble getting back into the dating game. Social occasions give them the opportunity to meet a great many interesting people, but they prefer the magic of meeting that special someone just by chance.

CHILDREN AND FAMILY

October 8 men and women need the security and love that comes from being part of a large family. Regardless of their place within that group, these people are often the emotional backbone of the family.

As parents, October 8 natives believe in setting high standards. They know that a little discipline, as long as it's fair and consistent, can go a long way. They have a great tenderness for their children.

HEALTH

Since October 8 individuals have problems handling stress, they may experience periodic indigestion, as well as poor sleep habits. Worry over financial or career decisions can often keep these people sleepless far into the night, eventually causing them to reach for the sleeping pills. But this recourse only exacerbates their problems.

October 8 individuals need to find holistic cures for sleep disorders. These can include chamomile tea or other types of herbal infusions just before bed. Drinking warm milk can also be helpful.

CAREER AND FINANCES

People born on this date thrive in careers related to the business aspects of artistic endeavors. They make excellent business managers or agents for actors, musicians, writers, and other artists. They also enjoy working with luxury goods in big-ticket retail.

October 8 men and women are exceptional money managers. They have creative ideas involving investments, and have the savvy needed to become effective financial counselors.

DREAMS AND GOALS

The people born on this date have the ability to achieve their goals without any showiness or ego. They have the patience to take each day as it comes.

October 8 folks believe in the importance of details. More than most people, these men and women understand that great goals hinge on details, and that if these are left undone there is little chance that even the most ambitious goal can be realized.

EMBRACE
Serenity
Honesty
An ability to share

AVOID
Greediness
Restriction
Love of power

ALSO BORN TODAY
Columnist Rona Barrett; comic actor Chevy Chase; actor Michael Dudikoff; novelist Frank Herbert; political leader Jesse Jackson; Argentine President Juan Peron; actress Sigourney Weaver; actress Stephanie Zimbalist.

OCTOBER 9

People born on October 9 have the natural gift of making peace. They possess a strong love of beauty, and love truth even more. Their unique and singular lives are spent in the search for truth, and in understanding both the material and spiritual aspects of their world.

October 9 men and women are controversial yet good-natured. They may display a sharp wit in their debates with others, but they are more ironic than sarcastic.

EMBRACE
Bold challenges
Maturity
Stability

AVOID
Impossible odds
Making enemies
A foolish heart

ALSO BORN TODAY
Actor Scott Bakula; singer/songwriter Jackson Browne; writer Miguel de Cervantes; French King Charles X; writer Jill Conway; musician John Entwhistle; Watergate figure/novelist Howard Hunt; singer/songwriter John Lennon.

FRIENDS AND LOVERS Those born on this date demand a lot from their friends. They desire respect as well as love, support as well as sympathy. Whether or not they want to hear the truth, they will always ask for it, knowing that once friends begin being less than honest with one another, the relationship is in trouble.

October 9 people have a complicated love nature. They may initially look for superficial attractiveness in a lover, but what they really want is a soul mate. When they are involved in a relationship that fulfills their spiritual as well as their emotional needs, they are perfectly content.

CHILDREN AND FAMILY October 9 natives are devoted to the memory of their childhood, even if what they remember is far removed from the truth. They go through life with a certain nostalgia related to their growing-up years, despite the fact that there may have been a great deal of turmoil going on behind the scenes. October 9 men and women make extraordinary parents. They have the unique talent of being able to enter a child's world, re-experiencing all the joy and fantasy of that period.

HEALTH The men and women born on this date have little interest in keeping fit if it means they have to follow a regimen of schedules and activities. These people like to do things their own way, and that often means overindulging in the good things of life once in a while.

October 9 people have spurts of energy but are not especially exercise-conscious. They enjoy being involved in physical activities that are conducive to daydreaming, such as long walks by the beach, or hikes in a beautiful and secluded area.

CAREER AND FINANCES People born on this date have a sincere interest in doing things of real consequence in the world—and not just to satisfy their own egos, either. These men and women are often drawn toward creative fields.

Although October 9 individuals have a definite talent for handling money matters, they aren't likely to be devoted to the subject. These people prize values more than cash.

DREAMS AND GOALS People born on this date need to feel they are living their life on their own terms. They will gladly throw off all the trappings of status in order to get to a point where nothing matters except their personal autonomy.

October 9 men and women want to find contentment in their personal relationships. Although frustrated and complex in youth, these matters usually work themselves out by middle age.

226

OCTOBER 10

October 10 men and women play by the rules. They have a good sense of self, and care a great deal about their personal reputation. Although they possess a pleasant temperament and a charming disposition, they may lack a certain level of humility. Yet true to their Libran nature, they are never gauche enough to show it.

These people have the ability to command respect from others. They do this by exerting their own brand of subtle charm in ways that are completely irresistible.

FRIENDS AND LOVERS
October 10 people do not enjoy playing the role of peacemaker. If they have a problem with a friend's opinion they will speak their mind, regardless of the possibility that their remarks could have a negative effect on the friendship.

They are equally forceful in handling matters of romance. These men and women usually take the initiative where love is concerned and aren't afraid to go after what they want.

CHILDREN AND FAMILY
People born on this date may not be able to come to grips with some of the unhappy incidents of their past. They may find it very difficult to forgive certain family members.

October 10 people make good parents, though they are likely to be somewhat unsure of just what they are bringing to the experience. It takes them a while to become accustomed to sacrificing so much of their private time for a child.

HEALTH
People born on this date take a strong stand in matters of health and nutrition. They are constantly exploring new ways to optimize their physical, spiritual, and emotional well-being. Further, they understand that each is dependent upon the others.

October 10 natives are big on exercise, especially competitive sports like tennis and racquetball. Occasionally, they prefer dangerous endeavors like rock-climbing and white-water rafting. Putting themselves "out there" gives them a real adrenaline rush.

October 10 individuals favor a varied diet and are usually fond of high-protein foods.

CAREER AND FINANCES
Because they prefer to be in positions of power, October 10 men and women often choose careers in business, middle management, and retail. They have an eye for knowing what the public wants and are therefore extremely adept at marketing, and research and development.

October 10 people are good money managers who are concerned about maintaining financial security. They are likely to take on an extra job if they feel they don't have enough money in reserve for unforeseen emergencies.

DREAMS AND GOALS
These men and women need to feel as if they are constantly moving forward in their lives. They rebel against emotional and spiritual stagnation, and embrace change.

Because they are exceedingly ambitious, October 10 people are sometimes forced to spend more time away from loved ones than they prefer. Yet once they have attained certain career goals they are careful to make up for lost time with the people they love.

EMBRACE
Wise use of power
Unselfish motives
Spontaneity

AVOID
Hesitation
Dishonesty
Losing faith

ALSO BORN TODAY
Actor Charles Dance; actress Jessica Harper; playwright Harold Pinter; stage actress Helen Hayes; musician David Lee Roth; singer Tanya Tucker; novelist Sheila Walsh; painter Jean Watteau.

OCTOBER 11

October 11 people have the ability to put other people at ease. Their exquisite manners contribute to an effortless grace of spirit that makes them unique and inspirational.

People born on this date have a sweet and sensitive nature, which in no way implies a lack of strength. In truth, they possess considerable grit and determination, and are often drawn toward adventure despite being somewhat afraid of what it will bring.

FRIENDS AND LOVERS
Friends accord October 11 people some of the greatest joys in life. Folks born on this date put a lot of effort and affection into friendship and only require that they be given the same treatment. Falling out with friends can be a bitter experience for these individuals.

October 11 people are vulnerable to the emotional ups and downs of love. They can be hurt easily, and when this happens they are sometimes afraid to give their heart again. Relationships mean everything to these people, and when they maintain a good one, they blossom spiritually.

CHILDREN AND FAMILY
People born on this date may have experienced significant restrictions in childhood. Perhaps one parent was extremely domineering, or absent, causing the October 11 child to seek an authority substitute. Because it's difficult for these people to break with the past, they may benefit from therapy once they reach adulthood.

Parenthood gives October 11 individuals the chance to work through some of their own childhood issues. Therapy is generally a positive experience, though feelings of loss and abandonment can arise when the past is revisited.

HEALTH
October 11 people need to break with tradition and start a health regimen that is present- and future-oriented. This way, these occasionally timid people can remake themselves in their own image.

Because they have a great deal of emotional strength at their core, October 11 people benefit from utilizing prayer and meditation.

CAREER AND FINANCES
October 11 natives love beauty in all its forms, but have a special talent for words. They make exceptional writers, lecturers, teachers, researchers, and attorneys. Because they go about their work in a quiet, unassuming way, it's amazing to witness how they are transformed by the exercise of their talents.

People born on this date are addicted to a luxurious lifestyle. Because of this, they concentrate more on spending money than on saving it. This will create problems if they are not conscientious about paying the bills on time and maintaining good credit.

DREAMS AND GOALS
October 11 people need to express themselves through artistic means, usually in words. Even if these men and women do not seek a professional writing career, they will always look to words as their way of showing others just who they are.

These folks desire a comfortable life in more ways than one. They like the goodies that money can bring, but they also realize that they need to find spiritual satisfaction, as well, which is most likely to come to them via relationships.

EMBRACE
Charity
Good conscience
Belief in self

AVOID
Emotionalism
Inner fears
Living in the past

ALSO BORN TODAY
Actress Joan Cusack; singer/songwriter Daryl Hall; musician Billy Higgins; actor David Morse; actor Luke Perry; choreographer Jerome Robbins; First Lady Eleanor Roosevelt.

OCTOBER 12

There are few individuals who possess the sort of generous spirit that October 12 individuals display. These men and women enjoy living large, and enjoy the respect and patronage of others.

October 12 natives love people. They enjoy spending money on those they care for, and may sometimes strive for an opulent lifestyle that is beyond their means. These people are high-spirited and fun-loving, always looking for ways to have a good time.

FRIENDS AND LOVERS October 12 individuals have a lot of friends. They usually have a well-filled social calendar, which allows them to meet people from many different walks of life.

People born on this date have a coquettish attitude in love matters. Although they may seem fickle, they simply enjoy variety and playing the field. Only someone very special will convince these good-time men and women to settle down to a life of domestic bliss. Even after marriage, though, October 12 people are likely retain their roving eye.

CHILDREN AND FAMILY October 12 people often come from a large or extended family group. Yet even among all these individuals they may be thought of as special in some way. This sense of being adored stays with them throughout life.

These men and women are indulgent of their own children, perhaps to an unwise degree. Eventually, when discipline becomes a problem, they will learn that it is better to be strict than sorry.

HEALTH There is no question that October 12 individuals love good food.

Unfortunately, these men and women possess the typical Libran disdain for regular exercise. If they play a favorite sport or sports, this isn't really a problem. But if they are heavily career-focused or unwilling for other reasons to work off the extra calories, they're likely to have weight problems in middle age.

CAREER AND FINANCES Like most people of their sign, October 12 individuals are in love with beauty and need to be surrounded with it, at work as well as in their personal lives. These men and women also crave a harmonious atmosphere, and function best in a work environment with a minimum of noise and emotional friction.

October 12 natives need to make a good salary in order to maintain the sort of lifestyle that appeals to them. If they do not, they may be tempted to spend heavily on credit.

EMBRACE
Financial restraint
An open mind
Inner voice

AVOID
Conflict
Struggle
Intemperance

ALSO BORN TODAY
Model/actress Susan Anton; actor Kirk Cameron; English King Edward VI; singer Sam Moore; opera tenor Luciano Pavarotti; actor Adam Rich; singer Dave Vanian; composer Ralph Vaughn-Williams.

DREAMS AND GOALS People born on this date have very specific goals. They may wish to get to the very top of their chosen profession, or at least receive the sort of notice and attention they believe they deserve.

October 12 individuals love to travel, and often experience some of their happiest and most fulfilling times while visiting foreign countries. These people have a cosmopolitan soul, which draws them to exotic cultures. Learning to look at the world through the eyes of other people is a cherished experience for October 12 individuals.

OCTOBER 13

The people born on this date have enormous inner strength. They may have a fragile or quiet exterior, yet underneath that reserve they are pragmatic and loaded with common sense. These people have the potential to be idealistic, yet they do not want to be caught off-guard.

October 13 individuals are true romantics at heart, and their need to feel sheltered and protected by loved ones is their only real emotional "weakness."

FRIENDS AND LOVERS

These men and women have a difficult time letting people into their life. They may struggle to completely trust others or may have a fear of intimacy that causes them to keep even the people they care about at arm's length. Often they feel truly close only to friends they've known for many years.

October 13 people face similar problems with lovers. They have a great deal to offer, and yet very few potential life-partners can give them the security they need. Even when they find the man or woman of their dreams, they suffer a sense of unease and a feeling that the relationship can't last.

CHILDREN AND FAMILY

Many October 13 people developed their emotional strength as children, when circumstances caused them to handle demanding challenges. Although this may have set the stage for positive accomplishments later in life, it can still exact a great emotional price.

October 13 men and women have a very protective attitude toward their own children. They do everything they can to keep them from being exposed to the harsh realities of life.

HEALTH

Those born on this date are very exacting about their health routine. They eat sparingly but well, and are very big on vitamin and mineral supplements. Exercise isn't something these people love, but they realize its value and pursue a workout plan with their usual common-sense attitude.

By following a program of exercise, meditation, and plenty of positive thinking, they are able to keep themselves looking and feeling great.

CAREER AND FINANCES

People born on this date are the ultimate professionals. Whatever their career choice, they are certain to do their job to the very best of their ability and with a minimum of ego. Because they are patient, they are very good at managing others. These people have the typical Libran interest in creative occupations, and make fine artists, writers, and dancers.

October 13 men and women have enormous financial acumen. They are very aware of their standard of living, and know that in order to maintain it they need to set—and meet—serious financial goals.

DREAMS AND GOALS

For these people, the destination isn't as important as the way they get there. Being able to withstand pressure and disappointment and even loss is the keynote to their character and helps them to grow spiritually.

October 13 people are incredibly focused and are able to endure a great deal of tribulation as they travel their road to success.

EMBRACE
Balance
Opportunity
Justice

AVOID
Guile
Inability to forgive
Need to dominate others

ALSO BORN TODAY
Comedian Lenny Bruce; figure skating champion Nancy Kerrigan; actor Yves Montand; British Prime Minister Margaret Thatcher; actress Kelly Preston; singer/songwriter Paul Simon; actor Cornel Wilde.

OCTOBER 14

People born on this date incorporate the very best traits of Libra. They are intelligent, diplomatic, and concerned with the sort of image they project to others. They have a flair for expressing themselves, and are masters of communication.

October 14 natives can appear lighthearted on the surface, yet they are extremely serious at their core. These men and women are introspective, but still manage to display a warm personality.

FRIENDS AND LOVERS

Those born on October 14 are devoted to making their relationships work. They are good friends who believe in sharing all the joys and problems of life with the people they love. Because they have natural leadership abilities, these men and women are often in the position of giving advice to pals.

Romantic love is everything to these individuals. They have an idealistic view of love and can feel hurt or betrayed if their lover or mate does not appreciate them in the way they need to be appreciated. These people want soul-to-soul communication, not just a love affair.

CHILDREN AND FAMILY

October 14 folks have a deep belief in family hierarchy, and an understanding of just where they fit into their own pattern of familial relationships. They're dedicated to living up to the values and ethics they were taught as children.

As parents, people born today are strict but sensitive. They want their youngsters to experience plenty of freedom, but feel that kids need to understand the limits and responsibilities freedom demands.

HEALTH

October 14 individuals have a great deal of unfocused energy and may suffer from nervous complaints such as headaches, sleeplessness, or the inability to concentrate for long periods. These are usually symptoms of overwork, yet can be related to dietary habits.

These people should stay away from caffeine, since it has a very unsettling effect upon them. Also, they should be very careful about the amount of sugar they consume. The best diet for them is basic dishes, prepared simply. In order to combat sleep disorders they need to exercise moderately at least five times a week.

CAREER AND FINANCES

People born on this date are talented in a number of ways. They have extremely good verbal skills and are able to make others understand their points of view with a minimum of explanation. October 14 individuals are very creative, yet they also have a strong analytical sense, October 14 folks handle their money sensibly, but may be somewhat uncertain when it comes to deciding on investment opportunities.

DREAMS AND GOALS

People born on this date believe in being conscientious about everything they do. When these men and women decide upon a course of action, they plan all their efforts in detail.

Getting to the top of their profession is a common goal for October 14 individuals, yet these people are equally concerned about making their personal relationships successful.

EMBRACE
Tranquility
Harmony
Sense of mission

AVOID
Mistrust
Depression
Unhappy love matches

ALSO BORN TODAY
Poet e. e. cummings; Watergate figure John Dean III; U.S. President Dwight D. Eisenhower; actress Lillian Gish; English King James II; fashion designer Ralph Lauren; fashion designer Isaac Mizrahi; actor Roger Moore.

OCTOBER 15

October 15 men and women are pleasure-seeking, luxury-loving individuals. These traits are generally assets, but there are times when they cause these freewheeling people to become their own worst enemies.

People born on this date are always quick to apologize for their real or imagined misdeeds but, unfortunately, they go on living their lives in a way that makes the recurrence of such actions not just possible but probable. While October 15 people are usually more sinned against than sinning, they often need to learn a higher level of discretion.

and may spend a good part of their adult life reacting to the feelings of insecurity this created. If there is little harmony in their lives they will opt to live on the surface of events, and avoid deep emotional commitment.

On the other hand, they'll go to any lengths to make their own children feel happy and safe.

HEALTH With a big appetite for life and all the good things that come with it, October 15 people may have a hard time maintaining a strict nutritional regimen. They are usually motivated more by cosmetic than health concerns, which may cause them to endorse fad diets rather than a sensible eating plan.

They're good competitors and enjoy playing sports, but this may not be enough to keep them fit.

CAREER AND FINANCES Involvement in a variety of projects is one way October 15 people tend to scatter their energies, and until they find a particular career that is right for them they're likely to be unfocused and underproductive. They may not have much confidence in their own abilities, so the validation of friends and colleagues is a major plus.

Money can be a source of problems in the lives of October 15 people until they learn to control it, instead of the other way around.

DREAMS AND GOALS The ultimate goal of October 15 people is to learn how to manage the highs and lows of life. These goodhearted but often misguided folks can get themselves in a real bind simply trying to be honest, only to discover that everybody else is playing by different rules.

People born on this date become more goal-oriented as they learn to trust themselves.

EMBRACE
Independence
Strength of character
Practicality

AVOID
Pretense
Social climbing
Superficiality

ALSO BORN TODAY
Former British royal Sarah Ferguson; economist John Kenneth Galbraith; actress Linda Lavin; actress/director Penny Marshall; author Mario Puzo; actress Tanya Roberts; playwright Oscar Wilde; writer P. G. Wodehouse.

FRIENDS AND LOVERS October 15 people make loyal and loving friends. They know how to have a good time, and how to make everyone around them feel as if there's a party going on. These men and women will do whatever it takes to help a friend in need, and will stand by them in times of crisis or moral dilemma.

Romance is one big roller coaster ride for October 15 people. Their fair-minded and forgiving qualities are virtues that sometimes work against their own best interests. They are flirty but not fickle, and once they make a commitment to one person they remain true.

CHILDREN AND FAMILY October 15 people may have experienced more than their share of tumultuous events while growing up,

OCTOBER 16

People born on October 16 are peace-loving individuals who nevertheless can meet tough challenges. These engaging men and women have an almost childlike love of the spontaneous gesture. Further, they have the ability to judge others in a wise yet kindly way. These folks have a strong humanitarian streak and display a great deal of concern for the welfare of other people.

FRIENDS AND LOVERS October 16 natives have no trouble making friends. Their sincerity and lack of pretense draw others to them easily. Though they have the power to be manipulative, the men and women born on this date refuse to act that way.

Like all Librans, October 16 people are extremely romantic in the most personal sense of the word. Yet they are more practical than many people of their sign and will never allow themselves to become so addicted to a relationship that they can no longer see the truth in it.

CHILDREN AND FAMILY October 16 natives understand how to make peace with the past. If there are issues from childhood that have the power to derail their adult lives, these men and women can put those issues into perspective and move on. Although they have exceptionally high ideals, they are not idealists—this gives them a useful ability to live in the now.

As parents, October 16 people are able to really let their hair down and get involved in every aspect of their child's life. They can play the role of authority figure and friend.

HEALTH While keeping active enough to remain healthy is rarely a challenge for these individuals, eating right can be a difficult assignment. October 16 people can be real junk-food junkies, and learning to divest themselves of this habit can be tough. The important thing for them to do is start learning more about what they're putting into their bodies.

October 16 people have a radiant zest for life and care more about how they feel than how they look. When they use this attitude to change their ideas about food, they'll gain amazing new perspectives.

CAREER AND FINANCES These versatile men and women can see themselves in a variety of professions, and even if they work long and hard toward a particular goal they are not afraid to suddenly change directions and pursue another path.

Because of their need for freedom in assessing career options, October 16 people are comfortable with the fact that their financial situation can change radically from one job or career to the next.

DREAMS AND GOALS People born on this date need to have fun. Whether that means having a good time on the job, playing a silly joke on a pal, or keeping the joy alive in their sex life with a long-time partner, these folks want to grab all the gusto from life that they can.

October 16 men and women can set specific goals for themselves without becoming obsessive. They have great organizational ability and know how to take a project one step at a time.

EMBRACE
People of substance
Information
Wise choices

AVOID
Shyness
Unrealized dreams
Lack of fulfillment

ALSO BORN TODAY
Actor Barry Corbin; playwright Eugene O'Neill; actress Linda Darnell; baseball star Tim McCarver; actress Angela Lansbury; film actor/director Tim Robbins; novelist Kathleen Winsor; actress Suzanne Sommers.

233

OCTOBER 17

Complex and complicated, October 17 individuals understand the need to suffer in order to obtain wisdom. These creative people seek expression through artistic means, though their head and heart may often be in conflict.

They must follow a circuitous route to their destiny, forced to learn important life-lessons along the way. These are generally related to the October 17 native's relationships with others, but include a great deal of personal soul-searching as well.

FRIENDS AND LOVERS October 17 natives are many things to many people. It's as if they are a prism through which others may obtain a brief but stunning glimpse of themselves. While people born on this date are likely to surround themselves with a variety of friends, it is just as likely that not one knows all aspects of their personality.

These men and women are equally inaccessible to their lovers and mates. Even when a love affair or marriage seems made in heaven, it is typical for October 17 individuals to hold something back. They have great emotional resilience, so if a relationship ends they are able to take stock of what made it fail, and move on.

CHILDREN AND FAMILY As with many Libra natives, the upbringing of October 17 individuals is unlikely to live up to their idea of perfection. Consequently, they may spend most of their adult life rationalizing what happened to them as children without ever really wanting to know the answer.

When October 17 people have their own children they are likely to experience a great sense of vulnerability regarding their new responsibilities. They are exceptionally loving people, and may be unable to draw the line between affection and authority.

HEALTH October 17 people understand that the only way to achieve a state of balance is to continually move back and forth between two points of opposition.

For this reason, October 17 individuals are likely to try many different diets and health regimens—some of them unusual and even bizarre—before they settle upon one that works for them.

CAREER AND FINANCES October 17 individuals have a creative spirit that usually dictates the direction their career takes. They have an artistic temperament that is likely to be displayed no matter what their professional status.

These men and women have a decisive nature that makes them good managers and supervisors. They have the ability to motivate people and bring out their full potential.

People born on this date are very careful about the way they handle their money.

DREAMS AND GOALS October 17 individuals have few illusions about life. They are savvy enough to realize that no matter how hard they work they may not receive the acclaim or status they want. That rarely deters them.

People born on this date are more concerned with their own efforts than the results. They realize that success is an arbitrary term.

EMBRACE
Empathy
Pure motives
Fidelity

AVOID
Scandal
Impulsive actions
Carelessness

ALSO BORN TODAY
Actor Sam Bottoms; author Elinor Glyn; actor Montgomery Clift; actress Beverly Garland; choreographer Doris Humphrey; actress Rita Hayworth; playwright Arthur Miller; actress Margot Kidder.

OCTOBER 18

People born on this date are dynamic, spirited, and energetic. Not as diplomatic as the average Libra native, they refuse to sugarcoat their opinions in order to please others. These truth-tellers are ambitious, even a little aggressive, but they wear it well.

October 18 people are not afraid to display their confidence. They are real self-starters who believe in taking control of their lives. Personality plays a big part in their appeal.

FRIENDS AND LOVERS October 18 men and women are very particular about whom they choose as friends. They don't concern themselves with superficial appearances and may surround themselves with unlikely types whose low-key personalities are very different from their own.

If it is possible for Libra individuals to be practical about romantic matters, it is October 18 people who fit this description. They aren't likely to be carried away by the frivolous aspects of love, preferring to judge a potential partner by more serious criteria. They are very sexual, however, and need to feel fulfilled by this aspect of the relationship.

CHILDREN AND FAMILY The men and women born on this date may have a habit of rewriting their background if it doesn't accord with their image of what it should be. They have a tendency to grow up too early. This could be the result of family circumstances when they were growing up; it's possible that they may have been given more responsibility than they were ready to handle.

October 18 individuals are very concerned about making life less stressful for their own children. With their tendency to go to extremes at times, they may offer a more protective influence than is necessary.

HEALTH People born on this date are highly motivated to keep themselves looking and feeling good. They don't have the typical Libra indolence, and may even be quite athletic. These men and women enjoy pushing the envelope and may favor dangerous pastimes like rock climbing or whitewater rafting.

Where nutrition is concerned, October 18 individuals are far more Spartan than most people of their sign. They like red meat and they benefit from drinking a glass of red wine each day.

CAREER AND FINANCES October 18 people don't like being in the background, so their career ambitions usually take them in the direction of leadership. Because they have great analytical intelligence, they do very well as engineers, architects, designers, city planners, teachers, and musicians.

People born on this date are extremely budget-minded and have the patience to save for big-ticket items.

DREAMS AND GOALS It is in the nature of October 18 individuals to attempt a reconciliation between the practical and the aesthetic sides of their personality. This can be a challenge for them, so they are accustomed to letting others see only their "sensible" side.

These men and women are organized and detail-oriented, so setting and meeting goals is second nature to them.

EMBRACE
Accountability
Commitment to causes
Spirituality

AVOID
Recklessness
Self-admiration
A quarrelsome nature

ALSO BORN TODAY
Musician Chuck Berry; U.S. Senator Jesse Helms; musician Keith Knudsen; actress Melina Mercouri; actress Erin Moran; actor George C. Scott; Canadian political figure Pierre Trudeau; playwright Wendy Wasserstein.

OCTOBER 19

The intensity that characterizes people born on this day marks them as unlike any other Libra. These broad-minded individuals find fulfillment through bringing together both the worldly and the spiritual sides of their nature.

October 19 men and women have strong, yet flexible opinions on many subjects. They are curious about life, have a fierce love for learning, and have the ability to transcend their own limitations.

FRIENDS AND LOVERS Although they have no trouble making friends, October 19 individuals often find themselves in controversial situations relating to friendship, which may severely test relationships. Being sensitive to the views and opinions of others can help mend misunderstandings.

Love relationships create their own problems in the lives of October 19 people. While these men and women possess the typical Libra idealism concerning romance, they also have a practical side that allows them to be objective about choosing a partner.

CHILDREN AND FAMILY October 19 natives are often the center of attention within their family circle. Their sunny personality and ability to see the positive side of any situation make them genuinely lovable.

People born on this date take their own roles as parents very seriously. They never allow their feelings to get in the way of good judgment, and may favor strict discipline, yet they instinctively know when a little indulgence is called for.

HEALTH Because October 19 men and women feel invulnerable to ill health, they are likely to be casual about their habits. This may be sufficient when they are young, but as middle age approaches these people need to start taking better care of themselves.

Individuals born on this date enjoy pursuing an active lifestyle, including a daily workout and competitive sports. They also respect the part that spiritual renewal plays in their daily lives.

CAREER AND FINANCES October 19 people need to feel that they are making a contribution to the world through the work they do. They have a strong humanitarian streak and are concerned with helping others. This may lead them to caring professions such as therapists, marriage and family counselors, and the clergy.

Money matters are in very good hands with October 19 people, who combine the instincts of sensible business practices with the willingness to take bold risks. These men and women have the potential to turn a very modest sum into a fortune merely by applying their own special brand of optimistic good sense.

DREAMS AND GOALS People born on this date are concerned with reaching their full potential in life. They are constantly making and meeting goals that will bring them closer to this reality.

Even though they are extremely focused, these men and women have the ability to withstand setbacks and disappointments. They realize that some of the greatest lessons they can learn come as a result of these seemingly negative situations.

EMBRACE
Virtue
Anticipation
Strength to dream

AVOID
Preoccupation
Dishonor
Fickleness

ALSO BORN TODAY
Actor Richard Dreyfus; pianist Emil Giles; novelist John Le Carre; actor John Lithgow; artist Peter Max; singer/songwriter Peter Tosh; actor Simon Ward; musician Karl Wallinger.

OCTOBER 20

People born on October 20 embody the yin-yang principle: Duality is their defining characteristic. Their attitudes, even their personality, may seem changeable, yet they are merely displaying both sides of their nature. At times, they may appear aloof.

October 20 people have profound intellectual potential, yet they may lack the discipline to study any one subject in depth. They have a habit of extracting the information they need, then moving on to something else.

FRIENDS AND LOVERS
October 20 men and women give a great deal of themselves to their friends, and demand a lot in return. Loyalty is a premier virtue in their eyes, and they will always be closest to people who retain their trust through acts of honesty and discretion.

October 20 people are idealists in romantic love, who always expect more from love than they receive. They can be drawn into tempestuous love affairs that seem doomed to fail.

CHILDREN AND FAMILY
The past is not a place that October 20 people feel comfortable visiting too frequently. There may have been a great deal of tension and unrest in the home when they were growing up, due to an unstable family situation or lack of money. It is important for these men and women to get past the sense of shame they may have regarding those days.

Having children of their own can be a big step for them, but before they can be effective as parents they need to reconcile their own image of themselves.

HEALTH
It isn't easy for October 20 men and women to adhere to a strict health program. These carefree individuals are accustomed to eating whatever they like without any unpleasant consequences.

The key to keeping fit for October 20 individuals is to commit to a rigorous exercise program that includes power walking, aerobics, and weight-training. Yoga or some other type of mind-body discipline can be equally helpful in maintaining emotional and physical equilibrium.

CAREER AND FINANCES
People born on this date have a hard time deciding which career to pursue, simply because they have so many choices open to them. October 20 natives enjoy being in the spotlight, so they may gravitate toward professions where they can showcase their talent as a performer.

Despite their many talents, October 20 people are not usually adept at handling money. This isn't from any lack of judgment, but merely because of bad habits that can be changed if they put their mind to it. Like all Libras, October 20 individuals will pay a high price for a life of luxury.

DREAMS AND GOALS
These men and women are always striving to bring the two sides of their nature together. This may be done through their relationships, love affairs, career choices, or even the way in which they present themselves to others.

In order for October 20 people to understand themselves, they must be willing to accept their dark as well as their positive side.

EMBRACE
Facts
Tradition
Persistence

AVOID
Illusion
Ego-issues
Flamboyance

ALSO BORN TODAY
Columnist Art Buchwald; writer Thomas Hughes; composer Charles Ives; actor Bela Lugosi; baseball star Mickey Mantle; singer Tom Petty; poet Arthur Rimbaud; architect Sir Christopher Wren.

OCTOBER 21

Bold and creative, October 21 people need their own space. Although they are far more mischievous than rebellious, they enjoy stirring things up so that others take notice of them. They're fun-loving and don't mind breaking a few rules now and then.

These folks may possess the antic demeanor of a typical Libra, but their sense of emotional loyalty is very real.

FRIENDS AND LOVERS

Nothing is as important in the lives of October 21 men and women as the people they love. This preoccupation is more than just social: October 21 people have a spiritual bond to their friends.

They are adventuresome in romance and invariably choose a mate who is fun and spontaneous. Together with such a partner, these folks live fully and see the world in a fresh way, as if through the eyes of a child. Under such circumstances, romance only grows better and more satisfying.

CHILDREN AND FAMILY

October 21 people have engaging, exuberant personalities and the ability to have a good time. They generally maintain close relationships with their siblings and other relatives. Although sensitive parents, they never withhold discipline when it's called for.

At the same time, though, their children respond to them in positive ways, regarding them not as adversaries but as fun-loving leaders and companions. Parent-child relationships may falter a bit during the kids' adolescence—they may perceive their parents' upbeat nature as being competitive with their own—but settle down later. Older October 21 parents and their children enjoy casual, warm relationships.

HEALTH

People born on this date often battle weight problems. This isn't usually because of a sedentary lifestyle but because they have too great a fondness for rich foods and sweets.

October 21 natives need to be intensely motivated in order to maintain a commitment to exercise. They benefit from long walks, especially in beautiful pastoral settings.

After a period of this sort of physical activity, they may surprise themselves by craving a more structured and disciplined approach to fitness. They're unlikely to go so far as to hire a personal trainer, but they may join a health club and make full use of its facilities and staff.

CAREER AND FINANCES

Smart, sassy, even a little sarcastic, these men and women know how to put their personality on display. Multitalented, they have a tendency to switch careers.

Because they place relatively little importance upon their earning power, these folks often spend carelessly.

DREAMS AND GOALS

October 21 people like to do things their own way and would rather fail at something than give up control of their destiny.

Despite a fierce devotion to career, they try very hard to make their relationships the most important aspect of their lives.

EMBRACE
Diplomacy
Family ties
The truth

AVOID
Empty praise
A false face
Frivolous ambition

ALSO BORN TODAY
Singer Charlotte Caffey; poet Samuel Taylor Coleridge; musician Eric Faulkner; writer/actress Carrie Fisher; baseball star Whitey Ford; playwright Simon Gray; writer Ursula K. le Guin; symphony conductor Sir George Solti.

OCTOBER 22

People born on October 22 are definitely something special. They combine personal charm and attractiveness with intelligence and talent. Although they shine effortlessly in the spotlight, those born on this day are natural loners who draw strength from privacy.

October 22 individuals want to make their mark on the world and may even feel that they are destined to do so. Although their expectations may strike others as being naive, these people definitely perceive all the possibilities available to them and ask "why not?"

FRIENDS AND LOVERS

October 22 individuals set great store by their personal relationships. Even though they understand that they must listen to their own inner voice when making life-decisions, they have a great need to connect with others on many levels. They may have many friends, but few close ones. It is to these intimates that October 22 natives confide their deepest hopes and fears.

Idealistic and romantic, people born on this date are easy targets for a broken heart. They love deeply, sometimes unwisely. Yet despite their mistakes in judgment, October 22 individuals live most completely through their own feelings and emotions.

CHILDREN AND FAMILY

It isn't unusual for people born on October 22 to occupy a special place in the family circle. They possess a quality of quiet leadership, which sets a powerful example for their siblings and other relatives.

With their own children, these individuals tend to be liberal and indulgent. Even though they are adamant about setting a good moral example for their youngsters, those born on October 22 are anxious to allow their kids more freedom than they themselves were allowed.

HEALTH

A preference for excesses is the key to understanding the health habits of October 22 people. They may equate a surfeit of food and drink with happiness, which could lead to the inevitable yo-yo dieting effect.

Since these traits could be very deep-rooted, they may benefit from professional advice and help; a transformation to good eating and exercise habits will be the result.

CAREER AND FINANCES

Because of their artistic nature, those born on October 22 often seek careers in the creative or performing arts. Expressing their personality through art allows these individuals to play out their inner drives, and make good use of their profound imaginative powers.

It is rare for someone born on this date to choose a career based on its earning potential alone. Money is not unimportant to these individuals, but it is definitely secondary to personal fulfillment.

DREAMS AND GOALS

With their optimism and enthusiastic flair for enjoying life, those born on October 22 don't put up any barriers to what they can accomplish in life. If these people want something they go after it with surprising tenacity. Even though they do not judge their level of success by how much money they make, these individuals want to be recognized for their talent and ability.

EMBRACE
Balance
Serenity
Being in the moment

AVOID
Loss of inspiration
Looking back
Loving not wisely but too well

ALSO BORN TODAY
Actress Sarah Bernhardt; figure skating champion Brian Boitano; actress Catherine Deneuve; novelist Doris Lessing; actress Joan Fontaine; actor Jeff Goldblum; composer Franz Liszt; songwriter Dory Previn.

SCORPIO

October 23 - November 21

S corpio is the eighth sign of the astrological year and is known by its astrological symbol, the Scorpion. Scorpio individuals are enigmatic, strong-willed, and passionate. With Pluto as the ruling planet, people born under this sign are considered to be dynamic and extreme in their opinions.

THE SCORPIO MAN Scorpio men are enigmatic and appealing. Even though they have a steely exterior, they also possess considerable sensitivity. Men born under this sign are extremely moody, and for this reason they need their emotional "space." No one ever really gets close to these men—they have a secretive nature that keeps everyone at a distance.

These men are not usually the playboy type. They prefer the stability of home and hearth, and they make exceptionally good fathers. Scorpio men have a deeply caring nature and enjoy being part of their children's upbringing. Although they can be very demanding, even obsessive, in their relationships with family members, their actions are generally motivated by love. Career success means a lot to these men, but they never mistake it for personal achievement—for that they look to their family life.

THE SCORPIO WOMAN She is truly a woman of mystery. Part tomboy, part femme fatale, this fascinating woman is capable of many moods and many emotional shadings. Though often not overtly sexual, she has a magnetism that is incredibly provocative. She is maternal, yet not smothering. Her persona transcends her many roles.

Scorpio women do everything with great zeal and dedication. Whether she has a satisfying career or a fulfilling family life—or both—the typical Scorpio woman gives everything she has to the job. Although she can be demanding with those around her, she is equally demanding of herself. Scorpio women are constantly reinventing themselves, always looking to transform themselves into even better versions of their original selves. Because of this they never seem to age, but merely grow in wisdom, maturity, and accomplishments.

THE SCORPIO CHILD The Scorpio child, even a docile one, can test a parent to the limits of patience. This little one may actually start playing power games in his cradle, and this only increases with each passing year. Parents may be astounded at the subtlety of this child's mind and actions. Everything is a game, a means of achieving power and mastery over others. It can be quite intimidating, even to a resilient parent.

As Scorpio children grow and develop they begin to "grow" into themselves and are better able to handle the extremes in their nature. They generally have positive motives in mind. They want to get to the bottom of things, to understand the way their world works, and they won't rest until they do. Raising this child can be like playing a game of chess—in order to win, the parent needs to stay several moves ahead.

THE SCORPIO LOVER Astrology has made the words "lover" and "Scorpio" virtually synonymous, and while there is every reason to believe that Scorpio individuals possess amazing skills in this department, it is misleading to think they are preoccupied with sex. The Scorpio nature is much more complicated than that, and the typical Scorpio is interested in marriage and long-term commitment. Without this type of stability in their lives, Scorpio individuals have a difficult time focusing their energy in a positive way.

It is also true that Scorpio men and women have a strong sexual appetite and may be tempted to stray if their mate does not provide the profound spiritual and physical attraction that they require.

THE SCORPIO BOSS The typical Scorpio boss is demanding and somewhat austere. He or she has the ability to give a reprimand by merely lifting an eyebrow. Many Scorpio bosses rule through intimidation, and even those who don't deliberately use this skill have enough steely determination in their nature to create fear in the breast of a fully grown man or woman.

Naturally, not all Scorpio employers are tyrants. They are not generally communicative however, and this in itself can cause problems. Gossip or rumors in the workplace have the power to create disharmony and doubt, and because of an attitude of remoteness, the Scorpio boss may not be aware of what is being said about him or his methods.

ELEMENT: Water
QUALITY: Fixed
PLANETARY RULER: Pluto
BIRTHSTONE: Topaz
FLOWER: Chrysanthemum

KEY CHARACTERISTIC: Endurance.

STRENGTHS: Intense, Powerful, Transforming
CHALLENGES: Jealous, Domineering, Violent

THE SCORPIO FRIEND As a rule, Scorpio individuals have very few friends, but they share an incredible closeness with the ones they do have. By nature, Scorpio men and woman are loners who look to themselves, not others, to solve problems and learn lessons. Although they may love their friends dearly, Scorpio individuals may not confide in them. It is often said that the Scorpio wants to know everyone's secrets but will never willingly divulge any of his own.

The typical Scorpio often acts as counselor to his or her friends. Because Scorpio men and women have great wisdom in both the worldly and spiritual sense, they are often sought out as life guides, even gurus.

241

OCTOBER 23

Individuals born on October 23 have the charismatic personality so often found in those whose birthday falls on the cusp between signs. These people have a definite flair for putting themselves into situations where they will be noticed, then are just as likely to pull back, vexed, when too much attention is accorded to them. This dichotomy has the power to put them at the center of controversy throughout life, but can be a source of emotional growth and transformation.

FRIENDS AND LOVERS Those born on October 23 are exceptionally romantic, even idealistic where love and marriage are concerned. Romances are likely to be conducted in a surreptitious manner, since these individuals are attracted to secrecy even when there is no need for it.

October 23 people demand complete loyalty from those they care about, and will leave a relationship impulsively if there is any suspicion of betrayal. These individuals value friends almost as much as lovers, and often enter into intense friendships that give them avenues to express their own unique personality and life-force.

CHILDREN AND FAMILY October 23 individuals have extremely close family ties. They regard their grown brothers and sisters more as friends than siblings, and may have forged equally close relationships with cousins or other relatives.

They make affectionate, protective parents who are concerned with giving their children a sense of self-reliance and independence even from a very early age.

HEALTH People born on October 23 often strike a cavalier attitude about their health and fitness. Since these individuals tend to be favored with a strong constitution and superior powers of physical and emotional endurance, they may feel virtually invulnerable to outside forces.

Because of their strong mental gifts, people born on this date benefit from practicing meditation before bedtime in order to promote deep sleep and productive dream patterns.

CAREER AND FINANCES October 23 individuals are drawn to careers that offer emotional and spiritual satisfaction, such as the arts and humanities. These people need to be challenged, and enjoy challenging others. A desire for friendly competition is an integral part of this personality.

Although skillful at handling financial matters, especially the art of negotiation, October 23 people are not very ambitious about making money. Realizing that they have the talent to do so is more important than exercising it.

DREAMS AND GOALS People born on this date think big. They are not interested in listening to the reasons why something cannot be done, only in how they can turn that negative into a positive. Although their goals may seem improbable, even impossible to others, October 23 individuals embrace them without fear. They enjoy living at a high pitch and would rather be in chaos than boredom.

EMBRACE
Artistic fulfillment
Finding your soul mate
A positive self-image

AVOID
Being overly secretive
Going to extremes
Self-fulfilling prophecies

ALSO BORN TODAY
Talk show host Johnny Carson; author Michael Crichton; actress Diana Dors; quarterback Doug Flutie; film director Philip Kaufman; author Emily Kimbrough; soccer player Pele; singer Dwight Yoakam.

OCTOBER 24

October 24 individuals have great personal magnetism. In love with life, these men and women possess a highly romantic and sensual nature that defines their personality.

People born on this date are extremely talented as well as fiercely competitive. They don't like to lose at anything and can be very intimidating to others. While these individuals have a haughty disposition, they are actually much nicer than they appear. Because they may lack confidence, October 24 people find it necessary to act as though they are in complete control of their lives.

FRIENDS AND LOVERS
October 24 people are able to command great love, even worship from their friends. These darkly charming individuals have the ability to treat people rudely, and still be loved for their magnetism alone.

The road to romance can be a difficult one for the men and women born on this date. Because they are addicted to excitement, they often end up with someone who is actually the antithesis of what they really want.

CHILDREN AND FAMILY
Even if there is not some deep, dark secret locked away in their past, October 24 individuals treat the memory of their childhood as if there were such a secret. These people make mysteries out of everything!

If they have learned the important lessons life has to teach them, October 24 men and women will not repeat the mistakes their own parents made with them.

HEALTH
Extremists in most areas of life, October 24 natives have some incredibly eccentric health habits. They are likely to banish certain foods from their diet and overindulge in other foods that are considered to be especially "healthy."

Fasting is a popular health habit of October 24 people because it fulfills physical and spiritual needs for them.

CAREER AND FINANCES
October 24 people enjoy work that has some possibility of danger attached to it. For this reason careers in police work, firefighting, or the military often appeal to them. They also enjoy professions that allow them to dabble in mystery or detection. Private investigator, undercover police officer, or industrial spy are jobs that are tailor-made to their interests.

October 24 folks are very careful about how they manage their money. They are much more taken with the idea of saving, even hoarding, money than with spending it.

DREAMS AND GOALS
People born on this day have difficulty deciding just what they want out of life. The talents they possess often make things easy for them. Still, these people want to strive, fail, then begin again. Only through this complicated scenario do they feel as if they've earned their place in the sun.

Making relationships work is a key goal, which may be why these people so often travel a circuitous route to personal happiness. If they can make complicated situations work, they know they've achieved nirvana.

EMBRACE
Experience
Activity
Subconscious will

AVOID
Carnality
Lordly behavior
Hidden agendas

ALSO BORN TODAY
Actor F. Murray Abraham; film director Merian C. Cooper; opera star Tito Gobbi; actor Kevin Kline; baseball star Juan Marichal; actor/director David Nelson; football star Y. A. Tittle; musician Bill Wyman.

OCTOBER 25

The past is never very far away from people born on this date. Whether pleasant or unpleasant, they compare each new experience to what they have known. With their extremely sensitive and highly imaginative nature, dreams and illusions are as concrete to these individuals as reality.

There is a certain ageless quality about these people. In youth they may seem far older than their years, while old age only seems to refine their unique qualities.

with their current situation. If childhood was a negative experience, they're likely to continually relive their familial relationships through new ones.

Because of their complicated history, whether or not to have children is a major decision for people born on October 25.

HEALTH Learning to vent their innermost feelings is a must for these people. They don't do anything halfway, and they are emotional extremists. The best health tip for these people is to act out their anger, rather than bottle it up.

These men and women need to be vigilant about their eating habits if they want to stay slim. Less red meat, starches, and sweets can help to keep their weight down.

CAREER AND FINANCES October 25 natives look for careers that will provide them with a sense of their own autonomy. These men and women do not like to answer to others, and prefer to be independent, both financially and spiritually.

Although October 25 people cannot be seduced by the idea of money, they are very cautious about maintaining the status quo. Security is an emotionally charged issue for these individuals. They need to feel as if they have the funds to support themselves, no matter what the situation.

DREAMS AND GOALS October 25 people strive to find their special place in the world. They don't believe in doing anything the easy way, and will gladly sacrifice in order to make their dreams come true.

These individuals know what they want out of life and are not afraid to take a few risks to claim it. They learn from their mistakes and can turn adversity into success.

EMBRACE
Poignant memories
Artistic expression
Peace

AVOID
Sadness
Regret
Addiction

ALSO BORN TODAY
Composer Georges Bizet; violinist Midori; actress Tracy Nelson; singer Minnie Pearl; artist Pablo Picasso; singer Helen Reddy; actress Marian Ross; composer Johann Strauss.

FRIENDS AND LOVERS A possessive streak shows up in the relationships pursued by these folks. Friends are expected to be unflinchingly loyal and singularly devoted. Because they don't like to "share," October 25 people may expect friends to choose between them and someone else.

This attitude is even more extreme in romantic relationships, where these folks can be very demanding with a partner or mate. This relationship is the most important factor in their lives—and their mate had better feel the same or there will be trouble.

CHILDREN AND FAMILY It's extremely difficult for water-sign individuals to let go of their childhood, even if it was far from idyllic. These men and women may have unresolved problems dating from childhood. If it was a happy time for them, they may feel unsatisfied

OCTOBER 26

October 26 people are easy to love, yet hard to know. They value power and know how to use it, yet are more concerned with using it to help others rather than to glorify themselves.

People born on this date are extremely self-disciplined. Personal honor means a great deal to them, and they are fanatics about keeping their word. Whenever an October 26 individual makes a promise, no one else in the world is more likely to keep it.

FRIENDS AND LOVERS Although October 26 men and women may have very few friends, this is the way they like it. To them it is quality, not quantity, that matters. Their best friends are often those who have been with them in a time of trouble or challenge.

People born on this date are intense in love matters and have the charisma to carry it off. They have a great deal of personal charm as well as the power to manipulate others. But manipulation is definitely not their style; they have far too much honor.

CHILDREN AND FAMILY On some level, October 26 people are always at war with their background. Past emotions still run high, and in order to resolve those feelings these people need to learn how to make peace with that time in their lives.

As parents, October 26 people have an almost psychic bond with their children. This closeness continues throughout life and can develop into extremely powerful relationships.

HEALTH October 26 men and women are very disciplined about health matters. They don't make a big deal about it, but they are careful to adhere to strict principles. These folks know enough to stay away from red meat and caffeine, and even if they indulge once in a while, they're careful to temper their diet with plenty of green leafy vegetables and legumes.

These people believe in natural exercise; rather than working out at a gym or even at home, October 26 natives like to take their exercise in the great outdoors.

CAREER AND FINANCES People born on this date have a genuine talent for research of any kind. Because they have a solitary nature they like to work behind the scenes, searching out answers from books and databases. They love learning, especially when they have a chance to dig into old facts, old mysteries.

October 26 people have a very circumspect way of handling money. They adhere to a strict code that requires them to save as much as possible, while spending mostly on necessities, with luxury items thrown in every once in a blue moon.

DREAMS AND GOALS October 26 men and women are interested in wielding power, though usually from behind the scenes. These people will go to great lengths to put their ideas out there for others to see, but aren't surprised to see them rejected. The very fact that they have such a specialized view of things is enough to make October 26 folks realize that they are usually in the minority as far as popular opinion is concerned.

These people are highly motivated and are willing to sacrifice to meet their goals.

EMBRACE
Cooperation
Commitment to excellence
Kindness

AVOID
Sadness
Regret
Addiction

ALSO BORN TODAY
First Lady Hillary Rodham Clinton; actor Cary Elwes; actor Bob Hoskins; singer Mahalia Jackson; film director/producer Ivan Reitman; composer Domenico Scarlatti; film director Don Siegel; actress Jaclyn Smith.

OCTOBER 27

October 27 natives are complicated individuals who like to walk on the wild side. Their quiet personality seems to hide something dangerous and volcanic.

The men and women born on this date have the ability to make others notice them. This is really a feat, since October 27 people are almost preternaturally quiet. But they're also magnetic, which is why others are attracted to them. While some people might use this power in order to manipulate those who care for them, October 27 people rarely attempt such a thing.

FRIENDS AND LOVERS

There are few people who make more loyal friends than those born on October 27. They give emotional support without question, always willing to do whatever it takes to help a friend.

The love nature of October 27 men and women is even more extreme. They love so deeply that they very nearly become the person they love. This attitude has its drawbacks, including fits of jealousy, which come to the surface whenever these individuals feel as if their feelings aren't being returned in kind. October 27 people are often involved in tempestuous love affairs.

CHILDREN AND FAMILY

October 27 people feel closely bound to their upbringing. Even though at one point or another they may have experienced an estrangement from family members, they inevitably mend fences and try to remake and improve the relationship.

These people make good parents, although because of busy professional lives, they will depend heavily on a spouse for help in child-rearing.

HEALTH

Given their nature, it's very difficult for October 27 people to banish their all-or-nothing attitude from health matters. Either they faithfully adhere to a fitness program, almost to the point of fanaticism—or they completely ignore a commitment to exercise.

Food and drink can be problematical for these individuals. The downfall of many October 27 men and women is their habit of taking huge servings. They need to learn that to eat five small meals a day is far better for them than three huge ones.

CAREER AND FINANCES

Because October 27 individuals understand the balance of power that exists in every relationship, they are canny judges of the skill levels of others. People born on this date make fine supervisors, mentors, teachers, and coaches.

October 27 men and women have better luck with money than many other Scorpio natives, perhaps because they refuse to be intimidated by it. They have a common-sense attitude about finances.

DREAMS AND GOALS

October 27 people are very complex individuals who walk the tightrope between excitement and high risk. They can be sensible, they can be daredevils. There's so much contradiction in their behavior, in fact, that it's difficult to know how they'll react from one moment to the next—and that's the way they like it.

Those born on this date have the energy to accomplish amazing things in their lifetimes.

EMBRACE
Intellect
Balance
Friendships

AVOID
Depression
Insecurity
Making demands

ALSO BORN TODAY
Comedian John Cleese; actress Ruby Dee; Watergate figure H. R. Haldeman; violin virtuoso/composer Nicolo Paganini; poet Sylvia Plath; actress Carrie Snodgress; poet Dylan Thomas; violin virtuoso Vanessa-Mae.

OCTOBER 28

People born on this date have a great need to exert authority over others. Though this is almost always done in a positive way, it can still result in almost continuous power struggles that negatively affect personal and professional relationships.

October 28 individuals are strong-willed, precise, and dedicated to doing a good job. They become very disgruntled with themselves if they can't live up to their own expectations—which are usually far too ambitious.

FRIENDS AND LOVERS October 28 men and women expect their friends to "be there" for them in good times and bad. They can be demanding and may often have brief periods of estrangement from people who have unwittingly displeased them. When they get along well with their pals, though, there's not a better friend on Earth.

Love rarely runs smoothly for these people. They can be very critical, and do not mince words when it comes to voicing their opinions. Anyone who falls in love with an October 28 native had better expect to take more than their share of emotional lumps.

CHILDREN AND FAMILY October 28 natives spend a great deal of their adult life puzzling over their childhood. Even if they enjoyed a relatively peaceful upbringing, they remember whatever darker undercurrents that may have prevailed.

Once October 28 people become parents, they're likely to begin to open up emotionally about their childhood years. This can help them to understand themselves, and to understand their own youngsters, as well.

HEALTH Staying healthy is rarely a priority for these individuals—that is, until something happens to make them question the notion of their own immortality. Once they realize that they're just as vulnerable to illness as anybody else, they begin to take stock of their habits.

When young, October 28 people are likely to have poor eating habits. They gravitate to fast food and convenience foods rather than to the home-cooked variety. But once they make the effort to alter their eating habits, they become easily habituated to leafy green vegetables and fresh fruit.

CAREER AND FINANCES October 28 natives have a great desire to wield power. They don't need to be in a highly visible position, nor do they hunger after compliments. What they want is the power to make decisions that will stick.

Money is seldom a key issue with these people, except in the way it gives them emotional and psychological leverage. People born on this date are very careful with the way they handle money.

DREAMS AND GOALS October 28 people perpetually try to hold it all together. They are tough on others and tougher on themselves. Getting to where they want to go is worth a lot to these scrappy types, yet they will not compromise their ethics to do so. October 28 people know that the race of life is won not by the sprinters, but by the long-distance runners.

EMBRACE
A generous spirit
Knowledge
Involvement

AVOID
Dictatorial attitudes
Perfectionism
Willfulness

ALSO BORN TODAY
Astrologer Nicholas Culpepper; actor Dennis Franz; actress Jami Gertz; singer Cleo Laine; actress Joan Plowright; actress Julia Roberts; novelist Evelyn Waugh.

OCTOBER 29

October 29 natives are quixotic, sprite-like individuals who possess a changeable nature and exciting personality. They always seem to be observing, rather than taking part. These men and women dislike being the center of attention, even though they have the ability to draw the spotlight to themselves.

People born on this date are the ultimate secret-keepers. Yet even though they're very careful about safeguarding their own secrets, they love to try to uncover the secrets of others.

FRIENDS AND LOVERS
People born on this day have a small and select group of friends. To be part of the inner circle of someone born on this date is something like belonging to a secret society.

These men and women can be extraordinarily jealous and will react strongly to any questionable behavior—either real or imagined—on the part of their mate. They want to know about exes in great detail, yet may feel angry and betrayed when they hear the facts. October 29 people will interpret anything less than being cherished and adored as a lack of sincerity.

CHILDREN AND FAMILY
October 29 men and women may have a great many regrets from the past, especially related to their adolescence. They're likely to have spent some of their most difficult times during this period, striving to be something they were never meant to be.

As parents, October 29 individuals are certain to stress the importance of autonomy to their youngsters.

HEALTH
October 29 men and women enjoy the challenge of testing themselves. They may push themselves in difficult physical activities, such as mountain climbing, or endurance sports like biking, long-distance running, or swimming.

These folks like to prove that they can get along on a very limited diet. They may enjoy fasting, and have little trouble giving up particular foods.

CAREER AND FINANCES
Whether or not they wish to be noticed, October 29 people don't remain hidden easily. Their personality is slightly off-center, a little prickly, but ultimately enchanting. They favor unusual careers, and often end up working for themselves. Their iconoclastic attitudes make them interesting writers, photographers, fashion designers, models, musicians, and conceptual artists.

These folks aren't interested in money, though they have a great potential for becoming very rich through their talents. They have a reputation for spending money casually.

DREAMS AND GOALS
People born on this date are very secretive about their goals. They don't really want anyone else to know their plans, for several reasons: Because they have a problem with intimacy, they don't like to answer to others, especially if they are expected to explain failure. Also, if they happen to change their minds, October 29 people don't want to have to explain why they did so.

These men and women sometimes give too much attention to their professional goals, while ignoring personal ones.

EMBRACE
Emotional stability
A hopeful heart
High ideals

AVOID
Envy
Blaming others
Troublesome love affairs

ALSO BORN TODAY
Animator Ralph Bakshi; writer James Boswell; comedienne Fanny Brice; singer Kevin Dubrow; astronomer Edmund Halley; actress Kate Jackson; singer Melba Moore; actress Winona Ryder.

OCTOBER 30

O ctober 30 people have an adventure-some spirit that manifests itself in a great love of travel and distant cultures. They may think of themselves as citizens of the world. These people seek knowledge in order to gain wisdom.

People born on this date are innovators in the way they live life. They understand that in order to progress they must be part of new experiences. To trust instinct over intelligence can be a challenge for them, but is generally a sound goal.

FRIENDS AND LOVERS October 30 individuals are about the least demanding and most fun friends on earth. Not only can they make friends with virtually anyone, they are able to build up the self-esteem of others. They want an active friendship that involves intense debate, travel, hobbies, and plenty of social life.

These men and women make equally engaging romantic partners. They aren't strictly marriage-minded and may prefer a relationship that is less constricting.

CHILDREN AND FAMILY People born on this date understand how to embrace their growing-up years, forgiving parents for any mistakes they may have made. They usually retain very close ties with family members.

As parents, October 30 natives are loving, affectionate, and full of fun. They know how to get into a child's world by taking part in the sort of imaginative fantasy that only young people have the ability to understand.

HEALTH People born on this date do everything the natural way. They adapt easily to an organic, low-fat diet, and may even like growing their own fruits and vegetables. These men and women understand the need to cut harmful toxins and additives out of their diet.

Although they pursue a generally active lifestyle, these folks are not particularly interested in exercise unless it's an extension of their daily routine.

CAREER AND FINANCES People born on this date are happy in professions that allow them to travel and experience other cultures. They also make great professors, teachers, counselors, and travel agents. Since October 30 people have little of the typical Scorpio need for privacy, they usually prefer to work with a large group of people.

These men and women think big. They aren't foolish with money but they do like to spend it. They have a generous nature and love to remember friends and loved ones with keepsakes and other thoughtful gestures. They have a good head for investments, and the potential to make a great deal of money.

DREAMS AND GOALS People born on this date want to learn as much as they can. Although not academically inclined, they think of themselves as life-long students.

October 30 natives are too broad-minded to think that they can have a successful personal life only if they have a spouse and children. They want to extend their horizons, and if that means having a family—fine. If not, they won't be disappointed.

EMBRACE
Self-discipline
Aptitude
Benevolence

AVOID
Pretense
Ambivalence
Insensitivity to others

ALSO BORN TODAY
U.S. President John Adams; England's King George II; film director Claude Lelouch; poet Ezra Pound; rock star Grace Slick; actor Charles Martin Smith; singer Otis Williams; actor Henry Winkler.

OCTOBER 31

October 31 individuals are searchers after truth and spiritual oneness. They are not rebels, but loners, and have no need of validation from others. Although their personal lives may often be characterized by many highs and lows, they have tremendous endurance and can always get past a disappointment or a setback.

People born on this date have a forthright attitude that allows them to display their honesty without seeming brusque or harsh. They get along well with others, but are careful about enforcing emotional boundaries.

October 31 men and women look to the past for answers. No matter what sort of upbringing they had, these people draw from their memories in order to come to grips with present-day problems.

Once they make peace with the past, October 31 natives are exceptional parents. They seek a spiritual bond with their children that transcends the relationship.

EMBRACE
Realization
Psychology
Self-understanding

AVOID
Questioning existence
Disorganization
Promiscuity

ALSO BORN TODAY
Musician Bernard Edwards; actress/director Lee Grant; poet John Keats; actress Sally Kirkland; actor Michael Landon; TV journalist Jane Pauley; TV journalist Dan Rather; actor David Ogden Stiers.

FRIENDS AND LOVERS These introspective people have difficulty relating to others on anything but a completely truthful level. They are incapable of having superficial relationships. Any friendship is as deep as a love relationship to them, and they expect to be treated the same way in return.

These men and women expect a great deal from their romantic life. Above all they seek stability, and will do anything they can to ensure that their marriage or relationship is permanent. Yet they cannot overlook the infidelity of a partner, nor will they allow themselves to be ignored or taken for granted.

CHILDREN AND FAMILY Because they are constantly searching for ways to bring the disparate parts of their nature into harmony,

HEALTH People born on this date have their own ways of dealing with health matters. They aren't comfortable with simply taking advice from others, but prefer to initiate a self-designed plan suited just for them.

Because October 31 people have a great deal of physical and intellectual energy, the system of Chinese exercise known as Qigong is a perfect way for these people to raise, rather than deplete, their energy levels.

CAREER AND FINANCES October 31 men and women are restless individuals who may frequently change their career aims. These people are very interested in the esoteric sciences and often seek out careers as astrologers, astro-therapists, Tarot-card readers, or hypnotherapists.

People born on this day don't have any particular system of handling their finances. When they have a positive cash flow, they spend. When they don't, they pull in the proverbial belt.

DREAMS AND GOALS October 31 men and women continually strive to learn more about themselves. They have great spiritual potential and usually see life from this perspective. They're not interested in worldly success, preferring to seek out the esoteric meaning behind the events and circumstances of life.

NOVEMBER 1

November Scorpios are far more intense than their late October cousins, but those born on November 1 are somewhere in between. These men and women have a restless, energetic spirit, yet they are far more people-oriented than many natives of their sign.

November 1 individuals want their place in the sun and are constantly striving for success. Even when they meet with serious obstacles, these people remain survivors with big plans about how to turn things around.

FRIENDS AND LOVERS

November 1 men and women look to their friends for inspiration and experience. People born on this date never take friendship lightly. They have a need to bond with their pals, sharing experiences on a truly soul-based level.

Love is always a combination of the simple and the complex with November 1 people. They often demand more love and attention than anyone can give, yet they give it back, and more.

CHILDREN AND FAMILY

People born on this date draw considerable strength from the values and beliefs they were taught as children. Even if the family situation was not particularly stable, they are able to see it in a basically positive light.

November 1 people are exceptionally good parents, though they are strict and even a bit closed-minded at times. They don't expect their children to be perfect, but they do demand that they become responsible at a very early age. These people are never shy about showing their affection, and will always let their children know how special and important they are.

HEALTH

People born on this date are not interested in pursuing a lot of complicated machinations in order to stay healthy. They believe in doing things the natural way: sensible diet, moderate exercise, and plenty of time for meditation and contemplation.

These people are equally pragmatic where food is concerned. They don't naturally gravitate toward fast food, but they don't deliberately avoid it, either. November 1 natives definitely believe in taking life as it comes.

CAREER AND FINANCES

People born on this date seek careers that give them ultimate satisfaction and a sense that they're someone important and worthwhile. They don't look for validation from their colleagues, preferring to live up to their own standards.

November 1 natives are experts at handling their personal finances. They are the sort who do their own taxes and make their own investment decisions.

DREAMS AND GOALS

Becoming successful in both the worldly and spiritual senses of the word is very important to November 1 individuals. These men and women have an almost unlimited ambition to succeed and will work hard to make their dreams come true.

Fortunately, they have their own timetable for success and won't allow arbitrary standards to put pressure on them. They go at a steady pace, taking one day at a time, not expecting success to come easily, though they never doubt it will happen eventually.

EMBRACE
Creative ambitions
Constancy
Taking ownership

AVOID
Negativity
Apprehension
Disenchantment

ALSO BORN TODAY
Actress Barbara Bosson; writer Stephen Crane; opera singer Victoria de Los Angeles; musician Keith Emerson; actor Robert Foxworth; singer Lyle Lovett; golfer Gary Player.

NOVEMBER 2

People born on this date are stubborn individuals who possess an incredible amount of emotional and spiritual stamina. Although they often seem quiet and somewhat introspective, November 2 natives are fighters who support the status quo and expect it to support them.

These men and women are the kings and queens of high drama. Every emotional scene in their lives is like something out of an opera. These are not people who enjoy being disagreed with, and because of that, they often get their own way.

FRIENDS AND LOVERS
People born on this date are intensely loyal to their friends, and they demand to be accorded similar loyalty in return. There are a great many control issues at work with these folks, which can be a challenge for all of the participants.

In love affairs or marriage, November 2 natives can be very jealous, even fanatically so. They love so deeply and possessively that they may not be aware of how controlling they can seem, even to those who love them just as much in return.

CHILDREN AND FAMILY
Like many Scorpios, November 2 people are truly plugged into their memories from childhood. These people cannot separate from their past any more than they can from themselves. The past is not dead to these men and women—it is alive and affecting their lives every single day.

Although November 2 natives want to see their own children become self-sufficient and independent, they may nonetheless be extremely clinging and demanding toward them. This is usually done out of love, yet it can create a rift between parent and child.

HEALTH
People born on this date are iconoclasts when it comes to taking care of their health. They understand the value of exercise and proper eating, and generally obey these rules, but on their own terms.

Men and women born on November 2 enjoy solitary sports, such as running, swimming, or hiking. They pursue these interests less for physical exercise than for a need to be alone with their thoughts.

CAREER AND FINANCES
People born on this date have a great talent for acting, speech making, speech writing, teaching, and creative work of all kinds. They are often extremely religious, and may seek to work within their faith.

Money rarely tempts these people to do something they prefer not to do. They're dedicated to ideas, not their pocketbook. Because they prefer to live simply, they may appear to be parsimonious. In truth, they possess a generous nature.

DREAMS AND GOALS
November 2 people are determined fighters who see every aspect of life as a battle to be won, a challenge to be overcome.

They have high standards and want to do everything on their own. While most people welcome a little good luck, November 2 people don't feel as if they have earned their goals unless they have been forced to suffer in order to attain them.

EMBRACE
Fairness
Good judgment
Tenacity

AVOID
Dogmatic attitudes
Hypocrisy
Possessiveness

ALSO BORN TODAY
Political commentator Pat Buchanan; U.S. President Warren G. Harding; actor Burt Lancaster; singer/songwriter k. d. lang; French Queen Marie Antoinette; film director Luchino Visconti; actress Alfre Woodard.

NOVEMBER 3

November 3 individuals are sarcastic, inventive, and extremely precocious. Their attitude of wry amusement seems to say that they know a few secrets about life that other people can't guess. Although they enjoy the good things that come their way, they never quite believe that their good luck will hold.

People born on this date are fond of gambling in all its forms, yet they are far too savvy to take unnecessary chances or draw undue attention to themselves. To the contrary, they place high value on their privacy.

FRIENDS AND LOVERS

November 3 natives have a habit of continually remaking their relationships. Nothing ever seems stable with these people. Friendships that last for many years may be perpetually on-again, off-again. November 3 natives demand unflinching loyalty from their pals, and will force a falling-out if they believe that their wishes are not being upheld. In order for November 3 people to be happy in their romantic relationships, they must first be happy with themselves.

CHILDREN AND FAMILY

These men and women have an extremely sensitive nature and a need to distance themselves from the pain of the past. Although they have the ability to get beyond unhappy memories, they may not choose to do so until they have assurance from the new people in their lives that there will be something to replace it.

Because of their background, November 3 individuals are extremely protective parents who may struggle to resolve their own abandonment issues through an unusually close relationship with their children.

HEALTH

November 3 people are full of enthusiasm and vigor for a fitness regimen—

then they may lose interest altogether. They are destined to struggle to adhere to any strict plan that demands blind obedience. These people like to make their own rules.

CAREER AND FINANCES

Many November 3 individuals do not have a specific career strategy. Instead, they often use their strong intuition to pick up on opportunities as they arise. They're usually talented people who can choose within a variety of occupations. Since they are exceptionally intelligent, their work often gives them the chance to show off their way with words.

People born on this date have some very careless money habits. Although quite capable of handling their own finances, they are often impatient with the details of bookkeeping.

DREAMS AND GOALS

November 3 men and women need to defy authority. These people want success, but it must be on their own terms. They are incapable of allowing themselves to be manipulated in any way.

Also, they have a hard time balancing professional success against personal happiness; at some point in life they may be forced to make a choice between the two. Although they may give the appearance of being career-oriented, they are actually more concerned with maintaining the integrity of their personal relationships.

EMBRACE
Deep feelings
Vulnerability
Faith

AVOID
Rivalries
A desire to rewrite the past
Cynicism

ALSO BORN TODAY
Singer Adam Ant; actor Charles Bronson; baseball star Bob Feller; writer Ludovic Kennedy; comedian Dennis Miller; singer Lulu; comedienne Roseanne; novelist Martin Cruz Smith.

NOVEMBER 4

The need of November 4 natives to create controversy exerts its will in every aspect of their lives. Quick-witted and talkative, these people tell the truth without fearing its consequences.

Eccentric, even bizarre, behavior is the norm with people born on this date. They don't worry about what others will say about them, and have the integrity to be themselves. These men and women are the real article, and will not deviate from their own standards for any reason.

FRIENDS AND LOVERS November 4 people are very specific about the sorts of friends they bring into their lives. Superficial relationships turn them off; meaningful and honest friendships are what they strive for.

Their requirements in love and romance are similarly honest. They aren't looking for a social companion or someone to keep them company in bed once the lights go out. These men and women want a passionate, committed life partner.

CHILDREN AND FAMILY November 4 people usually owe their uniqueness and special gifts to the way they were brought up. They generally had the sort of relationship with their family that allowed for differences of opinion.

People born on this date are adamant about giving their own children the same sort of freedom. While they understand the necessity of establishing guidelines, these progressive men and women don't want their children to feel as if they must conform to a specified standard of behavior in order to be loved.

HEALTH November 4 people know that, for them, staying healthy starts on the inside. Feeling good about themselves and being in touch with their emotions is the very best health habit they can endorse. A refusal to express their feelings and opinions can actually make these people ill.

People born on this date don't neglect exercise or a good diet, but they don't obsess over these things, either. These folks go about their regular activities without thinking about such things in detail. This casual attitude helps them to relax—another good health tip.

CAREER AND FINANCES November 4 people are intelligent and perceptive. They look for career choices that showcase their abilities with words and their outgoing personality. These men and women make excellent teachers, public speakers, computer programmers, writers, and media personnel.

November 4 individuals, seem to have a sixth sense about their finances. They are perceptive investors who are capable of turning a moderate income into a considerable fortune.

DREAMS AND GOALS November 4 men and women are definitely not the types to muse over "the good old days." They believe that whatever is ahead is better than what came before. For this reason, they are enthusiastic about setting personal goals, and even more energetic about achieving them.

People born on this date have very realistic ideas about what they can do in life, but that doesn't keep them from dreaming the "impossible dream."

EMBRACE
Discretion
Fair play
An intuitive nature

AVOID
Tedium
Feeling blue
Looking back

ALSO BORN TODAY
Actor Art Carney; TV journalist Walter Cronkite; actor Ralph Macchio; actress Markie Post; actress Kate Reid; rap singer Kool Rock; musician Mike Smith; actress Loretta Swit.

NOVEMBER 5

November 5 people have a love of things that can be proven by scientific fact. These people are natural researchers and students. They are constantly looking for answers, and cultivate knowledge and wisdom in order to better understand themselves.

Despite their admittedly serious side, these men and women have a great love of an active social life. Their clever sense of humor has a cutting edge, but they never deliberately hurt another person's feelings. If they wish, November 5 people can be the life of the party.

FRIENDS AND LOVERS
Although most Scorpios have a small, close-knit group of friends, November 5 natives need a lot of companions in their life.

November 5 men and women usually enjoy a stable but exciting love life. They often marry early in life, sometimes to their high school or college sweetheart. They are devoted to the idea of fidelity in marriage.

CHILDREN AND FAMILY
If there were some serious problems in the family during their growing-up years, November 5 people are wise enough to realize that they can get beyond whatever emotional scars they may have sustained.

As parents, November 5 people are encouraging and helpful. While they don't push their children to become achievers, they do understand their own part in helping their youngsters to feel good about themselves.

HEALTH
People born on this date take good physical care of themselves. They eat well but moderately, and are always looking for ways to maximize the efficiency of their workout schedule. One of the things that works best for them is to maintain their regular exercise plan on weekdays, and take weekends off. Pacing, then, is the key.

November 5 natives generally prefer simple fare: meat, potatoes, and unadorned vegetables. They also like rich desserts, which should be kept to a minimum.

CAREER AND FINANCES
November 5 people are doers as well as thinkers. They are intelligent, but are more likely to go with their instincts instead of analyzing everything before coming to a conclusion. These men and women usually seek careers that require, at minimum, an undergraduate degree.

Handling money is no problem for these practical people. They usually manage their own finances, and within their personal relationships they are generally the ones who set the budget rules.

DREAMS AND GOALS
November 5 people don't do anything halfway or recklessly. They understand their academic potential, so that's usually where they put their faith. These people are not career-driven, but they do believe in living up to their natural potential by working hard in their chosen field.

Where their personal life is concerned, November 5 men and women want the usual things out of life: love, partnership, and children. More than anything, they believe in being happy.

EMBRACE
Good fortune
Solace
Facts

AVOID
Questioning authority
Materialism
Sarcasm

ALSO BORN TODAY
Singer Bryan Adams; historian Will Durant; singer Art Garfunkel; actress Vivien Leigh; actress Tatum O'Neal; playwright/actor Sam Shepard; actress Elke Sommer; singer Ike Turner.

NOVEMBER 6

November 6 natives are passionate, romantic individuals who have the ability to communicate on many levels. Although relationships are the centerpiece of their lives, these men and women are nevertheless extremely self-sufficient. They may seem serious on the outside, but they know how to have a good time.

People born on this date are lovers of luxury who enjoy having all the familiar creature comforts. When they feel blue, they have a tendency to pamper themselves.

FRIENDS AND LOVERS
Honesty is the key to the relationships of November 6 people. They may not have a great many friends, but they are very close to a special few. These men and women prefer maintaining a strong sense of kinship with their friends. Superficial or social relationships are definitely not for them.

The happiness or unhappiness of November 6 people is often determined by the wisdom of their romantic choices. These folks fall in and out of love in a big way and are accustomed to having their hearts broken. But even when they face severe romantic challenges, they will not give up, and will continue to search for the person of their dreams.

CHILDREN AND FAMILY
November 6 people have a natural love of family life. They usually have close ties to family members, and enjoy reminiscing about their growing-up years. They are far too practical to worry over what may have gone wrong when they were children.

People born on this date may not feel as if they have truly "grown up" until they begin a family of their own. This gives them the opportunity to learn more about themselves than they ever believed possible.

HEALTH
November 6 men and women live an active lifestyle that ensures good health. They always seem to be aware of the latest facts and theories related to fitness, and, indeed, can be somewhat fanatical when it comes to diet.

Sufficient exercise is one of their major concerns. These men and women don't enjoy setting time aside from their schedules to work out on machines or at the gym. Instead, they prefer to be active in natural ways: walking instead of driving and doing their own yardwork and household chores.

CAREER AND FINANCES
Although they may not seem ambitious, November 6 people are always looking to extend the boundaries of their job descriptions. They want to make it to the top of whatever field they choose. Despite this, they do not possess the ruthlessness that many Scorpio natives display.

People born on this date are concerned with maintaining a secure lifestyle for their loved ones, but other than that they are not worried about making a lot of money.

DREAMS AND GOALS
Whether it is a friendship, a marriage, or parenthood, these men and women work very hard to make all of their personal relationships happy and honest.

People born on this date have high hopes for professional success, but are not willing to allow other areas of their lives to go unfulfilled.

EMBRACE
Comprehension
Ability to reason
Fate

AVOID
Secretive behavior
Overwork
Worry

ALSO BORN TODAY
Actress Sally Field; actor Nigel Havers; actor Ethan Hawke; novelist James Jones; film director Mike Nichols; model Jean Shrimpton; TV journalist Maria Shriver; composer John Philip Sousa.

NOVEMBER 7

Very few people have the potential of these amazing men and women. They possess intelligence and spirituality in equal measure—a marvelous combination. Although they have a strong sense of mission in life, they are also profoundly inner-directed, needing a lot of time to concentrate on their personal sense of fulfillment.

November 7 natives are often drawn to New Age studies and attitudes. They need to express themselves through spiritual and supernatural attunement.

FRIENDS AND LOVERS Few people have as much love to give as those born on this date. They take their friendships very seriously and will keep their word to a friend without fail. Being a mentor as well as a pal is second nature to these people.

Because they are deeply giving people, November 7 men and women usually experience the greatest joy in their lives through their marriage or other primary love relationships. These individuals are loyal and do not take any commitment lightly.

CHILDREN AND FAMILY Whatever their upbringing was like, people born on this date are able to use the experience in a positive way. They are totally guileless and will not blame their parents for any real or imagined mistakes.

They try to bring this same sense of balance to their roles as parents. November 7 men and women want to do the very best job that they can, but they realize that rearing children is a complex calling. They know that not all children will respond to their type of philosophy, and do not blame themselves if their youngsters do not choose to follow their way of life.

HEALTH November 7 people believe that a healthy body, mind, and spirit are interrelated. These men and women have a lot of natural energy highlighted by a positive attitude that allows them to greet each new day with enthusiasm.

Prayer and meditation play important roles in the lives of November 7 natives. They understand that too much activity can make people lose track of what is really happening in their lives.

CAREER AND FINANCES November 7 individuals do their best work in jobs that give them the opportunity to help others. November 7 men and women do not set themselves up as "experts." They see themselves simply as good listeners.

Although financial gain is seldom a major factor when November 7 individuals choose a career, these people are nevertheless very adept at handling money.

DREAMS AND GOALS November 7 natives are dedicated to doing good in their lives. Although their ideas and politics may conflict with those of their closest friends and relatives, no one can question their motives.

People born on this date know that for them, family must always come first.

EMBRACE
Fortitude
A pure heart
Innocence

AVOID
Absolutism
Conflict
Misunderstandings

ALSO BORN TODAY
Existentialist philosopher Albert Camus; explorer James Cook; evangelist Billy Graham; musician Al Hirt; actor Dean Jagger; singer Joni Mitchell; musician Johnny Rivers; opera diva Joan Sutherland.

NOVEMBER 8

November 8 people must walk their own path in life, and even if it is a difficult one, they will usually resist help at every turn. These people give advice rather than take it.

People born today see life on a broad, episodic scale. They have a quirky vision that—though it may not accord strictly with reality—is definitely their own. If they are bold enough to divulge that vision to others, they can be handsomely rewarded.

FRIENDS AND LOVERS

These individuals are extremely secretive and have a hard time allowing other people to be an intimate part of their lives. They like friends who are loyal, yet know how to keep their distance. This prickly approach makes it difficult for November 8 people to have a lot of friends, but the ones they do have are very loyal.

People born on this date combine a sultry sexuality with a romantic spirit. They fall in love deeply, and if something goes wrong with the relationship they are likely to suffer a great deal of emotional pain.

CHILDREN AND FAMILY

The standoffish attitude of November 8 people usually has its roots in their upbringing. If they grew up in a large family they may feel as if their privacy wasn't adequately protected, causing them to be obsessively demanding about it as an adult.

November 8 people do not take their parental duties lightly. They see it as their responsibility to teach their children not simply about the good things of life, but its hardships, as well. This may seem harsh, but people born on this date believe they owe it to their youngsters to send them into the world well prepared.

HEALTH

November 8 men and women generally take a common-sense approach to fitness and health. They eat a moderate diet, and if they have any bad habits, such as smoking or drinking, they rarely overindulge.

Sexually transmitted diseases are far too prevalent these days and November 8 individuals understand the need to take special precautions concerning their own sexual activities.

CAREER AND FINANCES

As they do with every other aspect of life, November 8 individuals treat their profession with great seriousness. Whatever they choose to do for a living, they put all their efforts toward making a success of it. These people prefer to work behind the scenes—large groups do not appeal to them. They make marvelous researchers, teachers, and scientists.

November 8 people are careful about money to the point where they may seem cheap to those who don't know better. They are in constant search of bargains, unwilling to part with money unless it is for necessities or infrequent frivolous pleasures.

DREAMS AND GOALS

November 8 men and women are determined to achieve success on their own, or not at all. These independent souls refuse to take any shortcuts toward their goals, feeling that they should succeed by hard work and talent and no other way.

These folks have amazing patience and can withstand delays and disappointments like few other people.

EMBRACE
Destiny
Spiritual love
One's true self

AVOID
Compulsive behavior
Spitefulness
Disrespect

ALSO BORN TODAY
Actor Alain Delon; TV personality Mary Hart; opera singer Jerome Hines; novelist Margaret Mitchell; singer Bonnie Raitt; novelist Bram Stoker; actress Courtney Thorne-Smith; actress Roxana Zal.

NOVEMBER 9

Those born on November 9 are extremely adventurous, and always on the lookout for new experiences. These high-energy people seem to be constantly in motion, continually involved in new tasks and challenges.

November 9 men and women have a definite need to live life on their terms. They don't mind making mistakes as long as they learn from them. They have a great curiosity about life and never stop investigating the world around them.

FRIENDS AND LOVERS November 9 people are good at making their relationships work. These men and women are much more relationship-minded than many Scorpio natives.

In romantic relationships, people born on this date have the boldness to take the initiative. They don't sit around hoping that true love will find them—they go out and look for it! Once settled in a committed relationship, they are content to remain in it forever, and usually do unless their partner seeks a change.

CHILDREN AND FAMILY November 9 people generally have a philosophical view concerning the past. They don't obsess over what may have been lacking in their childhood. If these people experienced a particularly difficult time growing up, they have some emotional grit to show for it.

People born today have the wisdom to understand that they can't fight their children's battles for them. They can only stand by and be supportive, allowing them to learn life's lessons the same way they did—on their own.

HEALTH November 9 people have a nicely balanced temperament, which has a lot to do with their good health. These people understand that letting out their emotions allows them to be free of anxiety. They know how to turn negative emotions into positive feelings.

Diet can be a problem for November 9 individuals, who have a tendency to overeat when feeling blue. Substituting low-calorie meals for sweets and junk food can provide just the necessary change in their nutritional program.

CAREER AND FINANCES People born on this date are interested in careers that provide excitement and new experiences. They often opt for work that involves physical labor and a constant change of scenery. They may change careers several times, always eager to expand their horizons and bring new people into their lives.

November 9 people are scrupulously honest and have the shrewdness needed to turn a modest investment into a healthy moneymaker.

DREAMS AND GOALS November 9 people are perpetually in search of new and interesting experiences. They understand that they cannot have the sort of life they want without taking a few chances, so they're more than willing to work without the proverbial net.

People born on this date never worry about failure, because they understand that anyone who has the ambition and drive to go after their dreams will eventually succeed, despite the odds.

EMBRACE
Adventure
Learning
Deep feelings

AVOID
Risks
A defensive attitude
Pipe dreams

ALSO BORN TODAY
U.S. Vice President Spiro Agnew; England's King Edward VII; baseball star Bob Gibson; novelist Ronald Harwood; actress Hedy Lamarr; silent film actress Mae Marsh; singer Phil May; playwright Ivan Turgenev.

NOVEMBER 10

The men and women born on this date have so much strength of will that when they put their minds to it there is nothing they cannot accomplish. These people possess a keen intelligence and brilliant insights.

However, November 10 people need to develop the spiritual side of their nature; if they do not, it becomes easier for them to be seduced by worldly attractions that bring them little satisfaction. When they overcome this weakness, these men and women have the potential to achieve great things.

EMBRACE
Sagacity
Purpose
Generosity

AVOID
Frivolity
Weakness
Squandering talents

ALSO BORN TODAY
Actor Richard Burton; film composer Ennio Morricone; actress Mackenzie Phillips; poet Vachel Lindsay; actor Claude Rains; actress Ann Reinking; painter William Hogarth; actor Roy Scheider.

FRIENDS AND LOVERS People born on this date retain a remarkable loyalty to their friends, even if circumstances seek to divide them. They have the ability to bond with others on a spiritual level, which leads to friendships that are meaningful and emotionally healing.

Romantic love is the most profound experience in the lives of November 10 people. Like most water-sign people, they seek a soul mate, not just a partner. Even though these men and women often have the misfortune to be hurt by the ones they love, they never lose their idealism.

CHILDREN AND FAMILY November 10 people are devoted to their families. They remain in touch with their childhood roots no matter what later life brings them. These individuals have a very strict moral compass and rarely deviate from the values they learned in their youth.

Those born on this date expect a great deal from their children. They don't believe in making allowances for society's foibles, feeling that whatever made good sense when they were children should still be respected today.

HEALTH November 10 people have so much natural good health and vibrancy that it can be undermined only by their own actions. If these people maintain a good health regimen throughout life, they are likely to live to a ripe old age.

Although likely to be slim in youth, these men and women need to increase their exercise level as they near middle age. They have an extremely low tolerance for alcohol and should refrain from drinking anything stronger than red wine.

CAREER AND FINANCES People born on this date have a need to be involved in work that challenges them intellectually. They have a deep understanding of philosophy, science, and religion, and make very fine teachers.

November 10 folks have their share of problems with money matters. Although they have the intelligence to handle their finances well, they have a generous nature and may often spend money foolishly.

DREAMS AND GOALS These individuals often have a hard time deciding on just which goals they wish to achieve—the spiritual ones or the material ones. This dichotomy plays out in their lives over and over again.

When November 10 men and women are in pursuit of a goal, they turn all their talents toward achieving it.

NOVEMBER 11

November 11 individuals are the world's true mystics. Unable to live life on a strictly material level, they depend upon knowledge and experience to take them where they wish to go. They have marvelous creative powers, which they put to use in even the most ordinary circumstances and everyday events.

Gifted with the ability to spin interesting tales, they are natural storytellers. An interest in all facets of human experience is an illuminating influence in the lives of November 11 people.

FRIENDS AND LOVERS
Superficial relationships are beyond the understanding of these people, who prefer the sometimes rockier road of intense friendships and love relationships.

When November 11 individuals fall in love it's almost as if they become the person who is the object of their desire. While this closeness can produce an amazing union, it also has the ability to create a relationship that's too complicated for its own good.

CHILDREN AND FAMILY
Whether or not they come from a large family, people born on November 11 have a singularity about them.

Where their own children are concerned, they neither possess nor allow themselves to be possessed, regardless of how deeply they love their kids. They may see their children as having been "lent" rather than given to them, and are usually able to keep ego issues out of parenting duties.

HEALTH
Because the will of men and women born on this date is so strong, it often has the effect of endowing a fragile constitution with good health. If the creative energies are acknowledged and expressed, there's every reason to assume that these people will enjoy a high level of vitality. If these channels become blocked, the individuals may become depressed, even depleted.

CAREER AND FINANCES
Those born on November 11 have a need to feel as if they are contributing something unique to the world. For this reason they may have a hard time settling on a career goal. It's not unusual for them to take up the same work as someone they admire. Writing, teaching, and scientific research are occupations well suited to people born on this date.

Although money is not likely to be a significant factor in selecting a career, November 11 natives have the ability to amass and administer a great fortune, since money has no emotional hold on them.

DREAMS AND GOALS
Despite their somewhat otherworldly demeanor, November 11 people are very concerned with meeting their practical responsibilities, especially to those whom they love. The urge to live up to the challenges they set for themselves is a common goal.

Their personal dreams are likely to be plotted on a grandiose scale—impractical but not impossible. Because of their powerful will, it's likely that if these goals do not come true it is unrelated to any lack of focus on their part—merely a whim of nature.

EMBRACE
Graceful words
Positive thinking
The will to win

AVOID
Inner fears
Petty details
Power trips

ALSO BORN TODAY
First lady Abigail Adams; actress Bibi Andersson; novelist Fyodor Dostoyevsky; astrologer Katina Theodosiou, novelist Howard Fast; actress Demi Moore; novelist Kurt Vonnegut, Jr.; comedian Jonathan Winters.

NOVEMBER 12

November 12 individuals possess a dual nature, and may be perceived as either a "saint" or "sinner." The penetrating intelligence of these men and women is almost unnerving because it seems able to decipher the motives of others.

People born on this date are essentially loners, yet they have a magnetic personality that forces others to take notice of them. They can use their appeal in a manipulative fashion, though if they do, they run the risk of alienating others.

EMBRACE
Enchantment
Self-reliance
Devotion

AVOID
Unkindness
Selfish motives
Vindictiveness

ALSO BORN TODAY
Composer Alexander Borodin; gymnast Nadia Comaneci; Monaco's Princess Grace; figure skating champion Tonya Harding; actress Stefanie Powers; film director Richard Quine; sculptor Auguste Rodin; actor Wallace Shawn.

FRIENDS AND LOVERS November 12 men and women arouse strong feelings—people either like them very much, or dislike them in equal measure. It's difficult for these people to make friends because they have a hard time trusting others.

Although they possess a passionate love nature, unattached November 12 people may often experience long periods of self-inflicted celibacy. They are happiest when in a close, committed relationship that allows them the physical and spiritual intimacy they treasure.

CHILDREN AND FAMILY As with almost everything else in their existence, November 12 people find that family life is a study in extremes. They may be forced to endure an unsettled, unsatisfactory home life—or they could be the beneficiary of an extraordinarily close and loving family. One way or the other, these impressionable people take the lessons of childhood into their adult life.

Although they love their children, November 12 natives may have difficulty showing their affection. This generally becomes easier as the children grow into adolescence and young adulthood.

HEALTH November 12 people require emotional and spiritual motivation in order to feel good about themselves.

If they are unhappy, November 12 individuals may seek relief in food, drink, or drugs. If they can get interested in a challenging workout routine, people born on this date are just as likely to become fixated on it, as on bad habits.

CAREER AND FINANCES These men and women are incredibly ambitious and eager to prove that they have what it takes to be successful in their field. Because they don't really get along well with others, they do best in a career that emphasizes and rewards solitary accomplishment.

November 12 individuals are often careless with money. This could be the result of indifference, or a lack of training in financial matters.

DREAMS AND GOALS People born on this date want their talents to be recognized. They often possess a great deal of sensitivity in this area, and are caught between wanting their dreams to come true and feeling certain that they won't.

When they're feeling good about themselves, November 12 men and women can accomplish amazing things. They simply need to believe in their own abilities.

NOVEMBER 13

People born on November 13 possess a powerful conscience and a strong desire for personal autonomy. They have the ability to go against the "crowd." Uniqueness is so important to them that they may actually adjust their opinions to deliberately conflict with those of others!

November 13 natives have a natural dignity in the way they carry themselves. They are humorous, spontaneous, and often lucky. These individuals see things from a quirky perspective.

FRIENDS AND LOVERS November 13 people have difficulty making friends. They aren't particularly generous in their view of people and are not easily pleased. When they do make friends, it is a long and complicated process.

November 13 men and women seem destined to draw criticism of their love affairs. They often pick unlikely partners who are very different from them in lifestyle, background, or religious beliefs.

CHILDREN AND FAMILY People born on this date have a powerful connection to their upbringing. It is possible that they experienced an emotionally transforming period in childhood, which forever marked their development. They may have felt extremely insecure about their appearance or social standing when they were little. Later, able to "grow" into their true nature, they are usually able to feel good about themselves.

November 13 men and women are strict parents. They never allow their more tender feelings to get in the way of what they perceive to be their parental duty.

HEALTH People born on this date believe in taking control of their physical and spiritual well-being. They often follow the advice of a healer, guru, or spiritual counselor to begin to understand the more esoteric nature of life.

With November 13 people, being healthy isn't just a part-time occupation—it's a lifetime quest.

CAREER AND FINANCES November 13 individuals often follow a circuitous path to career success. They may start out in one field, only to be lured into another through a series of unlikely circumstances. This appeals to their love of the unexpected.

People born on this date are very careful about money, to the point where they might even seem cheap. They aren't, but their careful handling of their assets is often born out of a fear that their prosperity will not last.

DREAMS AND GOALS November 13 individuals want to achieve success on their own terms; if forced to play by the rules, they are unlikely to make the effort. These people know the level of their own talents, but no matter what they have to offer they will resist if they cannot do things their way.

People born on this date are constantly striving to achieve a personal best, and have no concern for others' opinions of them. If they can't set their own standards, November 13 people would just as soon be out of the race altogether.

EMBRACE
Ethics
Appreciation
Desire

AVOID
Irreverence
Ill-will
Stress

ALSO BORN TODAY
TV journalist Peter Arnett; actress Hermione Baddeley; England's King Edward III; actress Whoopi Goldberg; actor Joe Mantegna; film director Garry Marshall; actress Jean Seberg; novelist Robert Louis Stevenson.

NOVEMBER 14

November 14 natives are deeply introspective people who refuse to conform to the worldly standards of success. Of particular interest is the possibility of their having healing powers or psychic talents.

These men and women have a deep affinity for nature, and are at their most spiritually fulfilled when communing with it. They regard themselves in an abstract, analytical way, and can make objective judgments regarding their motives and inner drives.

FRIENDS AND LOVERS November 14
people understand relationships at their most intimate level, yet it may be difficult for them to openly show their feelings. Because they are extremely sensitive, these men and women may appear aloof, even snobbish. Yet their friends know how kind and considerate they truly are.

November 14 people have a deep respect for commitment, and once they give their heart they are unlikely to fall out of love.

CHILDREN AND FAMILY People born on
this date have an especially close relationship with family members, which influences their attitudes and opinions throughout their lifetime. For this reason, November 14 natives are very liberal with their own children, giving them a chance to make many of their own

decisions in matters large and small. Although they are quick to discipline wayward youngsters, November 14 parents can differentiate between innocent mistakes and deliberate disobedience.

HEALTH November 14 native are scrupulous
about their health and nutritional regimen. They enjoy physical exercise because it gives them a chance to counterbalance the exhausting mental activity that consumes most of their working day.

These men and women are generally careful about what they eat, though their high level of nervous energy could promote a desire to smoke, or drink caffeinated beverages, which, of course, only promote greater nervousness.

CAREER AND FINANCES November 14
men and women may not decide upon a career path until well after they have grown into adulthood. Because they are highly intelligent, November 14 people often feel most comfortable in an academic setting.

A casual attitude about money marks many people born on this date. Although very good at handling it, they are not materialistic people who strive to become rich.

DREAMS AND GOALS People born on
November 14 seek to find their separateness within the bounds of their personal relationships. This is paramount to their physical, emotional, and spiritual well-being—in fact, to every aspect of life. If these people feel that too much is being demanded of them, they are unlikely to be happy or satisfied.

November 14 men and women strive to achieve a spiritual oneness with nature. This gives them the solace they need.

EMBRACE
Insights
Spiritual truth
Modesty

AVOID
Craftiness
Immorality
Unhappy heart

ALSO BORN TODAY
Silent film actress Louise Brooks; England's Prince Charles; composer Aaron Copland; actress Laura San Giacomo; socialite Barbara Hutton; actor Brian Keith; journalist Harrison Salisbury; actor MacLean Stevenson.

NOVEMBER 15

People born on this date are fun-loving individuals who are compatible with others and who enjoy being the center of attention. Their outward high spirits are something of a departure from the usual brooding Scorpio demeanor. These people have the same level of intensity, but with a lighter touch.

November 15 natives are great conversationalists who enjoy a lively debate on just about any subject. They are avid collectors of facts and trivia who treat their knowledge as a game, not an accomplishment.

FRIENDS AND LOVERS
November 15 men and women are not emotionally possessive. They love their friends and go to great lengths to nurture all of their relationships. They expect loyalty from their friends, and will expel from their lives anyone who fails to provide it.

People born on this date have a deeply sensual love nature. Extremely passionate, they often fall in love at first sight. They don't toy with a partner's affections, but give of themselves generously and with amazing sincerity.

CHILDREN AND FAMILY
Even though the upbringing of November 15 individuals is likely to be positive, these men and women do not care to live in the past. They may actually have few memories of being a child.

November 15 men and women may be similarly disinterested in their own children's upbringing. This arises not from a lack of love, but because they tend to better appreciate their children as the little ones grow into adolescence.

HEALTH
November 15 natives are very moderate in their health habits. They don't believe in "overdoing" anything, and seek a balanced approach. While they may have picked up some regrettable dieting habits during adolescence, their common sense usually points them in the right direction before very long.

These individuals like to work out their anxieties and aggressions through routine physical activity, especially swimming, gymnastics, or figure skating.

CAREER AND FINANCES
People born on this day have remarkable artistic sensibilities, and often gravitate to careers in decorating, fashion, art, filmmaking, or writing.

November 15 natives are not particularly concerned with their financial status. As long as they have the necessities of life—and a few little luxuries—they are content. These people are not the sort to hold out for a raise, or quit a job they like in order to find something that pays more.

DREAMS AND GOALS
November 15 men and women aren't especially goal-oriented, but they certainly have their dreams. These people like to feel that they are free to do anything they want in life. If they feel tied down or restricted in any way, they simply cannot be happy.

These individuals always look to get the maximum out of their personal relationships, but if these turn unsatisfactory they are unlikely to give up on happiness. November 15 people are too much the sensualists to believe that they can be happy with one person only.

EMBRACE
Self-control
Work ethic
Spiritual wholeness

AVOID
Hysteria
Gossip
Perfectionism

ALSO BORN TODAY
Actress Beverly D'Angelo; singer Petula Clark; actor Ed Asner; U.S. Senator Howard Baker; pianist Daniel Barenboim; actress Veronica Lake; painter Georgia O'Keeffe; actor Sam Waterston.

NOVEMBER 16

People born on this date have the ability to transcend their everyday experiences, gaining wisdom through encounters with others.

They may seem wise beyond their years, even as children. They have a solemn, almost stern attitude that makes them appear humorless, yet they actually have a wonderful personality. These men and women are quiet and self-effacing, though when they choose to display their less complicated side, they are extremely likable.

FRIENDS AND LOVERS

November 16 individuals have the rare ability to teach and learn from their friends. This isn't usually an obvious thing, since these people are wise and subtle in their approach.

People born on this date are among the most passionate and romantic of the year. Their love bridges a void between the complex and the simple. These people understand the spiritual aspects of love, and judge with their hearts more than with their minds.

CHILDREN AND FAMILY

Because of their great spirituality, November 16 men and women have the ability to look back upon their childhood years with philosophical understanding. Regardless of what may have taken place, or whatever the person's relationship with family members, November 16 people realize that they owe a great deal of their essence to their childhood.

Those born on this date have some unusual ideas about parenting. They don't believe in forcing their children to accept their views of life, but encourage them to form their own opinions as they mature, and find their own values.

HEALTH

November 16 natives are not particularly health conscious. They don't like to feel as if they must maintain a strict diet or exercise routine in order to stay healthy. They prefer an esoteric approach, by which they surround themselves with beautiful objects and beautiful thoughts.

It's important that people born on this date get enough exercise. Since they are basically sedentary people, they need to find a sport or an exercise that appeals to them.

CAREER AND FINANCES

November 16 individuals are interested in careers with spiritual significance. They are not generally the nine-to-five type, and may prefer working for themselves or at least within a small circle of people, where they can be semi-independent. These men and women make excellent researchers and writers.

Financial matters are sometimes complicated for November 16 people, who may not be very concerned with whether or not they make a good living.

DREAMS AND GOALS

People born on this date are always questing to get to the bottom of things. They want answers to everything

While November 16 men and women try very hard to make their relationships work, they understand the value of learning from their problems and disappointments. If a relationship fails, these people are usually able to console themselves with the knowledge that although they have lost something, they may have actually gained more.

EMBRACE
Accomplishments
Religious faith
Good will

AVOID
Frustration
Notoriety
Revenge

ALSO BORN TODAY
Actress Lisa Bonet; boxer Frank Bruno; journalist Elizabeth Drew; baseball star Dwight Gooden; musician W. C. Handy; playwright George S. Kaufman; journalist Mary Margaret McBride; actor Burgess Meredith.

NOVEMBER 17

People born on this date have the rare ability to read the hearts and intentions of others. Their great wisdom gives them a spiritual view of life; because of this they refuse to get caught up in the superficial aspects of life.

November 17 men and women carry themselves with great personal dignity. Although well known for their uproarious sense of humor, they know when to display it, and when it's not appropriate.

FRIENDS AND LOVERS People born on this date make excellent friends because they freely embrace relationships with individuals from entirely different backgrounds and personalities.

Romantically, November 17 people are very intense. They are believers in fate, and may feel as if only one perfect person exists for them. If their love is not returned by this individual, or if they're unable to find their soul mate, they're likely to sink into the doldrums.

CHILDREN AND FAMILY There often comes a time in the lives of November 17 men and women when they suddenly feel as if they must separate from their family in order to achieve ultimate autonomy. This has nothing to do with problems within the family circle. To the contrary, November 17 people are usually very close to their parents and siblings. Yet like other water-sign individuals, they may suddenly experience a need to reexamine family life.

November 17 people may be somewhat unsure of their abilities as parents, yet they are affectionate and caring in their attitude to youngsters.

HEALTH Although people born on this date are not necessarily health fanatics, they under-stand that if they fail to handle their lives in a certain way, they'll lack the vigor and energy they need to make their lives worthwhile. Therefore, they'll eat healthy meals even if they prefer junk food, and will exercise even if they detest working out and sweating.

Music has a healing effect on these people, who may use it to induce meditative states.

CAREER AND FINANCES November 17 natives gravitate to careers that offer them opportunities to indulge their introspective, contemplative side. These people are book lovers who are well suited to be teachers and professors, librarians, or researchers.

November 17 individuals have a very practical attitude toward money. They are usually the marriage partner who manages the family budget, and can be extremely critical of a mate who spends lavishly on items that November 17 people believe to be frivolous.

DREAMS AND GOALS People born on this date seek to strike a balance between the serious and comical sides of their nature. They know that a joke often makes unpleasant news or views go down easier, so they may use this approach with others.

November 17 men and women aren't hung up on labels of success. They have their own idea about what constitutes achievement.

EMBRACE
Evaluation
Principle
Acceptance

AVOID
Subjectivity
Resentments
False friends

ALSO BORN TODAY
Actor/director Danny DeVito; basketball star Elvin Hayes; actor Rock Hudson; baseball star Tom Seaver; actress/model Lauren Hutton; actress Mary Elizabeth Mastrontonio; film director Martin Scorsese; drama coach Lee Strasberg.

NOVEMBER 18

People born on this date possess amazing determination and an unbeatable will. They have a need to put their own personal stamp upon existence. Never satisfied with "the way things are" they seek to improve, and even perfect them.

These vibrant, energetic people have a strongly physical nature. They can be aggressive, even pugnacious at times, but only in a worthwhile cause. While it's nearly impossible to win an argument with these people, they make interesting, challenging opponents.

EMBRACE
Self-expression
Perseverance
Plenty

AVOID
Loss of faith
Preoccupation with details
Delays

ALSO BORN TODAY
Novelist Margaret Atwood; actress Linda Evans; actress Andrea Marcovicci; baseball manager Gene Mauch; lyricist Johnny Mercer; symphony conductor Eugene Ormandy; astronaut Alan Shepard; actress Brenda Vacarro.

FRIENDS AND LOVERS
People born on this date sometimes have a problem making friends. This is generally caused by their inability to step back from the relationship and allow the other person to be an equal partner. November 18 natives people have the need to control everything around them, and that includes their friendships. This doesn't make them "bad" friends, but it can inhibit their ability to help their relationships grow.

November 18 people inevitably look for someone who shares their temperament. These men and women don't want to be involved with someone weaker than themselves.

CHILDREN AND FAMILY
November 18 people often experience a great deal of emotional turmoil during their growing-up years. They may become unwittingly rebellious in order to balance what is happening to them, especially if the family is in disarray.

As parents, November 18 people are a mixture of strict and experimental. They demand respect from their children, but do not expect them to be perfect.

HEALTH
These men and women are active people who don't seem able to sit still. They have a high energy level and are always busy with a project of some kind.

As for diet, November 18 men and women take an old-fashioned approach. Because they're constantly on the go, they eat what they like. They are likely to have battled weight in years past, with disappointing results, but by making a few adjustments, they can take weight off and keep it off.

CAREER AND FINANCES
Unlike many people of their sign, November 18 people are not content to work behind the scenes. They need a hands-on position that allows them to make decisions and guide the careers of others.

November 18 people don't easily give control of their finances to anyone else. Although not financial risk-takers by nature, they will occasionally surprise themselves and everyone around them by making a bold move in that direction.

DREAMS AND GOALS
Few people are as goal-oriented as the men and women born on this date. They have a determined spirit and will endure a great deal of hardship and sacrifice in order to reach a chosen goal.

November 18 people are not the types to complain when the path they are traveling grows difficult. These are tough people, physically and mentally, and they understand that anything worth achieving is worth hardship and sacrifice.

NOVEMBER 19

People born on this date are likely to keep their own counsel. These self-controlled, taciturn individuals make good leaders, yet they do not mix well with others. One of their greatest talents, however, is the ability to make other people feel good about themselves.

November 19 men and women have a powerful, almost magnetic presence, which endows them with an attractive and lordly aspect. Although they may seem aloof, even unfriendly, they actually possess considerable charm.

FRIENDS AND LOVERS
People born on this date guard their emotions and are very cautious about letting people into their lives. They usually have only a handful of close friends, who provide all the support and emotional sustenance they require.

November 19 people are extremely cautious about letting themselves rely too heavily on a lover or mate. Because of this, they often unconsciously subvert their relationships.

CHILDREN AND FAMILY
Childhood is often a troubled time for November 19 people. They may live an unsettled existence that imbues them with a fear of change and distrust of those who are close to them.

Parenthood is a difficult decision for November 19 people because it forces them to relive the past in ways that are not comfortable for them. When they do choose to become parents, it's for disparate reasons, including a need to resolve the past.

HEALTH
People born on this date read all the latest literature about exercise and diet, and have an uncanny ability to discover which of these new approaches are just right for them. Although November 19 men and women are concerned about their appearance, they know their health must come first. They can be fanatics about their workout schedule and may spend more than an hour each day laboring with various machines.

CAREER AND FINANCES
November 19 men and women often seek career opportunities in business, law, local politics, or academia, where they can achieve a long-standing reputation through overall accomplishments, rather than the day-to-day office politics they find so hateful.

Finances are usually a stable factor in the lives of these individuals. If they have the good fortune to inherit money, they're perfectly capable of caring for it themselves. They have the potential to become enormously wealthy by their own wheeling and dealing.

DREAMS AND GOALS
November 19 men and women are success-oriented, yet with a difference. Because they have a strongly moralistic streak, these people will never compromise their beliefs in order to meet the worldly criteria of success. Instead, they're determined to do things their own way, achieving their goals regardless of the obstacles that may stand in their path.

People born on this date may not realize until later in life that their accomplishments, though laudable, are best when shared with someone close.

EMBRACE
Talent
Independence
Resoluteness

AVOID
Scarcity mentality
Blunt remarks
Injustice

ALSO BORN TODAY
Talk show host Dick Cavett; England's King Charles I; actress/director Jodie Foster; talk show host Larry King; designer Calvin Klein; actress Kathleen Quinlan; actress Meg Ryan; media mogul Ted Turner.

269

NOVEMBER 20

November 20 individuals are complex and complicated people who can be truthful to the point of recklessness. Loyalty is practically a religion to these men and women, whose actions stem from their own deep spiritual beliefs, which are inseparable from their character.

Although these people dislike change, they are often instrumental in bringing it about in the lives of others. They strive constantly for achievement, eager to prove that "good guys" finish first.

FRIENDS AND LOVERS

November 20 people make the best friends and the worst enemies. They have great protective loyalty to those they love, but can turn against those who hurt them or those close to them.

Marriage and family form the centerpiece of their lives. They are devoted to their spouse and will work hard to keep the romance and passion alive in their relationship.

CHILDREN AND FAMILY

The personality and character of November 20 people are closely allied to what they were taught as children. They have a deep reverence for family life, and frequently count siblings as their closest friends and role models.

People born on this date experience their greatest joy through parenthood. They adore their children and involve themselves in all aspects of their upbringing. Despite the closeness these people experience with their children, they're not clinging or demanding, and will never do anything to inhibit their kids' chances to become happy and functioning adults on their own.

HEALTH

Because of their strong emotional nature, November 20 men and women understand the value of daily meditation. These opportunities to listen to their inner voice help them to control the powerful emotions that rage within them.

Regular physical exercise helps to control their emotionalism. By working out every day and playing competitive sports on the weekend, they have the opportunity to expel their anxiety and the stress that comes with other areas of life.

CAREER AND FINANCES

November 20 people are driven individuals who gravitate toward high-powered careers where they can make a difference in their world. Success and money alone are not enough to pique their professional interest. The work they do may be related to environmental concerns, which is one of their favorite causes.

Though they are not motivated by money, November 20 people are expert at handling financial affairs. They save carefully, and can show a real flair for investing.

DREAMS AND GOALS

The most important achievement in the lives of November 20 people is to make their spouse and children happy. When they know they have achieved that, they will turn their attention toward other dreams, such as creating change. They refuse to let go of their dreams no matter how impractical they may seem. While other people grow out of their youthful idealism, these men and women become even more dedicated as the years go on.

EMBRACE
Moderation
Self-love
Priorities

AVOID
Showmanship
Bragging
Harsh judgments

ALSO BORN TODAY
Film director Henri-Georges Clouzot; TV journalist Alistair Cooke; actress Bo Derek; New Orleans D.A. Jim Garrison; novelist Nadine Gordimer; actress Veronica Hamel; U.S. Attorney General Robert F. Kennedy; actress Estelle Parsons.

NOVEMBER 21

People born on this date are humorous and infinitely practical. Quite simply, they're interested in getting the job done, and have a good time while doing it.

These individuals see themselves as movers and shakers. A strong belief in their own abilities keeps them actively involved in projects that would intimidate other, less confident people. These men and women have a head start in every endeavor because of their ability to see the big picture.

FRIENDS AND LOVERS Unlike most water-sign individuals, November 21 people have a need and desire to surround themselves with a great many friends. People born on this date are loving and thoughtful, and give enthusiastic support to those close to them.

November 21 men and women need to be happy in their romantic relationships. They're not the tragic lover types who think that suffering makes love more romantic. On the contrary, they like to feel content and connected, and will usually opt for marriage.

CHILDREN AND FAMILY People born on this date are always able to see the sunny side of things. If there were problems in childhood, these folks don't choose to remember them negatively. Instead, they believe that all experience contributes positively to character development.

These individuals make exceptionally good parents because they are true to their own values. They don't attempt to mold their children into miniature versions of themselves.

HEALTH November 21 individuals understand that by putting a positive spin on events they can keep their mind-body-spirit equilibrium. Happiness is the most important factor in the lives of these men and women, and it keeps them looking and feeling great.

People born on this date don't believe in restricting what they eat. If they put on a few pounds over the holidays, they're likely to cut back on calories for a week or so, but their attempts at dieting seldom go beyond that. As for exercise, they enjoy playing sports and may sometimes favor bike riding over driving a car.

CAREER AND FINANCES As with every other aspect of life, November 21 people look for enjoyment in their work. They're looking for professional pleasure, and pursue a career that they know can bring them happiness as well as success—but happiness comes first.

November 21 people have a natural talent for making their money go a long way. They never scrimp, but they can make one dollar do the work of ten, and can entertain lavishly on a shoestring.

DREAMS AND GOALS People born on this date have a great desire to bring joy into the lives of others. They can appreciate achievement in other ways, but unless happiness is attached to it, they aren't interested in hitching their wagon to the proverbial star.

November 21 men and women are hard workers who have the common sense to know what must be sacrificed for success, and what isn't worth tossing away as they reach for the brass ring.

EMBRACE
Details
Compliance
Actualization

AVOID
Hasty decisions
Instability
Pride

ALSO BORN TODAY
Magazine editor Tina Brown; novelist Marilyn French; actress Goldie Hawn; novelist Oliver Goldsmith; singer Lorna Luft; actress Juliet Mills; baseball star Stan Musial; actress Marlo Thomas.

271

SAGITTARIUS
November 22 - December 21

Sagittarius is the ninth sign of the astrological year and is known by its astrological symbol, the Archer. Sagittarian individuals are jovial, intelligent, and freedom-loving. With Jupiter as the ruling planet, people born under this sign are considered to be understanding and principled. They have an appetite for learning and travel.

THE SAGITTARIAN MAN The typical Sagittarian man is well-traveled, well-read, and thoroughly likable. He possesses a broad and all-encompassing view of life as well as boundless enthusiasm. Sagittarian men need to love, not just like, the work they do. Although their career concerns often take them away from family life, they aren't as driven and ambitious as other fire-sign types. They are philosophical and even a little old-fashioned, always putting a positive spin on events and looking for that proverbial pot of gold at the end of the rainbow.

Sagittarian men are often sports enthusiasts who enjoy showing off their athletic prowess by playing weekend sports with friends. The typical Sagittarian man keeps himself in good physical condition.

THE SAGITTARIAN WOMAN Sagittarian women are friendly, sociable, and outgoing. They also have a reputation for being incredibly blunt speakers and regularly speak their minds without worrying how their opinions will be received by others.

Like their male counterparts, Sagittarian women love to travel and are curious about other lands and other cultures. While they love to read about these things, the true Sagittarian woman also likes to experience them for herself. Like other fire-sign females, she is bold and never afraid of taking risks.

Physically, Sagittarian women are often tall and svelte, though they have a tendency to put on weight in middle age. These ladies have a fashion style all their own, and they manage to look fabulous without opting for the same look everyone else is wearing.

THE SAGITTARIAN CHILD Sagittarian children are adventurous from the moment they come into this world, and because they are so eager to explore its boundaries they often crawl, walk, and talk earlier than children of other signs. This little one thinks big. From the time he is in the playpen he's seeking to enlarge his world. From an early age he appreciates the value of things and the satisfaction that they can bring to his life. This child may group all his toys together, taking inventory even before he can count!

Sagittarian youngsters usually love school—both the academic and extracurricular activities. They love to participate in sports and are big on school spirit. Girls who aren't sports-oriented may become cheerleaders. Sagittarian teens need plenty of freedom, but they are likely to use it wisely.

THE SAGITTARIAN LOVER Sagittarians want romance in their lives—so long as it doesn't interfere with their personal autonomy. These freedom-loving people shy away from demanding or needy individuals who may seek to infringe upon their personal "space."

As soon as they fall in love, the typical Sagittarian begins to worry about what he or she is going to have to give up for it. For this reason they may put off making a definite commitment as long as possible. They may even break off a worthwhile romance just because the fear of giving up their freedom is too great. When they do decide to settle down, they adjust very well to domesticity. They refuse to let the relationship get stale and are always looking for ways to bring more excitement and romance into their union.

THE SAGITTARIAN BOSS It is difficult to find a better boss than the typical Sagittarian man or woman. These people combine all the traits necessary to be a worthwhile employer. Because they have an ability to see the big picture, they can see potential in even the most ordinary individual. They are also good judges of people. It is rare for this boss to play favorites. Most pleasing of all, the Sagittarian boss is likely to have an open-door policy. Workers can come to him or her for advice that goes beyond workplace concerns.

ELEMENT: Fire
QUALITY: Mutable
PLANETARY RULER: Jupiter
BIRTHSTONE: Turquoise
FLOWER: Narcissus
COLOR: Purple

KEY CHARACTERISTIC:
Benevolence

STRENGTHS: Optimism,
Generosity, Foresight
CHALLENGES: Intolerance, Self-righteousness, Ignoring details

THE SAGITTARIAN FRIEND Sagittarian men and women make excellent friends, and because they have so many interests they can accommodate friends of all sorts. Even though they have a great many intellectual pursuits, the Sagittarian isn't simply a meet-for-coffee friend. This man or woman is a doer. Think fun, think adventurous, think physical. Most Sagittarians love sports. That means getting together with pals for a friendly game of touch football on Thanksgiving Day, or Frisbee in the park on a lovely summer afternoon.

These people make the very best travel companions. Not only do they manage to be well-informed about their destination, but the typical Sagittarian traveler knows a dozen little side trips and interesting facts that make the journey even more enjoyable.

NOVEMBER 22

People born on this date are fun-loving, yet they have their serious side. These folks unhesitatingly put themselves on the line for the people they love and the causes they value, and manage to do all this without behaving in a self-righteous way.

November 22 people possess a great soul, which manifests their love of humanity and deep commitment to doing the right thing. These men and women have so much class that it's impossible for anyone to dislike them.

FRIENDS AND LOVERS November 22 people make friends in every area of life. They love to travel, and often find their truest, most memorable friendships with men and women from other countries and cultures.

People born on this date seek love affairs and relationships that combine true romantic love and potent sexuality. Since they are usually quite attractive, these people have their choice of potential partners. But because they value the sanctity of love, they are not likely to be promiscuous. They prefer long-lasting relationships; oddly, though, they sometimes find that inhibits their sense of autonomy.

CHILDREN AND FAMILY Like many natives of their sign, November 22 people are great believers in family closeness. They may not always agree with their relatives in philosophical matters, but on an emotional level they are consistently bonded with them.

People born today often put off having children until they're able to see and do things that are important to them. But while travel and professional goals usually come first with these people when they are in their twenties, by the time they have matured into their mid-thirties, they're ready to become parents.

HEALTH Good health on all levels is important to these men and women. They enjoy the challenge of a daily workout, and are likely to participate in sports.

Stress management is high on the list of things that November 22 people need to master. These people are so affable that even they may not always know when they are angry or annoyed. An ability to recognize the symptoms of potential emotional meltdown will help these folks handle life's negative moments.

CAREER AND FINANCES People born on this date are action-oriented and are likely to find exile behind a desk difficult to bear. Although they love study and reading, they usually feel the need to put their learning to practical use.

Money is usually viewed as a simple means of exchange for these folks, who have no desire to "keep up with the Joneses." They have a passion for gambling, which may need to be controlled through therapy.

DREAMS AND GOALS November 22 men and women are big dreamers. Yet they aren't likely to map out their goals step by step. These people like to go where the wind takes them.

They know how to maximize their level of enjoyment in life, but they are wise enough to know that material achievements don't always equal success.

EMBRACE
Redemption
Karma
Strength

AVOID
Procrastination
Nihilism
Divisiveness

ALSO BORN TODAY
Composer Benjamin Britten; actress Jamie Lee Curtis; novelist George Eliot; animator/director Terry Gilliam; novelist Andre Gide; tennis star Billie Jean King; actress Geraldine Page; actor Robert Vaughn.

NOVEMBER 23

People born on this date have a strong moral conscience, though they enjoy flouting convention and defying the status quo. These intelligent men and women seek diversity through everyday experience.

November 23 people have the ability to see and expose their own faults as well as the hypocrisy of others. Although not judgmental, they do have a talent for uncovering truth, and are able to size up people and situations with ease.

FRIENDS AND LOVERS
There's often a time in the lives of these men and women when they undergo a polarizing emotional experience that causes them to appreciate the value of their friendships.

November 23 natives are idealists about romantic love. They often experience disappointments because the people they attract may not share their need for total honesty in a relationship. Yet with characteristic resilience, folks born on this date bounce back from heartbreak to find their perfect mate.

CHILDREN AND FAMILY
November 23 natives are fairly casual when it comes to analyzing their past. They understand the need to take the good with the bad, and rarely point the finger of blame at a parent or sibling.

When they become parents, these men and women are usually liberal in their approach to discipline, although their attitude isn't likely to be a response to how they were treated as children. November 23 individuals simply feel their kids will learn more about life if they're allowed to explore it freely.

HEALTH
November 23 people derive a great deal of pleasure from golf, tennis, and volleyball. Not only do these sports help to keep them in shape, but they relieve tension and build self-esteem. Religion often plays a vital role in the lives of these people, giving them the inner peace they need in order to withstand the pressures of everyday life.

CAREER AND FINANCES
November 23 men and women are drawn to careers that give them a chance to deal with large numbers of people. They have enormous leadership potential and have the ability to make people appreciate their own talents. People born on this date make excellent teachers, sports coaches, motivational speakers, and middle-management supervisors.

People born today have a real talent for making money. Because they posses an entrepreneurial spirit, they often profit from their own ideas or products. Although the accumulation of a fortune is seldom their aim, these people often accomplish it when they simply follow their best instincts.

DREAMS AND GOALS
November 23 people are curious about life and use their goals as vehicles that take them on an unending journey of discovery. Although they appreciate the value of careful planning, they also have a knack for taking advantage of circumstances.

These folks live in the moment and prefer not to pursue scenarios that promise complications and a minimum of enjoyment. Whatever destiny has in store, they accept.

EMBRACE
Respect
Obeying the rules
Normalcy

AVOID
Ridicule of others
Sarcasm
Scattering energies

ALSO BORN TODAY
Actress Susan Anspach; outlaw Billy the Kid; newspaper publisher Otis Chandler; composer Manuel de Falla; actor Boris Karloff; comedian Harpo Marx; U.S. President Franklin Pierce; actress Diana Quick.

NOVEMBER 24

People born on this date seem to do everything by way of their personality. They attract others to them, project an aura of youth and charm, even have the ability to seem better looking than they actually are—all because of their extraordinary personality.

November 24 men and women may seem like "lightweights" but are actually emotionally and spiritually strong. They have an exceptional level of intelligence, yet don't need to be identified with it for purposes of ego.

FRIENDS AND LOVERS
November 24 natives have a need for many friends. They especially enjoy people who have their gift for conversation and ideas. These clever individuals have fun matching wits with others.

Love is a romantic idyll for November 24 people. They often fall for someone who is their mirror opposite, and thus force themselves to deal with thorny philosophical issues. They do not commit to a relationship easily, and sometimes have second thoughts when they do.

CHILDREN AND FAMILY
November 24 people have a strong connection to their family life. These men and women have a passion for tradition that is unusual for people of their sign, and may find it difficult to criticize their parents or other family members.

As parents themselves, November 24 people may not be able to live up to their doctrine of independence. Because they are very close to their children, they have difficulty letting go emotionally.

HEALTH
These people constantly change their ideas about what constitutes an intelligent health program. By the time they reach middle age they have tried just about everything there is to make themselves healthy, fit, and good looking.

Many November 24 men and women are expert cooks. They're convinced they can control their health through a good diet.

CAREER AND FINANCES
November 24 natives may not be aware of all the talents they possess. Since they are often academically inclined, they may overlook natural artistic abilities that may have been relegated to the role of hobbies. November 24 people are articulate, and make excellent writers, journalists, satirists, and comedians.

Finances are not a subject of great interest for most November 24 individuals, though they do enjoy expensive travel. They have the potential to react to money in an emotional rather than practical manner.

DREAMS AND GOALS
Individuals born on this date often set very exacting professional goals at a young age, then discard them later, when they realize that knowledge cannot take the place of wisdom.

These men and women may not be particularly interested in achieving personal goals until after they've made their mark professionally. They need to feel as if they're in control of their lives, though this may prove to be misguided if they become involved in a passionate love affair that tempts them to sacrifice personal liberation in the name of romance.

EMBRACE
Consistency
Seriousness
Unselfish motives

AVOID
Escapism
Impulsive behavior
Self-doubt

ALSO BORN TODAY
Columnist William F. Buckley Jr.; actress Geraldine Fitzgerald; composer Scott Joplin; politician John Lindsay; basketball star Oscar Robertson; novelist Laurence Sterne; U.S. President Zachary Taylor; artist Henri Toulouse-Lautrec.

NOVEMBER 25

November 25 people have the soul of a true visionary. Dreamers more than doers, these people are sensitive to the hurts and happiness of everyone they meet, and are governed more by emotion than by reason.

The men and women born on this date give the impression of being loners, but they are actually in a constant search to connect with others. Spirituality plays an important role in the lives of these people, affecting all their major decisions.

FRIENDS AND LOVERS
November 25 natives have more followers than they have friends, because even though they are quiet and introspective, their spiritual aura is very strong, and leads others to depend upon them.

Because of their high ideals, these folks are often destined for disappointment in love. Although they don't give their heart easily, they may project their own romantic notions upon the relationship, only to discover that their partner cannot understand their spiritual needs.

CHILDREN AND FAMILY
These men and women often find themselves deeply bound up with the lives of siblings and parents long after they are responsible for looking after their own families. There may be an element of self-sacrifice involved, such as taking care of an aged parent or lending money to a sibling in need.

There is also a feeling of being spiritually bound to their children, which makes it difficult for November 25 parents to cut the proverbial apron strings.

HEALTH
November 25 natives believe in achieving harmony among aspects of life. They feel that in order to be physically healthy they must first align their mind-spirit energies. This may be accomplished through any number of practices, especially by meditation.

These men and women often seek to cleanse their bodies through fasting. Modified fasts include fresh fruit and vegetable juice, while pure fasts include only water, and should therefore be used sparingly.

CAREER AND FINANCES
People born on this date have a great desire to share their views and ideas with others. They often gravitate toward careers that allow them the opportunity to act as a teacher or counselor, even if only by setting an example.

Despite their spiritual leanings, November 25 people have a rare gift for making and handling money—perhaps because the dollar is of little interest to them. They are incredibly generous to others.

DREAMS AND GOALS
November 25 people feel the need to spiritualize every aspect of life. It's virtually impossible for them to look at things from an opportunistic point of view. Far from losing out on success by this method, they manage to attract good things into their lives because of it (though this is definitely not their intent).

People born on this date seek empowerment through their close relationships, and are able to believe more in their own abilities if someone they care for is there to cheer them on.

EMBRACE
Diligence
Dedication to duty
Humanity

AVOID
Resting on laurels
Egotism
Shallowness

ALSO BORN TODAY
Actress Christina Applegate; philanthropist Andrew Carnegie; baseball star Joe DiMaggio; singer Amy Grant; magazine publisher John F. Kennedy, Jr.; actor John Larroquette; actor Ricardo Montalban; musician Percy Sledge.

NOVEMBER 26

People born on this date are achievement-oriented, and like to do things their own way. They have the ability to use practical means in order to bring about seemingly impractical goals. November 26 men and women give the impression of being hotheaded and stubborn, and it is true that they often demand their own way. This attitude doesn't come from ego, but from an innocent sort of self-confidence: They simply believe that their way is the best way. And if that turns out not to be true, they'll gladly try another approach.

FRIENDS AND LOVERS
November 26 natives are self-disciplined and centered. They trust their own judgment and rarely make choices or affect an attitude strictly to win friends or keep the ones they already have.

Practical in romantic matters, November 26 individuals don't really enjoy playing the field once they've set their sights on a potential mate. Unlike most Sagittarians, they are happy to settle down and start a family.

CHILDREN AND FAMILY
People born on this date are the bulwark of their family. Even if not the oldest, they often fill this role. Though they enjoy showing off the responsible side of their personality, the expectations of family members, especially parents, can be a burden at times.

These individuals make excellent parents themselves because they combine a sense of fun with a sense of discipline. They don't let their youngsters get away with much, but always explain why certain behavior will or will not be allowed.

HEALTH
The recipe for health and happiness as maintained by November 26 people is comprised of equal parts activity and indolence. They know that relaxation plays a big role in feeling good, and they also understand the need for regular exercise.

November 26 people are extremely disciplined in all areas of life and will make time to exercise on a regular basis no matter what other demands are placed on their schedule. They like to keep in shape with beach volleyball, rollerblading, or bicycling.

CAREER AND FINANCES
These men and women are often drawn to an academic life, or at least to careers that require a college degree. Knowledge is the linchpin of their nature, and this path is followed with dedication. Their goal?—ultimate wisdom.

November 26 people have a practical approach to handling money. They have the self-discipline to save and can usually resist spending on credit. This cash-only approach is important to them, and they have the ability to stick to their guns on it.

DREAMS AND GOALS
November 26 people would rather struggle than have things come to them easily and without challenges. They have a great deal of emotional toughness and feel that only through hard work and difficulty can they truly regard themselves as being successful.

Despite their common-sense attitude, November 26 natives don't necessarily strive to achieve practical goals. They're just as likely to wish for the impossible. The only difference is their ability to accomplish it.

EMBRACE
A joyful heart
Rewards
Adaptability

AVOID
Intolerance
Pessimism
Regrets

ALSO BORN TODAY
Actor Cyril Cusack; singer Robert Goulet; cartoonist Charles Schultz; TV journalist Eric Sevareid; singer Tina Turner.

NOVEMBER 27

There are few more independent thinkers than the people born on November 27. These people enjoy controversy and are apt to seek out an eccentric lifestyle. Plus, they successfully sway others to their point of view.

These go-getters have real leadership potential and seem to be always on the move. They possess the ability to inspire others with their mercurial attitude and explosive personal style. Their sense of humor makes them notorious for playing practical jokes.

FRIENDS AND LOVERS

November 27 natives are accustomed to being the center of attention among their friends. They are leaders, but even more than that, they have the ability to inspire awe among those who know them. These men and women don't always get along well with others, but they do seek out relationships with those who can teach them the lessons they need to learn.

People born on this date are likely to have a tumultuous love life prior to settling down with a committed partner. Once they choose that special someone, they are inclined to remain faithful.

CHILDREN AND FAMILY

November 27 natives are likely to possess the "firstborn" mentality, even if they are not the oldest child in the family. They mature early—both physically and emotionally—and quickly learn to take on family problems that their siblings may be unable or unwilling to handle.

People born on this date demand a great deal from their own children, expecting them to measure up to what they were able to accomplish as youngsters.

HEALTH

November 27 natives are given to extremes in just about everything they do. Their attitude toward keeping healthy generally revolves around being active and eating what they please. Because of their intensity, November 27 people are likely to struggle with food at some period in their life; this may take the form of anorexia or bulimia, especially among young women.

In spite of their seemingly addictive personality—or perhaps because of it—November 27 men and women have the potential to "reform" their habits at some point.

CAREER AND FINANCES

These individuals have absolutely no interest in working behind closed doors where no one can observe their talents. If this is egotism, it's egotism of a natural, unmalicious sort.

People born on this date have the potential to make a great deal of money, but not much ability to hold onto it. Ruthless, careless spending is their worst habit.

DREAMS AND GOALS

Despite their careless spending, November 27 people have the self-discipline to approach most of their goals with precision and hard work. They have the emotional and physical endurance to labor for long periods at a time without allowing outside distractions to take away their focus.

People born on this date have something to say and will not give up until they have a forum.

EMBRACE
Due process
Deliberation
Encouragement

AVOID
Superficial friendships
Combativeness
Conceit

ALSO BORN TODAY
Playwright James Agee; musician Randy Brecker; actress Robin Givens; rock star Jimi Hendrix; kung-fu champ/actor Bruce Lee; singer/songwriter Eddie Rabbit; actor Fisher Stevens; TV host "Buffalo Bob" Smith.

NOVEMBER 28

I t's often said that November 28 people are their own best friend as well as their own worst enemy. They certainly know how to break rules in order to gain attention. But they're also divinely creative, with the ability to be an inspiration to others.

November 28 people have a rare intelligence that exists on many levels. They have amazing bursts of creative energy, as well as periods of indolence during which they produce very little.

FRIENDS AND LOVERS

Because they often struggle to understand their own motivations, people born on this date rely upon trusted friends to help them understand themselves and interpret the things they do. For this reason, they generally have a large circle of friends who are relatively unknown to each other.

Despite their seeming accessibility, November 28 men and women are extremely private, and inevitably manage to keep something of their personality in reserve.

CHILDREN AND FAMILY

November 28 people seem to have sprung to life magically, without parents or family entanglements of any kind. Even from a very early age, they're continually reinventing themselves, constantly searching for the single truth within the patchwork of truths that explains them.

They bring the same sort of existential angst to their role as parents. They want to connect emotionally with their children yet may be unwilling to force their ideas upon their youngsters.

HEALTH

People born on this date believe in keeping their mental and physical energies in balance. Although they know that exercise and diet play big parts in good health, they also feel that such habits only provide a temporary solution to vitality.

These men and women are masters at achieving trance states through concentration. These meditative periods allow them to engage in a spiritual dialogue with their inner self.

CAREER AND FINANCES

November 28 people have a tendency to make unusual career choices. Even if their profession is conventional, these fascinating folks will seek out an offbeat area of expertise within their field. Unfortunately, they sometimes overlook a profession that's perfect for them, simply because it doesn't appear to offer potential for excitement and creativity.

These individuals change careers quite often, feeling that once they have accomplished or learned what they were looking for, no further challenge exists for them in that sector. Money is rarely a factor in making a career choice.

DREAMS AND GOALS

People born on this date want what they want, though exactly what that is has a tendency to change from one day to the next.

November 28 individuals are often uncertain about which path to take, generally because they have so many interests. They try hard to be more decisive about goals, which can become a goal in itself!

EMBRACE
The inner path
Serenity
Focus

AVOID
Lack of commitment
Banality
Mistrust

ALSO BORN TODAY
Poet William Blake; novelist Rita Mae Brown; actor Ed Harris; U.S. Senator Gary Hart; actress Hope Lange; composer Jean-Baptiste Lully; film director Michael Ritchie; composer Anton Rubenstein.

NOVEMBER 29

November 29 natives travel many paths but find their greatest self-realization through their love of others. These people are ruled by their emotions, but have the ability to be objective about their personal motives.

Personally charming and attractive, November 29 men and women have a dark side that even those closest to them may not understand or even realize exists. Their potential for self-discovery is great, but they must learn to tell themselves the truth in all things.

FRIENDS AND LOVERS Friends provide a mirror by which November 29 men and women decipher their own image. These individuals have a tendency to confide in those close to them, then immediately regret having done so.

In romantic relationships November 29 men and women are at their most vulnerable. They want to trust someone they love but may be unable to, due to insecurities in their own character.

CHILDREN AND FAMILY Childhood is often a precarious time for November 29 natives. They may feel as if they do not receive the nurturing spirit they require in order to feel good about themselves. Or they feel passed-over, especially if surrounded by siblings who are more verbal or clever.

When they choose to become parents, November 29 men and women are extra sensitive to their child's emotional needs. Remembering their own difficulty making friends, they will encourage their youngsters to become socially adept. Scheduled playtimes with other children, begun at an early age, are beneficial for kids of November 29 natives.

HEALTH Although they are generally healthy, people born on this date sometimes experience health problems related to emotional or psychological factors. As long as their attitude remains upbeat, these men and women are fit as a fiddle. Yet should a relationship go wrong or a career turn sour, they may lose all interest in pursuing a healthful lifestyle.

CAREER AND FINANCES In order to boost self-confidence, November 29 men and women need to seek out careers that give them opportunities to project their personality through the work they do. These individuals have enormous charm, yet their natural shyness sometimes keeps them from displaying it. Although they may be reticent to enter a career in retail sales, real estate, or teaching, November 29 people score high in all these pursuits after their first taste of success.

Like all Sagittarian natives, these people are generous with money, but possess a good head for business dealings.

DREAMS AND GOALS People born on this date are often unwilling to set firm goals for fear they'll be unable to achieve them. This attitude needs to be dispelled before any progress can be made.

November 29 natives are able to bring many of their dreams to fruition through partnerships, both romantic and platonic. By connecting with people they care for and who care for them, they gain considerable self-confidence.

EMBRACE
A self-nurturing attitude
Calm
Togetherness

AVOID
Chaos
Discord
Impossible goals

ALSO BORN TODAY
Novelist Louisa May Alcott; choreographer Busby Berkeley; actress Diane Ladd; comedian Howie Mandel; actor Andrew McCarthy; comedian Gary Shandling; poet Sir Philip Sidney; U.S. Senator Paul Simon.

NOVEMBER 30

Possessed with a razor-sharp wit and the personality of a stage star, November 30 individuals tend to live a flamboyant lifestyle. Yet despite their outrageous attitude, these men and women are loners at heart.

These are charismatic people who enjoy breaking conventional patterns. They're also moralists who believe that the common moral code applies to everyone—except themselves! They are apt to be egotistical, but have a rare ability to laugh at themselves.

FRIENDS AND LOVERS Forging friendships is not an easy thing for people born on this date, because they are extremely competitive and have a tendency to bring this attitude to the relationships. They generally prefer their own company, though their outgoing personality inevitably attracts others.

In romance, November 30 people have the need to continually test the boundaries of the relationship, sending a message of mistrust to their partner or mate. Once these people learn to accept their own vulnerabilities, they are apt to be more accepting of the person they love. Belief in themselves grows with their belief in the relationship.

CHILDREN AND FAMILY November 30 men and women often separate from their family at a relatively early age. This may be caused by their inability to withstand the pressures put upon them by family members who find their attitude or lifestyle in conflict with their traditional upbringing.

People born on this date make no such dictates to their own children, wanting their youngsters to express themselves according to their emotional needs.

HEALTH People born on this date have their own way of doing nearly everything—and that includes their health regimen. Because they are iconoclasts by nature, these men and women are unlikely to follow any prescribed plan.

November 30 natives like to make things simple for themselves. They may enjoy eating a plain diet made up of raw fruits and vegetables, and the occasional dairy product.

CAREER AND FINANCES People born on this day have unequaled sales skills, though they are likely to favor another line of work. Smart alternatives include comedy, education, or writing. They may also do well in advertising or law.

People born on this date have incredible luck with money but might be a little too eager to capitalize on that fact. Gambling can be a problem if they don't learn to resist the urge.

DREAMS AND GOALS November 30 natives have so much talent and personal appeal that they may find their goals come to them a little too easily. Many people born on this date are classic underachievers for this very reason.

When they do find something challenging to occupy their time and efforts, November 30 men and women become eager to attain their goals. But once they've accomplished what they set out to do, they move on to something new.

EMBRACE
Daring
Values
Self-expression

AVOID
Trendiness
Conflict with authority
Meddling

ALSO BORN TODAY
British Prime Minister Winston Churchill; actor Richard Crenna; Watergate figure G. Gordon Liddy; actor Robert Guillaume; singer Billy Idol; playwright David Mamet; film director Ridley Scott; humorist Mark Twain.

DECEMBER 1

People born on this date are theatrical and flamboyant, with all-too-human flaws. These individuals use their marvelous sense of humor to showcase their bubbly personality.

These men and women are extremely impulsive, sometimes to their own detriment. But despite warnings from loved ones and well-meaning friends, these feisty people are determined to live life on their own terms. That generally means plenty of laughs, a good dose of fun, and very few rules.

FRIENDS AND LOVERS December 1 individuals have a wide variety of friends, and because they generally have a very active social life, these men and women often collect friends from various walks of life.

December 1 people have exciting love lives. They see themselves as glamorous figures and may at times favor a somewhat superficial approach to love. It takes someone really special to get these people to settle down on a permanent basis.

CHILDREN AND FAMILY An unconventional note often characterizes the upbringing of December 1 natives. Either the family was constantly on the move or the parents separated when the children were very small. One way or another, people born on this date probably learned self-sufficiency at an early age.

Although parenthood may not be something that December 1 men and women naturally aspire to, once they settle into a domestic routine they have a real talent for the job.

HEALTH December 1 individuals are always conscious of making a good appearance. They work hard in in order to look fabulous, but eventually they learn that good health is more important than good looks.

Holistic and herbal medicine is the route that December 1 people usually choose once they decide to get healthy. These people may also opt for less conventional treatments such as colonic washes, chakra adjustments, and aura cleansing.

CAREER AND FINANCES People born on this date are lively fun-lovers who enjoy being in the public eye. They are not the sort who can labor in anonymity or behind closed doors. Instead, they enjoy professions that enable them to make use of their sparkling personality. They find interesting careers in marketing, advertising, modeling, show business, or real estate.

All Sagittarians have an open-handed policy about money, and December 1 people are no exception. They are extremely generous in the way they treat themselves and others. Money comes and goes in their lives, but it has little bearing on their happiness.

DREAMS AND GOALS People born on this date want to shine. They have a need to put their talents on display. Many December 1 individuals have theatrical aspirations, either professionally or as an enjoyable hobby.

Although these folks prefer spontaneity to goal-making, they do have a strong will and can achieve amazing things when they put their mind to it.

EMBRACE
Free will
Credibility
Self-control

AVOID
Self-promotion
The dark side
Controlling others

ALSO BORN TODAY
Writer/director William Allen; supermodel Carol Alt; singer/actress Bette Midler; musician Sandy Nelson; actor/comedian Richard Pryor; golfer Lee Trevino; singer/songwriter Gilbert O'Sullivan; actress Charlene Tilton.

DECEMBER 2

The mysterious men and women born on this date are very big on "image." They are highly romantic and greatly talented, often in matters relating to the arts. Their good looks and personality mark them as extraordinary individuals.

December 2 people sometimes use their talent to shelter themselves from the world. Although they seem strong, they are actually quite vulnerable to the emotional pressures that come their way, particularly in relationships. But they seldom show their wounds, putting a positive spin on even the most difficult events.

FRIENDS AND LOVERS Few people display the loyalty and affection to their friends that December 2 men and women show. These individuals are capable of great insight, and for this reason their friends often come to them with confessions or questions.

December 2 people love on an epic scale. Although they often fall in love unwisely, there is never any doubt concerning their sincerity. Learning to live with the romantic choices they make can be difficult, but these amazingly resilient people are up to the task.

CHILDREN AND FAMILY Because December 2 men and women are skilled at keeping their insecurities under wraps, they're far more sensitive than they may appear. In childhood, they may have imaginatively attrib-

uted great melodrama to events that, to other eyes, would seem perfectly reasonable, even ordinary.

Like most Sagittarians, December 2 natives are fun-loving, cheerful parents who know how to relate to children on many levels. They are very ambitious for their kids but never attempt to push them toward any particular goal.

HEALTH Emotions generally dictate the health of December 2 men and women. When these people are happy, they feel marvelous. But if depression or disappointment comes their way they often find themselves suffering from headaches, body aches, or general malaise.

While exercise can help dispel these feelings, December 2 people are more likely to rely on meditation techniques such as creative visualization. By picturing a positive conclusion to any question or dilemma they may have, they are able to affect the outcome.

CAREER AND FINANCES People born on this date often place their career goals above everything else. This is sometimes their way of coping with disappointments in other areas of life.

Living large is a habit of December 2 people. They make a habit of doing things in a big way and don't worry about the price tag.

DREAMS AND GOALS December 2 people believe that, with a little luck, any dream or wish can come true. These remarkable men and women are usually able to accomplish whatever they set out to do.

While it isn't easy for them to rebound from failure, they have the ability to turn their focus to another important goal if they must give up on their primary one.

EMBRACE
Drama
Courage
Commitment to excellence

AVOID
Rash choices
Envy
A broken heart

ALSO BORN TODAY
Symphony conductor Sir John Barbirolli; actor Steven Bauer; opera diva Maria Callas; fashion designer Robert Capucci; TV personality Cathy Lee Crosby; actress Julie Harris; tennis champion Monica Seles; radio personality Howard Stern.

DECEMBER 3

These folks have personality plus. Their charm, good looks, and sex appeal make them incredibly appealing. They enjoy living the good life, yet always manage to keep in touch with spiritual values.

December 3 people have a will of iron and can stand up for themselves in adversity and controversy. Although known for having a well-developed ego, this does not detract from their tremendous likability.

FRIENDS AND LOVERS

December 3 natives have a ceaseless interest in people, and because of this they are never without their supply of pals, friends, buddies, and confidantes.

These individuals are adventurous lovers. They thrive on the challenge of pursuing a love object, but may lose interest once the chase is over. Like most Sagittarians, they have a bit of trouble making an emotional commitment, since they are likely to equate it with giving up personal freedom, which is their most prized possession.

CHILDREN AND FAMILY

Though they may have had modest beginnings, December 3 people often credit early hardships with their competitive spirit. These people thrive on challenges from the time they are children.

December 3 men and women feel it is important to teach their own children the value of competition, but they have the good sense to know where to draw the line. They want their youngsters to try their best, but never shame or belittle them if they fall short of the mark.

HEALTH

Keeping fit is important to these men and women, who want to look great, feel great, and live to a ripe old age. Yet despite being active, many December 3 men and women find it difficult to keep weight off their "problem" areas.

December 3 natives have the usual Sagittarian love of fine dining. They are partygoers, which often implies an overindulgence in alcohol. Although this can be the case, it is usually confined to social occasions.

CAREER AND FINANCES

People born on this date may become accustomed to trading on their personality from the time they are very young, but their real talent is their creativity, especially in the performing arts. They make spectacular dancers, actors, and magicians.

December 3 people have the gift of attracting good luck, especially in finance, and have the potential to make a lot of money. This does not mean that they are particularly good at holding on to what they earn, since their generous nature gives them the impulse to spend, spend, spend.

DREAMS AND GOALS

Being able to make a living doing what they love is a priority in the lives of December 3 people. These folks work very hard to achieve their long-range goals, yet they may have problems with the short-term. This is because they see the big picture rather than small details.

It may be more challenging for December 3 men and women to achieve success on a personal level than in their professional lives.

EMBRACE
Experience
Direction
Thoughtfulness

AVOID
Frivolous romances
Moodiness
Belligerence

ALSO BORN TODAY
Race driver Bobby Allison; novelist Joseph Conrad; film director Jean-Luc Godard; cinematographer Sven Nykvist; composer Nino Rota; artist Gilbert Stuart; singer Andy Williams; figure skating champion Katarina Witt.

DECEMBER 4

R isk-takers who never play it safe is an apt description of December 4 natives, who typically have revolutionary opinions and a gift for being trend-setters. At the same time, they're excitable and can be difficult to get along with on occasion, especially when they refuse to back down from an argument.

People born on this date never attempt to be part of the crowd. They enjoy being different, as their eccentric attitude makes very clear. At some point in life they usually find themselves involved in New Age studies.

FRIENDS AND LOVERS
People born on this date have little interest in cultivating conventional relationships. They like living on the edge, and that means drawing interesting, even bizarre people into their orbit.

In romantic situations, December 4 people make their own rules. They often shy away from long-term commitment, preferring not only to stay single, but totally unattached.

CHILDREN AND FAMILY
December 4 men and women maintain a respectful distance from family members. This doesn't reflect a lack of love—merely their need to blaze their own trail from a very early age. Their ideas are usually far too unconventional to please their parents.

People born on this date don't believe in burdening their own children with too many rules. In fact, they may actually encourage their kids' opposition, just to help them learn independence.

HEALTH
December 4 men and women are extremists, and their attitude toward their own health often reflects this. They are either fanatics about maintaining good health, or extremely careless.

Constants are their love of learning and their curiosity for newness and exploration. To these iconoclastic folks, feeling young means *thinking* young. They don't believe in chronological age—one of the reasons they seem ageless.

CAREER AND FINANCES
December 4 individuals have a love of electronic gadgetry and often look for career options in communications, computer software or analysis, mathematics, accounting, or various scientific disciplines. Many people born on this date have a very high level of analytical intelligence.

Despite their brilliance, people born on this date are often careless about money matters. This usually reveals their disinterest, though they may expect a spouse or mate to handle these matters without ever really giving them over to that individual.

DREAMS AND GOALS
"Don't fence me in" could be the motto of December 4 men and women. These people are intense about their desire for personal freedom and will go to great lengths in order to achieve it. They will sacrifice anything—even love—to make this a reality.

People born on this date have a genius for taking advantage of the spontaneous twists of fate that come their way. An ability to capitalize on the vagaries of existence is something that few people other than December 4 individuals can fully implement.

EMBRACE
Rules
Structure
Inner dialogue

AVOID
Bad choices
Misrepresentation
Becoming sidetracked

ALSO BORN TODAY
Actor Jeff Bridges; novelist Samuel Butler; actor Horst Buchholz; critic/historian Thomas Carlyle; actress Deanna Durbin; artist Wassily Kandinsky; poet Rainier Maria Rilke; actress Marisa Tomei.

DECEMBER 5

December 5 people are dreamers as well as doers. They have a strong personal vision that informs everything they do, and which may become the focus of their lives.

These people have a great store of creativity and imagination: Elaborate, reachable dreams are particularly alluring to these folks. Their particular challenge is to stay true to their own ideas without being intimidated by the objections and negativity of those who don't possess their vision or ability.

FRIENDS AND LOVERS Sagittarians make the best friends, and December 5 people are even better in this role than most. These individuals possess an outgoing, sociable nature that draws people to them easily.

Love is generally a positive experience for people born on this date. They are true romantics who can fall in love at a glance, and change their feelings at a moment's notice. They tend to put off marriage until they are certain they can make a permanent commitment to one person—not an easy thing for them.

CHILDREN AND FAMILY December 5 natives never forget the magical moments of childhood. They have an uncanny ability to recapture that time in their life and use it as a form of emotional time-travel.

As parents, December 5 men and women attempt to connect with the spiritual aspects of child-rearing. This also enables them to study their own links with the past. They are careful to encourage their children to make the most of this remarkable period of life.

HEALTH Although they enjoy generally good health, December 5 men and women need to take a closer look at the bad habits that could put their health in jeopardy. Smoking is espe-

cially hard on these people and should be avoided at all costs.

People born on this date have a lot of nervous energy, which they need to manage through relaxation techniques.

CAREER AND FINANCES December 5 individuals have remarkable verbal skills that can translate to a career in journalism, television news, fiction writing, or teaching.

People born on this date may have to work very hard and for a long time before their proverbial ship comes in. But it is merely a question of "when," not "if." These men and women have an incredible ability to accurately judge the taste of others. Because of this gift, they have the potential to put their entrepreneurial skills to great use by marketing their own product or idea.

DREAMS AND GOALS Few individuals dream the impossible dream as fervently as December 5 men and women. These people have a great belief in their ability to maintain their focus as they work to achieve their goals.

If they must juggle personal happiness with professional acclaim, these folks always seem able to make the right choice at the right time. They understand that there are usually trade-offs to success, but are not willing to give up the personal life they have worked hard to manage in order to gain worldly or material rewards.

EMBRACE
Authenticity
Intensity
Readiness

AVOID
Confusion
Fear
Daydreaming

ALSO BORN TODAY
Actress Morgan Brittany; novelist Joan Didion; film producer Walt Disney; astrologer Robert Hand; football star Jim Plunkett; film director Otto Preminger; singer Little Richard; poet Christina Rossetti.

287

DECEMBER 6

These kind, soft-spoken individuals have a genuine love of people and are natural mediators. From childhood, they make peace between squabbling factions in the sandbox—and they never really lose this gift.

December 6 men and women understand the power of quiet persuasion. Their positive attitude and exquisite good manners make them pleasant to know and nice to be around. People born on this date raise sociability to an art form.

ALSO BORN TODAY
Musician Dave Brubeck; actor Tom Hulce; actress Elissa Landi; lyricist Ira Gershwin; actress Janine Turner; singer/guitarist Ben Watt; comedian Steven Wright.

FRIENDS AND LOVERS There is a sweetness inherent in the personality of December 6 people that ranks them high on anyone's list of potential friends. They have an understanding nature, which makes them the person everyone gravitates to for advice and compassion.

December 6 natives are old-fashioned romantics. They dream of finding their perfect mate, and when they do they're ready to make a lifelong commitment. If they suffer a broken marriage or other love relationship, they need a long time to pick up the pieces.

CHILDREN AND FAMILY Those born on this date may see themselves as a central figure in their family circle. They generally possess a traditional view of family life, and may continue to look at their childhood years in a naive way, even when old enough to know better.

December 6 people make good parents because they have the ability to transcend their own parochial views in order to understand the ways in which their own children may be different from themselves.

HEALTH December 6 people believe a positive attitude is necessary for good health. They also realize that physical health alone isn't enough. By working to incorporate a total mind-body-spirit harmony, these folks are able to achieve peak performance on many levels.

People born today often have problems with weight gain in middle age, when they cease to be as active as they were in youth. The obvious answer is to cut back on calories or change their style of eating, but this isn't easy for people who enjoy good food.

CAREER AND FINANCES December 6 individuals often carry their mediating ability into adulthood. This talent makes them excellent lawyers, judges, and corporate executives. As teachers, they have a great impact on students who might otherwise have little interest in schooling.

As with most Sagittarians, December 6 people have a talent for making money. Although this may not be an especially fervent goal for these people, they often end up living a luxurious lifestyle.

DREAMS AND GOALS People born on this date have a strong drive to help others. No matter what form this ability takes, it has the power to transcend both career and personal matters.

December 6 men and women have the rare ability to "go with the flow." If attainment of a cherished dream is beyond their reach, they will find something else to take its place.

DECEMBER 7

People born on this date have great wisdom and occult knowledge, which allows them to perceive life on many levels. These men and women have the ability to understand the complicated symbology of life.

December 7 people search for meaning through their important relationships, and generally express their true inner self via a creative outlet. These men and women know where the rough water is, and have the ability to maneuver through life's swift currents without losing their way.

FRIENDS AND LOVERS December 7 natives don't so much choose friends as they are chosen as a friend by others. These people have a natural ability to act as a counselor, and often dispense advice.

Romance is an extremely serious matter to December 7 men and women. These people have a profound, almost religious view of commitment to the one they love. There is often a strong karmic tie between December 7 individuals and their mates, since they're automatically drawn to someone through whom they can learn life's most important lessons.

CHILDREN AND FAMILY December 7 natives often grow up in an unusual family that not only understands their psychic leanings, but helps to foster them. If orthodox religious training or the absence of spirituality characterizes the home life, December 7 people are unlikely to develop their occult gift to its full potential.

When December 7 people become parents, they show a great deal of sensitivity to the emotional needs of their youngsters. The strong bond between parent and child lasts a lifetime.

HEALTH People born on this date are interested in a holistic approach to good health. They are often extremely well read in Eastern practices, such as Reiki and acupuncture.

Because these men and women understand the value of dispelling toxins from their body, they can benefit from a weekly juice fast, where for 24 hours they drink only fresh-squeezed fruit and vegetable juices.

CAREER AND FINANCES Although these folks have a great many talents, they generally gravitate toward work in the arts. They make talented musicians, photographers, painters, and dancers. If they seek to explore their psychic abilities further, they have the ability to become fine astrologers, palmists, and tarot-card readers.

Because people born on this day feel strongly that to do something strictly for money is unethical, finances are a tricky factor in their lives. Their idealism is laudable, but needs to be tempered with a more practical attitude.

DREAMS AND GOALS Continual use of their remarkable talents to the spiritual betterment of themselves and others is the goal of December 7 people. They have the ability to reach the highest levels of spiritual understanding—if they remain open to the positive influences that come their way.

Because they can make a difference in the lives of those closest to them, December 7 people take their relationships with utmost seriousness.

EMBRACE
Good intentions
Direction
Promises

AVOID
Artistic pretensions
Self-glorification
Denial

ALSO BORN TODAY
Baseball star Johnny Bench; composer Rudolf Friml; basketball star/coach Larry Bird; actress Ellen Burstyn; singer/songwriter Harry Chapin; novelist Rosemary Rogers; actor Eli Wallach; composer Pietro Mascagni.

DECEMBER 8

Headstrong and imperious, December 8 individuals also have a docile side; they express this duality via constant changes in personality. They may be a risk-taker one minute and a timid soul the next. Because they tend to extremes, it's not uncommon for these men and women to regret many of their choices.

December 8 people have creative talent, but seem to prefer the life of a dilettante. This attitude, if unchecked, can be their downfall. They also possess a weakness for flattery.

FRIENDS AND LOVERS

December 8 men and women have a gift for living the high life, and that means plenty of friends at their side. Because they possess a fascinating personality, December 8 individuals have no lack of people wanting to get close to them.

People born on this date fall in love easily, but may have trouble committing to a long-term relationship. They don't say "I do" easily.

CHILDREN AND FAMILY

December 8 natives project a certain arrogance, which tends to create problems with family members. These people often grow up in familial circumstances that invite an atmosphere of combativeness and competition. This can create long-term misunderstandings with siblings.

Even if they don't become parents themselves, December 8 people have an excellent rapport with youngsters. They make marvelous uncles and aunts, and enjoy spending time with the kids of good friends.

HEALTH

The phrase "if it feels good, do it" was probably coined by somebody born on December 8. These people have little use for rules and regulations that dictate how much they can eat and how often they need to exercise.

But these men and women are far from indolent. They simply prefer to stay healthy their own way. Their happy, can-do attitude has the ability to banish tension, keep their blood pressure low, and help them sleep well at night. When they do feel under the weather, December 8 people prefer a shopping trip to a spoonful of medicine.

CAREER AND FINANCES

People born on this date may give the impression of being unable to hold down a serious job, though this isn't the case. They use the force of their personality to further their aims at work, and prefer career choices that put them in the public eye, or allow them to meet the public.

December 8 folks are big spenders who enjoy showing their generosity to family members, friends, and even acquaintances. They like to gamble, and should take care to monitor their emotional attachment to this pastime.

DREAMS AND GOALS

Although December 8 men and women love to have a good time, they don't let it interfere with their more practical goals. These people have a naturally spirited personality that helps them achieve their goals. Note, however, that people born on this date have considerable integrity, and will not compromise it for personal gain. To them, winning counts only when it's achieved fairly and with dignity.

EMBRACE
Good advice
A nurturing spirit
Prudence

AVOID
Destructive behavior
Turmoil
Impatience

ALSO BORN TODAY
Mary, Queen of Scots; actress Kim Basinger; singer/songwriter Jim Morrison; actress Teri Hatcher; composer Jean Sibelius; actress Jennie Linden; writer James Thurber; actor Maximilian Schell.

DECEMBER 9

December 9 individuals find their identity through group involvement. These high-energy people enjoy being challenged and seem to have a knack for starting conflicts with authority figures. Loaded with a brand of self-confidence that would seem like conceit in others, they're unwilling to acknowledge the possibility of failure.

Although they have a jovial temperament, December 9 men and women also possess an edgy, somewhat sarcastic attitude that often draws them into controversy.

FRIENDS AND LOVERS

December 9 natives have personality to spare, and are the envy of all their friends. They collect friends, yet never seem to have enough. They enjoy surrounding themselves with a group of people that knows how to have a good time. Wherever December 9 folks go, a party inevitably follows.

People born on this date have a reputation for being fickle. They may remain single until late in life, or never marry at all, usually for fear that any relationship, once it concedes to matrimony, will dissolve in boredom.

CHILDREN AND FAMILY

Although December 9 men and women are unlikely to have a close relationship with family members, this does not imply troubled relationships. These people simply "graduate" from the family once they reach maturity, and may not feel the need to carry on a close relationship afterward.

This casual relationship often changes once December 9 people become parents, when they're likely to want to reconnect emotionally with their roots.

HEALTH

With the exception of childhood ailments and the seasonal complaints that every adult suffers, December 9 people can usually make the claim that they haven't had a sick day in their lives. These hearty individuals owe much of their good health to a positive attitude.

Exercise is the main component of any Sagittarian's health program. These people never seem to slow down. Playing competitive sports on the weekend is more to their taste than going to a gym or health club.

CAREER AND FINANCES

December 9 natives enjoy careers that allow them to travel. They're talkative, extroverted individuals who make good teachers, tour guides, or language instructors. They do very well in the hospitality business—hotel or restaurant management, food service, catering.

These folks love to spend money but don't like to keep track of it. They can be somewhat irresponsible in the way they handle even the most commonplace financial chores, such as paying the monthly bills. Still, their forgetfulness is one of their charms.

DREAMS AND GOALS

People born on this date have a great many goals, though they may not possess the self-discipline to see them through to the end. Fortunately, they're often the beneficiaries of good fortune, which helps to make their dreams come true.

December 9 people have the resilience to come back from disappointments and even the most spectacular failures. Their natural optimism plays a big part in their success.

EMBRACE
Dignity
Sociability
Meditation

AVOID
Safety risks
Deceit
Blasphemy

ALSO BORN TODAY
Actor Beau Bridges; football star Dick Butkus; actress Judi Dench; actor Kirk Douglas; comedian Redd Foxx; singer Neil Innes; actor John Malkovich; singer Donny Osmond.

DECEMBER 10

Analytical yet creative, people born on this date believe in getting things done. Because they have a very good self-image, they don't need to rely on ego to get the job done for them. They have a sunny, personable nature and always seem to be full of good humor and enthusiasm.

These men and women instinctively protect themselves from emotional pain. Although they can handle every other type of challenge extremely well, December 10 people flinch from touchy situations involving feelings.

FRIENDS AND LOVERS
December 10 people have a straightforward attitude about all their relationships. They don't like complications and will opt out of any friendship when too much is expected of them.

These men and women have a similar attitude where romance is concerned. Although they are capable of great love and affection, they don't like to feel pressured about the relationship. If a partner or mate doesn't respect the boundaries they put up, December 10 folks may lose interest, even if they're still very much in love. Even romance can't compete with their need for personal autonomy.

CHILDREN AND FAMILY
People born on this day feel connected to their family throughout their lifetime. They generally have an extremely close relationship with one or both parents, who may also have served as a role model or mentor.

As parents, December 10 men and women prefer the "pal" approach. They understand the value of instilling structure and discipline in their child's life, but are even more concerned with providing an atmosphere that promotes creativity and self-esteem.

HEALTH
These robust individuals prefer to keep healthy the natural way with plenty of outdoor exercise. Mountain biking, hiking, and long-distance running are favorite pastimes.

Learning to relax can be difficult for these people, but they can benefit from setting aside an hour each day for meditation and reflection. By injecting a spiritual element into their daily lives, December 10 people can achieve true emotional equilibrium.

CAREER AND FINANCES
December 10 people are decisive individuals whose ability to react coolly and intelligently under stressful conditions makes them perfect for high pressure jobs. These men and women excel as fire and police officers, air traffic controllers, paramedics, surgeons, and military personnel.

People born on this date handle their financial affairs with the same combination of forthrightness and common sense that marks all their other actions. They see the "big picture," and also are on top of all the little details that come with money management.

DREAMS AND GOALS
Living large is a goal of December 10 men and women, who dislike skimping on anything. Whether it's money, time, or personal relationships, people born on this date take everything to the limit.

December 10 natives pride themselves on being invincible, and will do whatever they must in order to keep that image intact.

EMBRACE
Sensation
Good work habits
Privacy

AVOID
Detours
Negative vibes
Disillusionment

ALSO BORN TODAY
Actor/director Kenneth Branagh; actress Susan Dey; poet Emily Dickinson; composer Cesar Franck; writer Rumer Godden; composer Morton Gould; TV journalist Chet Huntley; actress Dorothy Lamour.

DECEMBER 11

Intellectually gifted, people born on this date have the ability to transform their world into something quite amazing. They are ambitious, though not in the strictly material sense.

A strong emotional nature makes these people more intense than many Sagittarians. They are likely to be extremely passionate about their political views, especially in matters that affect the environment. They demonstrate a great deal of urgency in their need to "make a difference."

FRIENDS AND LOVERS

Men and women born on this date are usually the center of attention within their group of friends. Relationships are the center of their life, yet are just as likely to cause them pain as happiness. Close friendships can have a note of controversy.

These emotional folks can grieve for a long time when a love affair goes wrong. The fairytale aspect of romance inevitably attracts them. This is sometimes their unconscious way of setting themselves up for failure, since they don't always believe that they deserve happiness in love.

CHILDREN AND FAMILY

Although they may not completely understand their motivations, December 11 people have a great need to reconnect with their childhood years. Often it is only by coming to terms with their upbringing that these men and women are able to fully comprehend their inner self.

December 11 natives are ambivalent about having children, since career plans generally drive their lives. Yet once they commit to the "baby thing," these people amaze themselves with the level of their involvement.

HEALTH

Like most people of their sign, December 11 people can usually count on good health. Yet despite this, they may have some very bad habits that threaten to undermine it. Smoking or overindulgence in alcohol can be especially harmful to them.

Poor eating habits can rob these men and women of vitality. Excess sweets and starches promote sluggishness. Instead of filling up on all those carbohydrates, December 11 people need to eat more meat and dairy products, as well as taking calcium supplements.

CAREER AND FINANCES

These energetic and committed individuals need to believe in their ability to make the world a better place through their work.

When their resources permit, December 11 people contribute to charities and worthwhile causes. Although they enjoy their creature comforts, money isn't an important factor in their lives.

DREAMS AND GOALS

Making a difference is what it's all about for December 11 people, who are always ready to put their considerable talent to work in this way. If they have the chance to heal someone's emotional pain by giving them the benefit of their experience, they're willing to do it.

Personal goals often revolve around travel and learning. These men and women are life-long students who never pass up an opportunity to expand their horizons.

EMBRACE
Ecology
Redemption
Satisfaction

AVOID
Unhappy memories
Contradictions
Intimidation

ALSO BORN TODAY
Composer Hector Berlioz; novelist Ursula Bloom; actress Teri Garr; singer Jermaine Jackson; singer/actress Rita Moreno; film producer Carlo Ponti; film director Susan Seidelman; writer Alexander Solzhenitsyn.

DECEMBER 12

December 12 people are competitive in all aspects of life. No matter how much they are able to accomplish, these obsessive perfectionists inevitably feel bad about the opportunities that got away.

These folks have a great need to accumulate the tangible emblems of success in order to feel that they have truly "made it." It is often this same attitude of accountability that helps these focused men and women blaze their trail.

FRIENDS AND LOVERS
There are few people who treat their friends with as much pure love and show them as much affection as December 12 individuals.

In romantic matters, they show a great deal of forbearance and sophistication. Since friends are sometimes lovers and lovers are always friends, these men and women don't terminate a relationship if the affair or marriage ends. Being able to remain close friends with their exes is one of the most remarkable things about these individuals.

CHILDREN AND FAMILY
In childhood or as an adult, December 12 people are part of an extended family. They don't draw boundaries around their affections and can easily accept a cousin, a brother-in-law, or even a distant relative on the same terms as siblings or a parent.

December 12 natives are loving, if overly strict parents. Although not disciplinarians by nature, they take their parental responsibilities seriously, even if that means behaving against type.

HEALTH
December 12 people don't like to be curtailed in any area of life, and that includes their diet. These individuals love good food and don't take kindly to medical advice that suggests they give up red meat or rich desserts.

But despite their questionable eating habits, December 12 men and women aren't likely to pack on the pounds. These people have been likened to perpetual motion—always on the go. Their competitive nature revels in playing tennis, racquetball, or golf.

CAREER AND FINANCES
People born on this date are articulate and witty, and often choose to make their living with words. They are well suited to work as journalists, writers, comedians, and lawyers. Their talents can also be showcased in advertising, publishing, and academia.

Spending money comes easily to these individuals. They have a champagne taste that doesn't stop at the gratification of their own wishes. There are few people on the face of the earth who have the generous nature of these people.

DREAMS AND GOALS
Despite their ability to live in the moment, December 12 men and women want very much to leave something behind when they die. Whether this means money, accomplishments, or the fond memories in the minds of their best friends, December 12 people want something to show that they were here.

These individuals do many good deeds throughout their lifetime, demonstrating yet another goal—to help others.

EMBRACE
Ingenuity
Change
Foresight

AVOID
Defensive behavior
Danger
Scarcity

ALSO BORN TODAY
Actress Mayim Bialik; singer Connie Francis; political commentator Rush Limbaugh; painter Edvard Munch; playwright John Osborne; gymnast Cathy Rigby; singer/actor Frank Sinatra; singer Dionne Warwick.

DECEMBER 13

Eccentricity marks the personality of people born on this day. These people don't hesitate to put themselves "out there," and always see risks as major signposts to challenges.

These people have a strong belief in themselves and enormous confidence, yet they have the ability to admit when they are wrong. When it comes to leadership ability, these individuals are second to none, though that sort of role seldom appeals to their antic sense of fun.

FRIENDS AND LOVERS

Even though these fun-loving individuals love having people around them, they aren't big on making close friends. They feel that familiarity often breeds contempt and that casual friends often make the best friends.

These people are totally honest in all their relationships and never try to manipulate a mate or date. If they are unhappy with a relationship they simply say so—and move on without guilt.

CHILDREN AND FAMILY

Because of their unconventional ideas about life, December 13 individuals don't always get on well with family members who possess a more prudent view of the world. But true to their broad-minded nature, people born on this date never disparage the more conservative attitudes of others.

Nor do their liberal views change when they have children. These people want their youngsters to experience life on their own terms.

HEALTH

Anything goes regarding health maintenance for these quirky people. They may be hooked on bowling one day, espousing the values of colonic irrigation the next.

Nutrition is another source of endless change and challenge. They have probably tried every diet on the market, trying to lose the same ten or fifteen pounds each year. Yet they do have a serious interest in the values of good nutrition.

CAREER AND FINANCES

December 13 natives excel in technology-oriented careers. These science buffs may have a nerd reputation in high school, but are sure to blossom into brilliant men and women who not only know their way around a computer, but may even write code for them.

People born on this date are amazing in their handling of money matters. They are the original entrepreneurs, whose ideas are so far ahead of their time they can't help but succeed or fail in spectacular ways. It's not uncommon for December 13 individuals to market an idea and make a fortune from it, only to lose the same money in another equally risky enterprise. It's all the same to them. Money isn't lost, but simply exchanged.

DREAMS AND GOALS

December 13 people want to have it all and do it all, and don't mind if they have to suffer the consequences. These unique men and women value experience—not the weighty, tangible kind—but the airy, in-the-moment variety.

These brilliant people are powered by their ideas. Their minds are in a constant state of flux, churning out amazing and sometimes impossible concepts.

EMBRACE
Make-believe
Learning
Maturity

AVOID
Sensationalism
Imitation
Dissemblers

ALSO BORN TODAY
Novelist Gustave Flaubert; actor Van Heflin; poet Heinrich Heine; baseball star Ferguson Jenkins; First Lady Mary Todd Lincoln; actor Christopher Plummer; guitarist Ted Nugent; actor Dick Van Dyke.

DECEMBER 14

People born on this date have the ability to juggle a variety of tasks and responsibilities. Good-natured and friendly, they make wonderful cheerleaders for the goals and ambitions of others.

True to their Sagittarian nature, these men and women remain enthusiastic and full of optimism no matter what the circumstance. While others may be bemoaning a potential problem, December 14 people have already worked it out and moved on.

FRIENDS AND LOVERS
Men and women born on this date never differentiate between a good friend, an old friend, or a best friend. Friends simply are, and are what life is all about.

Love affairs and even marriage with December 14 individuals are firmly grounded in friendship. These individuals have a truly communal attitude about human relationships, and though that does not imply sexual practices, it does mean that these people are quite capable of grouping together everyone they love and considering the result one big collage of human happiness.

CHILDREN AND FAMILY
It's fairly typical for Sagittarian types to grow up happily in a family, rebel, separate, then make up later on. December 14 people fit this description. No matter what differences may divide them from siblings and parents,

they're always willing to give the relationships another try, even if history should have taught them better.

People born on this date have real talent for parenting, though they may shy away from it. They aren't big on commitment as a rule, though if they do become parents they often surprise themselves with the depth and intensity of their parental love.

HEALTH
December 14 people brag about never being sick, though they often take their robust vitality for granted, not really appreciating it unless a health condition strikes.

These men and women have a sincere interest in crystal balancing, aura cleansing, and chakra adjustment—and they couldn't care less how odd or trendy it may seem to others.

CAREER AND FINANCES
December 14 people are the original show people. They have a knack for getting themselves noticed, and deep down in the bottom of their soul they want someone to make them a "star." When this doesn't come true for them, they're likely to turn their interest to other creative endeavors, such as music, art, poetry, or magic.

True to form, they have an almost naive contempt for money, and refuse to let it influence their choices in life.

DREAMS AND GOALS
To be, to think, to do, to express—these are the goals of December 14 natives. They have little interest in putting together a linear plan of life and achievement. If it feels good, if it helps someone, if it creates beauty for even an instant, these people are all for it.

To unplug themselves from the workaday world is something that December 14 people don't merely enjoy—it's a positive necessity to them.

EMBRACE
Diversity
Sentiment
Enjoyment

AVOID
Stubbornness
Lack of control
Resistance

ALSO BORN TODAY
Actress Patty Duke; England's King George VI; actress Cynthia Gibb; novelist Shirley Jackson; bandleader Spike Jones; actress Lee Remick; U.S. Senator Margaret Chase Smith; actress Dee Wallace Stone.

DECEMBER 15

December 15 men and women are not as unconventional as some members of their sign, but they can appreciate the absurd and contemplate the impossible.

These people are success-oriented, yet have far too much integrity to ever go against their principles in order to get what they want. While they understand the trade-off between hard work and achievement, they never lose sight of what's going on outside the boundaries of their own commitments and interests.

FRIENDS AND LOVERS

Friends are not simply diversions in the lives of December 15 people; people born on this date constantly look to their pals for advice, counsel, and just plain sympathy.

Romance can be a complicated affair for these individuals, who may endure more than their share of unrequited love and bad choices. Yet they never stop trying to make their love life work. They are much more intense than they seem, and can suffer more pain because of a breakup than even those closest to them realize.

CHILDREN AND FAMILY

December 15 people believe that you really can go home again. Although they may have spent many years estranged from family members, they never give up hope that someday those differences can be mended, and a new understanding can emerge.

People born on this date can learn a great deal about themselves from parenthood. Often it's not until they have children of their own that these people are able to take stock of their upbringing.

HEALTH

The jovial attitude of December 15 people may hide serious food issues that they may be unwilling to face. These usually have their roots in childhood, when good behavior was rewarded with food and bad behavior punished in the same way.

December 15 individuals need to relearn how to appreciate food, how to choose food that's good for them, and most of all how to separate emotionally charged issues from the act of eating.

CAREER AND FINANCES

People born on this date are often drawn to fields that allow them to make their living in a semi-public way. Retail sales is a particularly rewarding field for them, since it allows them to make use of their people-skills and charming personality.

Money often comes to these individuals in odd ways. Even if they don't work very hard to acquire it, these men and women seem destined to easily draw material resources into their lives.

DREAMS AND GOALS

December 15 people know how to conceptualize a goal and make it come true. These folks have a strong work ethic and are delighted when rewards flow from their efforts.

People born on this date don't become discouraged by disappointments in their personal or professional lives, looking at these things as challenges that can only make them work harder and focus more intently on what they want out of life. They also understand the importance of remaining true to themselves.

EMBRACE
Spiritual transcendence
Facts
Belief

AVOID
Mood swings
Temperament
Lateness

ALSO BORN TODAY
Playwright Maxwell Anderson; singer Dave Clark; comedian Tim Conway; millionaire J. Paul Getty; actor Don Johnson; novelist Edna O'Brien; actress Helen Slater.

DECEMBER 16

December 16 individuals are singularly extraordinary. These men and women have such a disciplined nature that they can live on very little, as long as they have the opportunity to express their inner fire. Blessed with a truly artistic temperament, they understand that success equals creative accomplishment, not money.

People born on this date have so much wisdom that they may seem to be plugged into some cosmic energy source that the rest of the world can't see.

EMBRACE
Composure
Common sense
Fortitude

AVOID
Reclusiveness
Indulgence
Feeling superior

ALSO BORN TODAY
Novelist Jane Austen; composer Ludwig von Beethoven; TV producer Steven Bochco; playwright Noel Coward; guitarist/singer Billy Gibbons; composer Zoltan Kodaly; TV journalist Lesley Stahl; actress Liv Ullman.

FRIENDS AND LOVERS It's not easy to be a friend to December 16 people. They have a habit of pushing people away, especially when they need the help and reassurance of a friend the most.

Relationships are never easy for these folks because they refuse to accept the code of conventional behavior. Few people are as true to their own nature as these men and women. Unfortunately, this can create problems with their relationships. People born on this day have an intense love nature, though they may prefer abstinence if there is no one special in their lives.

CHILDREN AND FAMILY As children, these people never feel as if they fit in with the "group" and may develop a bad self-image during this time in their life. Later, when they grow into their personality, they learn to draw strength from their uniqueness.

Because they don't want their own children to experience the difficulties they faced, December 16 men and women can be very strict and rule-conscious. In a sense they are taking back the control they did not have as children.

HEALTH December 16 people are not particularly concerned with health maintenance. They're even more stubborn about it if they have a health condition! These individuals don't care to be told how they can behave, even by a doctor.

People born on this date may be reluctant to exercise. When they do, it's usually done for emotional rather than physical reasons: a walk on a windswept beach, a horseback ride along the surf, or a hike on a serene mountain trail.

CAREER AND FINANCES December 16 men and women are usually drawn toward creative enterprises, though this doesn't necessarily suggest their ultimate career path. Because artistry means something special to these folks, they may work at their talent for years without being compensated with money, while making a living at a job that means nothing to them other than a paycheck.

People born on this date have the good sense not to believe that money equals success.

DREAMS AND GOALS People born on this day live in a world of their own making. These people are not preoccupied with goals; they listen to their intuition rather than to conventional wisdom.

These men and women have high expectations for their talent, yet are willing to allow it to develop at its own pace. They understand that true art cannot be forced.

DECEMBER 17

People born on this date are material realists. Although they constantly aim high, they have the maturity to accept failure as part of the bargain. Their talent for leadership usually shows itself early in life, often through dramatic circumstances.

Although self-disciplined, December 17 natives enjoy breaking the rules from time to time. They may be self-conscious about their practical side, and keep that aspect of their personality hidden from all but those closest to them.

FRIENDS AND LOVERS December 17 people believe that friendships can't be formed overnight, but are forged through circumstances, both good and bad, over a period of many years.

December 17 people are the marrying kind. Although they may worry about retaining the same level of independence and autonomy after marriage, they prefer to go through life as part of a couple. They make exceptional mates, and strive to keep the romance alive in the relationship.

CHILDREN AND FAMILY Family matters are usually favorable for December 17 folks. As children, they become accustomed to receiving a great deal of praise and admiration, and may have shouldered considerable responsibilities at a very young age.

December 17 people may feel that their own children should be brought up in a similar fashion. They also believe in giving their youngsters the opportunity to make some of their own rules and regulations, in order to give them a sense of independence.

HEALTH Because people born on this date may have experienced a health condition as a

child, they may feel somewhat vulnerable in this area. As a result, these men and women may become health fanatics, especially about exercise.

December 17 people can benefit from weight-training, which helps them to build up physical endurance as well as muscle mass.

CAREER AND FINANCES In common with other Sagittarians, December 17 men and women possess an entrepreneurial spirit. These individuals have both the vision and the practicality to succeed in a self-owned or self-run business. They are likely to do well in publishing, graphics, pet care, and catering.

December 17 people were born to make money. Their ability is predicated upon a keen understanding of what the public wants. Their tireless research efforts back up their intuition.

EMBRACE
Impartiality
Organization
Social skills

AVOID
Destructive habits
Poor judgment
Ruthlessness

ALSO BORN TODAY
Novelist Erskine Caldwell; singer Sarah Dallin; conductor Arthur Fiedler; novelist Ford Maddox Ford; painter Jacob Landau; journalist William Safire; singer Tommy Steele; poet John Greenleaf Whittier.

DREAMS AND GOALS Goal-making is a specialty of people born on this date. They love everything that goes with it—the planning, the slow progress, even the setbacks. Once they've decided that a project must go forward, they put forth monumental efforts to succeed.

December 17 people seem to have a good deal of self-confidence, but they may not feel quite as positive about their own abilities as they seem. Success usually cures them of that problem.

299

DECEMBER 18

People born on this date are energetic go-getters, yet they are never aggressive or abrasive in their dealings with others. These likable folks have an open, generous nature and a sharp sense of humor.

When December 18 individuals are dedicated to an ideal or concept, they will fight with tireless diligence to protect and support it. These men and women are often extremely modest about their talents, while they may be unduly proud of lesser accomplishments.

FRIENDS AND LOVERS December 18
natives are capable of achieving dizzying heights of friendship. They give a great deal of loyalty to their close friends, and may feel extremely protective of them.

People born on this date have the potential to be powerfully committed in a love relationship or marriage. Whatever facade they may adopt, they actually possess a great deal of romantic sentimentality.

CHILDREN AND FAMILY When December 18 individuals succeed in life—in a profession or in a personal relationship—it's because of the understanding and emotional support they received as children. Even if they had little in the way of material possessions during their growing-up years, that "lack" was offset by the affection and sense of importance they received.

As parents, December 18 men and women are extremely sensitive and caring. Although these individuals are generally most concerned about the state of their relationship, they manage to give their children all the understanding and affection they received as little ones.

HEALTH Many December 18 natives retain
their youthful exuberance well into middle age and even beyond. Their "no worries" policy is one of their best-kept health and fitness secrets.

As long as December 18 folks take relatively good care of themselves, they can expect to enjoy health and vitality. The key is moderation. They generally believe that nothing done in moderation can hurt them, and that anything—even good habits—can be harmful if followed too slavishly.

CAREER AND FINANCES People born on
this date need to be excited about the work they do. Whatever it is, they want to wake up every day eager to go to work. If their career can't support that level of enthusiasm, they'll look for something that does.

Money matters in the lives of these men and women are usually stable. Although they don't equate making money with success, people born on this date are concerned with maintaining a good standard of living for themselves and their loved ones.

DREAMS AND GOALS An ability to
express themselves through their work and their relationships is one of the goals of December 18 people. These men and women don't believe in putting limits on what they can achieve.

At the same time, they don't expect anything to come to them without a lot of hard work and effort.

EMBRACE
Prestige
Determination
Inner power

AVOID
Lethargy
Indecisiveness
Lack of commitment

ALSO BORN TODAY
Baseball star Ty Cobb; playwright Christopher Fry; actress Betty Grable; painter Paul Klee; film director Steven Spielberg; composer Edward MacDowell; guitarist/singer Keith Richards; film director George Stevens.

DECEMBER 19

December 19 individuals walk an emotional tightrope, but are utterly fearless. These people revel in taking chances but never do it without a good reason. They often give the impression of being the strong, silent type.

People born on this date feel the need to make a contribution to society through their work or their ideals. A strong sense of commitment to personal goals marks them as certain success stories. Their talent may get them in the door, but it's their moxie that keeps them in the room.

FRIENDS AND LOVERS
Because they are such likable types, December 19 people make friends effortlessly. Friendly and sociable, these men and women have the ability to transform a frivolous relationship into a meaningful friendship.

December 19 natives have something of a reputation for being great lovers. They enjoy playing the field for a number of years before settling down, and usually gravitate toward good-looking, glamourous types, even though they may be somewhat plain themselves.

CHILDREN AND FAMILY
People born on this date believe in maintaining strong family ties. Despite a somewhat unconventional nature, they secretly relish the trappings of respectability and tradition that come with family life.

December 19 men and women could hardly be more different in their role as parents than their own parents were. They're inclined to give their children far greater freedom than they were allowed, though their academic expectations are likely to be higher.

HEALTH
People born on this date are in tune with the rhythms of their own body. For this reason they often subscribe to homeopathic or holistic treatments for wellness or for sickness.

December 19 natives can benefit from deep massage, reiki, or rolfing techniques, which provide psychological and emotional benefit in addition to physical therapy.

CAREER AND FINANCES
It's not uncommon for December 19 individuals to experience some success in their career very early in life. Although this may appear to be fortunate, it can actually be a mixed blessing. These individuals actually do better when they have to struggle for their success. If things come too easily to them, they're likely to lose interest.

The same holds true for money. December 19 people who are born to money or who have the good fortune to make it very early in their careers may lose their edge, inhibiting their ability to compete with others on professional and personal levels.

DREAMS AND GOALS
People born on this date are not particularly goal-conscious, but are happiest when they have opportunities to use their professional status in order to affect positive change.

December 19 individuals like to be noticed for their singularity of purpose. The more difficult the odds against them, the more likely it is that these men and women will succeed. They love a challenge, and will always respond positively to it.

EMBRACE
Willpower
Solidarity
True happiness

AVOID
Being insincere
Bias
Incredulity

ALSO BORN TODAY
Actress Jennifer Beals; playwright Jean Genet; baseball star Al Kaline; actress Alyssa Milano; singer Edith Piaf; symphony conductor Fritz Reiner; actor Sir Ralph Richardson; actress Cicely Tyson.

DECEMBER 20

The strong psychic and emotional nature of December 20 men and women belies an outwardly breezy attitude. Their's is a personality of subtle shadings, a chameleon that offers something different to everyone.

Attracted to tradition and the status quo, people born on this date retain strong ties to their past. They may struggle to break free of the image others have of them. Once they learn to see themselves as independent of their background or current situation, their true self can emerge.

FRIENDS AND LOVERS

As friends, December 20 natives choose people they admire and would like to emulate. There's often an element of hero-worship in their relationships, which is likely to be reflective of how they might have felt about an older brother or sister while growing up.

The typical December 20 person is often extravagantly romantic, and usually manages to have interesting love lives. These folks have a somewhat old-fashioned view of romance and may subconsciously seek to connect with individuals who favor their idea of true love and a happily-ever-after mentality.

CHILDREN AND FAMILY

Family relationships have important significance for December 20 natives. These people feel most complete when part of a group. They like to think of their siblings as friends, and are able to put aside any sense of competition that may have existed in their childhood years.

Many men and women born on this date are ambivalent about having children of their own because they fear a loss of personal freedom. Yet once they become parents, they fit into the role almost magically.

HEALTH

December 20 people eat what they want, exercise when they please, and generally do their own thing. Their notions about health maintenance are their own.

People born on this date can thank their positive attitude for their health and vitality. Whatever comes their way, they're able to adopt a philosophical approach, and refuse to let anything get to them.

CAREER AND FINANCES

People born on this date usually choose a career that allows them to use their natural curiosity and psychic intuition. They have great wisdom and sensitivity. If they seek a career in education it is generally teaching subjects that have an occult or New Age significance.

December 20 people are unlikely to be interested in money yet are singularly fortunate in drawing resources into their lives. They may choose a profession that picks up the tab for travel expenses.

DREAMS AND GOALS

December 20 people are fascinated with the world around them, and look for ways in which they can use their natural abilities to bring new experiences into their lives.

People born on this date have the rare ability to balance professional and personal goals without losing sight of either. They are able to deal with defeats and delays in a positive manner, and are always ready to try again.

EMBRACE
Self-determination
Strength
Ego

AVOID
Needy people
Fear of change
Pressure

ALSO BORN TODAY

Actress Jenny Agutter; singer/songwriter Billy Bragg; film director George Roy Hill; actor John Hillerman; singer Anita Baker; actor Chris Robinson; psychic Uri Geller; actor Kiefer Sutherland.

DECEMBER 21

SAGITTARIUS

THE

ARCHER

Few people have such power of self-determination as the men and women born on this date. They possess the ability to transform themselves from ugly duckling to beautiful swan, both physically and otherwise.

When an idea or concept grabs them, December 21 people are able to draw upon their incredible powers of concentration and discipline in order to make their dreams a reality. People born on this date are quick to spot intellectual dishonesty in others.

FRIENDS AND LOVERS
These men and women subconsciously seek out friends who can give them the validation they need. December 21 people often lack self-confidence, and need others to help them feel good about themselves.

The typical December 21 native seldom becomes romantically involved with a person who lacks the potential to become a friend. People born on this date place a great importance upon partnership in marriage, feeling that it is as valuable a component in a relationship as romance. They want a spouse who can appreciate them on many levels.

CHILDREN AND FAMILY
The relationships and alliances made in childhood affect lives of December 21 forever, particularly since these folks often have a complicated family history that puts them at an unfair disadvantage. Demanding parental figures, uncertain relationships with siblings, and all the baggage that comes with a difficult childhood can weigh heavily on the emotional health of those born on this date.

Despite their own difficult beginnings, these people are excellent parents who have the ability to transcend their negative experiences.

HEALTH
December 21 people have a sense of vulnerability about their health. They need to be fiercely motivated in order to begin a fitness routine, but once they start seeing a marked improvement in how they look and feel, they can become fitness fanatics.

It's important for these men and women to add a spiritual aspect to their daily life, in order to create harmony. They benefit from regular meditation sessions.

CAREER AND FINANCES
December 21 people bring a high level of enthusiasm to their work. Whatever the job, these energetic men and women need to feel personally involved and able to make a difference in their world.

People born on this date are well equipped to handle their own financial affairs, no matter how complicated these might be. They have a talent for making intelligent investment choices, and always seem to be one step ahead of the conventional wisdom.

DREAMS AND GOALS
These individuals have the ability to reach the very top of their field once they learn to have confidence in their own abilities. Enormously talented, they can nevertheless be hamstrung unless they appreciate their gifts. When they learn how not to be their own worst enemy, their goals are apt to materialize.

EMBRACE
Excitement
Emotional fulfillment
Blessings

AVOID
Depression
Sense of loss
Feeling blue

ALSO BORN TODAY
Ballerina Alicia Alonso; TV talk show host Phil Donahue; tennis champion Chris Evert; actress Jane Fonda; opera conductor Christopher Keene; actor Josh Mostel; symphony conductor Michael Tilson Thomas; musician Frank Zappa.

CAPRICORN
December 22 - January 19

Capricorn is the tenth sign of the astrological year and is known by its astrological symbol, the Goat. Capricorn individuals are controlled, conscientious, and practical. With Saturn as the ruling planet, people born under this sign are self-disciplined and hard-working. They are highly efficient and dedicated to becoming a success.

THE CAPRICORN MAN It isn't easy to get to know the Capricorn man because he is secretive and will often conceal things about his life or background for little or no reason. Being defensive comes naturally to him, for he actually feels very vulnerable and is afraid that if he allows himself to be open with people, somehow the mask he wears will crumble and he will be exposed. This is why he seems so serious, even at a young age.

Getting to know a Capricorn man is a rare treat. With those he trusts he shows his wicked sense of humor and wry good nature. He is generally a highly principled individual, though he keeps his beliefs and life philosophy to himself. Capricorn men are often devoted to their career aims, which can make them appear distant regarding their home and family responsibilities.

THE CAPRICORN WOMAN Capricorn women have a cool, standoffish charm. Elegant and glacial, they may seem unapproachable. Actually, this is just a mask to hide their feelings of vulnerability. Capricorn individuals are always afraid of "losing face." For this reason they are extremely cautious about how much of themselves they allow others to see and know. They fear criticism and can't abide situations that force them to be self-critical.

This woman is a highly competitive personality, though she is usually more interested in besting her own best efforts than those of her closest rivals. If she is not involved in a career outside the home, she will turn her home into her career and be better at it than anyone else. Capricorn women make good, if overly strict, mothers. They expect the best from their children and will set very high standards for them to follow.

THE CAPRICORN CHILD This child seems to turn family roles upside down: he is the adult, the parents are children. Capricorn children usually seem to be old beyond their years—miniature adults who are serious, conflicted, and even a bit world-weary. Although diligent and smart, these little ones may lag behind other children developmentally. They may have a fear of trying particular skills, because they are afraid to fail. For these sensitive children to succeed, parents must be gentle and supportive, inspiring them to try for the sake of trying, and no other reason.

As he or she grows, so grows the confidence level. By the time they reach high school age, most Capricorn youngsters have found their own way to fit in. They have natural leadership skills that can be especially helpful in allowing them to adjust to this phase of their development.

THE CAPRICORN LOVER

The Capricorn lover may seem cautious and even a little bit cold, but he or she holds more than a few degrees in naughtiness from the school of love. As in other areas of life, Capricorns' biggest problem is one of confidence. This individual is always worried that a chosen love interest will prove fickle or even faithless.

Capricorns respond very well to domestic life because it provides the order and stability they need. Once they fall in love and commit to a relationship, the typical Capricorn man or woman is unlikely to jeopardize the union in any way. Although there are times when career matters must come first, Capricorn men and women place great importance on their personal happiness and rarely lose sight of this objective.

THE CAPRICORN BOSS

This is the ultimate boss, the boss to end all bosses. He or she doesn't have to be the CEO of a multi-million-dollar conglomerate to take the role seriously. The Capricorn boss can be perfectionistic and demanding, but in most cases this individual is also fair. However, the Capricorn boss requires that absolute respect be given to him or her. So long as the employees understand just where the balance of power rests, the typical Capricorn boss will deal honestly and truthfully with those who work under him.

Because they are extremely ambitious by nature, the Capricorn employer tends to elevate those who share this trait.

ELEMENT: Earth
QUALITY: Cardinal
PLANETARY RULER: Saturn
BIRTHSTONE: Garnet
FLOWER: Carnation
COLOR: Grey

KEY CHARACTERISTIC:
Ambition

STRENGTHS: Discipline, Patience, Structure.
CHALLENGES: Inhibited, Depressed, Rigid.

THE CAPRICORN FRIEND

Although they may seem to lack many of the traits that attract friendship, Capricorn men and women make loyal and caring friends. Unlike some signs that see friendship as a mostly social exchange, Capricorn individuals value the deep personal ties that can be forged.

Capricorns often keep the same circle of friends over a period of many years, or even a lifetime. Because they have a great love of stability, Capricorn men and women gain something special from long-term friendships. Capricorns may not have a huge group of friends, but the ones they do have are very dear and precious to them.

DECEMBER 22

December 22 natives have great sensitivity under a tough shell of pretended indifference. These men and women are emotionally vulnerable, and are sometimes shy about letting others see who they really are.

Attractive and charming, people born on this day are often more complicated than those closest to them realize. They have a great deal of intelligence, though it may be as hard for them to accept their talents as it is to accept their limitations.

FRIENDS AND LOVERS
Although their circle of friends is likely to be small, people born today derive a great deal of happiness and emotional security from these relationships.

December 22 people have conflicted feelings about their romantic involvements. They want to love deeply, yet are afraid of the pain a broken relationship can inflict. It's only when they learn to blindly trust their feelings that December 22 folks find their perfect mate.

CHILDREN AND FAMILY
These men and women have a somewhat old-fashioned view of family life; their idealistic view of their upbringing is likely to stay with them for decades.

December 22 people have no trouble relating to children on an emotional level. They have a genuine love of family life and make excellent parents. These people find it difficult to be both disciplinarian and "buddy," and may depend on a spouse to hand out the punishments.

HEALTH
December 22 natives are constantly changing their views on nutritional and health issues. At one point they may endorse a thoroughly holistic regime, only to lose interest in it a few weeks or months later. Because they have a natural ability to remain slim no matter how they eat, they can misinterpret what constitutes a healthy diet.

Women born on this date may have issues with food, which lead them to problems with bulimia and anorexia. Learning not to be afraid of the emotions that food can trigger is something that requires therapy, not willpower.

CAREER AND FINANCES
December 22 people take their career responsibilities very seriously, and are likely to have a reputation for being workaholics. However, this isn't necessarily negative, unless those involved are working hard in order not to deal with other important issues in their lives, especially ones related to relationships.

To maintain the lifestyle that December 22 people are comfortable with takes considerable resources. Fortunately, these men and women have the ability to handle this part of their life perfectly.

DREAMS AND GOALS
December 22 natives are often shy about revealing their goals to anyone, preferring to keep them secret in case of failure.

Being able to "have it all" is the dream of December 22 people, who have seen too many others like them make sacrifices for career success that ended in unhappy personal lives. These people don't want to lose what they have at home but, at the same time, are unwilling to give up on career success.

EMBRACE
Hard work
Intensity
Truth

AVOID
Guilt
Self-centeredness
A lack of healthy ego

ALSO BORN TODAY
First Lady Lady Bird Johnson; actress Peggy Ashcroft; singer Robin Gibb; composer Giacamo Puccini; actress Barbara Billingsley; TV journalist Diane Sawyer; actor Hector Elizondo; singer Maurice Gibb.

DECEMBER 23

December 23 individuals have a great deal of emotional pluck. If plans fail, these amazing people will simply start again. Because of their good attitude and innate ability to motivate others, these men and women make excellent mentors.

Although they may seem scatterbrained at times, people born on this date have great organizational abilities. Witty and intelligent, they are exceptionally verbal for people of their sign, and can tell an enjoyable story or anecdote.

FRIENDS AND LOVERS
Because they have such a likable nature, December 23 individuals make friends effortlessly. Yet despite their penchant for closeness, people born on this date are unlikely to reveal confidences or ask for advice.

Love is a very permanent and practical factor in the lives of December 23 men and women. These people value stability in the life, and do not usually seek separation or divorce unless there is no other alternative.

CHILDREN AND FAMILY
December 23 natives love all of the traditions of family life, and typically have happy memories of their own childhood. Though their upbringing is likely to have been quite strict, these folks look at this as a positive thing.

December 23 men and women are good parents who do everything they can to provide stability in the life of their child. Though they promote an atmosphere of fun, they are strict on discipline.

HEALTH
People born on this date have a common-sense approach to good health. They believe that moderation is the key to their success. By not overdoing anything, they reap the rewards without losing out on the occasional need to indulge a few bad habits.

Health problems are typically minor, but problem skin is not unknown. December 23 folks are careful about the amount of fried food and sweets they eat, but may not be as careful about what they drink. If they make water their number-one beverage, any bothersome skin condition is likely to clear up.

CAREER AND FINANCES
People born on this date are very serious about their career ambitions. They work hard, learn quickly, and obey the rules. More importantly, they know that professional shortcuts can be deceptive, and that by following accepted procedures they are likely to be successful in the long run.

December 23 people often spend a great deal of money on home decorating, with an eye for antiques and other objects d'art that will increase in value as the years go on.

DREAMS AND GOALS
To climb to the top without fudging the rules is a common goal of December 23 people. These folks are honest, straightforward types who don't believe in cutting corners. They know what they want and are willing to work hard in order to get it, no matter how hard that may be.

These resourceful men and women never blame their setbacks on anyone but themselves. If a goal becomes impossible to fulfill, they simply replot their course.

EMBRACE
Details
Imagination
A personal agenda

AVOID
Stress
Demoralization
Indifference

ALSO BORN TODAY
Poet Robert Bly; archaeologist Jean-Francois Champollion; dancer Jose Greco; actor Corey Haim; singer Johnny Kidd; actress Susan Lucci; football star Paul Hornung; actress Ruth Roman.

DECEMBER 24

These quixotic, changeable individuals are as much an enigma to themselves as they are to everyone who knows them. Although they have a great deal of personal magnetism and the potential to lead, they are often confused about their own priorities and end up following someone far less talented than themselves.

December 24 people are one of a kind. They are totally unafraid of being themselves, and don't give way to the usual Capricornian obsession to follow the status quo. These people are different—and proud of it.

FRIENDS AND LOVERS

Because December 24 natives skillfully hide their feelings, it's impossible for others to understand them on an emotional level. They often have a secret agenda that they are unwilling to divulge to anyone, even their closest friends.

People born on this date develop romantic fascinations easily and may find it difficult to know what they really want from love. They enjoy being seen with an attractive partner, and may sometimes confuse this with true love.

CHILDREN AND FAMILY

There is a dark side to people born on this date that usually has its roots in childhood. These folks may feel that they failed to receive the nurturing they needed, and may be somewhat self-critical as a result. If they're lucky enough to have the sort of adult life-experience that can help them understand this problem, they can work through it and become more sure of themselves.

As parents, December 24 natives are usually quite indulgent, though they often display a pronounced ability to understand the emotional needs of their child.

HEALTH

People born on this date are fanatics about their appearance. They like to look their best, and if that requires following a complicated health and fitness regimen, these people are all for it.

Many Capricorn individuals have a love/hate relationship with food and December 24 people are no exception. Paradoxically, their amazing self-discipline often goes hand in hand with fad dieting, as they try to prove just how much willpower they possess.

CAREER AND FINANCES

Like other people of their sign, December 24 people are very hard workers who easily weather the sacrifices that come with success. These men and women can follow rules they don't agree with, because they know that their high level of self-discipline usually pays off.

December 24 people are good financial planners and money managers. They aren't afraid to take risks.

DREAMS AND GOALS

People born on this date are an interesting combination of free-wheeling and conservative. They know that by alternating their methods, they're most likely to meet with success—and success is the goal of every December 24 native.

For most, this has to do with business or career, but for others it can mean family life, personal power, or even a sense of spiritual enrichment. One way or the other, these people hitch their dreams to a star.

DECEMBER 25

People born on this date are soul-centered, and drawn to life's mysteries. New Age learning and holistic healing have special appeal for them. They are introspective people who can transcend their own emotional struggles by involving themselves in work that helps others to conquer personal problems.

December 25 natives have an ability to read other people, understanding their inner motives and divining what even they may not realize.

FRIENDS AND LOVERS
Men and women born on this day seem self-sufficient and capable, but they need their friends to step in once in a while and take over. This is one of the ways in which December 25 individuals "test" their friends: Do they care enough to take control when it becomes necessary?

In romantic relationships, December 25 people can be enigmatic. It's often difficult to understand just what they expect of a relationship, let alone a marriage. There is always a sense of the transitory, as if they aren't quite sure if they want to make things permanent.

CHILDREN AND FAMILY
No matter how close they may be to family members in an emotional sense, December 25 people are always a little outside of the circle. They're quiet rebels who have their own way of thinking and who refuse to be influenced by others.

With their own children, December 25 men and women do the best they can to show their affection and emotional support. They are quick to discipline their youngsters for deliberate wrong-doing, but can be forgiving about unintentional errors.

HEALTH
People born on this date have trouble committing to a full-time health regimen. They have great intentions, make preparations, and then suddenly the whole thing loses focus in their mind. These people need strong motivation to work out every day and watch what they eat.

December 25 individuals have to guard against brittle bones as they age. They can benefit from taking calcium supplements, and getting into weight-bearing exercise.

CAREER AND FINANCES
People born on this date are drawn to professions that allow them to indulge their love of knowledge. These men and women are fabulous researchers, and enjoy doing their work behind the scenes. They make excellent lawyers, academics, and medical researchers.

Pure knowledge aside, December 25 natives are concerned with making a good living. They are likely to inherit money from their family at some point in their life, and may come to depend on this rather than going out and making their own fortune.

DREAMS AND GOALS
People born on December 25 want to succeed but have trouble maintaining their motivation. They're ambitious, yet may lack the single-mindedness of other Capricorn natives.

Those born on this date are most likely to reach their goals if they have an emotional as well as material reason to succeed. If they experience a setback regarding a cherished goal, they are likely to try again, even harder, to achieve it.

EMBRACE
Tranquility
Desire
New beginnings

AVOID
Indolence
Lack of preparation
Impossible odds

ALSO BORN TODAY
Writer Quentin Crisp; football star Larry Csonka; singer Annie Lennox; singer Barbara Mandrell; musician Noel Redding; actress Hanna Schygulla; writer Rod Serling; actress Sissy Spacek.

DECEMBER 26

December 26 people possess a determined, exceptionally serious nature. They have a masterful ability to read the motives of others, and are exceptional judges of character.

These ambitious, career-oriented people have a pragmatic nature, yet they dream on a large scale. Although conservative, they possess a generous soul and the desire to be part of the crowd. Oddly, though, they may be unwilling to show this last aspect of their personality to others.

FRIENDS AND LOVERS The close friendships formed by December 26 people, often in youth, remain part of their lives for years. These folks are consistent, dependable, and very loyal. Even though they show their emotions quietly, there is never any doubt about how much they care for the important people in their lives.

December 26 natives often have more than their share of the emotional ups and downs of romantic love. They usually have their heart set on a firm commitment, though they may fall in love with people who do not. Finding just the right person can be a chore for them, but when they do, December 26 men and women want that person with them for a lifetime.

CHILDREN AND FAMILY There is often an unusual dynamic at work in the family lives of December 26 people.

This could relate to a difficult childhood that saw a great many changes and emotional upheavals, or perhaps they felt left out of the family group.

December 26 people are sometimes unsure in their role as parents. They believe in being strict disciplinarians, but do not want to restrict their children in the way they may have been inhibited by their own upbringing.

HEALTH The people born on this date are worriers, and often suffer from a worrier's ailments. Headaches, backaches, upset stomach, and sleeping disorders are all par for the course.

December 26 people benefit from learning how to handle stress. Meditation and prayer, practiced on a regular basis, can be a marvelous way to get rid of tension.

CAREER AND FINANCES People born on this date have a natural affinity for the business world. These are meticulous, intelligent individuals who may not be in touch with their creative potential. If they are, they may seek to work in a creative field, but in the role of business or corporate figure. December 26 people make excellent agents, business managers, corporate lawyers, and accountants.

Money is the centerpiece in the lives of December 26 people. This does not imply greediness, but rather a desire to see that all their family members and loved ones are secure.

DREAMS AND GOALS The men and women born on this date are eager to succeed in life. Whatever it takes to bring their dreams to life, December 26 natives are willing to do it.

As long as they make an effort to spend time with their loved ones, December 26 people can make both their professional and personal goals come true.

EMBRACE
Inner vision
Forgiveness
Kindness

AVOID
Overconfidence
Repression
An authoritarian attitude

ALSO BORN TODAY
Writer/composer/TV personality Steve Allen; singer/actress Toni Arthur; baseball star Carlton Fisk; entertainer Alan King; newspaper publisher William Loeb; actor Donald Moffat; novelist Henry Miller; actor Richard Widmark.

DECEMBER 27

There's something haughty and erudite about December 27 individuals. These people elevate style to an art, yet are remarkably practical and down to earth. When they achieve their personal aims, it's always the result of hard work.

The authoritarian nature of December 27 men and women makes them good at handling others, particularly in the workplace. These people are demanding and have a perfectionist streak—so much so, in fact, that at times they can seem intolerant of others' mistakes.

FRIENDS AND LOVERS

Practicality is a theme that runs through the lives of December 27 people, even in their relationships. They tend to choose friends who share their views and values. They're loyal to their friends and will unhesitatingly provide emotional support in times of trouble.

The pragmatism of December 27 individuals is displayed in romance by virtue of the fact that they have a very clear notion of what they want in a lover or mate, and seldom deviate from it. These men and women are highly sexual, but not very romantic, and have little patience with people who bumble into bad relationships.

CHILDREN AND FAMILY

Given their great appreciation for the status quo, December 27 individuals are happy to conduct themselves as part of a family group. Even though their upbringing may have been extremely strict, these men and women are grateful for the lessons they learned from that period.

December 27 natives are equally strict with their own children, though they strive to present a balance of love and discipline. They're keen on getting their children to accept responsibility at a very early age.

HEALTH

People born on this date are sticklers for staying fit. They follow a restricted diet and are careful to get their share of exercise. They have somewhat old-fashioned ideas about what kind of exercise is most helpful, feeling that it's better to keep fit by leading an active lifestyle than by going to a gym every day.

December 27 people like a natural diet, and may become vegetarians later in life.

CAREER AND FINANCES

People born on this date are excellent at getting others to work at their highest potential. For this reason, they make good supervisors and bosses. Although they prefer not to get involved in the personal lives of those who work for them, these men and women do understand the value of managing the "whole" person.

December 27 natives are about as good as it gets when it comes to handling money. Although conservative, they know there are times risks are unavoidable. The combination of these disparate attitudes makes these people expert financial planners.

DREAMS AND GOALS

Getting to the top of their profession is a natural goal for December 27 people. Yet even their ambition has a practical side. They know better than to ignore all other aspects of life.

December 27 people feel that their existence is fulfilled only if they can experience the joys of family life.

EMBRACE
Selectivity
Romance
Belief in the future

AVOID
Foolishness
Temptation
Inattentiveness

ALSO BORN TODAY
Actor John Amos; pianist Oscar Levant; actor Gerard Depardieu; actress Marlene Dietrich; sex therapist William Masters; actress Tovah Feldshuh; chemist Louis Pasteur; actor Sidney Greenstreet.

DECEMBER 28

December 28 people have a style all their own. Self-possessed and intelligent, they have great social skills, including the ability to make anyone feel at home in any situation. These men and women take great pride and enjoyment in performing everyday tasks, believing that it is through the minor, not major, events in life that character is both formed and tested. December 28 natives are personable and people-loving, and have a generally happy outlook on life.

FRIENDS AND LOVERS
People born on this date have a great capacity for friendship. They understand their own character best through relationships with others. Friends are not just social companions to these people, but true confidantes who provide both a mirror and a prism by which their own attitudes and aspirations are shown.

December 28 individuals are loving and tender companions. These people need the emotional support of a partner, and often marry early in life. Like most Capricorn natives, they support the status quo. They are always happiest in a committed relationship that offers emotional equilibrium; playing the field has little allure for them.

CHILDREN AND FAMILY
People born on this date are model sons and daughters. They are devoted to the idea of home and family, and do everything they can to venerate the family name by the way they live their life. December 28 people often have extremely close relationships with their parents, especially the father.

As parents, the men and women born on this date strive to provide for the material and spiritual needs of their youngsters. They understand the need of children to rebel, and therefore they do not punish these actions. Although they teach their kids to respect adults, December 28 people also teach their children to be unafraid to question authority.

HEALTH
December 28 people are active and manage to incorporate exercise into their daily routine by simply making a few adjustments, like taking the stairs instead of the elevator.

These lucky folks can eat almost anything and usually do; their diet is varied and interesting. They often are talented cooks who can prepare exotic foreign dishes.

CAREER AND FINANCES
People born on this date often choose careers that put them in the spotlight. They are sociable and do well in positions of power, where they meet and socialize with others.

December 28 people are good financial managers, with the talent to become financially well off by their own shrewd yet honest manipulation.

DREAMS AND GOALS
Those born on this date have a modest yet earnest desire to do the very best they can. Their goals tend to be carefully mapped out and may involve many years of trial and error. These folks don't expect to get to the top in a hurry—although they often do.

December 28 people are filled with self-confidence about their abilities, and can withstand their share of disappointments on the road to making their goals a reality.

EMBRACE
Political correctness
Sociability
Terms

AVOID
Dissemblers
Carnal appetites
Betrayal

ALSO BORN TODAY
Actor Lou Jacobi; film director F. W. Murnau; musician Charles Neville; actress Hildegard Neff; musician Johnny Otis; actress Maggie Smith; actor Denzel Washington; U.S. President Woodrow Wilson.

DECEMBER 29

The men and women born on this date have the ability to be transformed by spiritual significance, but only after experiencing a profound and transfiguring reality. These people may become the symbol around which others rally, though they have little in common with the image they represent.

December 29 people are often attractive and charming, with a devastating effect upon those who come under their spell. Unlike most Capricorns, these individuals enjoy taking risks.

FRIENDS AND LOVERS

December 29 natives tend to experience a great deal of emotional flux in their relationships. Although they want and need stability in their lives, the situations in which these people often find themselves can promote exactly the opposite. Oddly, these people have a tendency to "freeze out" even their closest friends at one time or another because of differences in opinion.

These people may have some serious disappointments in love during their youth, but once they get past them they are able to find a partner who can make them happy.

CHILDREN AND FAMILY

In the family, December 29 people are either the proverbial golden child or the black sheep. Other family members will find this quality lovable or infuriating, depending on the mood of the moment.

The latter is the trait that makes December 29 men and women such compassionate parents. They remember what it was like to be a child, and don't demand the impossible from their youngsters.

HEALTH

The same extremes that exist in other aspects of their lives often occur in health matters for December 29 people. They are either extremely careful about their health, or amazingly unconcerned. Their emotional condition often dictates just how well they take care of themselves.

When they are happy, people born on this date are likely to be very careful about what they eat. They favor a slim figure and may be on a perpetual diet.

CAREER AND FINANCES

Many of these people have great creative talent and opt for a life in the arts. If they choose another line of work, they're likely to have artistic hobbies that give them the chance to vent their creative abilities.

People born on this date may feel vulnerable about their financial situation, even if they make a good salary. This "scarcity mentality" can cause them to make a few foolish decisions about money until they learn to move beyond their fear.

DREAMS AND GOALS

People born on December 29 want to make their personal life work. Despite success in the professional arena, these men and women are often burdened with the consequences of mistakes in their youth. An ability to bear down and get past the fear that every love affair or relationship will fail is vital to their emotional well-being.

December 29 natives also have a great deal of resilience; despite their problems, they're usually able to pull themselves together and find a worthy love relationship.

EMBRACE
Belief
Long-range plans
Reality

AVOID
Sacrificial love
Addiction
Envy

ALSO BORN TODAY
Cellist Pablo Casals; actor Ted Danson; singer Marianne Faithfull; English Prime Minister William Gladstone; ballerina Gelsey Kirkland; actress Mary Tyler Moore; comedienne Paula Poundstone; actor John Voight.

DECEMBER 30

People born on December 30 are jovial individuals who promote the status quo. These men and women like the good life, and are willing to work long and hard in order to achieve it. They are very focused, and understand the need to make sensible sacrifices.

These individuals are happiest when they have a stable family and happy home life.

FRIENDS AND LOVERS

The men and women born on this date make wonderful companions. They treasure their close friends, and enjoy making the social rounds with acquaintances. They believe that no one can have too many friends.

December 30 people tend to have rather conventional attitudes about love and romance. They want a partner who shares their enthusiasm for life, as well as their philosophical and religious beliefs. Although they are not generally close-minded, December 30 natives do have a need to incorporate their own view of spirituality into their existence.

CHILDREN AND FAMILY

People born on this date are devoted to the ideals of family life. They are often part of a large or extended family group, and draw their ideas about family values and what a family should be from this experience.

People born on this date make wonderful parents. They don't see themselves simply as authority figures, but also as guides and friends.

HEALTH

December 30 people are generally vibrant, and stay healthy because they are happy. These men and women know the value of having a good attitude toward life. They don't take their successes any more seriously than their failures.

Because they have a healthy appetite for the good things in life December 30 folks need to become involved in a regular exercise regimen, and cut back on sweets and fatty foods. Single servings at every meal are wise.

CAREER AND FINANCES

People born on this date have great leadership ability. Because of this, and their love of people, December 30 natives make wonderful supervisors or bosses. They have the ability to bring out the hidden potential of others, and help them to reach their goals. They have real entrepreneurial talents, as well, and may do well for themselves in a business of their own.

Making money is definitely high on the priority list of these men and women, yet they aren't especially materialistic. They merely want to reap the rewards due to them.

DREAMS AND GOALS

December 30 individuals like to live a full and exciting life. They don't like to miss anything, and although they aren't known for taking risks, these men and women will walk on the wild side now and then if it means a chance to experience something marvelous that will bring them knowledge or pleasure.

These individuals have a genius for devising a balance between their personal and professional lives. This is an important factor for them, because they aren't content to be unfulfilled in either.

EMBRACE
Risk-taking
Adventure
Preparation

AVOID
Preoccupation
Self-indulgence
Greed

ALSO BORN TODAY
Actor Joseph Bologna; writer Rudyard Kipling; baseball star Sandy Koufax; actor Jack Lord; TV personality Bert Parks; film director Carol Reed; actor Russ Tamblyn; comedienne Tracey Ullman.

DECEMBER 31

December 31 natives respond to the demands of their heart, not their head. These utterly guileless people may be impractical in the extreme, but they also paint their world in vibrant and extreme colors.

A certain brilliance does not shield these men and women from a great deal of instability in their personal lives. This can be a drawback to their maturation, yet it also provides them with the intense emotional exhilaration they crave.

FRIENDS AND LOVERS

Even though December 31 individuals enjoy being surrounded by a large group of friends, they are anxious to have their time in the spotlight. This ego-issue is part of their character and is generally based on a certain lack of self-esteem.

December 31 men and women often experience a great deal of heartbreak in their love life. This is usually linked to their inability to make good romantic choices. They are inevitably drawn to flighty, good-looking people who treat them badly. If they are lucky enough to find the perfect mate, they may still experience a great deal of romance-related anxiety.

CHILDREN AND FAMILY

December 31 people love family life. Whether they come from a large or small family group, these people seek the validation of their relatives.

It's often the anticipated pleasures of starting a family that prompts December 31 people to settle down to married life or a committed relationship. Even though they may seek to work out issues from their own childhood in their relationship with their offspring, December 31 men and women brim with love and tenderness.

HEALTH

December 31 natives often ignore health issues until they begin to notice a problem. Luckily for them, they possess a great deal of natural vitality, which allows them to neglect exercise and nutrition without seriously affecting their health.

People born on this date may experience periodic problems with sleep, usually brought on because of worry. Warm milk or herbal tea before bedtime can bring relaxation and sleep.

CAREER AND FINANCES

It isn't uncommon for December 31 natives to change careers several times. They have a hard time settling on just what they want to do. Although they have an instinct to make money and lead a stable, productive life, they also possess an emotional instability that is constantly at war with their other instincts.

Money is equally problematic for these individuals. Although adept at making money, December 31 men and women are even better at spending it. They want a luxurious lifestyle, and that often means taking credit spending to the limit—and beyond.

DREAMS AND GOALS

People born on this date need to feel as if they are loved and valued. This is far more important to them than any professional success.

If they are able to conquer their personal insecurities, December 31 men and women can be very successful in their career choices. They have enormous creative talent and if they have the opportunity to tap into it, they are able to express their true selves.

EMBRACE
Receptiveness
Fantasy
The creative muse

AVOID
Willfulness
Flattery
Ego-issues

ALSO BORN TODAY
Actress Barbara Carrera; singer John Denver; actor Anthony Hopkins; actor Ben Kingsley; painter Henri Matisse; actress Sarah Miles; singer Donna Summer; fashion designer Diane von Furstenberg.

315

JANUARY 1

People born on January 1 have a truly aristocratic nature regardless of background or family connections. They demonstrate good taste in all aspects of life and know how to exist well, even on limited resources. January 1 natives expect a great deal of themselves and always strive to live up to their full potential. This attitude translates to a search for personal excellence, which can be rewarding but also exhausting, since these folks are perfectionists.

FRIENDS AND LOVERS Because the standards of January 1 natives are exceptionally high, it's sometimes difficult for them to find friends who share their values and general view of life. They are incredibly loyal, however, and retain friendships over many years.

January 1 people have regal appeal, and attract special attention in love and romance. Their screening process is very particular, and because of this they are unlikely to marry early in life. But when they do meet that special someone, they become eager to marry and settle down.

CHILDREN AND FAMILY Those born on January 1 set a good example for other family members, but even though they appreciate the closeness that family life provides, they tend to go their own way in personal matters. Siblings and relatives come to them for advice, not the other way around.

EMBRACE
True happiness
Your spiritual path
Emotional creativity

AVOID
Being overly sensitive
Emotional isolation
Anxiety

ALSO BORN TODAY;
Actor Dana Andrews; United States Senator and presidential candidate Barry M. Goldwater; baseball star Hank Greenberg; FBI chief J. Edgar Hoover; actor Frank Langella; actor Don Novello; novelist J. D. Salinger.

These people make good, if stern parents. They set high standards for their kids, and can be disappointed if their children don't follow their example of staunch personal responsibility. Although they don't interfere in the lives of grown children, January 1 natives are always ready to give advice when it is asked for.

HEALTH Since they may have a sedentary lifestyle, it's important that these folks maintain good eating habits and avoid overindulgence in rich desserts or alcohol.

Since they do not exercise on a regular basis, January 1 natives should take brisk walks, especially in a pastoral setting. Reliance on prescription medication should be kept to a minimum.

CAREER AND FINANCES January individuals have very conservative career aims. They may discover their "calling" at an early age, or be influenced in their career path by the example of an older relative or sibling. It's not unusual for someone born on this date to go into the family business.

Although January 1 people have great money sense, they aren't the entrepreneurial sort. They're far more at ease when they can make and manage their money in conservative and risk-free ways.

DREAMS AND GOALS Though not given to lofty aims, individuals born on January 1 are extremely concerned with meeting a series of goals they may have set for themselves very early in life. Because they possess strong powers of patience and endurance, these people understand that some goals take a long time to become reality.

Providing a secure emotional and financial future for loved ones is an important goal of January 1 people.

JANUARY 2

Secretive and quiet, January 2 individuals present a stern face to the world. This persona belies their actual nature, which is considerably more animated and joyous. A sense of being judged by others keeps them from revealing their sensitivity to all but their closest friends.

A certain level of personal detachment allows them to behave as spectators to their own actions, learning from each experience. January 2 natives don't credit others for their success, but neither do they blame anyone for their failures.

FRIENDS AND LOVERS

The guarded nature of January 2 individuals makes them difficult to know. They don't usually make friends easily—not from a lack of social skills but because of a desire to retain their sense of mystery. They seek quality in friendship, not quantity, and cultivate a small circle of close friends.

January 2 individuals experience many romantic disappointments before finding that special person. When they do connect with someone on an emotional level they invariably lose some of their natural cynicism and become more open with themselves and others. Marriage isn't a natural state for them but can be made successful with a little effort.

CHILDREN AND FAMILY

Because of their singular approach to life, people born on January 2 often have a powerful connection to one family member and virtually none at all with their remaining relatives. They may look up to an older sibling and see this person as a role model.

With their own children these individuals cultivate a loving yet autonomous relationship. From a very early age they urge their youngsters to assert their independence.

HEALTH

January 2 individuals can be obsessive concerning their health and fitness habits. With almost Spartan sensibility they keep themselves fit by adhering to a demanding exercise regimen. This is likely to include daily workouts and a careful eating plan.

Because of their adherence to good health measures, January 2 natives are likely to follow the latest fads in nutrition as well as holistic rather than conventional medical advice.

CAREER AND FINANCES

Organization and the dogged pursuit of excellence ensure that January 2 individuals will establish themselves in a profitable career. They do not necessarily seek success, yet they inevitably find it, often in professions favoring research and development.

Although January 2 people have considerable skill at handling money, they also have a tendency to play fast and loose with financial opportunities.

DREAMS AND GOALS

People born on this date are specific about their goals, often committing them to paper in a series of elaborate steps and carefully prescribed measures. They benefit from the experience and wisdom of a mentor who can help to delineate their path.

The possibility of failure can keep them from reaching their goals.

EMBRACE
Enthusiasm
Spontaneity
A sense of humor

AVOID
Melancholy
Self-pity
Being contemptuous of others

ALSO BORN TODAY
Writer Isaac Asimov; photographer David Bailey; evangelist Jim Bakker; actress Gabrielle Carteris; musician Chick Churchill; actress Joanna Pacula; Congressman Dan Rostenkowski; opera singer Renata Tebaldi.

JANUARY 3

People born on January 3 are resourceful and able to draw good things into their life without exerting much effort. They have a streak of originality, which is always evident in their personality and their work.

January 3 men and women are naturally acquisitive. Material objects are important to them, but only as an outward expression of how they feel about their circumstances and the world around them.

FRIENDS AND LOVERS Like most Capricorn natives, January 3 people are loners who have difficulty expressing their true feelings, even to those closest to them. Able to connect on a career rather than personal level, they're most likely to find friends within their professional circle.

Although they have a warm and loving nature, January 3 people often struggle to make a romantic relationship work because of intimacy issues. Learning to share their thoughts and feelings with a mate can be a real challenge for these people.

CHILDREN AND FAMILY Childhood is generally filled with good things for those born on this date. They may be the only child—or the favorite child—and in such cases there is a tremendous pressure put upon them to succeed. They generally thrive under such pressure, so this is likely to be a positive influence.

Men and women born on this date make exceptional parents. They favor a big family and revel in all the confusion and joyful mayhem.

HEALTH January 3 people have boundless energy. This is often more the result of their positive attitude than any special health regimen. Because they love to eat they may be a few pounds overweight, but their active schedule and zest for life keep them looking and feeling great.

Most January 3 people are far too busy to exercise. Instead, they manage to incorporate physical activity into their daily schedule. Also, these men and women understand the value of a good night's sleep.

CAREER AND FINANCES January 3 people are good at seeing the "big picture." They have a naturally ambitious nature and are unwilling to stay in the same job over a period of years. Even if they like what they are doing, they have an urge to move on. An entrepreneurial spirit makes them good candidates for working freelance or owner-operators of their own business.

Because they enjoy the good things in life, January 3 people are motivated to make a lot of money. Yet they enjoy the process more than the actual result.

DREAMS AND GOALS January 3 individuals have endless aspirations. After they achieve one goal, they turn their attention to another. These men and women never set any limits on what they can do, and because of this they usually succeed!

On a personal level, January 3 people strive to get closer to those they love. Despite their personable nature, this is not easy for them, and they may need to summon all of their emotional resources to accomplish this goal.

EMBRACE
Openness
Availability
Distinction

AVOID
Cover-up
Self-indulgence
Distractions

ALSO BORN TODAY
Film director Dorothy Arzner; actor Dabney Coleman; actor/director Mel Gibson; hockey star Bobby Hull; film director Sergio Leone; actor Robert Loggia; actress Victoria Principal; writer J.R.R. Tolkien.

JANUARY 4

January 4 individuals possess a quirky, quicksilver personality. They are dedicated to acts of kindness on a personal level, acts of humanity on a public level. They are extremely issue-oriented, and are not shy about expressing their opinions, even unpopular ones.

Those born on this date have a heartfelt sympathy for the unfortunate and unlucky. They feel it is their duty to draw attention to the plight of such people, and do so at every opportunity.

FRIENDS AND LOVERS

January 4 individuals are not merely opinionated—they are extremely vocal about their opinions, and this can be somewhat off-putting to friends and associates. People born on this date don't care what sort of message they send, as long as they speak the truth. Those who count themselves among the friends of these people must learn to live with that attitude.

The love life of January 4 individuals is usually quite colorful. These folks are attracted to eccentric types with a love of the spontaneous. However, settling down to married life may not be in the cards for these fun-loving souls.

CHILDREN AND FAMILY

January 4 men and women have a need to break with the past. No matter how happy or satisfying their childhood may have been, these people are not tied to its traditions. They believe in throwing off the conventions of their upbringing in order to find a truer, more meaningful identity.

People born on this date allow their own children this same sense of freedom. Understanding that it is necessary to discipline youngsters, January 4 men and women nonetheless use a light touch.

HEALTH

Although they are healthy in a general way, January 4 men and women often suffer from unusual complaints. These are exacerbated by the fact that these individuals are somewhat lax in their attention to health and fitness matters. They may begin an exercise plan with great enthusiasm, only to lose interest a few weeks later.

Migraine headaches, skin rashes, and periods of mild depression are often symptomatic of the moods of January 4 people.

CAREER AND FINANCES

January 4 people are not particularly career-oriented. They prefer taking a circuitous route toward finding what they want to do for a living.

People born on this date are often very fortunate where money is concerned, though they seem to take little interest in financial affairs. Gambling is a favorite pastime of these individuals, but should not be encouraged.

DREAMS AND GOALS

The chief goal of January 4 people is to experience life in all its variety. These people want to see and do things that most people miss because they are concentrating on the more mundane aspects of life.

January 4 men and women delight in the challenges and rewards that come to them unexpectedly. To them, achievement is a relative concept.

EMBRACE
Freedom
Precision
Gratitude

AVOID
Transgressions
Irreverence
Pessimism

ALSO BORN TODAY
Actress Dyan Cannon; psychic Jeane Dixon; writer Jacob Grimm; artist Augustus John; actress Ann Magnusson; boxer Floyd Patterson; football coach Don Shula; actress Jane Wyman.

JANUARY 5

Because they are so mentally focused, it is important for January 5 people to find ways to express their inner energy. For this reason, physicality becomes an important factor in the lives of these individuals.

These men and women may give the impression of being flighty or disorganized because they always seem to be in a hurry and are rapid-fire conversationalists. But they are actually brilliant people who simply trip over their own intelligence once in a while.

FRIENDS AND LOVERS January 5 individuals look for friends who share their love of communication. These talkative men and women have opinions on everything under the sun. They don't expect friends to always agree with them—in fact, they appreciate a rowdy debate now and then.

Romance is a complicated affair for these folks. They seem to attract people with whom a long-range relationship is impossible. Yet when they do manage to make a permanent union they become bored once the relationship settles into a regular routine. It takes a very special individual to keep someone born on this date satisfied and interested.

CHILDREN AND FAMILY January 5 individuals are rebels, and often show this trait early in life. They may have trouble getting along with their more placid siblings.

People born on this date aren't particularly adaptable to life as parents. They have a reputation for being impatient around children, though when they do make an attempt to get along with little ones they have an easy time.

HEALTH January 5 men and women depend upon exercise for more than physical fitness. They need it to maintain equilibrium between their physical and mental selves. Because they spend so much time focusing on intellectual pursuits, these people have a tendency to suffer bouts of mental exhaustion unless they relieve tension through exercise.

Because January 5 people have little interest in food, they may not get all of the vitamins and minerals they need through diet alone. Therefore they require extra supplements.

CAREER AND FINANCES People born on this date have the intelligence and curiosity to succeed in any career they choose. They usually gravitate toward occupations where their verbal and analytical skills can be put to use. They make fine teachers, lawyers, accountants, insurance agents, Realtors, actors, and speech makers.

January 5 people are in their particular line of work in order to satisfy their aesthetic, not material, needs.

DREAMS AND GOALS It is the goal of most January 5 individuals to express the world as they see it. These bright, articulate men and women are fascinated by small details and large events—the whole pattern of human existence.

January 5 people are constantly striving to learn more about their world. For this reason educational goals may be a part of the picture for them, although they never really stop being students, no matter how many advanced degrees they attain.

EMBRACE
Tenacity
Friendliness
Harmony

AVOID
Boredom
Pressure
Complaints

ALSO BORN TODAY
Actress Suzy Amis; pianist Alfred Brendel; actor Robert Duvall; novelist Umberto Eco; writer Stella Gibbons; actress Diane Keaton; U. S. Presidential candidate Walter Mondale; football coach Chuck Noll.

JANUARY 6

People born on this date are quite different from most Capricorn natives because they are totally uninhibited, socially and personally. These men and women express their true nature through action. They refuse to be bound by the rules of convention, though they have an innate sense of decorum that allows them to be rebellious in the most courteous way possible. Charming people, they nonetheless make their own rules.

FRIENDS AND LOVERS
Friendship is one big party for January 6 people. They are naturally sociable individuals who like nothing better than getting together with interesting individuals. Deep, committed friendships can be difficult for these people because they have a hard time establishing intimacy with others.

January 6 natives have a similar problem with romantic partnerships. They enjoy the flirting, the dating, the "chase." But when it comes to settling down with someone special, they have a blind spot. They're far too interested in having fun to give up their independence readily, unless they fall deeply in love.

CHILDREN AND FAMILY
People born on January 6 are devoted to family members and may play the role of benefactor to them. Because they are likely to have lacked material comforts as a child, these men and women are anxious to enjoy the good life once they start making a living for themselves.

January 6 people make delightful, if somewhat indulgent parents. They want their children to have everything they didn't have.

HEALTH
People born on this date are not particularly energetic. They enjoy sports, but a regular workout regimen is often more than they can handle. Because they have a weakness for sweets, January 6 people need to guard against diabetes and other disorders as middle age approaches.

Getting involved in holistic healing methods can be a great source of spiritual and emotional wellness for these individuals.

CAREER AND FINANCES
January 6 people have a great love of the arts and may be drawn to careers in acting, painting, writing, fashion, architecture, or music. Because they have an analytical streak, they do well in the business-related activities surrounding these professions, such as agent, manager, accountant, or public relations representative.

People born on this date enjoy leading a luxurious lifestyle that requires a hefty bankroll. Though naturally ambitious about making the green stuff, January 6 people realize that if they want to maintain their status, they're going to have to put forth extra effort and make their salary a priority.

DREAMS AND GOALS
January 6 individuals want to have fun. Even after they leave their teens and twenties behind, these party-hearty people aren't ready to settle down. There's nothing destructive in their attitudes or actions, merely a desire to live life to the fullest and on their own terms.

When these men and women settle upon a career goal they are almost completely single-minded in their efforts to succeed.

EMBRACE
True love
Opportunity
Popularity

AVOID
Defenses
Obsessions
Intrigue

ALSO BORN TODAY
Comic Rowan Atkinson; novelist E. L. Doctorow; musician Mark O'Toole; composer Alexander Scriabin; film director John Singleton; entertainer Danny Thomas; actress Loretta Young; guitarist Malcolm Young.

JANUARY 7

People born on January 7 have a sensitive, vulnerable quality that endears them to others. They have a strong spiritual nature as well as a social conscience, and are often drawn into political activism or humanitarian concerns.

January 7 men and women are likely to experience a conflict between their inner-life needs and their external responsibilities. This has the potential to create a powerful dichotomy in their lives, requiring frequent soul-searching and introspection.

FRIENDS AND LOVERS
January 7 people need the emotional security of a large circle of friends. These kind-hearted people inspire feelings of emotional and spiritual closeness, which bring wonderful and interesting people into their life.

Love is a magical event in the lives of these folks. They have an almost impossibly idealistic view of romance, and are, for that reason, often hurt by lovers who are insensitive or fickle.

CHILDREN AND FAMILY
These dreamy, introspective people are big on fantasy, and may have dealt with difficulties in their childhood by tuning in to their imagination. Their relationships with other family members are likely to be based on off-the-mark emotional projections.

January 7 people make nurturing and loving parents. They have the ability to bring out the creative aspects of a child's nature, and are quick to encourage a love of imagination and fantasy.

HEALTH
If anything is going wrong in their lives, January 7 people are likely to have trouble getting a good night's sleep. Although it's easy for them to use sleeping pills when this happens, they should think twice before doing so. These men and women have an extremely sensitive body chemistry, which reacts negatively to artificial depressants and stimulants.

Since January 7 people often suffer from indigestion, they should drink fresh melon juice in season to combat nausea.

CAREER AND FINANCES
January 7 natives are interested in expressing their inner thoughts and feelings, though they may not have sufficient mettle to withstand a career in the performing or creative arts, where their most deeply held and sensitive emotions are open to criticism by others. For this reason they may opt for other work.

January 7 people are not interested in making a great deal of money. These are people-oriented, issue-concerned individuals who base their values on spiritual rather than material concerns.

DREAMS AND GOALS
People born today are interested in exploring the spiritual avenues of life. At some point in life they are likely to get involved with New Age or occult studies in order to probe the mysteries of the world beyond their sight.

These men and women may have difficulty motivating themselves to attain a material goal, yet if they can find spiritual significance in it, they may be able to draw some relevance from the experience.

EMBRACE
Renewal
Rapture
Intuition

AVOID
Transient affections
Impermanence
Confusion

ALSO BORN TODAY
New Yorker cartoonist Charles Addams; novelist William Peter Blatty; actor Nicolas Cage; TV journalist Katie Couric; U.S. President Millard Fillmore; singer Kenny Loggins; TV personality Maury Povich; flutist Jean-Pierre Rampal.

JANUARY 8

January 8 individuals seek to balance worldly concerns with an expression of their soul-needs. Although these people strive for a pragmatic approach to life, they have an extremely superstitious nature.

People born on this date are very gifted, yet they may be riddled with self-doubts and profound questions about the nature of their place in the universe. These problems are exacerbated by the fact that January 8 people have difficulty expressing their feelings through words.

FRIENDS AND LOVERS

Because of their basic distrust of the motives of others, it is hard for January 8 people to make friends. These men and women need to feel as if they can rely on the love and support of their close companions. If this trust is breached, the friendship is likely to end.

People born on this date have an extremely powerful love nature. These people are romantics at heart who demand total devotion from a lover or mate. They have considerable charm. Even if they are not especially attractive they can manage to cast a spell over others, drawing lovers to them with ease.

CHILDREN AND FAMILY

Even when they do not feel closely bound emotionally to family members, people born on January 8 are loyal and generous to them. They may have experienced a morally strict upbringing from which they have lapsed in adulthood, creating a sense of guilt and dishonor.

January 8 people make doting parents, anxious to give their children material as well as spiritual riches.

HEALTH

Although January 8 people love food, they are not particularly interested in learning healthful ways to prepare it. They may have complicated food issues that date from childhood and need to be reconciled if their problems from the past are ever to be settled.

Exercise can be a physically as well as emotionally safe way for January 8 people to work out their aggressions and stress. Swimming helps them to release emotional tension, while weight-bearing exercise strengthens bones.

CAREER AND FINANCES

People born on this date need to feel as if they are in control of their own destiny. Unfortunately, these men and women sometimes take the easy way out, allowing family connections to dictate their path in life.

Although they know the value of a dollar, January 8 folks enjoy spending money in a lavish manner. They indulge themselves, and are generous with friends and loved ones.

DREAMS AND GOALS

January 8 people may dream big dreams, but their true goal is to understand their own motivations. This is not always easy because these people are seldom in touch with their core self. If they manage to integrate the two sides of their nature, they can achieve any goal.

These men and women usually look for some way to express their deep inner tension; once they find this outlet they will embrace it with great single-mindedness.

EMBRACE
Sensuality
Dynamism
Stamina

AVOID
Overindulgence
Greed
Self-pity

ALSO BORN TODAY
Singer David Bowie; writer Wilkie Collins; actress Butterfly McQueen; TV journalist Charles Osgood; actress Yvette Mimieux; singer Elvis Presley; novelist Alexandra Ripley; comic actor Larry Storch.

JANUARY 9

January 9 natives are extraordinarily complicated people who may seem to be at war with themselves. Brilliant and philosophical, they often strain to maintain a facade in order to appeal to others.

These men and women reach for the stars, striving for perfection on every level. Sometimes they are fortunate enough to achieve it. They are tireless workers who will sacrifice a great deal in order to prove their worth to others—and themselves.

FRIENDS AND LOVERS People born on this date are naturally shy, and look to close friends for the intimacy they may be unable to share with a spouse or other loved ones.

Once they meet the person of their dreams, they are happy to settle down for life. These men and women may have trouble with intimacy, no matter how devoted they are to the one they love. Only the ability to open themselves emotionally can result in a true bonding of souls.

CHILDREN AND FAMILY January 9 natives are often troubled by conflicts relating to the values they were taught as a child. These men and women may have been brought up in a strict environment. As adults they are likely to have completely different views, which can create a deep sense of guilt. Learning who they are independent of their upbringing can be the most valuable lesson they'll ever learn.

As parents, January 9 individuals are tender and involved. They seek to shield their children from the harsh realities of life and support all their efforts to become independent.

HEALTH More than most people, January 9 individuals experience the consequences of their emotions upon their health. The stress of trying to succeed, while striving to live up to the expectations of others can put enormous pressure on them.

Learning to deal with stress is an important issue for January 9 people. Through regular exercise, good eating habits, and involvement in the spiritual side of life, they are able to come to grips with who they are. These men and women need to integrate both the material and spiritual sides of their nature in order to feel healthy and energetic.

CAREER AND FINANCES January 9 individuals have a driving need to succeed in their chosen field. Ambitious and unusually hard-working, they often are content to sacrifice personal happiness in order to achieve career desires.

Although January 9 people have a good head for financial matters, they are not very interested in the day-to-day aspects of making money. Not big spenders, they are more concerned with the status value of money.

DREAMS AND GOALS People born today want to achieve as much power as they can. They may often experience feelings of deep insecurity on a personal level, which can only be assuaged by achieving worldly success.

Despite their very private nature, January 9 people have a great need to attract public notice. When they transcend their shyness, they may experience their most ambitious and satisfying successes.

EMBRACE
Spiritual values
Initiative
Ethics

AVOID
Hypocrisy
Extravagance
Dishonesty

ALSO BORN TODAY
Singer Joan Baez; actor Bob Denver; singer Crystal Gayle; novelist Judith Krantz; actor Herbert Lom; U.S. President Richard M. Nixon; football star Bart Starr; actress Susannah York.

JANUARY 10

People born on January 10 have heightened perception and fiercely held likes and dislikes. These strong-minded men and women are not shy about dealing with others in a direct and honest manner.

January 10 people have no secret agenda. They are proud of their forthright approach to life and may even flaunt it at times.

FRIENDS AND LOVERS
January 10 natives have a swaggering attitude that attracts others to them. These people always seem to give the illusion that they know best, and whether or not it's true, others believe it. People born on this date have the ability to make others see things through their eyes, change opinions, and change lives.

In the love department, these men and women possess a strongly sexual nature beneath their sunny facade. They have a type of animal magnetism that is fairly typical of this sign. Capricorns may not seem particularly sexy, but those who love them know differently.

CHILDREN AND FAMILY
People born on this date are proud of their family heritage, and are keen to preserve it. They have the ability to remember many details from childhood, and see themselves as a continuation of a tradition that goes back many years. Although they may have been particularly rebellious in adolescence, January 10 people usually return to the values of their upbringing as they approach middle age and the philosophy that comes with it.

Because of their good associations with their own upbringing, January 10 individuals make loving, caring parents who prefer appropriate discipline to harsh punishment.

HEALTH
January 10 men and women are robust and rarely suffer from ill health. They don't enjoy having to conform to any prescribed method of exercise or nutritional advice, although by doing so they unknowingly add years to their life.

People born on this date are uncomfortable with working out on a regular basis and prefer sports to "managed" exercise. They are unusually competitive, and take enormous satisfaction from besting friends or colleagues through competition.

CAREER AND FINANCES
January 10 people have potent leadership skills. Although their approach to projects may be somewhat unorthodox, they always manage to get the job done. They can think and act on the fly, which makes them especially valuable in high-pressure businesses like publishing, retail, and advertising.

People born on this date spend heavily on luxury items like antique furniture, art, and good clothes. But they could never be called spendthrifts.

DREAMS AND GOALS
January 10 natives put financial security and material success high on their list of priorities, yet they also appreciate personal goals. Relationships, especially romantic ones, are an important part of their lives.

People born on this date can be impatient about making their dreams come true. While they understand that delays can be part of the game, they have a sense of urgency about everything they do.

EMBRACE
Good manners
Peak performance
Duty

AVOID
Antagonism
Pretense
Misdirection

ALSO BORN TODAY
Singer Pat Benatar; singer Jim Croce; boxer George Foreman; actor Paul Henreid; sculptor Barbara Hepworth; actor Sal Mineo; singer Rod Stewart.

JANUARY 11

en and women born on this date possess great personal dignity. They are lovable people, yet can be totally inflexible where their religious or political philosophy is concerned. Attractive and personable, they are also brilliant—a fact they may hide if they feel it gives them more leverage.

January 11 natives have the ability to rise from seeming obscurity to achieve everything they desire. Their intractable determination is legend, and is by far their most remarkable characteristic.

FRIENDS AND LOVERS It may appear that January 11 people deliberately cultivate rich and influential friends, merely to become part of that august circle. This may be true to a certain extent, yet this jaundiced view does not take into consideration the fact that January 11 men and women have a genuine love for people, regardless of their backgrounds or prospects.

In romantic matters, these folks can take their pick of dates and mates. They're unlikely to be swept off their feet, since practicality dominates most of their thoughts and decisions.

CHILDREN AND FAMILY The traditions of family life are very important to the men and women born on this date, particularly if those traditions were not a part of their upbringing. January 11 people have a great need to bring respectability into every area of life. Even if they don't choose to live by especially strict standards themselves, they like to give the appearance of doing so.

January 11 people make loving, if strict, parents. They can be demanding regarding the standards they want their children to adopt.

HEALTH Keeping healthy isn't difficult for January 11 people, who work very hard to maintain their good looks and good health. These men and women are sticklers when it comes to physical exercise, and may incorporate many different types into a routine.

January 11 natives may sometimes suffer from a mild form of depression if they fail to pay attention to the natural rhythm of their moods. These individuals have a strong emotional nature, which they tend to either master or ignore.

CAREER AND FINANCES People born on this date need to take charge of every aspect of their career. For this reason they do best if they work as freelancers, or as soloists of some sort who can direct their career path.

Even if they have no background in handling finances, January 11 folks can become expert at it. They are sound money managers, and what they may lack in experience they make up for in good judgment.

DREAMS AND GOALS The achievement of personal and professional success against tremendous odds is the chief goal of January 11 people. They enjoy struggle, feeling that it adds to their sense of accomplishment.

January 11 men and women understand that some goals take a great deal of time to achieve—but then these people have a lot of patience, and manage to stay focused regardless of how long they have to wait for success.

EMBRACE
Inner strength
Sharing
Psychic healing

AVOID
Patronizing attitude
Coldness
Aloofness

ALSO BORN TODAY
Musician Clarence Clemons; American patriot Alexander Hamilton; philosopher William James; singer Naomi Judd; actress Eva Le Galliene; writer Alan Paton; guitarist Vicki Peterson; actor Rod Taylor.

JANUARY 12

People born on this date enjoy giving the impression that they are far more adventuresome than they are. They possess a good sense of humor and the ability to transcend their own limitations.

Bold, imaginative, and undisciplined, January 12 people have an intellectual sophistication that few people can appreciate. Although they may go to great lengths in order to prove their abilities, January 12 people are often the ones who need to be convinced. Despite their "who cares?" attitude, they are actually quite insecure.

FRIENDS AND LOVERS
People born on this date sometimes struggle to make friends. Although this is often brought on because of an inability to appreciate their own place in the scheme of things, it's also due to a natural shyness that they are anxious to hide at all costs.

People born on this date are not very comfortable in romantic matters. Insecurity and a fear of abandonment can create problems in their relationships. In order for them to feel loved and appreciated, these men and women must first learn to trust their mate. Once this has been accomplished, they are likely to lose some of their other fears and insecurities.

CHILDREN AND FAMILY
The attitude problems of some January 12 individuals are likely to be the result of their upbringing. They may have been raised in an atmosphere where criticism was the rule rather than the exception. Problems that may have existed in the relationship between January 12 people and their siblings can have repercussions in their adult life.

Parenthood allows January 12 people to tap into a whole different area of their psyche, promising positive emotional growth.

HEALTH
While those born on this date generally have a strong physical constitution, they may be nonetheless prone to injuries and ailments throughout their lives. They like to take chances because it gives them a feeling of power.

Getting rid of bad health habits can be a real challenge. Additional fresh fruits and vegetables, as well as vitamin pills, can work wonders for these people.

CAREER AND FINANCES
January 12 people seek the limelight, looking for personal validation through success. Although they have considerable talent, they don't always have the ability to recognize their own skills.

Sensible money-handling can be a challenge for people born on this date. Since they often equate success with the amount of money they earn, they feel good about themselves by spending the money they make. However, credit debt can be a problem for these people.

DREAMS AND GOALS
Conquest of their own doubt is the best goal January 12 people can have. These sensitive souls must learn to believe in themselves before they can make others believe in them.

Those born on this date usually have a well-conceived game plan for success. They're willing to work hard in the spirit of that plan, learning as much from episodes of failure.

EMBRACE
Bravery
Trust
Exuberance

AVOID
Self-delusion
Riding the moral high horse
Incompetence

ALSO BORN TODAY
Actress Kirstie Alley; writer Jack London; actor Anthony Andrews; TV personality Des O'Connor; actress Louis Ranier; cowboy personality Tex Ritter; painter John Singer Sargent; supermodel Vendela.

JANUARY 13

Fearless, reckless, eager to meet all of life's challenges—that sums up January 13 natives, who often lead a tumultuous existence. These people often give the impression of being emotionally unstable, but they have the power to learn from their own mistakes.

These men and women have a jovial sense of humor and can see the funny side of even the most difficult situation. They possess the virtues of their defects, and if they are unable to envision the possibility of failure, it's because they are stubborn as well as optimistic.

FRIENDS AND LOVERS
Blessed with a pleasing personality and a generally happy disposition, January 13 natives are the envy of their friends. They're sociable and witty, and have the ability to make others feel good about themselves.

Despite a reputation for being frivolous and fickle, these men and women actually possess the virtues of stability and faithfulness—they simply may not wish to acknowledge these virtues to others. Partnership is important to these people, and they are likely to marry young.

CHILDREN AND FAMILY
January 13 natives identify strongly with their background. Whatever their family situation, these individuals have extreme pride in what their family was able to accomplish. January 13 people bring mostly happy memories from childhood into their adult life—in this respect, they're unusually fortunate.

As parents, these career-driven individuals are able to see the necessity for changing priorities and coming to grips with their nurturing side. They make good parents because they're able to combine their own life-lessons with instinct.

HEALTH
Looking good and feeling good are important to January 13 individuals. These men and women are not especially robust, but they know how to compensate by doing everything right.

While it's difficult for these folks to get excited about exercise, they are very savvy about nutrition and are likely to count every calorie, every gram of fat or protein, that they put in their mouth.

CAREER AND FINANCES
Whichever career they may choose, January 13 individuals need to feel as if they are in control of the details. These are not the sort of people who can work at a job that fails to interest or involve them.

January 13 natives are very concerned with financial security for themselves and their loved ones. Although they have the ability to live well on very little money, it's not a talent they enjoy having to use.

DREAMS AND GOALS
January 13 men and women are capable of achieving amazing things in life if they stay focused long enough to bring their goals to fruition. The problem with this is that they constantly shift their allegiance from one plan to the next, losing valuable momentum.

If they can commit to a project or plan on mental and emotional levels, January 13 natives can generally achieve their goals.

EMBRACE
Transcendence
Intelligent choices
Values

AVOID
Failure
Tedium
Short-sightedness

ALSO BORN TODAY
Composer Richard Addinsell; actress Julia Louis-Dreyfus; guitarist Joe Pass; actress Penelope Ann Miller; entertainer Sophie Tucker; actor Robert Stack; dancer Gwen Verdon; actress Frances Sternhagen.

JANUARY 14

People born on this date are ambitious, and are happiest when they juggle a variety of responsibilities. A sense of "if I don't do it it won't get done" is fairly prevalent with these individuals, though they have a sense of humor about their obsessiveness.

Scholarly and verbal, January 14 men and women are classy individuals who have the ability to recognize their own limitations, but who prefer not to acknowledge them to others.

FRIENDS AND LOVERS
People born on this date treat friendships as rather noncommittal outgrowths of their social life. They aren't given to deep, introspective feelings about friendship, and may feel uncomfortable if someone feels exceptionally close to them, or confides a secret.

Even in romantic matters, January 14 people need to have their "space." Control issues loom large in the lives of January 14 people, and are often at the core of their romantic breakups.

CHILDREN AND FAMILY
January 14 natives are precocious, and often distinguish themselves as prodigies. Their childhood is usually unconventional, even gypsylike, with the family having many changes of location and the children attending many different schools.

Although their circumstances may be quite different, January 14 people try to give their own children a feeling of independence and adventure by exposing them to a variety of interests.

HEALTH
Because they usually have an especially hectic lifestyle, January 14 men and women may have some very bad health habits; proper nutrition is often neglected. These folks have a tendency to eat fast food or convenience food when in a hurry, or eat thoughtlessly while in front of the computer or television.

January 14 natives need to learn how to relax. An hour spent in meditation and seclusion before going to bed each night can help prolong life.

CAREER AND FINANCES
People born on this date are very clever when it comes to details. Because of their ability with numbers they make excellent accountants, financial planners, bank personnel, and merchants. The more enterprising of these individuals can do very well in their own business, especially if it deals with financial matters and involves the public.

Despite being expert at handling other people's money, January 14 people have a somewhat scatterbrained approach to their own finances. These are the people who have difficulty balancing a checkbook!

DREAMS AND GOALS
"Making it up as they go along" is the way January 14 people like to work. Their goal is to do things their own way, and still be every bit as successful as those who don't have the creativity to break the rules.

January 14 men and women set high standards for themselves, yet they know how to take delays and disappointments without losing their enthusiasm or sense of fun.

EMBRACE
An ability to apologize
Good judgment
Vigor

AVOID
Acrimony
An arrogant attitude
Sanctimonious behavior

ALSO BORN TODAY
Photographer/designer Cecil Beaton; novelist John dos Passos; actress Faye Dunaway; singer Jack Jones; writer/film director Lawrence Kasden; author/TV journalist Andy Rooney; film director Joseph Losey; actor Carl Weathers.

JANUARY 15

Comfort is a vital component in the lives of people born on January 15. They seek it at every level of existence, and are equally concerned with maintaining the comfort of others. Physically, emotionally, and spiritually, they do what they can to make the world a better place. They gravitate toward good feelings, good works, and good intentions. January 15 individuals enjoy living in the lap of luxury, but never lose sight of the intangible virtues that truly make life worth living.

EMBRACE
Laughter
Spiritual riches
Reachable goals

AVOID
Feeling blue
Secret agendas
Possessiveness

ALSO BORN TODAY
Actor Lloyd Bridges; singer Charo; civil rights leader Martin Luther King, Jr.; musician Gene Krupa; actress Margaret O'Brien; shipping magnate Aristotle Onassis; actor Julian Sands; actor/film director Mario Van Peebles.

FRIENDS AND LOVERS People born on this day are essentially loners, yet they possess a special magnetism that draws people to them effortlessly. They are concerned about making the important people in their lives feel needed. Because of this trait they are exceptionally loyal and supportive friends.

Love is a serious commitment for these individuals. They have trouble making sense of all but the most intense relationships, and usually give their heart only once in a lifetime. Because of their self-sufficient attitude, January 15 natives have little or no problem keeping their relationships separate from their personal expectations about life.

CHILDREN AND FAMILY Family matters have an exceptionally important place in the lives of those born on January 15. These folks have real leadership potential and are often regarded as the scion of the family, regardless of age. As parents, they encourage their youngsters to develop independence and self-sufficiency, yet are anxious to protect their offspring from the failures and disappointments that are natural parts of growing up.

HEALTH Although blessed with general good health, January 15 individuals possess an extremely sensitive nature that can sometimes negatively affect their physical well-being. They may work for hours on end without taking a break, then suffer from nervousness or even insomnia.

In order to retain emotional and physical equilibrium, it's important for those born on January 15 to practice meditation on a regular basis, especially shortly before bedtime.

CAREER AND FINANCES January 15 natives know how to take care of business. Career goals play a vital role in their lives, though it may take a long time for these people to discover just where their deepest interests lie. A love of life's variety is one reason for this dilemma.

When they do settle on a career, these individuals give it their all. They enjoy making money, although that isn't an especially important factor in their career choice.

DREAMS AND GOALS Although they wear the mask of practicality with conviction, people born on January 15 have a complicated nature. They want to create something lasting, a legacy. Their dreams may be far more fanciful and creative than those who know them might expect. For this reason, they often turn to the creative arts for personal expression. Painting, writing, or music made in private help them to achieve their inner potential.

JANUARY 16

Those born on this date have pronounced psychic ability and can channel their inner energy toward their facilitation of worldly goals. Although they have the temperament of a loner, they love people.

January 16 men and women have the capacity to indulge their materialistic needs without losing sight of the importance of spirituality in their lives. Something of an enigma to all who know them, these individuals have an inner intensity that fuels all their actions.

FRIENDS AND LOVERS January 16 individuals connect with others on many levels. When they cultivate friendships, they don't look for conventional relationships. They want to be challenged, both emotionally and intellectually, by the people who call themselves their friends.

These men and women are equally idealistic in their romantic involvements. They seem drawn to individuals who can expand their lifeview, or teach them the karmic lessons they need to learn. Even sexual attraction is infused with a spiritual imperative.

CHILDREN AND FAMILY January 16 natives have a feeling of ambivalence regarding their upbringing. While they can appreciate tradition, they have a need to break from patterns in their background that they may perceive as outdated and inconsequential.

People born on this date have a fondness for children but may not wish to have any of their own. Playing the role of aunt or uncle, as well as confidante to the children of their friends, suits them much better.

HEALTH January 16 natives do not see a division between mind, body, and spirit. For them, all three meld to create a seamless entity. For this reason, they put just as much emphasis on meditation as they do on proper exercise and nutrition.

People born on this date require at least eight hours of sleep each night. If their sleep patterns are disturbed or changed, they can become irritable, even ill. To draw upon the richness of their nightly dream states adds to their good health.

CAREER AND FINANCES People born on this date need to use their considerable imaginative power in the work they do. They have great creativity and are able to envision the totality of a project at its conception. They have incredible visual skills and make excellent photographers and artists.

These folks also enjoy spending money on beautiful things, but are not very good at managing their financial affairs. An overwhelming generosity is the real problem, with these people willing to loan money to friends and relatives.

DREAMS AND GOALS Learning to use their psychic awareness in a positive way can be a challenge to January 16 people, who have a tendency to be afraid of their abilities. Once they discover that their prescience can help themselves and others, these men and women are more likely to feel confident about using their special talents.

When people born on this day set their sights upon achievement, they have the heart to stick with it.

EMBRACE
High spirits
A joyful heart
Good health

AVOID
Escapism
Irrational behavior
Detachment

ALSO BORN TODAY
Film director John Carpenter; designer Gordon Craig; opera diva Marilyn Horne; supermodel Kate Moss; poet Laura Riding; singer Sade; writer Susan Sontag; musician Paul Webb.

JANUARY 17

People born on this date have incredible physical and emotional endurance, and grasp the strong correlation between mental and physical energy. They're devoted to the notion of "peak experience," which may or may not be physical in nature.

January 17 men and women operate on a level of almost primal instinct, trusting their intuition far above intellect in almost every situation. These people continually put themselves "out there" in order to prove their abilities are undiminished by age or negative experience.

FRIENDS AND LOVERS Despite their natural conservatism, January 17 people have an odd collection of friends. Rather than cultivate relationships with people who are very much like them, they enjoy looking outside of their realm of experience to find people who can show them life-lessons they may not otherwise learn.

Romance is often unfulfilling for these individuals. They demand unstinting loyalty from those they love, holding them to almost impossible standards.

CHILDREN AND FAMILY As with most of their other emotions, people born on this date may keep their feelings regarding their family members a secret. Yet January 17 men and women are far more sentimental than they want others to know, and may harbor an almost naive reverence for their growing-up years and those who were a part of that time. Challenging episodes from their childhood often become the building blocks of opportunity.

People born on this date have a tendency to overindulge their youngsters in order to make up for what they themselves did not have as little ones.

HEALTH Keeping healthy is not just a matter of common sense for the men and women born on this date—it's a spiritual quest. These individuals want to be at the very peak of their conditioning, believing that it affects every area of life, not only the physical aspects.

Since good health and achievement go hand and hand in their lives, January 17 people recognize the value of mastering creative visualization techniques that allow them to "build" their success via meditation.

CAREER AND FINANCES January 17 people are extremely career-oriented, and often begin to plan their professional goals when they are little more than children. Secretly and systemically, these focused individuals may spend years bending every effort toward a final goal.

Money rarely plays a part in career choices for these people, but they have considerable ability to handle financial affairs.

DREAMS AND GOALS January 17 people need to adopt goals that help them deal with their desires. Understanding that there is not just one path their life can take helps these overachievers deal more successfully with the possibility of failure.

Once they achieve a sense of balance between their personal and professional lives, January 17 natives are more likely to feel good about themselves.

EMBRACE
Noble motives
Intensity
High ideals

AVOID
Vanity
Negativity
Adulation

ALSO BORN TODAY
Boxer Muhammad Ali; comedian Jim Carrey; American patriot Benjamin Franklin; boxer Joe Frazier; actor James Earl Jones; hair stylist Vidal Sassoon; ballerina/actress Moira Shearer; actress Betty White.

JANUARY 18

With these appealing people, the accent is always on personal charisma. January 18 people can literally charm anyone, and have the potential to be extremely manipulative if they choose. In most instances these men and women are forthright, and seek to be honest in their emotional dealings with others.

January 18 natives need excitement and variety in their lives, constantly craving new experiences and the chance to alter their professional and personal circumstances from time to time.

FRIENDS AND LOVERS January 18 men and women understand the politics of making friends. They often use important friendships as a springboard to professional success, though not in a strictly opportunistic sense.

As lovers and mates, January 18 people are anxious to project an attitude of sophistication that may only represent one part of their personality. They are naturally adventuresome and make a habit of falling in love with people who don't suit them except for the short-term.

CHILDREN AND FAMILY People born on this date may come from a perfectly ordinary background that may not accord with their view of themselves. Because of this, it isn't uncommon for January 18 people to reinvent their past.

January 18 people are concerned with giving their children all the status symbols that they themselves may have wanted but could not have. To be able to provide handsomely for their children's material needs is important to people born on this date.

HEALTH Because January 18 people are concerned with the image they project, they're likely to take good care of their health. Like many Capricorns, they combine a few bad habits—smoking, fast food—with a love of vigorous outdoor exercise.

People born on this date have a great love of food and may enjoy putting together gourmet meals that showcase their culinary talents and nutritional good sense. They favor plenty of fresh vegetables and protein-rich fish and poultry.

CAREER AND FINANCES January 18 natives are among the most career-oriented individuals of the yearly cycle. They often know what they want to do with their lives from a very early age, and begin laying plans on how to train for it. They have amazing faith in their talent, and often appear egotistical or even foolish about the way in which they are able to visualize all the wonderful things that are going to come their way.

Although intelligent enough to realize that making a lot of money doesn't necessarily indicate success, January 18 folks are also concerned with the luxuries of life.

DREAMS AND GOALS January 18 people live for their plans. Goals are the apex of their life, and even after the goals have been reached, new goals are likely to be set right away.

Although it may seem that these people are always in the right place at the right time for success, their preparation and hard work has a lot to do with the good things that come their way.

JANUARY 19

The intelligence of January 19 individuals is rooted in an awareness of their psychic understanding. These people recognize the strong connection between conscious and unconscious thought, which come together in dreams and creativity.

January 19 men and women have an excellent grasp of worldly and esoteric wisdom. They can present themselves in many different guises, but their true nature may not resemble any of them.

EMBRACE
Brilliance
Musical ability
Security

AVOID
Excesses
Instability
Divine madness

ALSO BORN TODAY
Actor Desi Arnaz, Jr.; painter Paul Cezanne; singer Michael Crawford; novelist Patricia Highsmith; singer Janis Joplin; actress Tippi Hedren; singer Dolly Parton; author/poet Edgar Allan Poe.

FRIENDS AND LOVERS People born on this date put their whole heart and soul into friendships. They depend upon the advice of those close to them, and are just as likely to return the favor. These men and women are not by nature sociable, yet if they have a supportive group of friends who can help them to feel self-confident about their social skills, they're happy to plunge into the social scene.

These people need to feel that they control any romantic relationship. This usually is a reaction to their possible abandonment in childhood, or because of an earlier romantic relationship that went awry.

CHILDREN AND FAMILY The childhood of January 19 people is often complicated by relationship problems with parents and siblings. These individuals are loners and may not fit into the emotional structure laid out by their family. Instead of trying to work things out, feelings of alienation and misunderstanding can cause January 19 natives to simply stop trying to get along with family members.

January 19 people make very good parents because they combine sensitivity with common sense.

HEALTH People born on this date will manage their health well—if they feel in control of the issue. This isn't an easy thing for these men and women, and explains why they must often make radical changes in their thinking before they can take care of their physical well-being.

It's wise for these folks to immerse themselves in positive image reinforcement, either through classes, seminars, or a reading program.

CAREER AND FINANCES People born on this date have many talents, including artistic and creative abilities that may not have been discovered until adulthood. It often takes an initial success early in their career to give these people a level of self-confidence that encourages them to accept and meet challenges.

Though January 19 people have a talent for numbers, they may not feel confident about handling financial matters. Yet this is another area where, once they prove to themselves that they have the talent, they are capable of amazing things.

DREAMS AND GOALS To learn to trust their incredible intuition on a level that can help them make life-choices is an important goal for January 19 people. These men and women are eager for professional and personal success, but are often confused about how to achieve it. They are wise enough to look to valued friends and associates for assistance.

AQUARIUS
January 20 - February 18

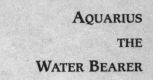
Aquarius is the eleventh sign of the astrological year and is known by its astrological symbol, the Water Bearer. Aquarius individuals are intelligent, progressive, and independent. With Uranus as the ruling planet, people born under this sign are considered to be free-thinking and unconventional. They will fight avidly for the rights of others.

THE AQUARIUS MAN Aquarian men are something of a puzzle. They may seem distant and unapproachable, or warm and welcoming, depending on their mood. They have incredible charisma and have the ability to draw people to them because of it. Despite their intelligence and unique brand of creativity, these men are not complicated or difficult to know.

Though on some level they are dedicated to making their personal lives a success, Aquarian men are usually focused on something greater than themselves. They care profoundly about a number of issues: politics, the environment, the economy. But unlike others who may shake their heads and shrug their shoulders over the impossibility of effecting change, Aquarian men truly believe that they can make a difference.

THE AQUARIUS WOMAN She is unusual, startling, even unclassifiable. The typical Aquarian woman is *atypical,* unique. She doesn't have to try to be different—she started out that way!

Aquarian women have a need to live their lives on a large scale. They want to learn and experience as much as they possibly can, and are not afraid of what the consequences may be. To these women, every experience is valuable if it shows them something about themselves and the world that they didn't know before. Even though Aquarian woman are often very attractive, they are rarely concerned with the more superficial aspects of life. These intelligent and talented women would rather be judged for their contributions and abilities than for their unique glamour or sex appeal.

THE AQUARIUS CHILD There is nothing conventional about the Aquarian child. This youngster enjoys going his or her own way and is apt to rebel for seemingly no reason. Although this child is likely to be intelligent—even brilliant—he or she does not fit any prescribed image. As a toddler this child may have more than the usual amount of temper tantrums. But this frustration usually fades once the little one is given an opportunity to begin exploring the world. Curiosity is stronger than any other characteristic.

The Aquarian child needs parents who encourage his or her need to be different. This youngster needs to feel free.

THE AQUARIUS LOVER

The Aquarius lover is full of surprises. This liberated individual has unique ideas about love that have very little to do with conventional ideas or principles.

The most important factor in an Aquarian's life is freedom. These people simply cannot be happy or fulfilled unless they are free to do as they like. Although a new love interest or date may not recognize this attitude, he or she will eventually learn the truth if the relationship moves beyond the casual stage. No matter how deeply in love an Aquarius man or woman may be, they are never willing to sacrifice their autonomy to the relationship. This attitude has doubtless ended many a love affair or marriage for these people, but they will always put personal honesty ahead of romance.

THE AQUARIUS BOSS

The typical Aquarian boss is a worker's dream come true. Humanitarian and fair-minded, this individual never uses his or her position to intimidate an employee. Playing power games simply isn't something this individual feels comfortable doing. Aquarians have far too much integrity to demean themselves or those who work for them in this way.

But it would be incorrect to assume that just because they are broad-minded and tolerant, the Aquarian boss is a pushover. This individual believes in fairness on all levels, and that includes those who work for him. Aquarians make great entrepreneurs and therefore often end up being their own boss. Because of their ability to let their dreams flourish, Aquarians can understand just how important the dreams of others are.

THE AQUARIUS FRIEND

Aquarians tend to collect friends the way some people put together a wildly eclectic art collection. They have a tolerant attitude toward people and refuse to set up the barriers to friendship that folks born under most other signs concoct. Aquarians respond to the simple humanity in another person and can always find something to like or respect. They are genuinely interested in people and don't make unfair judgments about backgrounds or motives.

Unfortunately, the typical Aquarian may have so many friends that it is impossible to have an intimate personal relationship with any of them. Some Aquarians may even use this as a way to maintain an emotional distance from others. But those who use their talent for friendship in the purest form are the world's greatest friends.

ELEMENT: Air
QUALITY: Fixed
PLANETARY RULER: Uranus
BIRTHSTONE: Amethyst
FLOWER: Orchid
COLOR: Aqua

KEY CHARACTERISTIC:
Iconoclastic

STRENGTHS: Humanitarian, Modern, Analytical
WEAKNESSES: Unreliable, Extremist, Chaotic

JANUARY 20

J anuary 20 individuals have a deeply personal vision of what their personal and professional lives are meant to be. These men and women have a quiet determination that gets them through difficult times.

People born on this date are concerned about the image they project. They make excellent role models and are deeply committed to humanitarian causes. In their youth, they're usually involved in political activism.

FRIENDS AND LOVERS Unlike many Aquarian natives, January 20 individuals prefer to cultivate emotionally charged friendships that last a lifetime. These folks are very sure of themselves, yet they value the lessons that close friends can teach them.

January 20 natives are broad-minded about love and sexuality. They have a certain cynicism about romance and are unlikely to believe some of the more fanciful blandishments that come their way. Not content to give up their freedom at an early age, January 20 people often marry late in life, or not at all.

CHILDREN AND FAMILY Men and women born today prefer to maintain close contact with their family members. Siblings may be an especially important part of their life, and there may have been rivalry during childhood, and especially during adolescence.

People born on this date are very dutiful parents, though they have a tendency to be excessively strict with their children. They are careful to cultivate their youngsters' creative ambitions.

HEALTH January 20 people have boundless physical energy. Their recipe for good health is a combination of positive thinking and practicality. These men and women love to look great,

which is a huge motivation to exercise daily and eat right.

Once in a while they fall under the spell of a New Age style diet or fitness plan that encourages them to seek spiritual enlightenment. This can be an eye-opener to these generally analytical individuals.

CAREER AND FINANCES People born on this date often seek out very specialized careers. They can't be happy in just any job, because so much of their sense of self is bound up with what they do for a living. They often feel as if they were chosen, even anointed, to do something special in the world. If they're able to follow their intuition without second-guessing themselves, January 20 people can be amazingly successful.

People born on this date are very careful with their resources. They know the value of a good credit rating and prefer to pay cash.

DREAMS AND GOALS These men and women have an almost icy determination to succeed. While they are unlikely to compromise any deeply held beliefs or ethical principles in order to realize a goal, they do play hardball when they deal for the things they want.

January 20 people are extremely well organized and can accomplish extraordinary things by simply sticking to their game plan. Few people learn more from their own mistakes than these individuals.

EMBRACE
Versatility
Curiosity
Adventure

AVOID
Routine
Defeatism
Judgmental people

ALSO BORN TODAY
Conservationist Joy Adamson; astronaut Buzz Aldrin; film director Federico Fellini; figure skating champion Carol Heiss; actor Lorenzo Lamas; film director David Lynch; actress Patricia Neal; dancer Ruth St. Denis.

JANUARY 21

January 21 individuals are utterly unique. Cool on the outside, they nonetheless possess a magnetism that always seems to put them in the spotlight. Although they can appear somewhat egotistical at times, they are actually generous souls.

Sexual, spiritual, and highly intelligent, these fun-loving men and women seem able to have it all—and on their own terms. They have the ability to see the humor in things, even themselves.

FRIENDS AND LOVERS
Friends provide a great source of love and fellowship for these men and women. January 21 people are always willing to learn important lessons from their friends, though they are more likely to provide leadership within the relationship.

These men and women are more conventional in romantic matters than many Aquarians. They are interested in marriage rather than the pursuit of a series of uncommitted relationships. Yet despite their need to be involved, these individuals must retain a sense of their own independence apart from the marriage.

CHILDREN AND FAMILY
Many January 21 people grow up feeling in sync with their childhood upbringing, only to discover when they hit middle age that they're still carrying around a lot of anger and a great many unresolved issues.

January 21 men and women can be very demanding parents. They expect their children to follow a specific code of conduct and to handle responsibility at a very early age.

HEALTH
People born on this date see themselves as invulnerable to illness or injury, so it always comes as a tremendous surprise to them if they are suddenly faced with a serious health problem.

Weight can be an issue with January 21 natives, especially later in life. These people are known to be big eaters, but as long as they remain active there is very little chance of them putting on too many extra pounds.

CAREER AND FINANCES
January 21 men and women need to feel as if they call the shots in their professional lives. They have a certain amount of difficulty working for others, and may exhibit a rebellious streak on their very first job. A streak of perfectionism is part of the problem, and encourages them to oversee every detail.

They are equally fanatical about watching how every penny is spent. Although this in no way implies a miserly attitude—these folks are actually incredibly generous—it does reveal just how obsessive they can be.

DREAMS AND GOALS
January 21 natives can be disillusioned when their goals become reality: Once the dream comes true, their motivation vanishes. It's therefore necessary for these people to have a whole host of goals, some big, some small, to prevent them from becoming directionless when a major plan is realized.

People born on this date need to understand that it is their own best efforts, not simply success itself, which crowns their achievement.

EMBRACE
Perspective
Dedication
Familiarity

AVOID
Danger
Unpreparedness
Surprise

ALSO BORN TODAY
Actress Geena Davis; fashion designer Christian Dior; opera singer Placido Domingo; film director Clive Donner; actress Jill Eikenberry; golfer Jack Nicklaus; singer Billy Ocean; actor Telly Savalas.

JANUARY 22

People born on this date have it in their power to do amazing things. They are extraordinarily talented, and usually enjoy calling attention to themselves, though often to achieve something worthwhile than merely to satisfy their own egos.

These folks enjoy being the focus of any group, and may deliberately put themselves into controversial circumstances for this reason. Able to find the uniqueness in each experience, January 22 people enjoy the resonance of negative as well as positive emotions.

FRIENDS AND LOVERS

Although it may seem as if January 22 individuals cultivate friends who will adore and praise them for their talents, they are actually far more interested in being a friend than having friends.

The love life of these individuals is often tumultuous and even a little dangerous. These are men and women who are attracted to illusive, glamorous types who mirror their own dark side.

CHILDREN AND FAMILY

People born on this date may distance themselves from their childhood if it represents values they no longer espouse, yet they constantly look back on that time in their life with a sense of gratitude and affection. These men and women are likely to retain a close relationship with one particularly bizarre family figure.

Whether or not January 22 people become parents, they tend to be involved with children, often through a mentoring program, or a civic or sports group. The company of young people helps these folks retain their own youthfulness.

HEALTH

Like many Aquarians, January 22 people have unique ideas about keeping healthy. They go far beyond conventional methods like vegetarianism or fasting, and may often try an unusual weight loss regimen or holistic healing routine. While these things can sometimes be helpful for them, January 22 people need to become far more critical and selective about their health maintenance.

Where exercise is concerned, these men and women have a tendency to either overdo, or ignore it altogether.

CAREER AND FINANCES

Because their aspirations are generally artistic in nature, these talented men and women are usually able to console themselves with the knowledge that their side work is valid and important.

Money is often a critical factor in the lives of these people, especially during their early years. Happily, these folks have a tremendous potential for making money once their talents are recognized.

DREAMS AND GOALS

The ability to make a living from their artistic endeavors is the number-one goal of people born on this day. These courageous men and women may spend many years developing their talents, yet always believe in themselves, even if few others do.

When they are rewarded for all of their hard work and sacrifice, January 22 natives aren't content to revel in their good fortune. These amazing people set new standards for themselves, new heights to be reached.

EMBRACE
A good reputation
Discovery
Popularity

AVOID
Untruths
Denial
Neglect of self

ALSO BORN TODAY
Ballet choreographer George Balanchine; poet George Gordon, Lord Byron; film director Sergei Eisenstein; actor Balthazar Getty; film director D. W. Griffith; actress Piper Laurie; playwright August Strindberg; novelist Joseph Wambaugh.

JANUARY 23

People born on this date are hard-headed realists whose persona reflects a strong, silent type. They have a toughness about them that's at once laudable and useful: They seem able to handle anything.

Inside, though, they're tender souls, uncomplaining men and women who hide their vulnerabilities for fear they'll be considered weak. Although often put in the position of role model, these individuals do not generally regard their conduct as anything special.

FRIENDS AND LOVERS

January 23 natives enjoy the social elements of friendship. Whether it's a game of cards, an outing, or just a conversation, these men and women receive joy from connecting with others.

People born on this date make gentle, caring lovers. They have an aversion to commitment, though it's not uncommon for them to enter into a long-term relationship or marriage when they find someone who shares their unconventional views.

CHILDREN AND FAMILY

January 23 people have a great feeling of pride in their family background. Many of the ideals and traits they exhibit as adults were absorbed from their parents and older siblings. Even though they may also have a great many contrasting views, January 23 individuals have respect for the honesty and integrity of those who reared them.

When they become parents, these folks may feel pulled between providing their children with the discipline they need, and endorsing the freer, more liberated parenting style they believe in.

HEALTH

People born on this date like to do things their own way. They don't take kindly to health or nutritional advice of any kind and prefer to monitor their own well-being without the supervision of doctors. An annual visit to a health-care professional should not invalidate their sense of independence.

Because of the natural sensitivity of their systems, people born on January 23 should shun questionable habits like smoking and drinking.

CAREER AND FINANCES

Like many Aquarian people, January 23 natives are not the sort who can work at a job they find boring or uncreative. These people need to feel thoroughly plugged-in to the universe through the work they do.

These men and women have a potential to earn a good deal of money, though they usually spend it faster than they make it. Since they don't care about splendid surroundings, friends and relatives are often the beneficiaries of their generosity.

DREAMS AND GOALS

Not having to pretend they are something they aren't is one of the major goals sought by January 23 people. These men and women are highly motivated to achieve career success, and may not realize until later in life that they also want personal stability.

January 23 natives have a desire to be the best at what they do. They take criticism well, and are able to look at themselves objectively.

EMBRACE
Humor
Good luck
Acceptance

AVOID
Solitude
Antisocial attitudes
Grudges

ALSO BORN TODAY
Actor Humphrey Bogart; Monaco's Princess Caroline; musician Billy Cunningham; American patriot John Hancock; actor Rutger Hauer; painter Edourd Manet; actress Jeanne Moreau; singer Anita Pointer.

JANUARY 24

One of the most fascinating characteristics of January 24 people is their need to break patterns and shock those who are closest to them. These people have a flamboyant spirit, and need to demonstrate their eccentric nature.

Beneath the surface of their sophistication, people born on this day have a deep well of kindness. They have a genuine love for others and a willingness to reveal their vulnerabilities to the people they love.

FRIENDS AND LOVERS Friendship is a complicated matter for January 24 people. Although they have a great need to feel emotionally close to their friends, they have a tendency to strike a competitive pose. This is generally a result of insecurity on their part, and it can have a negative effect on even the most important friendships in the lives of these people.

January 24 natives exude glamour and respond to it in others. They often choose the wrong type of mate because they are fooled by glamour, glibness, and other superficial trappings. In the end, these folks are happiest when they find a soul mate.

CHILDREN AND FAMILY January 24 individuals are often the rebel within their family group. It may be difficult for them to adhere to rules that they find dishonest and stifling. Yet on some level these individuals may feel guilty for not conforming to the expectations their parents set for them.

People born on this date are sometimes insecure about their own abilities as parents. They want to avoid the mistakes that their own parents made, and yet wish to set standards that will help their youngsters develop into loving, worthwhile adults.

HEALTH The rebellious nature of January 24 men and women is often reflected in the on-again, off-again way they adhere to a health program. They are fascinated with health and fitness issues, but may be unable to commit to a program for any length of time. These men and women have great natural vitality, but may not take particular care to preserve it.

CAREER AND FINANCES January 24 individuals may experience their career success very early in life. Although this may seem desirable, it can actually be a drawback if they cannot summon the motivation to move on from that point.

Money comes and goes in the lives of these individuals, whose financial situation is never very stable. These people have the potential to win and lose a great deal of money in their lifetime, but may need some reality checks before they know how to manage it.

DREAMS AND GOALS People born on this date are devoted to career goals, but need to learn that there are other important dreams in their lives that require just as much nurturing and intensity.

January 24 men and women have the potential to do amazing things in life, but may require the validation of others in order to believe in themselves.

EMBRACE
True self
Dependability
Thrift

AVOID
Making demands
Physical excesses
Risks

ALSO BORN TODAY
Comic John Belushi; singer Neil Diamond; actress Nastassja Kinski; actor Michael Ontkean; gymnast Mary Lou Retton; ballerina Maria Tallchief; actress Sharon Tate; novelist Edith Wharton.

JANUARY 25

Despite their pleasing personas, those born on January 25 are difficult to know. These people are cloaked in mystery, always seeming to hold something of themselves in reserve. Dreamy and introspective, they have a special magnetism and charm.

These men and woman have a profound sense of their own destiny. Although they are intelligent and gifted, they may feel as if they are constantly being passed over by people who are far less talented.

FRIENDS AND LOVERS
People born on this date often become deeply involved in the lives of others. Because they are able to withhold criticism and judgment, January 25 people are likely to attract a large circle of friends.

Finding their true love is a spiritual quest. They have a need to find a soul mate, and may be disappointed in love until they find that special person.

Commitment is not easy for these people, who have a tendency to idealize love beyond recognition. In order to make a romance work, January 25 people need to come down to earth.

CHILDREN AND FAMILY
It is not uncommon for January 25 natives to feel rather strongly connected to their childhoods throughout their adult lives. This may be due to the influence of an imaginative and inspirational parent whose ability to transcend the role of authoritarian figure had a positive effect upon children.

In their own role as parents, January 25 men and women feel it's their duty to foster a spirit of individualism in youngsters, and fiercely support their kids' creative interests.

HEALTH
January 25 individuals have a tendency toward moodiness when their idealism collides with reality. In order to restore emotional equilibrium they need to engage in a vigorous regular exercise. Running and working out with weights helps.

People born on this date have a low tolerance for pills of any kind. They should also guard against use of alcohol or nicotine, both of which have an unpleasant effect upon them. A high-protein, low-fat diet is best for these folks.

CAREER AND FINANCES
January 25 natives are often unsure of what career path is best for them. They have a myriad of interests, particularly in artistic or creative fields, yet often lack confidence. They require a great deal of encouragement or they may never have the nerve to shoot for their goals.

People born on this date have unusual luck with money. At times they may receive money out of the blue, but may occasionally struggle to make ends meet.

DREAMS AND GOALS
January 25 individuals wish to retain their autonomy despite the personal and professional demands in their lives. The air of mystery they cultivate is a natural reaction to their need for privacy and introspection.

People born on this date continually shuffle their priorities, so their goals are likely to change. This is not due to a lack of interest or commitment, but their need to take life as it comes.

EMBRACE
Allegiance
Growth
Know-how

AVOID
Fair-weather friends
Petty dislikes
Crankiness

ALSO BORN TODAY
American Revolutionary War General Benedict Arnold; poet Robert Burns; actress Mildred Dunnock; football star Lou Groza; actor Dean Jones; actress Dinah Manoff; novelist W. Somerset Maugham; novelist Virginia Woolf.

JANUARY 26

Few people understand the dimensions of power in quite the same way as January 26 people. These individuals make their own rules, and are never afraid to strike out in unexpected directions.

Distinctive in both appearance and attitude, these men and women have the ability to set an example for others. Their strength of character and steely intelligence give them a unique persona; they are keenly aware of how they can use these talents to their own advantage.

FRIENDS AND LOVERS
Because of their standoffish personality, January 26 men and women are more likely to have admirers than friends. These people often act as mentors to their professional colleagues.

It is not uncommon for January 26 individuals to become romantically involved with someone who is either much older or much younger than themselves. These people don't believe that age has any drawbacks to romantic happiness. When they are in love with someone, January 26 people are unconcerned about how others might judge the relationship.

CHILDREN AND FAMILY
January 26 individuals believe wholeheartedly in tradition, which sets them apart from most Aquarius natives. These men and women have the insight to understand which aspects of their upbringing may have been too strict or old-fashioned, but they do not hold this against their parents.

With their own children, January 26 people take a slightly different tack. They are sticklers for discipline yet have the emotional flexibility to understand that the day will come when their youngsters feel a need to test the boundaries of the relationship.

HEALTH
The men and women born on this date have some very unusual ideas about staying fit, often endorsing peculiar or restrictive diets with a New Age slant.

These people have a natural understanding of what they need to do in order to stay healthy. They can indulge in a hectic lifestyle at times, then slow down to accommodate a period of rest and recuperation. A positive outlook has many good health implications.

CAREER AND FINANCES
People born on this date have a need to transcend the boundaries of their existence through the work they do. They are often drawn to professions that allow them to exert some measure of authority over others. Because they know the worth of power, these individuals are unlikely to misuse it.

These people do not trust their financial situation to anyone but themselves.

DREAMS AND GOALS
When January 26 individuals choose to plot a course goal by goal, they're likely to exhibit amazing reserves of will power and determination. They are more likely to succeed in bringing their dreams to reality if they have opposition lined up against them. These people thrive under pressure.

January 26 men and women have a need to prove what they're made of—both to themselves and to the important people in their lives.

EMBRACE
Appeal
Adoration
Romance

AVOID
Unhappiness
Unfocused energy
Spite

ALSO BORN TODAY
Cellist Jacqueline du Pre; actor Scott Glenn; hockey star Wayne Gretsky; singer Eartha Kitt; TV journalist Edwin Newman; actor Paul Newman; film critic Gene Siskel; film director Roger Vadim.

JANUARY 27

January 27 people have an excitable, magnetic personality. They may have trouble balancing the disparate sides of their nature, but this seeming instability is actually one of their most intriguing traits.

People born on this date are alternately focused and indifferent. What is an obsession to them on one day may be a subject of inconsequence the next. These men and women possess an attractiveness that has nothing to do with the way they look.

FRIENDS AND LOVERS People born on this date have a wide social circle that reflects their friendliness. But while they enjoy having people around them, January 27 individuals are extremely careful about which people they allow to occupy places of importance in their lives. These men and women don't give their trust to everyone, and even those who do qualify as close friends may find themselves ignored or sharply criticized at some point in the relationship.

January 27 natives have a taste for exotic romance and may have trouble being faithful to a mate. Their hearts are always true, but their spirits have a wandering nature.

CHILDREN AND FAMILY January 27 individuals have a love/hate relationship with family members—a state of affairs that usually lasts a lifetime. This may be played out on an almost operatic scale, with January 27 individuals constantly at odds with a sibling or parent figure.

Liberal and independent-minded as they are, January 27 people are willing to allow their children a chance to make up their own minds about things. As parents, they encourage a spirit of rebellion.

HEALTH People born on January 27 are sometimes careless about their health, feeling invulnerable to the threat of illness or injury. These individuals have a dislike of anything that is too firmly regimented and have problems committing to an exercise program.

Diet can be another source of friction in the lives of January 27 people. Their rebellious nature asserts itself in a desire to eat rich, sugary foods without experiencing any of the consequences.

CAREER AND FINANCES People born on this date have an ability to deal with individuals of all backgrounds, all temperaments. Their talent in perceiving the motives of others is nothing short of extraordinary.

It is not uncommon for January 27 men and women to embrace some bad financial habits. They may have an almost fanatical need to spend money, an attitude that is part of their rebelliousness.

DREAMS AND GOALS January 27 individuals have an overwhelming need to be free. They see their autonomy as something more than an expression of their personal needs—it is a quest for self-actualization.

These men and women are not especially goal-oriented, but they do set their sights on big dreams. Some of these may be extravagant or even foolhardy, but they characterize these eccentric people perfectly. Because January 27 natives refuse to set limits, they have the potential to scale the very heights.

EMBRACE
Sense of drama
Power
Graciousness

AVOID
Perplexity
Hoping against hope
Inertia

ALSO BORN TODAY
Ballet dancer Mikhail Baryshnikov; actor Troy Donahue; actress Bridget Fonda; writer Lewis Carroll; actress Donna Reed; actress Mimi Rogers; composer Wolfgang Amadeus Mozart; actress Ingrid Thulin.

JANUARY 28

People born on this date see themselves as a work in progress. For this reason they don't expect to assimilate all of the important experiences in their lives overnight. While they hope for perfection, and even strive toward it, these men and women have the good sense to realize that it isn't a likely achievement.

January 28 people have the common sense to be as tolerant and forgiving of their own faults as they are of those of others.

FRIENDS AND LOVERS
If there is one aspect of life in which January 28 people display a strong competitive streak, it is in their relationships. No matter how devoted they are to a friend or loved one, they need to compete on both a personal and professional level.

This spirit of mild antagonism is also part of their romantic nature. As kindhearted and tolerant as January 28 people are, they feel the need to continually push against the boundaries of the relationship, initiating a spirit of "me too-ism" that can sound the death knell to even the most rewarding union.

CHILDREN AND FAMILY
It is likely that their competitive nature has its roots in childhood or adolescence. Either it was fostered by unwise parents who thought to motivate them in this way, or it was the refuge of a lonely teenager, perhaps as the result of being unable to fit into the "cool" set.

Because of their own insecurities and sensitivities, January 28 people are very gentle with their children. They understand the negative role played by stress in the life of a child, and they do what they can to shield their youngsters from it.

HEALTH
If January 28 individuals develop good health habits early, they will keep them all their lives. If not, it's unlikely that they will ever acquire them. Like most Aquarians, January 28 men and women are extraordinarily stubborn. Despite an intellectual grasp of the importance of change, they don't like to be pushed in unfamiliar directions.

These people don't bring the office home with them any more than they take their personal life to work. Being able to compartmentalize their emotions can be a big factor in helping them maintain emotional and physical health.

CAREER AND FINANCES
January 28 individuals have a talent for seeing the analytical side of things. They have a natural affinity for math, science, and music, and may find a rewarding career in any of these fields. These men and women also show a great skill with languages.

Since January 28 people have a reputation for frequent career changes, their earning potential is always in flux.

DREAMS AND GOALS
January 28 natives aren't big on making plans. They prefer to take life as it comes, no matter the consequences. These folks are curious about life, and that is enough to keep them interested.

These individuals don't distinguish between professional and personal goals, knowing that in order to have a balanced life they need to concentrate on both.

EMBRACE
Honest mistakes
Inner voice
Attitude

AVOID
Fears
Chaos
Dictatorial behavior

ALSO BORN TODAY
Actor Alan Alda; novelist Colette; figure skating champion Sjoukje Dijkstra; actress Marthe Keller; painter Jackson Pollock; actor Nicholas Pryor; pianist Arthur Rubenstein; actor Elijah Wood.

345

JANUARY 29

People born on this date are remarkable individuals in many ways. They are never content to just watch the parade go by, but are spurred on by a powerful sense of mission.

January 29 people may appear somewhat prickly to others, but they are actually gentle and philosophical in nature, despite their strong political beliefs. These people will put their reputation on the line in order to bring about necessary change. This need to do something for others isn't fueled by ego, but by conscience.

FRIENDS AND LOVERS Friends, of whom January 29 people have many, help to define the lives of January 29 individuals. These men and women have a rare talent for being able to inspire and influence others in an amazingly powerful and positive manner.

Like many Aquarians, January 29 people suffer their share of romantic heartaches. They are frequently afraid of commitment because it represents to them the loss of their most prized possession—independence! These folks are capable of profound, spiritual love, yet they can't get past the need to hold back something of themselves.

CHILDREN AND FAMILY Whatever the drawbacks of their upbringing, January 29 men and women can find strength by transcending the challenges life sends their way. These people are human dynamos who refuse to be vanquished by any situation, no matter how painful or devastating it may be.

January 29 people have all the best traits for parenthood: intelligence, spirituality, humor, and patience. They take this role seriously, perhaps more than any other in their lives.

HEALTH Once these men and women understand the value of fitness, they are likely to be lifelong converts. Like many Aquarians, January 29 people generally keep up a hectic pace, yet may be unwilling to commit to anything more than the occasional trot around the block after dinner.

CAREER AND FINANCES There are no better teachers on Earth than the men and women born on this date. These people love learning and have a natural affinity for inspiring others to love it, as well. January 29 individuals are always looking to expand their horizons, and for this reason they may change their career plans several times.

Although they are unconventional in their thinking, January 29 individuals have a healthy respect for money. These people may not set out to increase their earning power, but somewhere along the way they are likely to do so.

DREAMS AND GOALS January 29 men and women want to help others see the power and beauty of life through personal accountability and wise choices. They have a love and respect for knowledge that surpasses anything else in their lives, and they wish to share this intense experience with others.

When it comes to personal goals, January 29 people want to know themselves and understand their own deepest motivations. These people have the courage and integrity to ask the hard questions.

EMBRACE
Ideals
Distinction
Irony

AVOID
Self-centeredness
Controversy
Destructive acts

ALSO BORN TODAY
Writer Anton Chekhov; actress Sara Gilbert; feminist Germaine Greer; actress Ann Jillian; diving champion Greg Louganis; author/patriot Thomas Paine; actress Katherine Ross; TV host Oprah Winfrey.

JANUARY 30

People born on this date have an aristocratic bearing, yet are extremely accessible and friendly. These men and women are great humanitarians: generous, but somewhat self-deprecating. It may be difficult for them to see their own good traits without first having them validated by friends and loved ones.

January 30 people may seem serious on the outside, but they definitely know how to have a good time. In youth, these folks are likely to be party animals.

FRIENDS AND LOVERS

January 30 natives need a lot of people around them, even though they never seem to reveal the same truths about themselves to each friend. By compartmentalizing their friendships, these men and women are able to attract the sort of affection they require without giving away too many of their secrets.

They are hardly more generous in their attitude toward lovers or mates. January 30 people need their emotional "space" and will not sacrifice their independence, even for the one they adore. These people are honest, and they let their romantic interests know their foibles.

CHILDREN AND FAMILY

People born on this date believe in honoring the family tradition regardless of what sort of upbringing they experienced. They may have a very close relationship with a parent or a parent figure.

People born on this date are strict disciplinarians and do not allow their children the wide margin for error they may have enjoyed in their own childhood. These individuals can be very good parents, but they believe that toughness, not an easygoing disposition, is the key to getting the job done right.

HEALTH

January 30 natives are believers in the holistic path to good health. They are likely to be averse to conventional medical treatment.

People born on this date understand that there can be no peace in their lives if they don't work to accomplish a realization of their inner drives and needs. Daily meditation and prayer help them to feel centered and spiritually whole.

CAREER AND FINANCES

Even though they have natural leadership ability, January 30 individuals may seek out occupations that allow them to withdraw from the world. This isn't because they can't handle reality, but because they have too clear an understanding of it.

Finances seldom define these individuals, who have the ability to live well no matter if they are rich or poor.

DREAMS AND GOALS

The goals of January 30 men and women are often far too complicated for the average person to understand. They don't care about the things that preoccupy others: money, relationships, a good job. These people have such a high soul-level that they constantly seek to undertake spiritual challenges that will push them to even greater heights.

People born on this date are so unconcerned with conventional goals that they often achieve great prominence because of their very indifference.

EMBRACE
Goals
Good taste
Fashionable appearance

AVOID
Lost opportunities
Misjudging others
Surliness

ALSO BORN TODAY
Baseball star Ernie Banks; actor Gene Hackman; actress Dorothy Malone; U.S. President Franklin D. Roosevelt; actress Vanessa Redgrave; financial analyst Louis Rukeyser; chess champion Boris Spassky; historian Barbara Tuchman.

JANUARY 31

People born on this date have an eccentric perspective, which makes them interesting and unique. They're extremely charismatic and have the ability to charm just about anyone.

January 31 natives are unusual people who have an instinct about their own specialness. What may appear to be egotism is actually a simple appreciation for their own gifts and talents. These people are extraordinarily intelligent, yet their brilliance is at times undermined by some very foolish personal choices.

FRIENDS AND LOVERS January 31 people forge powerful friendships, which help them to define their own nature. These men and women seem to draw into their orbit people who can add to their lives qualities that may be lacking. These folks do likewise with romantic partnerships, "expanding" their own personalities via their choice of lovers and mates. They are not particularly adamant that their relationships be permanent. Often, when they have learned the lessons they needed to learn, January 31 people move on.

CHILDREN AND FAMILY People born on this date are able to transcend the experiences of their upbringing. Despite their penchant for being unusual, these people have a practical side that's best seen in the way they rationalize difficulties they may have experienced as children. If they were not appreciated for their own uniqueness, or if they were unfairly and consistently measured against a more conventional sibling, these people are able to forgive and forget.

They take an equally practical approach when they become parents. January 31 natives don't push their children to succeed, but allow them to develop at their own pace.

HEALTH January 31 men and women may endorse a natural lifestyle that includes holistic healing, meditation, a diet of raw fruits and vegetables, and exercise.

January 31 individuals understand the need to promote a mind-body-spirit harmony. Taking time out for relaxation on a regular basis helps them maintain a high energy level.

CAREER AND FINANCES People born on this date are extremely intelligent and enormously talented. The one drawback to their potential success could be that they actually possess too many talents! Because of this, it may be difficult for them to settle on a single career option.

If January 31 individuals choose to take an active interest in financial affairs, they are extremely capable. But these people typically prefer to turn management of that part of their life over to someone else, generally a spouse or a trusted friend.

DREAMS AND GOALS Like many Aquarians, January 31 men and women have the ability to see beyond their own personal concerns and look at life on a global level. They maintain a humanitarian view of the world and are always looking for ways to affect society positively. When they are very young, it's easy for them to become disillusioned once they discover that this is not as simple to do as they had anticipated. Yet they'll always find time to help others, whether in big ways or little ways.

EMBRACE
Credibility
Enjoyment
Altruism

AVOID
Immaturity
Fatuousness
Addiction

ALSO BORN TODAY
Actress Tallulah Bankhead; singer Mario Lanza; novelist John O'Hara; baseball star Jackie Robinson; composer Franz Schubert; actress Jean Simmons; novelist Norman Mailer; actress Jessica Walter.

FEBRUARY 1

February 1 individuals are a rare breed: rebels who have respect for essential values. These impulsive people always seem able to meld the two diverse sides of their personality.

Men and women born on this date have an elusive glamour that makes them unforgettable. There is something in their nature that attracts danger. Although they know how to control this need, at times they come a little too close to the dark side of their personality and must confront it.

FRIENDS AND LOVERS

February 1 natives have the typically Aquarian trait of surrounding themselves with a great many friends while not really getting close to anyone. These individuals enjoy the social components of friendship, but are generally unwilling to let anyone too close emotionally. They have the same tendency to keep a lover or mate at a distance.

In general, February 1 men and women have a problem with intimacy, which can spell big trouble for their love relationships. In order to create a closer bond, these men and women need to learn how to trust the people they love.

CHILDREN AND FAMILY

Aquarian natives take interesting things from their childhood, and February 1 people are no exception. They have the ability to look beyond the shortcomings of parents in order to glimpse the characteristics that define the greater reality. They understand that they have the power to transcend their beginnings instead of remaining trapped in them.

As parents, February 1 men and women are surprisingly strict with little ones.

HEALTH

People born on this date usually take a casual attitude toward diet and exercise. Although they may go through periods when they adhere to a restrictive regimen, in general they trust their own instincts regarding what is and is not good for them.

February 1 people have a tendency to turn to food or alcohol as means of escape when things go wrong. Yet they also have the ability to bounce back from these unhealthful habits once their emotions are under control. These individuals should refrain from depending upon sleeping pills—herbal tea is a much better alternative.

CAREER AND FINANCES

People born on this date enjoy work that offers freedom of schedule, and that allows them to move around.

Although these men and women have a casual attitude about money, they often seek the kind of high-powered success that translates to a big salary.

DREAMS AND GOALS

People born on this date have a desire to show their independence in all things. Whether in a relationship, a financial arrangement, or a professional choice, these men and women have a real flair for demonstrating their liberated status.

February 1 natives are unwilling to compromise their high standards in order to succeed. When they are young they may not be aware of how many times they will have to weigh ethics against getting what they want out of life.

EMBRACE
Exploration
Confidence
Leisure

AVOID
Superstition
Losing interest
Disappointment

ALSO BORN TODAY
Actress Sherilyn Fenn; actor Clark Gable; model Margaux Hemingway; comic Terry Jones; famous daughter Lisa Marie Presley; TV journalist Jessica Savitch; Monaco's Princess Stephanie; opera diva Renata Tebaldi.

FEBRUARY 2

People born on this date have a thoroughly modern outlook on life, no matter what their age. These classy men and women seem ageless, and their physical attractiveness testifies to their need to present themselves in the most favorable way.

February 2 natives are sticklers for honesty and will tell the truth even if it shows them in a bad light. They need to display their unconventional personality and embrace controversial issues.

FRIENDS AND LOVERS Building close friendships isn't an easy process for people born on this date. February 2 people inevitably feel a need to hold something of themselves back. Even their closest friends do not know them as well as they believe.

For those born on this date, love can be problematic. No matter how deeply in love they may be, these people will always put their own concerns first. Sometimes they even unconsciously subvert a relationship because it interferes with what they may perceive to be their own best interests. This is not selfishness, but an instinct for emotional survival.

CHILDREN AND FAMILY February 2 people often bring a great deal of emotional baggage from childhood into their adult life. It's possible that they experienced an unsatisfactory relationship with a parent or sibling, which negatively affected their upbringing. While it's likely that these differences can be bridged in later years, February 2 people have a tendency to remain estranged from family members.

People born on this date may have to face the unresolved issues from childhood before they can undertake a parental role themselves. If this is not possible for them, they may choose to remain childless.

HEALTH February 2 individuals have a strong, healthy constitution, and for this reason they may take foolish risks with their own health and safety at times. They love the combination of high speed and danger.

Allergies can be a problem for February 2 people. Though they should not avoid conventional cures, these men and women should also seek holistic treatments. Acupuncture can be helpful.

CAREER AND FINANCES People born on this date look for careers that let them make their own hours. These folks don't like to be accountable to anyone. They would rather take a job that gives them all the freedom they want and little money.

Despite their seeming indifference to money, February 2 people have considerable talent for managing their financial affairs, as well as those of other people.

DREAMS AND GOALS Liberty and self-determination are the chief life-goals of February 2 people. They don't care what they have to do or what they have to give up, as long as it provides them with the autonomy they require.

People born on this date do not see achievement as a linear path. They are more concerned with amassing life experiences that will help them in their quest to reach their full potential—as they see it.

EMBRACE
Good choices
Lost causes
Quietude

AVOID
Subjugation of goals
Bad habits
Loose talk

ALSO BORN TODAY
Model Christie Brinkley; singer Garth Brooks; novelist James Dickey; actress Farah Fawcett; violinist Jascha Heifitz; novelist James Joyce; columnist Liz Smith; actress Elaine Stritch.

FEBRUARY 3

People born on February 3 are talented, modest, and completely charming. These men and women have the capacity to see both the big picture and life's small details.

February 3 natives are not as extreme as most Aquarians. They can be eccentric, yet may choose to shelter themselves beneath a personality that reflects rather conventional views. They put their faith in careful planning, knowing that sooner or later all their hard work and research will pay off.

FRIENDS AND LOVERS

Because of their tendency to cultivate impressive friendships, February 3 men and women are sometimes seen as opportunists who care more about appearances than they do about relationships between people. Although it's true that they have some very specific criteria for friendship, this in no way supposes that these people are only looking for well-connected friendships.

Love is a very serious matter for these people. They don't play emotional games and dislike individuals who do. When they are interested in someone they make their intentions clear, though in a very diplomatic way.

CHILDREN AND FAMILY

People born on this date are devoted to family life. They often have a very close relationship with family members, particularly a father or father figure. They love getting together with grown siblings.

February 3 natives make good, if somewhat demanding, parents. They have a very strict code of conduct and expect their youngsters to follow suit.

HEALTH

People born on this date have a very exacting nature that is revealed in the way they handle health matters. They're dedicated to keeping fit and looking good, no matter how much time and effort it takes. At some point they may decide to have surgery to enhance some part of their anatomy—but that's a big step, and people born today should closely examine their motives before making that sort of commitment.

Because they are so health-conscious, February 3 people usually eat moderately. They enjoy preparing food, since this assures them of its high-quality, low-fat content.

CAREER AND FINANCES

These very determined individuals enjoy working in careers that allow them to exercise power in a positive way. Since February 3 people have a strong sense of humanitarianism, they are always happy to use what power they have in order to shift the focus to those less fortunate.

Commanding a good salary is another way for February 3 men and women to contribute to the causes that matter to them.

DREAMS AND GOALS

February 3 individuals are expert organizers who are eager to use their talents for humanitarian aims. These caring people have a strong conscience, which balances their seemingly narcissistic side.

People born on this date can focus on a project to the exclusion of everything else in their lives. While they are involved with a particular enterprise, these men and women may be completely distracted and unable or unwilling to give attention to other tasks.

EMBRACE
Complex emotions
Wonders of nature
Happiness

AVOID
Emotional instability
Pretense
Self-interest

ALSO BORN TODAY
Comic Joey Bishop; actress Blythe Danner; actress Morgan Fairchild; football star Bob Griese; composer Felix Mendelssohn; illustrator Norman Rockwell; poet Gertrude Stein; football star Fran Tarkenton.

FEBRUARY 4

The men and women born on this date are so intelligent and quirky that they may give the impression of being "airheads"; in reality, though, they are much more practical than they seem to be.

February 4 people are inspired by their vision of what can be achieved through hard work. They have enormous self-discipline and can be extremely austere when it comes to cutting unnecessary encumbrances out of their life. These folks have little use for frivolous nonsense, and aren't ashamed to say so.

FRIENDS AND LOVERS

Strong friendships are among the greatest joys in the lives of February 4 people. Though they connect more on an intellectual than emotional level, these individuals don't rule out a spiritual component in their relationships.

Unfortunately, they are often less successful in their romantic relationships, though this is rarely their fault. These men and women often fall in love with people who don't live up to their own high standards.

CHILDREN AND FAMILY

February 4 natives learn many of their finest character traits from equally high-principled parents. Those born on this date often seem to be born into households where a valued tradition of ethics, morality, and humanitarianism is commonplace.

These men and women make the best-intentioned parents, though they have a tendency to be somewhat preachy at times. They are a very strong force in the lives of their children, and continue to play this role long after their youngsters are grown.

HEALTH

February 4 people often learn mental toughness through physical self-discipline. These men and women really enjoy putting themselves through the paces. Hiking, biking, wilderness training, and deep-sea diving all accord with their idea of what it takes to develop an edge.

People born on this date enjoy the sense of power that comes from feeling fit and derive considerable satisfaction from staying young in body as well as in mind.

CAREER AND FINANCES

Humanitarian and social issues are the chief concerns of people born on this date. These people often seek careers in medicine, law enforcement, human resources, marriage and family counseling, the clergy, social work, or government.

February 4 people are not interested in money for what it can buy, but for what it can accomplish for others through them. They are never frivolous spenders.

DREAMS AND GOALS

If only half of all the goals February 4 people envision come true, they will consider themselves extremely fortunate. These men and women realize that they are often tilting at windmills, yet their deep sense of commitment makes it impossible for them to behave any other way.

People born on this date are often less successful with making their personal dreams come true. They may not really know what they want out of life for themselves because so much of their time and effort is used to help others.

EMBRACE
Being at ease with oneself
Giving thanks
Daring

AVOID
A critical demeanor
Public opinion
Truculence

ALSO BORN TODAY
Singer Clint Black; feminist author Betty Friedan; symphony conductor Erich Leinsdorf; aviator Charles Lindbergh; actress/director Ida Lupino; Argentine President Isabel Peron; U.S. Vice President Dan Quayle; football star Lawrence Taylor.

FEBRUARY 5

People born on this date have an intense and magnetic personality. Paradoxically, perhaps, they also have a loner mentality and keep to themselves, though they do indeed possess an ability to shine socially.

These men and women are haughty yet lovable. They have a very strong code of behavior and generally have equally strong religious or spiritual beliefs. There is very little in their attitude that marks them as a "joiner." February 5 people have a thoroughly modern outlook, but are very set in their ways.

FRIENDS AND LOVERS
Because the men and women born on this date are intensely private, they regard their personal relationships as sacrosanct. They often learn a great deal about themselves from their friendships, choosing individuals who can expose them to attitudes they need to learn.

In terms of romance, February 5 individuals struggle to commit to a lasting relationship. This has nothing to do with faithfulness, but rather displays their constant need for variety. When they do become involved, it's often with a partner who can bring some much-needed stability into their lives.

CHILDREN AND FAMILY
February 5 natives often show signs of their introspective nature from a very early age. If they are not an only child, it's likely that there is a distance of more than a few years between themselves and another sibling.

These men and women are very good at parenting, infusing it with the same measure of fairness and equality they bring to all other important facets of life.

HEALTH
Since many people born on this date tend toward a sedentary lifestyle, they have a special need for a regimen that includes a healthy diet and a regular workout routine.

February 5 men and women are highly sensitive individuals who generally suffer from sleep disorders, especially if important areas of their lives are in flux. In order to restore a sense of calm, they need to refrain from caffeine.

CAREER AND FINANCES
People born on this date are drawn to careers that allow them to do their work in private. They excel as researchers in any field, though medicine and the sciences are high on their list. They also are well-suited to be musicians, writers, computer programmers, or mathematicians.

They're indifferent about handling their finances, and often turn that job over to a professional.

DREAMS AND GOALS
February 5 people like to establish emotional boundaries. They have a great fear of being hurt by others and feel safe only when they have control of the relationship.

Because they are often deeply engrossed in their professional career, February 5 men and women place less importance on their personal lives than most people. Yet when they manage to find a relationship that works for them, they are spiritually and emotionally energized, and better able to handle all aspects of life, without burying themselves in work.

EMBRACE
That special talent
Mental energy
Ecstasy

AVOID
Foolish risks
Envy
Co-dependency

ALSO BORN TODAY
Baseball star Hank Aaron; comic/actor Red Buttons; actor Christopher Guard; presidential candidate Adlai Stevenson; actress Barbara Hershey; actress Jennifer Jason Leigh; football star Roger Staubach; actress Charlotte Rampling.

FEBRUARY 6

February 6 natives possess a strong sense of personal integrity and the ability to act as a mediator between disparate factions. These likable individuals have so much natural charm that even their personal and professional rivals are willing to compliment them.

People born on this date have the potential to become legendary. They embrace humanity and use their talents and personal goodness for the benefit of others.

FRIENDS AND LOVERS

These folks have a true gift for friendship and are eager to invite others into their circle. They encourage close friendships, even though they don't need them in order to complete themselves as people.

When February 6 individuals fall in love, it's likely to be forever. They are extraordinarily loyal and devoted to the one they love. Aquarians are not known for being especially sentimental, but with the right partner, February 6 people find it easy to open their hearts.

CHILDREN AND FAMILY

It's not uncommon for February 6 individuals to "rewrite" their own history, generally because a mundane, colorless background does not fit with the carefully constructed persona they tend to build for themselves in later years.

As parents, February 6 individuals may see themselves more as authoritarian figureheads than as an actual hands-on mother or father. Although they set high standards for their children, February 6 natives may not be particularly accessible on an emotional level—in obvious contrast to their treatment of their friends.

HEALTH

February 6 natives generally endorse the natural approach to good health. In this area of life they are oddly conventional, even old-fashioned.

February 6 men and women pay very little attention to what they eat. They don't count calories or obsess over their cholesterol level. However, they're adamant about getting plenty of outdoor exercise. These folks don't get much satisfaction from a walk on a treadmill, and would much rather head outside to row on a lake or chop some firewood.

CAREER AND FINANCES

People born on this date are exemplary in their ability to help others. They want to do something positive with their lives, which usually means involvement in the caring professions—medicine, therapy, social services—or other humanitarian arts.

February 6 men and women have a brilliant understanding of business tactics. They not only handle their own financial interests with skill, but are equally capable of handling other people's.

DREAMS AND GOALS

February 6 natives have the potential for greatness, though they seldom realize this fact themselves and usually need to have it pointed out to them by those who love them best. These people are true idealogues and find it difficult to reconcile their strong beliefs with the practical methods that are needed to bring them into actualization.

February 6 men and women have high ideals, and their primary goal is to uphold that code no matter what may interfere with that aim.

EMBRACE
Ideals
Honesty
Spiritual harmony

AVOID
Capitulation
Self-interest
Wasting resources

ALSO BORN TODAY
Pianist Claudio Arrau; TV journalist Tom Brokaw; singer Natalie Cole; singer Fabian; actress Gayle Hunnicutt; actor/manager Sir Henry Irving; U.S. President Ronald Reagan; baseball star Babe Ruth.

FEBRUARY 7

February 7 natives are very private people. Although they have a need to express strong opinions, they always manage to do so in a gracious and nonthreatening way.

Others may sense that these individuals have their own private agenda that they are not willing to share with others. Although this may indeed be the case, their great personal charm and sweetness make them popular on many levels.

FRIENDS AND LOVERS
People born on this date have a secret side to their nature that they only show to those closest to them. They possess a high degree of integrity in their dealings with all individuals and place their friends on the same level as family.

February 7 people may be slow to commit to love, but once they do, the relationship takes on a spiritual significance in their life. These men and women are not romantic in the traditional sense, because they have a keen dislike for sentimentality.

CHILDREN AND FAMILY
February 7 natives may experience strong feelings of reincarnation in regard to their relationship with family members. There is likely to be an almost mystical closeness between February 7 people and their siblings—a closeness that continues into adulthood.

As parents, February 7 men and women are liberal in allowing their children to experience life at their own pace. They believe in establishing standards, but not emotionally intrusive ones.

HEALTH
People born on this date take charge of their health. Any condition that could cause them to require professional treatment at some point in life is always met with an adamant and obstinate disregard for conventional medical care.

February 7 men and women believe in taking the holistic path, whether for a common cold or a life-threatening illness. Because they have the courage of their own convictions, they are not shy about talking to their regular health-care provider about a natural approach to wellness. In diet, they prefer to eat as many raw foods as possible and to supplement their meals with occasional dairy products and lean meat.

CAREER AND FINANCES
These people truly "live" their profession, not because they are alienated from their personal lives, but because they value their work. Career choices made by these men and women are never random, but reflect whatever is valuable in their lives. Big money is seldom a focus for February 7 people, who take a relaxed attitude toward the dollar's importance.

DREAMS AND GOALS
People born on this date have a strong need to make their ideas and opinions heard. This attitude affects every important act of life and comprises their spiritual and intellectual base.

February 7 men and women do not pursue professional goals in a linear fashion, but are adventuresome, looking for life to provide some of the answers. They often make seemingly bizarre but smartly intuitive changes in their life-path—changes that inevitably turn out well.

EMBRACE
Morality
Truth
Transcendental awareness

AVOID
Bitterness
Emotional detachment
Lies

ALSO BORN TODAY
Actress Dora Bryan; novelist Charles Dickens; actor Miguel Ferrer; English statesman Sir Thomas More; actor James Spader; writer Gay Talese; musician Brian Travers; novelist Laura Ingalls Wilder.

FEBRUARY 8

A certain spookiness is evident in the personality of individuals born on this date. These people have an enormously powerful life-force, with marked evidence of psychic awareness. Although they may appear almost sphinx-like in their particular brand of emotional isolation, February 8 individuals possess intensity on all levels. But before these men and women can use all the talents and gifts they have been given, they must first master—and understand—their personal power.

FRIENDS AND LOVERS Friends play a special role in the lives of February 8 natives. But in order for their friendships to work, they need to feel a strong sense of trust in the other person and in the relationship itself.

Romance may not deliver all that these men and women expect when they are very young. Later, when they have experienced their share of pain and broken hearts, they are likely to be rewarded with the true love they've been looking for.

CHILDREN AND FAMILY February 8 people may be unhappy with the way they were raised. When these men and women are adults this can create a sense of separateness from the rest of the family, or a desire to be estranged from them.

There may not be a strong emotional impetus for February 8 individuals to become parents, at least until after they have made peace with their own past. Once this area of their lives has been put in order, they are certain to feel more confident about giving love to a child.

HEALTH February 8 natives are very much centered in their own time. Therefore, whatever health influences are adrift in the public consciousness are likely to attract their interest.

In true Aquarian style, February 8 individuals are creatures of extremes. They may endorse a health plan one day, then throw it out for something radical the next. They may take pills for everything that ails them, then turn around and express disdain for all but the most pure and natural lifestyle.

CAREER AND FINANCES February 8 natives often have difficulty settling on a career. Because their interests are generally philosophical, it may be hard for them to find a twentieth-century equivalent. They have the potential to be excellent teachers, but they may lack the discipline and energy to stay focused on the task.

Money has a great significance for February 8 men and women, who appreciate the status it bestows upon them.

DREAMS AND GOALS People born on February 8 are often confused about their life-goals. This is because they know that when they choose one road, they are obligated to give up their exploration of another.

When they do finally make choices, February 8 men and women have the heart to follow through, though, predictably, questions continue to haunt them. The perfect freedom that these people seek doesn't exist—and they know that. But it doesn't keep them from trying to force their will upon an uncaring universe.

EMBRACE
Karmic lessons
Sensitivity
Spiritual harmony

AVOID
Carelessness
Scattering energies
Indifference

ALSO BORN TODAY
English Queen Mary I; actress Brooke Adams; novelist Jules Verne; actor James Dean; TV journalist Ted Koppel; actor Jack Lemmon; composer/conductor John Williams; actress Mary Steenburgen.

FEBRUARY 9

February 9 men and women are a unique combination of childlike innocence and great wisdom. They have a need to communicate their ideas through action. They don't merely espouse their beliefs—they *live* them.

There is often a great deal of struggle in the lives of these men and women, but they accept it with grace, knowing that they can only become what they envision as their true potential through hard work or even sadness.

FRIENDS AND LOVERS

The influence of friends is threaded through the lives of all those born on this date. February 9 people readily turn to those close to them for advice and sympathy, and are always eager to return the favor. If asked, they have the courage and the integrity to become involved in the problems of their friends, but only when they know they can help.

The love life of February 9 men and women is seldom an easy path. They go where their emotions take them, which, if not always wise, is inevitably honest.

CHILDREN AND FAMILY

February 9 natives are highly attuned to their background, and usually retain strong ties to the people and things from years past. Although they may have trouble getting along with some family members who don't understand their need for breaking with tradition, these people are generally amenable to the rhythms of family life.

People born on this day make remarkable parents. They don't expect perfection from their kids any more than they expect it from themselves.

HEALTH

People born on this date tend to their health through a mixture of common sense and superstition. They seem to have a cure for just about every ailment under the sun, many of which are borrowed from herbal treatments and New Age symbology.

February 9 people are great believers in natural foods. They typically prefer organically grown produce because of the harm pesticides and other chemicals can cause.

CAREER AND FINANCES

These men and women have an aura of vitality that draws them to careers in the spotlight, despite their very private nature. They get along wonderfully with people and work well in partnership with others. Because they have a strong sense of moral obligation, February 9 people often pursue careers that allow them to showcase their political or philosophical alliances.

People born on this date are practical about money; they are extremely budget-conscious and have a gift for managing on a small amount of money.

DREAMS AND GOALS

February 9 folks have untold optimism about their dreams and goals. They might not have a linear plan, but their unconventional methods manage to make things happen.

People born on this date don't look at their humanitarian dreams as personal goals, but as logical progressions on their spiritual path. These men and women are not content to sit back passively and wait for things to happen, but rush headlong toward their dreams.

EMBRACE
Belief
Liberality
Ethics

AVOID
Hostility
Ill-wishes
Unpredictability

ALSO BORN TODAY
Astrologer Evangeline Adams; actor Ronald Colman; actress Mia Farrow; novelist Anthony Hope; singer/songwriter Carole King; poet/critic John Ruskin; actress Lana Turner; writer Alice Walker.

357

FEBRUARY 10

People born on this date are high-energy types whose ambition for worldly success is grounded in motives other than materialism. Although these men and women have a strong belief in their abilities, they have nothing of the egocentric about them.

True to their Aquarian roots, February 10 people use their own resources to help others. These individuals have a natural desire to fight for the underdog. Their ability to see beyond their own selfish concerns is one of the characteristics that makes them so praiseworthy.

FRIENDS AND LOVERS
When it comes to making friends, those born on February 10 are as good as it gets. These people have a real concern and love for others, and are able to look at the total person without any judgment or pettiness. Their criteria for friendship are high-minded, and include being able to share thoughts, feelings, and opinions without emotional rancor.

February 10 natives are anything but conventional in love and romance. Their reputation for fickleness isn't really deserved, as it's grounded in their inability to commit on a long-term basis.

CHILDREN AND FAMILY
It's not uncommon for people born on this day to keep their growing-up years a closely guarded secret. This is generally for a very specific reason, often related to their inability to resolve painful childhood issues. Until they learn to face these issues, they can't move successfully beyond them.

Often, it's not until they mature and have children of their own that these folks are able to put the ghosts of the past to rest. They are protective, nurturing parents who give their children what they feel they missed at that age.

HEALTH
February 10 people lead a fairly active life that frees them from the worry of weight gain. Yet these folks always seem to be on a diet, even when their weight is just fine.

Meditation can be a big help to those born on this date. If they learn to handle problems through stress-reduction techniques, they can make major strides toward an understanding of what is best for them.

CAREER AND FINANCES
February 10 people are clever, quick learners. They enjoy doing things on the fly and may not have the patience to pursue careers that require long years of training. They make excellent social workers, teachers, marriage and family counselors, hypnotherapists, or members of the clergy.

These folks are very generous with their money, but not in a frivolous way.

DREAMS AND GOALS
Smart use of their talents and resources to help others make their dreams come true is one of the chief goals of people born on this date. They see themselves as leaders who have it in their power to bring about change for the better.

In their personal lives, February 10 men and women seek to bridge the gap between the loneliness they may have experienced as a child and the sense of peace and contentment they seek in later life. They often turn to therapy or self-hypnosis in order to resolve these issues.

EMBRACE
Fellowship
Self-determination
Honesty

AVOID
Mediocrity
Worry
Irresponsibility

ALSO BORN TODAY
Writer Bertolt Brecht; actress Laura Dern; singer/songwriter Donovan; singer Roberta Flack; actress Joyce Grenfell; novelist Boris Pasternak; swimming champion Mark Spitz; actor Robert Wagner.

FEBRUARY 11

hese unique people understand the powerful forces that can be commanded with discipline and training. They have a single-mindedness that allows them to sacrifice in order to bring a life-goal to fruition.

Yet despite the seriousness of their commitment, these men and women have a sunny side. They're able to balance many different elements in their personal lives without losing focus or their emotional centeredness.

FRIENDS AND LOVERS February 11 natives seem to feel that no one can have too many friends. No matter how many people find their way into the intimate circle of these men and women, February 11 people manage to treat them all with the affection usually reserved for family members.

People born on this date may have a colorful love life, even if it must play second fiddle to their professional goals during their twenties and thirties. By the time these men and women finally settle down, they're ready for a permanent commitment. Despite their reputation for enjoying the good life, February 11 natives can show a decidedly domestic side to their personality.

CHILDREN AND FAMILY February 11 individuals grow up early. They have tremendous emotional resonance and often show a marked precocity in their childhood. If their parents were sensitive and supportive, February 11 men and women are living testaments to how parents can make a positive difference in the lives of their children.

People born on this date often put off starting a family until later in life because of career commitments. When they do become parents, they're more than equal to the task.

HEALTH Sleep isn't just a usual requirement for February 11 men and women—it's an emotional necessity. These folks depend upon their nightly dream activity for creative impetus.

Nightly meditation and prayer also help to facilitate that oh-so-necessary dream life. The physical health, too, of people born on this day responds very well to this regimen.

CAREER AND FINANCES These men and women are highly competitive by nature. Because they're determined to make it to the top of their profession, they'll go to great lengths and endure hardship in order to achieve their aims.

The typical February 11 native is adept at making money and even better at handling it. Even where there are considerable resources to look after, these people retain their budget-minded ways.

DREAMS AND GOALS February 11 people are among the most goal-oriented of the yearly cycle. They often begin to prepare for their chosen career while still children. During the intervening years, they learn lessons about sacrifice and focus.

Once they achieve major career goals, February 11 men and women are likely to set even greater goals. These people are all about commitment and find it hard to walk away from any sort of challenge.

EMBRACE
Sensitivity
Concern for others
Emotional high

AVOID
Perfectionism
Excessive temperament
Exhaustion

ALSO BORN TODAY
Singer Sheryl Crow; inventor Thomas Edison; actress Tina Louise; film director Joseph Mankiewicz; fashion designer Mary Quant; actor Burt Reynolds; novelist Sidney Sheldon; actress Kim Stanley.

FEBRUARY 12

Men and women born on February 12 have quiet strength. Their wisdom is based on karmic rather than worldly experience, yet they have the ability to live according to society's material constraints.

These men and women possess enough spiritual power to heal the psychic wounds of others. Although they may seem ordinary, even conventional, these people are cut from a different cloth. Their Aquarian nature helps to draw people from various walks of life into their circle, yet February 12 individuals remain loners at heart.

FRIENDS AND LOVERS
Although February 12 folks enjoy the company of others, they have a difficult time making close friends. They love people, yet there are times when they feel burdened by the responsibility of helping friends solve their problems.

The men and women born on this date like to feel as if they can attract the most eligible romantic partners. Despite their serious side, they possess a haughty personality, and enjoy showing off on the social scene.

CHILDREN AND FAMILY
It's not uncommon for February 12 men and women to idealize their family background. This attitude is usually related to an overwhelming love for family members, and happy memories that have grown sweeter with the passage of years.

February 12 people make good parents because they never really let go of their childhood innocence. Even with all their knowledge and wisdom, these remarkable people manage to retain an understanding of what it means to be a child.

HEALTH
People born on this date enjoy exercise and don't care how hard they need to work, or how often, in order to keep themselves in good physical condition. They also understand the emotional benefits that flow from an active lifestyle.

The desire to look good is another factor that keeps February 12 men and women on their toes. These people like to make a positive impression on others.

CAREER AND FINANCES
February 12 men and women can exhibit incredible single-mindedness in career choices. Although they possess a high level of intelligence, much of their energy is expressed through artistic or spiritual means.

People born on this date don't have a great deal of confidence in their ability to handle money. They may have been brought up to believe that the pursuit of money is wrong, or they may be fearful about not being able to provide for their family.

DREAMS AND GOALS
Smart use of their psychic awareness for practical applications in life is the chief goal of February 12 people. These men and women are capable of doing spectacular things, but they must first learn to assimilate the two sides of their personality and stop feeling uncomfortable with that disparity.

Emotionally, February 12 individuals are distance runners, not sprinters. When they set their sights on a goal, they have the grit and determination to see it through to the close.

EMBRACE
Positive attitude
Confidence
Destiny

AVOID
Depression
Disinterest
Failure

ALSO BORN TODAY
Actress Maud Adams; writer Judy Blume; naturalist Charles Darwin; TV personality Arsenio Hall; U.S. President Abraham Lincoln; actor Simon Mac-Corkindale; basketball star Bill Russell; film director Franco Zeffirelli.

FEBRUARY 13

People born on this date are go-getters. Overcoming odds is what these folks live for, and they may even invite a struggle when there's no need to do so! They're natural scrappers.

February 13 natives have incredible energy, though they may not always use it wisely. They find it easy to get through life on their charm and good looks, and often pick up a reputation for being superficial—that's misleading, since their glitter is only one side of their personality.

FRIENDS AND LOVERS For February 13
people, every day is a party. These good-hearted, fun-loving men and women don't expect a lot from their friends—only good companionship and an occasional shoulder to lean on.

Romantically, February 13 natives are in great demand. They have a hard time settling down, because they enjoy the free and easy lifestyle of being single. They're likely not to experience a grand passion until later in life. The attachment that results from this encounter can be galvanizing for them. Commitment isn't usually a part of their vocabulary—until the right mate comes along.

CHILDREN AND FAMILY People born on
this date may carry a lot of emotional baggage into adulthood. This could be the result of a troubled relationship with a parental figure—particularly a mother—who did not provide the nurturing that February 13 individuals need in order to feel good about themselves later in life. This is a governing factor that keeps February 13 natives from wanting to have children of their own, though when they do they are better able to resolve issues from their past.

HEALTH Many February 13 people are heavy
smokers. Alcohol can also be a problem for people born on this date, especially if they use it to cover up some perceived inadequacy in their personality. At some point, most February 13 individuals undertake a serious health regimen. Although their commitment is unlikely to last, it does provide an interlude of health consciousness.

CAREER AND FINANCES With their
clever chatter and dazzling personality, February 13 people seem as though they've just stepped out of an endless party. Yet they do possess a more serious side. Where professional matters are concerned, these charming people thrive in jobs that give them a forum for their considerable personal appeal. Their real star quality may lead them into the performing arts.

Although they give the impression of being unstable, February 13 men and women have a talent for handling money, particularly with smart investments.

EMBRACE
Wise choices
Moderation
Faithfulness

AVOID
Ignoring details
Insincerity
Gloating

ALSO BORN TODAY
Musician Peter Hook; actress Carol Lynley; actor David Naughton; novelist Georges Simenon; actress Kim Novak; actor Oliver Reed; First Lady Bess Truman; actor George Segal.

DREAMS AND GOALS Like other mem-
bers of their sign, February 13 men and women have an unconventional view of what constitutes worldly success. Their goals may be a bit unusual but can be achieved with determination and focus.

February 13 natives are concerned with life-goals. They don't generally put all their ambition into career aims, preferring to indulge the personal side of their life. These people are happiest when their relationships with others are successful.

FEBRUARY 14

These high-strung, interesting people possess an analytical intelligence that allows them to tackle complex problems without losing sight of the practical side issues. Their verbal skills are considerable.

February 14 men and women have a bold, sometimes reckless attitude toward life. They also have an edgy charm that makes them irresistible. But while it's their flamboyant attitude that gets them noticed, they really impress with their cleverness and way with words.

FRIENDS AND LOVERS People born on this date attract the spotlight with little effort. From an early age, they're able to pull people into their orbit. Friendship is an easy art for these men and women to master, and because of that fact they may not work at it as diligently as they could.

Romance is another area of life where February 14 people shine. They thrive in the dating scene, and yet—perhaps because of the romantic influence of their birthdate—they are more likely to fall passionately in love than others of their sign.

CHILDREN AND FAMILY February 14 natives often grow up in an unconventional family. Either there was a great deal of moving and changing of schools, or a step-family atmosphere. As parents, these men and women encourage their children to take chances and follow their own path. Drawing on the very best of their own upbringing, February 14 people provide a creative environment for their youngsters.

HEALTH Mental stresses and strains will have a negative impact on the health of most February 14 people. When they're relaxed and worry-free, they feel great. But when they experience a great deal of pressure at work or suffer under the weight of money worries, these individuals are likely to experience nightmares or sleeplessness, headaches, nausea, or simple fatigue.

February 14 people aren't devotees of exercise, but they do enjoy playing sports. A softball game or a round of golf with friends are their ideas of a workout.

CAREER AND FINANCES People born on this date are interested in careers that don't demand too much of their time and effort. They're accustomed to things coming to them with ease, and so a job that requires them to put in additional hours or sacrifice a great deal of their personal life is not generally to their liking.

Money is another matter. Even February 14 people who don't have considerable financial resources behave as though they were born to the silk. These men and women can run up tremendous credit card bills if they aren't careful.

DREAMS AND GOALS February 14 natives are not especially goal-oriented, yet they do have a passion for pursuing their dreams. The optimism of these men and women makes them believe that anything worthwhile can—and eventually will—happen.

If an especially cherished wish is not fulfilled, February 14 people refuse to look at it as a failure or even a setback; instead, they simply find themselves another dream to chase.

EMBRACE
Imagination
Romance
Sophistication

AVOID
Mental exhaustion
Prejudice
False hope

ALSO BORN TODAY
Journalist Carl Bernstein; TV personality Hugh Downs; writer Frank Harris; dancer Gregory Hines; union president Jimmy Hoffa; football star Jim Kelly; film director Alan Parker; actress Meg Tilly.

FEBRUARY 15

People born on this date exude sophistication and glamour, and they possess an aura of mystery and charm that easily impresses others. These men and women are the very picture of romanticism.

Yet despite their seemingly benign persona, these men and women possess a caustic wit. Their sarcasm is usually reserved for extreme situations, but most of their loved ones feel its sting at one time or another.

FRIENDS AND LOVERS From a very early age, February 15 people become aware of their talent to make friends and influence people. These men and women have incredible personality. Although they have the ability to manipulate people, they have far too much integrity to do so.

People born on this day give the impression of a quiet, smoldering temperament, even though they are likely to be very different. Their dreamy eyes and aristocratic good looks have the power to charm just about anyone. When they fall deeply in love, they let go of their reservations about romance.

CHILDREN AND FAMILY In contrast to their somewhat eccentric nature, February 15 people believe in tradition and are likely to carry a great many of their childhood illusions into adulthood.

February 15 natives are loving and nurturing parents. They're creative people who know how to fuel the imagination of their children. Since there may have been some discord in their childhood, these men and women do their best to give their youngsters a stress-free environment.

HEALTH Because they are naturally robust, February 15 men and women seldom experience any serious health challenges unless they experience an emotional problem in their lives.

Sleep disorders also can undermine their health. If they do experience problems in this area a safe, nondrug approach, such as raspberry leaf or camomile tea, will help.

CAREER AND FINANCES One of the weaknesses of the February 15 person is his or her inability to stick with a project long enough for it to become a career springboard. These men and women are accustomed to things coming easily to them and don't always respond well to challenges.

The situation is much the same with money. If they have ample resources, February 15 natives can become weak and unmotivated, with nothing to inspire them. Also, they can be very free with credit cards and need to learn some rules about cash-only spending.

DREAMS AND GOALS Maintaining their own legend without letting it get the best of them is a goal of February 15 people. These men and women have a great many gifts, but need to learn how to use them to their full potential.

February 15 natives are often dependent upon their love relationships to give them the satisfaction they want out of life. But in order to make this dream a reality they must be truthful about their feelings and not allow a false sense of happiness to prevail simply because they're afraid to look deeper.

EMBRACE
Practicality
Honest emotions
Credibility

AVOID
Shallowness
Frivolous emotions
Excesses

ALSO BORN TODAY
Activist Susan B. Anthony; screen legend John Barrymore; model/actress Marisa Berenson; actress Claire Bloom; cartoonist Matt Groening; comedian Harvey Korman; singer Melissa Manchester; actress Jane Seymour.

FEBRUARY 16

Easygoing and generous, February 16 natives give freely of their time and talents. These people have a relaxed, laid-back attitude toward life that endears them to everyone.

Yet despite their pleasant facade, February 16 men and women are perfectionists who have a commitment to excellence in every aspect of life. When they involve themselves in a project, they give it everything they have. Known for their ability to see the big picture, February 16 folks are equally at home with details.

FRIENDS AND LOVERS People born on this date have the kind of temperament that not only wins the affection of those around them, but respect, as well. Because they're secure enough in their relationships to let friendship take its own course, these men and women don't make emotional demands on their friends,

February 16 people are equally fair-minded in their attitude toward romantic partners. These people never encumber their relationships with petty jealousy or displays of temperament. If career conflicts arise, February 16 people are always ready to play the role of cheerleader for their mate.

CHILDREN AND FAMILY February 16 people are wise enough to understand their ties to the past. Indeed, they are dutiful sons and daughters, often taking on heavy responsibilities within the family when still very young. Yet

instead of becoming bitter, February 16 people manage to put a positive spin on events.

There are few people who make better parents than these men and women. Not only are they affectionate and caring, but they possess an uncanny ability to know exactly what each child needs from them, emotionally and spiritually.

HEALTH People born on this day are constantly in search of the newest information regarding health and fitness, and they take a very active role in nutrition. They are excellent cooks with a flair for combining great taste with good nutrition.

Also, they have a fondness for sports of all kinds, which fuels their competitive nature. Also, walking or running in a pastoral setting provides February 16 people with physical exercise that also enriches their spirit.

CAREER AND FINANCES These folks seek variety in the work they do. They lose interest in a job that doesn't challenge them intellectually. They constantly strive toward new horizons, putting past accomplishments and mistakes behind them with equal vigor.

People born on this date look for clever way to stretch the budget. They have a good head for business—and the makings of an entrepreneur.

DREAMS AND GOALS The goal of February 16 people is to never get so caught up in work or other serious matters that they forget to stop and smell the roses. These people are dedicated to getting the maximum amount of excitement out of life, and are bold enough to take chances in order to make that come true.

February 16 men and women are concerned with making their personal relationships work. Success in this area of their life rivals all other accomplishments.

EMBRACE
Versatility
Acceptance of change
Mastery

AVOID
Quitting
Discouragement
Lost opportunities

ALSO BORN TODAY
Congressman/entertainer Sonny Bono; actor LeVar Burton; ballet dancer Anthony Dowell; singer/songwriter James Ingram; actor William Katt; tennis star John McEnroe; film director James Schlesinger; musician Andy Taylor.

FEBRUARY 17

February 17 individuals subscribe to a "grand design" that formulates the basis of their actions. These people are stable and intense, with strong views. And yet they prefer to express themselves through nonverbal communication.

People born on this date have a need to keep their emotions in check, because they fear the intensity of their feelings. They give the impression of someone who is strong and capable, yet there are times when February 17 people feel very much on the edge. This repressed tension creates a persona that is tiring for them and exciting to others.

FRIENDS AND LOVERS
These men and women cultivate friendships only when the relationships promise meaningful emotional rewards. The superficial trappings of social relationships mean little to them.

Where romance is concerned, February 17 individuals may experience somewhat unusual circumstances. Periods of intense sexual activity may be followed by periods of enforced abstinence. Many February 17 natives avoid marriage for fear that it will not live up to their expectations.

CHILDREN AND FAMILY
There is a natural dignity about these people that marks them, even as children, as special. They are precocious emotionally and intellectually.

These people have a lot to offer as parents. Even though they adopt an authoritarian attitude at times, they also know how to be compassionate and loving.

HEALTH
People born on this date are often very careful about their health, especially if a family-related condition has them feeling vulnerable. It's important that February 17 men and women engage in frequent weight-bearing exercise in order to keep their joints limber and to avoid loss of bone mass as they grow older.

Diet can provide even more help. Spinach and other green leafy vegetables have much more calcium than milk or other high-fat dairy products. A daily "health cocktail" of freshly juiced spinach, carrot, and cucumbers gives February 17 people the calcium and vitamins they need, with very few calories.

CAREER AND FINANCES
When they do have a forum for their true personality, they can impress people with their charm and good manners. These people do well in any work that allows them to serve as a public spokesperson or to work with the public at large.

If these folks are blessed with considerable financial resources, they exhibit great generosity to others. While they do like to spend money on luxury items, they also like to invest in art, antiques, and other items with the potential for increased value.

DREAMS AND GOALS
February 17 men and women want to succeed even as they play by the rules. These straight-arrow individuals often start laying career plans in childhood.

While financial security and career success are high on the list of goals for February 17 people, they are even more concerned with maintaining the meaning and integrity of their personal relationships.

EMBRACE
Self-satisfaction
Dependability
Practice

AVOID
Derision
Dependence
Losing faith

ALSO BORN TODAY
Singer Marian Anderson; actor Alan Bates; actress Brenda Fricker; basketball star Michael Jordan; actor Hal Holbrook; novelist Ruth Rendell; actor Lou Diamond Phillips; singer/songwriter Gene Pitney.

FEBRUARY 18

February 18 individuals are dedicated to the art of perfection. These unique men and women have the ability to transcend the mundane trivia of everyday life in order to become something truly special.

These people not only attract controversy—they actually thrive on it! Quiet and introspective, they have what it takes to become emotionally self-sufficient. Leaning on others for support makes them feel weak and ineffectual. When challenges come their way, they bear up stoically.

FRIENDS AND LOVERS The men and women born on this date are very selective about the people they bring into their circle. While they have an open-minded, liberal style, February 18 people are far more critical than other members of their sign. Friends are often chosen for their discretion and ability to keep confidences.

February 18 people despise sentimentality in romance. To them, true love is the fusing of two souls, mated by a passion that is both physical and intellectual. These men and women are looking for a soul mate and are likely to remain unattached until they find exactly what, and whom, they are looking for.

CHILDREN AND FAMILY Whatever their beginnings, February 18 natives always seem to stand alone. As children they may have been forced to accept adult-size responsibilities, and this is likely to have affected their lives in powerful ways. Many of the issues they take into their adult lives are rooted in a dissatisfying relationship with a demanding parental figure.

They are strict disciplinarians as parents, but they are also loving and supportive.

HEALTH February 18 people are extremists in almost every aspect of their lives. Fasting is often a part of their health regimen. A diet consisting primarily of raw fruits and vegetables, augmented by grains, nuts, and legumes, offers February 18 people everything they need. If they've been compulsive dieters in the past, this regimen provides weight loss without unhealthy consequences.

CAREER AND FINANCES People born on this date do not make career decisions rashly. They often know from a very early age what they want to do with their lives. Because of their strong humanitarian streak, February 18 people often bring a high level of political consciousness to their work. It's not possible for them to find happiness in a simple nine-to-five routine with few challenges. These people need to live for their work.

They have good taste and like living well, but would never subvert their beliefs simply to make a good salary.

DREAMS AND GOALS February 18 natives look at every goal as a personal challenge. They're tough on themselves, always looking to make each challenge more meaningful than the one that came before.

When they turn their unstinting vision on personal goals, February 18 people are just as motivated to succeed. To be a good spouse, a good parent, and a good citizen are all equally important to these conscientious individuals.

EMBRACE
Wisdom
Empathy
Purpose

AVOID
Making demands
Psychological strain
Irritability

ALSO BORN TODAY
Novelist Jean Auel; singer Juice Newton; artist Yoko Ono; actress Molly Ringwald; TV personality Vanna White; actress Cybill Shepherd; film director Milos Forman; actor John Travolta.

PISCES
February 19 - March 20

Pisces is the twelfth sign of the astrological year and is known by its astrological symbol, the Fish. Pisces natives are keenly in touch with their emotions, though never to the point of mawkishness. With Neptune as the ruling planet, people born under this sign are apt to be idealists who may do best when paired with a person who is by nature more pragmatic. Although Pisces men and women are physically and emotionally strong, they may put their hardiness to the test if they try to resolve the emotional conflicts of others.

THE PISCES MAN The men born under this sign have great personal warmth and charm. They are not afraid to show their vulnerabilities—in fact, they display them with pride. These individuals have a real need to connect with others on an emotionally satisfying level. For this reason the Pisces man may seek closure to his relationship with a distant, seemingly unloving father or mother well into his own middle age. And through his own role as parent or guardian he may try to relive or even remake his early-life relationships in order to spiritualize them.

This man is far more complicated than he seems. If his work or profession does not provide the sort of self-expression that he needs, he will look for it by way of hobbies, especially those that allow him to show his artistic or creative side. Relationships make up the primary focus of this man's life.

THE PISCES WOMAN The Pisces woman is mysterious, but not aloof. She possess an ageless charm that is enthralling to those who know her. Though she may be extremely attractive, she need not be beautiful or even pretty in order to draw attention to herself. Her capacity for sympathy and understanding is enough to make her stand out.

Pisces women, like Pisces men, find their greatest fulfillment through personal relationships, both romantic and platonic. If these matters are complicated or unsatisfactory, they may be unable to reach their own potential for specialness. Even when these women are extremely talented, they may not respect their own gifts. Many Pisces women are very self-conscious and need a stronger individual, usually a partner, to bring out their own best qualities.

THE PISCES CHILD Pisces children are dreamers. At times they may seem completely caught up in their illusions and unable to tell reality from fantasy. Although this may alarm parents, it is important for them to understand that when this child tells a lie, he or she is doing so not to get out of trouble, but to test his ability to invent an interesting scenario.

These little ones should be allowed to explore the limitless boundaries of imagination without fear of ridicule. Playing games of imagination with them from a very early age allows Pisces children to feel safe in exploring their creativity.

THE PISCES LOVER Pisces men and women have an idealistic view of love and romance. They look at the world, and love, through rose-colored glasses. Because of their sensitivity it is often inviting for them to prefer a fairy tale scenario to the real thing. Pisces know their vulnerabilities in love and are sometimes afraid that the magic "bubble" will burst.

If a Pisces man or woman has an unfulfilled romantic life there is the tendency for them to become suddenly promiscuous or celibate. The natural Piscean attitude is to seek escape either through or from the emotional experience that is causing them pain. The Piscean individual who is deeply in love may have an exaggerated desire to sacrifice themselves for their lover or partner. This appeals to their egoless nature, as well as to their idyllic notions of what romance is all about.

ELEMENT: Water
QUALITY: Mutable
PLANETARY RULER: Neptune
BIRTHSTONE: Aquamarine
FLOWER: Water lily
COLOR: Violet

KEY CHARACTERISTIC:
Compassion

STRENGTHS: Idealism,
Spirituality, Transcendence.
CHALLENGES: Escapism,
Weakness, Self-deception.

THE PISCES BOSS Because of their gentle nature, many Pisces individuals are not especially well-suited to positions of power in their working environment. It is sometimes difficult for these kind-hearted individuals to reprimand employees, even if they deserve it.

Pisces men and women are admirably suited to the more positive aspects of delegating authority. They have the ability to bring out the very best in their employees, always encouraging them to reach their highest potential.

THE PISCES FRIEND Friendship comes naturally to Pisceans. Their strong commitment to easing the pain of others often draws them to less fortunate, less happy individuals. But there is never any pity involved. Pisces men and women lend a dignity of spirit to every relationship they encounter. Although they may seem weak or unfocused at times, Pisces natives actually possess a deep core of spiritual strength that makes them genuinely sympathetic listeners.

Pisces individuals have strong links to the past and are likely to keep the same group of friends over a period of many years. Also, because of their intense familial ties, Pisces natives may count a sibling or other relative among their closest friends.

FEBRUARY 19

The intrepid people born on this date are eager to learn, to discover. They are restless, eccentrically spiritual, and emotionally fragile. Charming and attractive, they are also easily managed by others and are unable to assert their authority.

Governed by their emotions, February 19 people have the habit of being their own worst enemy at times. Though they are kindhearted and generous to a fault, these men and women have a hard time feeling good about themselves, and rely on validation from friends and lovers.

FRIENDS AND LOVERS
February 19 natives are always seeking the love and approval of others. This is typically Piscean, but it can become a habit that undercuts their self-confidence if left unchecked. It's not uncommon for February 19 individuals to allow themselves to be manipulated by so-called friends, just to retain their apparent affection.

Unfortunately, these mild-mannered men and women behave in the same way toward love interests. They are so anxious to be loved and cherished that they may be drawn into an unsatisfactory love affair.

CHILDREN AND FAMILY
Many people born on this day cling to their past as a way of trying to understand the present. They're strongly tied to their childhood memories. Whether these memories are happy or unhappy, the people born on this date hold onto them with grim determination.

By nurturing their own children, February 19 people find a way to nurture themselves. Their sensitivity and imagination are excellent tools for dealing with their youngsters.

HEALTH
February 19 natives often rely on food and drink and even drugs in order to escape their feelings and fears. Initially, their attitude is the real problem, but if they cannot break their bad habits, the dependencies become the problems—and quite serious ones.

The best thing February 19 people can do for their health is learn to deal with their insecurities head-on, rather than look to a substance to help them deal with it. When food is strictly food to these people, the problem disappears.

CAREER AND FINANCES
People born on this date have an artistic sensibility that often makes itself known in their career choices. These folks make excellent photographers, painters, decorators, fashion designers, models, and actors.

Most Pisces individuals are better at making money than at taking care of it, and February 19 people are no exception. These luxury-loving souls enjoy spending money, and balk at keeping to a strict budget. Credit spending should be avoided.

DREAMS AND GOALS
Although not particularly goal-oriented, February 19 natives are devoted to their dreams. Learning to move beyond potentially destructive role-playing can liberate these people from the bondage of insecurity.

Because of their selfless nature, many of their dreams are for others. These individuals have incredibly high ideals.

EMBRACE
The joy of giving
Ethics
Leadership

AVOID
Predictability
Censure
Irresponsibility

ALSO BORN TODAY
England's Prince Andrew; actor Jeff Daniels; film director John Frankenheimer; singer Holly Johnson; jazz musician Stan Kenton; actor Lee Marvin; writer Amy Tan; actress Merle Oberon.

FEBRUARY 20

en and women born on this date are deeply attuned to the spiritual mysteries of life. For these psychically attuned men and women, religiosity can become a virtual obsession.

These people possess a phenomenal memory. Their intelligence—though considerable—is more of an esoteric understanding than an analytical skill. These men and women have high ideals, though they aren't necessarily practical creatures.

EMBRACE
A sense of wonder
Perfection
Emotional resonance

AVOID
Doubts
Pretense
Sleep disorders

ALSO BORN TODAY
Basketball star Charles Barkley; singer/songwriter Buffy Sainte-Marie; singer Kurt Cobain; supermodel Cindy Crawford; actress Sandy Duncan; fashion designer Gloria Vanderbilt; actor Kelsey Grammer.

FRIENDS AND LOVERS Loneliness and a lack of self-confidence often cause February 20 natives to choose the worst possible companions. They're eager to feel "included," and may be willing to sacrifice a great deal in order to have a large circle of friends.

This attitude is destructive when it relates to romantic partnerships. These men and women have a habit of holding on to people who are bad for them, and until they learn to transform their obsessive love into more rational love, they will be unable to make romance work.

CHILDREN AND FAMILY Letting go of the past is very difficult for February 20 individuals. They may want to believe that their familial relationships were far more satisfying than they actually were, and that fantasy may become incredibly real to them.

Because of all the emotional baggage they bring into their adult life from childhood, February 20 people may feel insecure about becoming parents. If they do, they're often pleasantly surprised to discover that they can let go of the unwise choices of the past.

HEALTH Destructive habits relating to food and alcohol are not uncommon among February 20 people, who sometimes seek to hide from the stresses and emotional strains of everyday life.

These men and women need to find new, healthy addictions. By turning their attention to exercise and good nutrition, February 20 natives can turn their attitude around and create the healthy lifestyle they need and deserve.

CAREER AND FINANCES February 20 people combine a natural artistic ability with a deep spiritual understanding. Those with a particularly high level of psychic ability can become experts at mediumship and tarot card divination.

Money is rarely an issue with these people. Though they may spend it freely, February 20 folks seldom give any real thought as to where it comes from, or where it will go.

DREAMS AND GOALS To understand themselves through the power of their own psychic talent is one of the most important goals February 20 people can have. These men and women are often emotionally adrift in a sea of confusion. Their great psychic sensitivity can be a hindrance as much as a help. Yet once they begin to understand their power, they can liberate themselves from fear and delusion.

February 20 men and women need to learn how to set limits in their personal relationships. When they do, they'll be considerably calmer than before.

FEBRUARY 21

People born on this date are acquisitive without being materialistic. Security-oriented, they seek social prestige but are generous with the resources available to them. People close to these individuals know that they can always come to them for help without fear of being rebuked.

February 21 people are generally fun-loving, yet they embrace responsibility wholeheartedly, always hoping to up the ante in the game of life.

FRIENDS AND LOVERS As with most Pisceans, February 21 individuals are kind and giving, almost to a fault. They will literally do anything to help a friend, and without any concern as to what they might receive in return.

Unfortunately, few people have as much integrity as February 21 individuals, who are often hurt by the insensitivity of fickle or uncaring lovers. The search for someone who shares their need for commitment is the focal point in the lives of February 21 people.

CHILDREN AND FAMILY February 21 natives are extremely impressionable, so they are likely to retain many memories from childhood—both good and bad.

People born on this date may feel unable to take on the responsibility of another human being, fearful of not being up to the task. It is typical of February 21 people to underestimate their abilities, but when they do make a decision to have children, they turn out to be wonderful parents.

HEALTH The men and women born on this date have a tendency to get involved in New Age health practices that may seem odd and extreme to others. Practices such as aura cleansing, chakra balancing, and healing with crystals may all be components of their spiritual health regimen.

February 21 people are careful about what they eat, often adopting a restrictive diet for philosophical as well as health reasons. These people have a great love for food, but they prefer to substitute vegetables, fruits, and grains for fatty, high-calorie goodies.

CAREER AND FINANCES People born on this date have a natural affinity for artistic endeavors. They make talented artists, photographers, dancers, fashion designers, decorators, and poets. But no matter which career they follow, these individuals are excellent managers or supervisors.

February 21 people enjoy the good things of life but aren't especially fervent about getting ahead financially. This may be because things come easily to these people, even money. They seem able to make all the right choices without seeming ruthless or opportunistic.

DREAMS AND GOALS People born on this date are constantly striving to reconcile their spiritual and worldly concerns. These men and women have a real desire to succeed in the conventional sense, but they aren't willing to check their ethics at the door in order to do it.

Although highly motivated, February 21 people are not single-minded about success. To them, achievement means doing their best, without sacrificing other aspects of their life.

EMBRACE
Restraint
Prudence
Fiscal responsibility

AVOID
Intrigue
Spendthrift habits
Tension

ALSO BORN TODAY
Actor Christopher Atkins; singer Mary Chapin Carpenter; writer Jilly Cooper; actress Tyne Daly; entertainment mogul David Geffen; writer/diarist Anaïs Nin; film director Sam Peckinpah; singer Nina Simone.

FEBRUARY 22

The complex personality of February 22 individuals is sheltered behind a quiet facade. But these people have a great deal of personal courage, and are always ready to make tough decisions.

The winsome glamour of these individuals makes them lovable as well as interesting. Although they are extremely conscious of personal achievement, they are equally aware of the long and circuitous road they must take to get there. February 22 people often feel as if they are being directed more by fate than by their own will.

FRIENDS AND LOVERS
February 22 individuals have a deep appreciation for friendship. Because these men and women may not be as confident as they seem to be, they value the comments and support of those who will tell them the truth and lend emotional support when it's needed.

However, people born on this date may be less discriminating in their choice of romantic partners. They have an unrealistic view of love and always look for the happy ending. It's not impossible for February 22 people to find lasting happiness, but they must come to terms with reality first.

CHILDREN AND FAMILY
The significance of family life is hardwired into the psyche of people born on this date, and they are likely to spend a good part of their life living up to the example that was set for them—or living down the baggage that came with it.

Yet it's not always possible for these people to raise their own children in a different way, since they may be unable to repudiate their own upbringing.

HEALTH
Though not particularly robust, people born on this date have a high energy level that reflects their enthusiasm for life. Since escapism is a part of life for most Piscean individuals, it is important that they learn to channel this need in a positive, life-affirming direction.

These folks are at their physical best when they exist on a diet of fish, seafood, and fresh produce. By cleansing their bodies of harmful toxins and preservatives, they boost their stamina and lower the risk of depression.

CAREER AND FINANCES
Despite some grandiose dreams in their youth, February 22 people soon come to realize that the "rat race" is not for them. They are much happier and healthier when they live a simple life where their needs are taken care of, instead of one that indulges their wants and wishes.

Although any honest work suits them, they are considerably more devoted to the idea of spare time than overtime. One of the worst mistakes February 22 individuals can make is to live their life in a way that pleases other people rather than themselves.

DREAMS AND GOALS
More than anything else, February 22 people want to be allowed to live their life in a way they find pleasing. These men and women are merely being true to their own instincts when they ignore the fast lane and choose to go through life at their own pace.

EMBRACE
Affection
Lightheartedness
Achievement

AVOID
Betrayal
Confusion
A disillusioned heart

ALSO BORN TODAY
Actress Drew Barrymore; composer Frederic Chopin; film director Jonathan Demme; "Profumo Scandal" party girl Christine Keeler; Senator Edward Kennedy; astrologer Sybil Leek; poet Edna St. Vincent Millay; U.S. President George Washington.

FEBRUARY 23

People born on February 23 seek to experience reality through a singular, if somewhat unrealistic way. Their artistic bent is likely to be the main determination in whether or not they are able to accommodate this tendency, or resist it. These people have the ability to reach emotional fulfillment on many levels and are not limited to the more orthodox understanding of spirituality that sustains others. They discover reality through a heightened sensitivity that can be difficult for all but those who are closest to them to understand.

FRIENDS AND LOVERS Relationships—both romantic and platonic—are the single greatest influence in the lives of February 23 people. From a very early age they seek to meld comfortably with others, seeking their own identity through the prism of interpersonal experience.

Often February 23 individuals "live" the same relationship over and over again, exchanging one friend or love interest for another in a series of emotionally demanding and very intense unions.

CHILDREN AND FAMILY Family issues continue to play a part in the lives of those born on February 23 long after they have reached adulthood. These people often pursue an idyllic version of their growing-up years, even if the reality was quite different.

Fanciful and imaginative, people born on February 23 have no difficulty identifying with their own children. Desiring to connect with their youngsters on all levels, they can easily repeat their own parents' mistakes if they aren't careful. The saving grace is an almost preternatural ability to sense their children's emotional and spiritual needs.

HEALTH The high-strung disposition of those born on this date can contribute to a certain amount of "nervous" conditions, especially among women. But if enough attention is paid to satisfying creative and artistic needs, these folks are normally happy and healthy.

Regular exercise is a good way for February 23 people to deal with the daily stresses of life. Long walks in a lovely pastoral setting have positive effects on mind and body.

CAREER AND FINANCES February 23 individuals often gravitate to careers in the "caring" professions, such as medicine or social work. Artistic endeavors like painting, photography, or music can also channel the incredible creative energy of February 23 people.

Seldom, if ever, will a February 23 individual pursue a career path solely for financial gain, although they do make exceptional money managers.

DREAMS AND GOALS People born on this date cherish their illusions and seek to make them come true. When this is not possible they will pursue a philosophy or spiritual path that approximates what they really want out of life. Because they are dedicated to helping others, it is sometimes hard for them to concentrate on their own concerns. Men and women born on February 23 will measure their life experience against those of their friends and loved ones.

EMBRACE
The strength to dream
Creative inspiration
Tolerance

AVOID
Self-pity
Intolerant people
Striking an attitude

ALSO BORN TODAY:
Film director Victor Fleming; actor Peter Fonda; composer George Frederick Handel; actress Kathleen Harrison; musician Mike Maxfield; author William Shirer; musician Brad Whitford.

FEBRUARY 24

People born on this date have a natural dynamism that sets them apart from other Pisceans. These folks are go-getters who enjoy a varied and interesting social life.

These men and women may have difficulty finding a focus in their lives, but when they do they are true to it. This often comes in the form of humanitarian concerns that provide them with just the sort of involvement they need in order to keep their life in balance.

FRIENDS AND LOVERS
People born on this date collect friends of all types and backgrounds. These are sociable people who enjoy, though they do not need, a large circle of friends.

February 24 people are extremely romantic. They have a tendency to fall in love many times, and no matter how often their heart is broken they have the ability to bounce back. They are far more concerned with looking forward than wondering what might have been.

CHILDREN AND FAMILY
February 24 individuals may have a somewhat contentious relationship with family members, usually caused by their own highly favored position within the family.

Although people born on this date have good intentions, they may be overindulgent as parents. Wanting to give their children everything, they can sometimes overstep the bounds of common sense. When this happens, they create a spoiled and unmanageable child. February 24 people quickly realize that discipline is the most valuable lesson they can give their youngsters.

HEALTH
Health problems experienced by February 24 people are generally due to a lack of consistent self-maintenance. These men and women have difficulty keeping their level of motivation high.

These people need to stop looking for a magical cure-all and embrace a common-sense approach that includes sensible eating and normal, everyday exercise, such as walking. Meditation before bedtime improves sleep states.

CAREER AND FINANCES
People born on this date are drawn to the humanitarian professions: counseling, health care, child care, or the clergy. Empathetic rather than just sympathetic, they have the ability to understand the pain of others.

Money doesn't equal status in their minds, and although they enjoy living well, they can get along on very little if their circumstances demand it.

DREAMS AND GOALS
It's often the goal of people born on this date to have a goal! These folks may be confused about which direction they want to take in life, and they often benefit from the example of a friend or loved one who shows them the way.

February 24 people are sometimes slow to recognize their own talents. Even when they do, they may find that their material goals conflict with their spiritual needs. Learning to reconcile these two aspects is the greatest goal February 24 men and women can achieve.

EMBRACE
Trust
Good intentions
Faith

AVOID
Resistance
Formality
Pride

ALSO BORN TODAY
Actor Barry Bostwick; fantasy writer August Derleth; actor James Farentino; folklore writer Wilhelm Grimm; composer Michel Legrand; actor Edward James Olmos; actress Helen Shaver; TV journalist Paula Zahn.

FEBRUARY 25

eople born on this date are in tune with the world around them. They may possess an amazing psychic sensitivity that causes them to be drawn to a study of supernatural and occult wisdom.

These men and women have the potential to do great things, but they are even more powerful when they put their talents toward a cause greater than themselves. They understand themselves best through group involvement.

FRIENDS AND LOVERS
February 25 people favor a small group of close friends. They are likely to be mistrustful of purely social relationships, and do not as a rule pursue work-related friendships. Many people born on this date keep the same circle of friends for years—even for life.

These folks need to experience at least one wild romance in their life. They are attracted to love interests who share their mystical sensibilities. Clandestine love affairs provide the thrills and sense of danger they find indispensable to romance.

CHILDREN AND FAMILY
February 25 individuals have scrappy but loving relationships with family members. Problems that exist may relate to strong differences of opinion but are not strong enough to cause any real dissension.

As parents, February 25 people strive to give their children more than just material advantages. They wish to show their youngsters life's limitless possibilities that wait to be explored.

HEALTH
As is the case with many Pisceans, February 25 individuals have a rather casual attitude toward keeping fit. Although they understand the need to keep their spiritual and physical energies in balance, they may lack the discipline to carry out this approach.

They are easily influenced by the mood of the times. When something becomes trendy, they're likely to get involved, notably with newly chic forms of exercise and diet.

CAREER AND FINANCES
People born on this date have an instinct for understanding and empathizing with the problems and concerns of others. Their sensitivity to subjects such as addiction, depression, weight control, and difficult personal relationships makes them ideal counselors and therapists.

February 25 people aren't particularly motivated to make a lot of money, though they often fret about their financial security.

DREAMS AND GOALS
February 25 people look for ways to reconcile their psychic sensitivity with common-sense goals. These folks are ruled by instinct and intuition, yet they appreciate the value of an intellectual point of view, as well. When they learn to balance these two approaches, February 25 people find what they want in life.

Because their goals often change with their moods, these men and women are on a constant search for new challenges and new horizons.

EMBRACE
Partnership
Joy
Living in the moment

AVOID
Instability
Conceit
Distractions

ALSO BORN TODAY
Opera singer Enrico Caruso; actor Tom Courtenay; football star Carl Eller; composer George Frederick Handel; singer George Harrison; TV celebrity Sally Jessy Raphael; tennis player Bobby Riggs.

FEBRUARY 26

People born on February 26 see life on a large scale, yet their ability to perceive details is nothing short of amazing. They are affectionate and gentle, and although their ambition to succeed is very strong, they never lose sight of the importance of personal relationships.

February 26 people have a romantic view of life that is mildly tinged with melancholy. They extract the maximum from experience, and never regret an opportunity taken, even if it doesn't bring them the happiness they expected.

FRIENDS AND LOVERS February 26
natives always seem to be surrounded by a group. Whether or not all of these individuals qualify as close friends is beside the point. People born on this date have a way of making everyone in their life feel indispensable.

These men and women have an exceptionally romantic nature and have a reputation for investing their lovers with far more virtues and charms than they actually possess.

CHILDREN AND FAMILY People born on
this date often harbor a great deal of anger and resentment toward their upbringing, which affects their adult life in more ways than they may be willing to admit. It is likely that in childhood they were expected to shoulder responsibility before they were ready to handle it. Therapy as an adult can help February 26 people learn to cope with their anger.

Although they have the potential to be very good parents, people born on this date may experience feelings of jealousy when they see how much easier things are for their own children in comparison to what they themselves experienced.

HEALTH February 26 people take great pride
in their appearance, which motivates them to exercise on a regular basis. They are concerned with retaining their youthful good looks and are likely to adapt their nutritional habits toward achieving this aim.

Exercise should be done in moderation several times a week. Walking, either outdoors or on a treadmill, provides exercise and a way to relieve stress.

CAREER AND FINANCES February 26
individuals like to master their own fates. They have the discipline to work for others, but prefer not to, feeling that they cannot achieve their desired level of success unless they go their own way. These people have the tenacity to start their own business or work in a freelance position.

People born on this date are careful with money, especially if they have an irregular income. Their conservative stewardship allows them to build up a respectable bank account over a period of time.

DREAMS AND GOALS February 26 people
are extremely idealistic in their hopes and perceptions, and many of their goals may seem wildly out of reach. But it is precisely the presumed unattainability that makes those goals so appealing to these folks.

People born on this date see no reason why their dreams can't be realized and are willing to sacrifice in order to make sure they do.

EMBRACE
Energy
Perception
Cooperation

AVOID
Egotism
Unpredictability
Anger

ALSO BORN TODAY
Singer Michael Bolton; comedian Jackie Gleason; singer Johnny Cash; novelist Victor Hugo; singer Fats Domino; actor Tony Randall; singer Mitch Ryder; singer Sandie Shaw.

FEBRUARY 27

The men and women born on this date have great empathy for others. They are especially protective of those they love and will go to any lengths to secure their happiness.

Although they may be somewhat lacking in analytical skills, February 27 people show their intelligence in other ways, often through the application of their intuitive talents. These people have great skill at managing the lives of others and often take charge of situations outside of their circle.

FRIENDS AND LOVERS February 27
individuals inspire great love and loyalty from their friends. Because of their sensitive approach to helping others handle their problems, these men and women have a "life mentor" reputation.

These people want more than a lover or a partner—they want to find a soul mate who will understand and cherish them for everything they are. Because this is asking a great deal, February 27 people often experience profound disappointment in love.

CHILDREN AND FAMILY February 27
people don't really come into their own until they leave childhood behind them. That period of their life is often a time of emotional suspended animation.

These men and women have a natural ability to understand the imaginative and secret world of their own children. Although they are strict with youngsters, February 27 people are as nurturing and loving as any parent can be.

HEALTH Many Pisceans are not physically robust, and February 27 people are no exceptions. They tend to lead a fast-paced lifestyle, however, and this sometimes gets them into trouble. Few people are as accident prone as

these individuals. But they have a hearty appetite for life and seem to sail through an illness or injury with aplomb.

February 27 folks need to adopt as healthy a lifestyle as possible in order to keep their physical and spiritual energies intact. Purified water, fresh-squeezed fruit and vegetable juices, and herbal tea instead of alcohol and coffee can do a lot toward making them feel younger and full of energy.

CAREER AND FINANCES Although
February 27 people have the ability to shine at almost anything they attempt, they often turn their talents toward helping others. They are fearless when it comes to stating their opinions on the most controversial matters, and they have the power to effect great change and understanding.

February 27 people have a deep respect for money but always put people before possessions of any kind.

EMBRACE
Good nutrition
Practicality
Wisdom

AVOID
Flightiness
Insecurity
Jealous rages

ALSO BORN TODAY
Actress Joan Bennett; presidential daughter Chelsea Clinton; consumer activist Ralph Nader; actress Elizabeth Taylor; ballerina Antoinette Sibley; novelist John Steinbeck; actress Joanne Woodward.

DREAMS AND GOALS It is the goal of
those born on February 27 to help people who are unable to help themselves. These remarkable individuals have an almost saintly quality to their devotion for doing good in the world.

On a personal level, February 27 individuals are on a constant path to find their true nature. They are not afraid to examine even the most difficult periods of their life in order to find the answers they need.

FEBRUARY 28

It is typical for February 28 men and women to strive for perfection. These people dream on such a lofty scale that their reach often exceeds their grasp.

February 28 people enjoy living in the limelight. They gravitate toward a fast-paced lifestyle that offers them the glamour and romance they are eager to experience. These individuals are in tireless pursuit of excellence in all areas of life.

EMBRACE
Talent
Sensitivity
Distinction

AVOID
Excesses
No-win situations
Enemies

ALSO BORN TODAY
Actress Stephanie Beacham; musician Brian Jones; film director Vincente Minnelli; actress Bernadette Peters; mob figure Bugsy Siegel; poet Stephen Spender; dancer Tommy Tune; actor John Turturo.

FRIENDS AND LOVERS People born on this date are able to distill their life-view through their experiences with friends. They possess a strong sense of loyalty and are never afraid to stand by a friend who is having problems.

Romance is a high priority in the lives of February 28 men and women. Because they enjoy the excitement of the dating scene, they may choose to marry late in life, or not at all. These individuals are not intentionally fickle, yet they do fall in and out of love quickly. Although they can appreciate the values of fidelity, they find it very difficult to settle on one person with whom to spend their life.

CHILDREN AND FAMILY Pisceans hold on to their memories from childhood, good or bad. Even if they feel burdened by the past, it is almost impossible for these sensitive souls to cut themselves off from family members.

February 28 men and women make conscientious parents. They take their responsibilities seriously, yet know how to foster an atmosphere of liberalism and good times.

HEALTH People born on this date require harmonious surroundings if they are to experience the peak of health. Maintaining a good attitude is crucial to the physical and emotional well-being of February 28 individuals.

Since February 28 individuals often have food allergies, these people may find the healthiest diet to be a simple one, with few additives or artificial ingredients. A vegetarian lifestyle is the best choice for these people.

CAREER AND FINANCES These men and women have an extraordinary ability to transcend the difficult balancing act that causes so much trouble for so many people: finding enough time for personal and professional concerns without giving preference to either. Many February 28 people choose an alternative: working from home.

These individuals have a natural instinct for making money. They always seem able to make the right decisions where investments are concerned, and they have the ability to stay within a tight budget.

DREAMS AND GOALS February 28 people have a love of bright lights and fame. Even if they do not aspire to be famous themselves, these men and women will always be drawn to those who are. Because they know the measure of their own abilities, they also feel as if they deserve some special attention.

Even if it is solely within their own circle, people born on this date seek recognition. Although their own self-worth is not determined by the validation of others, these men and women still gravitate toward it.

FEBRUARY 29

Owing to their unusual birthdate, these men and women have unusual talents and personalities. February 29 people are good-natured, friendly, and almost unbelievably optimistic. They have a brilliant talent for seeing the positive side of any issue, and while they are not naive, they do manage to retain a measure of their childhood innocence long after they have entered the worldly phase of their life. These individuals have a youthful exuberance that brightens their outlook no matter how bleak a situation may appear.

FRIENDS AND LOVERS
People born on this date are outgoing and friendly. They have a winsome, genuinely pleasant personality that draws people to them almost magnetically. They are good friends who set great store by loyalty. They will go to extremes to help a pal who needs their assistance.

These men and women are equally loyal to a spouse or lover. They work very hard to make even the most challenging relationship work and will not voluntarily give up on a marriage.

CHILDREN AND FAMILY
February 29 people are spunky and highly opinionated, and willing to stand their ground regardless of what family pressures are brought to bear upon them.

February 29 natives are well suited for parenthood because they combine sensitivity with an instinct for knowing when to discipline their children. They seek to engage their youngsters in projects that teach responsibility and that offer outlets for creativity and emotional growth.

HEALTH
February 29 people have a very healthy lifestyle. They understand that in order to get the maximum out of life they need to be vigilant about diet and exercise, while also making time to relax.

People born on this date know how vital it is to stop and smell the flowers. They need to feel connected to natural things in order to cultivate a relaxed frame of mind. This allows them to deal with the normal pressures of life without succumbing to them.

CAREER AND FINANCES
People born on this date are proud of their versatility. They don't like to lock themselves into a single life-option without having the freedom to change course at some point. These men and women have a great deal of faith in their ability to make the transition from career to family life, and this is often the reason for their change in focus.

Although many February 29 people spend their youth in a mad dash toward career success, this means less to them as time goes on.

DREAMS AND GOALS
Leap-year individuals insist on personal happiness. They have the ability to rise above any challenging situation and turn it into a success.

No one accepts setbacks with as much dignity and forbearance as these individuals. They never doubt their ability to overcome obstacles and go on to even greater success. To these plucky individuals, sticking with a goal despite problems is more of an achievement than the goal itself.

EMBRACE
Optimism
Enthusiasm
Happy days

AVOID
Trying too hard
Childishness
Making demands

ALSO BORN TODAY
Musician Richie Cole; bandleader Jimmy Dorsey; actor James Mitchell; hockey star Maurice Richard; composer Gioacchino Rossini; poet George Seferis; singer Dinah Shore; film director William Wellman.

MARCH 1

People born on March 1 have strong views on morality, yet do not confuse them with deeper, spiritual truths. Their need to understand their own motivations is very strong, and it defines their character on many levels.

March 1 people respect the status quo but rarely seek to live their lives in search of it. They are highly competitive people who give their best at every opportunity, always believing that attitude, more than ability, promises success.

FRIENDS AND LOVERS Friends are a vital part of life for March 1 people. These men and women are extremely sensitive and require continual emotional support from those close to them. They give the same in return.

People born on this date are unsatisfied in anything other than a long-term relationship. They need the security that commitment provides and will work hard to keep their union satisfying and exciting. If a relationship or marriage ends, these men and women are quick to seek out another.

CHILDREN AND FAMILY Few people are more sentimental than the ones born on this date. They extend this attitude to their family, with whom they are likely to experience a remarkable closeness throughout their lifetime. They look upon their parents as heroes and their siblings as close friends.

As spouses and parents, they try to foster an atmosphere conducive to happiness and security. They are puzzled when their children rebel, often taking the situation far too seriously and feeling as if they are to blame.

HEALTH Though Pisceans are not known for being especially robust or energetic, March 1 people generally pursue a very active lifestyle. Not only do they enjoy working out on a regular basis, but they love to play sports.

If March 1 people have a bad health habit it usually relates to diet. These busy individuals often take the easy way out at meal time, preferring to eat junk or convenience food rather than take the time to prepare a more healthful repast.

CAREER AND FINANCES People born on this date look at things from an artistic perspective. This is not to say that they will automatically look for a career in the arts, but they do bring an artistic sensibility to anything they do. They are particularly enamored of shape and color, and make first-class decorators.

Although not naturally materialistic, March 1 people have a healthy respect for money. They enjoy living with nice things, but prefer putting aside something for a rainy day.

DREAMS AND GOALS March 1 men and women seek to balance their life between the psychic and the practical. Because a constant ebb and flow of psychic energy in their consciousness is normal for Pisceans, these people understand both its value and its drawbacks. For this reason they often choose not to make anything special of it.

People born on this date have a deep respect for spiritual principles and try to incorporate them in their daily existence.

EMBRACE
Celebration
Improvement
Discipline

AVOID
Charlatans
Emotional instability
Needless worry

ALSO BORN TODAY
Singer Harry Belafonte; poet Robert Lowell; singer Roger Daltrey; actress Joan Hackett; actor/film director Ron Howard; actor David Niven; bandleader Glenn Miller; actor Alan Thicke.

MARCH 2

People born on March 2 have a perception that borders on genius. Although they may seem to clear everything through intellectual channels, they are really exercising their psychic sensitivity. Most of their major life-decisions are made in this way.

March 2 people are gentle souls who may lack self-confidence. This is unfortunate because they have many talents and can actually "find" themselves through judicious application of their abilities.

FRIENDS AND LOVERS People born on this date have a great deal of love and empathy for their friends. Although they have a shy nature, these men and women are very sociable and delight in having a large circle of friends.

The love nature of March 2 people is complicated but sincere. These men and women may sometimes have difficulty remaining focused on their partner, but not from lack of love—they simply have a hard time resisting the flattery of others. To become dependent on a committed relationship requires a great deal of emotional growth on their part.

CHILDREN AND FAMILY March 2 natives have happy memories of their childhood, preferring to set aside any negative issues in favor of the positives. They have especially close ties to their mother.

When they become parents, March 2 men and women put their whole heart and soul into it. They are loving and nurturing, with a deep understanding of the imaginative world of children.

HEALTH March 2 people are sometimes afflicted with nervous ailments that can be traced to lack of sleep or emotional exhaustion. They may suffer from headaches after a particu-larly stressful day at work, making sleep difficult or creating an emotional atmosphere in which bad dreams flourish.

March 2 people often prefer a natural diet that excludes meat, sugar, and dairy products. Light or moderate exercise is usually enough to keep these folks feeling and looking fit.

CAREER AND FINANCES People born on this date have many talents. They are analytical and aesthetic, and may seek to satisfy both within the boundaries of a single career. For this reason they are attracted to music, mathematics, or the theoretical sciences. They have a great love for photography and may seek this out as a hobby or avocation.

March 2 people like to surround themselves with beautiful things but understand the perils of credit spending.

DREAMS AND GOALS March 2 natives have a great need to display their intellect through practical means. They may not appreci-ate their talents until they experience external validation by loved ones or professional colleagues.

While people born on this date work very hard to make their dreams a reality, they have a sensible attitude toward setbacks and delays, understanding that nothing happens overnight. They have the emotional stamina to work toward their achievements one goal at a time.

EMBRACE
Self-worth
Independence
Meditation

AVOID
Insecure friends
Dilemmas
Scheming

ALSO BORN TODAY
Bandleader/TV personality Desi Arnaz; singer/songwriter Jon Bon Jovi; actor John Cullum; novelist John Irving; actress Jennifer Jones; director Martin Ritt; novelist Peter Straub; composer Kurt Weill.

MARCH 3

March 3 people are fairly aggressive and opinionated. Professional goals are a definite priority, and success is an important goal in their lives. But despite these attributes, they are also tuned-in to life's spiritual aspects.

People born on this date have an air of glamour about them. They are often drawn to the supernatural and may possess extreme psychic sensitivity, as well. These men and women approach life from a dreamer's perspective.

FRIENDS AND LOVERS March 3 natives are solitary people who have a natural reluctance to ask others for help. But when these men and women connect with someone in a meaningful friendship, it is likely to last for a lifetime.

March 3 people don't enjoy being the pursuer in a romantic relationship. If they feel that a love affair has little possibility of being a permanent factor in their lives, they are likely to move on.

CHILDREN AND FAMILY People born on this date have a hard time coming to grips with problems in their relationship with family members. Indeed, they may wish to gloss over circumstances that cry out for resolution. But this only complicates matters, and it may render March 3 people unable to stand up for their convictions during family squabbles.

It may not be evident just how untenable this position is until these men and women become parents.

HEALTH March 3 individuals have a generally upbeat disposition that keeps them physically, emotionally, and spiritually energized. They may not be especially careful about their diet, though, which can lead to unwanted pounds later in life.

People born on this date draw enormous emotional satisfaction from their nightly dreams, which bring them inspiration and opportunities for problem-solving. If they have periods when they are not sleeping well, or perhaps not dreaming, March 3 people are likely to notice the effect on their health.

CAREER AND FINANCES These men and women have great originality and often look for careers that give them opportunities to showcase this talent. They are adamant in their desire to put their achievements "out there" for the world to see.

March 3 people do not judge themselves according to how much money they make, though they can appreciate beauty and like to surround themselves with nice things. They may become budget-minded at a very early age.

DREAMS AND GOALS In order for March 3 people to achieve their goals, they must accept challenges. This can be difficult, especially their struggle to overcome their loner mentality. But reticence about showing their talents is a mistake, and so their doubts must be dealt with.

March 3 men and women are not averse to success, but they may have a different definition of the word than other people. To see things on a universal rather than strictly personal scale is paramount to these individuals.

EMBRACE
Allure
Great expectations
Sympathy

AVOID
Passivity
Fear of commitment
Personal obsessions

ALSO BORN TODAY
Actress Diana Barrymore; inventor Alexander Graham Bell; designer Perry Ellis; writer William Godwin; actress Jean Harlow; socialite Lee Radziwell; actress Miranda Richardson; cartoonist Ronald Searle.

MARCH 4

At times life may seem to be a battle-field to the courageous and icono-clastic people born on this date. They seem to attract upheaval and chaos, creating a never-ending cycle of change. Yet it is this very state of destabilization that gives these men and women their unique perspective.

March 4 natives hold themselves to a very rigid code of conduct, testing their character at every turn. They may practice a specific intellectual or spiritual discipline through which they express their true nature.

FRIENDS AND LOVERS People born on this date are very cautious when choosing people to trust. They usually have a small but loyal group of friends, and are apt to discourage casual acquaintances.

The love life of March 4 individuals is often operatic in its intensity. These men and women are attracted to kinetic people who share their love of spontaneity. It takes a very engaging individual to get these people to make a lifetime commitment.

CHILDREN AND FAMILY March 4 people often experience great turmoil in their childhood years. This may be the result of a family breakup or some emotional problems that affected the entire family. March 4 people may grow up with a distorted perspective regarding the importance of money.

Before they can become successful parents, March 4 men and women need to put their own house in order. When they deal with issues from their troubled past, they have an opportunity to wipe the slate clean and begin again.

HEALTH As in most other areas of life, March 4 natives experience frequent ups and downs in health matters. These are usually related to their own indifference, since people born on this date have a propensity for breaking the rules and doing things their own way.

Although March 4 people have boundless energy, they sometimes overtax themselves. All it takes for these people to recover their health is a few days of stress-free rest and relaxation.

CAREER AND FINANCES People born on this date have a great deal of nervous energy and are rarely comfortable in sedentary, nine-to-five jobs. They favor a career where every day offers something different, and where they have a chance to make their own hours. It isn't uncommon for March 4 individuals to start their own business just to accommodate these needs.

Although they have a reputation for playing fast and loose with money, March 4 men and women have some very good financial instincts.

DREAMS AND GOALS These people have an all-or-nothing mentality. If they cannot reach the highest goals they have set for themselves, they may not be interested in attempting anything on a more modest scale.

The challenge that awaits these folks is to work toward their lofty ambitions while also pursuing reachable goals. Small-scale success is a positive reinforcement for them, and it helps to strengthen their resolve to keep going.

EMBRACE
Mastery
Self-knowledge
Astrology

AVOID
Going to extremes
Deliberation
Blaming others

ALSO BORN TODAY
Actor John Garfield; England's King Henry II; actress Patsy Kensit; writer Alan Sillitoe; actress Paula Prentiss; musician Chris Squire; silent screen star Pearl White; singer/songwriter Bobby Womack.

MARCH 5

People born on March 5 possess considerable intellectual courage. These men and women are never afraid to take a stand or to own up to their controversial opinions. Even if they face stiff opposition to their ideas or plans, they will not allow dissent from others to sway them from their course.

March 5 natives have a great talent for using words to their own benefit. At times, this ability can land them in hot water, though things usually turn out well for all in the end.

FRIENDS AND LOVERS

Talkative and friendly, March 5 people treasure their friends. They put a great price on the opportunity to share ideas and feelings with those close to them, and care little whether friends agree or disagree with their beliefs.

An ability to communicate is one of the things March 5 natives look for in a companion or mate. These men and women have an affinity for lovers who combine intelligence with good looks, preferably someone who possesses interesting opinions. Nothing bores a March 5 person more quickly than a date or mate who has limited wit or interests.

CHILDREN AND FAMILY

March 5 people are likely to enjoy a special status within their family. They may be the oldest or youngest child, perhaps the only child. One way or another, they are sure to be the *favorite* child.

Unfortunately, March 5 parents have a tendency to play favorites among their own children. Though they love all their kids, they cannot help but be drawn to the one who possesses a unique intelligence or talent.

HEALTH

March 5 people often suffer from breathing-related ailments, such as sinusitis or asthma. These symptoms, though real, are likely to be stress-related. Learning how to deal with tension in their daily lives can have positive health benefits for these individuals.

People born on March 5, particularly young women, may suffer from a negative body image, which causes them to repudiate their appearance through poor eating habits or even anorexia. This has the potential to cause severe emotional as well as physical damage.

CAREER AND FINANCES

With their fascination for language and the written word, March 5 men and women make excellent novelists or journalists. Being able to construct graceful, even lyrical prose is a specialty of these people, who also have a gift for making images—especially photographic ones—speak.

March 5 people have very little talent for handling their own financial affairs. This should be left to a professional, or a spouse.

DREAMS AND GOALS

March 5 natives may not feel they have achieved their goals in life unless they have had to fight for them. These men and women have an instinct for controversy and enjoy the chance to overcome it through their own efforts and hard work.

People born on this date want to accomplish their aims on their own. The idea of accepting help, even in the form of encouragement from loved ones, makes them feel uncomfortable.

MARCH 6

March 6 individuals are free spirits who refuse to conform to ordinary standards. They are not rebellious, since they respect structure, yet they choose to live outside it. One of the quiet Piscean types, these people nevertheless communicate on a variety of levels.

Men and women born on this day possess a sense of destiny regarding their actions, and may often find themselves in odd or unusual circumstances at some point.

FRIENDS AND LOVERS March 6 natives have the ability to become deeply involved in the concerns of their friends while still managing to withhold judgment. They are inspirational types who often serve as wonderful mentors to their younger friends.

Because they are extremely particular, March 6 people have a difficult time finding their true love. These men and women are perfectionists who care about physical beauty and good manners.

CHILDREN AND FAMILY Like many Pisceans, the men and women born on March 6 feel incredibly connected to their childhood all of their life. This is not necessarily a positive thing; the ties could relate to unreconcilable differences between family members that continue into adulthood.

March 6 men and women have a surprisingly strict side to their personality and may be quite demanding as parents. Yet they know how to show affection, and they understand the importance of being friends to their children.

HEALTH People born on this day have many appetites. They enjoy indulging their love of fine food and wines, and may be quite the epicure. This is relatively harmless, unless these men and women resist daily exercise.

A love of beauty is the common unifier among March 6 individuals. Learning to draw aesthetic sustenance from art, music, poetry, and drama can help these people banish the strains and stresses of the day.

CAREER AND FINANCES March 6 individuals have a bold spirit when it comes to choosing their life's work. They are versatile, daring people who aren't afraid to extend the boundaries of their own perception. They may change careers several times or decide upon a course of action that's totally divergent from their initial training.

Since March 6 people enjoy financing their own projects, money can become a major part of their life. These people have grandiose ideas that may not always jibe with reality, so a more practical partner can be a definite plus.

DREAMS AND GOALS People born on this date are unafraid to take chances. They would rather fail grandly than be too timid to embark upon their chosen course. Of course, it's rare for a March 6 person to fail, because their positive outlook "channels" good things into their life.

These men and women are unique in the extreme, and they celebrate their traits, not caring if their sometimes outrageous behavior earns the disapproval of others.

EMBRACE
Curiosity
True emotions
Fellowship

AVOID
Snobbishness
Empty promises
Fatalism

ALSO BORN TODAY
Comic Tom Arnold; poet Elizabeth Barrett Browning; TV personality Ed MacMahon; sculptor Michelangelo Buonarroti; basketball star Shaquille O'Neal; film director Rob Reiner; baseball star Willie Stargell; singer Mary Wilson.

MARCH 7

March 7 individuals are among the most creative people of the entire year. These dreamy, artistic souls are true visionaries. Although they may appear malleable, even weak-willed to those who do not understand their nature, they actually possess an amazing ability to subjugate their own ego in order to comprehend reality in all its aspects.

People born on this date are empathetic to others. Their sensitivity can transcend relationships of all types and definition.

FRIENDS AND LOVERS

Friends are indispensable to March 7 people. These men and women collect friends the way other people collect art. Most March 7 individuals are eager to cultivate the closest possible relationships with their pals.

Where romance is concerned, March 7 natives are never fickle. They often seek out an impossible love situation, realizing that they can learn more through suffering than from a happy romantic relationship. Because these individuals are highly dramatic, they are particularly likely to fall in love with love.

CHILDREN AND FAMILY

Those born on this date have strong ties to their background. Even if they transcend their beginnings, through career or financial choices, they are still emotionally bound to their childhood years.

March 7 people make exceptionally good parents. They have the sensitivity to understand their children's need to rebel at times. Their nurturing skills are based upon instinct.

HEALTH

Although they may enjoy swimming or the occasional round of golf, these people have difficulty remaining true to a daily workout. They also rely too heavily on prescription or over-the-counter medication. This can affect them negatively, since they have an extreme sensitivity to drugs of any kind. The same goes for alcohol and nicotine. In order to remain truly healthy, they need to cut down on calories and drink at least 100 ounces of water each day.

CAREER AND FINANCES

Because March 7 people are lovers of antiques and beautiful things, they seek careers in well-paying fields. Although not materialistic, they do have a highly developed aesthetic sense. For this reason they often involve themselves in creative or artistic fields.

These men and women may have very little sense of responsibility about money. This doesn't necessarily reflect bad judgment on their part; these folks simply find it difficult to make objective financial decisions.

DREAMS AND GOALS

People born on this date have a profound need to experience life through the prism of their creativity. The insights they gain may not always be immediately recognizable, even to them, yet in time they come to know their value.

March 7 individuals do not need to receive worldly rewards in order to feel as if their efforts have been crowned by success. Highly evolved in every way, they are accountable only to themselves.

MARCH 8

People born on March 8 are a fascinating combination of cynic and mystic. They may possess a loner mentality, yet they love people. They have a deep psychic consciousness, and they may prefer to spend their time pursuing humanitarian aims in a worldly forum.

March 8 natives are puzzling, provocative men and women who, though they are able to see the very best in mankind, are deeply distrustful in their own personal relationships.

FRIENDS AND LOVERS

March 8 individuals may have few close friends, but the ones they do have are totally devoted to them. They do not reject social friendships but generally prefer to conduct all of their relationships on a much more emotionally intense level.

When March 8 people fall in love, they give their whole heart. There is more to these individuals than an ability to love deeply and well: They are interested in creating a relationship that will survive the test of time.

CHILDREN AND FAMILY

People born on this date may never quite fit into their family circle, and typically experience a certain level of ambivalence toward family members their whole life because of it. These people are the ultimate outsiders.

March 8 natives are aware of a considerable difference in temperament between themselves and their offspring. Not wanting to impose themselves on their kids, they may prefer to take a more casual approach toward childrearing.

HEALTH

March 8 men and women have a stubborn, extremist streak that often causes them to follow an unusual diet or health regimen. They're particularly devoted to fasting, which may be carried out on several levels:

modified fast (grains and water), juice fast (fruits and vegetables), or pure fast (water only).

People born on this date are not particularly devoted to exercise. They prefer to involve themselves in useful physical tasks rather than buy an expensive gym setup.

CAREER AND FINANCES

Because of the dichotomy in their nature, March 8 people may reach adulthood undecided about the path they wish to take. For this reason they often choose a lengthy academic career. Studying many different subjects gives these complicated individuals the chance to come up with a workable plan.

Financial security is extremely important to March 8 people. Although there can be an element of "I'll show them!" in their drive to accumulate money, it's generally a reaction to wanting the best for their loved ones and family members.

DREAMS AND GOALS

March 8 men and women may have a hard time admitting that they feel a need to reconcile the two sides of their nature. This can spring from a sense of incredulity that they can actually harbor such diverse opinions, or it may simply reflect the curiosity that drives their efforts.

Once March 8 folks select a lifestyle, they generally stick with it, allowing that side of their personality to "win out" over the other.

EMBRACE
Security
Providence
Gentility

AVOID
Fear
Compromise
An unforgiving nature

ALSO BORN TODAY
Dancer Cyd Charisse; singer Mickey Dolenz; musician Peter Gill; composer Ruggiero Leoncavallo; actor Aidan Quinn; actress Lynn Redgrave; baseball star Jim Rice; ballet dancer Lynn Seymour.

MARCH 9

People born on this date are devoted to the pursuit of excellence in all endeavors. These men and women are extraordinarily sensitive at the core, yet are outwardly strong and determined.

March 9 people are genuine and truthful. They have a great regard for spirituality in all its aspects and also possess a wicked sense of humor that infects even their most serious moments. These individuals have very little regard for artifice and will freely speak out against it.

EMBRACE
Positive actions
Goal-oriented achievement
Dynamism

AVOID
Caution
Pretense
Superstition

ALSO BORN TODAY
Composer Samuel Barber; chess champion Bobby Fischer; cosmonaut Yuri Gagarin; singer Mark Lindsey; actress Irene Papas; writer Mickey Spillane; singer/songwriter Jeffrey Osborne; actress Trish Van Devere.

FRIENDS AND LOVERS The concept of friendship is held reverentially by March 9 people. They treasure their friends and allow them the sort of emotional intimacy most people reserve only for mates and family members. But because they hold such great regard for their friends, March 9 people can be devastatingly hurt by them.

People born on this date are remarkably stable managers of their love affairs. Although deeply romantic, March 9 men and women are incapable of being fooled by a would-be lover. These people have the ability to judge character with pitiless accuracy.

CHILDREN AND FAMILY March 9 people are deeply, unalterably devoted to their family. They display great loyalty, even in the face of potential disagreements.

Because March 9 natives are sensitive to the resonances of their own upbringing, they have the potential to be nurturing, loving parents. They may find it difficult to impose rules or discipline upon their children and may need to relegate these matters to a spouse.

HEALTH People born on this date believe in their ability to create a healthy reality through concentration, meditation, and positive thinking. They generally go through several extreme health-related phases in their life, but eventually settle down to a philosophy that's practical and sensible.

Although March 9 people are quite careful about their diet, they do favor plenty of red meat and red wine. Far from being a detriment, this indulgence maintains their good looks and high level of fitness.

CAREER AND FINANCES Even from an early age, March 9 people have a very clear picture of what they want to do with their life. Whatever they aspire to, they lay careful and intricate plans for success. These men and women are especially drawn to pursuits requiring intensive training over a period of many years.

Money is often a source of controversy in the lives of March 9 people, who are apt to expect a spouse or mate to look after their financial interests while they devote themselves to more unusual pursuits.

DREAMS AND GOALS March 9 natives are constantly perusing their own character, searching for the one reality that will explore and explain the totality of their existence. These men and women often have a problem separating their personality identity from their work, though the relationships they seek out will help them to accomplish this.

MARCH 10

arch 10 individuals have attitude. They know how to draw the spotlight in any situation, and usually manage to keep it on themselves for as long as they choose.

Although these men and women display a flirty, semi-serious personality, there's considerable grit beneath the surface of their good humor. They can take care of themselves on just about any level and will never let anyone get the better of them.

FRIENDS AND LOVERS
People born on this date have a hard time knowing just who their friends are. This is usually because they have a highly charged aura that draws people to bask in its glow. While March 10 people are flattered by the attention, they also have grave suspicions regarding it.

Their love affairs and romantic relationships are similarly affected by this fact. March 10 men and women have a real need to believe that a lover finds them desirable for who they really are.

CHILDREN AND FAMILY
March 10 natives have a sunny attitude toward their past. Because they are basically philosophical in nature, they choose to see the positive side of things. Even if they retain unreconciled issues regarding a parental or sibling-based relationship, they are unlikely to obsess over the fact.

As parents, March 10 men and women are broad-minded enough to allow their children the chance to fail as well as succeed. They understand that by being overprotective they are actually keeping their youngsters from the life-lessons they need to learn.

HEALTH
March 10 people are near-fanatics about health and fitness. A natural grace marks their every physical effort, and they enjoy playing sports—a concession to their naturally competitive personality.

Although they go through periods when they are avid calorie-counters, for the most part March 10 people believe in allowing themselves to eat whatever they please. March 10 people enjoy cooking for friends and family—just one of the many ways in which they show their love and regard for the people they care about.

CAREER AND FINANCES
March 10 individuals have a great respect for learning and a reverence for wisdom. They have a strong belief in the transfer of knowledge, and for this reason they can make caring, even spectacular, teachers and mentors.

While money plays an important part in the lives of March 10 individuals, it is not likely to keep them from going into a modest-paying profession they love. They need to get satisfaction from the work they do, and a paycheck—even a big one—can't compensate if this is lacking.

DREAMS AND GOALS
March 10 natives need to feel that what they are doing is vital to others. They can be among the most committed artists, the most passionate teachers, the singularly enlightened scholars. These men and women are dedicated to passing their knowledge to others.

People born on this date believe in working to positively affect the next generation.

EMBRACE
Courage
Moral strength
Sensuality

AVOID
Inflexibility
An implacable nature
Coldness

ALSO BORN TODAY
Baseball star Johnny Callison; psychic Gerard Croiset; England's Prince Edward; actress Jasmine Guy; ballet dancer Tamara Karsavina; gymnast Shannon Miller; playwright David Rabe; actress Sharon Stone.

MARCH 11

Those born on this date have the temperament of a true artisan. These gentle yet determined souls follow a very personal path throughout life, which takes them on an amazing soul-journey. They are drawn to extremes, and whether or not these have a positive effect, March 11 people will learn the lessons they need to learn. These individuals are sticklers for truth who prize honesty.

FRIENDS AND LOVERS March 11 people command great love and affection from their friends. These men and women are experts at being able to bring disparate people into the same orbit.

As lovers, March 11 individuals can be somewhat demanding. They have very specific ideas about what they want in a partner and are not very flexible about change. If a romantic relationship breaks up, these people may have a hard time moving on.

CHILDREN AND FAMILY March 11 individuals maintain a cordial if somewhat distant relationship with family members. Because they may have felt like an outsider within their own family circle as a child, they may not be emotionally connected to their background. And yet, they possess a deep respect for the values that guided their own development as children.

March 11 men and women want to give their youngsters a strong spiritual base, as well as providing exposure to life's intangible values.

HEALTH March 11 men and women appreciate the need to protect their health by preserving harmony in all areas of life. They know that the stresses and strains of unfortunate relationships and unwise career choices can create severe problems, which can lead in turn to physical symptoms.

Putting aside some time each day for quiet reflection and meditation helps March 11 people retain their emotional and physical equilibrium. These individuals derive inner peace from getting in touch with their core self.

CAREER AND FINANCES People born on this date are not particularly career-driven, though they do have a need to express their values and views by way of their profession. These thoughtful individuals are dedicated to helping others discover their strengths and weaknesses. For this reason they make remarkable therapists, marriage and family counselors, or hypnotherapists.

March 11 people often have a careless, even irresponsible attitude toward money. This may be because they have a sense of vulnerability in this area of their life. Learning to accept ownership of their financial decisions is a must.

DREAMS AND GOALS March 11 individuals are committed to finding inner peace. These remarkable people have naturally pacifist tendencies, yet are quietly heroic. These folks want to succeed in life, yet are aware that success can be measured in many ways.

Remaining true to their spiritual compass is a major issue for March 11 people. No matter how much financial or worldly success they achieve, it can never mean to them what the satisfaction of simple decency provides.

EMBRACE
Fascination
Enchantment
Mystery

AVOID
Distractions
Pettiness
Worry

ALSO BORN TODAY
Novelist Douglas Adams; TV journalist Sam Donaldson; actress Dorothy Gish; singer Bobby McFerrin; newspaper magnate Rupert Murdoch; actress Susan Richardson; film director Raoul Walsh; bandleader Lawrence Welk.

MARCH 12

People born on this date bring astonishing creativity and grace to everything they do. They are particularly adept at physical endeavors, but can also impart their natural artistry to important life interests.

March 12 individuals possess a spiritually centered type of intelligence. They are incapable of acting from a strictly selfish perspective and are usually willing to sacrifice their own interests to accommodate those they love. In some cases, March 12 people take this attitude to such extremes that they surrender necessary prerogatives.

FRIENDS AND LOVERS March 12 natives are engaging, energetic people who have a special talent for friendship. Because they know they have a lot to give to others, these folks often become deeply involved in the lives of friends.

Individuals born on March 12 have great difficulty maintaining a sense of permanence in their romantic life. This is likely to change once they learn to reconcile their own emotional strengths and weaknesses. Romance is a high art to these people.

CHILDREN AND FAMILY Coming to grips with severe disappointments suffered in childhood can be a real challenge for those born on this date. Because of their natural reticence to criticize anyone they love, these individuals may never confront parents or siblings over unresolved issues from the past.

As parents, March 12 men and women are careful to support the creative aspirations of their youngsters.

HEALTH March 12 people understand the need to keep their life in balance, and that means plenty of physical exercise in addition to the pursuit of artistic ambitions. Also, these individuals need to spend a lot of time alone in order to recharge their emotional and spiritual batteries.

People born on this date are generally big eaters, but they understand the need to cut back on sweets and starches whenever they gain a few pounds

CAREER AND FINANCES With so much artistic talent at their disposal, March 12 individuals are often drawn to creative professions such as art, writing, photography, dance, film, and music. If they are unhappy or unfulfilled in the work they do, March 12 people cannot learn the lessons that are meant for them.

These men and women are not really concerned with how much money they make. Pressure from a spouse to make finances more important will only cause trouble in the relationship.

DREAMS AND GOALS March 12 individuals need to reconcile their creative aspirations with the profound spirituality that dominates their life. Although the these two aspects of life would seem to be naturally compatible, the creativity of people born on this date sometimes raises ego issues that undermine spiritual goals.

These men and women are fantasy-oriented and require periodic escapes from reality.

EMBRACE
Discipline
Direction
Preparedness

AVOID
Destructive impulses
Confusion
Guilt

ALSO BORN TODAY
Playwright Edward Albee; composer Georges Delerue; actress Barbara Feldon; writer Jack Kerouac; actress Liza Minnelli; dancer Vaslav Nijinsky; musician Bill Payne; singer/songwriter James Taylor.

MARCH 13

Talented yet erratic, March 13 natives have a reputation for being high-strung. Their highly kinetic personality masks a temperament that finds it difficult to "go with the flow." Although generous by nature, at times, these individuals may have trouble accommodating the views and needs of others.

March 13 men and women have their own way of doing things and refuse to be roped into the conventional approach. They are intelligent, even brilliant individuals who seldom question their own judgment.

EMBRACE
Popularity
Justice
Normalcy

AVOID
Resentments
Mistrust
Meddling

ALSO BORN TODAY
Philanthropist Walter Annenberg; astronaut Gene Cernan; actress Dana Delany; bandleader Sammy Kaye; actress Deborah Raffin; singer/songwriter Neil Sedaka.

FRIENDS AND LOVERS Even though they generally have a large circle of friends, March 13 people respect the emotional boundaries of others and demand that their friends give them the same courtesy. This may be related to a reluctance to become truly intimate, or could merely reflect a need to retain autonomy.

These men and women even manage to keep a certain emotional distance from a lover or mate. They need to feel that the relationship is equal on both sides, and will discourage any sort of dependency for that reason. March 13 people try hard to support the aims and goals of a partner.

CHILDREN AND FAMILY People born on this date often separate from their family at quite a young age. While these people may have many happy memories of their upbringing, they are unlikely to subscribe to any religious code that was taught to them as children.

March 13 men and women understand the need to provide a base of knowledge for their youngsters, but always stress the fact that parents aren't perfect beings, and that their judgment and opinions can be flawed.

HEALTH March 13 people have little interest in conventional exercise, preferring to lead an active lifestyle through more natural means. These people love to take long walks, and they enjoy sports.

March 13 people may embrace a fad diet or two during their lifetime, but generally prefer to eat what they like.

CAREER AND FINANCES It takes a lot to keep March 13 people involved and interested. These men and women need to be emotionally engaged in the work they do; once they become bored with it they are likely to start looking for another career path. They have a bold sense of adventure and are not afraid to strike out in a new and different direction.

These people have the ability to start their business or work from home in a freelance capacity. Getting it done in a new or interesting way is what it's all about to them. Although their financial situation is often in flux, March 13 people always seem able to ride out the lean times.

DREAMS AND GOALS March 13 men and women are not as committed to simply achieving their goals as they are to achieving goals in their own way. These people have a very strong sense of self and will not allow themselves to be managed.

March 13 people never concern themselves with the reasons they cannot succeed at a goal, only why they can.

MARCH 14

March 14 individuals combine intelligence with profound creative insight. These unconventional men and women have great sexual magnetism and are able to exert considerable control over others.

Prophetic and poetic, March 14 men and women seem at times to be on another plane of existence. They have a natural love of illusion and are drawn to the occult and the supernatural, often as a result of their own experiences.

FRIENDS AND LOVERS
People born on this date don't make friends easily, but once they do, it's for keeps. March 14 natives must feel needed and indispensable or they cannot give of themselves to others.

They are extremely vulnerable in romantic matters. When they fall in love they fixate upon the object of their affection, investing that individual with all the magical traits of their creative, romantic imagination.

CHILDREN AND FAMILY
Because of their sensitive nature, it may be difficult for March 14 natives to resolve issues from their past. They prefer to move beyond these matters, forgiving those who may have hurt them.

March 14 people may not feel as if they have what it takes to be a good parent. Naturally reticent, they may allow their spouse to be the strongest emotional influence upon the children, waiting until the kids are older to cement a more satisfying and personal relationship.

HEALTH
People born on this date are often more interested in their spiritual than physical health, but they eventually come to realize that each affects the other. When they feel depressed or unhappy, March 14 people find it almost impossible to commit to physical activity.

Because they have a sensitivity to alcohol, March 14 people should not drink. Healthful substitutes like fresh mango shakes or citrus juice provide a natural alternative that's full of vitamins and natural cleansers.

CAREER AND FINANCES
March 14 individuals have an artistic sensibility that is incredibly rewarding to themselves and others. Whatever they choose to do in life, that creative perspective will make itself felt. For some it will be their entire life, for others merely a hobby or pastime. But one way or the other, an artistic outlet will be a part of their existence.

People born on this date are rarely able to comprehend the importance of money. Even if they are financially successful, they may discount this fact as having any real impact upon their life.

DREAMS AND GOALS
Few people have the pure "art for art's sake" mentality of March 14 men and women. These folks need to express their inner drives and needs through an artistic medium at some point in their life. Even if their life diverges far from this path, the time will always come when only art can take them where they wish to go.

March 14 men and women rarely strive for success in any dollar-oriented way, yet they are likely to set personal goals that act as signposts on their journey through life.

EMBRACE
Realism
The life force
Tenacity

AVOID
Naivete
Impulsiveness
The blues

ALSO BORN TODAY
Actor Michael Caine; actor/comedian Billy Crystal; physicist Albert Einstein; composer Quincy Jones; cartoonist Hank Ketchum; poet Eric Millward; composer Johann Strauss, Sr.; actress Rita Tushingham.

MARCH 15

March 15 people are great mediators on the intellectual level and great mediums on the occult or spiritual level. These men and women are extremely idealistic in all aspects of life, often refusing to address the questionable motives of others.

Despite their intelligence, there is a certain naivete about these people, which instantly endears them to others. They really cannot comprehend selfish behavior and are put off by negativity of any kind. Even if they are not religious, March 15 people seem to radiate a spiritual aura. These individuals put their emotional and psychic energy at the disposal of those they love.

FRIENDS AND LOVERS People born on this date are very sincere about their friendships. They don't try to manage others, nor do they "court" people simply to make use of important contacts. To the contrary, March 15 natives are as straightforward as they come.

Owing to their sensitivity, trust, and tendency to take things at face value, March 15 people experience more than their share of heartbreak. Unfortunately, if they experience too much negativity from a lover or spouse, March 15 people simply stop trusting others, though it wounds them deeply to do so.

CHILDREN AND FAMILY The high level of idealism endorsed by most March 15 men and women has its roots in their upbringing. They often come from a background where one extreme or another is put forth as the absolute truth: People are considered to be "all good" or "all bad." This ability to see what they want to see is often carried into adulthood and passed on to their own children. This is almost always a mistake, and March 15 people usually come to realize that fact once their children begin to form their own opinions.

HEALTH Living a healthy lifestyle is second nature to March 15 people, who truly believe in the "body as a temple" theory. These men and women can benefit from relieving work-related stress through yoga and meditation, or even brief periods of seclusion and self-enforced silence.

Time spent satisfying their own needs is a habit they must develop in order to avoid serious spiritual burnout.

CAREER AND FINANCES Career stress can have a negative influence on the emotional and physical health of March 15 people, but they understand that laughter is the best medicine. An ability to laugh at themselves is a key component in the revitalization of sagging self-esteem.

These people are not usually able to deal with materialistic aims, and may suddenly feel the need to change gears in midlife.

DREAMS AND GOALS Successful management of their daily need for spiritual fulfillment and peace is the goal of many March 15 men and women. They wish to live a life that's simple and meaningful, honest and productive.

March 15 people can have a difficult time zeroing in on personal goals, since they may feel uncomfortable concentrating on their own best interests.

EMBRACE
Validity
Compassion
Fate

AVOID
Cynicism
Emotional obsession
Unreality

ALSO BORN TODAY
Film director Philippe De Broca; model Fabio; actor Judd Hirsch; singer Mike Love; U.S. President Andrew Jackson; bandleader Harry James; musician Phil Lesh; singer Sly Stone.

MARCH 16

March 16 individuals possess a profound inner vision and are able to integrate their psychic sensitivity with their everyday life and activities. Because these men and women have a natural affinity for metaphysical reality, they always seem to have a foot in both worlds. They are idealistic, yet have a wonderful capacity to understand and empathize with the day-to-day concerns of others. These people have a high-stakes attitude toward life.

FRIENDS AND LOVERS

People born on this date are great cheerleaders for their friends. They're unfailingly interested in the lives of their pals, and do what they can to participate.

March 16 people are loyal, dependable partners. They may have second thoughts about settling down, yet once they do they are in the relationship for keeps. These individuals have a very strong sexual nature and need to feel attractive to their partner.

CHILDREN AND FAMILY

Despite their metaphysical bent, March 16 people display a remarkably practical attitude toward their background. If they felt neglected or unloved during their growing-up years, they forgive whatever mistakes their parents may have made.

March 16 men and women know their youngsters' wants and needs instinctively. Their natural sensitivity allows them to transcend generational differences and focus on issues that really count.

HEALTH

The health of March 16 people is linked to their inner life. If they're able to indulge their need for a creative outlet, they'll maintain a harmonious balance between their worldly and spiritual realities.

March 16 people are very sensitive and may be unable to deal with the stresses that other people handle easily. There are times when the world is just too cruel a place for these folks. However, they can find themselves through meditation and asceticism.

CAREER AND FINANCES

People born on this date often have a hard time deciding which career to follow. They may be drawn to artistic occupations, though if these do not provide the necessary financial benefits, they could be forced to look for something more stable. In such cases, they may need to pursue their creative interests as a hobby, which may push them to the brink of emotional and physical endurance.

These men and women need to find a harmonious balance between their career and personal life. If they strive too hard to make money, this balance could be upset. They need to trust in their ability to live on what they make, whatever that may be.

DREAMS AND GOALS

March 16 individuals require a sense of security in their lives—which is not usually available to anyone. Learning to trust in the future can be a major breakthrough for these people, as it eliminates the stresses that do so much damage to their peace of mind.

If they can maintain belief in themselves and in their own ability to deal with daily stress, March 16 men and women can make all their other dreams come true.

EMBRACE
Sensitivity
Artistic integrity
Miracles

AVOID
Compromise
Being controlled
Sexual excesses

ALSO BORN TODAY
Film director Bernardo Bertolucci; actress Isabelle Huppert; First Lady Pat Nixon; actor/comedian Jerry Lewis; U.S. President James Madison; actor Leo McKern; actress Kate Nelligan; singer Nancy Wilson.

MARCH 17

There is a hard edge of reality to those born on this date, even though they are warmly sensitive to their environment and day-to-day situations. These men and women are often miraculously talented, yet they have the ability to emotionally transcend their greatness and see the practical side of life.

Rather than suffer confusion from this dichotomy, March 17 people are actually enlivened by it. They know that however complicated and demanding their life is, they have the option to turn a blind eye to the reality others wish to see.

FRIENDS AND LOVERS People born on this date often find their greatest challenges in relationships. Why this is the case may not be understood by these individuals, yet they know enough to bypass such controversy when it appears. Those who seem to be their friends are sometimes not as loyal as March 17 people have the right to expect them to be.

Being drawn into major conflicts revolving around love is fairly commonplace for March 17 people. They have a tendency to let themselves be managed in romantic matters.

CHILDREN AND FAMILY Those born on this date often spend their growing-up years in an extremely sheltered environment. Although this is meant to be a positive experience, it can actually have the opposite effect; Starting life as a "princess" or "fair-haired boy" has its privileges, but in most cases it merely delays maturation.

March 17 people want to expose their youngsters to a more realistic view of life and craft an upbringing that is short on fantasy, long on truth.

HEALTH March 17 people require a lot of calcium and iron in their diet. This means eating plenty of fish, poultry, lean red meat, and green leafy vegetables.

People born on this date already know the value of daily exercise. Though naturally slim, they may have concerns about an inherited condition, such as arthritis. To build bone mass and retain it late in life is vital and can be accomplished via weight-bearing exercises.

CAREER AND FINANCES March 17 people must follow the dictates of their heart when it comes to making career choices. These men and women have an overwhelming need to play out their innermost fantasies through the work they do. Career goals are likely to be a major force through which all other aspirations are filtered.

Financial security is a very serious matter to March 17 individuals. Although not materialistic, they do want to know that their loved ones have all the comforts of life.

DREAMS AND GOALS March 17 people are concerned with bringing together their dreamy side as well as their practical side.

Since relationships generally constitute the most challenging part of life for these individuals, they may need to set specific goals that address these conflicts. March 17 people vacillate between being incurable romantics and hard-boiled cynics.

EMBRACE
Objectivity
Fun
Appreciation

AVOID
Defensiveness
Fatalism
Wasting resources

ALSO BORN TODAY
Football star "Slingin'" Sammy Baugh; singer Nat King Cole; actress Lesley-Anne Down; artist Kate Greenaway; actor Rob Lowe; dancer Rudolf Nureyev; actress Mercedes McCambridge; actor Kurt Russell.

MARCH 18

People born on this date depend upon their strong psychic awareness to guide their actions, and for this reason they may appear to be caught up in compulsive, even reckless behavior. They are actually very centered, both emotionally and spiritually.

These men and women have a zest for life and are on a continual search for adventure. They are pioneers who are never afraid to embrace all of the personal and professional challenges that confront them.

FRIENDS AND LOVERS
March 18 people have a highly competitive nature, which can create unexpected rifts in their relationships.

People born on this date have a strong sexual appetite that often dictates the nature of their intimate relationships. They have criteria for love that are at once spiritual and practical.

CHILDREN AND FAMILY
People born on this date understand the value of coming to grips with their past. Memory is a powerful factor in the lives of all water-sign people, but March 18 natives know how to distill this in positive ways.

March 18 individuals are aware of the profound influence they have over their own children and wisely see fit to allow their young-sters to interact with siblings, parents, or close friends. March 18 men and women understand the value of allowing their children more than a single view of adulthood.

HEALTH
People born on this date look to physical activity for release from the stresses of everyday life. While they may favor a regular workout, they also enjoy playing competitive sports, which energize them on a variety of levels. March 18 folks like to demonstrate their subtle mastery over colleagues, and nothing gives them as much satisfaction as besting a coworker at tennis, racquetball, or touch football.

March 18 natives enjoy eating red meat and sweets, but understand the need to cut back on calories whenever they gain a few pounds.

CAREER AND FINANCES
With a strong work ethic and limitless ambition, March 18 people are destined for career success. These men and women have great organizational skills and will distinguish themselves in careers where their know-how can be accommodated.

People born on this date are not as concerned with how much money they make as with how well they manage it. They have the ability to make bold financial decisions without being reckless.

DREAMS AND GOALS
Because they're not afraid to push ahead into unknown territory, March 18 men and women are likely to feel as if they've achieved their goals. Although they want to get to the top of their profession, they're more interested in preparing the groundwork according to their own specifications.

March 18 individuals need to look at the spiritual side of life; if they do not, they'll never be completely happy.

EMBRACE
Values
Laughter
Premonitions

AVOID
Trade-offs
Psychic pain
Loss

ALSO BORN TODAY
Speed skater Bonnie Blair; psychic Edgar Cayce; film director Rene Clement; novelist Richard Condon; actor Robert Donat; writer George Plimpton; composer Nicolai Rimsky-Korsakov; novelist John Updike.

MARCH 19

People born on this date are sensitive and possess a sunny disposition and a positive outlook. Although they can easily give themselves over to impulse and intuition, they understand the need to ground themselves in common sense.

March 19 people are charming in a subtle, unassuming way. They don't attempt to use their charm in a manipulative manner, yet they may unconsciously do so when they feel as if a partner or colleague isn't "hearing" them.

FRIENDS AND LOVERS
March 19 individuals prompt feelings of intense love and protectiveness from their friends. These men and women are not as helpless as they may be perceived by their pals, yet this "nurturing from a distance" goes on throughout much of their life.

Despite their natural good looks and ability to attract the opposite sex, March 19 people experience a great deal of disappointment in romantic matters. This is partially due to their idealistic attitude toward romance. They expect every love affair to be a "forever" kind of thing, which is rarely the case.

CHILDREN AND FAMILY
Because what they remember and what they wish to recall are often in direct opposition to each other, March 19 people have a way of rewriting their childhood years to match their view of what their upbringing meant to them. Even if there was nothing very distinctive or unpleasant about how they were raised, these folks may need to revise that period of their life in order to lend it ego-pleasing glamour and a sense of mystery.

March 19 men and women believe in giving their own children free reign to let their imaginations take them where the youngsters wish to go.

HEALTH
March 19 natives take control of their health. Although they may have suffered from allergies or asthma as children, they are likely to be quite healthy as adults, unless they allow pills or alcohol to become part of their life.

By eating a healthy, low-fat diet, March 19 men and women can cut their chances of obesity and all its complications.

CAREER AND FINANCES
People born on this date instinctively understand their talents and weaknesses. They are often drawn to careers that allow them to conquer their inhibitions. For this reason, they make wonderful actors, writers, and magicians. If they find career satisfaction in more conventional situations, they are still likely to explore some means of artistic expression.

March 19 people seem to have contempt for money, though their attitude only illustrates their lack of patience with people who worship at the dollar's altar.

DREAMS AND GOALS
March 19 men and women need to feel as if they are striving toward something awe-inspiring that will change not only their life but the lives of those around them.

Despite their trademark sensitivity, people born on this date are extremely goal-oriented and will sacrifice for years in order to make a cherished dream come true.

EMBRACE
Emotional healing
Intellect
Caring

AVOID
Restrictions
Disparity
Turbulence

ALSO BORN TODAY
Musician Paul Atkinson; actress Ursula Andress; explorer Sir Richard Burton; actress Glenn Close; novelist Philip Roth; Supreme Court justice Earl Warren; novelist Irving Wallace; actor Bruce Willis.

398

MARCH 20

It's impossible to truly know March 20 individuals because no matter how emotionally accessible they may seem, there is always a veil drawn between the persona they allow others to perceive and the core self that is the reality.

These aesthetic individuals are naturally drawn to the past, whether as a fount of their unconscious desires or the pool of their conflicted memories. To transcend barriers to reality is their way of bringing both worlds together, but is not a task that these secretive individuals choose to share with others.

FRIENDS AND LOVERS

The illusive glamour of March 20 men and women has an almost mythological effect upon those who surround them. But there is a price. They can be the most loving and considerate people on Earth one minute, totally self-seeking and insensitive the next.

People born on this date demonstrate the same duality with romance. They seem at times to favor a spiritual intimacy with their lover or mate, but this can turn to stony indifference if they feel their partner is "pushing" them.

CHILDREN AND FAMILY

The men and women born on this date understand that love can have a profoundly healing effect on the their past pain, even if it resonates from long ago. Unfortunately, they carry around a great deal of resentment and confused feelings from their childhood, some of which is more perceived than actually remembered.

As parents, these individuals inevitably seek to resolve their own emotional issues by giving almost unlimited freedom to their own children.

HEALTH

As a rule, March 20 people are healthy, though they may suffer from periodic indolence and mild depression, conditions usually brought on by emotional rather than physical factors. March 20 people are healthiest when they eat a simple diet that offers high levels of protein and calcium. Drinking more than eight glasses of water each day is a must for these fish-sign people.

CAREER AND FINANCES

No matter which career March 20 people select, there is likely to be an element of creativity involved. These men and women are extremely artistic and need to address this fact on a daily basis. They make excellent commercial artists, copywriters, decorators, fashion consultants or designers, musicians, and dancers.

March 20 people often rely on others to take care of their financial affairs, since they have very little interest in this part of their lives.

DREAMS AND GOALS

Learning to manage the sometimes wild impulses of their own creative psyche can be a major life-goal for March 20 people. They need to understand that breaking the rules simply to be different isn't the same as breaking those rules in order to do something worthwhile.

March 20 men and women can have a hard time sustaining their drive toward success, because they're easily distracted. If they can achieve greater balance in life they are more likely to accomplish their goals.

EMBRACE
Gracious living
High style
Happy memories

AVOID
Controversy
Regret
Suspicion

ALSO BORN TODAY
Actress Holly Hunter; playwright Henrik Ibsen; actor William Hurt; film director Spike Lee; hockey star Bobby Orr; writer/actor/film director Carl Reiner; basketball coach Pat Riley; actress Theresa Russell.

FAMILY AND FRIENDS' BIRTHDAYS

Name	Birthday	Sign	Birthstone